**Business Skills**
ALL-IN-O
FOR
DUMMIES®

by Colin Barrow, Kate Burton, Peter Economy,
Clare Evans, Nick Graham, Tom Hopkins,
Ben Kench, Elizabeth Kuhnke, Malcolm Kushner,
John Marrin, Bob Nelson, Richard Pettinger,
Brinley Platts, Stan Portny, Romilla Ready,
John A. Tracy and Rob Yeung

Edited by Kate Burton

**WILEY**

A John Wiley and Sons, Ltd, Publication

**Business Skills All-in-One For Dummies®, UK Edition**

Published by
**John Wiley & Sons, Ltd**
The Atrium
Southern Gate
Chichester
West Sussex
PO19 8SQ
England
www.wiley.com

For general information on our other products and services, please contact our Customer Care Department within the U.S. at 877-762-2974, outside the U.S. at 317-572-3993, or fax 317-572-4002.

For technical support, please visit www.wiley.com/techsupport.

Wiley publishes in a variety of print and electronic formats and by print-on-demand. Some material included with standard print versions of this book may not be included in e-books or in print-on-demand. If this book refers to media such as a CD or DVD that is not included in the version you purchased, you may download this material at http://booksupport.wiley.com. For more information about Wiley products, visit www.wiley.com.

British Library Cataloguing in Publication Data: A catalogue record for this book is available from the British Library

ISBN 978-1-119-94162-0 (pbk); ISBN 978-1-119-94372-3 (ebk); ISBN 978-1-119-94374-7 (ebk); ISBN 978-1-119-94373-0 (ebk)

Printed and bound in Great Britain by TJ International, Padstow, Cornwall

10 9 8 7 6 5 4 3 2 1

WILEY

# About the Authors

**Colin Barrow** was, until recently, Head of the Enterprise Group at Cranfield School of Management, where he taught entrepreneurship on the MBA and other programmes. He is also a visiting professor at business schools in the US, Asia, France, and Austria. His books on entrepreneurship and small business have been translated into twenty languages including Russian and Chinese. He worked with Microsoft to incorporate the business planning model used in his teaching programmes into the software program, Microsoft Business Planner. He is a regular contributor to newspapers, periodicals and academic journals such as the *Financial Times, The Guardian, Management Today,* and the *International Small Business Journal.*

Thousands of students have passed through Colin's start-up and business growth programmes, going on to run successful and thriving enterprises, and raising millions in new capital. He is on the board of several small businesses, is a University Academic Governor, and has served on the boards of public companies, venture capital funds, and on Government Task Forces.

**Kate Burton** (see www.kateburton.co.uk) is an international NLP master coach who challenges individuals and organisations to create lives that are sustainable and fun. Her business career began in corporate advertising and marketing with Hewlett-Packard. Now she works with leaders and managers across industries and cultures to work at their best. She loves to deliver custom-built coaching programmes that support people to boost their communication skills, motivation, self-awareness, and confidence. She believes that people all have unique talents, abilities and core values: the skill is about honouring them to the full. In addition to co-authoring *NLP For Dummies,* the *NLP Workbook* and *Confidence For Dummies* she is the author of *Live Life. Love Work* published by Capstone, an imprint of John Wiley's. Her latest addition to the Dummies personal development range is *Coaching with NLP For Dummies.*

**Peter Economy, MBA** is associate editor of *Leader to Leader,* the award-winning magazine of the Peter F. Drucker Foundation for Nonprofit Leadership, and author of numerous books. Peter combines his writing expertise with more than 15 years of management experience to provide his readers with solid, hands-on information and advice. He received his bachelor's degree (with majors in economics and human biology) from Stanford University and his MBA at the Edinburgh Business School. Visit Peter at his website: www.petereconomy.com.

**Clare Evans** is a personal and business coach working with individuals and businesses to improve their time management, increase productivity, and create a better work life balance in these time-challenged times.

Clare worked in the corporate sector for a global company for many years. Managing IT projects and working with global teams, she understands the pressures today's working environment places on people's time and the difficulty of creating a better work–life balance.

Now running her own business, Clare coaches people one-to-one and runs workshops, seminars, and teleclasses on the subjects that challenge our time. She frequently writes and publishes articles for newsletters and magazines such as *Zest, Cosmopolitan,* and *New Woman* magazines, *Better Business Focus* (a monthly Internet magazine for business advisers), and *Financial Solutions* (the Personal Finance Society's magazine for financial advisers).

Everyone cares about the best use of their time. Clare specialises in enabling people to achieve what they want in ways that makes people master their use of precious time.

For additional information about time management, or to invite her to speak at your meeting or event, you can contact Clare at info@clareevans.co.uk. You can visit her website and sign up for her free newsletter at www.clare evans.co.uk.

**Nick Graham** is the founder and Managing Director of Inspirandum Ltd, a small and specialised company focused on achieving excellence in project management. In his company he has set very clear objectives to teach all project approaches and methods in a practical way so that they can be applied intelligently and productively.

With a career that has covered both the public sector and the private sector, Nick is able to communicate readily with managers in both communities and he's been involved in project consultancy and training for more than 15 years. Nick's experience with structured methods in projects goes back much further, and in the PRINCE method it goes back to before it was even called PRINCE.

Nick is an experienced project practitioner and trainer and he's also a qualified teacher. His work has taken him world wide and those attending his courses have described his style as energetic, lively, fun, very practical, and very informative. Nick's consultancy work has ranged from helping to plan individual projects to advising senior managers on how to implement PRINCE2 throughout their organisation. He teaches regular open PRINCE2 courses in London UK and in Hong Kong as well as running courses 'in-company' for clients in the UK and world wide.

When not away on consultancy or training assignments, Nick lives in Weymouth in Dorset. His company's offices are on the tip of the Isle of Portland overlooking the sea and the famous Portland Bill lighthouse. His wife Kath also works for Inspirandum.

Nick is a member of the Association for Project Management (APM) and the Institute of Directors (IoD).

www.inspirandum.com

**Tom Hopkins** is the epitome of sales success. A millionaire by the time he reached the age of 27, Hopkins now is Chairman of Tom Hopkins International, one of the largest sales-training organisations in the world.

Thirty years ago, Tom Hopkins considered himself a failure. He had dropped out of college after 90 days, and for the next 18 months he carried steel on construction sites to make a living. Believing that there had to be a better way to earn a living, he went into sales – and ran into the worst period of his life. For six months, Tom earned an average of $42 a month and slid deeper into debt and despair. Pulling together his last few dollars, he invested in a five-day sales training seminar that turned his life around. In the next six months, Tom sold more than $1 million worth of $25,000 homes. At age 21, he won the Los Angeles Sales and Marketing Institute's coveted SAMMY Award and began setting records in sales performance that still stand today.

Because of his unique ability to share his enthusiasm for the profession of selling and the successful selling techniques he developed, Tom began giving seminars in 1974. Training as many as 10,000 salespeople a month, he quickly became known as the world's leading sales trainer. Today, he presents approximately 75 seminars a year to over 100,000 people throughout the world.

Tom was a pioneer in producing high-quality audio and video programs for those who could not attend the seminars or who wanted further reinforcement after the seminars. Recognised as the most effective sales-training programmes ever produced, they're continually updated and are now being utilised by more than 1 million people.

Tom Hopkins has also written nine other books, including *Sales Prospecting For Dummies* and *Sales Closing For Dummies,* as well as the best-selling *How to Master the Art of Selling,* which has sold over 1.3 million copies in 8 languages and 27 countries.

Tom Hopkins is a member of the National Speakers Association and one of a select few to receive its Council of Peers Award for Excellence. He is often the keynote speaker for annual conventions and is a frequent guest on television and radio talk shows.

**Ben Kench,** 'The Can Can Man', is Britain's number one small business growth specialist, enjoying a reputation for delivering quite incredible results.

Ben's pedigree and character have been formed over a lifetime of adventure and achievements that culminate in a rich spectrum of knowledge that's life-based with family values and an underpinning of integrity and honesty.

His selling career began with an early foray into double glazing sales as an impressionable 19-year-old and while his initial success was nationally recognised he also learned hard lessons about life, success, and attitude, eventually falling out with family and loved ones as arrogance overcame the youth. A few months taught lifelong lessons.

Moving on and learning, Ben's first major role in selling was to industry selling air compressors and related tools. Aged 20, he learned to face the 'we've been doing it this way for longer than you've been alive, lad' rejection.

Over the years Ben has enjoyed success in roles selling higher value equipment to corporate clients, selling to the small business market, and selling to the home owner. He's experienced in selling in the consumer marketplace in industries as diverse as unregulated timesharing to heavily regulated financial services. Each have presented their particular challenges and each has added their own unique refinement to the art of selling.

Ben also raised his daughter from the age of 20 months as a single parent and knows well the struggle to balance work and family while also appreciating the real value and meaning of family life. Ben is first and foremost a family man, with old-fashioned values, where truth and integrity are non-negotiable and where business relationships become friendships that last. Those sentiments echo throughout the advice in this book to help you succeed in your selling career.

Ben's programme, 'The Business Booster', is gaining national recognition and his company is often approached by major institutions to assist with their performance objectives. He's approved as a member of The National Consultants Register and is often asked to speak at conventions for The Institute of Sales and Marketing Management (ISMM), and The Federation of Small Businesses (FSB), as well as major business to business exhibitions nationally.

Ben has also written a book on small business growth entitled *How to Grow Your Business and Enjoy More Money, Less Stress!*

Today Ben's time is spent dedicated to helping individuals improve their performance through a variety of sales and business education programmes.

**Elizabeth Kuhnke** holds a Bachelor's degree in Speech and Communications from Northwestern University, and a Masters degree in Theatre Arts. For over 20 years, Elizabeth has worked with individuals and groups to bolster their personal impact and communication skills.

Before moving to Britain, Elizabeth acted throughout the United States on the stage, radio, and television. In addition to designing and delivering university programmes in voice and movement, she also taught acting skills to students and professionals.

In the United Kingdom, Elizabeth applies her theatrical expertise and psychological insight with a rock-solid business approach. She works at top level with FTSE 100 companies and leading professional firms to provide both one-to-one and group coaching in key areas relating to interpersonal communication and image projection. Coming from diverse backgrounds including accountancy, law, construction and telecommunications, Elizabeth's clients consistently achieve their goals and have fun getting there. Her keys to communication are based on the simple principle of demonstrating respect, establishing rapport, and achieving results.

A highly entertaining speaker, Elizabeth is a popular choice on the conference circuit, and is often quoted in the media addressing issues concerning confidence, voice, body language, and communication skills – all the ingredients that create a positive impact.

For further information about Elizabeth, visit her Web site at `www.kuhnke communication.com`.

**Malcolm Kushner,** 'America's Favourite Humour Consultant', is an internationally acclaimed expert on humour and communication and a professional speaker. Since 1982, he has trained thousands of managers, executives, and professionals how to gain a competitive edge with humour. His clients include IBM, Hewlett-Packard, AT&T, Chevron, Aetna, Motorola, and Bank of America.

A popular speaker, his Leading With laughter presentation features rare video clips of US presidents using humour intentionally and successfully. He has performed the speech at many corporate and association meetings, as well as at the Smithsonian Institute.

A Phi Beta Kappa graduate of the University of Buffalo, Kushner holds a BA in Speech-Communication. His MA in Speech-Communication is from the University of Southern California, where he taught freshman speech. He also has a JD from the University of California Hastings College of the Law. Prior to becoming a humour consultant, he practiced law with a major San Francisco law firm.

Kushner is the author of *The Light Touch: How To Use Humor for Business Success* and *Vintage Humour for Wine Lovers*. He is also a co-creator of the humour exhibit at the Ronald Reagan Presidential Library.

Frequently interviewed by the media, Kushner has been profiled in *Time Magazine, USA Today, The New York Times,* and numerous other publications. His television and radio appearances include CNN, National Public Radio, CNBC, *Voice of America,* and *The Larry King Show*. His annual 'Cost of Laughing Index' has been featured on *The Tonight Show* and the front page of *The Wall Street Journal*.

Need a great speaker for your next meeting or event? Contact Malcolm at P.O. Box 7509, Santa Cruz, CA 95061, call 001-831-425-4839, or e-mail him at mk@ kushnergroup.com. Visit his Web site at www.kushnergroup.com.

**Dr John Marrin** is an expert on how leaders of organisations totally engage their directors, managers and employees to enhance their commitment and achieve higher levels of individual, team and business performance. He is a leadership coach and organisation development specialist to a wide range of clients including large multinationals, privately owned businesses and public sector organisations. While working primarily with organisations throughout the United Kingdom, John is also experienced in supporting clients in Europe and South America.

John is intensely enthusiastic about engaging people to work better together through enhancing mutual understanding and establishing shared commitment and accountability for achieving success: he redefined the meaning and practice of engaging through his DPhil. John is a Chartered Fellow of the Chartered Institute of Personnel and Development, and holds a Master of Arts in Management Learning from Lancaster University.

John is founder of Marwel & Co. which specialises in leadership development and employee engagement. To find out more about the services of Marwel & Co., visit his website: www.marwel-co.com. John's email address is jmarrin@marwel-co.com.

**Bob Nelson, PhD** is founder and president of Nelson Motivation, Inc., a management training and products firm headquartered in San Diego, California. As a practising manager, researcher, and best-selling author, Bob is an internationally recognised expert in the areas of employee motivation, recognition and rewards, productivity and performance improvement, and leadership.

Bob has published 20 books and sold more than 2.5 million books on management, which have been translated in some 20 languages. He earned his BA in communications from Macalester College, his MBA in organisational behavior from UC Berkeley, and his PhD in management from the Peter F. Drucker Graduate Management Center of the Claremont Graduate University.

Visit his website at www.nelson-motivation.com or contact Bob directly at BobRewards@aol.com.

**Richard Pettinger, MBA** has taught since 1989 at University College London, where he is principal teaching fellow (reader) in management education and director of the Information Management for Business courses – part of a UK national initiative to bring about the required quality of management and technology education demanded for the future. Richard teaches general, strategic and operational management, change and organisational behaviour to a wide variety of domestic and international students on undergraduate, postgraduate and executive programmes.

Since 2005, Richard has been visiting professor at the Jagiellonian University Business School in Krakow, Poland, developing a wide range of teaching, learning and research initiatives.

Richard is the author of over forty books on all aspects of business and management. He also produces professional, conference and study papers.

**Brinley Platts** is a leading executive coach, researcher, and consultant to FTSE 100 companies. He is one of the UK's leading authorities on CIO and IT executive careers and works with international companies on the integration of senior executive life and career goals. He is a behavioural scientist by training, and his passion is to enable large organisations to become places where ordinary decent people can grow and express their talents freely to the benefit of all stakeholders. He is a co-founder of the Bring YourSELF To Work campaign, which aims to release the pent-up talent and passion of today's global workforce to create the better world we all desire and want our children to inherit.

**Stan Portny,** president of Stanley E. Portny and Associates, LLC, is an internationally recognised expert in project management and project leadership. During the past 30 years, he's provided training and consultation to more than 150 public and private organisations in consumer products, insurance, pharmaceuticals, finance, information technology, telecommunications, defence and healthcare. He has developed and conducted training programmes for more than 50,000 management and staff personnel in engineering, sales and marketing, research and development, information systems, manufacturing, operations and support areas.

Stan combines an analyst's eye with an innate sense of order and balance and a deep respect for personal potential. He helps people understand how to control chaotic environments and produce dramatic results while still achieving personal and professional satisfaction. Widely acclaimed for his dynamic presentations and unusual ability to establish a close rapport with seminar participants, Stan specialises in tailoring his training programmes to meet the unique needs of individual organisations. His clients have included ADP, ADT, American International Group, Burlington Northern Railroad, Hewlett Packard, Nabisco, Novartis Pharmaceuticals, Pitney Bowes, UPS, Vanguard Investment Companies and the United States Navy and Air Force.

A Project Management Institute-certified Project Management Professional (PMP), Stan received his bachelor's degree in electrical engineering from the Polytechnic Institute of Brooklyn. He holds a master's degree in electrical engineering and the degree of electrical engineer from the Massachusetts Institute of Technology. Stan has also studied at the Alfred P. Sloan School of Management and the George Washington University National Law Center.

Stan provides on-site training in all aspects of project management, project team building and project leadership. Web site www.StanPortny.com.

**Romilla Ready** is the creator and architect of Relationship Wizardry®, her own brand of training and coaching, which combines the two potent technologies of Neuro-linguistic Programming and Huna (the ancient knowledge from Hawai'i). Relationship Wizardry® evolved from the realisation that the common denominator in any interaction, be it one that causes distress or one that gives pleasure, is people and the way they think and communicate. Her product offerings are:

- Relationship Wizardry®, which is aimed at people (usually singletons) who want to create their perfect relationship,

- Relationship Wizardry® in Business, which helps companies build profitable stakeholder relationships through improved employee and customer engagement as well as through enhanced salesmanship.

- Relationship Wizardry® Coaching, which enables time paupers to experience fast, powerful, life-enhancing results in their personal and business lives.

- Applied NLP for Business Results™ networking events, where business owners discover how to apply NLP to create the specific results they want for their business.

Romilla has worked in high-stress, customer-facing environments for multinational companies and across cultural boundaries, has provided training in the UK, Europe, and Africa, and is the MD of her company, Ready Solutions Ltd.

**John A. Tracy** is Professor of Accounting, Emeritus, in the College of Business and Administration at the University of Colorado in Boulder. Before his 35-year tenure at Boulder he was on the business faculty for four years at the University of California in Berkeley. He has served as staff accountant at Ernst & Young and is the author of several books on accounting, including *The Fast Forward MBA in Finance* and *How To Read a Financial Report*. Dr Tracy received his MBA and PhD degrees from the University of Wisconsin and is a CPA in Colorado.

**Dr Rob Yeung** is a director at business psychology consultancy Talentspace. He is often asked to coach teams and individuals on presentation skills – in particular on developing their presence and charisma when presenting. He travels extensively around the world, running workshops, participating in panel discussions, and giving presentations to audiences of up to many hundreds of people at a time.

He has written for *Guardian, Daily Telegraph,* and *Financial Times* and contributed to publications ranging from *Men's Health* and *New Woman* to *Accountancy* and *Sunday Times.* He has published twelve other books on career and management topics including, in 2006, *The Rules of Office Politics* and *The Rules of EQ* (Cyan/Marshall Cavendish) and *Answering Tough Interview Questions For Dummies* (Wiley).

He is often seen on television including CNN and Channel 4's *Big Brother's Little Brother.* He is also the presenter of the highly acclaimed BBC television series *How To Get Your Dream Job.* A chartered psychologist of the British Psychological Society with a Ph.D. in psychology from the University of London, he has also lectured at a number of business schools and universities.

Need one of the UK's leading psychologists to work with you, your team or your organisation? Drop Dr Rob an email at rob@talentspace.co.uk or visit www.talentspace.co.uk.

## Publisher's Acknowledgments

We're proud of this book; please send us your comments at http://dummies.custhelp.com. For other comments, please contact our Customer Care Department within the U.S. at 877-762-2974, outside the U.S. at 317-572-3993, or fax 317-572-4002.

Some of the people who helped bring this book to market include the following:

### Acquisitions, Editorial, and Vertical Websites

**Project Editor:** Jo Jones

**Commissioning Editor:** Claire Ruston

**Assistant Editor:** Ben Kemble

**Proofreader:** Melanie Assinder-Smith

**Production Manager:** Daniel Mersey

**Publisher:** David Palmer

**Cover Photos:** © iStock / Skip ODonnell

**Cartoons:** Ed McLachlan

### Composition Services

**Project Coordinator:** Kristie Rees

**Layout and Graphics:** Amy Hassos, Laura Westhuis

**Proofreader:** Jessica Kramer

**Indexer:** BIM Indexing & Proofreading Services

---

**Publishing and Editorial for Consumer Dummies**

**Kathleen Nebenhaus,** Vice President and Executive Publisher

**Kristin Ferguson-Wagstaffe,** Product Development Director

**Ensley Eikenburg,** Associate Publisher, Travel

**Kelly Regan,** Editorial Director, Travel

**Publishing for Technology Dummies**

**Andy Cummings,** Vice President and Publisher

**Composition Services**

**Debbie Stailey,** Director of Composition Services

# Contents at a Glance

# Table of Contents

# Introduction

**W**elcome to *Business Skills All-in-One For Dummies*, your launch pad to developing the interpersonal, organisational and commercial strength so essential for business success. In order to compete in the uncertain and challenging economic environment you face, it has never been more important to be well informed on every aspect of business. Whatever organisation you work in, the higher you go, the more pronounced your people skills will need to be. That's why in every section of this book, you'll find strong guidance on taking people with you on your business journey as well as building on your own abilities.

This book draws together information on the key areas of successful business life – communicating effectively and confidently, developing powerful presentations, getting the right employees on board, budgeting wisely, engaging with technology, developing strong teamwork, motivating and managing resources as well as managing your time to achieve inspirational goals – all in one bumper guide.

With help from this book, you can make your business life even better and lead those around you to succeed.

## About This Book

This book is the ultimate business skills developer, providing expert guidance for the constant challenges managers and leaders face on a daily basis.

*Business Skills All-In-One For Dummies* draws on advice from several other For Dummies books, which you may wish to check out for more in-depth coverage of certain topics (all published by Wiley):

- ✔ *Body Language For Dummies, Second Edition* (Elizabeth Kuhnke)
- ✔ *Coaching with NLP For Dummies* (Kate Burton)
- ✔ *Confidence For Dummies, Second Edition* (Kate Burton, Brinley Platts)
- ✔ *Leadership For Dummies* (John Marrin)
- ✔ *Management For Dummies, Second Edition* (Richard Pettinger, Bob Nelson and Peter Economy)

- ✔ *Neuro-linguistic Programming For Dummies, Second Edition* (Romilla Ready and Kate Burton)
- ✔ *Persuasion and Influence For Dummies* (Elizabeth Kuhnke)
- ✔ *Project Management For Dummies* (Nick Graham, Stanley E. Portny)
- ✔ *Public Speaking and Presentations For Dummies* (Malcom Kushner, Rob Yeung)
- ✔ *Selling For Dummies (*Tom Hopkins, Ben Kench*)*
- ✔ *Time Management For Dummies, Second Edition* (Clare Evans
- ✔ *Understanding Business Accounting For Dummies, Second Edition* (John A. Tracy and Colin Barrow)

# Conventions Used in This Book

To make your reading experience easier and to alert you to key words or points, we use certain conventions in this book:

- ✔ *Italics* introduces new terms, and explains what they mean.
- ✔ **Bold** text is used to show the action part of bulleted and numbered lists.

# Foolish Assumptions

This book brings together the elements of knowledge that are essential for understanding the world of business organisations. As a consequence, to keep the book down to a reasonable number of pages, we've made a few assumptions about you (we hope you don't mind!). Maybe you're:

- ✔ A new manager or team leader looking for a fool-proof guide to check out what you don't know
- ✔ An experienced manager looking to raise your game
- ✔ A business owner with aspirations to grow your company
- ✔ A coach or business adviser working to support your clients

# How This Book Is Organised

We've divided *Business Skills All-in-One For Dummies* into four separate books. This section explains what you'll find out about in each one of these books. Each book is broken into chapters tackling key aspects of that part of the business world.

# Book 1: Communicating Effectively

One of the fundamental skills of business is connecting with people appropriately. This book is the one to turn to first if you're technically good at your job, and now find yourself needing to build rapport quickly with a range of different people. You may want to project yourself more confidently and negotiate rather than hiding behind the scenes getting on with your work. This book encourages you to listen to what different audiences would like from you, ask powerful questions and build presentations to get you off to a flying start.

# Book II: Building Your Commercial Acumen

You may have come into work with a particular skillset and now find you're running a mini-profit centre with the need to budget, sell products or services and manage people as well as business risks. This book will guide you to making a wise investment in the right people and save you from feeling foolish around accounting jargon. This book walks you through the commercial matters you'll need to know and stay on top of including the ability to deal with that sure fire constant in business - change.

# Book III: Managing and Leading Others

Unless you're intending to run your department or company single-handed, you need to master the essentials of managing and leading staff. This book tackles the 'people management' section of business, looking at how to build up teams of people who work at their best. You'll see what it takes to motivate and inspire even in the toughest times, overcoming the inevitable office politics and conflict using a coaching approach.

# Book IV: Increasing Productivity and Performance

Ultimately, the pressure is always on to perform better than ever before, and that means being focused on where you're going and organised in your approach. In this book, you'll see how to create clear goals that can be achieved and develop your skills at performance managing others. Most importantly, paying attention to what and how to delegate. Navigating the line between pushing people on to achieve while ensuring no-one gets over-stressed means keeping a sound perspective and knowing how to relax easily. In this book you'll get practical expertise so you can organise your time and tasks, keep meetings productive and stop email getting out of control.

# Icons Used in This Book

When you flick through this book, you'll notice some snazzy little icons in the margin. These pick out key points to recognise in business, and present you with important nuggets of information for your success:

Want to hone your business skills? Check out the text highlighted by this icon to pick up some sage advice.

They say elephants never forget and nor should good managers. This icon focuses on key information you should never be without.

The business world comes with dangers and the text beside this icon points out common pitfalls to avoid. So take special care here.

This icon gives real-life specifics on how to perform a specific task.

# Where to Go from Here

*Business Skills All-In-One For Dummies* can help you succeed no matter what kind of assistance you're looking for. If you're faced with confusing budgets and accounting terms for the first time, you may want to head straight into familiarising yourself with some accounting jargon that keep the financial controllers happy. Or maybe you'd like to get savvier with technology so you can speak with the Information Technology guys, (turn then to Book II). If you're ready to step up to a management or leadership role you may want to build a high performing team with shared values and a passion for what they're doing (head over to Book III). If you need to raise everyone's game to be more productive and effective, then you'll find ways to block out time wasting and get everyone aligned (check out Book IV). Remember that a good starting point is always rapport with your colleagues and customers so you get on the same wavelength quickly. (Book I takes you firmly by the hand.) This *All-In-One* is set up so that you can dip in and out of it, just one section at a time, depending on the situation you face today. Have fun learning on the way.

# Book I
# Communicating Effectively

'Aaaargh!!– emails, answer phones,
fax machines and now even the alphabet
soup is trying to communicate.'

# In this book...

**S**tart here when you want to boost the fundamental skills of connecting with people rather than tasks. As a manager or leader, it's not enough to be good at the technical side of your job, you'll need to navigate personalities and negotiate with all kinds of folks who bring their own needs to work. Dive right in now to focus on building strong rapport and confident communication skills.

Here are the contents of Book I at a glance:

# Chapter 1

# Creating Rapport

## In This Chapter

▶ Getting people to listen to you in challenging situations

▶ Handling difficult people

▶ Increasing your options in how you respond

▶ Gaining insights into other people's experience

**R**apport sits at the heart of Neuro Linguistic Programming (NLP) as a central pillar, or essential ingredient, which leads to successful communication between two individuals or groups of people. Rapport is a mutually respectful way of being with others and a way of doing business at all times. You don't need to like people to build rapport with them. Also, rapport isn't a technique that you turn on and off at will, but something that should flow constantly between people.

Rapport is like money: you realise that you have a problem only when you don't have enough of it. The first rule of communication is to establish rapport before expecting anyone to listen to you. And this rule applies to everybody and in every situation, whether you're a teacher, pupil, spouse, friend, waitress, taxi-driver, coach, doctor, therapist, or business executive.

Don't kid yourself that you can pull rapport instantly out of the bag for a particular meeting, conversation or problem-solving session. True rapport is based on an instinctive sense of trust and integrity. This chapter helps you to spot situations when you do (and don't) have rapport with another person. We share some special NLP tools and ideas to enable you to build rapport and encourage you to do so with people where it may prove valuable for you.

# Knowing Why Rapport is Important

The word rapport derives from the French verb *rapporter*, translated as 'to return or bring back'. The English dictionary definition is 'a sympathetic relationship or understanding': rapport is about making a two-way connection. You know that you've made such a connection when you experience a genuine sense of trust and respect with another person, when you engage comfortably with someone no matter how different the two of you are, and when you know that you're listening and being listened to.

Although you may want to spend your time with people who are just like you, the world is full of a huge variety of different types of people to meet, all with special skills, opinions, and backgrounds. Rapport is the key to success and influence in both your personal and professional life, because it's about appreciating and working with differences. Rapport makes getting things done much easier and allows you to provide good customer service to others and enjoy being on the receiving end of it, too. Ultimately, rapport preserves your time, money, and energy. What a great stress-free way to live!

## Recognising rapport when you see it

You can't take a magic pill to acquire rapport instantly; it's something you develop intuitively. So, in order for you to understand how you personally build rapport and what's important to you in different relationships, carry out the following steps:

1. **Think for a moment about someone with whom you have rapport.** What signals do you send out to that person and receive back that allow you to know that you're on the same wavelength? How do you create and maintain your rapport?

2. **Think for a moment about someone with whom you don't have rapport, but would like to.** What signals do you send out to that person and receive back that allow you to know that you're not on the same wavelength? What gets in the way of creating and maintaining rapport with that person?

3. **Think about your experience of the first person.** What can you do differently in your behaviour with the second person to help you build a stronger relationship?

You may think that the first person (with whom you have rapport) is simply easy to get on with and the second (with whom you share no rapport yet) is just a difficult person. Yet, by being more flexible in your behaviour and in your thoughts about the second person, you may find that you can build rapport through some simple actions.

You need to take time to get to know people and what's important to them instead of expecting people to adapt to you and your style. Throughout this chapter we provide tips for doing just that.

# *Identifying people with whom you want to build rapport*

By now you may be getting curious about the people around you – those with whom you work, share a home, or socialise. Perhaps you want to get to know some key individuals better, such as the manager of a project or your new partner's family. Maybe you want to influence your bank manager, or the recruiter at that all-important job interview.

Below we provide a template to help you think about anyone with whom you desire better rapport. We ask you to write down your ideas to make you stop and think, and so that you can come back to revisit your notes at a future date. Good relationships take serious investment – time to build and nurture. You can see that the questions require you to think about your needs and those of the other person. Rapport is a two-way street.

Name:

Company/group:

What's your relationship to this person?

Specifically, how would you like your relationship with this person to change?

What impact would this change have on you?

What impact would this change have on the other person?

Is the change worth investing time and energy?

What pressures does this person face?

What's most important to the person right now?

Who do you know that you can talk to who has successfully built rapport with this person? And what can you discover from this other person?

What other help can you get to build rapport?

What ideas do you have now for moving this relationship forward?

What's the first step?

Sometimes you have limited information about the intended person. If so, use this situation as your prompt to go out and do your research. Get curious about what makes that person tick, and who can help you find the information you need. Maybe you have a friend or colleague in common that you can identify with the help of a social networking site such as Facebook or LinkedIn.

# Having Basic Techniques for Building Rapport

Having rapport as the foundation for any relationship means that when tough issues arise, you can more easily discuss them, find solutions, and move on. Fortunately, you can find out how to develop rapport.

Rapport happens at many levels and you can build rapport constantly through the following:

- ✔ The places and people you spend time with
- ✔ The way you look, sound, and behave
- ✔ The skills you develop
- ✔ The values you live by
- ✔ Your beliefs
- ✔ Your purpose in life
- ✔ Being true to your natural identity

## Sharpening your rapport with eight quick tips

For starters, try the following immediate ways to begin building rapport:

- ✔ Take a genuine interest in getting to know what's important to other people. Start to understand them instead of expecting them to understand you first.

- ✔ Pick up on the key words, favourite phrases, and manner of speaking that an individual uses and build these aspects subtly into your own conversation.

- ✔ Notice how a person likes to handle information: lots of details or just the big picture? As you speak, feed back information in this same portion size.

✔ Check how a person uses the representation systems with visual, auditory, and kinaesthetic language (which you can read more about in Book I Chapter 2), and use similar words during your conversations.

✔ Breathe in unison with the person. You can do this discreetly by watching their neck and chest to see when they inhale and exhale, and then matching your breathing to the other person.

✔ Look out for someone's overall intention – the person's underlying aim – as opposed to the exact things done or said. People may not always get it right, but work on the assumption that people's hearts lie in the right place.

✔ Adopt a similar stance to another person in terms of your body language, gestures, voice tone, and speed of talking.

✔ Respect people's time, energy, friends and favourite associates, and money. These items are important resources for you.

The next four sections contain some more advanced rapport-building techniques.

## *Viewing the communication wheel and developing rapport*

Classic research by Professor Mehrabian of the University of California at Los Angeles (UCLA) looked at how people receive and respond to live communication. He suggests that when an incongruity exists between what you say and how you say it, 7 per cent of the message is conveyed through your words, 38 per cent comes through the quality of your voice, and a massive 55 per cent comes through gestures, expression, and posture (check out Figure 1-1).

Although opinion is divided on the actual percentages, most researchers are in agreement that messages aren't just conveyed in words, but that the tone of your voice and body language has a strong impact. If you've ever heard people say that 'everything's fine' when clearly they aren't well, you know that the impact of what you see in the other person influences you more than the words spoken.

Clearly, first impressions count. Do you arrive for meetings and appointments appearing hot and harassed or cool and collected? When you begin to talk, do you mumble your words in a low whisper to the floor or gaze directly and confidently at your audience before speaking out loud and clear?

In terms of building rapport – *you* are the message. And you need your words, image, and speech all working in harmony. If you don't look confident – in other words, as if you believe in your message – people aren't going to listen to what you're saying.

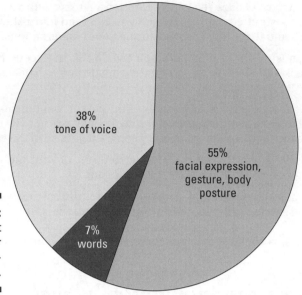

38%
tone of voice

55%
facial expression,
gesture, body
posture

7%
words

**Figure 1-1:**
The impact
of your
commun-
ication.

Rapport involves being able to see eye-to-eye with other people, connecting on their wavelength. A large percentage of the perception of your sincerity comes not from what you say but how you say it, and how you show an appreciation for the other person's thoughts and feelings.

When you have rapport with someone, you can each disagree with what the other says while still relating respectfully to each other. The important point is to acknowledge other people as the unique individuals that they are. For example, you may well have different political or religious views from your colleagues or clients, but you don't need to fall out about it. People prefer all sorts of different foods to eat for supper, and yet you manage to agree to differ with your family on that point.

Hold on to the fact that you simply differ from the person's opinion and that this difference is no reflection on that person. People are more than what they say, do, or believe.

## *Matching and mirroring*

When you're out and about in bars and restaurants (or even the staff cafeteria, if you're lucky enough to get meals at work), have you noticed how two people look when a rapport exists between them? Without hearing the details of the conversation, you can see that the interaction is like a dance: people naturally move in step with each other. A sense of unison informs their body language and the way they talk – elegantly dovetailing their movements and speech. NLP calls this situation matching and mirroring.

*Matching and mirroring* is when you take on someone else's style of behaviour and their skills, values, or beliefs in order to create rapport.

In contrast, think of a time when you've been the unwilling witness to an embarrassingly public argument between a couple, or a parent and child, in the street or supermarket: not quite a punch-up, but almost. Even with the volume turned off, you soon notice when people are totally out of sync with each other, just from their body posture and gestures. NLP calls this situation *mismatching*.

Matching and mirroring are ways of becoming highly tuned to how someone else is thinking and experiencing the world: it's a way of listening with your whole body. Simple mirroring happens naturally when you have rapport.

NLP suggests that you can also deliberately match and mirror someone to build rapport until it becomes natural. To do so, you need to match the following:

- ✔ Body postures and gestures
- ✔ Breathing rates
- ✔ Rhythm of movement and energy levels
- ✔ Voice tonality (how you sound) and speed of speech

Beware of the fine line between moving in rhythm with someone and mimicry. People instinctively know when you're making fun of them or being insincere. If you decide you want to check out mirroring for yourself, do so gradually in no-risk situations or with strangers you aren't going to see again. Don't be surprised though if it works and the strangers want to become your friends!

## *Pacing to lead other people successfully*

Building great relationships requires that you pace other people. As a metaphor, NLP compares pacing people with running alongside a train. If you try to jump straight on to a moving train, you're likely to fall off. In order to jump on a moving train, you need to gather speed by racing alongside it until you're moving at the same speed, before you can jump.

In order to lead people – to influence them with your point of view – remember to pace them first. This approach means really listening to them, fully acknowledging them, truly understanding where they're coming from, and being patient about it.

To build rapport NLP advises you to pace, pace, and pace again before you lead. Pacing is how NLP describes your flexibility to pick up and match, respectfully, other people's behaviours and vocabulary, and where you actively listen to the other person. Leading is when you attempt to get the other person to change by subtly taking that person in a new direction.

In business, companies that succeed in introducing major change programmes do so in measured steps, allowing employees to accept changes gradually. People are unwilling to be led to new ways of working until they have first been listened to and acknowledged (that is, paced). The most effective leaders are those who pace the reality of their people's experience first.

When you watch effective salespeople in action you can see how they master the art of pacing the customer and demonstrate genuine interest. (By effective, we're thinking of those who sell a genuine product with integrity rather than the shark approach.) They listen, listen, and listen some more about what the customer's needs are – what the person really wants – before trying to sell anything. People resent being sold to, but they love to be listened to and to talk about what's important to them. An antiques dealer friend has perfected this art over many years, gently guiding his customers through his genuine affection for the articles he sells from his own home, and sharing his expertise.

When Kate bought a family car several years ago, she went to six different showrooms where salespeople rushed to sell the virtues of their car without showing any interest in how it fitted in with her lifestyle. At the time she had a young family and went on long trips with the children in the car.

The salesperson who was successful displayed superb interpersonal skills and presented a practical, family estate car. He paced Kate well, listening carefully, treating her with respect (unlike those who assumed the buying decision would be made by her husband), and trusted her with the keys so she was able to take it for a spin immediately. As she drove along, he gently gathered the information he needed to match the right model of car to her buying criteria, realising she wasn't going to accept a hard direct sell. Within half an hour she bought the car and became a firm advocate of the brand and the garage.

## *Building rapport in virtual communication*

Twenty years ago, the Internet and email tools were confined to research labs and computer geeks. Regular business transactions involved cheques, letters, and faxes, mostly filed in hard copy: jumping in the car to visit suppliers and colleagues was all part of a day's work. Today, life's different. Of course, people still write and phone – the paperless office remains elusive – but the percentage of electronic transactions has shot through the roof. People are tweeting, blogging, and managing their lives online. If you lose your computer connection or have no access to email, you can feel lost and helpless very quickly.

Virtual teams who hold virtual meetings haven't just entered the workplace; you're as likely to join teleconferences for sharing information and speaking to social groups. People are comfortable with the virtual management of multi-cultural project teams that sit across global networks and work remotely thanks to technology – conference calls, email and videoconferencing. Expecting to get to manage our finances online or through an international support system is the norm, instead of seeing local bank staff or postal workers.

In this environment of reduced face-to-face contact, you lose the nuances of facial expressions, the body language, and the subtlety of getting to know the colleague at the next desk as you work closely with others. At its best, the virtual team spells freedom and flexibility of working practices, diversity, and a richness of skills: at its worst, it's lonely, isolated, and ineffective.

The challenge of building rapport through virtual working is now greater than ever. Little wonder that people are being recruited more for soft skills – the ability to influence and negotiate – than for technical competence.

Here are ten ways to develop rapport over the phone and in teleconferences:

- ✔ Make sure that all the locations are connected and can hear each other on the phone. Introduce and welcome people with a roll call.

- ✔ Work to a clear agenda. Set outcomes for the call and agree them with all participants.

- ✔ Check that you've had input from a mix of people. If necessary, encourage the quieter individuals to take part; say, for example, 'Mike, what are your thoughts on this?'

- ✔ Discourage small talk or separate chats at different sites: keep to one discussion, one meeting, one agenda.

- ✔ Speak more slowly and precisely than in face-to-face meetings. Remember you can't get clues from the body language.

- ✔ Listen for the style of language – check whether people have visual, auditory, or kinaesthetic preferences, and match your language style to theirs as we suggest in Book I Chapter 2.

- ✔ Get attention before making your point (otherwise the first part of the message gets lost). Begin with phrases along the lines of 'I have something I'd like to mention here . . . it's about. . .'

- ✔ Use people's names more than in face-to-face meetings. Address questions to people by name and thank them for their contribution by name.

- ✔ Visualise the person at the other end of the phone line as you listen to the conversation (you may even like to have a photo of the person in front of you).

- ✔ Summarise and check your understanding of points and decisions continually.

# Knowing How to Break Rapport and Why You May Want To

At times you may choose to *mismatch* people for a while in order to break rapport deliberately. Mismatching is the opposite of matching or mirroring (which we describe in the earlier section 'Matching and mirroring'). To mismatch someone, you aim to do something dissimilar to that person, such as dressing very differently, speaking in a different tone or at a different speed, adopting a different physical posture, or behaving quite differently from the other person.

We worked with a team of doctors who were suffering from an increase in patient workload due to the long-term sickness of one partner. In the initial assessments with them, we noticed how most of the meetings with patients were completed within the allotted one hour, and yet meetings with one partner took nearly twice as long. This particular doctor had a reputation for being especially kind and helpful with her patients; she topped the popularity bill in a patient survey. Indeed she is a great listener, and patients loved her approach. However, in order to get through her case load during normal surgery hours, she had to discover how to limit the time with each patient in a more disciplined way. She found a way to mismatch sensitively and get through her patient list.

## Discovering how to break rapport sensitively

Three particular changes to your behaviour can enable you to break rapport in the short term:

- ✔ **How you look and move physically:** You can move physically away from someone, break eye contact, or use a facial expression to communicate your message. Raised eyebrows say a lot. Turning your back is even more powerful, so beware of doing this action inadvertently!

- ✔ **How you sound:** You can change your voice intonation or volume: make it louder or softer, high or low, and remember the power of silence.

- ✔ **The words you say:** Remember that useful little phrase, 'no, thank you'. Sometimes it can be the hardest to say, so practise for when you need it. In multi-cultural settings, switching to your native language when you've been working in a common language is another clear way of saying, 'I need a break now.'

You're going to want to say 'thank you' and 'goodbye for now' plenty of times. Notice which situations are easier for you to handle and those that need some practice:

✔ **You're closing a deal:** Salespeople momentarily break connection with a customer at the point of signing a contract. They walk away and leave the customer to look at the paperwork alone instead of becoming connected to that final signing in the customer's eyes. This approach helps to maintain rapport in the long term if a buyer's remorse sets in.

✔ **You have enough information:** Maybe your brain has filled up for the moment and you're heading into sensory overload. You want time to think and digest what you've heard and come back for the next instalment later.

✔ **You see someone else you want to talk to:** Perhaps you're at a drinks party and become stuck with the ultimate bore and someone much more attractive is at the other side of the room.

✔ **You're tired:** All good things come to an end, and you need to know when the time has come for the party to end and head home.

✔ **You're busy:** At any one time you're going to experience a number of demands on your energy. Focus and hold on to your own outcome rather than satisfying someone else's.

✔ **You're getting into tricky subject areas:** Sex, politics, and religion are all good subjects to avoid in a business negotiation. They also cause overly lively dinner-party conversations where you may want to blow the whistle, call time out, and agree to differ when discussions get heated.

Discovering how to break rapport and end a conversation is a real skill, particularly if your best friend or mother wants to chat. Do it with consideration. Give clear feedback that you'd love to talk so long as it's at the right time of day, place, and length of time. You care about them as a person, and so try and arrange a time to talk that suits you when work's over for the day.

## *Grasping the power of the word 'but'*

Sometimes a tiny word can make a huge difference between your ability to keep rapport and break it. NLP pays attention to such details in the pattern of conversation and so offers some useful clues for you to influence communication. Work by Robert Dilts on sleight-of-mouth patterns has demonstrated the power of words to frame people's experience: NLP calls this *verbal reframing*. Even simple connective words such as 'and' or 'but' make listeners focus their attention in different ways. When you adopt the word 'but', people tend to remember what you say after it. With the word 'and', people tend to recall what you said before and after it. When you use the connection 'even though', the effect is to focus attention on the first statement, as in: '*It is snowing today* even though the weather men said it would be clear.' By changing the order of words in a sentence, you can change people's experience.

Be aware that when you make a comment to someone, that person may only notice part of what you say. Consider the following example: 'The company has returned £5 million profit this financial year, but we're closing the San Francisco operation.' If you phrase the news in this way, people may only remember what you said after the word 'but'. Now consider the following: 'The company has returned £5 million profit this financial year, and we're closing the San Francisco operation.' Phrased in this way, people may well remember what you said *before* and *after* the word 'and'.

Find out just how much difference little words can make in your daily communication with the 'Yes, but. . .' game for three or more players.

1. **Get your friends into a circle.**

2. **Round one starts with Person A offering 'a good idea'.** For example, 'It's a sunny day, how about we take the afternoon off and head out to the beach?'

3. **Person B replies 'Yes, but. . .', and offers another 'good idea' in return.** For example, 'Yes, but we have work to finish.'

4. **Person C and all the other players offer their ideas in turn, always starting with 'Yes, but. . .'.** For example, 'Yes, but we'll miss lunch.'

5. **Round two continues with Person A offering a good idea; it can be the same as in round one or a different idea.** For example, 'It's a sunny day, how about we take the afternoon off and head off to take a walk by the river?'

6. **Person B replies 'Yes, and. . .', and offers another 'good idea' in return.** For example, 'Yes, and we can have a picnic on the way.'

7. **Person C and all the other players offer their ideas in turn, always starting with 'Yes, and. . .'.** For example, 'Yes, and I'll check the footpath map.'

Notice the difference? In spite of the instruction to come up with a good idea, the use of the word 'but' seems to naturally lead the conversation to a negative place and detract from the original good idea. By contrast, the word 'and' builds one good idea upon another.

# Understanding Other Points of View

Successful people enjoy the flexibility of being able to see the world in different ways. They take multiple perspectives, enabling themselves to explore new ideas. NLP offers various techniques to help people build rapport in very challenging relationships, especially where some kind of emotional conflict is happening. These techniques are also used to explore new ways of building rapport, even in relationships that are only mildly troublesome or confusing.

# *Exploring perceptual positions*

One of the ways that NLP helps you to build rapport with others is by distinguishing at least three different points of view. NLP calls these *perceptual positions*. This approach is rather like looking at a building from all angles – coming in at the front entrance, moving round to the back door, and then looking down with a bird's eye view from a helicopter overhead:

- ✓ **The first position** is your own natural perspective, where you're fully aware of what you think and feel regardless of those around you. This position can be one of strength – when you're really clear about what you want and your own beliefs and values – but also one of incredible selfishness, until you consciously become aware of what other people want.

- ✓ **The second position** is about shifting into someone else's shoes – imagining what a situation looks like for them. You may already be really good at always considering the needs of others: for example, mothers rapidly develop this skill in caring for new offspring. You put someone else's view first.

- ✓ **The third position** involves taking an independent view, where you act as a detached observer noticing what's happening in the relationship. At its best, this position is one of maturity from where you appreciate a situation from both sides. Sometimes, however, it can mean that you're reluctant to engage fully in a situation – you merely sit on the fence.

Mastering all three perspectives puts you in a wise place that allows you to enjoy life more fully.

Get into the habit of mentally shifting your thinking into the second and third positions when you're in conversation.

# Chapter 2

# Seeing, Hearing, and Feeling Your Way to Better Communication

· · · · · · · · · · · · · · · · · · · · · · · · · · · · · · · · · · · · · · · · · · · · · · · ·

· · · · · · · · · · · · · · · · · · · · · · · · · · · · · · · · · · · · · · · · · · · · · · · ·

*O*ne of the upstanding elements of NLP is *sensory awareness*, the ability to understand how people make meaning of the world and create their own reality through their senses.

Just for a minute, imagine a special creature with highly developed personal antennae. Well, actually that's you. You come tumbling into the world as a new human baby ready to discover all about the surrounding world. Unless you're born with difficulties in some way, you arrive as a mini learning machine with eyes and ears, and a sense of smell, taste, and touch, plus that most distinctly human quality – the ability to experience an emotional connection with others.

As you develop, you form mental maps of the world and get into habits of thinking and behaving during childhood. You discover how to learn about the world in certain ways that work best for you, by looking at, touching, tasting, and smelling things, and hearing words.

NLP encourages you to become curious about how you form these mental maps. Understanding how you use your senses to represent your experience enables you to notice how your perceptions are shaped, thus influencing your ability to communicate with other people.

Ever heard the term 'use it or lose it'? Through your life experiences, you become conditioned, which can make you a bit lazy about learning. When you find that you're good at one way of doing things, that's the method you continue to use. So, assume that as a child you draw a picture, sing, or dance, and you enjoyed doing so and received positive reinforcement from a teacher. Clearly, you're most likely to concentrate more attention on that successful area, in which you show promise, to the detriment of other endeavours.

The same thing can happen with your sensory awareness. You get very good at using one method of thinking, processing, and indeed, sharing information in a particular context, until it becomes more natural to focus consciously on that one sense to the detriment of the others. You use your other senses, of course, but aren't consciously aware of them. For example, when you watch a film in vivid 3D, you may not be as aware of the soundtrack as the visual images in front of your eyes.

Leonardo da Vinci mused that the average human 'looks without seeing, listens without hearing, touches without feeling, eats without tasting, moves without physical awareness, inhales without awareness of odour or fragrance, and talks without thinking.'

What an invitation for personal improvement!

In this chapter, we invite you to try out some new ways of engaging with the world, fine-tuning your incredible senses, and noticing what a difference doing so makes to your life. You can look forward to fun and self-discovery along the way.

# Getting to Grips with the Senses

The NLP model describes the way that you experience the external world – which by the way is called real life – through your five senses, of sight, sound, touch, smell, and taste.

Notice what happens inside your head and body, for example, when we write: 'Think about a delicious meal you've enjoyed.' You may see a picture of the table spread with colourful dishes, hear the sound of knives and forks, a waiter telling you about today's specials, or a friend chatting in the kitchen. Perhaps you notice a warm and pleasant anticipation inside as the aromas of food drift your way, you hear the uncorking of a bottle of wine or feel a cool glass of water in your hand, and then you taste the first mouthful: a delicious, multi-sensory experience. And you're only thinking about it.

Until now you may not have thought about *how* you think (the process), only *what* you think about (the content). However, the quality of your thinking determines the quality of your experience. So the *how* is just as important, if not more important, than the *what*.

This section introduces you to some dimensions of your thought processes that you may never have considered before. As you open up your own awareness as to how you think and make sense of the world, some interesting things happen. You begin to notice that you can control how you think about a person or situation. You also realise that not everybody thinks like you do about even the most mundane, everyday events, which seem so clear and obvious to you. You may well decide that life can be more rewarding when you begin to think differently by paying attention to different senses.

## *Filtering reality*

As you experience reality, you selectively filter information from your environment in three broad ways, known in NLP as visual, auditory, and kinaesthetic, or VAK for short (or VAKOG if you include the olfactory and gustatory aspects):

- **Visual dimension:** Some people see clear *pictures* of the *sights.*

- **Auditory dimension:** Other people tune in to *hear* the *sounds.*

- **Kinaesthetic dimension:** A third group grasp the *emotional* aspects or *touch* – they experience a *body awareness* (for our purposes we include in this group the sense of smell (olfactory) and taste (gustatory)).

Think for a moment about the way you experience using this *For Dummies* book. Everybody who picks it up notices the look, sound, and feel in different ways. Take three individual readers. The first one chooses the book because of the friendly layout and amusing cartoons. The second likes the sound of what's said and discussed in the text. The third enjoys the feel or smell of the paper or has a gut feeling that this book is interesting to get hold of. Perhaps you experience the book as a mix of all three senses.

Check it out for yourself. As you use this book, start to notice how you prefer to take in information. Begin to check which pages make you sit up and pay attention. What works best for you? Are you most influenced by the words, the pictures, or the feel?

In everyday life, you naturally access all your VAK senses. However, in any particular context, one sense may dominate for you. As you become more sensitive to the three broad groupings of visual, auditory, and kinaesthetic at work and play, we promise that you're going to benefit from this exercise.

Imagine, for example, that you want to change a room in your home. You may have been thinking about this task in purely visual terms – what paint colours to choose or patterns for the fabrics. If you begin to engage in the auditory dimension, you may think about the sounds of objects in the room, those squeaky floorboards, the music or conversations you want to take place, and how to cut out the noise of the external traffic or let in the birdsong. Or what happens if you consider this space in terms of textures – the kinaesthetic dimension? Perhaps then you choose a plush, velvety carpet or rush matting. You may expose some brickwork or prefer a new smooth plaster finish on the walls, depending on the feel that appeals to you.

In the context of learning, when you know about VAK you can start to experiment with different ways of taking in information. Say, in the past you've studied a language by listening to CDs in your car. Perhaps now you may make faster progress by watching foreign films or plays instead, or by playing sport, sharing a meal, or learning a dance routine with native speakers of that language. When people discover how to develop their abilities to access pictures, words, and feelings, they often discover talents of which they were previously unaware.

## Hearing how people are thinking

Human beings naturally blend a rich and heady mix of the VAK dimensions, and yet people tend to have a preference for one modality over the others.

How do you decide whether you or others have a preference for the visual, auditory, or kinaesthetic dimension? To discover more about your primary modality, try out the following fun quiz on yourself and with friends and colleagues – we don't claim that the test's scientific, but it takes only a couple of minutes to do:

1. For each of the following statements, circle the option that best describes you.

    **1) I make important decisions based on:**

    a) Following my gut feelings

    b) The options that sound best

    c) What looks right to me

    **2) When I attend a meeting or presentation, I consider it successful when people have:**

    a) Illustrated the key points clearly

    b) Articulated a sound argument

    c) Grasped the real issues

    **3) People know when I'm having a good or bad day by:**

    a) The way I dress and look

    b) The thoughts and feelings I share

    c) The tone of my voice

**4) If I have a disagreement, I'm most influenced by:**

a) The sound of the other person's voice

b) How that person looks at me

c) Connecting with that person's feelings

**5) I'm very aware of:**

a) The sounds and noises around me

b) The touch of different clothes on my body

c) The colours and shapes in my surroundings

2. Copy the letters of your preferred statements onto the following grid.

| 1a K | 4a A |
| 1b A | 4b V |
| 1c V | 4c K |
| | |
| 2a V | 5a A |
| 2b A | 5b K |
| 2c K | 5c V |
| | |
| 3a V | |
| 3b K | |
| 3c A | |

3. Add up how many Vs, As, and Ks you got.

4. See how you did!

Did you get mainly V, A, or K, or was your total evenly mixed? Check your preferences below and see whether our explanations make any sense for you:

✔ **V – visual:** A visual preference may mean that you're able to see your way clearly, keep an eye on things, and take a long-term view. You may enjoy visual images, design, watching sport, and the symbols involved in studying physics, maths, or chemistry. You may need to live or work in an attractively designed environment.

✔ **A – auditory:** An auditory preference may mean that you're able to tune into new ideas, maintain harmonious relationships, and that you're happy to sound people out and listen to the opinions of others. You may enjoy music, drama, writing, speaking, and literature. You may be highly tuned into the sound levels in your environment.

> ✔ **K – kinaesthetic:** A kinaesthetic preference may mean that you're able to get to grips with new trends, keep a balance, and hold tight on to reality. You may enjoy contact sports, athletics, climbing, and working with materials – electronics, manufacturing, hairdressing, or construction. You may be sensitive to the textures and feel of your environment.

Within Britain and America, researchers estimate that visual is the dominant style for approximately 60 per cent of the population; which is hardly surprising given the daily bombardment of our visual senses.

Beware of labelling people as visuals, auditories, or kinaesthetics – a gross generalisation. Instead, think of people as having a preference or habitual behaviour in a particular context, rather than identities. Be mindful, too, that no one system is better or worse than any other. (You can't help but operate in all the different modes, even if this happens unconsciously.) The systems are simply different ways of taking in, processing, and outputting information, as you experience the world around you. After all, everyone's unique.

# Listening to the World of Words

The notion of sensory awareness isn't new, and dates back at least to the days of the Ancient Greek philosopher Aristotle, who talked about the senses in his book *On The Soul*. The nineteenth century psychologist William James was the first to discuss the primacy of modalities, which NLP refers to as the visual, auditory and kinaesthetic representational systems (check out the earlier section 'Getting to Grips with the Senses').

In the early days of NLP, the founders Richard Bandler and John Grinder, became fascinated by how people used language in different ways. The whole NLP notion of modalities came out of their seminars and study groups when they identified patterns of speech linked to the VAK senses. People represent their experience through their senses, and so NLP came to call the senses representational systems (or modalities).

The representational systems are much more than information channels coming in through the eyes, ears, or hands. The term refers to a whole complex system of activity that includes input, processing, storage, retrieval, and then output.

For example, you may take in information through your eyes – such as the image of a favourite person's face – and mentally process that information, store it for the future, retrieve the memory of it the next time you're feeling a bit blue, and say to yourself 'Never mind, things will look better tomorrow.' All of this happens outside of your conscious awareness.

## *Building rapport through words*

In our own training sessions, we often test out the method of representational systems and observe how easily and quickly groups with the same preferences can build rapport. Such people find that speaking to those who 'speak their language' is naturally easier.

So what can you do when you feel that you're speaking a 'different' language and the conversation is harder? Begin by listening more carefully and identifying other people's language preference. Then you're in a great position to adjust your language pattern so that it aligns with those around you and therefore build rapport through the similarity of your language pattern.

Table 2-1 lists some of the sensory-specific words and phrasesthat you hear people say. You can start to build up your own lists and notice which words you say or write frequently. When you have difficulty getting through to certain people, check whether you're stuck in a rut with your own language.

| Table 2-1 | VAK Words and Phrases | |
|---|---|---|
| *Visual* | *Auditory* | *Kinaesthetic* |
| Bright, blank, clear, colour, dim, focus, graphics, illuminate, insight, luminous, perspective, vision | Argue, ask, deaf, discuss, loud, harmony, melody, outspoken, question, resonate, say, shout, shrill, sing, tell, tone, utter, vocal, yell | Cold, bounce, exciting, feel, firm, flow, grasp, movement, pushy, solid, snap, touch, trample, weight |
| It looks like. . . | It sounds like. . . | It feels like. . . |
| A glimpse of reality | So you say | We reshaped the work |
| We looked after our interests | I heard it from his own lips | Moving through |
| This is a new way of seeing the world | Who's calling the tune? | It hit home |
| Now look here | Clear as a bell | Get a feel for it |
| This is clear cut | Important to ask me | Get to grips with |
| Sight for sore eyes | Word for word | Pain in the neck |
| Show me what you mean | We're on the same wavelength | Solid as a rock |
| Tunnel vision | Tune into this | Take it one step at a time |
| Appears as if. . . | Music to my ears | Driving an organisation |
| What a bright day | That strikes a chord | The pressure's on |

A few olfactory and gustatory words also exist, such as the following: fragrant, fresh, juicy, odour, pungent, salty, smell, smoky, sour, spicy, sweet, and whiff.

Many words in your vocabulary don't have any link to the senses. These words are non-sensory, and because they're 'neutral' you neither connect nor disconnect with somebody else's modality. Neutral words include the following: analyse, answer, ask, choose, communicate, complex, educate, experience, favourite, imagine, learn, question, remember, transform, think, understand, use, and wonder.

When people's thoughts and words are highly logical, conceptual, and devoid of sensory language, NLP calls this style *digital processing*. Documents from insurance companies are typical of digital language, as in the following example: 'The obligation to provide this information continues up to the time that there is a completed contract of insurance. Failure to do so entitles the Underwriters, if they so wish, to avoid the contract of insurance from inception and so enables them to repudiate liability.'

## Bringing on the translators

Two people can sometimes struggle to communicate, despite sharing similar viewpoints, because they speak with different language styles. One may use an auditory style, for example, and another a visual or kinaesthetic style. To be an effective communicator, you need to be able to do two things: know your own preferred style or modality and also practise using other ones.

Have you ever heard a dispute that goes something like the following one between a manager and a team member in the office? To demonstrate the different language styles, we show the predicates (the sensory-specific words and expressions) in italics:

Manager: (Betty) 'I can't *see* your point of *view* about your appraisal'(visual).

Employee: (Bill) 'Well, can we *talk* about it further?'(auditory).

Betty: 'It's perfectly *clear* to me – just *black and white*'(visual).

Bill: 'If you would discuss it, it may be more *harmonious* around here' (auditory).

Betty: 'Just have a closer *look*. I'm sure you'll get a better *perspective*' (visual).

Bill: 'You never *listen*, do you? End of *conversation*' (auditory).

Betty, the manager, stays with visual language, and the employee, Bill, is stuck in auditory mode: they're disconnected and not making progress.

Here's how a third person – maybe Bob from human resources or another department – can help to shift the dispute:

1. **Bob sums up the situation in *visual* mode to Betty and *auditory* mode to Bill.** The conversation goes something like:

   'So, Betty, it looks like you have a *clear picture* of the situation (visual). And Bill, you've still got some important questions to *talk through* (auditory).' (Heads nod in agreement.)

2. **Then Bob shifts into the third system (kinaesthetic), which is neutral ground for both arguing parties.**

   'You both want to *get this moving* and *off the agenda*. So how about we all *kick around the stumbling blocks* for an hour in my office, *reshape* the problem, and finally *put it to bed*.'

# *Acknowledging the Importance of the Eyes*

Body language offers wonderful clues to people's preferred representational systems. How they breathe, stand, move, their tone of voice, and tempo of speaking all tend to vary according to visual, auditory, and kinaesthetic styles. In particular, in the early days of NLP, Bandler and Grinder observed that people move their eyes in systematic directions depending on which modality they're accessing. These movements are called *eye-accessing cues*.

Therefore, when people move their eyes in response to a question, you can pretty much guess whether they're accessing pictures, sounds, or feelings. Why is noticing these movements helpful, you may wonder? The answer is that you have a great chance of knowing, even without them uttering a word, which system they're going to use and how you can talk to them in a way that makes them respond positively to you. Table 2-2 outlines what eye movements are associated with which modality.

| Table 2-2 | | Accessing Cues | |
|---|---|---|---|
| *Pattern* | *Eyes move to the subject's* | *What's happening inside* | *Sample of language* |
| **Visual** constructed | Top right | Seeing new or different images | Think of an elephant covered in pink icing |
| **Visual** remembered | Top left | Seeing images seen before | Think of your partner's face |
| **Visual** | Blank stare ahead | Seeing either new or old images | See what's important |
| **Auditory** constructed | Centre right | Hearing new or different sounds | Listen to the sound of your name backwards |
| **Auditory** remembered | Centre left | Remembering sounds heard before | Hear your own doorbell ring |
| **Auditory** internal dialogue | Bottom left | Talking to oneself | Ask yourself what you want |
| **Kinaesthetic** | Bottom right | Feelings, emotions, sense of touch | Notice the temperature of your toes |

Figure 2-1 shows the kind of processing that most people do when they move their eyes in a particular direction. A small percentage of the population, including about half of all left-handers, are reversed – their eye movements are the mirror image of those shown.

The illustration in Figure 2-1 is drawn as if you're looking at someone else's face and shows how you see their eyes move. So, for example, if they're moving up and to your right into the *visual remembered* position, your own eyes would be shifting up and to your left if you're trying it out on yourself in a mirror.

By developing your sensory awareness – spotting those little details – you can become more attuned to how people may be thinking at different times. When you know this information, you can select your words so that they listen to you.

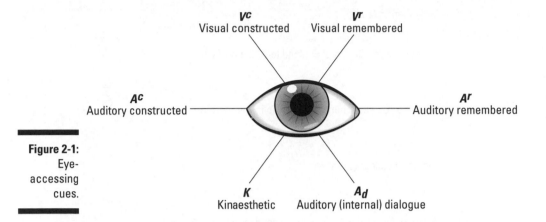

**Figure 2-1:**
Eye-
accessing
cues.

In the following exercise, your aim is to notice how people's eyes move so that you can calibrate them and decide whether they're thinking in pictures, sounds, or feelings. Find a willing friend, and then use the instructions, questions, and diagrams on the Eye Movements Game sheet in Figure 2-2. Each statement on this game sheet is phrased to engage with the senses – in the past or future. Follow these steps:

1. **Get your friend to think about something neutral so that you can check what their face looks like in a neutral state.**

    Washing up or sock-sorting may be a pretty safe and mundane subject to suggest.

2. **State one instruction or question at a time from the Eye Movements Game sheet. As you do so, pay full attention to their eyes.**

3. **Pencil in arrows on Figure 2-2 to record the direction in which your friend's eyes move.**

    Your arrow marks should match up with the positions on the eye-accessing cues (shown in the earlier Figure 2-1, in the 'Acknowledging the Importance of the Eyes' section), so that they move to top, centre, or lower positions, and to the left or the right. When you've recorded your friend's eye movements, see whether their eyes go to the position that you expect based on the eye-accessing cue pattern outlined in Table 2-2 (in the earlier section 'Acknowledging the Importance of the Eyes').

*Eye Movements Game*

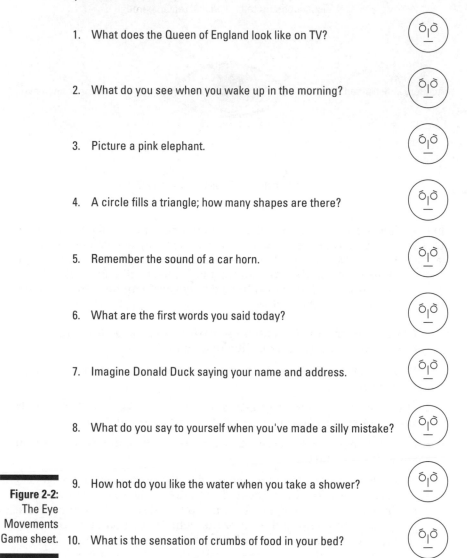

1. What does the Queen of England look like on TV?

2. What do you see when you wake up in the morning?

3. Picture a pink elephant.

4. A circle fills a triangle; how many shapes are there?

5. Remember the sound of a car horn.

6. What are the first words you said today?

7. Imagine Donald Duck saying your name and address.

8. What do you say to yourself when you've made a silly mistake?

**Figure 2-2:**
The Eye
Movements
Game sheet.

9. How hot do you like the water when you take a shower?

10. What is the sensation of crumbs of food in your bed?

# Making the VAK System Work for You

When you become aware of the VAK dimensions (which we describe in the earlier section 'Filtering reality'), life becomes more interesting. Here are some ideas on how you can pull this technique out of your new toolkit and use it to your advantage:

✓ **Influencing a business meeting, training session, or presentation.** Remember that when you speak to a room full of people they all have a preference for how they take in information and you don't know what that is. Unfortunately, people don't have a label on their foreheads to inform you about what they want to know and how they want to receive it – give me the picture, tell me the words, share your feelings about this subject. So, you need to ensure that you connect with each and every person in the room by presenting your ideas with a variety of media. Vary your presenting style and aids to help the visuals see the information with pictures, the auditories to hear it loud and clear, and the kinaesthetics to experience it with feeling.

✓ **Making home projects fun for all.** Recognise that each family member has a different way of thinking about a major project. Perhaps you want to extend the house, redecorate a room, or redesign the garden. Not everybody wants to spend hours talking it through, with discussions that stretch late into the night. Your partner may want to pore over the drawings, whereas your children are motivated by the chance to get stuck in and get their hands dirty with paint or earth.

✓ **Developing your goals so that they're more real for yourself.** When you set goals in your personal or professional life, they come alive if you use all your senses effectively. Think of what the goals look, sound, and feel like when you've achieved them and at every step along the way. NLPers get proficient at imagining all the fine details of their future experiences – you may hear the phrase 'putting up a movie screen' to describe how people can create their own dream. Therefore, if you want to motivate someone (or yourself) to push out of their comfort zones, help them to explore what things may look like when the task is complete and the hard work done.

✓ **Helping children to learn better.** Thank goodness education has changed dramatically since we were at school, and teachers now recognise that pupils learn in different ways. As parents and/or teachers, you need to support children to understand how they learn at their best – and appreciate that the method may be different to the way you were taught or prefer to learn. Visual learners benefit from pictures, wall displays, and diagrams. Auditory learners need to hear what they're learning – through discussions, lectures, and music. Kinaesthetic learners benefit from practical sessions and role playing: they prefer a 'hands-on' approach. Teachers of groups of pupils need to provide a multi-sensory approach that caters for all styles. Children may be labelled as 'slow' when in fact the dominant teaching style doesn't fit with their preferred way of learning. All these principles apply to adult learners, too.

✓ **Increasing the impact of the written word.** When you put pen to paper and words to screen – from a job description, to customer proposal, charity letter, product advertisement, or article for your local community newsletter – you need to broaden your vocabulary to cover all the representational systems. To appeal to every reader, select words that include all three dimensions.

✔ **Connecting with clients and colleagues on the phone.** Nowadays more and more business happens on the phone and through email rather than face-to-face. You may never get to meet some of your clients or colleagues. Keep a pad by the phone and make a note of the kind of language they use – can you hear visual, auditory, or kinaesthetic language? As you listen, and then reply, phrase your sentences to match their preference.

# Chapter 3

# Pushing the Communication Buttons

*W*hen you're engaged in a dialogue, for what percentage of the communication do you think you're responsible? Did you say 50 per cent? After all, two people are involved in a dialogue, and so logically each of you has half the responsibility to make and elicit responses, right?

If you're familiar with the following NLP presuppositions, you'd reply that you're 100 per cent responsible:

✔ The meaning of the communication is the response it elicits.

✔ If what you're doing isn't working, do something different.

✔ The person with the most flexibility within a system influences the system.

This chapter shows you how to take total responsibility for any communication in which you're involved. We provide tools to help you become more aware of how the people with whom you're communicating are transforming what they receive through their senses: what they hear you say and what they see and feel. When you understand their thinking process, you have the means to adapt your words, deeds, and actions to get the response you want.

What you intend to communicate isn't necessarily the message that the recipient understands.

# Introducing the NLP Communication Model

The NLP communication model is based on cognitive psychology and was developed by Richard Bandler and John Grinder.

According to the NLP communication model, when people behave in a certain way (their *external behaviour*), a chain reaction is set up within you (your *internal response*), which in turn causes you to respond in some way (your *external behaviour*), which then creates a chain reaction within the other person (their *internal response*), and the cycle continues. Figure 3-1 shows this chain reaction.

The internal response is made up of an *internal process* (consisting of self-talk, pictures, and sounds) and an *internal state* (the feelings that are experienced).

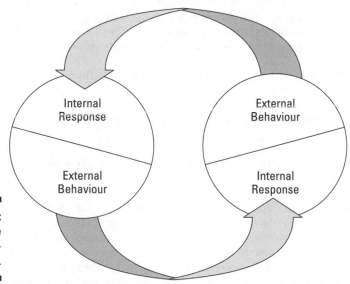

**Figure 3-1:**
The circle of communication.

The following sections present two scenarios, showing the NLP communication model in practice.

# Scenario 1

For some people, today has been a lovely, hot summer's day. But the air-conditioning in the office wasn't working and Dan had an awful day. He gets in the car and with a sigh of relief puts on the air-conditioning to battle his weary way home. His son, Drew, had promised he would cut the grass. Dan's looking forward to sitting out on a tidy, freshly mown lawn with a glass of chilled lager. As he drives up he notices the grass is *uncut*.

Dan storms into the house, so caught up in his emotions that all he can feel is bitter resentment welling up. He starts ranting at Drew, who retreats into his sullen teenage shell muttering about the broken lawnmower, a statement that Dan doesn't hear. Finally, Drew yells 'Cut the damn grass yourself,' as he storms off. Neither person is willing to communicate any more and both slide down the spiral of shouting, slammed doors, and finally silence.

In this example, when Dan explodes, the uncut grass is the trigger for setting up an internal state of anger, resentment, and frustration in him. The internal process may be a monologue such as, 'He promised. I knew I shouldn't expect anything from him. We always give him the best and he always lets us down.' This monologue is accompanied with pictures from the past when Drew didn't live up to Dan's expectations.

Dan's external behaviour of ranting at Drew, in that particular tone of voice or with that look on his face, provokes an internal state in Drew. Drew may experience feelings of anger, resentment, and frustration very similar to those felt by Dan. He may make pictures of previous altercations with his father and know that he isn't going to be heard, just like all those other times. Drew's external behaviour of adopting his usual, sulking manner and muttering may then further inflame his father . . . and so the process continues.

# Scenario 2

Now imagine scenario 2. Dan drives up and sees the uncut grass. Instead of exploding, he recognises his internal state and how that can affect his behaviour. So he takes a deep breath and asks Drew why the grass hasn't been cut. Drew, expecting recriminations, gets defensive as he explains that the mower broke down. From past experience, Dan realises that Drew is likely to retreat into his shell and so he offers to show Drew how to mend the mower.

He chills out with a glass of lager before helping Drew carry out the repairs. Drew mows the lawn before the family sits down to a companionable meal.

In this scenario the father changes his internal process and makes a conscious effort to remember when he was a teenager himself, in need of guidance and a firm hand. He decides on the result he wants from his interaction with the teenager and, having disengaged his emotions, is able to proceed down the path that keeps communication channels open in order to achieve the desired outcome: to get Drew to mow the lawn.

This scenario illustrates how, by putting the NLP presuppositions into practice, Dan is able to achieve his outcome of having Drew mow the lawn. (For example, the presupposition that 'the person with the most flexibility in a system is the winner'.) The male bonding is an added bonus. The response he gets from Drew when the teenager starts to become defensive is obviously not the one Dan wants. Dan has the flexibility to recognise Drew's behaviour patterns and modify his own responses in order to get his outcome, thereby controlling the system.

# Understanding the Process of Communication

John Grinder and Richard Bandler discovered that master communicators have three sets of capabilities:

- They know what they want.
- They're very good at noticing the responses they get.
- They have the flexibility to modify their behaviour until they get what they want.

Simon taught Kate some valuable lessons about dealing with people. Simon always manages to keep his cool and usually achieves his outcome even in the most difficult situations. He does so by distancing himself from his emotions and keeping his focus on the result he wants. He also attempts to understand the other person's point of view in order to arrive at a win–win result.

Everybody processes information differently and so reacts to situations differently. Wouldn't it be really useful to understand how another person's brain works? Read on for some clues.

Book I

Communicating
Effectively

## *Processing pieces of information*

Professor George Miller conducted research into how many bits of data people can process at any given time. He came to the conclusion that a person can hold seven, plus or minus two, bits of information; that is, nine bits if they're feeling good or have an interest in a subject and as few as five if they're feeling a bit low or aren't particularly interested in what they're trying to remember. If you're not into multi-tasking, you may have trouble coping with more than one!

Every second you're hit by millions of bits of information. If you tried to deal with this vast array of input, you'd go mad. In order to preserve your sanity, you filter the incoming information before your brain processes it and makes internal representations from this information.

In addition, all your different experiences and filters influence the processes by which you create these internal representations of the external events you perceive through your senses.

The way in which the external stimuli of the world are converted into internal representations in your brain involves three fundamental processes: deletions, distortions, and generalisations. The following sections give you a brief overview of these processes.

### *Deletion*

Deletions happen when you pay attention to some information coming in through your senses but are completely oblivious to other stimuli. Think of a nutty professor, so caught up in his work that he leaves home wearing his bedroom slippers.

Kate's story about her mother-in-law illustrates nicely how your unconscious mind makes deletions. Her mother-in-law used to travel by bus to Kennington in London to work for The Children's Society, a British charity. Normally she put her rubbish out before returning for her handbag and briefcase. One morning, however, she was running a little late and grabbed all three bags together – handbag, briefcase, and rubbish bag. Only when she found herself sitting on the bus, thinking that it was really whiffy that morning, did she realise that she'd taken her rubbish bag on to the bus with her!

### *Distortion*

A distortion occurs when you misinterpret information coming in through your senses and create meaning from a situation that's not necessarily true: for example, when a wife complains that her husband 'didn't help me and so that means he doesn't care'. You may see what you want to see to reinforce your viewpoint instead of what's in front of your eyes. Distortion can also involve deletion of information.

A cynic may say that being in love is a form of distortion, where you go all starry-eyed behind your rose-tinted glasses (to mix metaphors), completely oblivious to the faults of your 'perfect' partner. Perhaps you're so keen to find your true love that you ignore aspects of the person's behaviour that can ruin the relationship in the long term.

Romilla was driving down a dual carriageway late one night, when it started to rain: a very fine, misty drizzle. She could see a white, ethereal figure in the distance, by the side of the road. With a pounding heart, the conversation with herself went something as follows:

'Oh my goodness, it's a ghost.'

'Don't be stupid, there's no such thing as ghosts.'

'You know you're being idiotic. It isn't a ghost.'

'Yes it is. What if it's a ghost?'

'But it isn't.'

'Yes it is.'

And so on. To her extreme relief, but also in another sense bitter disappointment, the figure turned out to be a tramp in white plastic sheeting looking really spooky in the misty rain.

This anecdote involves distorting an image, but you can also distort the meaning of another person's actions.

Jacqui had a male boss, Tom, who because of his cultural background, found dealing with women at work very difficult, and was very abrupt in his interactions with female employees. Jacqui misunderstood Tom's behaviour and decided Tom didn't like her; she distorted the facts. The situation may have spiralled out of control if Jacqui hadn't confided her misgivings to another colleague. When Jacqui understood that Tom's upbringing was responsible for his behaviour, she no longer reacted emotionally. As a result her behaviour changed to reflect her confidence in herself, which resulted in an improvement in the way Tom treated her.

### Generalisation

You make a generalisation when you transfer the conclusions you came to from one experience to other similar situations or occurrences. Imagine that you gave a very good speech that was well received. Afterwards, you may form a generalisation that you're good at public speaking.

Generalisations can be useful; they help you to build a cognitive map of the world. If you didn't generalise, for example, you'd need to relearn the alphabet and how to put together individual letters every time you read a book. Generalisations allow you to build on what you already know, without reinventing the wheel.

They can be limiting, though. The beliefs you hold about your world are generalisations and you delete and distort to the best of your ability to hold them in place. So, in other words, your generalisations can become restrictive because they can make you less likely to accept or trust actions and events that don't fit with your preconceived notions.

This tendency can in turn lead to self-fulfilling prophecies. Confidence and self-doubt are two sides of a coin. When you feel confident about doing something, the chances are that you're usually successful because you expect a positive result. Even on the odd occasion when things don't work out quite as you'd wanted, you move on. If you're riddled with self doubt, however, and convinced something isn't going to work out or no one's going to talk to you when you go to an event, a very high chance exists that your experience goes on to reflect your beliefs. Do you experience a slight disappointment when someone or a situation fails to meet your worst expectations? And do you feel a little triumphant when you're duly disappointed? Sometimes, having your negative generalisation confirmed is more satisfying than a situation going better than expected. How self-defeating is that!

## Getting to grips with individual responses

When different people are exposed to the same external stimuli, they don't remember the event, and react to it, in the same way. The difference is because all people delete, distort, and generalise differently based on their own meta programs, values, beliefs, attitudes, memories, and decisions: we discuss these aspects in the next few sections.

### Meta programs

*Meta programs* are filters. They are the way in which you reveal your patterns of behaviour through your language. For instance, someone who's inclined to take charge and get things done (meaning that they display more proactive tendencies) may be heard to say, 'Don't give me excuses, just give me results.' Whereas someone who's likely to take their time to think things over before acting (a reactive tendency) is likely to be heard saying, 'Don't rush, think about all the factors and make sure that the results are right.'

If these leanings are abused and combined with a tendency to generalise, you may end up pigeonholing people: for example, 'you mean Tom, that geeky introvert?' (distortion) or 'yeah, typical salesman, always in your face' (generalisation). Remember, however, that people can change their behaviour patterns, depending on the environment and situation in which they find themselves.

Table 3-1 contains a little taster about introvert/extrovert tendencies and how they affect your filtration process. Both of these tendencies are basic meta programs. Although your meta programs are there in the background, you tend to have a proclivity to focus on certain aspects of particular meta programs, depending on different situations. For example, think of social interactions and how a gregarious person behaves as opposed to someone who's more solitary.

**Table 3-1     Comparison of Introvert and Extrovert Meta Programs**

| *Introverts* | *Extroverts* |
| --- | --- |
| Want to be alone to recharge their batteries | Need to have people around when in need of rest and relaxation |
| Have a few friends with whom they have a deep connection | Have a lot of friends with whom they connect at a more superficial level |
| May take a real or imagined slight to heart | May not notice the slight and if they do may attribute it to the other person having a bad day |
| Are interested in a few topics, which they know in great detail | Know about a lot of things, but not in as much detail as an introvert |
| Tend to be more solitary | Tend to be more gregarious |

An introvert isn't superior to an extrovert and an extrovert is as good as an introvert.

A useful way to think of how meta programs work is to imagine a sliding scale with a tendency towards one aspect or another at a certain time and in a particular setting (as illustrated in Figure 3-2).

At work, where you're confident and enjoy the environment, you may find yourself behaving like an extrovert. This tendency allows your antennae to pick up a broader band of information and has you noticing contacts and opportunities that help you in your job. When meeting your colleagues in a social setting, however, you may feel very uncomfortable and slide along the scale to display more introverted tendencies. As a result of your discomfort, you may delete subtle messages that would be very obvious to you in your familiar office environment.

Figure 3-2:
Meta
programs
work along
a sliding
scale.

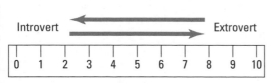

 Extroverts can really annoy their more introverted friends and acquaintances. So, extroverts, please take care to tone things down when you meet people who aren't as responsive as you are, and be careful not to encroach on their body space!

 An extrovert NLP nerd (who plays at NLPing with everyone and everything, all the time) danced a poor introvert that they met at a party all around the room, invading the body space of the introvert who kept moving away only to have their body space encroached upon again.

Some people with an extrovert preference may have a very strong bond with their pets and seek out the company of their four-legged friends instead of other humans when recharging!

### Values

Your values are also filters that are unconscious, although less so than the meta programs that we describe in the preceding section. You learn your values, almost by osmosis, from your parents and close family up to about the age of seven, and then from your peers and friends. Values are what motivate you to do something, but they can also work as brakes, stopping you from achieving your desires. They are the factors that are important to you and let you assess whether something that you're considering doing, or have done, is good or bad. They influence how you delete, distort, or generalise data from incoming stimuli.

Values are arranged in a hierarchy, with the most important at the top of the ladder. Examples of values are health, wealth, happiness, honesty, friendships, job satisfaction, and so on.

 James worked for a charity helping to organise an education programme in Africa. He had a young family and loved his work. Although he was as poor as a church mouse, the charity took care of all his day-to-day living needs. His values hierarchy was satisfied by his work and looked something like the following:

1. Happiness

2. Enriching lives

3. Being with my family

4. Freedom

5. Variety

6. Support network

These values were obtained by asking James 'What's important to you about your work?'

Because James's values were being satisfied he didn't pay attention (deletion) to any job advertisements that would offer him greater monetary reward, thinking they'd detract from the other aspects of his work that he valued. He admits that he bought into the distortion that all (generalisation) Western interests in Africa were aimed at exploiting the local people. Although, later, he did realise that in some cases this view was simply an excuse by some people not to take responsibility for their own lives.

Values are very contextual, which means that some of your values apply only in certain areas of your life and that their importance in the hierarchy also changes depending on which aspect of your life you're examining. James's values were relevant only in the area of his work.

During a deep relaxation, James remembered, when he was about six, his parents having a discussion about their landlord increasing the rent on their house. He recalled how worried his parents sounded. He realised that he'd formed a belief then that rich people were greedy and bad.

## Beliefs

Beliefs are really powerful; they can propel you to the heights of success or drag you to the depths of failure because, to paraphrase Henry Ford, 'whether you believe you can or whether you believe you can't . . . you're right'.

Your beliefs are formed in all kinds of unconscious ways. You learn that you're gifted from your parents, that you can't draw from your teacher, that you must support your friends from your peers, and so on. In some cases, as with the teacher, when you're told that you can't draw, you delete any opportunities you may have to find out how to draw. After all, one teacher told you that you can't draw.

Beliefs can start off like a 'splinter in your mind' (remember Morpheus talking to Neo in the film *The Matrix*?) and, as it irritates and niggles, you begin to find instances that validate the splinter and over a period of time you develop a concrete belief.

Choose your beliefs very carefully because they have a tendency to become self-fulfilling prophecies!

### Attitudes

Your attitude is your way of thinking about a topic or perhaps a group of people: it tells others how you're feeling or your state of mind about someone or something. Your attitude is a filter of which you're very conscious and is formed by a collection of values, beliefs, and opinions around a particular subject. Changing an attitude is challenging because your conscious mind is actively involved in building and holding on to attitudes.

You can get some awareness of other people's attitudes from what they say and how they behave. At work, someone who goes the extra mile and has a positive frame of mind is considered to have a good attitude to their work, whereas a dodger or malingerer may be seen as having a bad attitude to work.

Because your attitude is based on your values and beliefs, it affects your abilities by making you behave in certain ways. Someone with a positive attitude may always expect to get a positive outcome, and by demonstrating a pleasant and helpful demeanour, that person influences others to behave in a similar vein.

### Memories

Your memories determine what you anticipate and how you behave and communicate with other people. Memories from your past can affect your present and your future. The problem occurs when your memories don't stay in the order in which they were recorded. When memories get jumbled up, they bring along all the emotions of when they actually happened. By this we mean that your current experience invokes old memories and you find yourself responding to memories and emotions of the past rather than to the experience you're currently having.

### Decisions

Your decisions are closely linked to your memories and affect all areas of your life. This ability is especially important as regards decisions that limit the options you feel you have in life – what NLP calls *limiting decisions*. Examples of limiting decisions include: 'I can't spell', 'money is the root of all evil, so to be good I mustn't be rich', and 'if I go on a diet I won't be able to enjoy my food'.

Many of your limiting decisions are made unconsciously, some when you are very young, and may be forgotten. As you grow and develop, your values may change and you need to recognise and reassess any decisions that may be hindering you.

In the earlier section 'Values', we tell you about James who worked in Africa for several years. Well, when he returned to England, he was even poorer than a church mouse, because he now had to provide for his family, without the help of the charity for whom he'd worked. On thinking about their circumstances, he drew up a new hierarchical set of values as follows:

- ✔ Happiness
- ✔ Enriching lives
- ✔ Being with my family
- ✔ Security
- ✔ Financial freedom
- ✔ Variety

When he decided that he needed financial freedom, he realised that the decision he'd made (rich people = greedy = bad) when he was little was hampering him from providing for his family. He thought about how he may be able to earn good money, help people, and stay close to his family. Today, James is extremely happy, very wealthy, and enriching lives. How? He topped up his MSc in Business Management with a PhD in Psychology. He runs workshops around the world, travelling with his wife.

# Giving Effective Communication a Try

As the earlier sections in this chapter show, much of the way you think and behave is unconscious; your values, beliefs, memories, and so on, form and impact upon your responses. Fortunately, you don't have to be at the mercy of your unconscious mind.

With awareness, you can take control of how you communicate with people, which is a liberating and empowering thought in itself! Just keep these pointers in mind:

- ✔ **Engage your brain before your mouth:** Think of the result you want when you're interacting with people, and speak and behave with that desired outcome in mind.

- ✔ **Tread softly:** Having this knowledge gives you power, and of course power can corrupt. On the other hand, power can also free you from fear. Power allows you to work with generosity and kindness, so that with the knowledge of someone else's model of the world you can come to a win–win conclusion.

# Chapter 4

# Exploring Body Language

· · · · · · · · · · · · · · · · · · · · · · · · · · · · · · · · · · · · · · · · · · · · ·

*In This Chapter*

▶ Finding out how body language speaks for you

▶ Gesturing for a purpose

▶ Understanding what you're communicating

· · · · · · · · · · · · · · · · · · · · · · · · · · · · · · · · · · · · · · · · · · · · ·

**T**he science of body language is a fairly recent study, dating primarily from around 60 years ago, although body language itself is, of course, as old as humans. Psychologists, zoologists and social anthropologists have conducted detailed research into the components of body language – part of the larger family known as non-verbal behaviour.

If you're quiet for a moment and take the time to pay attention to body language movements and expressions that silently communicate messages of their own, you can cue in on gestures that convey a feeling and transmit a thought. If you pay close attention, you can identify gestures that you automatically associate with another person, which tell you who she is. In addition, you may notice other types of gestures that reveal a person's inner state at that moment.

In this chapter you discover how to interpret non-verbal language, exploring the gestures and actions that reveal thoughts, attitudes and emotions. Also, you have a quick glance at some of the research into this unspoken language and recognise similarities and differences throughout the world. In addition, you find out how you can use gestures to enhance your relationships and improve your communication.

# Discovering How Body Language Conveys Messages

When cave-dwellers discovered how to decipher grunts and to create words to convey their message, their lives became a lot more complex. Before verbal communication, they relied on their bodies to communicate. Their simple brains informed their faces, torsos and limbs. They instinctively knew that fear, surprise, love, hunger and annoyance were different attitudes requiring different gestures. Emotions were less complex then, and so were the gestures.

Speech is a relatively new introduction to the communication process and is mainly used to convey information, including facts and data. Body language, on the other hand, has been around forever. Without relying on the spoken word for confirmation, the body's movements convey feelings, attitudes and emotions. Like it or not, your body language, or non-verbal behaviour, says more about you, your attitudes, moods and emotions, than you may want to reveal.

According to research conducted by Professor Albert Mehrabian of the University of California, Los Angeles, 55 per cent of the emotional message in face-to-face communication results from body language. You only have to experience any of the following gestures or expressions to know how true the expression is, 'Actions speak louder than words':

- Someone pointing her finger at you
- A warm embrace
- A finger wagging in your face
- A child's pout
- A lover's frown
- A parent's look of worry
- An exuberant smile
- Your hand placed over your heart

## Projecting an image in the first 30 seconds

You can tell within the first seven seconds of meeting someone how she feels about herself by the expression on her face and the way she moves her body. Whether she knows it or not, she's transmitting messages through her gestures and actions.

You walk into a room of strangers and from their stance, movements and expressions you receive messages about their feelings, moods, attitudes and emotions. Look at the teenage girl standing in the corner. From her slouching shoulders, her lowered head and the way her hands fidget over her stomach, you can tell that this little wallflower is lacking in self-confidence.

Another young woman in this room of strangers is standing in a group of contemporaries. Her eyes twinkle, she throws her head back as she laughs, her hands and arms move freely and openly and her feet are planted firmly beneath her, hip width apart. This woman is projecting an image of self-confidence and joie de vivre that draws people to her.

How you position your head, shoulders, torso, arms, hands, legs and feet, and how your eyes, mouth, fingers and toes move, tell an observer more about your state of being, including your attitude, emotions, thoughts and feelings, than any words you can say.

## *Transmitting messages unconsciously*

Although you're capable of choosing gestures and actions to convey a particular message, your body also sends out signals without your conscious awareness. Dilated or contracted eye pupils and the unconscious movements of your hands and feet are examples of signals that reveal an inner emotion that the person signalling may prefer to conceal. For example, if you notice that the pupils of someone's eyes are dilated, and you know that she's not under the influence of drugs, you'd be correct in assuming that whatever she's looking at is giving her pleasure. If the pupils are contracted the opposite is true.

Be careful though when ascribing feelings and attitudes based on body language as individual signals can be easily overlooked or misidentified if they're taken out of their social context, or if they're not identified as part of a cluster of gestures involving other parts of the body.

At times in life you may want to conceal your thoughts and feelings, so you behave in a way that you believe hides what's going on inside. And yet wouldn't you know it, out pops a slight giveaway gesture, often invisible to the untrained eye, sending a signal that all's not what it appears. Just because these micro gestures and expressions are fleeting doesn't mean that they're not powerful.

In the 1970s, Paul Ekman and W V Friesen developed the Facial Action Coding System (FACS) to measure, describe and interpret facial behaviours. This instrument is designed to measure even the slightest facial muscle contractions and determine what category or categories each facial action fits into. It can detect what the naked eye can't and is used by law enforcement agencies, film animators and researches of human behaviour.

Arthur is the chief executive of a global telecoms company. Highly accomplished and rewarded for his successes, he still harbours some self-doubt and insecurity. This uncertainty is particularly evident when he's making formal presentations. He holds a pad of paper in front of himself, as if it were a protective shield. When he's unsure of the word he wants to use, he quickly and briefly rubs the skin under his nose with his index finger. When he moves from one point to the next in his presentation, he quickly taps his forehead with his left index finger as if to remind himself that he's about to move to the next point. Seeing himself on DVD he recognised how these meaningless gestures were revealing his lack of security, and how uncomfortable he feels in front of a large audience. By visualising himself presenting at his best and modelling specific behaviours of presenters who Arthur thinks are excellent, he developed ways of eliminating his unconscious negative gestures.

## Substituting behaviour for the spoken word

Sometimes a gesture is more effective in conveying a message than any words you can use. Signals expressing love and support, pleasure and pain, fear, loathing and disappointment are clear to decipher and require few, if any, words for clarification. Approval, complicity or insults are commonly communicated without a sound passing between lips. By frowning, smiling, or turning your back on another person, your gestures need no words to clarify their meaning.

When words aren't enough or the word mustn't be spoken out loud, you gesture to convey your meaning. Some examples are:

- Putting your index finger in front of your mouth while at the same time pursing your lips is a common signal for silence.
- Putting your hand up sharply with your fingers held tightly together and your palm facing forward means 'Stop!'.
- Winking at another person hints at a little secret between the two of you.

When Libby, the well loved and highly successful Artistic Director of the Oregon Shakespeare Festival was honoured for her years of service, she felt proud and humbled. Looking around the room filled with colleagues, friends and major financial contributors, Libby placed her right hand over her heart as she thanked them all for their years of support, belief and dedication. Around the room, many people's eyes were moist and they held their fingers to their lips to prevent themselves from crying out loud . Libby's hand to her heart reflected her deeply felt appreciation.

## Gesturing to illustrate what you're saying

When you describe an object, you frequently use gestures to illustrate what the object is like. Your listener finds it easier to understand what you're saying when you let your body create a picture of the object rather than relying on words alone. If you're describing a round object, like a ball, for example, you may hold your hands in front of yourself with your fingers arched upward and your thumbs pointing down. Describing a square building you may draw vertical and horizontal lines with a flat hand, cutting through the space like a knife. If you're telling someone about a turbulent ride on a boat or plane, your arms and hands may beat up and down in rhythmic fashion. Describing a large object may entail holding your arms out wide. If you're illustrating a small point you may hold your fingers close together. The point is that gesturing is a useful means of conveying visual information .

Because some people take in information more effectively by seeing what's being described, illustrating your message through gestures helps create a clear picture for them. To help a blind person experience what you're describing, hold her hands in the appropriate position.

Lotsie, my daughter's God mother, is a world explorer and frequently speaks to students about her adventures. As Lotsie was describing her climb up Mount Kilimanjaro she acted out those moments when the air felt so thin that she was hardly able to breathe and when she struggled to put one foot in front of the other. She mimed leaning on her walking stick, bending over with the weight of her equipment, gasping for air and pausing between shuffled steps as she put one foot in front of the other. Her gestures painted the combined picture of a woman who was both fit and exhausted.

## Physically supporting the spoken word

Gesturing can add emphasis to your voice, clarify your meaning and give impact to your message. Whether your point requires a gentle approach, or a firm telling off, your body's instinct is to reflect and move in harmony with the emotion.

In addition to reinforcing your message, hand signals especially reflect your desire for your message to be taken seriously. Watch a well-schooled politician standing at the podium. See how their hands move in a precise, controlled manner . No wasted gestures, just those specific ones that paint a clear picture and accurately convey the message.

When you're making a formal presentation, use illustrative gestures to help your audience remember the points you're making.

During the introduction to your presentation, as you establish the points to be covered, list them separately on your fingers. You may hold your fingers up in front of you, or touch them individually on one hand with a finger from your other hand as you say the point. (Note: Most British and American people begin counting with their index finger. Many Europeans begin counting with their thumb.) When talking about point one in your presentation, point to the first finger, or gesture to it; when you reach point two, point or gesture to your second finger, and so on.

Experienced lawyers, celebrities and anyone in the public arena are also adept at emphasising their messages through considered movements and gestures. By carefully timing, focusing and controlling their actions, moving in synchronicity with their spoken words and responding appropriately to the atmosphere in their environment, they court and woo the people they want, and dismiss others with aplomb.

Observe movie stars and celebrities at red carpet events as well as politicians at global conferences and notice what messages they're conveying through their body language.

When you're giving bad news and want to soften the blow, adapt your body language to reflect empathy. Move close to the person you're comforting and tilt your body towards hers . You may even touch her on the hand or arm or place your arm around her shoulder.

## Revealing thoughts, attitudes and beliefs

You don't have to tell people how you're feeling for them to know. Look at Rodin's sculpture of *The Thinker*. There can be no doubt about that person's state of mind: thoughtful, serious and contemplative. Equally so, a child throwing a tantrum with stomping feet, clenched fists and a screwed up face is letting you know that she's not happy.

Think of your body as if it were a movie screen. The information to be projected is inside you and your body is the vehicle onto which the information is displayed. Whether you're anxious, excited, happy or sad, your body shows the world what's going on inside. Here are some examples:

> ✔ People who feel threatened or unsure of themselves touch themselves as a means of self-comfort or self-restraint. Gestures, such as rubbing their foreheads, crossing their arms and holding or rubbing their fingers in front of their mouths, provide comfort and protection.

✔ People who perform specific gestures reserved for religious rituals reveal their beliefs and values. Upon entering a Catholic church, the congregation dip their fingers into holy water and cross themselves. Before entering the home of many Jewish people, you may touch the mezuzah by the front door. Muslims bow in prayer facing east. By performing these gestures, people are demonstrating their respect for the culture, its traditions and values.

✔ People in a state of elation often breathe in deeply and gesture outwards with expanded arms. Pictures of winning sportspeople frequently show them in the open position with their arms extended, their heads thrown back and their mouths and eyes opened in ecstasy.

✔ Footballers who miss the penalty kick and city traders who get their numbers wrong often walk dejectedly with their heads down and their hands clasped behind their necks. The hand position is a comforting gesture and the head facing downwards shows that the individual's upset.

✔ People in despair, or feeling down and depressed, reveal their thoughts and attitudes by the slouch in their step, their drooping heads and their downward cast eyes. Positive people, on the other hand, reveal their thoughts and attitudes with an upright stance, a bounce in their step and eyes that appear lively and engaged.

✔ Not every bent head signals depression. Sometimes it just means that you're reflecting, thinking or absorbing information. If you're demonstrating the behaviour of someone who's thinking hard, your head most likely rests in your hand or on your fingertips, like Rodin's *The Thinker*. You can find out more about body language and mental states in *Persuasion and Influence For Dummies* (Wiley).

At Peter and Louise's wedding anniversary celebrations, Peter stood up to toast his wife and children. As he raised his glass to the family members, his feelings for them were clear. By the way he slightly leaned forward toward his son, Sebastian, you were able to sense the great warmth and tenderness he held for him. As he turned to his daughter Olivia, to express his amazement at her joyous spirit, he slightly lifted his head and tossed it back. When he turned to gaze at his wife Louise, his eyes softened and a gentle smile played at the sides of his mouth. He stood upright, held his arm forward and raised his glass high in a display of love and appreciation for his family.

Holding your hands over or near your heart, is an expression of how much something means to you.

## Noticing your own body language

My husband suggested that people may only demonstrate body language when someone else is around to see and respond to it. I found that an interesting thought and retired to my office to consider the implications on my own. As I sat at my desk reflecting on what he said, I noticed I was leaning back in my chair with my head tilted upwards, one arm folded over my body supporting the elbow of my other arm. My chin was resting lightly on my thumb as my index finger gently stroked my cheek. I couldn't help but think of the saying about falling trees in the forest making noise if no one's around to hear it.

# Key Types of Gestures

Humans are blessed with the ability to create a wide variety of gestures and expressions from the top of the head to the tips of the toes. Gestures can show intention, such as leaning forward just before rising out of a chair; as well as showing no intention, such as crossing arms and legs. Some gestures belong to you, because you've become identifiable by them. Some gestures are displacement gestures: you perform them for no reason other than to shift some energy. Some gestures are specific to local customs and some are universal gestures that everyone does.

## Unintentional gestures

Unintentional gestures are behaviours that inhibit your ability to act. They're like the fright part in the 'fight or flight' syndrome.

The unintentional gestures imply that you have no intention of moving from where you are. They hold you back, won't let you go and your body says that you're not budging. And no amount of outside influence to get you to move is going to succeed.

Examples of unintentional gestures are:

- ✔ Folded arms
- ✔ Lips pressed together
- ✔ A hand or finger in front of the mouth
- ✔ Crossed legs

These actions all keep you in place. You can't walk when your legs are crossed. You can't speak with your hand in front of your mouth. Crossed arms say that you're holding back.

Standing or sitting with your legs crossed is no position to take if you want to get somewhere quickly. The scissor stance is a prime example of a gesture that keeps you in your place. One leg is crossed over the other, rendering you immobile. When someone adopts this position you know she's staying put.

Because the scissor stance contains no sign of impatience, the gesture can come across as submissive. The person has no forward movement in her body as does the body of a person about to take action. The person who acts is usually considered to be dominant. Therefore, the person who stays put is usually considered to be submissive.

## Signature gestures: Gestures that define who you are

A signature gesture is one that you become known by, a common gesture that you perform in a particular way. Some examples are:

- Twirling your hair around your finger
- Thumb sucking
- Eyebrow patting
- Throat stroking

These gestures give us clues into the person's personality.

Signature gestures set you apart from all others. Think Napoleon Bonaparte and his mighty stance – on the canvas, not the battlefield. Standing with his hand tucked into his waistcoat, he looks the picture of pride and authority. Who knows if he ever really stood in that position. The artist created the image and we believe the artist.

One of Diana, Princess of Wales's most vividly remembered signature gesture's was the lowered head with her eyes looking upward from underneath her eyebrows. This look is commonly referred to as the Shy Di look.

Sophie is a delightful woman in her early twenties. Pretty, vivacious and polite, Sophie's signature gesture is thumb-sucking. I first noticed this gesture when she spent several days at our home. Curled up on the couch, Sophie slipped her right thumb into her mouth, lightly rubbing her nose with her index finger. Claire, a woman in her forties, also sucks her thumb. Her variation on this gesture is a small piece of soft fabric that she rubs in the palm of her cupped hand. Both women are indicating a need for nurturing and succour by this gesture.

Martyn is a quiet, thoughtful, focused man. His boss, Annie, is highly energetic with a mind that skips and leaps from one project to the next. Frequently, Annie asks Martyn to do one task, only to interrupt his concentration by asking him to do something else, often unrelated. When Martyn pats his eyebrows with the tips of his fingers Annie knows that the time's come for her to back off and let him get on with what he has to do.

Some examples of signature gestures can be seen in a person's:

- ✔ Posture
- ✔ Smile
- ✔ Hand clap
- ✔ Pointing finger
- ✔ Clothes tugging

Some sportspeople perform specific actions as an anchor to get them grounded and focus their energy. Before serving, the tennis player Rafael Nadal, tugs at the back of his shorts. This gesture is so closely associated with this gifted sportsman that other players have been known to mock him on the courts and in the dressing rooms by performing it in front of him.

By recognising signature gestures you can tell what kind of person you're dealing with. Certain gestures, like clapping the hands together once, show a mind that's organised. The hair twirling gesture indicates that the person may be a day dreamer. When you successfully read the signs you can figure out how best to interact with the person.

If you want to be easily identified and remembered you can create your own signature gesture. Victoria Beckham's sexily defiant pout has become her signature gesture, as has Hugh Grant's foppish head toss.

## Fake gestures: Pulling the wool

Fake gestures are designed to camouflage, conceal and fool. They deliberately point you in one direction to make you believe something that isn't so. Fake gestures pretend to be something when they're actually something else.

You're able to tell a fake gesture from a real one because some of the real gesture's parts are missing.

Some gestures that are commonly faked are:

- ✔ Smiling
- ✔ Frowning

✔ Sighing

✔ Crying

✔ Holding your body as if in pain

Anna is a highly motivated recently qualified lawyer in a large London firm. She knows that, in part, her success depends on her ability to get on well with clients and colleagues. One day her supervising partner invited her to attend a client meeting and to put together the remaining briefs that a previous trainee had begun and hadn't had time to finish. Anna, already overloaded with work, stayed at the office until well past midnight. In spite of little sleep and over an hour's commute that morning, she arrived, shortly before the meeting's 8 a.m. start looking smart and ready to go. At one point during the session the client remarked that some information seemed to be missing. The partner shot Anna a glance of annoyance before covering up his feelings with the hearty remark, 'Well, she's new on the job. We'll let her get away with it just this once.' To cover her fury and shame, Anna put on what she calls her 'smiley face', a big toothy grin, and offered to find the missing materials. Anna's teeth were clenched, and her eyes didn't crinkle (a sign of a sincere smile). She was tired, hurt and humiliated and anyone paying attention would have seen she was giving a fake grin.

You can't spot a true emotion by one gesture or expression alone. Look for all the signs. Fake gestures are meant to deceive.

## Micro gestures: A little gesture means a lot

Teeny weeny, so small that they sometimes take highly specialised equipment to see them, micro gestures are flashes of emotion that flicker across your face faster than a hummingbird, revealing feelings that you may prefer to keep to yourself. These gestures aren't ones that you purposely choose. Micro gestures give a brief hint of what's going on inside. You choose to smile, wave and rise from a chair. You don't choose to have a micro gesture flicker across your face. No one is immune to them.

A list of the more common micro gestures include:

✔ Movement around the mouth

✔ Tension at the eyes

✔ Flaring of the nose

Mark and Liz met at a party. They were immediately attracted to one another. They stood easily in the other's intimate space. Their facial gestures were controlled, but the occasional flicker around Liz's eyes and hint of a smile around Mark's mouth gave the impression that a frisson existed between the two. Friends and family members recognised the signs and frequently ask about how the relationship between Liz and Mark is progressing.

## *Displacement gestures*

When you're feeling conflicting emotions, you may engage in gestures that have no relation to your immediate goals. These behaviours are mostly self-directed and serve to release excess energy and gain a feeling of comfort, even if only temporary. Drumming fingers, flicking feet, going for a glass of water when you're not even thirsty – these are the behaviours of someone who's looking to burn some pent up energy, or at least, refocus it. Called displacement activities, they're a conduit for excess energy that's looking for a place to go.

Some examples of displacement gestures are:

- Fiddling with objects
- Tugging at your earlobe
- Straightening your clothes
- Stroking your chin
- Running your fingers through your hair
- Eating
- Smoking

Some smokers light up a cigarette, take a puff or two and then put it out or leave it in the ashtray barely smoked. These people may not actually want the cigarette, but need a gesture to take their mind off something else.

I knew the time had come to stop smoking when I had three cigarettes on the go in a four-room apartment. I was working in New York, living on my own, making barely enough to pay my monthly bills and wondering what I was doing with my life. I was frustrated and feeling anxious. One morning, while I was in the kitchen making coffee, I lit up a cigarette. When the phone rang, I answered it in the living room, leaving the cigarette burning in the kitchen. While speaking on the phone to my soon-to-be ex-husband I lit another cigarette which, after a drag or two, I stubbed out in the ashtray on my desk. I went to the bathroom to get ready for work. Here, too, I lit a cigarette, which I occasionally puffed on as I applied my make-up. In the course of less than ten minutes I had lit three cigarettes, none of which I was interested in smoking and all of which were props for displacing nervous anxiety.

Rather than stating their feelings verbally, people demonstrating displacement activities are letting their gestures reveal their emotion.

Prince Charles is noted for fiddling with his cufflinks. He crosses his arm over his body and touches his cufflinks in a protective and reassuring gesture.

The Prince is displacing his anxiety by making contact with his cufflinks. On honeymoon with Diana, the late Princess of Wales, Charles is purported to have worn cufflinks given to him by his true love and now wife, the Duchess of Cornwall. No wonder that his young bride was upset when she discovered this wedding gift of gold cufflinks with entwined Cs. Especially when she saw him fondling them.

Words convey information. Gestures reveal attitude. If someone's feeling anxious she may fiddle with her keys, twist the ring on her finger or pull at her clothes to compensate for her anxiety.

If you see someone under pressure and being scrutinised, look to see what her hands are doing. If she's gently rubbing her stomach, you may assume that she's feeling the pressure and is calming and comforting himself, the way you comfort a baby or sick child.

## Universal gestures

Universal gestures, such as blushing, smiling and the wide-eyed expression of fear, mean the same thing across world cultures. These gestures stem from human biological make-up, which is why you can recognise them spanning the globe.

### Smiling

From the sands of Iraq to the shores of Malibu, humans are born with the ability to smile. From the earliest days in an infant's life, her facial muscles can form the upward turn of the lips and the crinkling around the outer edges of the eyes to create a recognisable smile.

Sure, each person may have her own unique way of smiling. The point remains that anyone with working facial muscles who's conveying a positive message lifts her lips in pleasure

When you see the sides of the lips turned up and the eyes crinkling at their outer edges, count on that smile being genuine in showing pleasure.

The Japanese smile in embarrassment as well as pleasure. Young women giggle behind their hands. Don't expect the Japanese to respond to your humour with a raucous, belly laugh.

### Blushing

If you blush, your embarrassment's showing. The blood flows to your chest and cheeks,and you want to drop down and hide. Whether you're in Thailand, Afghanistan, the United Kingdom or another country across the globe, when you see someone blush you know they're being consumed with embarrassment.

To control the blushing take several slow, deep breaths from your diaphragm to steady your nerves and control the blood flow. For more about how breathing can help control nervous energy, see *Persuasion and Influence For Dummies (Wiley).*

My Aunt MarNell lives in Dallas, Texas and is the perfect combination of cowgirl and southern belle. When Dad, MarNell's only sibling and adored brother, raised his glass in special toast to her at a recent family reunion, her cheeks flushed like a shy young girl's.

### Crying

Crying is a universal sign of sadness. One of a healthy infant's first actions is to let out a walloping great cry when she first enters this world, having been torn from the comfort and safety of her mother's womb. No one had to teach her how to cry, she was born with the innate ability to express her upset.

If you feel tears well up in your eyes and you want to stop them from flowing down your face, fix your gaze at that point where the ceiling and wall meet. This action focuses your attention onto a meaningless and unrelated subject and frees your mind of upsetting thoughts. You can also press your tongue firmly against the roof of your mouth as you remind yourself that in a few moments what's troubling you will be over. If you feel the salt of your tears about to splash down your face you could acknowledge what's happening and move on. Sometimes accepting what's about to occur is enough to make it stop.

### Shrugging

Shrugging is a gesture that people use when they need to protect themselves in some way. The full shrug is when your head dips into your rising shoulders, the sides of your mouth turn down, your palms turn upwards and you raise your eyebrows.

The shrug can indicate:

- Indifference
- Disdain
- Lack of knowledge
- Embarrassment

To know which attitude is being expressed, you have to look to see what the other body parts are doing.

## Television versus radio

In the early 1960s there was little knowledge of body language. Yet, John F Kennedy intuitively knew how to use it. Prior to their first televised debate in 1960 JKF and Richard Nixon posed for a media photo call. Kennedy placed himself to the right of Nixon and shook Nixon's hand. The resulting photograph showed Kennedy applying the upper-hand position causing Nixon to appear diminished in stature. This was one of Kennedy's favourite gestures. The Nixon-Kennedy election debate which followed this photo call was a further testimonial to the power of body language. Most of the Americans who only heard the debate on the radio believed that Nixon out-performed Kennedy. However, the majority of those who saw the debate on television believed Kennedy was the victor. Kennedy knew how to use his body to manipulate public perception and did it with grace, charm and unconscious expertise.

Robin was invited to speak at an industry event. She made the mistake of sitting at the panel table before making her presentation, rather than joining the other invited speakers afterwards. When the host introduced Robin, his comments were so glowing that Robin felt embarrassed. She'd set herself up for all to see and, rather than squaring her shoulders and lifting her head with pride, she dropped her head and lifted her shoulders in a humble shrug, as if seeking protection. What saved her from looking like a complete idiot was the sparkle in Robin's eye and the bounce in her step when she took to the stage.

# Getting the Most Out of Body Language

Successful people know how to use their bodies for greatest effect. They stand tall, with their chests opened like a well loved book, smiles on their faces and when they move, they move with purpose. Their moderate and carefully chosen gestures reflect their sense of what they want to project and how they want to be perceived.

Successful people also know where to position themselves in relation to other people. They know that if they stand too close they can be perceived as overwhelming or threatening. They know that if they stand too far away they can be perceived as distant. They know how to anticipate movements – theirs and another's – to avoid (or not) bumping into someone else, depending on their motives and their relationship with the other person. They know that the gestures they use and how they use them have infinitely more of an impact than the words they say.

The people who demonstrate respect for others, who think before acting and who develop the necessary skills to create their desired outcomes, are the ones who feel good about themselves. You can tell by the way they move. Their gestures and actions have purpose and meaning.

If you want to succeed in your career or relationship, using effective body language is part of your foundation. Once you're aware of the impact – of what works and what doesn't – you can move and gesture with confidence, knowing that you and your message are perceived the way you want them to be.

## Becoming spatially aware

Understanding how to position yourself in relation to other people is a skill that some people just don't seem to have. Someone is either so up close and personal to you that you can smell their morning coffee breath, or they stand just that bit away that makes them appear uninterested, unengaged or slightly removed. Others, however, know just how to get it right. They understand and respect the different territories and parameters that people have around themselves, and being with them is comfortable.

You have a personal, individual space bubble that you stand, sit and move around in, and it expands and contracts depending on circumstances. Although you may have grown up in the country and have need for a lot of space around you, people who grew up in cities need less.

The study of *proxemics*, how people use and relate to the space around them to communicate, was pioneered by Edward T Hall, an American anthropologist in the 1960s. His findings revealed the different amounts of personal space that people feel they need depending on their social situation. Robert Sommer, an American psychologist, coined the term 'personal space' in 1969. He defined it as the 'comfortable separation zone' people like to have around them.

## Anticipating movements

Movement can be equated to dance. It's more than just the gestures themselves, it's about the timing of them as well. Anticipating an action and registering that it's about to happen before it does, gives you information that others may not grasp.

The American anthropologist, Ray Birdwhistell, pioneered *kinesics*, the study of body movement and verbal communication. Replaying, in slow motion, films of people in conversation Birdwhistell was able to analyse people's actions, gestures and behaviours.

Consider these examples:

- Spotting the subtle gestures a person makes in preparation for rising from a seated position previews what's about to happen.

- Recognising when a person's about to strike out in anger gives you enough time to protect yourself and others.

- Feeling your dancing partner shift his weight indicates that a change in movement is about to occur.

Anticipating a movement can save your life. It can keep you from harm. It may also bring you great happiness, like a lover's first kiss which, had you missed the movement, you may have lost. By anticipating gestures, you gain the upper hand in knowing how to respond before the action is completed.

## Creating rapport through reflecting gestures

When you talk about establishing rapport you're talking about accepting and connecting with other people and treating one another with respect. Rapport assures that your communications are effective and lead to results that satisfy both parties' needs.

You have many ways of creating rapport, through touch, word choice and eye contact. Another way is to reflect another person's movements. By mirroring and matching the other person's gestures and behaviours you're demonstrating that you know what it feels, sounds and looks like to be in her shoes. If connecting with others and behaving respectfully is important to you, mirroring and matching their behaviour helps you achieve that goal.

## Becoming who you want to be

How you present yourself, how you move and gesture, how you stand, sit and walk all play their part in creating the image you present and in determining people's perceptions. By adopting a cluster of postures, positions and gestures known for the attitudes they effect, you can create any attitude and make it your own. Positive body language looks and feels strong, engaged and vibrant. Negative body language communicates weaknesses, dullness and a disconnectedness. Sometimes you want to project one image over another. Whatever image you want to project – moving your head, face, torso and limbs with confidence, control and commitment, or creating desired effects with the flick of your wrist or a furrow of your brow – being perceived and responded to in the way you want helps you to achieve your desired results.

Actors know the technique of creating a character from both within and without. Working from the outside in, actors consider how their character sounds, moves and gestures. They ask themselves:

✔ How would the character walk, sit and stand? Would the character move like a gazelle, lumber along like a sleepy bear or stagger in a zigzag pattern like someone who's had one drink too many? Is the posture upright and erect or slouched and limp?

✔ What gestures would be required for conveying a particular mood or emotion? Slow, deliberate and carefully timed gestures create a different impression from those that are quick, spontaneous and unfocused.

By adopting the appropriate behaviours, the actor creates an attitude, emotion or feeling that the audience recognises and understands. It's the same for the lay person. By acting in a particular manner you can create an image and become that character. As Cary Grant said, 'I pretended to be someone I wanted to be until I finally became that person.'

The behaviour you adopt and the gestures that you make leave an impression. How you're perceived – dumb or sultry, champion of the people or chairman of the board – is up to you. The key is to adopt/exhibit/display the right gestures. To do that, keep these points in mind:

✔ **Make sure that your gestures reinforce the impression you want to make:** For example, the higher up the command chain, the more contained the gesture (which is why you never see the chief executive run down the hall).

✔ **You can modify your gestures to suit the situation:** When Charlotte, my PA and I, are working in the office and no one else is around, our body language is loose and relaxed. When a client or another colleague arrives, the body language changes. We both become more formal, the degree of formality depending on how the other person behaves.

Decide what attitude you want to project. If you struggle to project that attitude, model the gestures of a person who you think successfully emulates the image you want to portray.

I recently experienced my first tax audit, which had me in a bit of a state. Tom, my financial director , and my accountant Rashmi, tell me how much and where to sign and I do it. I trust them and Tom's been teaching me about the finances. Tom arrived at the office, wearing a suit and tie, for the meeting with the VAT lady. Our office is normally quite informal and Tom's change of clothes told me that we were to leave out the jokes. Although I was dressed informally I adjusted my behaviour to mirror Tom's, which was thoughtful, serious and open. We wanted to create the impression that not only does the business have a strong creative base, but also that its financial backbone is firmly in place.

## Reading the signs and responding appropriately

Being able to read other's signals is a stepping stone to effective communication. By observing how people move and gesture, you get a glimpse into their emotions. You can tell, for example, the intensity of someone's feelings by the way she stands. You can see what kind of mood a person's in by the speed of her gestures. By having an insight into someone's feelings you're forewarned and forearmed for whatever may happen next.

Say that you're at a party with a friend. You notice her sitting dejectedly by herself. Seeing her in this position, with her head hanging down and her arms wrapped around her body, you know that she needs a little tender loving care. You gently put your hand on her arm and she begins to feel a bit better.

Later at the party you observe that some of the younger guests – who have had more than their fair share of drink – are beginning to go from jovial to rowdy. You notice the lads pushing and shoving one another, which is your sign to leave.

By reading body language effectively, you can tell when to stay and when to go.

Edith unexpectedly popped around to have a chat with her neighbours, Tim and Sarah, who were in the middle of a busy morning and had little time to stop for a gossip. Although Tim smiled warmly at Edith, he stood by the entrance without inviting her in. His arms were crossed over his chest, his legs were held closely together and rhythmically he rocked backwards and forwards on his toes. Edith sensed from Tim's closed position that now was not a convenient time for them to speak, and she quickly left.

# Appreciating Cultural Differences

How much more exciting, interesting and stimulating it is to live in a world with difference and diversity, rather than one in which everything's the same. Even though you appreciate the differences between cultures and nationalities, you may sometimes find yourself confused, scared or even repelled by displays of body language that are very different from what you're used to.

Because people in one culture act differently than people in another doesn't suggest that one is right and the other is wrong. When it comes to cultural differences, the operative verbs are 'to respect' and 'to value'. Valuing behaviours that vary so much from those that you grew up with, and were taught to believe in, can be hard. To create respectful, positive relationships between different cultures and nationalities, you need to expand the way you think and work, from an attitude of respect. That doesn't mean having to agree with all the behaviours you see in your travels. Instead, accept that differences do exist, and then decide how best to respond.

 Different nationalities and cultures use their bodies differently. An acceptable gesture in one country may land you in jail in another. Before visiting or moving to another country, do your homework and find out what's suitable and what's not. Before making a gesture, think whether it's appropriate and acceptable before doing so.

# Chapter 5

# Demonstrating Confidence in the Workplace

........................................................

## In This Chapter

▶ Finding your confident work self

▶ Asserting yourself

▶ Dealing with everyday work situations

▶ Coping confidently with your boss

▶ Promoting yourself

▶ Tackling big changes with confidence

........................................................

The most confident version of you will be immediately recognisable in the workplace. You will be at ease with yourself and others, straightforward and generous in your dealings with your fellow workers, cooperative and pleasant to work with, ready to laugh at the odd joke, and *very* effective in getting your job done.

So, now it's time to consider how you are in your place of work, and to apply your confidence in your job. This chapter helps you explore your relation to your work and the impact this has on your confidence. You find many ways to increase your confidence and be able to use this to your advantage both in your work and in other parts of your life.

## Developing Confidence in Your Professional Life

When you're introduced to someone new, and they ask you the age-old question, 'And what do you do?' how do you answer? So much of your sense of who you are is bound up in your work that the description you offer is a powerful indicator of the meaning that work has in your life and the degree of success you can expect.

Your workplace gives you a constant bombardment of influences, both positive and negative, from the physical environment, the people in it, the tempo and nature of the work, and how closely you identify with what is getting done.

Keep in mind that it is your own responsibility to maintain an attitude that helps you to get everything you need from your work: including a confident sense of pride and well being from doing your job well.

## Realising that your job isn't you

Although you may protest that your job doesn't bear any direct relation to who you really are, what is important to you, or what you want to achieve in your life, it nonetheless exerts a powerful influence on your sense of identity. It is possible to hold down a job that seems at odds with your true sense of self in the world, but this is unusual and takes a lot of confidence and self-belief.

If you hate your job, or your employer, this can become a drag on your deeper beliefs about yourself and your value in the world. It is very difficult to take action with confidence from this position, because you have so little affinity with who you are being when you are working and where this is leading you.

But your *work* isn't the same thing as your *job*. Your work can be a much fuller expression of your values and beliefs about yourself than any single job can be, even a good job that suits you. Your work in the world can be something very close to your spirit, something almost sacred. But to find your true work you have to be prepared to think beyond the job you are doing.

The place to start is with you. This can help you to think out your true sense of who you are, perhaps at a deeper level than you have ever thought about it before. As you increase your self-knowledge, you're in a far better position to decide upon the work you want to do in the world. Then, as you make the changes you find necessary, you become far more confident and better able to live powerfully a life that is balanced and fulfilling.

## Defining your professional identity

If you're a lawyer, or a medical doctor, then in the absence of any other information about you, people can reasonably accurately assume a whole lot of things about your ethics, values, social standing, and so on. This is because your identity in society is defined by the work you do. For members of the professions, the magic is in the job title; it defines them to themselves and to others.

**Book I**

**Communicating Effectively**

If you're not a member of a recognised profession, you don't have all the accoutrements of a professional identity. But it's still essential for you to recognise that you do a professional job that people need and value. In order to feel and act with total confidence, you must get clear about the contribution of the work you do and how it fits into the wider value chain in your organisation and beyond into society.

Try drawing a diagram of your job in its broadest context; like Figure 5-1 filling in the details. No job operates independently of everything else, so how does your role at work fit into the greater scheme of things in your business? Does your company make something, or provide a service that enables others to do their work? Perhaps you help to maintain the home or work environment that enables others to do their work. All of these things are essential for the economy to be successful.

Include and think about everything you could take pride in around your work. Do you work alone or in a team? (Both need special qualities.) Do you supervise others, do you work remotely from the main office, do you work in the home providing care for your family to allow them to engage fully in the world? All of these are essential for a healthy society.

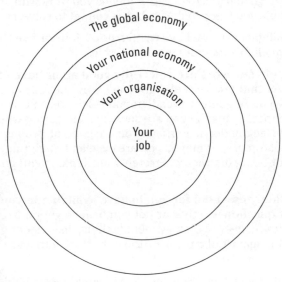

**Figure 5-1:**
The broader
context of
your work.

## *Uncovering what you want to do*

Of course, it is unlikely that you can step straight into the work of your dreams. You need to build up your skills and experience, make the contacts, gain the profile, and earn the opportunity to make the break. This is quite normal; but if you have no sense of these things, if you cannot see your way ever to getting the work you want, then you have a problem that you need to deal with.

At its highest, your *work* in the world is an expression of your being; something powerful and close to your core. But your job doesn't automatically give you the opportunity to do your chosen work. You need to manage this: take steps to acquire the skills you need and balance your life with voluntary work closer to your ideal as you take the time to develop your career.

Answer the following questions to get a clearer vision of your ideal work:

- ✔ **What do you absolutely love about working?** This is an unusual question and you may, like many people when asked it, find it easier to come up with an immediate list of what you don't like about working. Persevere, you will find there are many things you love about working, from a reason to go to town, to the great friends you work with, from the interesting people you meet, to the problems you get to solve, and so on.

 Don't stop thinking until you have written down four or five things, even if they're not available in your current job role.

- ✔ **What aspects of your work are you really good at, or have other people told you that you're really good at?** Wow! Include all the things that you know you're good at even if nobody else does. Perhaps you are a good timekeeper, or maybe you are sensitive and caring when your co-workers are feeling down. Perhaps you are good at dealing with the boss, or the customers, or maybe you are excellent at getting on with the job without being distracted. Stretch your thinking and go for four or five things.

- ✔ **What is absolutely essential for you to have available in your work?** This is a great question whether or not you believe your current role gives you what you need. You may include things like meeting people, good money, being part of a team, or the opportunity to learn new things, or the chance to make a real difference.

 Think about what *you* need. How much of it would be available in your current role if you came at it a little differently?

- ✔ **What do you feel you really ought or would like to be doing?** Many people who want to change jobs lack clarity in their ideas about the work they wish they were doing. So, what is it for you? How much more of the things you really need would be available in the job you would prefer to be doing?

✔ **Finally, what is the truth that your answers whisper to you?** Bring all your other answers to mind. Should you be doing something else? Would it make any difference? Other than giving you more money, do you have clear insight into how you will ensure that your next role supports you better?

After answering all these questions, you will have a clearer idea than ever before of how you see your work in the world and what about it is most important to you. Now you need to look at the kind of jobs you have been doing. Have they given you what you need? Will they ever? When your work aligns with your values, you can be fully confident and fully empowered in your job. What do you need to change to make it so?

This powerful exercise can help you get in touch with your deeper need for work. You are most powerful and confident in your work when you are able to find jobs and roles that match your developing sense of vocation and purpose.

## Finding value in what you do

Uncovering the hidden value in your work is important for your self-respect and contributes to your confidence.

Whether what you do is something you simply fell into, or whether it was a planned and conscious choice, your job defines you in the world more than almost anything else. You should always ask yourself what is valuable about the work you do in the larger scheme of things, and be sure you bring to mind all the hidden value.

If you work for a large company or a well-known branded business, you can take pride in that. Maybe you work for the government, or the local authority. Take a pride in that. If you work with children, or with sick people, or people with special needs, you may also have some sense of vocation and you can take pride in that.

Whatever you do, take pride in your professionalism. *Professionalism* is about knowing what needs to be done and going about it competently. When you adopt a professional approach to your work, you demonstrate your confidence to others that you know what you are doing, which in turn inspires others to be confident in you.

Eleanor Roosevelt said that the future belongs to those who believe in the beauty of their dreams. A key to confidence is having dreams. Connecting your work with your growing sense of your life's purpose and your dreams is a very powerful means to having that work sing to your soul.

# *Becoming Assertive*

The key to effective communication and relationships with most colleagues in your organisation (including your boss) is a set of personal skills that are usually lumped together and called assertiveness. Assertiveness is one of those acquired skills you need training and practice to acquire.

Assertiveness specialist coaches claim that this skills set is more powerful than any other in business. It can protect and boost your self-esteem, build your confidence, and reduce your stress levels.

Assertive people are generally liked and respected, they respond well in tight spots, and they are not afraid to say 'no'. You know where you are with an assertive person; they don't get put upon.

So what is this miracle skills set called assertiveness? At its core, *assertiveness* is the conviction that every person is equal to every other and that each person has the responsibility to take care of his or her personal needs and rights. There is an implicit acceptance that this applies to all of us, so in claiming it for yourself you also claim it on behalf of all your colleagues.

The fundamentals of assertiveness are

- You value yourself and others as equals.

- You have the ability to say 'yes' or 'no' to anyone when you choose, and you do not always choose to offer a reason for it.

- You embrace and protect your human rights. You stand up for yourself and this is something that you are unafraid to be known for doing.

- You take responsibility for your own needs and ensure you have them met.

- You take responsibility for your own contribution and the value you create. You are not afraid to admit to mistakes nor to ask for help when you need it.

- You express your thoughts and feelings honestly, whether positive or negative, and with due respect for others.

- You are able to handle conflict when it arises. You are prepared to confront difficult people when necessary or appropriate.

- You give and receive feedback honestly and in a straightforward manner. You take the trouble to do this effectively and completely.

- You respect these rights in others and understand that they have the same rights as you.

Don't worry if you don't feel you match up to all these points yet. It is important first that you know what they are. As you grow in confidence you will naturally become more assertive and powerful.

# Showing Confidence in Specific Work Situations

Several common work situations may test your confidence. This section offers advice on how to manage your confidence in meetings and during presentations.

You can develop new skills, or *competencies* as they are often called in business, through training and practice. Nothing in business is impossible to master (certainly nothing is as difficult as learning to walk and talk, and most of us manage that).

If your employer is asking you to do something for which you do not yet have the requisite skill, you should insist on the training. And if you find yourself struggling with any task at work your first question should always be: How can I acquire the skill to do this better or faster? This will take you forward into growth and confidence, rather than shrinking backward into fear and avoidance.

## Demonstrating power and presence in meetings

Have you ever sat in a meeting just bursting to make a telling point only to find that the discussion has moved on before you are able to get it in? Or have you come up with a brilliant idea after the meeting is over and felt if only you could go back in time and make the point everyone would acknowledge you for solving the problem or pointing up the unnoticed flaw in the argument? If you have, then congratulations, you are a fully functioning, normal human being. We've all done it.

The main cause of such missed opportunities is the lack of balance between the *two* conversations that are going on in the meeting: the one in the room and the one in your head. When you are *fully present* and engaged in the meeting conversation, the conversation in your head fades into the background where it belongs most of the time. When you are feeling nervous or self-conscious, the dialogue in your head becomes predominant and prevents you from being fully engaged in the meeting.

You may feel self-conscious just because you're in unfamiliar territory. Take a few deep breaths (from your abdomen) to ease the tension, focus on who is in the room and the details of what they're wearing, just to bring yourself fully into the present.

Understand that this is normal, and ease up on yourself. Accept that the more natural you can be in the meeting situation the more balance you will achieve between your inner and outer dialogues.

If you can become curious about how the external conversation is developing and how the meeting will turn out, you will find yourself naturally focused on the outer discussion. From this position your own ideas and comments come up more naturally and more appropriately, it will be easier for you to make your points and you will grow in confidence.

Above all, relax. Whether the meeting is highly formal and large, or small and routine, the more engaged you become in the business of the meeting, the more effective your contribution becomes.

## Shining during presentations

Making effective presentations, like most other things in your professional life, is an acquired skill. Nobody is a born orator, just as no one grows up being able to read a balance sheet or create a budget. In order to give effective presentations, you need to get proper instruction from a training course, books, or tapes. There's no shortage of material to help you. And while the subject is too big to go into much detail here, we offer a few of the key things you need to bear in mind.

- ✔ Basic as it sounds, the very first thing to ask yourself is 'what is my point?' Many beginners and even many experienced speakers forget that if their talk has no point it is quite literally pointless. It's difficult to give a pointless talk with confidence and conviction. So determine your point of view and what you want your audience to do as a result of hearing what you have to say.

- ✔ Next, who are you talking to? You need to know the composition of your audience before you can start to think about how to pitch your talk. Are they knowledgeable or novices in your subject? Will you have to spell things out for them or can you assume they will know what you are talking about, jargon included?

After you consider the basics, turn yourself to the vexed question of whether you need slides. Just because a projector is available, or even habitual, consider whether slides would really add anything to your message (getting the audience's attention off you and giving yourself a crib-sheet to read off are not good enough reasons). If you decide to use a projector follow these top guidelines:

✔ Your slides are there for your audience. Make sure that they are legible from the back of the room and that the information on them is crisp and to the point.

✔ Assume your audience can read and don't treat your slides as cue cards. If you want your audience to take in what is written on the slide, shut up and let them read it.

✔ Unless you're a graphic artist, don't be tempted by fancy fonts or colour schemes, any kind of animation, or even clip art. And use slide-builds sparingly. What looks great on your laptop when you are preparing all too often looks awful when projected onto a big screen.

✔ Always test your presentation on the actual equipment you will be using. Never, ever attempt to use external links to the Internet or to some kind of live demonstration unless you are a specialist, and even then only with caution.

✔ Have a contingency plan in case your equipment fails or won't behave itself. Have copies of the slides to hand out, but don't do this before you speak unless you don't mind people flicking through the pack while you are talking.

✔ Rehearse, rehearse, and rehearse. Time yourself and get your script down onto a few cue cards. This will ensure you are confident in what you are going to say, and in your timings.

Always bear in mind the golden rules of technology when making any kind of presentation involving projection or sound equipment: *what can go wrong will go wrong* sooner or later, and *less is more* in the balance of complexity versus clarity. Keep things simple and allow yourself the chance to connect with your audience.

You will improve your skills most effectively through practice and feedback. So seek out opportunities in non-work situations to hone your developing skills. Adult education classes in local colleges, women's groups, and your local church are always on the lookout for speakers. Offer yourself up for the experience and do your learning where you won't have to live with the consequences.

## *Rejecting manipulation and bullying*

Bullying is all too common in the workplace. Surveys show that millions of people feel bullied every day at work, which takes a heavy toll on confidence. If you feel you are a victim of serious bullying at work, seek professional help from your HR or union representative, or perhaps your functional director. Bullying is never acceptable, by anyone, in any circumstances.

Whilst the unacceptability of bullying is perfectly clear in cases of physical intimidation or sexual and racial harassment, the less dramatic, lower-intensity form of bullying by shouting, verbal abuse, and manipulation can sap your self-esteem just as surely as a flagrant assault.

The manipulative bully's techniques include sarcasm, unjustified criticism, trivial faultfinding and humiliation, especially in front of others. It can also include your being overruled, isolated, and otherwise excluded from team activities. All this is calculated to sap your self-confidence to make you more of a target.

You protect yourself best by refusing to play the victim. Recognise that it is the bully who is inadequate and needs fixing, not you. Don't be taken in by criticism, even though it may have a grain of truth in it. No amount of improvement in your performance will satisfy your bully; a bully isn't interested in improving you, only in having control over you.

If you seem to attract such people either into your professional or your private life, it may be because you exhibit certain personality traits that mark you as a target for someone with a bullying personality. *This is not your fault.* Table 5-1 contains practical tips on how to offset tendencies that make you easy prey for bully boys (and girls).

| Table 5-1 | Personality Traits and Being Bullied |
|---|---|
| *Tendency* | *Counter Behaviours* |
| You want to please. | Accept that you will never be able to please everyone, especially a bully. |
| You take on more and more to gain approval. | Set yourself sensible limits. |
| You find it hard to say "no". | Learn how to be more assertive. |
| You have a strong desire to think well of others. | Be more objective; ask others' opinions. |
| You want things to be perfect. | Realise that perfection isn't possible |
| You have a strong need to feel valued. | Learn to value yourself . |
| You tend to discount your own contributions. | Ask yourself whether what you are expected to do is fair and reasonable. |

Your first step in dealing successfully with a bully is to take control. Acknowledge your need to be more assertive, and look at that section in this chapter. There is almost certainly something you can do to stop yourself being victimised. Consider the following actions. Don't think for too long though, you need to take decisive action quickly:

- ✔ Let your union or staff representative know about the problem. Take any advice they offer you, and if this is inadequate check out any help-lines or consult your local Citizen's Advice Bureau.

- ✔ Talk about the situation to your colleagues (if they will discuss it). Find out if anyone else is suffering and if others are aware of what is happening to you. Others may be suffering in silence.

- ✔ Start a diary and keep a written record of all incidents. You may need this detailed evidence later if things come to a head but more likely it will act as a strong disincentive on your bully.

- ✔ Confront your bully in person if you feel you can, otherwise do it by e-mail or memo. In firm but non-aggressive language, make it clear what you are objecting to in their behaviour. Keep a copy and any reply. This may end their bullying.

- ✔ If you decide to make a formal complaint take advice first from HR or your union and follow your company's procedures. Ask your representatives to help you; this will cut down greatly on the stress on you.

  If you have made a formal complaint, be aware that your bully's job could now be in jeopardy. You need to be able to substantiate your allegations through witnesses or written records, and you may have to confront your bully in an investigation.

If you are not satisfied by the outcome of the internal investigation, take advice on your legal rights. If you leave your job and subsequently make a claim to an employment tribunal, they will expect you to have first tried to resolve the situation using the internal procedures. Any records you have will be heard when the tribunal hears your claim.

## Managing Your Boss

Complaints about the boss are commonplace in work life and pretty much inevitable. It will help your confidence to remember that however big and scary your boss may appear to you now, he got that way by having to cope with difficult situations on her own and that underneath he is as vulnerable as you are.

The bottom line with bosses is that they need to get the job done and meet their performance targets. They need their team members to perform effectively and they have strategies for getting the required performance out of their subordinates.

When the pressure is on, bosses become anxious and scared just like anyone else, and that is when problems often show up most.

Anyone who is persistently out of sorts or bad tempered is almost certainly stressed and needs help whether they know it or not. There may be nothing you feel you can do to help your boss with his issues, but you can certainly manage your own.

# Dealing with feedback

It is important for your self-confidence that you learn how to manage feedback. If you can receive and give feedback effectively, and especially turn even poorly delivered feedback to your advantage, you will grow massively in confidence and effectiveness at work.

The next sections offer tips for giving and getting feedback.

### Giving effective feedback

When giving feedback, whether positive or negative, things generally go most smoothly if you follow a few simple rules:

- **Be very clear about the information you are imparting and own the responsibility of making the point.** You don't want any grey areas at the end, and you want to make sure that your receiver knows this clear information is coming from you.

- **Focus on the action you want to take place.** Describe the facts of the situation and how you want them to change. Do not judge or offer opinions about why the problem is arising, you might get it wrong.

- **Be as specific as possible.** Take a keyhole or laser surgery approach to your intervention. Deal as precisely as possible with the situation and avoid generalisations like *always* and *never*. If your feedback deals with some aspect of behaviour, ensure that it is the behaviour you address and not the character of the person.

- **Emphasise the positive aspects of the situation.** This helps the person receiving your input to keep his receiving channels open. If you're correcting an error or making another point that he may receive as criticism, it can be helpful to the receiver if you sandwich the negative point between something positive, both before and after. This is not manipulative if you do it honestly; it is helpful to the person who has to take your point on board.

### Turning negative feedback around

Input from your boss that you receive as criticism, nit-picking, or nagging is just an inadequate form of feedback. The information it contains may be valuable to you though, and important to your organisation, so it is worth understanding what your boss is trying to communicate.

If you can see that your boss's criticism of you is just his inadequate way of giving you information, you retain more power in the relationship. You can do two things that may surprise his and turn things around:

✔ Take on board any feedback that may be useful to you in improving your performance and let your boss know what this is.

✔ Ask permission to give your boss feedback on how he can communicate with *you* more effectively. If you do this, follow all the rules on being specific, focusing on the action, and so on from the preceding 'Giving effective feedback' section. Remember, you both share the goal of improving performance.

## Getting your boss to keep his promises

The frustration of being offered some benefit or reward but not receiving it can corrupt your relationship with your employer and erode your confidence.

Unfulfilled promises generally fall into one of two cases:

✔ **Case 1:** You believe your boss has promised you something that he didn't. He may be surprised that you feel a promise has been made.

✔ **Case 2:** You both know full well that the promise has been made and yet it is being delayed for reasons that have not been made clear to you.

In both cases, you feel maligned or abused and your self-esteem and self-confidence will suffer unless you do something about it.

At the root of both cases is a problem with communication. In Case 1, you may have unintentionally translated a good intention by your boss into a promise. In Case 2, the ambiguity may be deliberate. Your boss may simply have made the promise to keep you quiet without intending to fulfil it any time soon. Fortunately, the remedy for both is simple and it is the same action.

What you do, as a professional person of integrity, is put down in writing in the form of an email or memo any important exchanges. In clear and straight-forward language, write down what you believe has been agreed. Figure 5-2 gives an example.

**Figure 5-2:**
Putting
an under-
standing in
writing.

Dear Boss

Thanks for seeing me yesterday to discuss my pay rise. I'm obviously delighted that you have agreed to my request and I'm looking forward to receiving it. When will this be by the way? (This is the first question my wife will ask me). Do please confirm a date and let me know if there is going to be any delay.

Thanks and regards

Of course, if you have the presence of mind in the discussion to ask when the reward will take effect, you will already know the promised date and you can include it in your note.

How will your boss react to this written input? In the majority of cases, your note simply confirms what your boss agreed to do, and your confirmation acts as a reminder. If you send it as an email, your boss can forward it to his PA, HR, or payroll with a confirmation that he has agreed to your note and a request for action. Then it will be done – easy for everyone.

But what happens when your boss doesn't agree or doesn't take action? In the case of a misunderstanding, your note is likely to evoke an immediate response from your boss pointing up the mismatch. Will he be annoyed? Maybe, a little bit, since the issue has returned so quickly, but it is far better to identify his mistake in communication immediately and give him the chance to rectify it. You can apologise if necessary to maintain rapport, and immediately ask when you can expect the reward. If he can't give you any indication, then you are probably being fobbed off, which is Case 2.

So what will be your boss's reaction to your note if he is using delaying tactics? You will catch him out and force his hand. If he continues to be evasive, then you know he is simply stringing you along. You won't have your reward, but you will have your integrity restored. You may be annoyed, but it will not be directed at yourself. You may use your annoyance to give you the motivation to do something about changing your dishonest boss by changing your job.

## Telling your boss he's wrong

At the heart of confidence is trust: Trust in yourself, trust in others, and trust that things will turn out okay. Telling your boss that he's wrong requires that you feel all three, so let's take a look at the structure and dynamics of the situation.

First, bear in mind that neither you nor your boss is infallible. Everyone makes mistakes from time to time; everyone makes errors of fact and judgement. This is perfectly human. What matters most in business is what you do to remedy the immediate problem and what you can then do to stop the situation occurring again.

If you are sure that you are correct about your boss's error or misjudgement, then you owe it to him to point it out before the damage gets worse. Here is where you need trust in yourself. No matter what gap there may be in age, prestige, salary, experience, or levels in the hierarchy, you are just as valuable a human being as your boss and you owe it to him, person to person, to point out his error. If you do this with respect and a little care (for example, not in front of your colleagues or in the middle of a meeting), your boss will remember and respect you for your honesty and tact.

If you have some evidence ready to support your judgement that he has made an error, use it discreetly. It can help your boss to come to terms with him error more quickly but spare his blushes with others. If you point out your boss's errors in public, he won't thank you for it.

If you have an honest and straightforward remedy, offer it to help fix his mistake quickly. Don't become wedded to your solution, though, as he may choose another.

Fundamentally, being assertive and acting to inform your boss of the error is what counts. You will grow in confidence from your taking the action and so, if he is any good as a leader at all, will your boss.

# Casting Off Your Cloak of Invisibility

More often than not, the reason nobody is acknowledging the great job you are doing is because your superiors and colleagues are too busy worrying about their own performances. Don't be afraid to seize the opportunity to take powerful action to bring your excellent work to the attention of your boss and colleagues.

The following formula creates a winning situation for everyone. If you use it, you set yourself apart as the one in a thousand employees who cares enough about performance to take it on.

Follow these steps:

1. **Ask your boss to define exactly what he wants from you in order for you to get a five-star annual appraisal.**

   The more detailed this is the better. Get him to spell out, from his point of view, what *good* looks like, then play it back: 'So if I do this, this, and this, and avoid that and that, you will think I'm doing an excellent job, right?' Once you have agreement, write it down (but don't send it anywhere just yet).

2. **Ask the same question of others who depend on you or are affected by your performance.**

   These may be customers or a group of colleagues who use your output in some significant way. Find out, from their perspective, what good looks like, play it back, get their agreement, and write it down for your own use later.

3. **Pull it all together into job objectives that you can realistically achieve.**

   You have a lot of detailed input on how other people depend on you and what they need you to do well in order to be happy with your performance.

4. **Spell out what you feel you can reliably deliver to your boss, colleagues, and customers.**

   Present them with a document that outlines the objectives you're committed to achieving (perhaps with training or some other assistance) and get their agreement to it (you may need to negotiate and compromise).

Doing the work to put together an action plan helps you achieve a number of really important objectives:

- Composing a job specification that is relevant, detailed, achievable, and creates value.

- Letting your boss and colleagues know what to expect from you and that they can rely on you to deliver.

- Laying a solid basis for renegotiating expectations and outcomes should anything change.

You have a perfect right, a duty even, to check in with your colleagues periodically to ensure they are happy with your performance. And each time you do so it will remind them of what a good and dependable job you do.

# Dealing Confidently with Corporate Change

As change managers know, change tends to trigger a cycle of reactions and feelings. These fall into a sequence of predictable stages, irrespective of whether the change is planned or unplanned. Figure 5-3 shows a simple change curve.

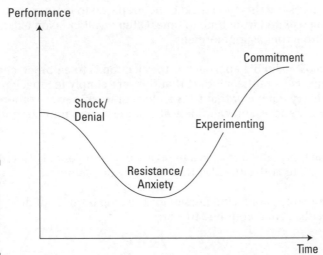

**Figure 5-3:** Changing with the change curve.

The time you spend at each stage and the intensity of your reaction depends on your personality and the nature of the change. To make a successful transition, however, you have to work through all the stages. The stages are:

- ✔ **Shock or Denial:** At this initial response, your natural response may be to minimise the impact of the change by trivialising it or denying that it exists.

- ✔ **Resistance and Anxiety:** This stage is characterised by your strong emotions and also feelings of flatness, accompanied often by a loss of confidence. You may have difficulties in coping with the new circumstances, which makes it hard to accept the changes.

- ✔ **Experimenting:** Activity now increases as you test new ways and approaches towards the change. You may have firm ideas of how things should be in relation to the new situation and feel frustration as the inevitable mistakes are made.

- ✔ **Commitment:** By this stage, you will have adopted new behaviour and accepted the change. Youll be working well and confidently with the new situation. You may reflect on how and why things are different, and attempt to understand all the emotion and activity of the previous stages.

## Getting through rejection

One of the messages coaches give out loud and clear is that it's a normal part of growth *not* to be chosen for every role or assignment. If you set out your stall to be successful then you need to be prepared to learn from the experience of being rejected from time to time. Often a valid reason exists and you can benefit from the disappointment.

One of the most valuable approaches to rejection is to embrace change and disappointments from the mindset that they are simply feedback rather than failure. For every company that wins a piece of work, several others lost the work. For every successful candidate at an interview, a number got a rejection call.

The rejection is not about you as a person, but about your skills and style not being appropriate at this time for this company or customer.

Winners stay professional and persist for the long term. Confident people welcome feedback and continue to learn.

## Taming the threat of redundancy

Since it is jobs or roles that get made redundant, and not people, you can only be made redundant if you see yourself as your job. You may find yourself out of work for a while, and it certainly won't be of your choosing, but you will avoid the quite ridiculous and yet soul-destroying label of being redundant yourself.

Fully embrace the notion of work being something you choose to do for yourself and sometimes – often – you pursue this through a job role. Now you have a clear distinction between the work you have taken on in the world and the medium through which you are currently engaged in your work. This is a far healthier relationship to your job and one that allows you to have much more personal power.

The way forward is to hold on to who you are and your true purpose and find the work or lifestyle that fits for you right now. Hold on to the idea that this is merely a transition in your life. Confidence is about accepting and embracing the energy of the change and finding the positive lesson for you. Ask someone who has been made redundant six months after the event, and many will tell you that it was the best thing that happened to them – it gave them freedom to move on and was a catalyst for change.

Here is a good example: When the British heavy industries of coal mining and shipbuilding were closed down over a 20-year period, hundreds of thousands of workers lost their jobs. Many of these workers had been miners or shipbuilders all their lives, and their fathers before them. Their identity was bound up in being a miner, and since the government had no more use for miners it had no further use for them. Many saw themselves as literally without use and useless; they were finished. Many of them reached retirement age without ever working again.

In stark contrast, thousands of others took their redundancy pay and used it to build new lives, either starting their own businesses or moving away to parts of the country where there were more and different jobs.

The ones who moved on saw the problem for what it was: Their heavy-industry jobs were gone forever and they needed to find different kinds of jobs. The rest embraced prolonged unemployment with their proud industrial identities intact but never worked again.

# Chapter 6

# Asking the Right Questions and Listening with Intent

*W*hen you know the 'right' questions to ask, you get the results you want much faster. In the true spirit of NLP, we deliberately aim to be non-judgemental, and so you can quite legitimately say that no 'right' or 'wrong' questions exist, only different ones.

So, we need to be more precise. When we talk about asking the 'right' questions, we're looking specifically for incisive questions – those that put your finger precisely on the nub of an issue, those that have a positive effect in the shortest possible time. In this context, the 'wrong' questions are those that send you off-course, meandering down dead ends, and gathering interesting but irrelevant information.

In this book, we explain and demonstrate that your language is powerful; it triggers an emotional response in you, as well as others. Therefore, you can make a difference as you begin to choose your language with increasing awareness. In this chapter, we bring together some of the most useful questions you can ask in different situations to make things happen for yourself and for others. Knowing the right questions to ask may make a difference for you when you want to do the following:

✔ Set your life going in the right direction

✔ Make the best decisions

✔ Help others to take more responsibility

✔ Select and motivate people

✔ Coach others to overcome their limitations

# Question-Asking Tips and Strategies

Before rushing on to the critical question you probably want answered – 'what are the magic questions that do make a real difference?' – take a quick breather and consider *how* to ask questions when you're working with people, which is just as important as *what* to ask.

In this section, we encourage you to challenge your personal style and assumptions and adapt your own behaviour in order to function at your best, whether you're the client or in the coaching seat.

## Cleaning up your language: Removing bias

Have you ever wondered how many questions you ask that make assumptions based on what *you* want, and *your* personal map of reality, rather than what other people want? Human beings find that not projecting their ideas, needs, wants, and enthusiasms on to others is difficult – especially on to those closest to them. You influence other people all the time; you just can't help it. For that reason, most questions aren't what we call *clean* – in the sense that they assume something, as in the famous 'when did you stop beating your wife?' question.

Even the one small word *beating* has different meanings for different people. Did you think of *beating* in the context of physical violence, or in the competitive sense of winning at a sport or game, or something else entirely?

Therapists go through many years of training in order to work with their clients like a clean mirror, which can simply reflect the issues back to clients so they can deliberate on them. Some mirrors get to shine brighter than others! After all, you know how much you can communicate just through one raised eyebrow or a suppressed giggle. (This is the reason why Freud had his clients lying on a couch while he, as the therapist, sat behind the client's head!)

If you want to be respectful of other people's views, make a point of noticing how well you can avoid prejudicing the result of a discussion. Are you telling somebody else what to do based on what you would do yourself?

Beware of making generalisations or limiting decisions. Listen to what you say, and if you hear yourself issuing instructions that begin with words such as you 'must', 'should', 'ought to', and 'can't' – the time is right to stop directing the action and imposing your stance on others.

Imagine that you're a manager coaching or mentoring a colleague or employee at work. In a coaching session, beginning with a clear aim in mind is essential. Therefore, you may quite reasonably ask 'What do we want to work on today?'

The question is simple, direct, and focuses attention on the shared understanding that you're *working* on something. Your words set out the intention for the type of interaction you're sharing: this isn't just a friendly chat, we have work to do today. This question is a 'better' opening in the context of this section than asking 'Shall we work out why you haven't finished the project as fast as Fred?', because you're giving the other person some space to think and bring real live challenges to the discussion.

Coaching is about exploring and challenging clients, leading them on to take responsibility and commit to action. Clean questions help you achieve these aims. Any suggestions you include must be phrased in such a way that people think for themselves, instead of being influenced by your own bias.

So, an even cleaner opening question that directs a client to think carefully for themselves may be: 'What would you like to have happen?'

Curiosity may have killed the cat, as the saying goes, but a different perspective may be that curiosity is the pathway to understanding. You choose which saying suits you best.

### Discovering Clean Language questions

The counselling psychologist David Grove created a body of knowledge known as Clean Language, in which he perfected the art of asking clean questions. This work continues to be developed and now forms part of some NLP practitioner training modules.

Grove created a set of questions that can be used in a variety of applications; in psychotherapy and coaching, of course, but also in health, business, and education. The questions come in three types and work in different ways:

- **Current perception questions:** Expanding the client's understanding of a situation.

- **Moving time questions:** Working with the client's sense of time.

- **Intention questions:** Concentrating on the outcome the client wants.

The overall aim of Clean Language is to remove the bias inherent in the questioner's language by exploring people's model of the world from their own perspective. Although the questions can look strange out of context, just consider the subtle difference between asking a really clean question such as 'And is there anything else?' compared with 'What are you going to do now?' The latter question clearly includes the expectation from the questioner that the person must do something.

### Starting the Clean Language process

Penny Tompkins and James Lawley suggest that one way to begin the Clean Language questioning process is to put the client into a resourceful state, by developing a *resource metaphor*. You can start the process of developing a resource metaphor by asking the following question:

> And when you're at your best, that's like what?

You can ask this question generally, as it stands above, or you can make it more specific by placing it in a specific context, as we do by adding the following words in square brackets:

> And when you're [working] at your best, that's like what?

> And when you're [collaborating] at your best, that's like what?

> And when you're [focusing] at your best, that's like what?

Or try adding a personal quality:

> And when you're most [patient], that's like what?

> And when you're most [loving], that's like what?

> And when you're most [content], that's like what?

When the person has created a resource metaphor, you can then ask the following clean question that begins the process of developing a desired outcome (goal, objective) metaphor:

> And what you would like to have happen, is like what?

When the person has spoken, written, or drawn a metaphor in answer to these questions, you can ask the first five developing questions listed in the next section, so as to bring the metaphor to life. We want the person to be living in their personal metaphorical landscape (to use several metaphors!).

### Developing current perception questions

Here are some examples of asking clean questions that increase a person's understanding of a situation:

- **Attributes:** And is there anything else about. . . ?

  And what kind of. . . ?
- **Location:** And where/whereabouts is. . . ?
- **Relationship:** And is there a relationship between . . . and. . . ?

  And when what happens to. . . ?
- **Metaphor:** And that's . . . like what?

### Trying out moving time questions

These clean questions are great when working with a person's sense of time:

- **Before:** And what happens just before. . . ?
- **After:** And then what happens/what happens next?
- **Source:** And where does/could . . . come from?

### Working on intention questions

The following clean questions are useful to explore a person's desired outcome:

- **Desired outcome:** And what would you like to have happen?
- **Necessary conditions:** And what needs to happen for their desired outcome?

  And can . . . ?

In order to work well with these questions, you can benefit from formal training in Clean Language. However, you can begin to make small adjustments to clean up your questions yourself, so that you act as an unbiased facilitator instead of unwittingly influencing another person's thinking.

Imagine that someone describes a problem to you, such as having too much work, and requests your help. If you ask the person 'And that workload is like what?', you're inviting them to work with their own metaphor. The person may come up with a metaphor such as, 'It's like a brick on the back of my neck.' You can then simply ask, 'And what would you like to have happen when there's a brick on the back of your neck?', so that you pace the person's experience and lead them towards coming up with their own solutions.

As with all the suggestions in this chapter, just try it and see how it works.

## Recognising that the way you behave is what counts

Own up now . . . have you ever shouted at someone, 'Stop shouting at me!'? Nonsense, isn't it, expecting someone else to do what you clearly aren't demonstrating in your own behaviour. Yet people do it all the time. You can easily see in someone else the negative qualities that you want to change in yourself.

The art of encouraging somebody else to change is to model that behaviour yourself. If you want somebody to become curious, be curious yourself. If you want someone to be positive and helpful, you too need to model that behaviour. If you think that someone just needs to lighten up, inject some fun into the proceedings.

Instead of expecting other people to change, lead the way yourself. One of the best lessons we can pass on is 'The way you behave with other people determines the way people behave with you.'

So when you ask questions, do so with awareness of how you're behaving as much as what you say.

## Pressing the pause button

Silence is golden. Pausing for a moment when one person has finished speaking is helpful, and in turn lets you think before you speak.

Alan Whicker, presenter of the fascinating *Whicker's World* television series, has a unique style of interviewing people. He asks a question and leaves a long pause after he gets an answer. The interviewees, feeling the need to fill the silence, elaborate with details that give far greater insights into their personality than the initial answer did.

Pauses give other people critical space to process what you said and to consider their reply.

Simply giving people unhurried time to think within a structured framework of questioning is a huge benefit in business and family situations. Listening to others is a generous act and an undeveloped, undervalued skill in most organisations, which is why coaching is so powerful. Trained coaches understand the power of listening and the importance of powerful questioning combined with silence so that clients can process their thoughts. They listen not only to what's being said, but also to the message beneath the words, paying acute attention to what they see as well as recognising the importance of getting clients into the most resourceful state to solve their own issues.

Great listeners create productive meetings, build strong relationships, and find the insights to solve complex issues.

## *Testing your questions*

If you have any doubts about whether your question is appropriate to help a person or situation move to a better place, stop and ask yourself the following:

- ✔ 'Is my next question going to add value in this conversation? Is it taking us closer to where we want to go? Is it going to move us further apart?'
- ✔ 'What is the outcome or result I'm looking for here?'

If in doubt, stay silent until a more powerful question comes into your head. You may then find yourself asking the person to take the lead by asking something like 'What's the most useful question to ask yourself here?' or even 'Can you tell me the most useful question I could ask you?'

## *Making positive statements the norm*

When we say to you, try really hard and don't think of a pink elephant, what happens? Yes, of course, you immediately think of a pink elephant, you just can't help it! Similarly, if you say to a child 'Don't eat those sweets before tea.' What happens? The child is compelled to *eat the sweets* – you've inadvertently issued a command.

The brain doesn't distinguish the negatives – it ignores the 'don't' and thinks 'do'. Better to say to the child 'Tea's coming, so save your appetite for just two minutes'

## *Figuring Out What You Want*

Knowing what you want can be the greatest challenge, because it's a constantly moving feast. Sometimes you can get what you *think* you wanted and yet be disappointed, because in fact that wasn't what you really wanted at all! To figure out what you really want, you have to ask yourself two questions: 'What do I want?' and 'What's that going to do for me?'

## What do I want?

If one great question comes out of NLP, it's 'What do I want?'

Sometimes you know very clearly what you don't want, which is a good starting point. When you know what you don't want, flip it over and ask yourself what's the opposite. And then check with yourself again, 'So, what is it that I do want?'

As you begin to articulate your answers, explore some details and allow yourself to dream a little. Imagine yourself in the future; fast forward your personal movie to a time when you have what you want and maybe more besides. Employ all your senses and ask yourself what that feels like, sounds like, and looks like? Are any smells or tastes associated with getting what you want? Check inside with yourself as to whether it seems right. Does it energise and excite you? If you feel anxious or exhausted, that's a clue that something's wrong.

## What's that going to do for me?

When you've thought about what you want, and some words and ideas have come to you, the next question is 'What's that going to do for me?' Perhaps you have a goal to achieve – to bid for a new business project, take up a new sport, or quit your work and go trekking in Nepal.

Ask yourself what achieving that aim is going to do for you. And ask the same question three times – really drill down until you hit some core values that make sense for you. Otherwise you may be choosing to do things that take you meandering down side roads, instead of staying on track for where you want to get to.

# Asking Questions to Help Make Decisions

You make decisions all the time: whether to go to work or stay at home; what to have for lunch and supper; whether to accept an invitation to see a film; how much you should spend on a new computer or holiday; whether to lay on a Christmas party with your family or not.

Imagine that one sunny day you're happily working at your job and a call comes in from a business head-hunter: a new job is on offer, you're the person the company wants, and by the way, it means moving your home to a town by the sea 300 kilometres away. You weren't even considering a change, but you're flattered, and so you go and talk to the company. The deal looks pretty attractive and you think, wouldn't it feel good to be working near the sea in hot weather like this? But a niggling little voice inside you is saying: 'Is this the right thing to do? Are you sure?'

Should you go for it or should you stay doing what you know best? How can you decide this one?

Here are four key questions that you can ask yourself, or someone else, to guide in making a decision – a life-changing one or something smaller:

✔ What will happen if you do?

✔ What will happen if you don't?

✔ What won't happen if you do?

✔ What won't happen if you don't?

These four questions are based on Cartesian logic and you may find them referred to as *Cartesian co-ordinates*. All you need to remember is that they offer some powerful linguistic patterns that enable you to examine a subject from different angles.

We often talk clients through these questions, and the decisions can be major – shall I leave my wife, move house, change career direction, have a baby, recruit a new team? The questions focus your attention and challenge your thinking. When you reach the last question, you may stop and think, 'that's confusing'. Good. This reaction means that you're arriving at a breakthrough in your thinking.

If you make a change in one area of your life at the expense of another area, the chances are that the change isn't going to last. So, for example, if you move jobs but have to give up important interests or friendships where you currently live, the change isn't going to make you happy in the long term and you probably won't stick with it. Don't take our word for it; try the questions out now on something about which you're deliberating. You can see that the questions encourage you to check out your decision based on the impact on the whole of your environment, in a healthy way – what we call an *ecology* check.

# Challenging Limiting Beliefs

When someone's thinking is stopping them from achieving a much sought-after goal, you can ask three simple questions in order to challenge such thinking. To help others (or yourself) overcome a limiting belief, ask the three questions set out in this section.

When asking the questions, give the person plenty of time to talk about an issue, and move on only when you sense that they've 'got it off their chest':

- ✔ **Question 1: 'What do you assume or believe about this issue that limits you in achieving your goal?'**

  Ask this question three times until you're sure that you've reached the heart of the matter – what NLP describes as a limiting belief. As you delve deeper, you may say: 'That's right, and what else about this limits you?'

  For example, the person may be thinking 'I'm not good enough,' or 'Nobody will let me,' or 'I just don't know how.' When you hold a negative position like these ones, you stop yourself from doing what you need to do to achieve what you want.

- ✔ **Question 2: 'What would be a more empowering belief, one that's the positive opposite of the one holding you back?'**

  This question flips the limitation over to the positive side. For example, the positive opposite of the assumptions and beliefs above would be stated positively as 'I am good enough,' or 'Somebody will let me,' or 'I do know how.'

  With this second question, your colleague or client may get confused or even cross because it's challenging to answer. Yet, this question's critical to hold on to if you're going to get a switch in perspective and come up with a more empowering belief that helps someone shift forward. So stick with it.

- ✔ **Question 3: 'If you knew that [your new freeing belief] . . . what ideas do you now have to help you move towards your goal?'**

  This question completes the process. At this point, the person comes up with their own ideas on how to move forward: 'Oh well, if I knew that I was good enough, I'd do X, Y, and Z.'

This questioning works by putting somebody into an 'as if' way of thinking. If you act with the belief that something can happen, you can then find the behaviours to achieve the aim.

# Finding the Right Person for the Job: A Question of Motivation

Getting the right people in the right jobs at the right time can be a tricky problem. Asking the right questions can help you to match people to the qualities needed to succeed in particular roles.

To get somebody lined up in the right job, you need to ask yourself about the *personal qualities* that are necessary to do that job well, as well as the *technical skills* involved. How is that person going to behave? The following questioning begins before you recruit:

- ✔ What are some of the essential criteria for someone to perform this job well? Come up with about five key words, which may include things such as teamworking, self-starter, clear processes, creativity, customer service, learning, variety, stability, flexibility, well organised, intellectual challenge, good product, attractive environment, travel.

- ✔ Does the person need to be motivated to achieve results or sort out problems?

- ✔ Does the person need to be primarily self-motivated or get consensus from customers or a team?

- ✔ Does the style of working mean that the person must follow processes or does the person have freedom in how things get done?

The next four sections contain questions that you can ask at the interview in order to gain specific information on how people are likely to behave in a given context, as well as their technical skills to do the job you have in mind.

The same questions apply when you check in with members of your team to see how things are going and what adjustments you can make to keep people motivated.

## *What do you want in your work?*

This question enables you to match the criteria or hot buttons that you're looking for with those that are important for the individual. When you hear that someone wants lots of freedom and flexibility, they may do well in a creative environment but not if required to tightly project-manage an implementation of a new system. If they thrive on change, they may be good for a short-term contract, but are unlikely to stay more than a year or two unless you can provide new roles.

## *Why is that important?*

Taking each of the applicant's criteria in turn, ask 'Why is that important?' This question enables you to identify the direction in which the person is motivated: *away from* a problem or *towards* a solution. A person with an *away-from* preference may say that 'Salary is important so I don't have to worry about not being able to pay my mortgage.' A person with a *towards* preference may say that 'Salary is important so I can buy my own home easily.'

The clues to understanding people are in the language style they adopt, for example:

- ✔ If someone is motivated *towards*, you may hear words such as attain, gain, achieve, get, include.
- ✔ If someone is motivated *away from*, you may hear words such as avoid, exclude, recognise problems.

## How do you know that you've done a good job?

This question enables you to identify the source of a person's motivation.

If people are *internally focused* – that is, they pay more attention to what's happening for themselves than for other people – you can motivate them by using phrases such as 'only you can decide', 'you may want to consider', and 'what do you think?'.

If they're *externally focused* – that is, they need to be convinced by other people and through gaining facts and figures – you can motivate them by using phrases such as 'others will notice', 'the feedback you'll get', and 'so and so says so'.

If you're employing somebody in customer service, that person needs to value external approval, instead of being internally focused. However, if you want to give a person a project to get on with on their own, someone with a strong external focus is likely to struggle without regular approval from others.

## Why did you choose your current work?

This question is a great one to ask when you want to know whether someone is motivated by having options or by being told what to do. If somebody has an *options style*, you're going to hear words such as opportunity, criteria, choice, unlimited possibilities, and variety. On the other hand, if somebody has a strong *procedures style*, they're likely to give you a step-by-step response, the story of how they got into their current line of work. You're likely to hear such people talking about processes and using phrases such as 'the right way' and 'tried and true'.

Both styles can work in the same team quite happily together. To motivate your options people, build in as many choices as you can offer them. Get them to brainstorm new ways to do things. To motivate your procedures people, get them to focus on the necessary systems and processes to bring more structure and controls to the team.

# Checking In with Yourself

In order to keep on track to where you want to get or what you want to achieve, on a daily basis or longer term, questioning yourself can be very helpful. Therefore, check out the following list of questions to ask yourself every day:

- ✔ What do I want?
- ✔ What will that do for me?
- ✔ What's stopping me?
- ✔ What's important to me here?
- ✔ What's working well?
- ✔ What can be better?
- ✔ What resources will support me?

If you accept the NLP presupposition that 'There's no such thing as failure, only feedback,' you aren't going to be afraid of asking questions from the fear that you may get answers you'd prefer not to hear. Tune into the feedback you get for yourself as well as others as you ask the right questions.

# Listening Intently

Listening is potentially the most difficult skill in life, let alone in coaching. How often do you think you're listening carefully to someone only to realise that your mind has wandered off? Inevitably, a word or phrase from another person makes a connection in your brain, setting a trail of memories or possibilities in motion.

The International Coach Federation defines active listening as 'the ability to focus completely on what the client is saying and not saying to understand the meaning of what is said in the context of the client's desires and to support the client's self expression.' What a tall order to listen for – what isn't being expressed, as well as what is!

Listening requires you to know when to be silent and when to intrude with a question or comment that moves the client forward. Listening is an important skill so that you create the space to pick up on your client's:

- ✔ Concerns
- ✔ Goals
- ✔ Values and beliefs
- ✔ Non-verbal clues

And you must do all of this without judgement to cut to the heart of your clients' challenges and growth.

## Listening at four levels

In my coaching skills workshops, I(Kate) teach the following model of listening that combines NLP perceptual positions with the work of Adam Kahane.

One of the ways that NLP encourages you to build rapport with people is by distinguishing three points of view, known as perceptual positions. First position is your own viewpoint; second position is about shifting into someone else's shoes and third position is taking an independent position.

In workshops, we practise the following four types of listening in small groups so people can really feel the way they normally operate and what it might take to raise their level of listening. Ultimately coaches need to find the creativity of the highest level of listening – meta position listening – for powerful coaching.

- ✔ **Downloading.** When you download, you say what you always say. You're stuck in what NLP calls first position, where you just state your viewpoint without noticing the other person. At this level you're basically dumping data.

- ✔ **Debating.** When you debate, you begin to recognise another person in the interaction, listening openly to the other (you're aware of this second position). You allow time for the other to talk and wait your turn, listening with your rational mind.

- ✔ **Empathy listening.** At this level, you open your heart to listen from the position of the person telling the story. The quality of dialogue improves as you empathise and truly get into second position, able to understand others' issues and reflect them back in your dialogue.

✔ **Meta position listening.** At this level, you take on the third NLP perceptual position where you listen from an independent fly-on-the-wall position, yet you stay connected with the other person. You're witnessing the whole picture from all points of view and listening with your full heart and soul to all elements of the system in which your client operates. This level of listening is where you can generate the most creative solutions.

## Listening beyond words

Research suggests that only a very small proportion of communication is affected by the actual words said – maybe as little as 7 per cent. The implication is that you can listen even better when you concentrate on your nonverbal skills of matching and mirroring the body language and tone of voice of your client.

In a coaching master class, I had the opportunity to coach a client who's language I couldn't understand. Although he understood English, the exercise involved him responding in his native language. This experience proved to be wonderfully informative and proof that the quality of listening is an important part of coaching. I couldn't comprehend his actual words, yet I picked up on the rhythm of the conversation, his physiology and emotion, and responded intuitively.

I never knew what the client's specific challenge was, only that this content-free coaching made a huge shift for my client because I concentrated on listening at the deepest possible level. If you'd been a fly on the wall documenting the session, you'd note that my questions for a 20-minute session were minimal, while the client's answers were extensive.

Following is a summary of coaching questions and statements made by the coach in a typical content-free session. (The responses are omitted because they're in a language that the coach doesn't understand.)

*You have something you'd like to be coached on?*

*And is it OK for me to coach you in English and you respond in your native language knowing that I don't understand the words?*

*Would you like to give me some sense of what's happening for you?*

*And is there anything more about this?*

*I can tell this is very significant.*

*Ah, interesting.*

*OK, I can feel that too.*

*And what's truly possible for you in all this?*

*Something's blocking your way?*

*What do you need most of all right now?*

*And you know where to access that?*

*Who do you become when this is resolved?*

*And anything else?*

*It feels purposeful and complete. Are we done?*

*Thank you.*

To pace this kind of content-free coaching frees the coach to say very little and hold the space for the client to express her thoughts and feelings. The coach needs to tune in and decide when the client has said what she wants to say and when to respond. The session is like a dance in which you feel your partner move and you respond only when you're invited to move. Learn the dance by getting out there and experimenting!

If you have a client who speaks a language that you don't understand, invite her to respond in her own language. You can also use it with the client giving responses in gobbledegook, which is a useful technique for sensitive subjects that a client doesn't feel comfortable talking about.

# Chapter 7

# Gearing Your Approach to Your Audience: Understanding Different Decision-Making Styles

..........................................................

..........................................................

**S**imply put: people are different, particularly in the ways in which they make decisions.

Some people have strong aversions to risk, while others can't get enough. You meet individuals who are suspicious of any data that doesn't match their pictures of the world, whereas others just rely on their instincts. Some base their decisions on what worked in the past, whereas others focus on facts and analysis, afraid to make independent decisions.

If you apply a one-size-fits-all approach as you attempt to influence others, you're in for a rough ride and, most likely, failure. Instead, you can craft an approach tailored to how the person you want to persuade makes his decisions.

This chapter describes the subtle differences between five familiar decision-making styles. We show you how to identify and persuade each type, including specific buzzwords you can use to appeal to each style, as well as the best types of information and presentation formats that win over your listeners.

# Knowing Who's Who and What's What

Knowing how to interpret and respond to the words, actions and attitudes of people who make decisions that impact on your life leads to secure and effective relationships. Whether you're influencing your boss, a colleague or members of your family, knowing how to convert your suggestions into compelling cases can turn your proposals into winning propositions.

For their 2004 book, *The 5 Paths to Persuasion*, which explores how leaders make decisions, executive consultants Gary Williams and Robert Miller interviewed nearly 1,700 executives across a wide range of industries. They identified five predictable types of decision-making processes: charismatics, sceptics, thinkers, followers or controllers. Persuasion works best when adapted to fit one of the five. Their findings show that to be a successful persuader you need to:

- **Customise your proposals.** Organise your information in the way that appeals to your listener. You must direct your arguments to your decision-makers' preferred styles, otherwise you don't stand a chance of persuading them to accept your proposals.

- **Become adept at interpreting behaviour.** People only make major decisions after collecting and processing information in their preferred style. As a persuader, you must carefully observe the person you want to persuade in order to know which style you're dealing with.

- **Assemble a full toolkit to draw from.** In order to influence the different types of decision-makers, you need to know what tools to use, as well as when and in what order.

Williams and Miller stress that their research is based on how people make decisions and is not influenced by personality types. Furthermore, while most people's decision-making styles change according to circumstances, when making difficult choices involving complicated issues and significant consequences, people revert to type. In other words, when the pressure's on, you use what worked in the past.

Williams and Miller also note that while some of the names for decision-making types may sound negative, they're simply descriptive terms to explain the main way each group of people makes decisions. No style is better than another. All can produce both good and bad decisions.

Also, like human beings themselves, the five different types can sometimes be tricky to decipher because every person contains elements of all five styles. That being said, Williams and Miller offer a starting point for considering different styles and strengthening your persuasive skills.

As you read through the following sections, consider which style you may belong to. Look for characteristics that resonate and sit naturally with you. While this approach isn't an exact science, it can give you insights into how you go about making decisions.

# Convincing the Charismatics

*Charismatic decision-makers* are identified as *charismatic* because they encompass certain charismatic qualities – such as passion for bold, innovative thinking, out-of-the-box approaches and a deep-seated desire for knowledge. Big picture thinkers, risk-seeking and responsible, a *charismatic decision-maker* needs to see what you're talking about as well as hear what you say. At work, canned Power point slide shows bore them to distraction so come to a meeting with a few prepared charts that can be modified in your head and redrawn on a whiteboard. Away from the office, be prepared to sketch out your ideas on a piece of paper. Although they're initially enthusiastic about a new idea or proposal, they require a balanced set of information before making their final decision.

Charismatics often have short attention spans and thrive on interaction. Start with the most critical information first. Be prepared for them to get up and walk around while you're talking. When they do, stay seated. Charismatics rely on you to refrain from joining in their excitement and count on you to stay grounded. They like to think out loud and get things moving. In addition, they like to bat ideas around and scribble down their thoughts, leaving it up to others to fill in the details later.

You know when you're interacting with a charismatic decision-maker because the person's face lights up with exuberance and enthusiasm when you present your big idea. You feel like you can comfortably introduce bold, even revolutionary thinking. The person may actually jiggle on the edge of his chair with excitement.

While charismatics typically embrace your idea when you first propose it, getting a final decision can be tough. Charismatics have likely experienced past mistakes in which their impulsiveness led to sorrow. Without having enough facts to support their emotions in the early stages of the process, they made previous decisions too quickly, often leading to unfortunate outcomes.

As a result, just when you believe you've persuaded them to commit to your plan, follow your lead or do as you suggest, and you're ready to crack open the champagne, they up and vanish. They may not take your phone calls or respond to your emails. They may delay making the decision to proceed in spite of their initial enthusiasm. To prevent this from happening, begin your persuasion process by giving charismatics the most critical information up front and make sure that you provide enough facts to support whatever information you give. Make sure that you back up your proposals with supporting data and a balanced set of information (see the following section 'Offering balanced information').

If you want to persuade a charismatic, be patient. While they loathe wasting time gaining consensus and can't be bothered with introspection, they avoid acting rashly and can take a long time making their decisions, frequently turning to trusted advisors to help them come to conclusions. While they may appear independent, and believe that they are, they're usually not. Charismatics rely on strong number two people to help them see the forest for the trees. These devil's advocates help keep the charismatics grounded and weigh in with their opinions, helping to think through the details the charismatics undoubtedly overlook or simply can't be bothered with. A charismatic can draw from a stable of trusted advisors – from business partners to life partners. The point is, charismatics seek advice from people they trust. When you're putting your arguments together, consider who they turn to for advice and support. Factor these important advisors into your overall approach.

David is always on the lookout for new and exciting investment ventures. When Stewart approached him with the chance to invest in his film distributorship, David leapt at the opportunity. He had always been fascinated by the film world and, although he was already a multi-millionaire, he saw this as another opportunity to make more money and have fun in the process. Stewart advised David that to gain an equity stake in the company he would have to invest £500,000 with an initial investment of £100,000. David agreed without hesitation and promised the funds would be transferred into the company account by the end of the week. When David got home that night and told his wife, Tina, what he had decided to do, she came in with probing questions including challenging him about his knowledge of the film industry, the people he was dealing with, anticipated returns on investment and other details David, in his excitement for the opportunity, had failed to ask. By triggering doubts in David's mind, Tina got him to think more carefully about his plan and put an end to the deal.

The following sections explore the key strategies for effectively influencing charismatic individuals.

## Offering balanced information

Charismatic decision-makers must have supporting data in order to make their decisions. They do want facts to support their emotions and lose their initial enthusiasm quickly if you don't have the details at hand. However, if you hit a charismatic decision-maker with tons of exhaustive facts and number-crunching exercises in the early stages of your persuasion process, you can say goodbye to your proposal.

In spite of seeming exuberant and enthusiastic at first, charismatics are methodical when making decisions and only take educated risks, relying on research and market studies to support their instincts. Having made mistakes in the past, they try to control their initial burst of excitement and douse themselves in reality. With this in mind:

- ✔ **Don't bog down charismatics with minutiae, particularly in the early stages of the process.** You quickly temper a charismatic's keenness if you muddy his thinking with too much data and detail.

- ✔ **Always know your back-up plans and strategies.** Although charismatics may seem uninterested in the finer details, they want to know that you've a well-developed plan in the background, ready to support any and every recommendation you're making. Because they've been burned in the past, they wait to act until they feel secure that you've crossed every *t* and dotted each *i*.

- ✔ **Plan for supporting visuals.** While charismatics can easily absorb a lot of information and can move from the big picture to the details without batting an eye, have visuals on hand to back up your proposal. A lot of verbal or written information often overwhelms and causes this type of decision-maker to lose enthusiasm. See the later section 'Providing visual aids to strengthen your position' in this chapter.

## Acknowledging and discussing risks

Risk averse? Not the charismatics. 'Bring it on!' can be their slogan. However, don't take that to mean that you can be rash and reckless when persuading a charismatic. They fight their urge to make on-the-spot decisions and usually have a wing-man close by to hold them back from plunging head first into unknown waters.

Give your charismatic listener supportive data to sustain their interest or they're likely to lose enthusiasm quickly. Be upfront when persuading charismatic decision-makers, telling them the bottom line, including the risks. Keep your arguments simple and straightforward – and explain upfront how you plan to minimise any risks and what measures you're prepared to take. By being truthful and direct, you're more likely to gain their acceptance than if you make the mistake of joining in with their initial excitement.

When you're persuading charismatics, slightly undersell the parts of your proposal that are likely to arouse their curiosity. For example, if a client has a dilemma he believes you can solve, avoid getting caught up in his enthusiasm by pointing out potential obstacles and gathering as much information as you can before committing to a deal. Frequently, and without necessarily being aware of what they're doing, charismatics try to pass a problem onto someone else in order to get rid of it. Simply acknowledge the points they're interested in. You don't need to hype something they're basically on-board with. Then lay out the inherent risks. This reality check makes you come across as honest and as someone who can be trusted.

Don't attempt to conceal any latent threats or dangers. A charismatic is going to discover them later – when you're not around to address any concerns that pop up. Despite their initial enthusiasm for an idea, charismatics are thorough and rely on others – especially those who understand the full implications of a proposal – before making a decision. While charismatics appear to be independent thinkers, they defer to experts – such as a chief financial officer, head of IT or a lawyer – who understand the implications of their choices before making their final decisions. Follow through rigorously, making sure that you do all the work that's requested and turn it over to the charismatics' key lieutenants, or else you may sabotage yourself. When the charismatics' trusted advisors are satisfied and you've followed through on your end of the bargain, all will be plain sailing. If you fail to follow through, you can expect to be seen as untrustworthy, ill-prepared and a questionable character.

## Providing visual aids to strengthen your position

When you're making your persuasive pitch to a charismatic, make sure that you've got plenty of pictures, images, diagrams and charts at hand. Because charismatics tend to see the world in visual terms, drawings and objects help clarify their thinking. For more information about learning styles and sense preferences, have a look at *Neuro-linguistic Programming For Dummies* by Romilla Ready and Kate Burton (Wiley) and *Business NLP For Dummies* by Lynne Cooper (Wiley), which deal with this topic in detail.

In addition to visual aids, fill your speech with visual metaphors. Compare abstract ideas and concepts to concrete objects. Use words such as 'What I see here is . . . ', 'Focusing on this point . . . ', 'Imagine that . . . ' and 'The big picture we're looking at is like . . . ' in your speech and writing.

Kiera scheduled a meeting with her boss, Nicky, to discuss ideas for a restructuring programme that Kiera believed would save her department more than £50,000 annually. Kiera prepared several visual aids for the meeting – for her own reference as well as for Nicky, who was visually orientated. Before the meeting, Kiera reviewed her visuals and thought about how she could modify and redraw them on the spot if necessary, based on Nicky's reaction to the information. Kiera began the actual presentation by drawing a diagram showing the current financial state of her department. She then presented another chart, outlining her proposal for the new structure and how it addressed current problems. When she saw that Nicky was captured by what she was seeing, the two of them stood at the flip chart, coloured pens in hand, drawing further charts and diagrams together.

Visually orientated charismatics pay careful attention to how they look and are usually smartly turned out. They expect others to dress in a similar fashion. If you want to impress a charismatic, make sure that you're well groomed, and that you add an elegant accessory – a good-quality watch, beautiful piece of jewellery, stylish tie or a smart handbag or briefcase. You don't need to compliment the charismatic on his notably attractive clothing items or office decor as charismatics habitually present themselves well.

## Tying arguments to bottom-line results

When you're persuading a charismatic, always link your arguments to the bottom line, be it a financial result, an emotional connection or a desired relationship. Charismatics are results-driven and keen competitors, whether they're working in business, at home or building a relationship with a potential partner.

Even if they don't ask straight away, charismatics want results-orientated information. If you fail to provide it, they become frustrated and annoyed, particularly when they want to explore your proposal in more detail after the initial discussion. Don't waste their time with extraneous niceties or chitchat that may be interesting to some but hold no fascination for charismatics.

When you're persuading charismatic decision-makers, include any (or all) of the following written and spoken words in your proposal in order to capture their interest:

- **Nouns:** *results, actions*
- **Verbs:** *show, watch, look, focus*
- **Adjectives:** *proven, bright, easy, clear*

# Swaying the Sceptics

With their strong personalities and what some consider to be antisocial behaviour, *sceptics* tend to have a highly suspicious nature and look for reasons to distrust people and their recommendations. When they do act, their decisions are based on their belief in your credibility. In order to establish your credibility, you can gain endorsement from someone the sceptic trusts, but ultimately you have to earn it through your own behaviour.

Others often describe sceptics as demanding, disruptive and disagreeable; they can also be rebellious. They can be tough – but not impossible – to persuade. They like to take charge and have a combative style. They look for reasons *not* to agree to your proposals; reasons *not* to do business or make agreements with you. Above all, with their suspicious nature, they question everything and accept nothing at face value.

While sceptics are straightforward, make decisions quickly and hop on board with ground-breaking ideas (as long as they trust you), they can also be unruly in meetings by taking phone calls or engaging in side conversations. They may just get up and leave if your argument seems full of holes or unsubstantiated.

Sceptics leave you in no doubt about where you stand. When you first meet sceptics, they always find rationales to be suspicious of you. They look for reasons to distrust you and only if they fail to find them do they begin to perceive you as credible. They don't ever give the benefit of the doubt to someone who's unproven but once you've stood up to their scrutiny and have gained their trust, you're on a winner. They're quick to tell you what's on their minds and don't hesitate to lock horns any chance they get. When they attack with volleys of questions, you're likely to feel as though they're attacking you personally (although that's not really the case). See the following section 'Allowing them their clout', for more about sceptics' questioning.

When you go to persuade a sceptic, be prepared – be very prepared. They can demand a lot of your time and energy, questioning every bit of data you place in front of them, especially those facts that challenge the way they view their world. Ultimately, most sceptics are willing to alter their positions – if you're patient with them, answer all their questions, back up your responses with credible sources and then allow them to draw their own conclusions. Although they can seem challenging, the key is to keep calm and carry on. The following sections cover the best ways of persuading sceptics.

## Establishing credibility through similarities

Credibility scores high on a sceptic's list of important attributes, so fill your arsenal with as much credibility as you can.

Sceptics trust people who are similar to them. If you didn't go to the same university, work for the same companies or belong to the same clubs, you need to find another way of proving that you're similar if you're to have any success in persuading them to accept your point of view. While a colleague can vouch for you, ultimately a sceptic only trusts you after you prove that you're credible. If the sceptic has no prior experience of you, prepare yourself for lengthy and aggressive questioning to establish that you're reliable and trustworthy. Earning credibility with a sceptic takes time and for a sceptic to believe in you, you have to stand your ground without getting defensive. If you're able to do that, the sceptic will give you his stamp of approval.

## Gaining endorsement from trusted sources

If you haven't already proven your credibility with a sceptic, solicit the endorsement of someone he trusts. Sceptics are more prepared to listen to you if someone they believe in has bought into your proposal. In fact, you may want to ask the trusted person to co-present your proposal with you, transferring their credibility onto you.

However, while this endorsement approach may work for a while, ultimately you have to prove yourself to a sceptic if you're to gain their trust and confidence.

Whether prior to your meeting or during it, gaining the support of someone the sceptic knows and counts on for honest assessments allows you the freedom of having an open discussion of the issues on their level, while the sceptic continues to maintain his superior position. You can get buy in from someone the sceptic already trusts by floating your thoughts by this person before having the discussion with the sceptic. You can also suggest that this person presents any information that may be controversial, as he's already established his credibility with the sceptic. That way your ideas are heard without you being in the firing line.

## *Allowing them their clout*

Persuading sceptics is a risky business. They're like attack dogs and have no compunction about challenging your integrity or your data. Put on your kid gloves, your steel-plated vest and handle sceptics with care.

When you're persuading them to see your point of view and they go on the attack, don't fight fire with fire, no matter how tempted you may be. Aggressive counterattacks only lead to more aggression.

Don't try to examine a sceptic's reasons for behaving the way he does. That's just the way things are. Rather than withering under a sceptic's challenge or putting him on the defensive, accept that sceptics rarely trust anything that doesn't fit into their worldview. They may want to move forward with a good idea – they just need to be certain that the person offering the idea is credible and can be trusted.

Avoid going on the defensive. While sceptics' accusations and criticisms may sting, you're not the only one to feel the pain of their assaults. They're critical and suspicious of everything and everyone. Stay cool, calm and collected as a sceptic flexes his muscles. Stand firm in your ideas and keep your emotions in check as you respond rationally and patiently to the sceptic's concerns. In addition, make sure that when you present data to back up your proposal, it comes from a reliable source and not hearsay.

To persuade sceptics, you must establish trust by allowing them to safeguard their reputation and protect their ego. Whatever you do, don't confront them as you may cause offense, which may just heighten their negative feelings toward you. Whatever criticisms or accusations they fling your way, depersonalise them. Their attacks have nothing to do with you personally – they're suspicious of everyone and everything until they're given clear reasons not to be. Even when they're coming at you with a full frontal attack, remain cool as a cucumber, biting your tongue, breathing deeply from your core or counting inwardly to ten if necessary.

Tread lightly around a sceptic's ego by acknowledging the sceptic or someone they respect. For example, when you present supporting information, preface your remarks with a comment like 'You're probably already aware that . . . ' or 'As you know, Apple succeeded by taking a similar approach to . . . '. Be sure that any example you share shows how the company's reputation was enhanced or tainted as a result of the decision made. Away from the office, this approach works equally well. For example, comments like 'Undoubtedly you know how valuable your contribution was when . . . ' or 'When your son shared his experiences of . . . ' provide supporting evidence to your observations.

Sceptics want to be seen as knowing everything. They don't like being helped, and they *really* don't like being contradicted. That said, they're not infallible, and you may need to correct inaccurate information that they hold to be true. While you risk offending them if you correct their thinking, they won't respect you if you acquiesce or back down. A tricky situation, indeed, so proceed with caution. Never accuse them of being wrong or not knowing what they're talking about and do everything you can to avoid judgemental language. Instead, present your case in a neutral, dispassionate way, allowing sceptics to draw their own conclusions and maintain face while you prove your credibility.

When Paul accused his wife, Anne, of grossly overspending on decorating and refurbishing their house and being personally accountable for spiralling costs, Anne remained calm. She asked if Paul was testing her, because she thought that when they had discussed the project several months earlier, Paul had told Anne to spend what she needed to make the house more to their liking. Anne then asked Paul if the situation had changed. Paul re-established the trust he had originally placed in Anne because Anne allowed him to save face.

Sceptics have a little bit of rebelliousness under their stern exteriors. They like to buck the trend and always like taking credit for new or innovative ideas. Whatever you propose, always tie it back into points they've made in the past or accomplishments you know that they're proud of.

## *Grounding concrete facts in the real world*

Sceptics are uncomfortable with abstracts. Like meat and potato people, they like hard facts and concrete reasoning. If something can go wrong, they want to know about it from the start and they insist upon verification of all your information sources.

The more reputable sources you can provide, the better. Be prepared to refer them to the successes of people they admire and put them in touch with other experts.

Craig was in charge of a major restructuring programme that required relocating 500 employees. As he presented his case to Don, his managing director, he included specifics, consisting of how he planned to close the premises in Loughborough and how the company may benefit. Craig suggested subleasing the space, including parking and recreational areas. He also made suggestions for how the building could be used, seeing it as an ideal site to turn into serviced office space, which was much in demand in that area. He provided data of how other companies had taken a similar approach, adding in examples of companies that had failed as well as those that had succeeded. Because Craig approached the situation with concrete examples of what was possible and had data to back up his proposal, he was able to persuade Don to act on his suggestion.

Appeal to the sceptics by including the following words when you speak with or write to them:

- **Nouns:** *power*, *action*, *trust*
- **Verbs:** *feel*, *grasp*, *look*, *focus*, *demand*, *disrupt*
- **Adjectives:** suspect, agreeable

# Appealing to the Thinkers

Logical and intellectually astute, *thinkers* can be difficult to understand and tough to persuade. They tend to make decisions primarily from their heads, not their hearts. They explore every nook and cranny of your proposal before making a decision. Picky is a word you can use to describe thinkers because they take apart problems and work their way back through a course of logic-based solutions.

When you're persuading a thinker, pretend you're speaking to an academic. (You may very well be doing just that.) Appeal to their brain power. Present them with intellectual arguments and clever lines of reasoning.

'Bring on the data!' may as well be their cry to arms. Thinkers are ravenous readers and choosy with their words, and don't talk a great deal. If you really want to please and impress them, come armed with a plethora of measurable arguments.

Thinkers are turned on by anticipating change and winning the chase. They get a real buzz from out-thinking and out-manoeuvring the competition. If they think that a bargain's to be had – a relatively risk-free prospect of saving time or money – they side-step their usual decision-making process in the interests of time and money. (Thinkers share this bargain-mindedness with followers; see the following section.)

Thinkers like being in control and don't care about being innovative. They keep their emotions under wraps and play their cards close to the chest, giving nothing away as they meticulously process arguments and ideas. Most of all, thinkers don't like risk.

Thinkers like to be included in the decision-making process, so after presenting your recommendation, ask for their help in filling in any possible blanks. Provide them with all the relevant information, as much as you can muster, and then sit back and wait while the thinker processes your proposal. This waiting period can be a matter of minutes, hours or days. Be patient. Thinkers need time to thoroughly analyse a problem as they explore all the potential pros and cons of every possible solution. Encourage them to solicit the help of others, as thinkers like to work through things with trusted advisors to make sure that they've not missed anything.

## *Telling your story sequentially*

When you're persuading a thinker, present your proposal by starting at the very beginning – a very good place to start – and finishing up at the end. Do everything you can to maintain a logical, sequential order.

Think of the process like feeding them a meal; begin with the appetiser and finish up with dessert. Jumping into the main course – for example, presenting your solution before introducing your proposition – is no way to persuade a thinker.

To persuade a thinker, allow them to confirm that every step in the process is free of error. As my lawyer brother says, 'Never assume facts that haven't been placed in evidence.' Thinkers like to be in control, so don't try to hide any information that would jeopardise that need.

- ✔ If you know of a hole in your proposition, a flaw in your thinking, an aspect that's open to interpretation or a point of contention, address the problem on the spot and encourage the thinker to get involved in analysing the situation before moving onto your next item.

- ✔ If you've made any assumptions based on inklings and intuition, admit it upfront. Thinkers are quick to spot your sixth sense at work.

- ✔ If a thinker doubts your judgement or reasoning on a point you're making and you're not able to defend it satisfactorily, stop and explain yourself. Your entire proposal can become suspect when thinkers disagree with you on an important bit of information.

If you've any concerns about the viability of what you're proposing, tell the thinker at the beginning of your conversation. Being risk-averse, thinkers need to know the possible downsides upfront. They need to explore and understand all the perils inherent in your proposition and may come at you with a battery of questions. Unlike the sceptics, these questions aren't personal and are only intended to challenge your process or data.

Explain your processes and data sources from the very beginning to gain a thinker's attention. If you have to limit the amount of information you offer the thinker to one piece, make that your methodology. They want to know most of all *how* you got from point A to point Z. You do this by defining the problem, highlighting the pros and cons of different options and explaining how they can minimise risk by choosing what you believe is the optimum solution.

Begin your presentation by presenting a slideshow of the project's history to provide thinkers with a framework for your proposal. Away from the office, begin your conversation by giving the thinker background information about the subject you want to discuss and offer them a few options of how to address the situation. Then discuss the pros and cons of each option including the risks involved. Be prepared for thinkers to ask a barrage of questions. They need to understand a situation from all angles before committing to a solution. You can even play devil's advocate to help the thinkers look at every perspective.

Like elephants, thinkers never forget. Bad experiences remain at the forefront of a thinker's mind, so whatever recommendation you make, be sure – beyond a doubt – that your option is the best option. (Of course, always be certain of your recommendations whenever you're persuading someone – but make a special effort when you're dealing with thinkers.)

## Providing abundant data

Thinkers hunger for comparative data and aren't satisfied until they consume as much as is available. Burn the midnight oil and do your homework. Fill your proposal with mountains of information, including market research, customer surveys, case studies, cost–benefit analyses and any other substantiating evidence you can muster. The more the merrier. Thinkers thrive on data and do their upmost to understand all perspectives on the subject at hand.

Rather than flood a thinker with options, shape your argument. Highlight the benefits and drawbacks of each option you offer. Supply thinkers with pertinent examples, drawing your data from different situations. Balance the data you provide with examples of wins and losses to avoid seeming prejudiced and deliberately trying to steer the final decision. See the following section 'Letting them draw their own conclusions' for more on the importance of putting a thinker in the driver's seat of the decision-making process.

Because of their need for as many facts and figures as you can provide, you may need to take more time persuading thinkers than you do other types. My advice? Be patient. Let them gorge themselves on facts and figures. Then give them time to digest the information and consider all the ramifications, no matter how long the process takes. The good news is, because thinkers are generally people of their word, when they tell you they'll have an answer by next Thursday morning, they do. Agree to a time frame and let them get on with it. You don't need to micro-manage as long as the thinkers feel engaged with the process. You can bring them on board by openly discussing your worries and concerns about the weaknesses in your proposal and your approach. Thinkers like honesty and being up front with them increases your credibility.

No matter how much information you provide, the chances are a thinker's going to ask for more. You'd be hard-pressed to over-anticipate a thinker's desire for data, but don't let this desire for information worry you. When presenting your proposal, you don't have to have all your arguments firmly in place. Thinkers like to be part of the process and want to help tweak and tune your thinking. That said, once they give you their input, they expect you to come up with the goods.

Present your data in big chunks over two meetings – or more, if needed. This way, the thinker can absorb and make sense of the information. After your first meeting, take on board the thinker's input and incorporate it into your to do list for gathering more data or backing up your arguments in preparation for your follow-up meeting. Let the thinker add his input in order to make him feel he has ownership of the methodology.

Thinkers abhor surprises. After adjusting your proposal based on the thinker's amendments and modifications, point out anything new and different from your first presentation, such as revised data.

## Letting them draw their own conclusions

Thinkers like to, well, think, and because they don't like being helped, you have to grant them the right to draw their own conclusions. Steering their responses jeopardises your credibility in their eyes, so keep your thoughts to yourself and give them plenty of time and space to reflect on what they hear and to figure out things for themselves.

Because thinkers like to play their cards close to the chest and often appear inconsistent in their views, you may struggle to detect how they feel about any of your suggestions. Thinkers are a tough lot, concealing their intentions until they're ready to render their decision. Simply remain silent as they digest your information and draw their own conclusions.

Always focus on open communication and involve the thinker as much as possible when you're seeking solutions. Besides engaging them, this approach makes them feel that they own the process, which ultimately helps you by getting their buy-in. Always be candid with thinkers and gain their input about your method. Thinkers like being part of the process and want to know that their input has been acted on. After you first present the process you're using to come up with a solution, schedule another discussion, perhaps a week later, to show the thinker how you're getting on. Holding regular meetings and keeping them in the loop helps the thinker become familiar and comfortable with your approach.

If you're working with a thinker on a major decision, keep him informed of the process you're using to arrive at your solution. Before a meeting, send him a report so he has a chance to review it and, during the meeting, talk him through the details. The bigger the decision, the more you must keep the thinker involved along the way.

Words and phrases that appeal to thinkers include:

- **Nouns:** *quality, numbers, data, plan, competition, proof*
- **Verbs:** *think, makes sense, plan*
- **Adjectives:** *academic, intelligent, expert*

# Urging the Followers

Followers are highly conscientious decision-makers. They tend to make decisions in the same ways they did in the past, based on how other, respected people came to their conclusions.

In some ways, followers seem contradictory:

- They fear making mistakes (so don't expect them to be early adopters of a proposal). They're turned on by known brands and bargains appeal to them because both represent less of a gamble.
- They're good at grasping others' points of view, and despite their cautious nature, they can be surprisingly spontaneous.

Identifying followers can be difficult because they share characteristics with charismatics, thinkers and sceptics (see the preceding sections for more on each of these decision-making types) – and they don't see themselves as followers. If you get into a discussion with them about their cautious nature, they'll flatly deny it. Followers are likely to prefer describing themselves as creative thinkers, innovative pioneers, rebels and mavericks – about as far away from their actual decision-making type as possible. The reason for that is simple. Followers don't want to be thought of as followers because of the negative connotation to the word 'follow'. They associate following with weakness and would rather be perceived as leaders, which connotes strength. What some followers tend to forget is that too many cooks spoil the stew and that followers are frequently dynamic and highly effective.

If you struggle to identify the type of person you're dealing with, look at their past decisions rather than what they say about themselves. Actions speak louder than words.

Still can't identify a person's decision-making type? You can safely assume that the person is a follower unless you find evidence to the contrary. Regardless of a person's preferred decision-making style, you can't go wrong by taking the persuasive approach of supplying lots of proof that your solution has a proven track record because everyone likes knowing that.

While you may not think of people in leadership roles as followers, you can find them, particularly within large, traditional corporations. In fact, research shows that 36 per cent of executives are followers and that only 6 per cent of sales presentations are targeted to their decision-making style.

## Helping them understand through successes – their own and others'

Because followers are adept at seeing things from other people's perspective, they like examples of success, especially case studies. By offering them examples of where others succeeded – and purposely leaving out the failures unless they ask for them – followers can often see themselves succeeding in similar ways.

Unless you've got a solid track record of success, don't take the path of persuading a follower based on your own recommendation. Instead:

- ✔ **Refer to past decisions they themselves made that support your position.** Remind a follower of how a similar approach that he took in the past worked. You can say something along the lines of, 'This is the way you've always approached this kind of problem. The only difference now is . . . ', 'This reminds me of when you . . . " or 'Remember when you were faced with a similar situation and you . . . '. Followers need to feel comfortable knowing that what you're suggesting has succeeded in the past.

- ✔ **Share winning stories of other successful leaders.** Prove that people they trust and respect did well by pursuing a certain strategy, and most followers go down the same route.

- ✔ **Draw from examples *outside* of the follower's profession.** Followers are likely to become even more excited about the prospect of following these types of winning strategies because they get to rely on proven ideas while seeing themselves as being the first to pioneer the 'new' strategy within their own industry.

Unlike sceptics, whom I describe earlier in this chapter, followers are not intrinsically suspicious. When they're struggling to understand a point, they gladly turn to you for help. You can comfortably challenge a follower and chances are they'll yield as long as you've got back-up data they respect.

## Minimising risk

Followers are keen to hold onto their hats and keep their jobs. While they want to be associated with solutions that are ground-breaking, original and even revolutionary, they desire answers that are reliable, proven and safe.

Don't expect a follower to adopt blue-sky thinking or out-of-the-box ideas. Unless you present a follower with information they can't ignore, they're most comfortable maintaining the status quo.

If you want a follower to accept a bold, new strategy, show how someone else has succeeded by following the same plan.

When you present your ideas, give the follower options to choose from – three's a good number; neither too many nor too few – and link each option to fully fleshed-out case studies. As you undoubtedly have one option that you think is best, link most frequently to your strongest case study. Even if your listener cottons onto one of your other suggestions (perhaps because he sees a chance for a bargain), you can be prepared to point out that your comprehensive analysis of the data shows that, on a risk-adjusted basis, your preferred option is the most cost-efficient. Presenting your proposal as part of your comprehensive analysis is sure to persuade a follower that you've worked through all permutations of possibilities and identified a winning strategy.

---

## Thrifty followers

If, in spite of all the proof you provide, you're still having trouble persuading a follower to go for your proposal, remember that followers love bargains. More than any other decision-making style, followers have the strongest desire for a good deal. If you want them to try something new – something they usually find risky – lower your price. If a follower thinks that he's getting a bargain, he may get to the point where he thinks that he can't afford *not* to take a risk.

Additionally, followers like to haggle. They like a bit of a tease and can be impulsive. Get yourself into a negotiating mood by thinking of yourselves as two people at the souk, each trying to wrangle a better price. The follower should enjoy the lively interchange, and if you put a time-sensitive element into your proposal, the follower is likely to say 'Okay'.

## *Keeping it simple*

Although followers like to be seen by clients, colleagues and anyone else who's looking as innovative – even though they're not – they really don't like being taken out of their comfort zone. Hit them with too much novelty, and you can kiss goodbye to your chances of persuading them.

Persuading followers is an easy prospect, as long as you give them what they need and nothing more. While followers like you to present them with profuse amounts of evidence that something is proven, avoid the temptation of thinking you need to include further amounts of information unless this information is relevant and explains how your proposed solution has worked in the past. Don't waste your time giving them too much information. They're likely to feel overwhelmed by too much information that they didn't really ask for.

Bottom line: keep your proposal simple, substantiated and straightforward.

Reframe your ideas with new references that affect your specific followers. Relate your proposal to something that's worked in the past that they're familiar with. Use phrases such as, 'Remember when you . . . ' or 'When we took this approach with . . . ' or 'You may recall from past experiences that . . . '. Each of these phrases puts your new suggestions into context for them.

John's an old-fashioned kind of guy who owns a successful property business, but he struggles to understand why the marketing and advertising campaigns that have worked well in the past aren't working so well now. Several years ago, his marketing director Louise suggested that they take a new approach to working with their customers. Rather than sending out costly four-colour printed brochures, Louise suggested undertaking more Internet activity. John baulked at the proposal, leading to a bit of tension in the office. Words and phrases such as *innovative*, *new*, *better* and *leading edge* threatened his perceptions, and he resisted her proposal. Louise was only able to persuade John to take a new approach by showing him how similar her suggestion was to what he was already doing, adding that making use of the Internet simply meant that what they were doing could be done with more ease and less cost.

Incorporate the following words and phrases into your speech and writing in order to persuade followers:

- ✔ **Nouns:** *expertise, experience, good deal, cost saving*
- ✔ **Verbs:** *innovate, expedite*
- ✔ **Adjectives:** *swift, bright, just like before, similar, previous, proven, what works, as in the past*

# Winning Over the Controllers

Love them or loathe them, *controllers* provoke strong reactions: on the one hand, they're demanding and frustrating to work with; on the other hand, they elicit fierce loyalty because of their candid way of communicating and their unswerving commitment to standards. When business is in turmoil, however, controllers are the ones you want at the helm because no one's better at getting the job done on time and within budget.

Logical, emotionally contained and detail-orientated, controllers are objective observers. They tend to have strong personalities and can come across as domineering. Whatever they do – whether sales, marketing, strategising or surfing the net – they're the best. At least, that's what they tell you.

Controllers see things only from their own perspective, unlike followers (see the preceding section) who can easily see things from another person's point of view. Snap judgements come easily to controllers and they're known for their cutting and scathing remarks. Loners by choice and tending to be rather egotistical, controllers make unilateral decisions with the possibility of leaving you standing there feeling rather redundant. Oh, sure, they may talk to you about a decision, but they seldom genuinely care about what you say.

Keep two main points in mind when persuading controllers:

- ✔ **Fear drives their decisions.** Controllers are always on the lookout for whatever can go wrong. They're never going to sit back on their laurels with smiles of contentment on their faces.

- ✔ **They need a lot – and I mean copious amounts – of time to make up their minds.** Persuading controllers is not so much persuading them, as letting them persuade themselves.

The following sections cover the essentials of influencing controllers.

## Overcoming internal fears

In spite of their bravado, controllers are inundated with fears and anxieties that they keep safely tucked away. They live in a state of constant tension between their private terrors and timidities, which they deny (even to themselves), and the persona they present to the world.

Because of their fears, they struggle to let go of even the smallest points. They question you about price, fearing that if they don't, you'll perceive them as weak negotiators. They demand that you come in ahead of schedule, dreading that their staff may see them as too soft. As well as doubting them-selves, controllers doubt other people and can even appear somewhat para-noid when interpreting other people's motives.

Like wounded animals, controllers may attack with aggressive comments and questions, and you may want to take their fury personally and react defen-sively. Don't. Instead:

- ✔ **Remain calm, composed and comforting.** I'm not saying this approach is the easiest way of dealing with a controller, I'm just saying it's the best way.

- ✔ **Patiently reassure them that you've worked through all possible per-mutations of the problem at hand.** Minimise any fears or anxieties they may have about your proposals by providing them with all the informa-tion they need; then back off and wait for them to respond.

In order to persuade controllers, you need to help them overcome their fears – without pointing them out. If you were to say something along the lines of, 'What are you so worried about?' most controllers would eat you for break-fast. Instead, patiently respond to their demands – they're bound to have many – while remaining calm and reassuring. Meeting their aggression with your own simply fans the flames and heightens their fears.

## Flooding with pure facts and analytics

You can spot controllers by the excessive amount of attention they pay to convoluted processes and procedures. They're likely to thrive on having you chase down further facts and figures as the mood strikes them. When you go to persuade a controller, make sure that you've got your data in place and that you absolutely, unconditionally and without a doubt know what you're talking about. Controllers only credit experts.

Controllers are frequently afraid of making decisions, especially when situa-tions involve lots of unknowns. Prepare for these individuals to become more aggressive and demanding, insisting that you provide them with more and more detailed information. Avoid becoming frustrated as that only adds fuel to their fire. Even when they've got you huffing, puffing and sweating buckets as you source obscure materials that they probably won't even look at, keep dancing to their tune.

Knowing what they want and when they want it, controllers leave nothing to chance and focus on the tiniest details in all proposals.

## Making your arguments structured, linear and credible

Controllers look for accuracy and facts presented in a structured and linear way. No jumping in at the middle or presenting your conclusions at the beginning if you want to persuade them. Controllers are persuaded by proposals that are strict and strong. They like discipline, authority and a command-and-conquer approach supported by highly analysed data. Present controllers with information that's ambiguous and open to interpretation, and watch their faces flush in fury. Give them unadulterated facts and clear analytics, and they're smiling. Submit proposals that seem preordained and destined to win, and they sign them off willingly.

You can't really persuade controllers to do anything because they always need to be in control. They draw their own conclusions, reach their own decisions and make up their own minds in their own sweet time. All you can do is give them all the information they need and keep your fingers crossed that they convince themselves to go with your proposal.

Controllers like to own the proposal, regardless of who suggested it. Let them think that your idea is theirs by tying your suggestion back to something they said or did in the past.

Because controllers need to be involved in all aspects of the decision-making process, they can slow things down. They can go beyond their remit or change the rules after negotiations begin. When they pull these punches, stand your ground. Be patient with them – as well as firm. 'That's not what we agreed but if you want to add extras we're prepared to do that at an additional cost' shows that you're both willing to work with the controller as well as resolute in your position.

Avoid aggressively pushing any decision when working with controllers. If you force their hands before they're ready to make up their mind, they see you as the problem and happily put the blame on you for anything that may go wrong. To avoid this from happening, you have to be absolutely clear from the beginning about what is – and isn't – negotiable and hold to your bottom line. Get everything in writing, and if you can, work through the controller's trusted advisors. Like all other decision-making types described in this chapter, controllers have their lieutenants who are invaluable resources of useful information and helpful suggestions.

## Working through others

Working directly with controllers can be tricky. They may try to avoid dealing with you, waiting to make up their minds and avoid taking responsibility in case something goes wrong.

If you're able to work with someone a controller trusts rather than the controller himself, go for it. Sometimes you can get lucky and the controller tells you not to deal with him directly, but instead to work with his colleagues – second-in-commands, trusted advisors, lieutenants, call them what you will – who report back to him. If that doesn't happen, suggest it yourself. You can also recommend that you work with the controller in pairs, thus avoiding one-on-one meetings where the controller may feel sanctioned power to do and say whatever he wants, including having an abusive go at you. Having another person present keeps the controller in check. Whatever you do, be diplomatic when dealing with a controller to prevent him from feeling cornered or that he's being kept in the dark.

Meetings with controllers can be fraught. Because of their need to be right and their demand for perfection, they can be ruthless in casting blame, especially if something doesn't fit their vision.

Seek allies when working with controllers. Because of the controller's need to be in charge, he may unwittingly sabotage your every effort. When you can, work with a partner. Two people together can often keep the lid on a controller's tendency to bully and act abusively.

If you do choose to work with a partner, make sure that you frame the meeting as a discussion and put the controller in charge. You don't want to look as though you're setting up a situation of two against one. You can perhaps say that you and your colleague were batting around ideas and wanted the controller's input. That way the controller feels valued and knows that nothing is going on behind his back.

Keep the following strategies in mind:

- Controllers need a lot of time to make up their minds. Be prepared for long silences as they draw their conclusions.

- Encourage controllers to make up their minds by giving them deadlines that are imposed by external factors – something out of their control – like new government regulations or a competitor's upcoming launch date.

- In meetings, controllers tend to be self-absorbed, focusing on their own thoughts. Because of that I suggest you schedule as few meetings as possible with controllers, working instead through their lieutenants who can do your persuading for you. If that's not possible, make sure that your meetings are highly structured and that you present your information in a linear way with the implication that your proposal is both unbeatable and unstoppable, thus matching the controllers' tendency to be clear, precise and straightforward.

Incorporate the following words into your speech and writing in order to persuade controllers:

- **Nouns:** power, details, facts
- **Verbs:** handle, grab, just do it, make them pay
- **Adjectives:** reasonable, logical, physically

For an outstanding example of how to persuade a group of people, watch the classic film *12 Angry Men*, in which juror number 8 – through incessant and logical probing, and by questioning the credibility of some of the witnesses – convinces his fellow jurors, all of whom have different decision-making styles, to change their votes.

## Persuading the masses

As I say in the beginning of this chapter, people are different with different decision-making styles. This makes persuading a group composed of various types of decision-makers an interesting challenge. Knowledge of the five different styles outlined in this chapter provides valuable clues on how to approach a mixed group.

When persuading a mixed group, begin your presentation with a quick summary of how your presentation is going to progress. As long as your overview makes logical sense, you can grab the attention of the thinkers because they respond favourably to rational thinking. When you've got the thinkers hooked, you can turn your attention to the other styles while the thinkers work through your arguments. As long as you continue to speak in a logical manner, the thinkers will stick with you. As for the controllers, you can't do much with them because they dance to their own tune and are all but impossible to sway in a group setting. Don't despair. As you hook the other styles, you may find some of the controllers get behind you, too.

The three styles you need to concentrate on are the sceptics, charismatics and followers because more people fit into these categories than into the others. Make the sceptics and followers comfortable by establishing your credibility and proving that you know your stuff.

More than most, these two styles rely on your personal integrity and track record to convince them that your proposal merits their attention. When you've got the followers and sceptics settled down, get into your ideas quickly to avoid losing the attention of the charismatics.

Having given your brief overview and established your credibility with examples of what you've done, provide bullet points of how you're going to proceed to satisfy the charismatics. When the time comes for you to burrow into those points – in a coherent, meticulous way – the charismatics, thinkers, sceptics and followers will be with you. Who knows, by this point you may have the controllers interested, too.

You may notice that this formula is like the approach: Tell them what you're going to tell them; tell them; tell them what you told them. The reason this approach works for a mixed group is that you hook the charismatics with your big idea. The thinkers join in because of your logical methodology and the followers come on board because others are. You may struggle with intransigent sceptics and controllers. The good news is that once you establish your credibility, you can persuade the sceptics and most people aren't controllers. As for those who are, turn to people they trust and work through them.

# Chapter 8

# Getting Ready to Make a Presentation

etting started is always the toughest part of any activity, including writing a speech or presentation – especially if you don't want to give one in the first place. But don't worry. Speechwriting doesn't have to be torture and can even be fun – well, at least more fun than getting poked in the eye with a sharp stick.

This chapter shows you several simple techniques for getting started with your speech or presentation.

## Making Important Preparations

Giving a speech or presentation doesn't start when you step in front of an audience. Giving a talk doesn't even start when you begin writing it. The entire process begins before you even accept the invitation to speak or present. The sections that follow discuss issues you should consider before you even commit yourself to a speaking engagement and things to think about prior to writing the content of your speech or presentation.

### Deciding whether you should speak

Just because you're asked to speak doesn't mean you have to. Of course, if your boss asks you to give a talk, you'd better do it, but we're referring to voluntary situations. Unfortunately, most people give little, if any, thought to whether they want to or should speak. Before you accept your next invitation to speak, consider the following issues so you can make the right decision:

- **Whether you have the time in your diary.** Remember, just because you're asked to speak for 30 minutes doesn't mean that's all the time it takes. You have to get to the event and back, of course, but you also need to leave time to answer questions and be available after you're finished. And you may need to engage in a bit of chit-chat either before or after your talk with the hosts who invited you. So, a 30-minute presentation can easily take up half of your day.

- **Whether you have the time to prepare.** Make sure that you have enough time to prepare a presentation that you're proud of and that meets the expectations of your audience – you want to create a great impression. While having an exact formula to follow would be great, in reality, preparing a 30-minute presentation can take hours, days, weeks, or months depending on whom you're speaking to and how important the presentation is. For example, if you need to put together a slide presentation, that could take hours to write. And then, of course, you may need to practise the presentation until you feel comfortable with it. You're the only one who can decide how much time is necessary for preparing your talk.

- **Whether you have something to say.** Just because someone asks you to present doesn't mean you have anything to say. Sometimes your best talk will be the one you don't give.

- **Whether to accept immediately.** You don't have to decide the moment someone asks you and you probably shouldn't. Take your time. Sleep on it. Get back to the person after you've had time to think about the considerations above.

Although we're sure you are a great speaker, bear in mind that some people resort to all forms of flattery just to get you to accept their invitation, especially if they're desperate to fill a speaking slot. Don't be swept away by their praise. Even if you truly are the perfect person for their engagement, it may not be something you want to or can do. Politely declining is okay if, after you've considered all the issues, you've concluded that this speaking engagement is not for you.

## *Figuring out why you're speaking*

Three types of speaker exist: Those who make things happen, those who watch things happen, and those who wonder what happened.

To avoid wondering what happened, you should definitely find out why you're speaking in the first place. Here are two effective ways to discover why you're giving a talk:

- ✓ **Figure out the goals of your talk.** Are you trying to inform, persuade, inspire, or entertain?

- ✓ **Examine your motivation for speaking and the audience's motivation for listening.** Have you been asked to speak? Have you been ordered to speak? Do you want to speak? Does the audience want to hear you? Have they been forced to hear you? Will they listen to you?

However you analyse your goals and motivation, the purpose remains the same – to know why you're speaking so you don't end up wondering what happened after it all goes horribly wrong.

## Setting specific goals

Most people either set no goals when they decide to give a presentation or set goals that are vague, such as wanting to be a hit, wanting to impress a co-worker or management, or wanting to get the talk over with. However, deciding what you hope to accomplish through speaking – your goals – makes developing yourpresentation easier.

Some examples of goals you may have are

- ✓ Wanting to build your credibility

- ✓ Wanting to get the audience to agree with your position

- ✓ Wanting to make the audience understand something

- ✓ Wanting to make the audience laugh

Write out your goals before you write your presentation. Then you can easily decide what material to include and exclude. Anything that doesn't further your goals o should be excluded.

## Getting the essential information

No matter what type of presentation you've been invited to deliver, certain information is basic and essential. You must first know the name of your contact person. Armed with that knowledge, you can ask your contact to provide the rest of the information that you need. The following lists show some of the questions you want answered.

Ask these questions about the event so you'll know the tone of the meeting and what will be expected from you:

- What's the purpose of the meeting?
- Is it a regularly scheduled meeting or a special event?
- Is it a formal or informal event?
- What's the atmosphere – very serious or light?
- Will your talk be the main attraction?

Ask these questions about the format to make sure your presentation content is the right length and style to fit properly into the meeting:

- What's the agenda for the day?
- What should the format be for your presentation:
    - A general session?
    - A breakout session?
    - A panel discussion?
    - Before, during, or after a meal?
- What time will you begin speaking?
- How long will you be expected to speak for?
- Will there be other speakers?
- When will they be speaking?
- What will they be speaking about?
- Will any of them be speaking in opposition to your views?
- What occurs before your presentation?
- What occurs after your presentation?

Ask these questions about the location to make sure that everything you need is available and arranged the way you prefer:

- Where will you speak?
    - Inside or outside?
    - What type of room: banquet, meeting, auditorium, and so on?
- How will the room and seating be set up?
- What audio/visual and sound equipment will be available for you?
- Will there be a podium/table/platform?

Ask these questions about the audience to get an idea of the mood they'll be in when you speak and how they'll react to you:

- ✔ What's the size of the audience?
- ✔ Is the audience required to attend?
- ✔ Are the people there to hear you or for some other reason?
- ✔ How much do they know about your topic?
- ✔ Will they be in a rush to leave?
- ✔ Will they be drinking?
- ✔ Will they be walking in and out as you speak?
- ✔ How have they responded to other speakers?
- ✔ What other speakers have they heard?
- ✔ What do they expect from you?

See the section 'Analysing Your Audience', later in this chapter, for a detailed discussion of how to suss out your listeners.

## Agreeing on a topic

You have a lot more control over your topic than you may suspect. Being asked to speak about a certain subject isn't the end of the discussion but just the beginning. If you don't like the topic, ask to change it. Many organisations will quickly accommodate your request. If you can't completely change the topic, try to slant it in a way that suits your needs.

Even when you're locked into a particular topic, you still have a lot of leeway in how to proceed. Suppose that you're a computer guru and you've been asked to speak about the latest upgrade to some software package that everyone wants to use. Will you give a broad overview? Will you give a list of specific tips for using it most effectively? Will you give a history of how it was developed? You can still essentially pick your topic because you can choose elements about the topic that was assigned to you.

Sometimes you may have free rein over the topic because the sponsoring organisation doesn't mind what you speak about. You may be given only the vaguest of guidelines – such as 'speak about business'. The organisation may just want you to show up and talk. (For more ideas on selecting a topic, see the next section 'Analysing Your Audience'

# Analysing Your Audience

How do you relate to an audience? You start by discovering as much about the people in the audience as possible – who they are, what they believe in, and why they are listening to you. This process is known as *audience analysis*.

The more information you can get, the more you can target your remarks to reflect your audience's interests. And by homing in on their concerns, you increase the likelihood that members of the audience will listen to you. Displaying your knowledge about an audience usually scores some points with them: They feel complimented that you bothered to learn about them.

Audience analysis also helps you develop your message. Such analysis structures the content of your presentation by shaping what types of arguments you should make; what the most effective examples will be; how complex your explanations can be; what authorities you should quote; and so on.

## Discovering demographics

The first thing we always want to know about an audience is its size. Will it be 10 people, 100 people, or 1,000 people? The size of the audience determines many aspects of a presentation. For example, a large audience eliminates the use of certain types of visual aids and requires the use of a microphone. A smaller audience is often less formal. Certain gimmicks that work with a large group will seem silly with a small one. (Telling the audience to 'Turn around and shake hands with the person behind you' just doesn't work when the entire audience is seated in one row.)

The second thing we want to know is the general nature of the audience: What's the relationship of the audience members to each other? Do they all come from the same organisation? Do they share a common interest? We use this information to shape our presentations at a very basic level. If the audience have a lot in common, our presentations can use terms and concepts that they all understand. We won't have to explain as much as for an audience with more diverse backgrounds.

The next thing we want to find out is specific demographic data about audience members. Depending on the circumstances, you may want to check out some of the following details:

- Age
- Gender
- Education level

✔ Economic status

✔ Religious affiliations

✔ Occupations

✔ Ethnic mix

✔ Political inclinations

✔ Major cultural influences

# Discovering what the audience is thinking

While speakers tend to focus on audience census data, they tend to over-look audience beliefs, attitudes, and values. The reason is simple: Gleaning information about what the audience is thinking is difficult. Yet their beliefs, attitudes, and values will colour their interpretation of every aspect of your presentation.

What exactly do you need to know? In essence, you want to compose a mental profile of your audience – to know 'where they're coming from'. And the person who asked you to speak should help you find out. Here are some of the questions you want that person to answer:

✔ What is the audience's attitude to the subject of your talk?

✔ What is the audience's attitude toward you as the speaker?

✔ What stereotypes may the audience apply to you?

✔ May anyone have a hidden agenda?

✔ What values does the audience find important?

✔ Does the audience share a common value system?

✔ How strongly held are its beliefs and attitudes?

The answers to these questions may determine your approach to the subject.

# Finding out what the audience knows

Here are some questions to ponder before you make your presentation:

✔ How sophisticated are the audience members about your topic?

✔ Will any experts be in the audience?

✔ Have the audience members heard other speakers talk about your topic?

> ✔ Why are they interested in your topic?
>
> ✔ Will they understand jargon related to your topic?
>
> ✔ Do they already know the basic concepts of your topic?
>
> ✔ Do they think they know a lot about your topic?
>
> ✔ How did they get the information that they already have about your topic?
>
> ✔ Are they familiar with your approach and attitude toward the topic?

The answers to these questions play a major role in how you construct your presentation. What your audience knows determines how much background you need to provide, the sophistication of the language you can use, and the examples you include.

## Relating to Your Audience

Establishing rapport with your audience is your primary goal – a feeling of mutual warmth and a sense that you're on the same wavelength. The following sections present a few ways to achieve that goal.

## Putting yourself in the shoes of your audience

Imagine that you're one of the members of the audience. What do they already know? What might they be interested in? Putting your audience at the heart of what you do – considering their needs and interests ahead of your own – is a great way to make them relate to you. In the following sections, we discuss some brilliant techniques for working out what your audience needs from you.

### Focusing on what interests the audience

You don't have to ignore your own needs, but your needs won't be served if no one is listening. For instance, if your audience has been sitting and listening to hours of presentations all day, give them a break and cut your 60-minute speech down to 30 minutes – they'll thank you for it.

### Discussing the world from the audience's point of view

Let the audience know that you can see the world or issue their way. Look for common experiences that both you and the audience share. For example, if your job has ever encompassed any of the duties of your audience, you could describe work situations that create a rapport and allow you to see the world from your audience's point of view. Or describe frustrating universal experiences such as traffic jams or dealing with faceless helplines.

People like to hear data related to what they do. So if you don't have an experience to share, you can substitute a study. But first acknowledge that you don't have the experience – or you'll lose credibility.

### Making personal experiences universal

Although an audience wants to hear about a speaker's personal experience, using 'I' all the time can turn them off. You can end up sounding like a raging egomaniac. So go ahead and describe that experience – just find and emphasise the universal aspects of your personal experience.

### Customising your remarks

Customising grabs the audience's attention and gets the audience involved in your speech. Tailoring your speech or presentation to a particular gathering makes the speaker a bit of an insider and lets the audience know that you went to the trouble of learning about them. And the good news is, a little (and we mean very little) customisation goes a long way. Many of us have given speeches where we made half a dozen references geared specifically to a particular audience and were showered with praise afterwards for the research we did to learn about the group. Make comments – humorous comments, praise, or just simple observations – about local businesses, the people you're speaking to, an organisation's history, or local news, events, or customs.

Use your imagination and consider what may impress you if an outsider referred to it.

Don't be offensive! If you're going to use a name of someone in or related to the group, clear it with a senior person at the organisation first. If you plan on poking fun at anything else local, discuss it with someone first to avoid inadvertently offending someone in the audience.

### Pushing their buttons

Purposely work in a reference to a hot topic – a source of minor controversy with the audience. Find an issue that affects the entire audience, not one that only affects key players and that no one else would understand. In addition, make sure that the issue isn't too controversial to mention – your contact will probably be reliable here.

A favourite example is when one of us suggested that an audience ease up on memo and report writing. 'You're wasting too much photocopy paper,'

Malcolm explained. The room burst into laughter and applause. Why? The people in the audience, employees of a big business, had been ordered to reduce their use of copier paper as a cost-saving measure. The comment wouldn't have been funny anywhere else. But here the audience thought it was ridiculous and appreciated the joke.

### Acknowledging what the audience is feeling

If you're speaking under any special circumstances, acknowledge those circumstances. Is the audience sweltering in a hot, stuffy room? Would the audience prefer to be anywhere but listening to you? Has the audience made certain assumptions about you? Get the issue out in the open or it will remain a barrier between you and your audience.

### Identifying and addressing audience subgroups

Keep in mind that an audience may be made up of numerous subgroups – each with its own special needs and agendas. To create rapport with your entire audience, you need to include something for each of them.

A common example of this situation is the convention dinner attended by spouses. Half the audience is made up of people with the same occupation – engineers, doctors, whatever. The other half – the spouses – fall into two major categories: Those who have careers outside the home and those who perhaps look after the family full time. So you immediately have three subgroups. The spouses with careers can probably be even further subdivided.

## Highlighting the benefits of what you've got to say

Make sure that the audience knows what they're going to get out of your speech. Identify and emphasise the benefits early in your talk and issue frequent reminders.

All audience members subconsciously ask themselves how a speech benefits them. They wonder if they will hear anything to help them save or make money; save time; or reduce stress, anxiety, ambiguity, and confusion. Sex and health are also topics of universal interest. These subjects span age, gender, culture, and geographic boundaries.

# Chapter 9

# Using Great Visual Aids in Your Presentations

*Y*ou've heard the saying, 'A picture's worth a thousand words'. If that saying were literally true, then the average 20-minute presentation could be reduced to two overheads, and we'd only need to spend 40 seconds looking at them before we could all go home. But of course the reality doesn't quite work that way. A picture is worth a thousand words only under certain circumstances. This chapter explores the nature of those circumstances – when visual aids help, when visual aids hinder, and what visual aids can really do for you – get the picture?

## Creating Charts and Graphs

Charts and graphs are commonly used to depict numerical data. They're also useful for expressing non-numerical relationships such as organisational structure, procedures, and lines of authority. Although charts and graphs appear most often on overheads and PowerPoint slides, they're becoming increasingly easy to print out in hard copy form for placement on an easel or flipchart stand.

## Choosing a type of chart or graph

The following points list some of the most common types of charts and graphs and how you may want to use them:

- **Bar graphs:** These are handy for comparing all kinds of data – sales of widgets versus gadgets, defect totals under various quality management programmes, drug reactions in infants versus adults.

- **Flow charts:** These are good for depicting any series of steps – company procedures, how a bill becomes a law, the pathway that an emergency phone call has to make to get through to the right service.

- **Line graphs:** These are great for showing changes over a period of time. Any kind of trend data works well – share prices, voting patterns, productivity gains.

- **Organisation charts:** Who reports to whom? What's the exact relationship between the telecommunications department and the information services department? Is the French operation an independent unit or part of the main plc? These types of questions can be answered with organisation charts.

- **Pie charts:** These are good for showing percentages in relation to each other. (The west of England region generated 7 per cent of the revenue; the east 10 per cent; the south 80 per cent; and the north 3 per cent.)

- **Tables of numerical data:** This is your basic spreadsheet layout. The format's boring, but sometimes the numbers are so dramatic that the format doesn't matter. ('As you can see from the numbers in column three, half of you are going to be made redundant next week. Surprise!')

## Making effective charts and graphs

The following are a few tips to keep in mind when you're using a chart or graph:

- **Limit the data.** If you include too many items on a chart or graph, you make it more difficult to understand. If you have a lot of items that must be represented, rethink the graph. Maybe you can split the data into several graphs.

- **Size pie slices accurately.** The audience gets confused when you show a pie chart with a slice labeled '10 per cent' that looks like a quarter of the pie. If you use a pie chart, make sure the slices of the pie correspond to the real numbers.

✔ **Make absolutely sure that the numbers are correct.** Check the numbers. Recheck them. And check them again. Correct data is a credibility issue. Someone in the audience is bound to be a stickler for detail and is certain to point the error out to the entire roomful of people. If one number is incorrect, it can undermine your entire presentation.

✔ **Avoid three-dimensional bars.** Don't make bar charts with three-dimensional bars. Because it's often difficult to figure out where the bars end, the audience may not know what the numbers represent. If in doubt, keep it simple.

# Making Use of PowerPoint and Overheads

You can't attend a business presentation these days without tripping over projector and computer wires. This section ensures that your audience doesn't trip over your visual aids.

## Using PowerPoint

Perhaps the greatest public speaking innovation in the past couple of decades, PowerPoint has grown rapidly from a novelty to a standard. Business speakers have treated it like the greatest thing since sliced bread (or the microphone). And many people now feel unable to speak without an accompanying PowerPoint presentation.

That reliance on PowerPoint is, of course, the problem. Although PowerPoint is undoubtedly a fabulous visual aid, the medium is often treated like an abused miracle drug. People overuse it, use it improperly, or become addicted to it. Because of this abuse, PowerPoint has spawned the following three major, negative side effects:

✔ **The presentation is underdeveloped.** Many speakers now spend more time preparing their PowerPoint slides than what they plan to say. They think that PowerPoint *is* their presentation. It's not! You still need a compelling message with an introduction and conclusion in order to hold the attention of an audience. Throwing up a load of PowerPoint slides isn't a presentation.

✔ **The speaker doesn't connect with the audience.** Ever heard speakers read their speech word-for-word from their PowerPoint slides? A presentation doesn't get much more boring than that. The audience can read the slides, too. So, if you plan on just reading the slide, you may as well not show up and just send the PowerPoint presentation for the audience to read themselves. Make sure you have something that is not written up on the PowerPoint slides to say to add colour to the presentation.

✔ **The message is lost.** While PowerPoint can add sparkle to a presentation, it can also overwhelm your message. Be careful not to animate every single slide, add too many graphics, or have too much text popping up all over the place. Your message disappears in the gimmickry.

Fortunately, the first two PowerPoint problems are easily solved just by being aware of them. That means the next time you are giving a presentation, remember to prepare an actual speech. PowerPoint should support your material, not replace it. Remember also to talk to your audience – not read slides to them. The third problem, of losing your message, can also be easily avoided. Just follow the advice in the section 'Discovering simple design rules'.

## Using overhead transparencies

Overhead transparencies are useful because you can project them without turning down the room lights. (So the audience isn't invited to snooze.) You can also write notes to yourself on the cardboard frames around the transparencies. And most important, you can reorder them as you speak.

However, overheads don't work well for a large audience because not everyone can see them clearly.

## Discovering simple design rules

Whether you're using overhead transparencies or PowerPoint slides, a few basic design rules can ensure you leave your audience dazzled not dazed. Just keep the following in mind:

✔ **Check for spelling mistakes.** Nothing is more embarrassing than a typo projected onto a large screen. So make absolutely sure that you eliminate all the spelling mistakes from your slides and overheads. With dictionary functions on most word-processing packages, you really have no excuse not to.

✔ **Use relevant graphics.** Graphics are good, but only if they support a point. Too many speakers use graphics just to fill space or because they look pretty. Big mistake. If the image doesn't relate to one of the points on your slide, don't use it.

✔ **Be consistent.** Visually, being consistent is very important. It shows that you're organized. Don't mix and match slides or overheads from different presentations if they have different fonts, colours, or design styles. Using a mix of styles and designs is jarring, and it distracts the audience from your message.

✔ **Take advantage of templates.** Many software programs for creating slides and overheads include predesigned templates. You just choose a style, and the program cranks out all your slides in that design.

✔ **Keep the text style simple.** Many speakers feel compelled to 'pretty up' their visuals with fancy text. Don't fall prey to this temptation; too much detail makes your slides and overheads difficult to read.

✔ **Use builds.** A *build* is a series of slides or overheads in which each successive slide contains the bullet points from the preceding slides plus a new bullet point. Builds have become a standard part of business presentations. Builds provide a good way to emphasise key points. The downside is that you need more slides. For example, say you want to make six points. You can put all six points on one slide. Or you can do them as a build, which means using six slides.

Using builds for more than just key points can result in overkill.

✔ **Keep the use of your logo to a minimum.** A logo should simply be a little element that says this is a presentation from your company or organisation. If you're going to put a logo on every slide, keep it small and tuck it away fairly discreetly into a corner somewhere. Otherwise it may distract from your message.

✔ **Use a mixture of uppercase or lowercase text.** Varying cases makes your overheads or slides easier for the audience to read. Using all uppercase text may be acceptable for headings or subheadings, but don't use it for the body of the text.

✔ **Use fewer rather than more words.** A common mistake is to put too much text on a slide or overhead. You don't have to include every word that you're going to say – and you shouldn't. The audience won't read all of the text and it makes you appear amateurish. Instead, just use key words or phrases that outline your ideas. Some designers refer to this as the 4 x 4 rule: Don't put more than four lines on a slide or four words in a line. Other authorities place the numbers as 6 x 6. Of course, you can exceed these guidelines, but only if you're certain that your presentation still looks coherent.

✔ **Use only two different fonts.** Using more than two fonts gives your slides a cluttered look. But an exception exists: Overheads or slides that display a logo, product name, or similar item identified by a specific font. Those items don't count toward your limit of two fonts.

✔ **Emphasise major points – not everything.** Have you ever seen students using a yellow highlighter pen to mark up 95 per cent of every page in a textbook? What are they trying to emphasise – the stuff that's not highlighted? If you want to visually direct attention to certain points, go ahead. But don't dilute your message by emphasising too much.

✔ **Use a maximum of four colours per visual.** At most, allow yourself one colour for the background, another colour for headlines, yet another colour for body text, and perhaps a fourth colour for emphasis. However, many people use fewer colours to create a sleeker, more coherent look. So remember that four colours is the absolute maximum – and not what you should automatically aim for. (You can make an exception for graphs and complex images because you may need more colours to make a pie chart or line graph understandable.)

✔ **The colours on your computer screen may look different from the colours on your overheads.** The colours you see on your computer monitor aren't always going to be the exact colours that appear on your overheads or any printouts you do of your PowerPoint presentation. Colours have a tendency to appear slightly differently depending on the brightness of a projector, the colour of the background you project on, and so on. If you're concerned about the colours, run samples to check out how they look.

# Flipping for Flipcharts

A flipchart is a very large pad of paper that sits on an easel (more commonly known as the flipchart stand). Flipcharts are very common at business meetings – and for good reason. The flipchart is a very versatile visual aid. You can write on it as you speak or have pages prepared in advance. A flipchart's easy to use, too. You don't have to find any on/off switches, electrical outlets, or replacements for burned out light bulbs. A flipchart always operates properly (unless your magic marker goes dry) and is easy to transport. This business tool's also very inexpensive. However, flipcharts aren't really effective for audiences larger than 40 to 50 people. The people seated toward the back can't see what's on the chart, and many presenters misuse flipcharts so badly that even people in the front row can't decipher what the chart is supposed to say. If you plan on using a flipchart in your next presentation, check out the sections below so you can use this versatile tool properly.

## Avoiding common flipchart mistakes

To make sure you avoid common flipchart mistakes, follow these guidelines:

✔ **Use as few words as possible.** We've seen flipcharts covered with writing from top to bottom. The paper looks like a cave wall crammed with hieroglyphics, and the text's about as easy to read as a cave wall, too. So do your audience a favour and leave some white space.

✔ **Write on the top two-thirds of the sheet.** Doing so makes the text easier for the audience to see. More important, by not writing on the bottom you don't have to bend down and give the audience a view of *your* bottom.

✔ **Write with large letters and plenty of space.** Maybe some people in your audience can read the bottom line of an eye chart, but testing them isn't your job. Make your letters large enough so that they can be read easily from the back of the room, and leave a couple of inches between lines.

✔ **Use a thick pen.** Even when the letters are large, they can be difficult to see if they're written in biro. So don't write using letters that look like stick figures. Use a thick-nibbed marker pen so that your letters can be read easily from the back of the room.

✔ **Use colours people can see easily.** Something about flipcharts brings out the artist in speakers. Control the urge. Don't use a magenta marker to write notes on the flipchart. Yellow, pink, and orange are also bad because they don't stand out enough from the white paper. In fact, if you want to make sure that your audience can see what you're writing, stick with black or blue. Those two colours can always be seen from the back of the room. The occasional bit of red for emphasis may be okay, too.

✔ **Use just two colours.** A rainbow is nice to look at in the sky, but not on a flipchart. You can use a few different colours to highlight various points and add emphasis. But if you use too many colours, they lose their impact and become distracting. Stick to either blue or black for your main text, and perhaps red or one other colour for titles or key words.

## Using flipcharts effectively

Want to turn your flipchart into a powerful presentation tool? Try these tips that separate the masters from the disasters:

✔ **Use flipcharts with paper divided into small squares.** Each page should look like a piece of graph paper. The advantage is that you can use the boxes as a guide when you write. That way you know your writing will be large enough to see. The boxes can also help you keep your writing evenly spaced.

- **Correct mistakes with correction fluid.** Have you ever spent a lot of time preparing a very detailed page in your flipchart presentation only to make a minor mistake when you were just about done? Don't pull out your hair and *don't* throw away the page. Put some correction fluid over the mistake just like you would on a sheet of printer paper. Then make your correction. No one in the audience will be able to see it.

- **Write secret notes on the flipchart pages.** If you're worried that you'll forget to discuss important points, use your flipchart pages as cheat sheets. Lightly pencil in a few key words or phrases on the appropriate page. No one in the audience will be able to see your notes. This technique can also improve the text and drawings that you do want the audience to view. If you need to write or draw something as you speak, draw it lightly in pencil beforehand. When you come to that point in your talk, you can just trace over it with a marker. The outcome will look a lot better than if you start it from scratch while you're speaking.

- **Copy pictures from colouring-in books.** If appropriate, drawing simple pictures can add a lot of interest to your flipcharts. If you can't draw, use children's colouring-in books because they have simple drawings that are easy to copy and modify.

- **Use human figures.** If you're drawing pictures on your flipcharts, use human figures whenever possible. People respond to humans. (We're a narcissistic species.)

- **Leave a blank sheet between each sheet you use.** If you prepare your flipchart in advance, don't use every page. The paper is so thin that the audience can see through to the next sheet. So leave a blank sheet between each page that you use. Doing so also gives you room to manoeuvre if you need to add some content suddenly.

- **Save your flipchart pages.** You put a lot of work into the ones you prepare in advance. So use them again. If you've torn them off the flipchart, don't worry. You can tape the pages up on a wall when you reuse them. No rule exists that the sheets have to be on a flipchart stand.

# Creating Great Video (and Audio)

Video is a very powerful, yet overlooked, visual aid. Today's audiences are supposed to have a short attention span due to the influence of television. So why not capture what little attention they possess with the medium they love – video? This section also discusses how to use audio to break through the attention barrier. (Although audio isn't technically a visual aid, it can create pictures *in your mind*.)

## Using video

Video is so powerful that it should only be used in small doses or it may take over your presentation. A video clip can make the non-video portions – you talking – seem boring by comparison, which is exactly what you *don't* want.

Use video clips in short bursts to emphasise key points and heighten audience interest. If you're speaking to a small group, bring a video player and a TV monitor. Or most laptops these days have built-in DVD players. You can work them like an overhead projector, turning them on and off when appropriate. If you're speaking to a large audience, you need to arrange for the video to be projected onto a large screen. (That task may require some professional help.)

### Using testimonials

No matter what you're selling – yourself, your ideas, or your products – you'll be hard pressed to top the persuasive power of third-party credibility. Suppose that we're going to give you a sales presentation. Hearing about the greatness of our products from some of our customers is much more persuasive than hearing it from us. Unfortunately, they usually have better things to do than accompany us on sales calls. (Video comes in here). You can videotape a customer or client singing your praises and show it to your audience.

### Tapping into other video ideas

When commercial television first took root in the 1940s, one Hollywood executive reportedly said that TV wouldn't last more than six months – people would get tired of staring at a box. He didn't realise that television then video would evolve into a wide variety of imaginative forms – all of which are designed to capture audience attention. Unless you're an imagination-impaired Hollywood executive, you should be able to work video into your presentation in lots of clever ways. Try these options:

✔ **Television adverts:** We once saw someone give a presentation about creativity. The speaker talked about different types of creativity and various techniques for being creative, and he illustrated the techniques with TV ads. (We assume he obtained permission to show them – see the section 'Getting permission to use content', later in this chapter.) The audience loved watching the ads (they were very funny) and they did a good job of bringing home the points about creativity. The speaker appropriately spaced the adverts throughout his presentation and they helped maintain audience interest and energy till the end of the talk. Given the range of subject matter covered in TV ads, you can probably find one or two (hundred) that can illustrate some points in your next presentation.

✔ **Filmed vignettes:** A speaker made a speech about cross-cultural communication. He emphasised how Brits could avoid gaffes when doing business with people from other countries. He covered the usual stuff, but he made his message more interesting by introducing each segment with a short video. Actors, portraying businesspeople from the UK and another country, acted out a brief scene of a business meeting. The actor portraying the Brit would make every gaffe possible. The audience responded with laughter to each gaffe. So the videos were entertaining, as well as educational.

✔ **Person-on-the-street interviews:** We've seen these used for comic relief in various types of presentations. You ask a four-year-old what he or she thinks the CEO of your company does all day and videotape the answer. Or you ask people at a trade show unrelated to your industry (gourmet coffees) what they think of your latest product (a hydraulic pump). Or you ask people in your organisation to sing happy birthday to someone. You get the idea.

If you plan to use clips from television shows, films, or adverts, you must first obtain the appropriate permissions. (See 'Getting permission to use content' later in this chapter.) Of course, you could always just try to 'get away with it' – but don't say that we didn't warn you!

## *Including audio in your presentations*

Music and sound effects can greatly enhance your presentation or speech, no matter what you're discussing. They can energise your audience, set a mood, and emphasise a point. Consider these ideas:

✔ **Set the mood with music.** Audience members are walking into the room where they'll hear you give a presentation. You have a choice. You can arrange for them to hear the theme from *Rocky* as they enter. Or they can hear nothing. Do you think it makes any difference? Yes, it does. If you play the theme from *Rocky*, your audience will get pumped up and energised (and perhaps laugh a bit at your cheesiness). Do you want your audience in a contemplative mood? Try some new age, cosmic music. Want them inflamed with patriotism? Play the National Anthem. Music can provide a wonderful warm-up act if used appropriately. Take advantage of it.

✔ **Add a beat to PowerPoint presentations.** People love to look at themselves. Meetings and conferences taking place over a couple of days often conclude with slide shows of photos taken earlier in the meeting for just this reason. (The meeting participants see themselves arriving, attending sessions, partying, and so on.) These PowerPoint shows are inevitably accompanied by loud music with a heavy bass beat (disco music is popular) because it generates energy and enthusiasm. The music makes the slide show come alive. (The slides seem to synchronise with the beat of the music.) You can adapt this technique to your own presentations. Are you giving a talk about the completion of some project (completion of a new building, graduation from school or a course, release of a new product, and so on)? Do you have photos documenting the project's progress? Put together a short PowerPoint show and add some music. Doing so's simple and very effective.

✔ **Fill time when people are thinking or writing.** Do you have a spot in your presentation when everything comes to a halt? Maybe you ask the audience to do some exercise in which they have to think about something or to take a few minutes to write something. You stop talking and silence fills the room. The silence can become oppressive after a while, and it definitely lowers the energy level of your audience. A simple solution is to play some music during this interlude. (Whatever you feel is appropriate.) Music helps maintain a minimal energy level and is also appreciated by audience members who finish early. They'll have something to listen to while the rest of the crowd finish.

# Making an Impact with Multimedia

*Multimedia* refers to the combination of video, text, graphics, and sound. In this section, we provide a quick overview of how you can enhance your presentations and public speaking with multimedia. And we give you a few easy-to-use techniques. But this section definitely does *not* provide in-depth coverage. (See *Multimedia and CD-ROMs For Dummies* by Andy Rathbone or *PowerPoint 2003 For Dummies* by Doug Lowe, both from Wiley, for an extensive discussion of this topic.)

## Getting the right multimedia equipment

You need three basic types of equipment to stage a multimedia presentation: A computer, an input device, and a projector. You also need software (see the section 'Using software for multimedia presentations' later in this chapter). You also need some kind of audio set-up.

### Computers

Computers are so fast and affordable these days that you don't need to spend thousands of pounds. Amazingly, you can pick up a great laptop that will do all the multimedia you're likely to need for around £500. Any computer built in the last three years will have a sound card, a video card, and a CD-ROM/DVD drive. But if you want to get fancy with video, then you may need a video capture card to record and digitise video from television, video tapes, and camcorders.

### Input devices

Input devices allow you to get sound and images into your computer in a digitised format – everything from music and video images to photographs and business cards.

- ✔ **Images:** Still images, such as slides and photographs, can be input to your computer from a digital camera or scanner. Moving images can be transferred from a video tape or camcorder with a cable you can find at any decent electronics goods store.

- ✔ **Sound:** The cables you get for video also usually work with audio devices – such as a cassette player, CD player, stereo, or radio. You run a cable from the 'headphone out' jack directly to the 'audio in' jack on your computer's sound card. Or plug in a microphone and record interviews or voiceovers directly in digitised form.

### Projectors

You also need hardware that projects the sound and images of your multimedia presentation. The sound part is easy. If the room where you're speaking has a sound system, you can just plug your computer into that system. If the room doesn't contain a sound system, you may have to bring your own speakers. For image projection, you need an LCD projector. This is a special projector that allows anything displayed on your computer screen to be projected onto a large screen or wall. The latest-and-greatest models are small enough for easy portability and bright enough that room lights don't have to be turned off. (They may need to be dimmed.) Most LCD projectors also have an input for video directly from a video player – although you don't really want to fiddle with both a video player and a computer, especially as most computers have DVD drives nowadays.

## Using software for multimedia presentations

The basic software requirements are Windows and Video for Windows or Windows Movie Maker. Beyond that, you need software to develop the individual pieces of your presentation and authoring software to put it all together.

### Creating and editing images, sound, and text

Your first task is to construct the various images, video clips, audio clips, and slides that will make up your presentation. The following list shows you the software you need:

✔ **Graphics:** Graphics software ranges from simple tools, such as Paintbrush (which comes with every copy of Windows), to high-powered packages such as Photoshop and CorelDRAW. Two of the more popular programs for image creation are Persuasion and PowerPoint. Both offer lots of help for the nonprofessional designer – so your slides won't end up with words written in 12 different fonts and 8 different colours.

✔ **Audio and video:** You also need special software for capturing and editing the audio and video clips that you want to use in your presentation. Almost any sound card or video capture card comes with recording and editing software that covers your basic needs. Adobe's Premier is among the better-known software products for editing video clips.

✔ **Text:** Most word-processing packages are capable of tagging your word-processing files for multimedia access. Your multimedia-authoring tool determines how this should be accomplished.

### Authoring systems

After you assemble the various pieces of your multimedia presentation, you need a method of putting them all together and controlling them. Software known as an *authoring system* performs that function. It allows you to choreograph all the other programs – sound, video, graphics – into a coherent presentation. One of the more popular systems is Macromedia Director MX.

If using an authoring program is too much of a challenge (they do take some time and effort to learn), don't worry. Use PowerPoint or any similar program. Many people use PowerPoint to make and show slide presentations. But adding sound and videos is very easy. (See *PowerPoint 2003 For Dummies* for more help.)

## Getting permission to use content

The good news about multimedia presentations is that you *can* use text, graphics, video, and audio. The bad news is that you need the rights to use that stuff.

A widespread misconception exists that you can use anything you want in a multimedia presentation. People tape stuff off the telly, capturing video clips of news items, sports events, and scenes from their favourite films. They record audio clips of music from CDs or the radio. They digitise photos and images found in books and magazines. Technically those activities are known as *copyright infringement* – an illegal activity punishable by fines and imprisonment.

So where can you get the materials you need for a multimedia presentation? Remember these two magic words – *public domain*. When an item is in the public domain, anyone is allowed to use it. No permission is required. Alternatively, just get a cassette recorder or camcorder and create your own audio and video.

# Wowing Your Audience with Simple Multimedia Techniques

To get started fast, try one of these three easy suggestions. They'll knock the socks off your audience (assuming that your audience wears socks).

- ✔ **Use a testimonial from someone in your audience:** Video- or audiotape people from the organisation that you'll be addressing. Then include the clip in your presentation. Nothing is more impressive to a group than suddenly seeing one of their own members talk about how great you are.

- ✔ **Throw in a clip or image of something that just happened:** If you're speaking at an event, get there a few hours early, record people on audio or video, and work them into your presentation.

- ✔ **Use a customised effect:** The speed with which you can change a multimedia presentation creates one of its biggest advantages – you can customise it really easily. Put in as many images and audio and video files related to the audience as you can. Are you talking to car dealers? Scan in some pictures of cars.

Get a business card from someone in the company that you'll be addressing and scan in his company's logo. Then you can make it appear in the corner of every screen with your own logo. Customise as much as possible.

# Being Handy with Handouts

Just as kids like to have little goodie bags to take away with them after they've been to a friend's birthday party, the members of your audience would probably like something to take away, too. When you make a presentation, bear in mind that your audience may want handouts. Consider the following things when you prepare and distribute handouts.

## *Making an impact with handouts*

If you're going to make handouts, make them look good. Creating effective handouts isn't hard to do. Desktop-publishing programs give you lots of options for making your handouts look professional. Reproduce them on good quality paper. If you can afford it, put the handouts in a binder. Everyone likes to receive handouts. But giving out a few good-looking ones is better than a lot of hard-to-read, poorly designed ones. Remember, the handouts represent *you*.

## *Including the right information*

Are you using PowerPoint slides or overheads in your presentation? Your audience would probably appreciate hard copies of them. Put some copies in the handouts. (If you don't, you inevitably receive requests for them.) Reprints of relevant articles, by you or others, are always popular items. Checklists are also very good. Your audience also wants to be able to contact you, so make sure you include your phone number, address, or e-mail.

Generally, if you provide more contact information, your audience will appreciate your handouts more. If you recommend products or services, talk about sources of information for a particular topic, or discuss getting in touch with an MP or a local councillor to voice concern about some issue, include lists of contact names and numbers.

## *Knowing when to give them out*

The appropriate time to distribute handouts depends on their function. If the handouts summarise your points and present supplemental information, then distribute them *after* your talk as people will read them instead of listening to you. But if your handouts include audience participation exercises or other materials that you want to refer to while you're speaking, give them out *before* you begin. Handouts distributed before you speak can also encourage the audience to take notes – especially when properly designed. Here's a handy hint: Instead of reproducing your PowerPoint slides or overheads to full-page size, print them so they occupy 25 to 50 per cent of a page. Then the audience can use the rest of the page to take notes while you speak about each slide or overhead. (Check out the automatic printing format for handouts in PowerPoint.)

# Chapter 10

# Negotiating Powerfully from the Outset

*H*ow you perceive and project yourself determines how people perceive and receive you. If you want to be seen as positive, powerful and influential at work, you have to act the part. Your gestures, actions and expressions need to celebrate and reflect your strengths and abilities. Based on what you reveal in the way you appear and move, people want to know more – or close the door on you.

From the moment you enter the work environment to your last day on the job, you're being watched. Make sure that the way you're moving, gesturing and behaving projects the image you want. The higher up the hierarchy you go, the more focused your actions and the more contained your gestures need to be, in order to project the expected authority.

Self-awareness is paramount if you're to work your way successfully through the office maze.

In this chapter we look at how you can make a positive impact from the first impression through to the final exit. You discover that how you position your body impacts upon how people perceive you, and you gain skills to display confidence, commitment and credibility.

# Making the First Impression: The Interview

I know, I know, you've heard it a hundred times or more, but here it is again: you never have a second chance to make a first impression. Make a good one and you're on a winner. Make a poor one and you're going to struggle long and hard to be invited back.

Going for an interview involves being on show. People begin making evaluations from the moment they first see you. From top to toe, how you groom, dress and accessorise yourself sends out signals about who you are and the message you want to convey. Add to those ingredients your body language, your manners and your demeanour, and in less than seven seconds the impression you make is set. Although you may appeal to some, others may be less than impressed. This section describes how to push the odds in your favour.

## Gaining Instant Rapport

When you're in rapport you feel a harmonious connection between yourself and others. All's right in the world and communication flows. You can find yourself smiling and nodding in agreement as you converse.

The word *rapport* derives from the French word *rapporter*, which translates as 'to return or bring back.' English dictionaries define rapport as 'a sympathetic relationship or understanding'. The result is that people in rapport can create outstanding results. Two useful ways to develop and increase rapport are *mirroring* and *matching*.

## Mirroring to get the ball rolling

People who are in rapport tend to reflect one another's physical patterns. They move in time with each other and mirror behaviour that they observe.

Research on rapport indicates that, from an evolutionary perspective, mirroring body language facilitates interaction between people. When you mirror people – whether in the way they speak or move – you're unconsciously reproducing their state of mind within yourself. The more effectively you can do so, the more able you are to understand the other person's perspective.

## Mirroring and matching effectively

People attempting to create rapport through mirroring and matching without attempting to understand and convey the state of the people around them come off like the worst of used-car salesmen. Those best at creating rapport match the *state* of the other person, feeling it within themselves much as the other person does. The goal in matching and mirroring behaviour isn't to replicate the behaviour, but that ability comes naturally when you adopt and replicate the state of the other person you're interacting with. Mirroring and matching the behaviour enhances communication only when the adopted physiology assists in replicating emotional state. For more about creating rapport through mirroring and matching see *Neuro-Linguistic Programming For Dummies* by Romilla Ready and Kate Burton (Wiley).

When you're reflecting other people's behaviour back to them, be sure to avoid mimicry. If you recreate muscle movement for muscle movement and replicate exact gestures and expressions with precision, the other person feels mocked and disinclined to engage in a meaningful conversation with you.

## *Matching to create similarities*

Matching someone's behaviour indicates that you're in sync with one another, experiencing similar feelings and emotions. When you're matching someone's behaviour you create a similar state to the other person that helps you understand their point of view.

When you match someone, look to match their:

- ✔ Body postures and gestures
- ✔ Breathing rates
- ✔ Rhythm of movement and energy levels
- ✔ Voice tonality including pitch, pace and volume

## *Showing you're glad to be there*

Before setting off for your interview, visualise yourself at your best. Only enter the interview room when you're looking, sounding and feeling like you do when you know you're in top notch form.

How you move signals how you perceive yourself and expect to be treated. When you're invited to enter the interview room, do so with focus and energy. If you want to be perceived as someone with an upfront, upbeat and positive attitude, move confidently, smoothly and purposefully. And smile. Put down whatever you're carrying, shake the interviewer's hand if offered and take a seat. You're demonstrating that you're comfortable coming into another person's territory.

### Smiling to engage

Smiling at someone you're meeting for the first time makes you appear approachable, prompting the other person to open up and to relate with you. When you smile you're indicating that you're willing to share yourself and connect at an emotional level. Smiling also lightens and relaxes a potentially tense atmosphere; it costs you nothing and yet enriches the lives of people who are at the receiving end. Although it may not last long, the memory of a genuine smile can last forever.

When the time comes to leave, move calmly and focus on what you're doing. Smile, shake hands with your interviewer, turn and head towards the door. When you reach the door, slowly turn, look your interviewer in the eye and smile again

When you smile, make sure that you mean what you're doing. A fake smile is easy to spot and leaves the impression that you're not genuine.

### Keeping them in your sights [eye contact]

When you're invited to sit, make sure that your body is at a 45 degree angle from the other person . Move the chair to this angle, if you can. If you can't, shift your body. (The later section 'Creating a relaxed attitude with the 45 degree angle' contains lots more info on the importance of the 45 degree angle.)

Look them in the eye as they speak, and appear interested. Pay attention to people's facial expressions – are they frowning or smiling, are their lips taut or trembling? Refrain from multi-tasking when someone's speaking: fiddling with your phone and playing with paper, pens or pencils is rude and potentially distracting. If you don't agree with what you hear, keep your facial expressions and gestures neutral.

### Firm handshake

Instead of shaking hands across the desk, which puts a barrier between you and the other person, move to the left of the desk to avoid receiving a palm down handshake and being put in a subservient position. Hold your palm straight and return the same amount of pressure that the other person gives. Let the interviewer decide when the handshake should end.

When you match the force of the interviewer's handshake, you're showing that you're sensitive and flexible and able to reflect that person's approach. If you crush the other person's fingers or offer a wet fish handshake in return for a firm one, you're showing that the two of you are mismatched and out of sync.

**Book I**

**Communicating Effectively**

Include the person's name in your remarks twice within the first 30 seconds of having introduced yourself, including when you first meet. Speak for no longer than 20–30 seconds at one time.

## Leading to get them to come to you

Short, sharp gestures hold more authority than open hands waving in the air. By keeping your fingers closed and your hands below chin level when gesturing, you look confident, in control and so command attention.

If you want to appear caring, approachable or subservient, also keep your hands below chin level but gesture with open fingers.

## Carrying only what's necessary

Keep your accessories slim and compact. Bulging briefcases indicate that you're the worker bee and not the one making the strategic decisions. They give the impression that, although you may be buzzing away very hard, you're not in control of your time.

Accessories are meant to enhance your image. Decide what image you want to project and choose your accessories accordingly. Also, to make a positive impression, invest in good quality accessories.

## Standing tall and holding your ground

Having a superior position carries with it an implied authority. The same goes for tall people: they can command respect because of their height. Others have to look up to them and because of their physiological make-up, they look down on others.

Some people don't feel comfortable being taller than others, however, and so they stoop or slouch. They diminish themselves in size and statue, giving away their authority. Shorter people have to create an image of height and stature. They do so by standing with their centre of gravity deep in their loins while lifting their upper torsos upwards and outwards. Nicholas Sarkozy, Tom Cruise and Al Pacino are no taller than 1.7 metres (5 feet 7 inches), and yet with Cruise's bright smile, Sarkozy's purposeful stride and Pacino's brooding passion all exude the aura of powerful men.

To experience what being in control feels and looks like, try this short exercise, practising from both the seated and standing positions:

- ✔ Visualise another person who's challenging you, at an interview, in a meeting or at an assessment.

- ✔ Place your feet firmly underneath you, hip width apart.

- ✔ Maintain flexibility in your knees and ankles to avoid becoming stiff.

- ✔ Keep your head upright and maintain eye contact with the other person.

- ✔ Let your arms and hands be visible.

- ✔ Keep your chest open.

- ✔ Keep your mouth closed while you're listening.

- ✔ Inhale from your abdomen. Breathing deeply from your core grounds you and provides a firm foundation from which you can move, gesture and position yourself.

- ✔ Reflect on what you're going to say before speaking.

- ✔ Remind yourself of your strengths and how you want to be perceived.

- ✔ Respond.

Stooped shoulders, caved-in chest and hands in the fig-leaf position (covering your private bits) are protective signals and indicate that you're subconsciously feeling defensive.

Cecile stands at just over 1.82 metres (6 feet) tall. As an athlete, she was used to being with people of equal height, and felt comfortable with them. When her sports career ended, she obtained her law degree and joined a city firm. After several months, Cecile noticed that she was hunching her shoulders and sinking into her hips. Her chest caved inward, her head sunk into her neck and she was looking at people from under her eyes.

As we explored the reasons for this new behaviour, we discovered several issues. Cecile was experiencing a lack of confidence and low self-perception because she was still learning the job. Highly competitive, she was uncomfortable, fearing that she was being perceived as lacking in her work. In addition, the male partner she reported to was shorter than Cecile. She discovered that she was purposely making herself smaller to make him look bigger. With practice, Cecile regained her stature. We explored her mental attitude and made the necessary self-perception adjustments. Her new way of thinking and perceiving herself was reflected in the way she stood and gestured. Now, when Cecile sits and stands using her full stature she feels confident, looks credible and commands respect.

## Matching mood and movements for results

I recently attended two training events led by two different trainers and the contrast was highly informative. At the first one, the trainer bounded into the room like a basket of puppies. Feeling overwhelmed by her exuberance – it was 6 p.m. and I was tired from a long day's work – I struggled to engage with her and left the session feeling disappointed, like I hadn't gained anything.

The second training session took place early in the morning, and again I was tired – this time from a long journey to the venue. Here, the trainer established rapport (check out the earlier section 'Establishing rapport') by matching my mood and movements. Instead of imposing her energy onto me, she allowed me to set the tone until I was ready to become more engaged and energised. By noticing my movements and purposely matching them to enhance our communication and build our relationship, I left the training singing the trainer's praises, having gained a valuable experience while enjoying the process.

## *Moving with purpose*

Whether you stride into a room with focus and direction, or wander in as though you've forgotten why you're there, you're going to create an impression. Unless you're purposely playing the role of someone from La-La Land, I suggest that if you want to be noticed in a positive light, put your muscles into your movement and propel yourself into the fray with focus, direction and positive energy. Other people then perceive you as vibrant, interesting and engaging.

Before projecting yourself into other people's territory, test the waters. Moderate your movements to mirror those of the people you're with (we discuss mirroring in the earlier section 'Gaining Instant Rapport'). If you come bounding into a room full of silent, contemplative folk, you may be perceived as a bit of a buffoon, if not an outright annoyance. Reflect back the energy you observe in the room and adapt your behaviour to match what you notice, still moving with focus and direction.

Positive energy draws people, whereas negative energy repels them. You don't have to bounce like Tigger or Tony the Tiger to demonstrate focus and energy. Slow actions performed with integrity project authority and command attention.

An intentionally deliberate movement draws attention to the action and highlights the meaning behind the gesture.

# Pointing Your Body in the Right Direction

How you position your body in relation to other people impacts upon their perception of you, which is particularly relevant in the work environment. If you stand directly in front of them, face to face, hands on hips and jaw jutted forward, you become a threatening force. Turn your shoulder to people, cross your arms and look down your nose at them, and you indicate that you think they aren't up to scratch. Turn your back completely on people and you better pray that they don't stick anything in it as a response to your dismissive attitude!

To create a more positive interaction, stand facing another person at a comfortable distance – with your arms open, your hands visible and a welcoming expression on your face – and see how constructive the mood becomes. Sit or stand side by side at a distance that feels right for your relationship, and sense the connection. Both consciously and subconsciously you're adjusting your body position in response to what's happening in your environment.

People who sit side by side tend to work in a collaborative way. People sitting across the table from one another are often at odds, relying on the furniture to act as a defensive barrier.

To make a positive impression, hold your head up, keeping your chin parallel to the ground. Let your eyes engage and sparkle. Allow yourself to smile. Free your shoulders and permit your chest to open as if it were a plane about to take off (but don't puff it out, which overeggs the pudding and reveals vulnerability not strength). Breathe from your abdomen. Ground yourself.

If someone you're engaging with seems distracted, uninterested or even annoyed, aim to match that person's movements and energy as a means of creating rapport. When the person feels that you're more connected, you can more easily lead the conversation to where you want it to go by making subtle changes to your movements and gestures that are in line with your feelings and attitudes.

## Creating a relaxed attitude with the 45 degree angle

The angle at which you position yourself in relation to another person affects the outcome of your communication. If you want your interaction to be comfortable, cooperative and congenial, place yourself at a 45 degree angle to the other person.

The benefit of sitting at a 45 degree angle to another person is that the position encourages openness and trust. By positioning yourself at this angle, you form a third point where you avoid being perceived as aggressive or flirtatious. Whereas face to face is confrontational, and side by side is intimate, placing yourself halfway between the two creates an atmosphere of confidence and equality. Neither confrontational nor intimate, the 45 degree angle allows people to see one another, gesture freely and maintain a comfortable space between themselves.

The 45 degree angle is a cooperative space that encourages discussion and the flow of ideas: it's perceived as a neutral territory. The third angle allows another person to join you in the space, creating an equilateral triangle. If a fourth person enters the group the group can form a square, and if one or two more people join, they can form a circle or divide themselves into two triangles.

### Positioning yourself for cooperation

Say that you're the newly appointed head of a well-established and successful team. One by one you invite your new colleagues into your office for a 'getting acquainted' session. They may feel a little wary of you and watch to see how you manage the meeting. By placing yourself in the neutral 45 degree zone you encourage openness and honest discussion. No threatening aspect is associated with this position. Turn 10 degrees in either direction and the dynamics change. If you turn inwards, you indicate that intimacy is in the air. If you angle your body away, you shut out the other person.

### Sitting with subordinates

When you want to create a relaxed, informal atmosphere when speaking to a subordinate in your office, open the session with both of you sitting in the 45 degree angle position, directing your bodies to a third point forming a triangle, suggesting agreement. From this position you can reflect the other person's gestures, creating a sense of ease and rapport.

If you want a direct answer to a question and you feel you're not getting it in the 45 degree pose, shift your position to face directly towards the other person . This action says that you want a direct answer to your direct question.

### Taking the pressure off

Positioning your body at a 45 degree angle relieves the potential stress of the meeting. When a sensitive issue needs addressing, go for this position. It takes the pressure off and encourages more open answers to your open questions.

## *Facing directly for serious answers*

If someone asks you a direct question, look at the person directly – that is, if you want to be taken seriously. If you drop your head, avert your eyes and peer over your shoulder, you're conveying that you're unsure, doubtful and perhaps even scared; you've lost your power.

Serious questions require a serious attitude and so you need to reflect that attitude in your pose. When you're asked a direct question, follow these steps (which you can do seated or standing):

1. **Close your mouth.**

2. **Breathe deeply from your lower abdomen.**

3. **Hold your head vertically as if your chin is resting on a calm lake.**

4. **Square your hips and shoulders with your knees.**

5. **Place your knees directly over your ankles, with your feet planted firmly on the ground.**

6. **Open your chest as if it's a treasured book.**

7. **Look the questioner in the eye.**

8. **Pause.**

9. **Answer.**

Emma worked in the HR department of a city law firm. She was ambitious and wanted to progress in her career. She received feedback telling her that her superiors weren't taking her seriously. She was told that, although she was a very pleasant person to have around and worked well organising events behind the scenes, as regards working directly with clients, she seemed unorganised, flighty and unsure of herself.

She had an abundance of nervous energy that was creating the image the clients described. She shifted her weight from leg to leg and slouched into her hips. Her shoulders stooped and her hands fidgeted. She tossed her head and frequently giggled. She had difficulty establishing and maintaining eye contact. Her words said that she wanted to progress in her work, but her body language conveyed that she wasn't up to the job. Working with a video camera – positioned so that she was able to see herself – Emma discovered how her gestures and behaviour were impacting upon people's perceptions of her. By adjusting her stance she stood taller. By controlling her breathing her actions calmed down. By opening her chest she filled her space. Her fidgeting lessened and she began to project the image she wanted. Emma's new presence looks, and sounds, confident and credible, and she's now working in the position she sought.

# Picking the power seats

As regards seating at work, and without beating around the bush, the message is simple: stay away from seats that make you look small, awkward and insignificant. These seats are the kind where you're forced to look upward, lifting your chin and exposing your neck, which happens to be one of the most vulnerable parts of your body. The person on the other chair is sitting upright and in control. Even if he's leaning back in his chair he's still in a higher position than you. He can look down on you along the length of his nose. He can lower his glasses, looking over the top at you, all cramped, awkward and feeling uncomfortable.

### The height of the back of the chair

The higher the back of the chair, the higher the status of the person it belongs to. The person with the support behind his back, the protective shield and frame that surrounds him, holds a more powerful position than the person sitting on a stool at his feet. Kings and queens, popes and prime ministers, chief executives and oligarchs, sit in chairs that reflect their power and position. The higher the back of the chair and the more luxurious the fabric, the higher the status of the person.

On the reality television show *The Apprentice,* Sir Alan Sugar sits in a black leather chair with a high back. The back of the chair frames his face and gives him authority. The would-be apprentices sit in front of him. The backs of their chairs are lower. Before a word is spoken, the positioning makes clear who holds the authority in the room.

High status people prefer to sit on high backed chairs.

### Rolling on casters

Chairs on casters have a power and mobility that fixed chairs lack. The person sitting in a chair that swivels has more freedom of movement and can cover more space in a shorter time than someone sitting in a fixed chair. When a person is under pressure, being able to move quickly expels energy and expedites the process.

The person who's sitting in the chair on wheels, with the arm rests and the high, reclining back, tends to be the person in charge.

### Gaining height advantage

Height is associated with status and power: the higher you are, the more authority you hold. Savvy business types know that by adjusting the seat height of their chairs they gain a competitive advantage.

If someone invites you to sit in a chair that puts you at eye level with the other person's desk, decline, saying that you prefer to stand.

### Placing the chair

When you seat yourself directly across the desk or table from another person, face to face, the atmosphere is immediately confrontational. But place the chair at a 45 degree angle in front of the desk and you create a welcoming environment . If you want to reduce a visitor's status, arrange for the person to be seated as far away from your desk as possible, into the public zone at least 2.5 metres (8 feet) away from where you're sitting.

# Negotiating Styles

When crunch time arrives and you're at the final stage of a work or business negotiation, you want to win, right? The best negotiations result in everyone feeling like a winner. And to feel that you're a winner you have to look, sound and behave like one (in other words, act the part). If you want to know more about how to position yourself when negotiating, persuading and influencing, pick up a copy of *Persuasion & Influence For Dummies* (Wiley).

Before you go into any meeting where you want to be seen performing well (interview, negotiation or assessment), find yourself a quiet spot in which you can gather your thoughts in peace. Five minutes is ample. Reflect on how you want to be perceived and visualise yourself behaving in that manner. See and hear yourself performing at your best and experience the feeling. By creating your desired image you're able to act the part and convince others that you really are like that. Who knows, you may actually be that person.

## Acting the part

The Russian director, Constantine Stanislavski, popularised a style of acting that became known as *method acting,* which requires actors to base their characterisations on the emotional memory process. The actors immerse themselves in their characters' lives, to experience that life as the characters would. Actors draw upon memories and incidents from their own lives and incorporate them into their roles, enriching and enhancing the portrayal. Devotees of method acting include Dustin Hoffman, Jane Fonda and Robert DeNiro. Although some people believe that method acting produces the most realistic results, it can annoy other actors who follow a more traditional approach to character portrayal. During the filming of *Marathon Man,* Dustin Hoffman went for several days without bathing, in order to immerse himself in the character's psyche. Upon seeing Hoffman's condition, his co-star Laurence Olivier asked him, 'Why don't you just act?'

# Claiming your space

When you enter a negotiation, you need to claim your space right from the beginning. If you don't, the competition is going to have you for breakfast. *Claiming your space* means that you're taking responsibility for yourself and your actions, and that you act as though you've got the right to be where you are, doing what you're doing. When you walk into a space and make it your own, you're telling others that this territory's yours and woe betide anyone who tries to take it away from you. Dogs spend much of their time marking out their territory in order to let the rest of the pack know that they've been there and the same applies with people (although I suggest that you mark your territory differently!). Your intention is to let people know that you own this space and you're to be taken seriously.

When you claim your space successfully you can act as if you belong there. Your gestures appear fluid, your posture's upright and you engage in eye contact with ease. You send out positive signals indicating that you're comfortable and in control.

## Getting acquainted with the environment

One way of demonstrating that the space you're in belongs to you, is to make contact with an item in the area. Say, for example, that you've been invited to speak at an event attended by many influential people, some of whom you know, others you don't. You want to appear confident and in charge of yourself and your material. To do that, follow these suggestions for getting comfortable in the space and making it your own:

- Walk into the room where the negotiation is taking place as if you own the space. Move with purpose and authority.

- Pull your chair out and sit down without waiting to be invited.

- Place your notes and pen in front of you with confidence and authority.

- Establish eye contact and open the discussion clearly and concisely.

Tracy is a highly qualified and respected lawyer. Practising for her partnership interview, Tracy felt nervous and awkward, as though she didn't belong. She fidgeted with her clothes, avoided eye contact and played with her jewellery. Her behaviour began shifting as she practised entering the room and taking her seat at the table in front of the imaginary panel. Before Tracy sat, she let her hands rest on the top of the chair's back as if staking her claim to that seat. By making contact with this object, she established a sense of ownership with the room. Her nerves steadied, and she gained an appearance of confidence and credibility.

### Choosing a good seat

Arrive at the meeting early enough so that you can pick your spot. Sitting facing the door gives you the upper hand. Research shows that people seated with their backs to the door experience stress, increased blood pressure and shallow, rapid breathing as the body prepares itself for a possible attack from behind. Save this weak and defensive position for your competition.

### Filling your space

People who fill their space look more commanding and in control, which can be a challenge for small or slim people, who may appear to be devoured by space. The following tips can help people of smaller stature appear more in command of their territory:

- Hold your elbows slightly out from your sides, when standing or sitting. (People who hold their arms close to their bodies look subservient, timid and fearful.)

- Lean forward when seated behind a table, letting your hands, elbows or lower arms rest on the table's surface.

- Never pull your arms in close by your sides at a meeting; you're reducing your stature and diminishing your influence.

Large people also need to consider the amount of space they fill, because lolling and ambling along, spreading across their space, can be perceived as invasive. You don't need to draw your shoulders and arms in towards yourself. Just be aware that you take up more space than smaller people and that you may need to adjust your position to allow others in.

To avoid overwhelming others with your large presence, contain your gestures, making them concise and precise.

## Displaying confidence

The way you stand and sit, your gestures and expressions, the actions you choose and the way you perform them, all reveal who you are and what you're about. Captains of industry, masters of the universe and doyennes of the theatre instinctively know, and are well trained, in projecting a confident countenance. With eyes clear and focused, posture erect and facial muscles engaged, they reveal a look of positive expectancy.

# Book II
# Building Your Commercial Acumen

'A great advertising gimmick, George, but who's
going to see it up here on top of Everest?'

# In this book. . .

**B**udgeting, creating sales and profits, managing risks and investments are the day to day skills required in a commercial environment. Stop by here whenever you want to check out accounting jargon and make wise decisions, especially in changing and uncertain economic times.

Here are the contents of Book II at a glance:

# Chapter 1

# Get the Right People on Board: Making the Million-Pound Decision

**G**ood employees are hard to find. If you've had the recent privilege of advertising for a job opening, you know that good employees aren't easy to come by. Here's the scenario: you place the advertisement and then wait for the applications to come flooding in. In just a day or two, you're pleased beyond your wildest dreams as you see the stack of applications awaiting your attention. How many are there – 100? 200? Well done indeed, what a response!

Your glee quickly turns to disappointment, however, as you begin your review. 'Why did this guy apply? He doesn't have half the required experience!' 'What? She's never even done this kind of work before.' 'Is this man joking? He must have responded to the wrong advertisement!'

Finding and hiring the best candidates for a job has never been easy. Unfortunately, with all the streamlining, downsizing and rightsizing going on in business nowadays, a lot of people are looking for work – and the chances are that very few of them have the exact qualifications that you're looking for. Your challenge is to work out how to pluck the best candidates out of the sea strewn with the wreckage of corporate cast-offs. The lifetime earnings of the average British worker can be as high as £1,000,000. Recruitment and selection really is, therefore, a million-pound decision!

# *Asking for the Right Stuff*

Your mission is to locate the most highly qualified suitable candidates for your job opening. When you locate your candidates, your task is to narrow your selection down to one person and to ensure that recruitment leads to his successful entry into the organisation. This process isn't always as easy or as straightforward as it sounds.

Employers look for many qualities in candidates. What do you look for when you interview? The following list gives you an idea of the qualities that employers consider most important when hiring new employees. Other characteristics may be particularly important to you.

✔ **Hard working:** Hard work can often overcome a lack of experience or training. You want to take on people who are willing to do whatever it takes to get the job done. Conversely, no amount of skill can make up for a lack of initiative or work ethic. Although you don't know for sure until you make your choice, careful questioning of candidates can give you some idea of their work ethic (or, at least, what they want you to believe about their work ethic).

✔ **Good attitude:** Although what constitutes a 'good' attitude is different for different people, a positive, friendly, willing-to-help perspective makes life at work much more enjoyable and makes everyone's job easier. When you interview candidates, consider what they'll be like to work with for the next five or ten years. Skills are important, but attitude is vital. 'Hire for attitude, train for success' is the mantra of US low-cost airline Southwest Airlines – apply it to your own organisation.

✔ **Experienced:** If you're asking for experience, be specific. In many cases, someone with 20 years' experience has in fact only had one year's experience – 20 times. So specify the things that you want the person to have done; and if you ask for '5/10/15 years' experience', spell out what you expect the candidate to have done during that period of employment. Make it clear that you're not seeking people of a particular age – age discrimination is illegal, and you can be prosecuted for unlawful discrimination. So be careful!

✔ **Initiative:** Everyone prefers somebody who takes the initiative to get work done. You're not going to get anything – from the new employee or from existing staff – if you take people on who are going to sit around waiting until you allocate tasks to them.

✔ **Team player:** Teamwork is critical to the success of today's organisations, which must do far more with far fewer resources than their predecessors. The ability to work with others effectively is a definite must for employees today.

✔ **Smart:** Smart people can often find better and quicker solutions to the problems that confront them. You need people who are going to do things for you, not say things to you.

✔ **Responsible:** You want to recruit people who are willing to take on the responsibilities of their positions. Questions about the kinds of projects that your candidates have been responsible for, and the exact roles they played in their success, can help you determine this important quality. Little factors, like showing up for the interview and remembering the name of the company they're applying to, can also be key indicators of your candidates' sense of responsibility.

✔ **Stable:** You don't want to hire someone today and then find out that he's already looking for his next position tomorrow. You can get some indication of a person's potential stability (or lack of) by asking how long he worked with his previous employer and why he left. Not only that, you can also enjoy listening to your candidates explain how they're ready to settle down.

# Defining the Job and the Person

Whether the position is new, or you're filling an existing post, before you start the recruiting process you need to know exactly what standards you're going to use to measure your candidates. The clearer you are about what you need, the easier and less arbitrary your selection process becomes.

Draft a job description and person specification that fully describes all the tasks, responsibilities and characteristics of the position, and the minimum necessary qualifications and experience. And if the job requires a driving licence, for example, then say so! Otherwise, you start making mistakes right from the start.

If you're filling an existing position, review the current job description closely and make changes where necessary. This is a good opportunity to rearrange workloads and make changes if you need to. Again, make the job description reflect exactly the tasks and requirements of the position. When you hire someone new to fill an existing position, you start with a clean slate. For example, you may have had a difficult time getting a former employee to accept certain new tasks – say, taking minutes at staff meetings or filing travel vouchers. By adding these new duties to the job description before you begin recruitment, you make the expectations clear, and you don't have to struggle to get your new employee to do the job.

Finally, before you start recruiting, get the desired qualities and characteristics into a priority order. If necessary, consult with colleagues to make sure that you give yourself the best possible chance of getting the right candidate for the job.

Additionally, when you come to interviewing, by law you have to give everybody the same chance. So use the characteristics in their priority order as the basis for your interviewing and selection methods. If you fail to do this, unsuccessful candidates can question the basis on which you turned them down for the job, and if any doubt at all exists that they were given fair treatment, they can (and in many cases, do) make representations to employment tribunals. So get this right – now!

# Finding Good People

People are the heart of every business. The better the people running your business, the better your business.

Some people are just meant to be in their jobs. You may know such individuals – someone who thrives as a receptionist or someone who lives to sell. Think about how great your organisation would be if you staffed every position with people who lived for their jobs.

Likewise, bad staff can make working for an organisation an incredibly miserable experience. The negative impacts of hiring the wrong candidate can reverberate throughout an organisation for years. If you, as a manager, ignore the problem, you put yourself in danger of losing your good employees. We can't overemphasise the importance of recruiting and retaining the right people. Do you want to spend a few extra hours up front to find the best candidates, or do you want to devote countless hours later trying to straighten out a problem employee? And if you still need convincing, a recent survey by the Chartered Institute of Personnel and Development estimates that replacing an employee costs up to twice their annual salary.

Of course, as important as the interview process is to selecting the best candidates for your jobs, you don't have anyone to interview if you don't have a good system for finding good candidates. So where can you find the best candidates for your jobs?

The simple answer is everywhere. Certainly, some places are better than others – you probably won't find someone to run your lab's fusion reactor project by advertising on the backs of matchboxes – but you never know where you can find your next star programmer or award-winning advertising copywriter. Who knows, he may be working for your competitors right now!

As you maximise your chances of success, you also minimise your chances of failure. The most effective recruitment and selection processes take place when you have plenty of time to evaluate all the candidates; and when you're not pressed to take on someone if you haven't so far attracted anyone of the calibre you want.

The following list presents some of the best ways to find candidates for your positions. Your job is to develop a recruitment campaign that can find the kinds of people that you want to take on. Don't rely solely on your human resources (HR) department to develop this campaign; you probably have a better understanding of where to find the people you need than they do, so work with HR to best advantage. And make sure that your contribution is noted.

- ✔ **Taking a close look within:** In most organisations, the first place to look for candidates is within the organisation. If you do your job in training and developing employees, then you probably have plenty of candidates to consider for your job openings. Only after you exhaust your internal candidates should you look outside your organisation. Not only is taking on people from within less expensive and easier, but you also get happier employees, improved morale and a steady stream of people who are already familiar with your organisation.

- ✔ **Personal referrals:** Whether from existing work groups, professional colleagues, friends, relatives or neighbours, you can find great candidates by referrals. Who better to present a candidate than someone whose opinion you already value and trust? You get far more insight about the candidates' strengths and weaknesses from the people who refer them than you get from applications alone. Also, research shows that people hired through current employees tend to work better, stay with the company longer and are happier. When you're getting ready to fill a position, make sure that you let people know about it.

- ✔ **Temporary agencies:** Taking on *temps*, or temporary employees, has become routine for many companies. When you simply have to fill a critical position for a short period of time, temporary agencies are the way to go. And the best part is that when you hire temps, you get the opportunity to try out employees before you take them on. If you don't like the temps you get, no problem. Simply call the agency, and they send replacements before you know it. But if you like your temps, most agencies allow you to employ them at a nominal fee or after a minimum time commitment. Either way, you win.

- ✔ **Professional associations:** Most professions have their accompanying associations that look out for their interests. Whether you're a doctor (and belong to the British Medical Association), or a lorry driver (and belong to the Transport and General Workers' Union), you can probably find an affiliated association for whatever you do for a living. Association newsletters, journals and magazines are great places to advertise your openings when you're looking for specific expertise, because your audience is already pre-screened for you.

✔ **Employment agencies:** If you're filling a particularly specialised position, are recruiting in a small market or simply prefer to have someone else take care of recruiting and screening your applicants, employment agencies are a good, albeit pricey alternative (with a cost of up to one-third of the employee's first-year salary, or more). Although employment agencies can usually locate qualified candidates in lower-level or administrative positions, you may need help from an executive search firm or *headhunter* (someone who specialises in recruiting key employees away from one firm to place in a client's firm) for your higher-level positions.

✔ **The Internet:** Every day, more and more companies discover the benefits of using the Internet as a hiring tool. Although academics and scientists have long used Internet newsgroups to advertise and seek positions within their fields, corporations are now following suit. The proliferation of corporate web pages and online employment agencies and job banks has brought about an entirely new dimension in recruiting. Web pages let you present almost unlimited amounts and kinds of information about your firm and about your job openings – in text, audio, graphic and video formats. Your pages work for you 24 hours a day, 7 days a week.

✔ **Recruitment advertising:** Recruitment advertising can be relatively expensive, but it's an easy way to get your message across. You can choose to advertise in your local paper or in nationally distributed publications such as the *Financial Times*. On the downside, you may find yourself sorting through hundreds or even thousands of unqualified candidates to find a few great ones. But that's what your HR department's for, right?

# Being the Greatest Interviewer in the World

After you narrow the field down to the top three or five applicants, you need to start interviewing. What kind of interviewer are you? Do you spend several hours preparing for interviews – reviewing applications, looking over job descriptions, writing and rewriting questions until each one is as finely honed as a razor blade? Or are you the kind of interviewer who, busy as you already are, starts preparing for the interview when you get the call from your receptionist that your candidate has arrived?

Spending some serious time preparing for your interviews is the secret to becoming the Greatest Interviewer in the World. Remember how much time you spent preparing to be interviewed for your current job? You didn't just walk in the door, sit down and get offered the job, did you? You probably spent hours researching the company, its products and services, its financial position, its market and other business information. You probably brushed up on your interviewing skills and may have even done some role-playing with a friend or in front of a mirror. Don't you think that you should spend at least as much time getting ready for the interview as do the people you're going to put through their paces?

## Asking the right questions

More than anything else, the heart of the interview process is the questions that you ask and the answers that you receive in response. You get the best answers when you ask the best questions and actively listen to the answers. Lousy questions often result in lousy answers – answers that don't really tell you whether the candidate is going to be right for the job.

A great interviewer asks great questions. 'How do I ask great questions?' you may want to know. According to Richard Nelson Bolles, author of the perennially popular job-hunting guide *What Color Is Your Parachute?* (Ten Speed Press, 2010), you can categorise all interview questions under one of the following four headings:

- **Why are you here?** Really. Why is the person sitting across from you going to the trouble of interviewing with you today? You have just one way to find out – ask. You may assume that the answer is because he wants a job with your firm, but you may be surprised at what you discover.

- **What can you do for us?** Always an important consideration. Of course, your candidates are all going to dazzle you with their incredible personality, experience, work ethic and love of teamwork – that almost goes without saying. However, despite what many job seekers seem to believe, the question isn't 'What can your firm do for me?' – at least not from your perspective. The question that you want an answer to is: 'What can you do for us?'

  One manager tells a story about the job applicant who slammed his hand on her desk and demanded a signing bonus. And this was before the interview had even started! We're not surprised that this particular candidate landed neither the job nor the bonus.

- **What kind of person are you?** Few candidates are going to be absolute angels or demons, but don't forget that you spend a lot of time with the person you hire. You want to take on someone you enjoy being with during the many work hours, weeks and years that stretch before you (or at least someone you can tolerate being with for a few hours every once in a while). You also want to confirm a few other issues: are your candidates honest and ethical? Do they share your views in regard to work hours, responsibility and so forth? Are they responsible and dependable? Of course, all your candidates answer in the affirmative to bland questions like these. So, how do you find the real answers?

When Bob used to recruit, he'd try to 'project' applicants into a typical, real-life scenario and then see how they thought it through. This way, no right answer exists and the applicants are forced to expose their thinking process, for example the questions they'd ask, strategies they'd consider, people they'd involve and so forth. Ask open-ended questions and let your candidates do most of the talking. Your candidate should talk for at least 70 per cent of the interview.

✔ **Can we afford you?** It does you no good if you find the perfect candidate, but at the end of the interview, you bring up the topic of pay and find out that you're so far apart that you're actually in a different country. Keep in mind that the actual wage you pay to workers is only part of an overall compensation package. Although you may not be able to pull together more money for wages for particularly good candidates, you may be able to offer them better benefits, longer holidays, more development opportunities or, ultimately, a faster career track.

## Interviewing do's

So what can you do to prepare for your interviews? The following handy checklist gives you ideas on where to start:

✔ **Review the applications of each interviewee the morning before interviews start.** Reading your interviewees' applications during the actual interview is not only poor form; it also means you miss out on the opportunity to tailor your questions to those little surprises that you invariably discover (such as gaps in employment).

✔ **Become completely familiar with the job description.** Are you familiar with all the duties and requirements of the job? Really? Telling interviewees that the position requires duties that it really doesn't is poor form. Surprising new staff with duties that you didn't tell them about – especially when they're major tasks – is definitely not good practice.

✔ **Draft your questions before the interview.** Make a checklist of the key experience, skills and qualities that you seek in your candidates and use it to guide your questions. Of course, one of your questions may trigger other questions that you didn't anticipate. Go ahead with such questions as long as they provide you with additional insights regarding your candidate and help to illuminate the information that you've outlined on your checklist. And remember, equality of treatment and employment law demand that you give all candidates the same opportunities to shine at interview.

✔ **Select a comfortable environment for both of you.** Your interviewee is likely to be uncomfortable regardless of what you do. You don't need to be uncomfortable too. Make sure that the interview environment is well-ventilated, private and protected from interruptions. You definitely don't want your phone ringing or employees barging in during your interviews. You get the best performance from your interviewees when they aren't thrown off track by distractions.

✔ **Avoid playing power games during the course of the interview.** Forget asking trick questions, turning up the heat or cutting the legs off their chairs (yes, some managers still do this game playing) to gain an artificial advantage over your candidates. Get real – you're in the twenty-first century, for heaven's sake!

✔ **Take lots of notes.** Write down the key points of your candidates' responses and their reactions to your questions. For example, if you ask why your candidate left his previous job, and he starts getting really nervous, make a note about this reaction. Finally, note your own impressions of the candidates; and make sure that you have a form to work on with columns allocated to each candidate. And when you write anything down about the candidates, make sure that you stick to the professional and occupational issues. If you then use phrases such as the following, make sure you can say why:

> • 'Top-notch performer – the star of her class.'
>
> • 'Fantastic experience with developing applications in a client-server environment. The best candidate yet.'
>
> • 'Not right for this job.'

If you write anything disparaging or overtly disrespectful about a candidate, you *have* to be able to say why. If an unsuccessful candidate decides to take you to an employment tribunal, you don't want your notes coming back to haunt you. So avoid one-word statements such as 'Hopeless'; if someone isn't right for the job, briefly note why and move on. Your candidates have the right to see any notes that you may have made, so always write them as if you were going to share them anyway.

✔ **Don't rely on your memory when it comes to interviewing candidates.** If you interview more than a couple of people, you can easily forget who said exactly what and what your impressions were of their performances. Not only are your written notes a great way to remember who's who, they're also an important tool to have when you're evaluating your candidates. And if there's any comeback (see the previous bullet point), you have your notes to refer to.

As you've no doubt gathered by now, interview questions are one of your best tools for determining whether a candidate is right for your company. Although some amount of small talk is appropriate to help relax your candidates (*as sweat poured down the candidate's face, the interviewer asked the opening question with razor-like sharpness: 'Hot enough for you?'),* the heart of your interviews should focus on answering the questions just listed. Above all, don't give up. Keep asking questions until you're satisfied that you have all the information you need to make your decision.

## Interviewing don'ts

Interviewing don'ts could probably fill a whole chapter. If you've been a manager for any time at all, you know that you can run into tricky situations during an interview and that certain questions can land you in major hot water if you make the mistake of asking them.

Some interviewing don'ts are merely good business practice. For example, accepting an applicant's invitation for a date probably isn't a good idea. After a particularly drawn-out interview at a well-known high-tech manufacturer, a male candidate asked out a female interviewer. The interviewer considered her options and declined the date; she also declined to make Prince Charming a job offer.

Then you have the blunders of the major legal type – the kind that can land you and your firm in court. Interviewing is one area of particular concern in the hiring process because it pertains to the possibility of discrimination. For example, although you can ask applicants whether they're able to fulfil job functions, you can't ask them whether they're disabled.

Always ask whether the organisation needs to make any adjustments or provisions in order for a candidate to gain an equal opportunity in their application. This includes access to your place of work, application forms and directions in Braille, and any other specific issues.

Because of the critical nature of the interview process, you must know the questions that you should absolutely never ask a job candidate. Here's a brief summary of the kinds of topics that may, depending on the exact circumstances, get you and your firm into trouble:

- ✔ Applicant's ethnicity or skin colour
- ✔ Applicant's national origin
- ✔ Applicant's gender
- ✔ Applicant's sexual orientation
- ✔ Applicant's marital status
- ✔ Applicant's religion (or lack of)
- ✔ Applicant's height and weight

✔ Applicant's debts

✔ Applicant's disability

✔ Applicant's age

✔ Applicant's arrest and conviction record (with statutory exceptions)

You can take into account offences involving money, theft, fraud, physical and psychological abuse, violence, vandalism and damage to property – even if the convictions are spent (or, in other words, the person has served their time). In the case of other spent convictions, you need to be prepared to justify why you have taken them into account, whether or not you do make someone a job offer.

Legal or illegal, the point is that none of the preceding topics is necessary to determine the applicants' ability to perform their jobs. So, ask questions that directly relate to the candidates' ability to perform the tasks required. To do otherwise puts you at risk. In other words, what *do* count are job-related criteria; that is, information that's directly pertinent to the candidate's ability to do the job (you clearly need to decide this *prior* to interviewing).

# Evaluating Your Candidates

Now comes the tricky part of the recruitment process – evaluating your candidates. If you've done your homework, then you already have a good selection of candidates to choose from, you've narrowed your search down to the ones showing the best potential to excel in your position and you've interviewed them to see whether they can live up to the promises that they've made in their applications. Before you make your final decision, you need a little bit more information.

## Checking references

You've just interviewed the best candidate on Earth. What an application! What an interview! What a candidate! Now, would you be surprised to find that this shining employee-to-be didn't really go to Oxford? Or that he really wasn't the account manager on that nationwide marketing campaign? Or that his last supervisor wasn't particularly impressed with his analytical skills?

Applications, curricula vitae and interviews are great tools, but you do need references. However, getting references can be tricky – for although you're entitled to ask previous employers specific questions about the candidate's performance, they may choose whether or not to answer them.

The primary purpose of checking references is to verify the information that your candidates provide. If you want further insights into how your candidates really performed in previous jobs, then you need to ask specific questions about absence records, achievements and jobs or positions held.

When you contact a candidate's referees, limit your questions to those related to the work to be done. As in the interview process, asking questions that can be considered discriminatory to your candidates isn't appropriate.

Here are some of the best places to do your reference checking:

- ✔ **Check academic references.** A surprising number of people exaggerate or tell lies when reporting their educational experience. Start your reference check here. If your candidates didn't tell the truth about their education, you can bet that the rest of their experience is suspect too, and you can toss the candidate into the discard pile before you proceed.

- ✔ **Call current and former supervisors.** Getting information from employers is increasingly difficult. Many businesspeople are rightfully concerned that they may be sued for libel or defamation of character if they say anything negative about current or former employees. Still, it doesn't hurt to try. You get a better picture of your candidates if you speak directly to their current and former supervisors instead of to their firms' HR department, especially if the supervisors you speak to have left their firms. The most you're likely to get from HR is a confirmation that the candidate worked at the firm during a specific period of time.

- ✔ **Check your network of associates.** If you belong to a professional association, union or similar group of like-minded careerists, you have the opportunity to tap into the rest of the membership to get the word on your candidates. For example, if you're a member of the Chartered Institute of Personnel and Development (MCIPD) and want to find out about a few candidates for a position in HR, you can check with the members of your professional association to see whether anyone knows anything about them.

- ✔ **Surf the web.** Especially for top, senior and specialist positions, type your candidate's name into a search engine such as Google (`www.google.co.uk`), along with the name of the company where he last worked or the city in which he lives. You never know what can turn up!

What a reference won't do is tell you how a candidate will perform in the future if you appoint him. However good he's been in the past, this doesn't mean that he'll make an excellent employee in the future. By the same token, if he receives a bad or average reference from a previous employer, you need to find out why, so that you have the fullest information before deciding whether to accept or reject him. You do have to be careful with references!

## Reviewing your notes

You did take interview notes, didn't you? Now's the time to drag them back out and look them over. Review the information package for each candidate – one by one – and compare your findings against your pre-determined criteria. Take a look at the candidates' applications, your notes and the results of your reference checks, such as they are. How do the candidates stack up against the standards that you set for the position? Do you see any clear winners at this point? Any clear losers? Organise your candidate packages into the following piles:

**Book II**

**Building Your Commercial Acumen**

- ✔ **Winners:** These candidates are clearly the best choices for the position. You have no hesitation in hiring any one of them.

- ✔ **Potential winners:** These candidates are questionable for one reason or another. Maybe their experience isn't as strong as that of other candidates, or perhaps you weren't impressed with their presentation skills. Neither clear winners nor clear losers, you hire these candidates only after further investigation, or if you can't hire anyone from your pool of winners.

- ✔ **Losers:** These candidates are clearly unacceptable for the position. You simply don't consider hiring any of them.

Make sure that you can justify your choice for each pile on the basis of capability, willingness and availability to do the job alone.

## Conducting second (or third) interviews

When you're a busy manager, you're under pressure to get things done as quickly as possible, and you're tempted to take shortcuts to achieving your goals. It seems that everything has to be done yesterday – or maybe the day before. When do you have the opportunity to really spend as much time as you want to complete a task or project? Time is precious when you have ten other projects crying out for your attention. Time is even more valuable when you're hiring for a vacant position that's critical to your organisation and needs to be filled right now.

Recruitment is one area of business where you can't take shortcuts. Finding the best candidates for your vacancies requires a very real investment of time and resources to be successful. Your company's future depends on it.

Depending on your organisation's policies or culture, or because you're undecided as to the best candidate, you may decide to bring candidates in for several rounds of interviews. In this kind of system, lower-level supervisors, managers or interview panels conduct initial screening interviews. Candidates who pass this round are invited back for another interview with a higher-level manager. Finally, the best two or three candidates interview with the organisation's top manager.

But keep in mind that the timescale for an offer is very different depending on the job you're interviewing for. Lower-level job hunters can't afford to be unemployed (if they are) for long, and they often get and accept job offers quickly. A higher-level position – say, a general manager – gives you more time.

The ultimate decision on how many rounds and levels of interviews to conduct depends on the nature of the job itself, the size of your company and your policies and procedures. If the job is simple or at a relatively low level in the company, a single phone interview may be sufficient to determine the best candidate for a job. However, you may need several rounds of testing and personal interviews if the job is complex or at a relatively high level in the organisation.

# Engaging the Best (and Leaving the Rest)

Ranking your candidates within the groups of winners and potential winners that you established during the evaluation phase of the process is the first step in making a recruitment decision. You don't need to bother ranking the losers because you wouldn't take them on anyway – no matter what. The best candidate in your group of winners is first, the next best is second and so on. If you've done your job thoroughly and well, the best candidates for the job should be readily apparent at this point.

Getting on the phone and offering your first choice the job is the next step. Don't waste any time – you never know whether your candidate has had interviews with other employers. Investing all this time in the recruitment process is wasted if you find out that he just accepted a job with one of your competitors. If you can't reach an agreement with your first choice within a reasonable amount of time, then go on to your second choice. Keep going through your pool of winners until you take someone on, or exhaust the list of candidates.

The following sections give you a few tips to keep in mind as you rank your candidates and make your final decision.

## Being objective

In some cases, you may prefer certain candidates because of their personality or personal charisma – regardless of their ability or work experience. Sometimes the desire to like these candidates can obscure their shortcomings, while a better qualified, albeit less socially adept, candidate may fade in your estimation.

Be objective. Consider the job to be done and consider the skills and qualifications that being successful requires. Do your candidates have these skills and qualifications? What would it take for your candidates to be considered fully qualified for the position?

Don't allow yourself to be unduly influenced by your candidates' looks, champagne-like personalities, expensive haircuts or dangerously named colognes. None of these characteristics can tell you how well your candidates can perform the job. The facts are present for you to see in your candidates' applications, interview notes and reference checks. If you stick to the facts, you can still go wrong, but the chances are diminished.

And one more thing: diversity in all staffing practices is positive for any organisation – both for the business and for society in general. Leave your bias at the door!

## Trusting your instincts

Sometimes you're faced with a choice between two equally qualified candidates, or with a decision about a candidate who's marginal but shows promise. In such cases, you've weighed all the objective data and you've given the analytical side of your being free rein, but you still have no clear winner. What do you do in this kind of situation?

Listen to yourself. Unlock your heart, your feelings and your intuition. What do you feel in your gut? What do your instincts tell you? Although two candidates may seem equal in skills and abilities, do you have a feeling that one is better suited to the job than the other? If so, go with it. As much as you may want your hiring decision to be as objective as possible, whenever you introduce the human element into the decision-making process, a certain amount of subjectivity is naturally present.

In reality, rarely are two candidates equally qualified, although often one or more people seem to have more to bring to the job than anticipated (for example, industry focus, fresh ideas, previous contacts and so forth). Your preliminary work can be invaluable here in keeping you focused. Can they both do the job? If so, the bonus traits can tip the scale.

Other options:

- ✔ Take one or the other (or both) on for a trial period.
- ✔ Have them both back for a round of interviews (and if this seems expensive, remember the consequences of a bad decision).

A further review of two more or less equally qualified candidates may draw you to the conclusion that, in fact, neither is good enough; in that case, advertise again.

One more thing: be sure to keep in touch with other top candidates as additional needs arise in case your first choice doesn't work out.

## Adjusting after the offer

What do you do if, heaven forbid, you can't hire anyone from your group of winners? This does happen; but no one said that management is easy. Take a look at your stack of potential winners. What would it take to make your top potential winners into winners? If the answer is as simple as a training course or two, then give these candidates serious consideration – with the agreement that they take the necessary training soon after engagement. Perhaps they just need a little more experience before you can put them in the ranks of the winners. You can make a judgement call as to whether you feel that their current experience is sufficient to carry them through until they gain the experience you're looking for. If not, you may want to keep looking for the right candidate. After all, this person may be working with you for a long time – waiting for the best candidate only makes sense.

If you're forced to go to your group of almost winners, and no candidate really seems up to the task, don't hire someone simply to fill the position. If you do, you're probably making a big mistake. Taking people on is far easier than getting rid of them. The damage a bad choice can cause for colleagues, customers and your organisation (not to mention the person you hire) can take years and a considerable amount of money to undo. Such a situation is also extremely stressful. You can also consider whether to redefine the job, re-evaluate other current employees or give someone a temporary contract to see whether a potentially risky candidate really works out.

# Chapter 2

# Feeling Confident with Accounting and Budgeting

**M**ost medium to large businesses employ one or more accountants. Even a very small business could find value in having at least a part-time accountant. Have you ever wondered why? Probably what you think of first is that accountants keep the books and the records of the financial activities of the business. This is true, of course. But accountants perform other very critical, but less well-known, functions in a business:

✔ Accountants carry out vital back-office operating functions that keep the business running smoothly and effectively including payroll, cash receipts and cash payments, purchases and stock, and property records.

✔ Accountants prepare tax returns, including VAT (value-added tax) returns for the business, as well as payroll and investment tax returns.

✔ Accountants determine how to measure and record the costs of products and how to allocate shared costs among different departments and other organisational units of the business.

✔ Accountants are the *professional profit scorekeepers* of the business world, meaning that they are the ones who determine exactly how much profit was earned, or just how much loss the business suffered, during the period. Accountants prepare reports for business managers, keeping them informed about costs and expenses, how sales are going, whether the cash balance is adequate, what the stock situation is and, the most important thing, accountants help managers understand the reasons for changes in the bottom-line performance of a business.

✔ Accountants prepare *financial statements* that help the owners and shareholders of a business understand where the business stands financially. Shareholders wouldn't invest in a business without a clear understanding of the financial health of the business, which regular financial reports (sometimes just called *the financials*) provide.

In short, accountants are much more than bookkeepers – they provide the numbers that are so critical in helping business managers make the informed decisions that keep a business on course toward its financial objectives.

Business managers, investors, and others who depend on financial statements should be willing to meet accountants halfway. People who use accounting information, like spectators at a football game, should know the basic rules of play and how the score is kept.

# Accounting Everywhere You Look

Accounting extends into virtually every walk of life. You're doing accounting when you make entries in your cheque book and fill out your income tax return. When you sign a mortgage on your home you should understand the accounting method the lender uses to calculate the interest amount charged on your loan each period. Individual investors need to understand some accounting in order to figure the return on capital invested. And every organisation, profit-motivated or not, needs to know how it stands financially. Accounting supplies all that information.

Many different kinds of accounting are done by many different kinds of persons or entities for many different purposes:

✔ Accounting for organisations and accounting for individuals

✔ Accounting for profit-motivated businesses and accounting for non-profit organisations (such as hospitals, housing associations, churches, schools, and colleges)

✔ Income tax accounting while you're living and estate tax accounting after you die

✔ Accounting for farmers who grow their products, accounting for miners who extract their products from the earth, accounting for producers who manufacture products, and accounting for retailers who sell products that others make

✔ Accounting for businesses and professional firms that sell services rather than products, such as the entertainment, transportation, and health care industries

✔ Past-historical-based accounting and future-forecast-oriented accounting (that is, budgeting and financial planning)

✔ Accounting where periodic financial statements are mandatory (businesses are the primary example) and accounting where such formal accounting reports are not required

✔ Accounting that adheres to cost (most businesses) and accounting that records changes in market value (investment funds, for example)

✔ Accounting in the private sector of the economy and accounting in the public (government) sector

✔ Accounting for going-concern businesses that will be around for some time and accounting for businesses in bankruptcy that may not be around tomorrow

**Book II**

**Building Your Commercial Acumen**

Accounting is necessary in any free-market, capitalist economic system. It's equally necessary in a centrally controlled, socialist economic system. All economic activity requires information. The more developed the economic system, the more the system depends on information. Much of the information comes from the accounting systems used by the businesses, individuals, and other institutions in the economic system.

# The Basic Elements of Accounting

Accounting involves bookkeeping, which refers to the painstaking and detailed recording of economic activity and business transactions. But *accounting* is a much broader term than *bookkeeping* because accounting refers to the design of the bookkeeping system. It addresses the many problems in measuring the financial effects of economic activity. Furthermore, accounting includes the *financial reporting* of these values and performance measures to non-accountants in a clear and concise manner. Business managers and investors, as well as many other people, depend on financial reports for vital information they need to make good economic decisions.

Accountants design the *internal controls* in an accounting system, which serve to minimise errors in recording the large number of activities that a business engages in over the period. The internal controls that accountants design can detect and deter theft, embezzlement, fraud, and dishonest behaviour of all kinds. In accounting, internal controls are the gram of prevention that is worth a kilo of cure.

An accountant seldom prepares a complete listing of all the details of the activities that took place during a period. Instead, he or she prepares a *summary financial statement,* which shows totals, not a complete listing of all the individual activities making up the total. Managers may occasionally need to search through a detailed list of all the specific transactions that make up the total, but this is not common. Most managers just want summary financial statements for the period – if they want to drill down into the details making up a total amount for the period, they ask the accountant for this more detailed backup information. Also, outside investors usually only see summary-level financial statements. For example, they see the total amount of sales revenue for the period but not how much was sold to each and every customer.

Financial statements are prepared at the end of each accounting period. A period may be one month, one quarter (three calendar months), or one year. One basic type of accounting report prepared at the end of the period is a 'Where do we stand at the end of the period?' type of report. This is called the *balance sheet.* The date of preparation is given in the header, or title above this financial statement. A balance sheet shows two aspects of the business.

One aspect is the *assets* of the business, which are its economic resources being used in the business. The other aspect of the balance sheet is a breakdown of where the assets came from, or the sources of the assets. The asset *values* reported in the balance sheet are the amounts recorded when the assets were originally acquired. For many assets these values are recent – only a few weeks or a few months old. For some assets their values as reported in the balance sheet are the costs of the assets when they were acquired many years ago.

Assets are not like manna from heaven. They come from borrowing money in the form of loans that have to be paid back at a later date and from owners' investment of capital (usually money) in the business. Also, making profit increases the assets of the business; profit retained in the business is the third basic source of assets. If a business has, say, £2.5 million in total assets (without knowing which particular assets the business holds) you know that the total of its liabilities, plus the capital invested by its owners, plus its retained profit, adds up to £2.5 million.

In this particular example suppose that the total amount of the liabilities of the business is £1.0 million. This means that the total amount of *owners' equity* in the business is £1.5 million, which equals total assets less total liabilities. Without more information we don't know how much of total owners' equity is traceable to capital invested by the owners in the business and how much is the result of profit retained in the business. But we do know that the total of these two sources of owners' equity is £1.5 million.

The financial condition of the business in this example is summarised in the following *accounting equation* (in millions):

£2.5 Assets = £1.0 Liabilities + £1.5 Owners' Equity

Looking at the accounting equation you can see why the statement of financial condition is also called the balance sheet; the equal sign means the two sides have to balance

*Double-entry bookkeeping* is based on this accounting equation – the total of assets on the one side is counter-balanced by the total of liabilities, invested capital, and retained profit on the other side.

Other financial statements are different than the balance sheet in one important respect: They summarise the significant *flows* of activities and operations over the period. Accountants prepare two types of summary flow reports for businesses:

**Book II**

**Building Your Commercial Acumen**

- ✓ The **profit and loss account** summarises the inflows of assets from the sale of products and services during the period. The profit and loss account also summarises the outflow of assets for expenses during the period leading down to the well-known *bottom line,* or final profit, or loss, for the period.

- ✓ The **cash flow statement** summarises the business's cash inflows and outflows during the period. The first part of this financial statement calculates the net increase or decrease in cash during the period from the profit-making activities reported in the profit and loss account.

The balance sheet, profit and loss account, and cash flow statement constitute the hard core of a financial report to those persons outside a business who need to stay informed about the business's financial affairs. These individuals have invested capital in the business, or the business owes them money and therefore they have a financial interest in how well the business is doing. These three key financial statements are also used by the managers of a business to keep themselves informed about what's going on and the financial position of the business. They are absolutely essential to helping managers control the performance of a business, identify problems as they come up, and plan the future course of a business. Managers also need other information that is not reported in the three basic financial statements.

## The jargon jungle of accounting

Financial statements include many terms that are reasonably clear and straightforward, like *cash, debtors,* and *creditors.* However, financial statements also use words like *retained earnings, accumulated depreciation, accelerated depreciation, accrued expenses, reserve, allowance, accrual basis,* and *current assets.* This type of jargon in accounting is perhaps too common: It's everywhere you look.

# Accounting and Financial Reporting Standards

Experience and common sense have taught business and financial professionals that uniform financial reporting standards and methods are critical in a free-enterprise, private, capital-based economic system. A common vocabulary, uniform accounting methods, and full disclosure in financial reports are the goals. How well the accounting profession performs in achieving these goals is an open question, but few disagree that they are worthy goals to strive for.

## The emergence of International Financial Reporting Standards

The most important financial statement and financial reporting standards and rules are called *generally accepted accounting principles (GAAP),* which describe the basic methods to measure profit and to value assets and liabilities, as well as what information should be disclosed in those financial statements released outside a business. Suppose you're reading the financial statements of a business. You're entitled to assume that the business has used GAAP in reporting its cash flows and profit and its financial condition at the end of a financial period – *unless* the business makes very clear that it has prepared its financial report on a comprehensive basis of accounting other than GAAP.

The word *comprehensive* here is very important. A financial report should be comprehensive, or all-inclusive – reflecting all the financial activities and aspects of the entity. If not, the burden is on the business to make very clear that it is presenting something less than a complete and comprehensive report on its financial activities and condition. But, even if the financial report of a business is comprehensive, its financial statements may be based on accounting methods other than GAAP.

If GAAP are not the basis for preparing its financial statements, a business should make very clear which other basis of accounting is being used and should avoid using titles for its financial statements that are associated with GAAP. For example, if a business uses a simple cash receipts and cash disbursements basis of accounting – which falls way short of GAAP – it should not use the terms *profit and loss account* and *balance sheet.* These terms are part and parcel of GAAP, and their use as titles for financial statements implies that the business is using GAAP.

In brief, GAAP constitute the gold standard for preparing financial statements of business entities – although the gold is somewhat tarnished. Readers of a business's financial report are entitled to assume that GAAP (and any accounting standards that have evolved from GAAP) have been followed in preparing the financial statements unless the business makes very clear that it has not complied entirely with GAAP. If the deviations and shortfalls from GAAP are not disclosed, the business may have legal exposure to those who relied on the information in its financial report and suffered a loss attributable to the misleading nature of the information.

The Accounting Standards Board, the body responsible for setting accounting standards in the UK, is undertaking a programme of gradually ripping up UK GAAP and replacing it with international financial reporting standards. Today, companies with outside shareholders in the UK and across Europe have bitten the bullet and are adopting international accounting standards, known as International Financial Reporting Standards (IFRS). International standards sound like a great idea – especially with the introduction of a single European currency and the emergence of pan-European equity markets. In fact most financial directors of public companies want to be able to adopt IFRS ahead of time. The UK's Accounting Standards Board is pressing ahead with a programme to 'converge' UK accounting standards so that they match the international standards – almost. You can keep track of changes in company reporting rules on the Institute of Chartered Accountants' website at http://www.icaew.com (click on Accounting and corporate reporting and then on UK GAAP).

You could ask if the move to IFRS is such a big deal? In reality, this programme is not an accounting revolution, but a journey from one comprehensive basis of GAAP to another. GAAP remains the preferred option for the majority of the 1.4 million private companies and 3 million partnerships and sole traders in the UK. Only the 3,500 or so companies listed on UK stock markets are changing to IFRS.

## *Why accounting rules are important*

Business managers should know the basic features of GAAP – though certainly not all the technical details – so that they understand how profit is measured. Managers get paid to make profit, and they should be very clear on how profit is measured and what profit consists of. The amount of profit a business makes depends on how *profit* is defined and measured.

For example, a business records the purchase of products at cost, which is the amount it paid for the products. *Stock* is the name given to products being held for sale to customers. Examples include clothes in a department store, fuel in the tanks in a petrol station, food on the shelves in a supermarket, books in a bookstore, and so on. The cost of products is put in the stock asset account and kept there until the products are sold to customers. When the products are eventually sold, the cost of the products is recorded as the cost of goods sold expense, at which time a decrease is recorded in the stock asset account. The cost of products sold is deducted from the sales revenue received from the customers, which gives a first-step measure of profit. (A business has many other expenses that need to be factored in,.)

Now, assume that before the business sells the products to its customers, the replacement cost of many of the products being held in stock awaiting sale increases. The replacement cost value of the products is now higher than the original, actual purchase cost of the products. The company's stock is worth more, is it not? Perhaps the business could raise the sales prices that it charges its customers because of the cost increase, or perhaps not. In any case, should the increase in the replacement cost of the products be recorded as profit? The manager may think that this holding gain should be recorded as profit. But GAAP accounting standards say that no profit is earned until the products are sold to the customers.

What about the opposite movement in replacement costs of products – when replacement costs fall below the original purchase costs? Should this development be recorded as a loss, or should the business wait until the products are sold? As you'll see, the accounting rule that applies here is called *lower of cost or market*, and the loss is recorded. So the rule requires one method on the upside but another method on the downside. See why business managers and investors need to know something about the rules of the game? We should add that GAAP are not all crystal-clear, which leaves a lot of wriggle room in the interpretation and application of these accounting standards. But first a quick word about GAAP and income tax accounting.

## *Income tax and accounting rules*

Generally speaking (and we're being very general when we say the following), HM Revenue & Customs' income tax accounting rules for determining the annual taxable income of a business are in agreement with GAAP. In other words, the accounting methods used for figuring taxable income and for figuring business profit before income tax are in general agreement. Having said this, we should point out that several differences do exist. A business may use one accounting method for filing its annual income tax returns and a different method for measuring its profit, both for management reporting purposes and for preparing its external financial statements to outsiders.

## Flexibility in accounting standards

An often-repeated accounting story concerns three accountants being interviewed for an important position. The accountants are asked one key question: 'What's 2 plus 2?' The first candidate answers, 'It's 4', and is told, 'Don't call us, we'll call you.' The second candidate answers, 'Well, most of the time the answer is 4, but sometimes it's 3 and sometimes it's 5.' The third candidate answers: 'What do you want the answer to be?' Guess who got the job?

The point is that GAAP are not entirely airtight or cut-and-dried, and are being updated. Many accounting standards leave a lot of room for interpretation. *Guidelines* would be a better word to describe some accounting rules. Deciding how to account for certain transactions and situations requires flexibility, seasoned judgment, and careful interpretation of the rules. Furthermore, many estimates have to be made.

Sometimes, businesses use what's called *creative accounting* to make profit for the period look better. Like lawyers who know where to find legal loopholes, accountants sometimes come up with inventive solutions but still stay within the guidelines of GAAP. Articles in financial newspapers and magazines regularly focus on such accounting abuses.

# Enforcing Accounting Rules

As we mentioned in the preceding sections, when preparing financial statements a business must follow generally accepted accounting principles (GAAP) – the authoritative ground rules for measuring profit and for reporting values of assets and liabilities. Everyone reading a financial report is entitled to assume that GAAP have been followed (unless the business clearly discloses that it is using another so-called comprehensive basis of accounting).

The basic idea behind GAAP is to measure profit and to value assets and liabilities *consistently* from business to business – to establish broad-scale uniformity in accounting methods for all businesses. The idea is to make sure that all accountants are singing the same tune from the same hymnbook. The purpose is also to establish realistic and objective methods for measuring profit and putting values on assets and liabilities. The authoritative bodies write the tunes that accountants have to sing.

GAAP also include minimum requirements for *disclosure,* which refers to how information is classified and presented in financial statements and to the types of information that have to be added to the financial statements in the form of footnotes.

How do you know if a business has actually followed the rules faithfully? We think it boils down to two factors. First is the competency and ethics of the accountants who prepared the financial reports. No substitute exists for expertise and integrity. But accountants often come under intense pressure to massage the numbers from the higher-level executives they work for.

Which leads to the second factor that allows you to know if a business has obeyed the dictates of accounting standards. Businesses have their financial statements audited by independent chartered or management accountants. In fact, limited companies are required by law to have annual audits and many private businesses hire accountants to do an annual audit, even if not legally required. The Companies Act 2006 has introduced some tough rules on how auditors, amongst others, should report on company accounts.

## Protecting investors: Sarbanes-Oxley and beyond

A series of high profile financial frauds in US-based businesses such as Enron and Worldcom in the mid–late 1990's badly shook people's confidence in US businesses. In response, the US government introduced the Sarbanes-Oxley Act, known less commonly but better understood as 'the Public Company Accounting Reforms and Investor Protection Act – 2002'.

The central tenet of the Sarbanes-Oxley Act is to ensure truthfulness in financial reporting – a quest the accounting profession has been pursuing since Pacioli set out the rules of double-entry bookkeeping five centuries ago. The act closes the loopholes that creative accountants opened up, which made it difficult (and sometimes impossible) for shareholders to see how a business was performing until after the baddies had made off with the loot. The act applies to any business with shares listed on an American stock market that does business in the US – not just to US companies. The act is extremely complicated, so check out www.sarbanes-oxley.com for the lowdown on that act.

The British version, 'the Companies (Audit, Investigations, and Community Enterprise) Act – 2004', is causing the accounting profession to clutch their collective heads. This knock-on effect from Sarbanes-Oxley means that all companies selling shares to the public have to make changes to their accounts and accounting standards. You can read up on the UK rules at the Office of the Public Sector Information website (go to `http://www.opsi.gov.uk` and click on 'Legislation', 'UK', 'Acts', 'Public Acts 2004', and finally on 'Companies (Audit, Investigations and Community Enterprise) Act 2004').

# The Accounting Department: What Goes On in the Back Office

**Book II**

**Building Your Commercial Acumen**

As we discussed earlier in this chapter, bookkeeping (also called *record-keeping*) and financial reporting to managers and investors are the core functions of accounting. In this section, we explain another basic function of a business's accounting department: the back-office functions that keep the business running smoothly.

Most people don't realise the importance of the accounting department. That's probably because accountants do many of the back-office, operating functions in a business – as opposed to sales, for example, which is front-line activity, out in the open, and in the line of fire.

Typically, the accounting department is responsible for:

- ✔ **Payroll:** The total wages and salaries earned by every employee every pay period, which are called *gross wages* or *gross earnings,* have to be determined. In short, payroll is a complex and critical function that the accounting department performs: the correct amounts of income tax, social security tax, and other deductions from gross wages have to be calculated.

- ✔ **Cash inflows:** All cash received from sales and from all other sources has to be carefully identified and recorded, not only in the cash account but also in the appropriate account for the source of the cash received. In larger organisations, the *Chief Accountant* may be responsible for some of these cash flow and cash-handling functions.

- ✔ **Cash payments:** A business writes many cheques during the course of a year to pay for a wide variety of items including local business taxes, paying off loans, and the distribution of some of its profit to the owners of the business. The accounting department prepares all these cheques for the signatures of the officers of the business who are authorised to sign cheques, and keeps the relevant supporting documents and files for the company's records.

✓ **Purchases and stock:** Accounting departments are usually responsible for keeping track of all purchase orders that have been placed for stock (products to be sold by the business) and all other assets and services that the business buys – from postage stamps to forklift trucks. The accounting department also keeps detailed records on all products held for sale by the business and, when the products are sold, records the cost of the goods sold.

✓ **Capital accounting:** A typical business holds many different assets called *capital* – including office furniture and equipment, retail display cabinets, computers, machinery and tools, vehicles, buildings, and land. The accounting department keeps detailed records of these items.

The accounting department may be assigned other functions as well, but we think that this list gives you a pretty clear idea of the back-office functions that the accounting department performs. Quite literally, a business could not operate if the accounting department did not do these functions efficiently and on time.

# Focusing on Business Transactions and Other Financial Events

Understanding that a great deal of accounting focuses on business transactions is very important. *Transactions* are economic exchanges between a business and the persons and other businesses with which the business deals. Transactions are the lifeblood of every business, the heartbeat of activity that keeps the business going. Understanding accounting, to a large extent, means understanding the basic accounting methods and practices used to record the financial effects of transactions.

A business carries on economic exchanges with six basic groups:

✓ Its **customers,** who buy the products and services that the business sells.

✓ Its **employees,** who provide services to the business and are paid wages and salaries and provided with a broad range of benefits such as a pension plan and paid holidays.

✓ Its **suppliers** and **vendors,** who sell a wide range of things to the business, such as legal advice, electricity and gas, telephone service, computers, vehicles, tools and equipment, furniture, and even audits.

✓ Its **debt sources of capital,** who loan money to the business, charge interest on the amount loaned, and have to be repaid at definite dates in the future.

✔ Its **equity sources of capital,** the individuals and financial institutions who invest money in the business and expect the business to earn profit on the capital they invest.

✔ The **government** agencies that collect income taxes, payroll taxes, value-added tax, and excise duties from the business.

Figure 2–1 illustrates the interactions between the business and the other parties in the economic exchange.

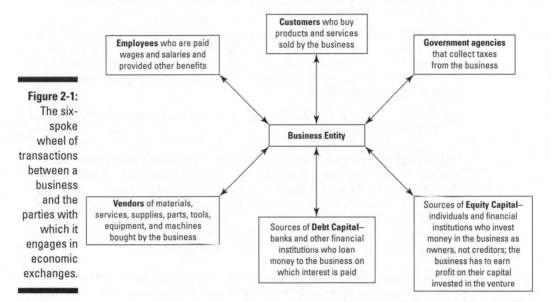

**Figure 2-1:** The six-spoke wheel of transactions between a business and the parties with which it engages in economic exchanges.

Even a relatively small business generates a surprisingly large number of transactions, and all transactions have to be recorded. Certain other events that have a financial impact on the business have to be recorded as well. These are called *events* because they're not based on give-and-take bargaining – unlike the something-given-for-something-received nature of economic exchanges. Events such as the following have an economic impact on a business and have to be recorded:

✔ A business may lose a lawsuit and be ordered to pay damages. The liability to pay the damages should be recorded.

✔ A business may suffer a flood loss that is uninsured. The water-logged assets may have to be written off, meaning that the recorded values of the assets are reduced to nil if they no longer have any value to the business.

✔ A business may decide to abandon a major product line and downsize its workforce, requiring that severance be paid to laid-off employees.

# Taking a Closer Look at Financial Statements

As we mention in the preceding sections, accountants prepare certain basic financial statements for a business. The three basic financial statements are the following:

- ✔ **Balance Sheet:** A summary of the financial position of the business at the end of the period.

- ✔ **Profit and loss account:** A summary of sales revenue and expenses that determines the profit (or loss) for the period just ended. This is also called the *income statement,* or simply abbreviated down to the *P&L statement.* (Alternative titles also include the *operating statement* and the *earnings statement.*)

- ✔ **Cash flow statement:** A summary of cash inflows and cash outflows for the period just ended.

This section gives you a description of these statements that constitute a business's financial centre of gravity. We show you the general format and content of these three accounting reports. The managing director and chief executive officer of a business (plus other top-level managers and financial officers) are responsible for seeing that the financial statements are prepared according to financial reporting standards and that proper accounting methods have been used to prepare the financial statements.

If a business's financial statements are later discovered to be seriously in error or misleading, the business and its top executives can be sued for damages suffered by lenders and investors who relied on the financial statements. For this reason, business managers should understand their responsibility for the financial statements and the accounting methods used to prepare the statements. In a court of law, they can't plead ignorance.

We frequently meet managers who don't seem to have a clue about the three primary statements. This situation is a little scary; a manager who doesn't understand financial statements is like an aeroplane pilot who doesn't understand the instrument readouts in the cockpit. A manager *could* run the business and 'land the plane safely', but knowing how to read the vital signs along the way is much more prudent.

In short, business managers at all levels – from the board of directors down to the lower rungs on the management ladder, and especially managers of smaller businesses who have to be a jack-of-all-trades in running the business –

need to understand financial statements and the accounting methods used to prepare the statements. Also, lenders to a business, investors in a business, business lawyers, government regulators of business, entrepreneurs, employees who depend on the continued financial success of the business for their jobs, anyone thinking of becoming an entrepreneur and starting a business, and, yes, even economists, should know the basics of financial statement accounting. We've noticed that even experienced business journalists, who ought to know better, sometimes refer to the balance sheet when they're talking about profit performance. The bottom line is found in the profit and loss account, not the balance sheet!

# *The balance sheet*

The balance sheet is the essential financial statement that reports the main types of assets owned by a business. Assets are only half the picture, however. Almost all businesses borrow money. At the date of preparing the balance sheet, a business owes money to its lenders, who will be paid sometime in the future. Also, most businesses buy many things on credit and at the balance sheet date owe money to their suppliers, which will be paid in the future. Amounts owed to lenders and suppliers are called *liabilities*. A balance sheet reports the main types of liabilities of the business, and separates those due in the short term and those due in the longer term.

Could total liabilities be greater than a business's total assets? Well, not likely – unless the business has been losing money hand-over-fist. In the vast majority of cases a business has more total assets than total liabilities. Why? For two reasons: (1) its owners have invested money in the business, which is not a liability of the business; and (2) the business has earned profit over the years and some of the profit has been retained in the business. (Profit increases assets.) The sum of invested capital from owners and retained profit is called *owners' equity*. The excess of total assets over total liabilities is traceable to owners' equity. A balance sheet reports the make-up of the owners' equity of a business.

**Book II**

**Building Your Commercial Acumen**

### Basic Format of the Balance Sheet

**Assets,** or the economic resources the business owns: examples are cash on deposit, products held for sale to customers, and buildings.

**Liabilities,** which arise from borrowing money and buying things on credit.

**Owners' Equity,** which arises from two sources: money invested by the owners, and profit earned and retained by the business.

One reason the balance sheet is called by this name is that the two sides balance, or are equal in total amounts:

Total Recorded Amount of Assets = Total Recorded Amount of Liabilities + Total Recorded Amount of Owners' Equity

Owners' equity is sometimes referred to as *net worth*. You compute net worth as follows:

Assets – Liabilities = Net Worth

*Net worth* is not a particularly good term because it implies that the business is worth the amount recorded in its owners' equity accounts. Though the term may suggest that the business could be sold for this amount, nothing is further from the truth.

## The profit and loss account

The profit and loss account is the all-important financial statement that summarises the profit-making activities (or operations) of a business over a time period. In very broad outline, the statement is reported like this:

### Basic Format of the Profit and Loss Account

**Sales Revenue** (from the sales of products and services to customers)

**Less Expenses** (which include a wide variety of costs paid by the business, including the cost of products sold to customers, wages and benefits paid to employees, occupancy costs, administrative costs, and income tax)

**Equals Net Income** (which is referred to as the *bottom line* and means final profit after all expenses are deducted from sales revenue)

The profit and loss account gets the most attention from business managers and investors – not that they ignore the other two financial statements. The very abbreviated versions of profit and loss accounts that you see in the financial press, such as in *The Financial Times*, report only the top line (sales revenue) and the bottom line (net profit). In actual practice, the profit and loss account is more involved than the basic format shown here.

## The cash flow statement

The cash flow statement presents a summary of the sources and uses of cash in a business during a financial period. Smart business managers hardly get the word *profit* out of their mouths before mentioning *cash flow.* Successful business managers can tell you that they have to manage both profit *and* cash flow; you can't do one and ignore the other. Business is a two-headed dragon in this respect. Ignoring cash flow can pull the rug out from under a successful profit formula. Still, some managers become preoccupied with making profit and overlook cash flow.

For financial reporting, cash flows are divided into three basic categories:

### Basic Format of the Cash Flow Statement

(1) **Cash flow** from the profit-making activities, or *operating activities,* for the period (***Note:*** *Operating* means the profit-making transactions of the business.)

(2) **Cash inflows and outflows** from *investing activities* for the period

(3) **Cash inflows and outflows** from the *financing activities* for the period

You determine the bottom-line net increase (or decrease) in cash during the period by adding the three types of cash flows shown in the preceding list.

Part 1 explains why net cash flow from sales revenue and expenses – the business's profit-making operating activities – is more or less than the amount of profit reported in the profit and loss account. The *actual* cash inflows from revenues and outflows for expenses run on a different timetable than the sales revenue and expenses which are recorded for determining profit. It's like two different trains going to the same destination – the second train (the cash flow train) runs on a later schedule than the first train (the recording of sales revenue and expenses in the accounts of the business).

Part 2 of the cash flow statement sums up the major long-term investments made by the business during the year, such as constructing a new production plant or replacing machinery and equipment. If the business sold any of its long-term assets, it reports the cash inflows from these divestments in this section of the cash flow statement.

Part 3 sums up the financing activities of the business during the period – borrowing new money from lenders and raising new capital investment in the business from its owners. Cash outflows to pay off debt are reported in this section, as well as cash distributions from profit paid to the owners of the business.

The cash flow statement reports the net increase or net decrease in cash during the year (or other time period), caused by the three types of cash flows. This increase or decrease in cash during the year is never referred to as the *bottom line.* This important term is strictly limited to the last line of the profit and loss account, which reflects net income – the final profit after all expenses are deducted.

Imagine you have a highlighter pen in your hand, and the three basic financial statements of a business are in front of you. What are the most important numbers to mark? Financial statements do *not* have any numbers highlighted; they do not come with headlines like newspapers. You have to find your own headlines. *Bottom-line profit* in the profit and loss account is one number you would mark for sure. Another key number is *cash flow from operating activities* in the cash flow statement, or some variation of this number. Cash flow has become very important these days.

# Exploring the Wonderful World of Budgets

A *budget* is an itemised forecast of an individual's or company's income and expenses expected for some period in the future. Budgets provide the baseline of expected performance against which managers measure actual performance. Accounting systems generate reports to compare expected performance against actual performance to provide financial information on an organisation's financial status. With this information, managers with budget responsibility act as physicians to assess the current financial health of their businesses.

When you receive the latest accounting report, it says that sales are too low compared to budget. What does that mean? As a responsible manager (this means you!), you need to work out why. Maybe your sales force is having problems getting the product delivered to your customers quickly. Or perhaps your competition developed a new thingamajig that's taking sales away from your product. Whatever the problem is, you can't know if you don't understand the basics of budgeting.

Because business is changing all the time, you may wonder why you bother having a budget. Without a long-term plan and goals, your organisation lacks focus and wastes resources as employees wander aimlessly about. A budget isn't just an educated guess that reflects your long-term plans and allows you to act on them; it's a personal commitment to making a designated future happen. The best budgets are flexible, allowing for changes in different key assumptions, such as income results. Of course, planning becomes more difficult as the world changes all around you, but plan you must.

Budgets also fulfil another important purpose: they provide a baseline against which you can measure your progress towards your goals. For example, if you're 50 per cent of the way through your financial year but have actually spent 75 per cent of your budgeted operating funds, then you have an immediate indication that a potential problem exists if you don't see any significant change in your expenditure. You've under-budgeted your expenses for the year, or you're overspending. Whenever budgeted performance and actual performance disagree, or are in *variance*, the job of responsible managers is to ask why, and then to put right any problems that they find.

Depending on your organisation's size, the budgeting process may be quite simple or very complex. Regardless of your organisation's size, you ought to budget for everything. Following are examples of budget areas that just about every organisation needs:

- ✔ **Sales budget:** The sales budget is an estimate of the total number of products or services that the organisation will sell in a given period. Determine the total turnover by multiplying the number of units by the price per unit.

- ✔ **Staff budget:** Staff budgets consist of the number and name of all the various positions in a company along with the salary or wages budgeted for each position.

- ✔ **Production budget:** The production budget takes the sales budget and its estimate of quantities of units to be sold and translates those figures into the cost of labour, material and other expenses required to produce those units.

- ✔ **Administration and overheads budget:** Administration and overheads budgets contain all the different expenses that a department may incur during the normal course of operations. You budget for things like travel, training, office supplies and so forth as expenses.

- ✔ **Capital budget:** This budget is a manager's plan to acquire *fixed assets* (anything your organisation owns that has a long useful life), such as furniture, computers, facilities, physical plant and so forth to support the operations of a business.

**Book II**

**Building Your Commercial Acumen**

# Making a Budget

You have a right and a wrong way to do a budget. The wrong way is simply to make a photocopy of the last budget and submit it as your new budget. Some people simply add a bit here and there, and then hand the slightly revised budget in, hoping it's good enough.

The right way is to gather information from as many sources as possible, review and check the information for accuracy and then use your good judgement to guess what the future may bring. A budget is a *forecast* – a commitment to the future – and is only as good as the data that goes into it and the good judgement that you bring to the process.

Review the basic steps in putting together a budget:

1. **Closely review your budgeting documents and instructions.**

   Take a close look at the budgeting documents you're working with and read any instructions your accounting staff provide with them. Although your organisation may have done something the same way for years, you never know when that procedure may change.

2. **Meet with staff.**

   When you're starting the budget process, meet with your staff members to solicit their input. In some cases, you need the specific input of your employees to forecast accurately. For example, you may need to know how many trips your salespeople plan to make next year and where they plan to go. In other cases, you can simply ask for employee suggestions. One employee may ask you to include a pay increase in the next budget. Another may inform you that the current phone system is no longer adequate to meet the needs of employees and customers and that you should budget for a new one. Whichever the case, your staff can provide you with very useful and important budget information.

3. **Gather data.**

   Pull out copies of previous budgets and accounting reports and then compare budgeted figures to actual figures. Work out whether you over-spent or underspent and by how much. If no historical data is available, find other sources of information that can help guide the development of figures for your budget.

   Determine how much business you plan to bring in during the next budget period, and what it will cost to bring it in. Consider whether you need to hire more people, lease new facilities or buy equipment or supplies. Furthermore, consider the possibility of large increases or decreases in sales or expenses and what effect they would have on your budget.

4. **Apply your judgement.**

   Hard data and cold facts are very important in the budgeting process; they provide an unbiased, unemotional source of information on which to base your decisions. However, data and facts aren't everything – not by a long shot. Budgeting is part science and part art. Take the data and facts and then apply your own judgement to determine the most likely outcomes.

5. **Produce a draft.**

   Depending on how your organisation does business, either fill out your budget forms and send them to your budget people for processing, or enter them in the budget model yourself. The result is a budget draft that you can review and modify before you finalise it. Don't worry if the draft is rough or is missing information. You have a chance to fill in the gaps soon enough.

6. **Check results and redraft as necessary.**

Check over your draft budget and see whether it still makes sense to you. Are you missing any anticipated sources of revenue or expenses? Are the numbers realistic? Do they make sense in a historical perspective? Are they too high or too low? Will you be able to support them when you present them to upper management? The fun part of budgeting is playing with your numbers and trying out different scenarios and what-ifs. When you're satisfied with the results, sign off on your budget and turn it in. Congratulations! You did it!

The accuracy of your budget hinges on two main factors: the quality of the data you use to develop your budget and the quality of the judgement you apply to the data you're working with. Although judgement is something that comes with experience, the quality of the data you use depends on where you get it. You can use three basic approaches to develop the data for building a budget:

- **Build it from scratch.** In the absence of historical data, when you're starting up a new business unit or when you just want a fresh view, you want to develop your budgets based strictly on current estimates. In this process, widely known as *zero-based budgeting*, you build your budget from scratch, determining the people, facilities, travel, advertising and other resources that you require to support it. You then cost out each need, and the budget is complete. Perhaps not too surprisingly, the answer that comes out of building a budget from scratch is often quite different from one that results from using historical data. Funny how that works; and funny, too, how many errors and omissions building from scratch can show in some cases.

- **Use historical figures.** One of the easiest ways to develop data for your budget is to use the actual results from the preceding budget period. Although the past isn't always an indication of the future – especially when an organisation is undergoing significant change – using historical data can be very helpful in relatively stable organisations and you may have an interest in seeing which numbers have gone up and which have gone down.

- **Use the combination approach.** Many managers do both. They use a combination of zero-based budgeting and historical figures for determining which data to include in their budgets. To use this approach, gather historical data and compare the figures to the best estimates of what you think performing a particular function costs. You then adjust historical data up or down, depending on your view of reality.

# Budgeting and the Real World

In any organisation a certain amount of mystery and intrigue – some call it smoke and mirrors – hovers around budgets and the budgeting process. Indeed, whether your organisation is a one-person operation or the central government, you can use many tricks of the budget trade to ensure that you get all the resources you need and desire. *Note:* In these days of big-business scandals and shenanigans, we definitely aren't suggesting that you do anything illegal, immoral or unethical. The tricks we suggest in this section are quite legal, and they're time-honoured techniques for budgeting that all kinds of organisations around the world use every day.

You can play the budget game up front, when you develop the budget, or during the course of the budget period. The following sections tell you how to develop a solid budget.

## Producing real budgets

This section lists some of the games that the pros play when they develop budgets. Again, these aren't immoral or unethical; they're simply what's necessary to survive and prosper in the real world. Although these techniques are most appropriate for new or unstable departments or projects, you can use them when developing any budget. We may be exaggerating just a bit on some of these points, but most of them have a very clear ring of truth.

- **Do some selective padding.** Simple, but effective. The idea is to pad your anticipated expenses so that your budget targets are easy to achieve. You end up looking like a hero when you come in under your budget, plus you get some extra money to play with at the end of the year. This situation is known as win–win. Do be careful, though – most senior managers have worked their way up and know how the game is played. If you go really over the top, they'll think that you're pulling their leg, and will reject your budget accordingly!

- **Tie your budget request to your organisation's values.** This is the 'Everything in the organisation is rosy' approach to budgeting. If you want to beef up your budget in a particular area, just pick one of your organisation's values – for example, quality – and tie your request to it. When your boss asks you to justify why you've tripled your office furniture budget, just tell him that your employees can't do quality work without large, hand-crafted walnut desks.

✔ **Create more requests than you need, and give them up as you have to.** You don't want to appear unreasonable in your budget demands – don't forget, you're a team player! When you draft your budget, build in items that are of relatively low priority to you overall. When your boss puts on the pressure to reduce your budget (and bosses always do), give up the things you didn't really care so much about anyway. Doing so ensures that you get to keep the items that you really do want.

✔ **Shift the time frame.** Insist that the budget items are an investment in the company's future. The secret is to tie these investments to a big pay-off down the road. 'If we double our staff budget, we'll be able to attract the talent that we need to expand our operations.'

✔ **Be prepared.** The best defence is a good offence. Know your budget numbers cold and be ready to justify each budget item in intimate detail. Don't rely on someone else to prepare for you – this can be your finest hour as a manager. Be a star and go for it!

## *Staying on budget*

After your new department or project starts up, you need to monitor your budget closely to make sure that you don't exceed it. If your actual expenditure starts to exceed your budget, you need to take quick and decisive action.

Following are some of the ways that experienced managers make sure that they stay on budget:

✔ **Freeze non-essentials.** Some expenses, such as staff, overheads and electricity, are essential to an operation or project and you can't stop them without jeopardising the organisation's performance. Others, such as purchasing new carpeting, upgrading computer monitors or travelling first-class, are discretionary and you can postpone them without jeopardising performance. Freezing non-essential items of expenditure is the quickest and least painful way to get your actual expenditure back in line with your budgeted expenditure.

✔ **Freeze recruitment.** Although you may have budgeted for new staff, you can save money by imposing a recruitment freeze. Not only do you save on the cost of hourly pay or salaries, but you also save on the costs of fringe benefits, staff accommodation and overheads expenses. And because you aren't tinkering with your current employees' pay or perks, generally everyone is happy with your decision. Of course, you may need to fill some critical positions in your organisation, budget problem notwithstanding. You can determine which positions you have to fill if they become vacant, and which jobs other employees can cover.

# The make-or-buy decision

One of the most common decisions that a business makes is whether to make – that is, build or perform with in-house staff – or buy-in goods and services that are necessary for the operation of the business. For example, say that you need a security guard for your reception area to ensure the safety of your clients. Do you take on someone new as an employee, or does contracting with a company that specialises in providing security services make more sense?

When you consider such a make-or-buy decision, the first point to think about is the cost of each alternative to your firm. Say that in Case A, you hire your security guard as a full-time employee for £6.00 an hour. In Case B, a security services firm provides a guard for £8.00 an hour. On the surface, hiring a security guard as an employee seems to make the most sense. If the guard works 2,000 hours a year, then in Case A you spend £12,000 a year for your guard and in Case B you spend £16,000 a year. By employing the guard yourself, you stand to save £4,000 a year. Right?

Maybe not. See why.

**Case A: Hire in-house security guard**

| | |
|---|---|
| Hourly pay rate | £6.00 |
| Fringe benefits rate (pension, employer's health care) @ 35% | £2.10 |
| Overheads rate (including NI, holiday cover, accommodation) @ 50% | £3.00 |
| **Total effective pay rate** | **£11.10** |
| Hours per year | × 2,000 |
| **Total annual staff cost** | **£22,200** |
| Annual liability insurance increase | £4,000 |

| | |
|---|---|
| Uniforms/cleaning | £1,000 |
| Miscellaneous equipment | £500 |
| **Total annual cost** | **£27,700** |

**Case B: Contract with security firm**

| | |
|---|---|
| Hourly pay rate | £8.00 |
| **Total effective pay rate** | **£8.00** |
| Hours per year | × 2,000 |
| **Total annual cost** | **£16,000** |

Surprise, surprise. Instead of saving £4,000 per year by hiring an in-house security guard, you're actually going to spend almost £12,000 more each year because more costs are involved in hiring an in-house employee than just his hourly pay. You have to add all the fringe benefits, national insurance, any pension contributions and more, plus the employee's share of overheads – facilities, electricity, air-conditioning and so forth – to the basic wage rate to get a true picture of the cost of the employee to your organisation. Furthermore, you need to purchase additional liability insurance, uniforms, uniform cleaning and any other additional equipment.

On the other hand, when you contract with a security services firm, the firm bears the cost of fringe benefits, overheads, insurance, uniforms and equipment. You simply pay the hourly fee and forget it. Furthermore, if the guard isn't any good, you just make a phone call and a replacement is sent immediately. No messy dismissals or potential tribunal cases to worry about.

Now, which deal do you think is the better one? On the face of it, no contest; contracting with the security organisation makes more sense.

However, you have to remember that you lose control over the quality of service provided; the guard isn't your employee, but the contractor's; and the security firm may have nobody who's any better to send to you if this one doesn't work out.

Second – and this applies to all sorts of outsourcing – you may find that the contracting organisation no longer wishes to do business with you at some time in the future; or else it goes broke. In both cases, you face having to find a new contracting organisation or take on your own employee in any case. Also, you may prefer simply to have everyone who works on your premises as an employee, and so you accept the increased cost in return for better overall control.

✔ **Postpone products, services and projects.** The development and production phases of new products and projects can burn up a lot of money. By postponing the start-up and implementation of these new products and projects, you can get your budget back on track. Sometimes it only takes a few weeks or months to make a difference.

✔ **Delay payments to suppliers.** Instead of paying right on time, you can delay your payments over a longer period. If you're going to go down this route, you're generally best off working this out with your suppliers in advance (that is, if you want them to continue to be your suppliers in the future).

Delaying payments to suppliers used to be a manager's favourite for improving cash flow. Of course, you do have to balance your decision to delay payments against the supplier's ability to remain in business without being paid! Otherwise you may find next time that you've got no supplies – because you've got no supplier!

✔ **Hammer suppliers.** If you're in a powerful position and take a large volume from a particular supplier, you can use this to drive the price down. Again, however, you do have to balance such a decision against the supplier's capability and willingness to continue to do business with you on this basis. And if suppliers find outlets that are prepared to do business with them on more favourable terms, they may refuse to do business with you.

✔ **Freeze wages and perks.** These kinds of savings directly affect your employees, and we can guarantee that they aren't going to like that at all. Most employees are used to regular wage and salary increases. Although increases aren't as generous as they were a decade ago, employees still consider them to be essential. However, if you've made cuts and still need to cut more, then you really don't have any choice but to freeze your employees' wages, salaries and other things such as overtime and bonuses at their current levels.

✔ **Lay off employees and close facilities.** You're in business to make money, not to lose money. When sales aren't sufficient to support your expenses – even after enacting cost-savings measures such as the ones in this list – you must take drastic action. Action doesn't get much more drastic than laying off employees and closing facilities. However, if your budget is as far off as it must be if you reach this point, then cut you have to.

# Chapter 3

# Harnessing the Power of Technology

Like everything in life, technology has good and bad points. With computers, for example, managers and workers alike have more ways to waste time than ever before. When all you could do with a keyboard was type, you couldn't get managers anywhere near one – they had secretaries to do that kind of stuff. Now, call it a computer, add email and the Internet, and you can't get managers away from it. Research shows that managers spend up to five hours of their working day on the computer. When you add the average of three hours a day in meetings, this doesn't leave much time to do the real work. And do you really need to spend half an hour typing, editing, spellchecking and colour printing a gorgeous, 64-shades-of-grey memo when a handwritten note or quick phone call works just as well? You may automatically assume that your employees are more productive simply because they have computers at their fingertips, but are you (and your organisation) really getting the most out of this innovative and expensive technology?

In light of this question, in this chapter we explain how to harness *information technology* – technology used to create, store, exchange and utilise information in its various forms. We examine the technology edge, and consider how technology can help or hinder an organisation. We look at how technology can improve efficiency and productivity, and how to get the most out of it. Finally, we describe how to create a technology plan.

# Using Technology to Your Advantage

You can easily get the impression that information technology is taking over the world. Certainly, computers and telecommunications technology are ever more important. CEOs and senior managers all use computers and mobile phones exactly the same as everyone else, because they too (some would say above all) need to be instantly responsive when required. Overall, information technology can create tremendous advantages for you and your business, and you must capitalise on them – before your competition does.

Information and telecommunications technology is only as good as the people who use it. So whatever technology you implement, make sure that your staff know and understand how to use their equipment. Also ensure that they understand what they're *not* allowed to use the technology for – such as booking holidays in the firm's time, or downloading material from controversial or obscene websites.

First, understand the technology and what it can do for you, your organisation, and your staff. You need to take the decision whether to let technology use you or you use it to facilitate more effective, productive and high-quality work. Next, make sure that your staff are fully trained. Using expensive technology to less than full capacity simply because employees don't know what to do with it is wasteful. Finally, recognise that technology is a 'sunk cost', as well as an investment on which you're looking for returns. This means that, whenever it becomes necessary, you have to be prepared to junk your technology and replace it in order to stay competitive. So you need to make sure that your technology works as effectively as possible for you before it becomes obsolete.

## Get some help

If you're a fan of technology and expert in it, that's great – but beware! Don't get drawn down the line of being blinded by technology for its own sake; always keep in mind its use in your organisation and how people less expert and enthusiastic than you are going to use it. Involve everyone, and if necessary engage a technician or technology consultant to advise on the process. If you do bring in a consultant, make sure that you involve the staff affected in making the changes.

# Evaluating the Benefits and Drawbacks of Technology

Think for a moment about the incredible progress of information technology just in your lifetime. Can you believe that three decades ago the personal computer had yet to be introduced commercially? Word processing used to mean a typewriter and a lot of correction fluid or sheets of messy carbon paper, but computers have revolutionised the way in which business people can manipulate and deliver text, graphics and other elements in their reports and other documents. The mobile phone, the laptop, the iPad, the Blackberry and other business technology essentials are all recent innovations; and they're all certain to be developed greatly over the next few years.

So how can technology help your business? Information technology can have a positive impact in these very important ways:

- ✔ **By automating processes:** Not too many years ago, most business processes were manual. For example, your organisation's accounting and payroll departments most likely did their calculations entirely by hand, using only calculators to assist them. People can now accomplish in minutes what used to take hours, days or weeks. Other commonly automated processes are stock tracking, customer service, call analysis and purchasing.

- ✔ **By automating personal management functions:** Managers can now make available their personal schedules and diaries to everyone who needs them.

- ✔ **By creating the ability to carry personal data around at all times:** Managers can now keep abreast of everything that they need as the result of portable information technology.

- ✔ **By keeping in contact around the clock:** Managers can now be accessed at any time, for any reason. Although managers need to preserve their work–life balance, this ease of contact means that things such as crisis management can be engaged much more quickly.

Before you run off and automate or upgrade everything, keep this piece of information in mind: if your present system is inefficient or ineffective, simply upgrading the existing system won't necessarily make it perform any better. In fact, upgrading it can make your system perform worse than the manual version. Whatever you do, review and evaluate all processes in detail. Cut out any unnecessary steps as you go along, and make sure that your system is designed for the future and not the past. And if that sounds a time-consuming process, it's time well spent.

Just as information technology can help a business, it can also hinder it. Here are a few examples of the negative side of information technology:

- ✔ Widespread worker abuse of Internet access has reduced worker productivity by 10 to 15 per cent. Forrester Research, an American think tank, estimates that 20 per cent of employee time on the Internet at work doesn't involve their jobs; other studies in the UK by the Chartered Management Institute, put the figure as high as 30 per cent of time.

- ✔ Hackers have sent periodic waves of computer viruses and malicious attacks through the business world, leaving billions of pounds' worth of damage and lost productivity in their wake.

- ✔ Non-experts spend inordinate amounts of unproductive – and expensive – time trying to make things work, in spite of the fact that they're not qualified to do so.

- ✔ Email messages can be unclear and confusing, forcing workers to waste time clarifying the intention or covering themselves in case of problems.

- ✔ Employees are forced to wade through an ever-growing quantity of spam and junk email messages.

- ✔ The slick, animated and sound-laden computer-based full-colour presentations so common today often tend to drown out the message you're trying to get across. People lose sight of what they're supposed to absorb, do or act on as the result of the presentation.

If you're in any doubt about the amount of time that information technology can consume, consider the findings of Patrick Glynn. He surveyed his own organisation, the headquarters of one of the largest UK banks, and found that providing a substantial answer to an important email took about 20 minutes. At that rate you can process only three emails an hour; so if you have 30 important emails to answer, they effectively take up a whole day's work.

You have to take the bad with the good with information technology. But don't take the bad lying down. You know the problems and difficulties – so recognise them at the outset, and take active steps to prevent them occurring. You can do this by:

- ✔ **Staying abreast of the latest information technology innovations and news.** Although you don't need to become an expert on how to install a network server or configure your voice-mail system, you do need to become conversant in the technology behind your business systems.

- ✔ **Hiring experts.** Although you must have a general knowledge of information technology, plan to hire experts to advise you on the specifics. Always seek expert advice on the design and implementation of critical information technology-based systems.

> ✓ **Managing by walking around.** Make a habit of dropping in on employees, wherever they're located, and observe how they use your organisation's information technology. Ask them for their opinions and suggestions for improvement. Research and implement changes as soon as you discover a need.

One point is certain: everyone's lumbered with the present state of technology and the great speed at which it develops. Therefore, you have to know and understand what current technology can do for you, as well as keep an eye on what new innovations or inventions can offer. So you have to become an expert in assessing and evaluating the potential of technology, the amount that it costs and the returns that it can (and can't) deliver for your organisation.

# *Improving Efficiency and Productivity*

British industry has shifted from primary manufacturing and engineering activities to domination by the service sector. The service sector – whether public services, commerce, financial services, leisure, travel, tourism or retail – depends on the speed and quality of information and data processing to maintain, secure and develop competitive advantage.

The idea that businesspeople who manage information best have a competitive advantage in the marketplace seems obvious enough. The sooner you receive information, the sooner you can act on it. The more efficiently you handle information, the easier you can access it when and where you need it. The more effectively you deal with information, the fewer expenses you incur for managing and maintaining your information.

Managers often cite the preceding reasons, and others like them, as justification for allotting vast amounts of corporate resources to buying computers, installing email and voice-mail systems and training employees to use them. Unfortunately, for years researchers found no evidence to prove that office automation resulted in measurable productivity gains. This led many to label the phenomenon the *productivity paradox*, meaning that technology that's supposed to make it easier for someone to do a job, more quickly, to a higher standard and with fewer errors actually produces fewer results, less quickly. The problem now is that work is done at the machine's speed, rather than the speed at which the individual works.

Author Eliyahu Goldratt defined information as 'the answer to a question'. Many information systems are great at providing data, but not so hot at providing information (at least within this definition). As a manager, you need to first identify the questions that need answers, then who needs the answers (customers, suppliers, employees, management), how fast (now, within one minute, one hour, one day) and how frequently (daily, weekly, monthly). When the answers to these questions become clear, you have a rational basis on which to evaluate alternative technologies. A great deal of technology seems to be designed to provide an immediate answer to a question that you only need to ask once a month.

The key to effective planning and implementation of information technology systems is understanding what they're supposed to do for you. You also need to know the environment and context within which they're to be implemented and, above all, the results that they're supposed to deliver. For example:

- ✔ Ryanair and easyJet have transformed air travel in Western and Central Europe. They cut out the cost of employing travel agents to make bookings, requiring people to book online or, at a premium rate, through their own call centres. However, the online booking facility isn't an end in itself; it's underpinned by the major cost and price advantages that each of the companies delivers, relative to the competition, including European flag-carrier airlines. And when Michael O'Leary, the CEO of Ryanair, was asked whether by getting customers to book online he was eliminating those who didn't have computer access, he simply replied: 'We are the largest volume carrier in Europe; and we carry more passengers than British Airways.'

- ✔ Honda UK at Swindon has a fully automated supply-side process. As parts are removed from the shelves to go on to the production lines, they're automatically deducted from the stock level; when the stock level reaches a particular point, a request to suppliers is automatically generated. The supply-side contract means that suppliers must dispatch within two hours, and Honda must receive their requirements within four hours.

Other companies have taken an enlightened view of 'the technology in its environment' to great effect. Especially, they've recognised the limitations of what technology does. For example:

- ✔ Semco, a Brazilian manufacturing company and globally iconic organisation, closed down one computerised accounting and billing system because it did the job more slowly than clerks working with calculators.

- ✔ Mobile communications retailer Carphone Warehouse forbids its staff to send emails to each other unless, and until, they've first talked face to face, or unless the particular member of staff isn't on the premises for some reason. The company takes the view that far more gets done, far more quickly, when people talk to rather than write to each other.

## Technology projects

If you're installing new technology in your organisation, you need to address the following questions: What do you want the technology to do for you? How will it be integrated into the rest of the organisation and its work? Which staff will use it? How much will it cost? How will we get our money back?

The answers to these questions must be your guide. The technology itself – both hardware and software – is of no consequence; what does matter is its use and value to the organisation. This and no other is the basis for choosing your equipment, computers and any other technology – they're working tools, not fashion items or 'must haves'.

Information technology projects can, and do, overrun on cost and installation times, and underperform when it comes to usage and value, particularly if you're driven by the technology itself rather than the answers to the questions above. The public sector, commerce and industry alike are riddled with major technology projects that have been under-designed, under-costed and under-evaluated. The UK's National Health Service national database was costed originally at £440 million; to date, it has cost £2.7 billion and is still not fully functional. This situation can happen to anyone, at any level. So be careful, and don't get sidetracked by the brand and cachet of the technology itself, especially when they're driven by fashion and fad rather than value.

So merely installing computers and other information technology doesn't automatically lead to gains in employee efficiency or product and service performance. As a manager, you must take the time to analyse and evaluate the environment in which the work has to be done. To be fully effective, the technology must integrate fully with the aims and objectives of the business, the ways in which it delivers products and services, and the capabilities and qualities of the staff doing the work.

# Getting the Most Out of Information Technology

The personal computer shifted the power of computing away from huge mainframes and onto the desks of individual users. Now, computer networks are bringing a new revolution in business. Although the personal computer is a self-sufficient island of information, when you link these islands together in a network, individual computers have the added benefit of sharing that information with every other computer on the network. A computer network can create huge benefits for you and your organisation, for example:

✔ **It can improve communication.** A network will allow all employees in your organisation to communicate with each other quickly and easily. At the click of a button they can send messages to individuals or groups of employees, and they can reply just as easily. Furthermore, employees can use the network to access the financial, marketing and product information they need to do their job, from anywhere in the organisation.

✔ **It can save time and money.** In business, time is money. The faster you can get something done, the more tasks you can complete during your business day. Email allows you to create messages, memos and other internal communications, to attach documents to them if necessary, and to transmit them instantaneously to as many colleagues as you want. And these colleagues can be located across the room or around the world – and they all get the same message at the same time.

✔ **It can improve understanding of markets, products and services.** Information communicated via a network is timely, direct and standardised. Everyone gets the same message and so can develop the same understanding of the company's vision and values. Everyone receives the same information on the company's products, services and markets, and on how they're performing. As a result, all staff should have a much clearer understanding of the business environment than was previously possible.

✔ **It can improve and underpin staff cohesion.** Because everybody has the same access to information, and receives the same messages in an unfiltered way, much greater potential exists for mutual cohesion and commitment, provided that you use the network to support the organisation's core values and staff management practices. However, problems always occur if you deliver different messages to different groups of employees. Because so many people have access to so much more information, this practice will be revealed very quickly. Make sure your network communications are transparent and ethical (see Book III Chapter 6 on behaving ethically).

Obviously setting up a computer network involves expense, but it will underpin the culture, values, product and service knowledge of your organisation and reinforce its very foundations.

Whatever information you publicise or communicate online or via email must also be available to anyone who doesn't have a computer link to you. Make sure you always provide hard copies too. Also ensure that vitally important information is still posted on company notice boards or distributed to everyone in paper form.

# *Planning and Implementation*

In the fast-changing world of technology, having a *technology plan* – a plan for acquiring and deploying information technology – is a must. Many businesses buy bits and pieces of computer hardware, software and other technology without considering what they already have in place, and without looking very far into the future. Then, when they try to hook it all up, they're surprised that their thrown-together system doesn't work.

Managers who take the time to develop and implement a technology plan don't have this problem, and aren't forced to spend far more money and time fixing systems problems. Follow these steps to ensure a smooth implementation process:

**Book II**

**Building Your Commercial Acumen**

1. **Create the plan.** You provide the vision of the chosen technology – what it's supposed to deliver, how, when, where and to whom. In order to give this vision life, you have to be able to present it in ways that your colleagues and staff can understand, so get them involved. Without doubt, they'll be able to see potential that you haven't thought of, and also spot glitches or problems; after all, they'll be implementing and using the technology in the pursuit of your grand vision.

2. **Cost the plan.** You need to know how much your investment in technology will cost and what returns on your investment you're likely to get. You then need to relate this information to your departmental or organisational budget. Also consider a timescale for predicted returns.

3. **Screen and select suppliers.** Visit potential suppliers yourself. Take your technology plan – drawn up in step one, in consultation with your staff – with you. Show potential suppliers what you want, and ask them if they can deliver it. If they respond, 'No, we can't deliver this; but we can deliver something much better', listen to them, evaluate their proposal and go back to your staff to discuss it. Alternatively, if they respond, 'No, we can't deliver this; we'll deliver what we always deliver regardless of customer requirements', then just walk away.

4. **Implement the plan.** So everyone has agreed on the technology plan and you've chosen your supplier. Now comes the tricky part – implementation. Be in absolutely no doubt that glitches, delays, overruns and teething troubles will occur – they always do. At the implementation phase build in as much slack and leeway as necessary to allow for problems to arise and for you to resolve them.

5. **Monitor performance.** And so finally your system is up and running. Congratulations all round! However, this is crunch time as you determine whether the system is really going to deliver what you planned. Teething troubles are inevitable, so make sure that you have a watertight service agreement with your supplier, committing them to sorting out any problems as soon as they occur. Make sure that your supplier's support staff are completely familiar with your system; if they aren't, insist that the supplier provides training for them.

   If the worst happens and the system doesn't deliver what you and your staff expected, you must acknowledge the problem and deal with it. Don't respond like many large corporations and public service bodies by trying to make the unworkable work.

6. **Train your staff.** Train your employees so that they can use the technology to its maximum advantage, getting the best possible returns before it becomes obsolete. Repeat this process each time that you change or upgrade your technology; don't assume that just because your staff can use one form of equipment, they can use all forms of it.

Remember that any technology is only as good as the people who use it.

'Everything takes twice as long as you think, and costs twice as much.' While never an excuse for organisational slackness or waste of resources, this truism underpins the point that nothing ever goes completely according to schedule.

Technology is a strategic expense; all organisations and their managers need to see technology projects as investments on which there are demonstrable and quantifiable returns. Make sure that whatever you do is guided by the business, product, service and market drivers of the organisation, and the results that the organisation expects you, as a manager, to deliver.

---

# Top five information technology websites

You can find loads of IT info on the web, but these sites are the cream of the crop:

- *Wired* magazine: www.wired.com

- **Computerworld:** www.computerworld.com

- **IBM:** www.ibm.com

- **Accenture:** www.accenture.com

- **InternetWorld:** www.internetworld.co.uk

# Chapter 4

# The Seven-Step Selling Cycle

*W*e like to think of selling as a cycle because, if done properly, the last step in the cycle leads you back to the first. Your new, happy client gives you the names of other people she feels would benefit from your product or service, and then you have your next lead or prospect to work with.

Selling breaks down neatly into seven steps. You can remember seven things, can't you? And if you can't or don't want to, you can always come back to this chapter.

Each step is equally valuable to you. Rarely can you skip a step and still make the sale. Each step plays a critical role and, if done properly, leads you to the next step in a natural, flowing manner.

## Step 1: Prospecting

*Prospecting* means finding the right potential buyer for what you're selling. When planning where to sell your product or service, ask yourself, 'Who would benefit most from this?' If the end user is a corporation, you need to make contacts within corporations. Larger companies often employ several layers of buying personnel – indeed they sometimes even outsource the process, especially in the earlier stages, so to spend some time researching your chosen target and discovering how best to approach them is critical. If your end user is a family with school-aged children, you need to go where families are (for example, local football groups, school fundraising events, dance classes, the park, and so on). You can also purchase a list of targeted prospects from a list broker and start contacting those prospects at home.

To make an informed decision about which prospects to approach, you need to find out some information about the people or companies you've chosen as possibilities. Do some research about any prospective client company at the local library or online. This legwork is sort of a prequalification step in prospecting. You'll do even more qualification when you meet a prospective client, but why waste time on an appointment with a company or person who wouldn't have a need for your offering? *Prequalifying* helps you just like market research helps companies determine their best target markets. In fact, one of the best places to begin your research in finding the most likely candidates for your product or service is your company's marketing department. The marketing department may do research during the product development stage to determine what people want in the product or service you sell. If they have done so, study their results to get a better idea of where to begin.

If your company does advertising to promote your products, you're likely to receive *leads* – names of people who called or otherwise contacted the company for more information about the product. Treat any client-generated contact like gold dust! If this person has taken the trouble to contact you, she's most likely seriously interested. Probably the best person to contact is the one who has called you for information first!

Other valuable assets are your friends, relatives, and business acquaintances. Tell them what type of product or service you're selling. See what suggestions they come up with. Who knows, one of them just may know people at one of your prospect companies who'd be happy to talk with you.

Never begin any selling cycle until you've taken a few moments to put yourself in the shoes of the other person and think about why you might want to buy or not buy if you were in her place. Take yourself out of the picture and look at the entire situation through the eyes of the buyer. Mentally put yourself in her shoes and think about what would motivate *you* to invest your valuable time reading a letter about your product or taking a salesperson's call. If you can't come up with solid answers, you may not have enough information about your product to even be selling it in the first place. Or, you may not know enough about your potential audience to sell to them. If you do lack information, go back to your research task. Study more about both areas until you're comfortable with being in that person's shoes. In other words, don't go out prospecting until you have something of value to share with your prospects – something that's worth their while to investigate and, hopefully, purchase.

We know from all our years of enjoying selling careers that being genuine is a major factor influencing success. If you haven't really found that what you're offering is a huge help to the prospect, then the chances are that she won't be so easily persuaded to purchase and you simply won't enjoy the process so much. Selling's no fun if it's always a battle.

You may need to take a somewhat unusual approach to get noticed by your prospects or to bring about a positive response. Some ideas include:

- **Enclosing a photograph of your warm, smiling, professional self.** If your goal is to arrange to meet these people in their home, they'll need to feel a little trust and liking for you before they invite you in and warmly engage with you. A picture and some contact points will make them feel more at ease.

- **Using humour.** If at all possible use humour to break the ice and have the prospect warm to you and your cause a little more.

  We remember a cartoon of a leader focusing on the job in hand fighting an army with bows and arrows whilst a salesperson is tapping him on the shoulder to sell him a machine gun. The leader shouts, 'Go away, can't you see I'm busy?' without even turning around to see what's on offer! This superbly illustrates the benefits of a time- or labour-saving device!

- **Adding a clever quote or anecdote to the bottom of your cover letter.** You can find books containing quotes for nearly every occasion, along with several websites such as Quotations Page (`www.quotations page.com`) or U-inspire.com (`www.uinspire.com`). Taking a few moments to find this kind of attention-grabber can be just enough to make your letter stand out from the rest and get you in the door.

- **Sending a small toy to the target prospect with a note attached.** Here's an example that worked well for a colleague: She discovered that the prospect was extremely keen on classic cars and sent him a vintage model along with a note saying, 'They don't make them like they used to – but some things are actually made better!' She followed up with a telephone call, was remembered, and a meeting and sale followed.

- **Sending a lottery ticket attached to the front of a mailer.** Use a headline: 'Is this your best bet for a brighter future?' or 'If this one doesn't win, what plans do you have for making your fortune?' The headlines in each case indicate the common unspoken thought that winning the lottery is the only way we truly believe we can become wealthy. However, we all want wealth, and so if you attached the ticket to an offer from you involving money-making training or investment, the missive would neatly introduce the thought that maybe, aside from the lottery, your offer should be seriously considered. Without a doubt (whether it's perceived as gimmicky or not), the recipient will remember you and will definitely talk to you when you call.

  If you sell a product, merely sending a sample is a blatant pushing of your product and many people won't like that or be impressed by your lack of creativity. Think laterally and send a quirky attachment. You'll be remembered and doors will open.

Book II

Building Your Commercial Acumen

These ideas may be a bit gimmicky if you're selling very top-end products that have a more serious and longer-term sales cycle, but they've worked well for many colleagues and acquaintances who were marketing everyday products and services to the average consumer. The idea is to open your creative mind to unusual ways of reaching people and capturing their attention.

To ensure that your name gets in front of the prospective client more than once, send a confirmation letter after you speak to her and make an appointment to further your conversation. Use this brief letter to remind her of the subject you were talking about and wish to discuss further and add a human comment, such as wishing her well on her holiday or with another family activity that falls between the time of the letter and the appointment date.

In addition, send a thank-you note after you enjoy your first sales visit. Thank the prospective client for her time and recognise that this is the most precious commodity she could afford you. Thank-you notes always get read, and if the prospect hasn't had the time to review your sales offering when she receives your thank-you note, she'll definitely have another look and remember you on her to-do list. You'll have made a positive first impression that will very likely bring you closer to getting a sale.

## Step 2: Meeting and Greeting

You've found the people, and now you actually get to meet them. To persuade another person to give you her valuable time, you need to offer something of value in return. To gain entrance to someone's home or office, a good idea is to offer a free estimate or gift in exchange for her opinion on the demonstration or explanation of your product.

With a business-to-business appointment, you always face the challenge that your prospect is hugely under pressure and thinks she cannot spare the time. Being mindful of your prospect's time constraints and being thoughtful in choosing a more ideal time of the day can and will help the situation. Your goal is to make agreeing to an appointment as easy as possible. We strongly recommend giving your prospect two options – an either/or – with regard to dates and times. Say something like, 'I have an appointment opening on Tuesday at 9.30 a.m., or would Wednesday at 3.00 p.m. be better for you?' This makes the prospect look at her calendar and consider the open blocks of time in her schedule, whereas if you just say, 'When can we get together?' she's likely to look at how busy she is and hesitate to commit. Suggest meeting 'first thing in the day before it all gets too busy' or 'last thing at night when everyone else has gone home', because many people feel they can see you then without creating pressure on their day's schedule.

When you get a commitment, confirm all the details, such as where the meeting will take place, and get directions if you haven't been there before. Also, get a commitment as to who'll be present. You ideally want all decision-makers present so that if you've done your job correctly and your product or service is suitable for them, they're in a position to purchase on the spot. If you sell products to consumers and know you need the agreement of both spouses, for example, you need to confirm that they'll both be present. If you're talking with a young, single person, she may decide to have a parent or other adult there to help her make a decision.

You've passed the first hurdle and been invited to visit a potential client. Be sure to appear at ease so your prospect is comfortable with you. Ensure that the prospect doesn't interpret your nerves as an indication that you have a poor product or service to offer. A key driver in the buying process is the need to feel safe with the purchase, and your nerves may make her feel uncomfortable and at risk; so be very careful as you make arrangements not to put your prospect off.

If nerves are an issue for you, here are some things that you can do to help minimise the negative impact or incorrect perception nerves can give:

- ✔ Do something with your hands that disguises the shaking. Try simply holding your pad and pen showing that you're prepared to take notes on the discussion. This appears professional and you can keep your hands on your knee, which hides or suppresses the trembling.

- ✔ Consciously breathe deeply immediately before going into the call and deliberately relax your muscles by practising going limp – flopping your arms like they're made of jelly! Doing so is good fun and breaks your thoughts, shifting focus away from nervousness.

Often your nerves are a result of your own fear of not saying your spiel right rather than the fear of your clients not receiving it well. Avoid this by constantly reminding yourself that they don't know what you're supposed to say. Even if you 'say it wrong', they won't know! You simply have no need to get nervous!

Overcoming any tension at this point in the selling cycle takes a bit of doing on both sides. If you don't defuse the tension, you can end up turning a potential win-win into a lose-lose situation. You won't make the sale, and the potential client will miss out on benefiting from your talents and the fantastic product.

First and foremost, you need to consider what you look like to your prospect. You know the old saying, 'You never get a second chance to make a good first impression.' When in doubt about what to wear to an appointment, err on the side of conservatism. Don't be too fashionable or flash. You want to look your best, but also remember to be comfortable. If your new shoes are too tight or they squeak, you'll be conscious of that fact and won't be able to put all your concentration into the visit.

Think twice before you apply your aftershave or perfume too liberally. Subtlety is the motto here. You never know if you'll meet someone who is allergic to your added scents. If the potential client opens the window, goes into a sneezing frenzy, or simply stops talking and falls over, you went a bit heavy on the fragrance – and you probably lost the sale!

Of special concern is the jewellery you wear to an appointment. If your bling could be considered distracting – a glitzy diamond necklace, for example – you may have gone over the top! These days jewellery is no longer solely the domain of women; many men wear earrings, bracelets, and rings. Whilst these may be perfectly acceptable for socialising, consider the reaction if you were to wear these items in your professional role. You don't want to be remembered as 'that woman we talked with who had a stud in her nose' or 'that man who was quite nice but wore an earring'. You want your prospects to remember your competence and professionalism.

Because this is a business situation, be prepared to shake hands, make eye contact, and build rapport. Building rapport is the getting-to-know-you stage that comes with any new contact. You need to immediately begin building trust. People buy from people they like and trust. Your prospect should feel your trustworthiness as early as possible in the contact you make.

# Step 3: Fact Finding

When you finally sit down with your prospect, you need to find out if she's qualified to be your client of choice. In selling, *fact finding* with your prospects means finding out who they are, what they do, what they have, and what they need.

You don't have to take on every client who qualifies for your product or service. If one particular client looks like she could become your biggest client, and that in turn makes it likely you'll be spending a large amount of your time with her, then it really isn't very good if you can't stand the person after your first meeting! In the real world you cannot expect to bond absolutely with every potential client. Sometimes you may have to pass a client to a colleague who is better able to deal with her.

If you've done your homework and looked up information about the prospect, you'll know what questions to ask. You'll eventually have to know a lot of information about the prospect, providing you get the account, so if you're truly convinced this is a good match for you, you may as well ask questions now. The more specific your questions, the more impressed your potential client will be with your expertise. Asking pertinent questions now shows that you're interested in more than just a closed sale and that you're looking into the future as a valued business partner of your client.

Your prospects will be assessing you too, so be aware of what you're showing them. Most clients are looking for people who are dependable, loyal, trustworthy, intelligent, competent, and even a little fun. Do your prospects see those characteristics when they look at you? If you need to communicate a character trait of yours that's difficult to see, work out how you can bring appropriate images to mind in the answers you give to their questions and the information you offer in your discussion of their needs. For example, if you're keen to demonstrate your attention to detail in order that your prospect may see how thorough you'll be when dealing with her, you may deliberately display material illustrating how you've taken it upon yourself to research her competitors.

The goal of your fact-finding discussion is to determine how well suited your product or service is to your prospect's situation. Whether you're selling to businesses or individuals, ask questions to get them talking about what they have now, how it's not fulfilling their current needs, and how much of a budget they have for making an improvement.

**Book II**

**Building Your Commercial Acumen**

# *Step 4: Presentation*

Your presentation of your product, service, or idea requires the most preparation. In your preparation, practise your answers to common questions with a family member or close friend. Make a list of the benefits you think are your strongest persuaders in placing your product. Then try to figure out a way to work those points into responses to the common questions.

For example, suppose you're selling a brand-new home-delivery grocery service based upon telephone ordering and a same-day local delivery. Your prospects are busy professional people who are cash-rich but time-poor and to whom the convenience angle outweighs the slightly higher cost of the groceries. Because the service is new, you don't have a track record of success to brag about. So here's where you may start:

> PROSPECT: Well, it sounds like a good idea, but you haven't proven it to be successful. I'd hate to be a guinea pig and end up having to do my shopping anyway because it didn't work out.

> SALESPERSON: Because this is a new service, we're paying special attention to the orders that we receive. In fact, we have two people who listen to the recording of each call to confirm that your verbal request is what shows up on our shopping list. One of them will give you a quick call to let you know your list was received in good order and to arrange the best delivery time for you.

The real issue is not that the service is new, but that the client doesn't feel totally confident that the service won't let her down, and perhaps more importantly, she feels if she were let down she wouldn't have the time to shop. By showing that you have backup systems in place to ensure the order is handled properly, you've answered the quality control question that triggered the prospect's 'guinea pig' reference.

To demonstrate personal dependability, tell the prospective client a story of how an issue with a previous client was proved to be the client's fault, but that you personally ensured the satisfactory delivery of the additional items nevertheless.

Your clients buy more than your product – they buy you. Possibly they place more emphasis on how they feel about you personally than on your product or service. They could probably purchase your offering or something very similar from a competitor if they were sold on the item but not you.

# Step 5: Handling Objections

One question that always haunts a person in a selling role is how best to handle any negative comments or qualifications your prospect raises during or after your presentation. To keep the answer simple, handle them with a brief acknowledgement of the prospect's statement and then ask a non-combative qualifying question to discover if the point raised is critical to the potential purchase, or even is worthy of note at all. (Often clients raise objections because they subconsciously feel obliged to make intelligent comments and that they have to appear to at least offer some resistance.) For example, if your product is only available in certain colours, and none of them quite fit the decor of your prospect's office, be prepared to recommend the least offensive colour suggestion. If the comment was to the effect that you don't have the exact colour the client had in mind, you might say, 'I fully appreciate your comment Ms Prospect. Can I just ask, will you be looking to change the blinds or the chairs from time to time over the next few years?' The answer is probably yes, so whatever colour you initially provide for your product, the prospect will eventually have a colour change issue, and she may think, why make an objection to it now?

If you sidestep obstacles during your presentation, a good chance exists that they'll come back to haunt you if you do get the sale. Find a way to bring up and elaborate on any concerns about fulfilling the needs of the buyer as early in the presentation as is appropriate. Don't let unfulfilled expectations bring your long-term relationship with a potential client to a bitter end. Cover all her concerns and make sure that she understands how those concerns will be handled – and that she's comfortable with your methods for doing so.

The most common concern you'll encounter in your entire selling career is the good old standby stall: 'I want to think it over.' When someone says she wants to think it over, that means she's interested. And if she's interested, you need to strike while the iron's hot. Find out exactly what she wants to think over. In the majority of cases, you'll find that her concern is the money involved. Surprise, surprise! Everyone wants a bargain. Unless your product or service is severely underpriced, most of your potential clients will want to bargain or are hesitating just to see if you'll offer to include something else to get them to buy.

# Step 6: Closing the Sale

If you've researched your prospect properly, given yourself enough valuable preparation time, and handled all the previous steps in a professional manner, you'll probably close the sale. Closing should follow naturally and smoothly after you address your prospect's concerns. But if your prospect doesn't automatically pick up a pen to approve your paperwork or write a cheque, don't panic. You don't have to turn into a stereotypical high-pressure salesperson and start leaning on her to get what you want. Getting your prospect's business can be as simple as saying, 'How soon do we start?' At this point, if you're confident about being able to give her what she needs, you should begin taking verbal ownership of your future business relationship with assumptive statements and questions.

You may also want to use analogies, quotes from famous people, or today's news to persuade people to go ahead and do it today. Use similar-situation stories about other clients who got involved with your product or service and are happy they did. Be prepared to show the potential client how she can afford this product or service if cost is her area of hesitation. Often, doing so's just a matter of breaking down the costs and the potential savings to show her how affordable the item is compared to the benefits she'll receive.

By the point of closure, you've hopefully reduced any sales resistance your new client had early on, covered all of the salient points, and reached her level of sales acceptance, so that agreeing on the finer details is all that remains. These may be delivery or pricing issues, but they're not threatening and a sale is the effective outcome.

# Step 7: Getting Referrals

After you close the sale with your client, take a moment to ask for referrals. Doing so can be as simple as asking, 'Because you're so happy with this decision today, would you mind if I ask you for the names of other people you know who may also be interested in learning about this product?' If the client has mentioned other family members in the area, ask, 'Who in your family would also enjoy the benefits of our fine lawn service?', or, 'Which of your neighbours would you say shares your desire for a hassle-free garden maintenance programme?'

In a larger corporate situation, ask about other departments within the company that may need the same service. In a smaller business environment, ask which other business owners the prospect meets up with.

In today's business environment, a great deal of work is passed via referrals and recommendation, much of it via networking. So ask if your new prospect is an active networker. If she is, then you're in line for a great referral situation.

In conversation, after having established a level of rapport, ask the client what professional organisations she belongs to where networking takes place. However, doing so too early can make the prospect feel that you're using her as a feeder channel and that you care more about who she links you to than about her.

If for some reason you and the prospective client find that this isn't the best time to go forward with the sale, instead of just walking out the door and saying goodbye, make the contact a part of your network of people who can help you find *more* people who may benefit from your product or service – if the prospect genuinely likes your offering, you have a good chance of meeting other prospects through her. Don't ever just walk away from an opportunity to network. And immediately upon leaving the premises, post a card to the person thanking her for her time. Doing so guarantees that your discussion will stay fresh in her mind for at least a few days. During that time, the right lead for you may come her way and if you've left a good impression, she'll be more likely to give you the referral.

# Chapter 5

# Easing Into Change

'Nothing endures but change' is an oft-quoted truism. Change can happen in one of two ways:

✔ You can initiate and plan for change. This type of change can be something relatively minor such as buying a new car or getting a new kitchen, or it can be life-changing – for example, when you decide to get married, move house, have kids, or change jobs: in these cases, you feel as if you have some control, although external agencies can throw a spanner in the works and leave you feeling helpless and stressed.

✔ You can have change imposed on you, for example, by your employer or through events such as an unexpected pregnancy or loss of a loved one: change is harder to accept when you feel as if you're the victim.

The NLP approach is that no single correct map of change exists at any one time. To survive and thrive, you need to acknowledge and embrace the fact that change is happening and put strategies in place to work with change rather than against it.

Because NLP is about how people think and behave, this chapter focuses on the *people aspect* of change and not on the project management of change in the workplace. We aim to show you how to deal with change in a way that allows you to maintain your equilibrium through choppy times, whether you initiate the change or a change is imposed on you. Should you come across someone for whom change isn't going as smoothly as they would like, we hope the insights you gain here enable you to ease their way a little. You could do this as simply as listening sympathetically, by lending a helping hand, or just explaining what they are experiencing.

To do all this, we pull together NLP tools and techniques to illustrate how you can apply NLP to the changes that happen in your everyday life, be they relatively small or life-changing and whether they are created by you or other people. For example, think about the presupposition, 'if what you're doing isn't working, do something different' . Change is all about doing something different when what you're already doing isn't working.

The premise in writing this chapter is that whatever the change, you can handle it humanely and compassionately – for example, when dealing with redundancies in a corporation. This chapter is also about enabling you to make change easier for yourself by understanding what you experience. Instead of beating yourself up, if you think you could have done better at something, you can show yourself some kindness and focus on what you've done well.

Keep a notebook to hand, and as you read through this chapter note what you're going through or how you're anticipating change, and think about how the change can be made easier by applying specific NLP techniques.

# Finding Clarity and Direction

Knowing where you want to go is crucial, because without clear direction you can end up expending a lot of energy chasing what you don't want and waste a lot of time achieving nothing.

For maximum results, you need to be sure about exactly what outcome you want from the change you choose to create. For example:

- I want to weigh 57 kilograms (126 pounds) by 30 September 2012.
- Our attrition rate is 27 per cent and we want to reduce that to 15 per cent.
- We want to outsource our services.
- I want my wedding day to be perfect.

Imagine that you're experiencing change in your work life. You're a manager who needs to keep a change process on track while making sure that your staff are engaged and motivated (so that productivity loss is kept to a minimum), and also ensure that you can keep yourself upbeat and healthy. The big problem when change like this happens in an organisation is that people feel powerless. The perception of lack of control leads to negative stress and lack of motivation. Very little room exists for manoeuvre in big-change objectives set by top management. The people who have to implement the change can get some sense of control and stay engaged in the change process if they can decide the steps of how to actually put the change in place. Teams and individuals can apply goal-setting techniques and experience less stress.

 Take some time out to sit your team around a table and brainstorm any impending changes (and team in this sense can be your family or a larger social group). This process is a good way for the whole team to find out what each other's concerns are as regards the change. If the team is too big to fit around a table, break the team into several groups and allocate one point to each group. The team then comes together and one group talks about what it discussed, thus bringing more valuable insights.

# Understanding the Structure of Change

In order to make change easier to understand, we use two models to illustrate what you may be experiencing and what you may allow for when you find that change is making you feel uncomfortable or making you behave in a way that's out of character.

## The Kübler-Ross Grief Cycle

Dr Elisabeth Kübler-Ross wrote about the 'Five Stages of Grief' in her famous book *On Death and Dying*. Although originally designed to deal with death, her model is useful in helping to understand change.

You don't come across this model in standard NLP courses. However, people are fairly familiar with the Kübler-Ross 'Five Stages of Grief' as applied specifically to corporate change. The reason we include it here is to pace anyone who doesn't know much NLP but who has used this model for organisational change, as a lead-in to applying NLP to change.

When change strikes, people try to maintain the status quo because it's secure and stable. When a change occurs in the status quo of any system, even when it's expected, people can experience the different stages shown in Figure 5-1. This model can forewarn and forearm you to deal with change more effectively, and help other people in the organisation manage change better. Understanding what you're going through helps you to manage yourself by managing your emotional state, so Table 5-1 examines these stages further. It offers ways of helping you to behave more resourcefully by having rapport with other people through an awareness of how change is affecting them.

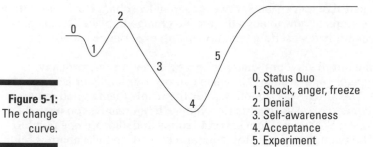

**Figure 5-1:**
The change
curve.

0. Status Quo
1. Shock, anger, freeze
2. Denial
3. Self-awareness
4. Acceptance
5. Experiment

When involved in corporate change, the manager's job is to keep the dip of the curve as low as possible and to keep the time frame from point 1 (the start of experiencing change) to point 5 (a new status quo begins to emerge) as short as possible, because that gets people back into full performance mode as soon as possible.

| Table 5-1 | The Stages of Grief in the Change Curve for Change in the Workplace | |
|---|---|---|
| *Stages in the Change Curve* | *How People May React* | *What Actions Help* |
| 1. Shock and anger | People may procrastinate when they experience shock. Feelings of shock and anger can be fleeting or last for a long time, depending on how resilient someone is. People feel trapped and respond fearfully. | Allow people to let off steam and reassure them that the change is temporary and things are going to get better. *Stress that the change is not personal.* Subtly work to help people change their map of the world, because people react based on their existing map and the depth of their reaction depends on what their map tells them to do or how to react. |

| Stages in the Change Curve | How People May React | What Actions Help |
|---|---|---|
| 2. Denial | People may have a false perception about their ability to cope. They may think they can handle things. They think everyone else is to blame. People can stay here and become dinosaurs who can't cope with change, which can result in their losing their job or being sidelined. | Coaching helps. The tool is to give feedback, because without feedback people don't realise that they're in denial and deluding themselves. |
| 3. Self-awareness | People feel worse as they realise their toolkit of skills and knowledge isn't good enough to cope with the change. They go into survival mode. The state of feeling bad and inadequate can spill into other areas of people's lives. | Here people need support and to know where they are on the curve and why they're feeling bad. People feeling like this need to tell their spouse, colleagues, and manager and ask for leeway to be grumpy and scared. They need to be given permission to feel bad and behave unre-sourcefully. |
| 4. Acceptance | People start to take personal responsibility for dealing with change as they realise they have finally stopped resisting the change. People's perception of their abilities is incorrect because they feel useless. | This stage is where people are shown how other people coped with change by giving them case studies, providing coaching and exemplars to model. |
| 5. Experiment | This stage is the learning and integrating of new tools, so people start modelling others to see how they deal with change. They feel more capable and competent. | Training people to acquire new skills and give them room to make mistakes. At this stage, managers must have done sufficient risk analysis and contingency planning, so that mistakes aren't detrimental to the company. A high-risk management is necessary at this point so that mistakes can be handled and dealt with appropriately. A blame culture only kicks people back to stage 2. |

**Book II**

**Building Your Commercial Acumen**

As you emerge from the change, *integration* then follows. You settle into the new way of doing things and are more flexible because you've had to learn to cope with a new environment. Your perception of your own competence rises and is likely to be measured more accurately. The change can be incorporated into the identity of the company by constantly referring back to it, until it becomes unconscious.

People react differently to change. Each person spends different lengths of time at each stage and each person has to be dealt with differently by teammates and manager. A manager's role, therefore, needs to change as they deal with the different stages that different people are at.

When you're leading or facilitating a team, experiencing the team's emotions is quite normal. For this reason, managers can feel a rollercoaster of frustration, fear, and anxiety as they experience the different phases themselves. So they may need coaching, mentoring, going for a beer, or whatever their release mechanism is, to gain space and perspective.

When people are under stress, their behaviour may need to be excused. Before reacting to someone, adopt the second position to, metaphorically, 'walk in that person's shoes' in order to get a better understanding of how the person is feeling (check out Book I Chapter 1 on understanding other people's perspective). This process gives you the ability to move up and take the bird's eye view when 'trouble's on the ground'.

## NLP logical levels

The *NLP logical levels* (sometimes known as neurological levels) are a powerful way to think about change by breaking it down as a model into different categories of information.

As you begin to consider the kind of changes that you experience, you find that logical levels can help you to find a route forward in confusing times. To do this, having alignment through all the logical levels of identity, belief and values, capabilities and skills, behaviour and environment is particularly important, because having an incongruity at one or more levels stops the desired result from happening. This model can be as useful when experiencing personal change as for understanding corporate change. The model's key value is that it provides a structured approach for understanding what's happening. This enables people to make a decision about choosing how they want to feel about the change and how they're going to behave.

In whichever case, changing at the lower levels of the diagram is easier than at the higher levels. So, for example, a company may find making changes to the building (environment), such as painting the walls a brighter colour, is easier than changing the culture or creating a new identity for itself. Changes like these at a higher level have an impact on people below it; changes at lower levels can impact people above, but this isn't a given.

Jas, a very bright, well-educated 30-something, booked herself on to a programme of Relationship Wizardry® coaching, as she'd had a series of relationships but she couldn't settle into anything permanent. Jas is the daughter of very successful parents, and as a result of the coaching, she realised that she'd modelled herself on her strong, very independent mother. Unfortunately, her identity as a strong, independent woman prevented her from accepting anything from people, and this affected all areas of her life. She admitted that some of her relationship problems were because she found it hard to accept love and would push her partner away (behaviour) if they came too close emotionally. Jas also realised that she had some self-esteem issues (beliefs) because she didn't feel she measured up to the success her mother had achieved by the time she was Jas's age, and she didn't feel she deserved a successful, dynamic man like her father.

Romilla helped Jas to 'design' her ideal relationship using the well-formed outcome process . One of the first steps Jas incorporated was to change the environment where she met people. She joined groups where she was more likely to meet people with whom she had interests in common. Before the coaching, the misalignment through Jas's logical levels stopped her attaining her goal of a long-term relationship.

### Creating alignment in logical levels

Alignment in any venture makes things flow more smoothly and helps you to attain your target more quickly. When you think about the logical levels , if you have alignment through all levels, you're going to find success easy.

Elaine is 45, married with young children, and climbing the IFA (UK's International Financial Advisors) ladder. She's extremely bright and very ambitious (one aspect of identity). She's also passionate about women having an understanding of how to attain financial security (values) and believes in educating women to this end, because she 'knows' (belief) that every woman has the right to financial independence.

Elaine has a string of letters after her name (capabilities and skills) but is striving to get more qualifications. This aim is completely congruent with her ambition of where she's taking her business, and the way she acts and talks about women's finance (behaviour) engenders complete trust. She has a lovely office at home (environment) where she can keep an eye on her children. When she needs to think, she goes into the garden for a spot of meditation. Because all the areas for her business are aligned, she's making good progress.

**Book II**

**Building Your Commercial Acumen**

Although this second example recounts what Jim experienced when his wife died, it can apply to anyone who goes through loss: of a marriage when a split occurs or the loss of a job due to redundancy, sacking, or retirement.

Jim, an accountant, and Alicia had been married for almost 30 years. The first couple of weeks after Alicia died were tied up with making the funeral arrangements and Jim functioned on autopilot, but then he went through huge change:

✔ **Environment:** Jim found that he was rattling around their bedroom after he took Alicia's clothes to the charity shop. A bed that had been comfortable for two felt very big and the king-size quilt was too heavy.

Obviously, depending on the loss, different aspects apply when adjusting to or creating a new environment for a new life.

✔ **Behaviour:** Jim had always been very playful and men and women enjoyed his company because he was such fun. In fact, Alicia would tease him for being an outrageous flirt. Some months after Alicia died and life began to stabilise, Jim realised that his sense of humour had started to return. He was surprised to notice that his interaction with the women he was meeting had changed dramatically. Although he was his playful self with women who were Alicia's and his old and trusted friends, he was much more reserved with women he was meeting for the first time. He realised that he'd seen Alicia as a guard against women who may misconstrue his playfulness.

✔ **Capabilities and skills:** Alicia had managed all the household affairs because she enjoyed the element of control and juggling funds and utilities to get the best rates and deals. Jim didn't want to think about numbers when he was at home. Suddenly, Jim had to organise the running of the home as well as manage his work.

Jim was extremely organised at work but both Alicia and he had given him tacit permission to be less than organised at home. Jim decided to bring his organisational skills into his life at home; he modelled his time keeping and organisational behaviour at work to manage himself at home.

Jim also found himself at a loss with leisure time and holidays. He slowly developed new strategies for deciding where to go and how to organise trips. Initially, he took holidays where he was able to acquire new skills. Jim had always enjoyed cooking and so his first holiday was to book a week in Tuscany to learn authentic Italian cooking and discover the flavours of Tuscan wine. Eventually, he was able to go on tours and see parts of the world Alicia and he hadn't got around to seeing.

Jim had to force himself to do things on his own, like going to the cinema. He took up hobbies that kept him interested in life, but his biggest thrill was to help a charity with its accounts.

✔ **Beliefs and values:** Jim found his beliefs around the future were shattered. Initially, all he saw when he looked into his future was darkness and loneliness. As the weeks became months, Jim began to see small glimmers of light as he forced himself to keep busy and engage with people. Interestingly, he says, on re-examining his values around his work and relationships he found that they hadn't changed although his values around 'life' had shifted dramatically. Before, they had focused on what was important to him about his life with Alicia – companionship, love, laughter, fun. He discovered that although he believed intellectually in love, he was too frightened to even contemplate the consequences of finding it again. He decided his highest value is leaving a legacy that's going to help people live more joyfully and 'add happiness to the collective unconscious'.

✔ **Identity:** What frightened Jim most was the loss of part of his identity. For 30 years, he'd been Alicia's husband. His role in life was to look after her. He said he felt adrift, rather like Scarlett O'Hara saying, 'Where shall I go? What shall I do? Whom do I look after now?' This stage is the hardest part of rebuilding his life but he has discovered that he has to do this a piece at a time. Two years on, holes still exist and can catch him out, but he recites the litany he found that gives him comfort, 'This too shall pass.'

Book II

Building
Your
Commercial
Acumen

We offer Jim's anecdote to help you understand what you're likely to experience when you encounter change in your life, so that you find it easier to work through the change instead of fighting it and making change harder.

Make a copy of Table 5-2 and use it to record the insights you get as a result of change that is happening in your life and to write down things you could do differently to make change easier.

| Table 5-2 | The Effects of Change on Your Logical Levels | |
| --- | --- | --- |
| *Logical Level* | *Insights* | *What You Can Do to Facilitate the Change* |
| Identity | | |
| Values and beliefs | | |
| Capabilities and skills | | |
| Behaviour | | |
| Environment | | |

### *Identifying the strongest level for change*

Depending on your journey and circumstance, changing one of the logical levels may have the greatest impact on what you're trying to achieve.

Tom was highly ambitious but found himself living a life of mediocrity; he was extremely frustrated and blamed everyone and everything for his bad luck. In fact, he was lucky to have a manager who engaged a coach to work with Tom. During a coaching session that involved a time-line exercise, Tom discovered that he was carrying a lot of emotions around the death of his mother when he was 11 years old. He realised he had very deep-seated beliefs around life being unfair and him being unlucky. Doing some work on his time line to let go of limiting beliefs worked at the level of Tom's beliefs and changed his life dramatically.

When Tom shifted his beliefs around the unfairness of life and reviewed his sense of being unlucky, he discovered that his identity shifted from that of a person who saw himself as a victim to someone who was successful. He felt brave enough to ask to go on a management training programme (capabilities and skills) and he engaged his manager and colleague to share ideas (behaviour), which was something he'd felt too fearful of doing in the past.

Although you may need to strengthen a level, perhaps by adding new skills, or redecorating your office, you may find that you need to remove something too. For example, if you're always late for meetings, you may need to improve your time-management techniques but, more importantly, you may have to remove unconscious, emotional blocks, causing the unhelpful behaviour, as in Tom's case.

Where are you experiencing change in your life? Do you want to make a big change but keep putting it off? Think about Elaine in the above example. She had five opportunities presented to her where she could have become an IFA, but she held on to her job as project manager because it felt safe. She eventually took the plunge when her environment didn't support her circumstances. She had a baby and wanted to work from home to have more time with him. Doing the following exercise helps you to get clarity about which of the logical levels you may need to develop or change:

1. Make a note of the change you're going through or want to make.

2. Copy out and complete the logical level matrix (Table 5-3).

3. Identify the logical level that will have the most impact.

4. Write down the change you're going through or the change you want to make.

| Table 5-3 | The Logical Level Matrix | |
|---|---|---|
| *Logical Level* | *How This Level Supports the Change* | *How This Level Doesn't Support the Change* |
| Identity | | |
| Beliefs and values | | |
| Capabilities and skills | | |
| Behaviour | | |
| Environment | | |

Now make a list of what you're going to do differently in order to make change easier or to instigate change. For example, Elaine (see the earlier section 'Creating alignment in logical levels') realised that she needed to add IFA qualifications to her capabilities and skills. She realised that, as a woman working from home, she was at a disadvantage in relation to other IFAs who could travel easily to clients and some of whom had offices and an infrastructure to support them. She wanted to stand out by being one of the most highly qualified IFAs.

# Holding On to Values

Your values are important because they support your identity; a value of honesty and kindness may result in you knowing that you're a 'good person'. The way you measure your values is by the criteria you give them. People can share a common value but can measure them differently. For example, two managers who espouse efficiency as a corporate value may measure efficiency with different criteria. One may see efficiency in purely monetary terms and only look at the bottom line. The other manager may measure efficiency in terms of people engagement.

Because values lie in the realms of the unconscious mind, until you understand them consciously, you hold on to them with a fervour, verging on the religious, which leaves very little room for manoeuvre. You may think that this strength is good, perhaps when training puppies, husbands, and children! However, as regards the workplace, some flexibility can be efficacious. The criteria for measuring the effectiveness of values can give room for negotiation.

In the example of the managers with the efficiency value, a mediator may be able to show how employee engagement benefits the bottom line or how a healthy bottom line gives job security and leads to employees engaging more fully. Understanding how to address people's values makes any change easier, be it getting all the members of a team to pull together or a husband and wife to work towards a common goal.

# Grasping the Importance of Clear Communication

The success of any change programme depends on everybody in a team pulling together; the team can be the whole corporation or part of a department, or indeed, a family. In this situation, rapport really comes into its own. The person with rapport can influence and bring on-board the people who can make or break the change process. The idea is that your communication reaches out to everybody so that they understand very clearly what you want from them. This section pulls together techniques to build rapport, especially in the written form.

If you think about the perceptual positions (which we discuss in Book I Chapter 1) and remember to create communication from the perspective of the person you're addressing, you find that carrying people along with you is much easier. This process is where you need to understand at least some of the values of the people involved in the change process.

Knowing your own values is important in choosing a job or a partner, be it a business or life partner. You need to understand other people's values when trying to succeed in achieving a common goal. You can make an assumption about common values in a company if you're careful in choosing who you employ. If the corporate values are repeated time and again, the people who stay and flourish understand these values and are in tune with them. As a manager or an individual wanting to build a long-lasting relationship, knowing the values of the person you want to motivate is very useful; sometimes, you simply need to ask, 'What's important to you about x?', where 'x' can be, 'working for this company', 'a relationship', or 'working together'. Having everyone working to fulfil common values makes change so much easier than if individuals work to their own agendas dictated by their individual values.

Using visual, auditory, and kinaesthetic (VAK) language allows your audience to more easily understand your message. Book I Chapter 2 tells you more about these aspects.

Like values, the meta programs are some of the most abstract filters that you use to filter the data your senses pick up about your world. Because of their abstractions, using the meta programs with a person shows a preference, and helps you to build rapport more easily. We suggest you start with the 'towards/away from' and 'big picture/detail' meta programs'.

When creating any communication, keep a cheat sheet to hand with points for remembering how to write. It may look something like this:

- ✔ Values
- ✔ VAK
- ✔ Towards/away from
- ✔ Global/detail

Leave space to insert anything that you think may be a good addition to your aide mémoire.

Keep in mind that some people feel overwhelmed if they're given too much information, and so a useful practice may be to provide a short overview followed by more detail. For example, if you're easily overwhelmed by too much detail, buying a new car or washing machine, or even choosing a holiday, can be difficult. A useful strategy is to ask someone you trust who understands your needs to give you a list of two or three cars, washing machines, or holidays that fit your 'must-have' criteria. Having fewer options from which to choose makes decision-making quicker and easier.

During an IT department restructuring, the well-meaning management wanted the change process to be an inclusive experience for the department so kept everyone apprised of the smallest detail regarding the change. Productivity hit rock bottom, however, because the programmers were extremely distressed by the barrage of information they were being sent several times a day. Productivity rose only when the manager realised he needed to filter the incoming flood of information to only that which would affect the programmers.

# Creating the Mindset for Change

The concept of behavioural flexibility is one of the pillars of NLP. This idea is crucial in dealing with whatever life throws at you. When you can develop the mindset that allows you to deal with these variables, you have the means to maintain equilibrium for most of the time. Why most of the time? Well, we're very conscious that when, with something like bereavement, life gets very tough, perhaps all you can do is go into survival mode. But remember, even managing to crawl through the day is a testament to your ability to be flexible in the face of such a harsh reality.

Every day remind yourself of something that you have achieved, however small it may seem to you.

## Letting go of fear

Fear incapacitates. People aren't so much afraid of making a mistake; really, the fear is about the consequence of an action. Fear is people reacting to their existing model of the world. So if you've been in an environment where you were constantly criticised or mistakes weren't tolerated, you're likely to be fearful of being criticised if your actions aren't in line with what is expected. This may force you into a state of procrastination or inactivity.

An urban legend pertains to a top salesman at IBM who reputedly lost a very large amount of money on a project. When the salesman was summoned to see Thomas J Watson Snr, one of IBM's most influential leaders, he offered his resignation, which was rejected. Watson said that IBM had just spent a vast amount of money on the salesman's training and didn't want to waste it.

If you're holding yourself back because you're afraid to do something, for example, you may be afraid to move to a different job, accept a marriage proposal, move house, accept a promotion, and so on, the following exercise may help you to uncover your hidden fears.

This exercise helps you with your decision-making. Even if afterwards you decide to do nothing, you've still made a conscious decision. This process itself can dispel a lot of your fears:

1. **Ask yourself the questions below Here 'x' relates to taking some action, such as the ones we mention above.**

   What will happen if I do x?

   What won't happen if I do x?

   What will happen if I don't do x?

   What won't happen if I don't do x?

2. **Make a list of the pros and cons of making your decision.**

3. **Make a list of everything that you think may go wrong and how you'd deal with the arising problems.**

4. **Decide that you're going to learn from the situation, no matter what happens.**

5. **Release any fears that haven't gone away using submodalities (see the following anecdote about David).**

In the world of business, the fact is that companies sometimes set up change programmes to improve efficiency for survival – which often means cutbacks in hours or people – or to improve the bottom line. Departments can be merged or closed down or a problem – such as strong competition, high attrition rates, low morale, or low productivity – may need to be addressed. NLP techniques can help you through such difficult times.

When David and his colleagues faced another swathe of cuts at work, he felt the old dread of losing his job dogging his waking moments. He'd been through several changes and states of feeling 'not good' and realised that his motivation and well-being had both suffered. He decided enough was enough and adopted the following strategies to stay productive:

Book II

Building Your Commercial Acumen

1. **David applied the 'what if' reframing process and asked himself, 'What's the worst that can happen?'**

   David knew that he may be out of work for several months but because he'd built a financial 'war chest' after the last cuts, he could survive for six months without work. This realisation went a long way to alleviating the feeling of dread he felt when he thought of being made redundant; the frequency declined but the intensity was still there. David decided to release the fear that he felt each time he thought of the changes that were being incorporated (see point 3 below).

   He decided he didn't like his work defining his identity, as in 'I am a salesman.' He asked himself what he'd do if he didn't have to work to pay his mortgage and remembered how much he'd loved working with wood at school. David decided that regardless of the outcome at work, he'd take classes in woodwork.

2. **He recognised he had a choice about how he dealt with the change.**

   Instead of letting the change get to him, he decided to treat each day as a learning experience. At the end of each day, he listed what had been difficult. He then reframed the difficulty by asking himself, 'What can I learn from this?' and 'How can I use it in the days ahead?'

3. **Most importantly, David decided to take charge of the way he reacted to the negative conversations around him and the fear he felt.**

   He began employing a pattern interrupteach time his colleagues began talking about the problems they were experiencing. He discovered how to differentiate between when the talk was negative, simply because his colleagues felt good about feeling bad, and when a need arose to solve a genuine problem. When the talk was meaningless negativity, David held his hand up and said something along the lines of 'Let's stop wallowing; we know things are tough and they're likely to get tougher but we've got to stay strong.' After a while, just having David hold his hand up switched his colleagues into problem-solving mode.

David found out that dread, for him, had two components. He felt the fear as heaviness descending, sliding down from his shoulders, and saw a solid, black cube encasing his torso. The cube was a metaphor for the way he felt in his body. Each time the dread returned, David changed the picture of the cube by introducing pockets of silver into it. The cube turned into a honeycomb of grey and then silver until it disappeared. While he worked with the image, David also did some breath work with an affirmation that he said out loud, if he was by himself. He drew a breath deep into the centre of the cube and on each exhalation he said, 'I'm relaxed, strong, and confident, and I feel good.'

A *pattern interrupt* is when a break occurs in a pattern of thought or behaviour. For example, when a coach asks a client, 'How can I help?', the client may take a deep breath, link into feeling bad about a problem, and burst into tears. These steps constitute part of the sequence in the programming that the client has with regards to the problem. The coach may break the flow in the pattern by doing or saying something unexpected. Anecdotally, Richard Bandler has been said to have tipped water over a client to break her pattern. The aim of the unexpected interruption is to break the neurological links that a person has built into a sequence.

The sword of Damocles of job cuts is still hanging over David, but he no longer allows himself to become incapacitated. He realises that he has a life away from work and that he'd rather have a 'whole life' than put his life on hold until he can get away from work at the end of the day.

One rather interesting side-effect occurred as a result of David's acceptance of the change. His manager noticed that he was far more productive than other members of staff and decided to offer him a promotion when the cuts were done. Now David feels that he's more secure if/when future cuts are announced and is more engaged with his work. His productivity is better now that he doesn't feel the dread that was his constant companion before he decided to change the way he thought. He gets more recognition for his work, and so he's more engaged and finds himself in an upward spiral.

## *Being willing to experiment*

When a section of an IT department was being outsourced, some of the people who were going to lose their jobs buried their heads in the sand and waited for the inevitable. A couple of people, however, were willing to experiment with new ways of working and developed their hobbies into potential businesses. The difference in mindset gave this pair the flexibility to move forward. The other group was stuck in inactivity and helplessness because they were unable to think beyond 'I've always worked in IT' and hope they'd find work in a diminishing market.

Part of this healthy mindset is accepting that nothing's permanent and that the person with the most flexibility in a system survives and may even thrive. Being fearful stops you experimenting and creating options for yourself.

# Getting Help on the Way

You may find that managing simple change on your own is easy. For introducing bigger changes, however, getting help facilitates the process. For personal change, you can get relevant help, such as that of a coach, a nutritionist, a financial advisor, an estate agent, or if you think of a holiday as a temporary change, you may employ the services of a travel counsellor.

For making change at work, using *change champions* is essential. A department of 500 people was being restructured. The staff were broken up into groups of 20. Each group was assigned a staff manager and all information was funnelled through that manager. The 20 managers bought into the change and went out and sold the change to their teams. They were in effect the 'change champions'. This reorganisation turned out to be one of the more successful, with minimum disruption and loss of productivity. Another reason given for the success of the project was that the management team and the top 200 people out of 500 all had individual one-on-one coaching sessions. Management placed a high value on clear communication and timely support systems for employees.

## Strengthening resources

Throughout this chapter, we talk about the need to be flexible. Being willing to experiment is an aspect of being flexible and you're more likely to experiment if you're in a resourceful state. When you feel resourceful, you can find ways around problems more easily. This mindset, in turn, makes change a lot easier for you to deal with than if you were to feel resentful.

Alan, a salesman, was unstoppable when he felt well and energetic. Other days he just couldn't cut the mustard. He decided to make a memory of himself on one of his unstoppable days. To do this, he picked a day on which he'd been really successful and wrote down, in graphic detail, exactly what he'd seen, heard, and done to make himself feel so energetic and unstoppable. He used his notes to create an anchor of being unstoppable. Initially, Alan did the exercise with a friend who helped him follow each step of the exercise correctly. When he could remember the steps, he was able to do the exercise by himself. His sales went up by 15 per cent in the first three months after he started employing his 'unstoppable anchor' before seeing a sales prospect.

Book II

Building
Your
Commercial
Acumen

## Future pacing

Even when you've chosen to introduce some change into your life, you may at times find that your resolve wavers. A useful exercise for staying on track is to mentally take yourself into the future to the time when you've achieved your goal to remind yourself of what you want to achieve. This technique is particularly good when you start a programme of healthy eating and are being tempted by a chocolate bar whispering your name. You can use this process to break the unhelpful strategy of instant gratification by building an extra step into developing a strategy for developing awareness of what you eat; in fact, being mindful of all your actions.

## Planning the road map

As Billy Wilder is reputed to have said, 'Hindsight is always twenty–twenty.' One way of achieving your goals is to know where you're at, where you want to go, and then logically work out the steps you have to take to get to your goal. An even better way to do this is to pretend 'as if' you've achieved your goal and work backwards, with hindsight, following the steps in this exercise.

This exercise can show you a different way of using time lines:

1. **Find yourself somewhere safe and quiet to relax deeply and think about your goal.**

2. **Draw a line and write down the starting point and endpoints for your goal at each end of the line.**

3. **Think about what the steps are for getting you from start to finish and jot these down on the line.**

4. **Float way above your time line so that you can see your past and your future stretching below you.**

5. **Still above your time line, float forward along your time line until you're above the time where you have successfully achieved your goal.**

6. **Turn and look back to now and allow your unconscious mind to fill in any gaps you hadn't thought of for your road map and add these to the sheet you've created.**

7. **Allow all the events along your time line to align so that they support your goal, noting any actions you may have to take along the way.**

8. **When you're ready, float back to your present and back down into the room.**

# Taking One Step Forward

The decision to make a change takes just a moment, but the change itself can take anywhere from a few minutes to a lifetime. What's important to recognise is that in order to incorporate change you have to do something actively. This section looks at the importance of the first and last steps in a change project.

## Making that initial move

The first step is the most important because it starts the momentum that takes you to the second and subsequent steps of your journey. Often, breaking down a goal into smaller, manageable chunks keeps you motivated on the path to success.

Susan, a drug addict for 24 years, was walking home from a nightclub very early one morning, when an encounter with an acquaintance turned her life around. When she tried to talk to him, all he said to her was, 'Go home, look in the mirror, and make some different choices.' Susan went home and looked in the mirror and saw that she looked terrible. Her skin was grey, she had dark shadows under her eyes, she was bedraggled and emaciated, and she acknowledged that she looked and felt dreadful.

She decided then and there, 'I don't want to do this anymore. I don't want to look like this anymore.' This decision, although all stated in the negative was the first step Susan took in taking back control of her life. She had a strong 'away-from' motivation pattern, recognising what she didn't want.

The next thing she did was to change her environment. She stopped seeing her drug-taking friends and got a job. During her clean-up phase, a neighbour suggested that Susan attend teacher-training college. This suggestion started Susan on her path to learning to become an excellent coach and get her MA degree in humanistic psychology.

## Celebrating and closure

Many goal-setting processes go into great depth, talking about well-formed outcomes, planning the road map, and taking the first step. Not many talk about the last step or *closure*. Admittedly, closure isn't the last step in the grand scheme of things, but integrating a last step to signal the end of a phase in a project or the project itself can be very useful.

Any change requires focus and the expenditure of huge amounts of physical and emotional energy and puts people under considerable stress. This stress can be *distress* (bad stress) or *eustress* (good stress, what Mihaly Csikszentmihalyi, the author of several inspirational books, calls *flow*). In either case you need a period to recharge your batteries. Getting closure releases the tension of concentrated work, signals the end of a phase, and gives you permission to move on to the next challenge.

End a project – which could be work at home (such as having your garden landscaped) or at work (where you're involved with improving productivity within a team) – with a debrief. You could examine the following:

- ✔ What went well?
- ✔ What could have been better?
- ✔ What lessons were learned?
- ✔ What will you do differently next time?

Remember to congratulate the team (even if that team has only one member – you) and finally make sure that you *celebrate*!

# Chapter 6

# Dealing with Risk and Uncertainty in Key Projects

---

---

*I*t's sad to hear about good projects that have failed – but it happens. It's even sadder when you find out a bit more and see that a project was killed off by a problem that the Project Manager could easily have foreseen, controlled or even prevented. Don't let your project be unnecessarily damaged or even destroyed by something that with a bit of effort – and sometimes not that much effort – you can get a handle on. This is the realm of risk management. The good news is that the basics aren't that difficult; in fact, you do risk management nearly all the time just to get through the day.

All projects need risk management, even the very small ones. However, some projects are clearly higher risk than others and justify more effort. Often the larger, more complex and longer your project is, the more risk management you need, but that doesn't let small projects off the hook. The highest-commercial-risk project the author Nick Graham has ever encountered was also one of the smallest: a six-week project with just two staff in a finance company in the City of London. If that project had failed, it would have seriously damaged the company's reputation in the City and threatened its whole business.

This chapter discusses risk when you're deciding whether you'll undertake your project and are simply evaluating the main risks, when you're developing your Project Plan, and while you're performing your project's work. We show you how to identify and assess the impact of project risks, and we explore strategies for minimising their consequences. We also offer pointers for preparing a risk management plan, and outline a few risk techniques.

# Understanding Risks and Risk Management

*Risk* is the possibility that you may not achieve some or all of your objectives because something unexpected occurs or something planned doesn't occur. All projects have some degree of risk because predicting the future with certainty is impossible. However, project risk is generally greater:

- ✔ The longer your project lasts
- ✔ The more unusual and groundbreaking the project is
- ✔ The less experience you, your organisation or your team members have with the type of project
- ✔ The more vulnerable the project is to things happening outside (such as in the wider business or due to change of government policy, change in the marketplace, activity of competitors or dependency on other projects)
- ✔ The newer your project's technology is

The current professional view of risk in projects is that it's about uncertainty, and that individual risks can be either positive or negative:

- ✔ *Negative risks*, also referred to as *downside risks* or *threats*, potentially have a detrimental effect on one or more of the project objectives, such as causing you to miss a deadline.
- ✔ *Positive risks*, also referred to as *upside risk* or *opportunities*, potentially have a beneficial effect on project objectives, such as allowing you to complete a task with fewer staff than you originally planned.

In other words, anything that can cause you either to fall short of or to exceed your established project targets, if it occurs, is considered a risk. Some approaches for analysing and responding to both types of risk are similar, but this chapter mostly focuses on approaches for identifying, evaluating and managing negative risks, because most (and maybe all) of your project risks will be negative.

## Seeing why you need risk management

Risk in projects is mostly negative: things that can go wrong. That's in line with dictionary definitions of risk, of which one is: 'The adverse consequences of future events.'

It's a no-brainer that wherever you can, you want to try to stop things going wrong and thereby increase the chances of success. The difference between project risk management and most of the risk management you do as part of daily life, like when crossing a road, is that you think out project risk management up front and handle it in a methodical way. Don't worry about a methodical approach here, and please don't confuse method with bureaucracy. We just mean that you need to think about the handling of the risk, consider all the possibilities for dealing with it, plan and carry out actions, and then check that the actions have indeed been carried out. It may well be that the chosen action for a particular risk is to not do anything about it, but even that's a considered decision that you should normally record.

On low risk projects, the answer may be that you don't do very much risk management at all, but you should always do some. For some projects, that may just mean gathering one or two people together for 20 minutes around a flip chart to look at what could go wrong with the project and how that might be controlled.

## Managing, not necessarily avoiding, risk

It's important to take on board the exact wording of the subject area of this chapter, which is risk *management*. Managing risk doesn't necessarily mean avoiding it. Clearly, a positive risk (an upside risk) is something that you want to happen, and your management action includes making it more likely. However, even negative risk may be a good option in the project.

In the project setting, a negative risk may be very high but worth taking, not for the buzz but for the business advantage. So, running the project very quickly and missing out some parts that are normally seen as essential could lead to more mistakes and higher costs. However, it's worth taking the risk in order to get to market faster and beat a competitor that you know is developing a similar new product.

## Keeping people informed

Throughout the project, and whatever part of the risk cycle you're in (see the later section 'Working Through the Risk Cycle', you need to keep people informed about risks involved with your project. You'll probably need to adjust your Communications Management Plan , if you're using one, as a reminder. As you consider who you need to keep up to speed with risk on your project, think about:

- ✔ **Corporate management,** including organisational risk systems or your organisation's risk manager, if you have one

- ✔ **Other projects** inside and outside your own organisation that need to know because they may be affected by the risk happening on your project or because a newly discovered risk may also need recording and managing on those projects

- ✔ **Programme management** if your project is one of a group of projects in a programme

- ✔ **Project sponsor** or steering committee members who need to know about new risks and changes in status to existing risks because they're authorising the countermeasures, including any finance needed for those countermeasures

- ✔ **Team leaders and team members,** so they know what to look for as they do their work, and can report relevant things that affect the risks

- ✔ **Statutory bodies** that need to know of a problem, when reporting an incident may be mandatory

People often share information about project risks ineffectually or not at all. As a result, their projects suffer unnecessary problems and setbacks that may have been avoided with proper communication.

You may be reluctant to talk too much about risk, because it looks like you're identifying excuses for failure rather than ways to succeed. Some organisations have a strange reaction to risk and think it's all very negative. 'We're a can-do company' may be a bit of management-speak imprinted on your brain from frequent repetition, and imprinted all the more deeply if your manager is about to start work on your annual report. Risk management isn't negative, though: it's positive. It's giving the project the very best chance of success by taking control of things that may cause problems. It's worth some effort to get people to understand that perspective.

Communicate about project risks from the beginning and regularly. In particular, share information at the following points in your project:

- ✔ **Starting the Project:** To support the process of deciding whether to undertake the project

- ✔ **Organising and Preparing:** To guide the development of all aspects of your Project Plan

- ✔ **Carrying Out the Work:**

    • To allow team members to discuss potential risks and to encourage them to recognise and address problems as soon as they occur

- To deal with any risks discovered during the delivery stages
- To reassess risks in the light of changing circumstances and if necessary modify parts of the current approved Project Plan

## Keeping risk in focus throughout the project

Risk management is ongoing, not just something you do at the start of the project. Here's a summary of the main stages in a project and what risk work you do at each of them (see Book IV Chapter 4 for a detailed discussion of these stages):

**Book II**

**Building Your Commercial Acumen**

✔ **Starting the Project:** Here you look at any large and obvious risks to help decide whether it's even worth taking the project idea on to planning. If the benefits of the proposed project are quite low, but the risk is huge, it's probably not worth going any further.

✔ **Organising and Preparing:** Here you do the main risk analysis and planning work. If you didn't open a Risk Register (see the section 'Identifying risk') when you were doing the start-up stage, you'll open it now to record the risks and the action you intend to take to control them.

✔ **Carrying Out the Work:** In the delivery stages, you carry out risk actions and monitor known risks, but you also deal with any new risks that you find or that others report to you in the project.

✔ **Closing the Project:** At the end of the project, you pass on any ongoing risk management actions that affect products in their working life, such as actions relating to dangerous machinery. You also evaluate how the risk management went on the project in order to learn and pass on any lessons for future projects.

# Working Through the Risk Cycle

Different approaches to risk management offer different cycles, but the example in Figure 6-1 is from Inspirandum's publication *The Project Techniques Toolbox,* by Nick Graham.

A cycle provides a framework to show how you analyse, decide actions and then manage the risks that may affect your project. As shown in Figure 6-1, the steps after the initial identification of a risk go on continually, with regular review, right through the project. Clearly, if something about the risk has changed, such as it has become more severe, you may need to make changes in the way that you're handling that risk. It could be that a course of action that wasn't justified when the risk was low severity is now fully justified because the risk has become high severity.

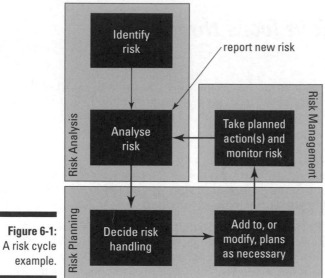

**Figure 6-1:**
A risk cycle example.

Here's an outline of the steps:

1. **Identify risks.**

   Determine what the risks are that may affect your project. You want to look at things within the project but also things that can come in from outside, such as changes in the marketplace or new laws. During the project, in particular, some new risks may also be reported to you by other people involved in the project.

2. **Analyse risks.**

   This is where you get to grips with each risk to make sure you really understand it and how it may affect your project. You normally put some measures on each risk at this point, such as the probability of the risk happening and the impact if it does.

3. **Decide risk handling.**

   This is where you think what to do and how you can protect your project from negative risk while trying to take advantage of positive risks. It may be that for some risks you decide not to take any action at all, but that's still a decision.

4. **Add to or modify plans as necessary.**

   Having decided what to do, if action is needed you're going to have to build that into the plan. For example, there may be risk actions that you'll need to include in the activity plans. Because this step is part of the cycle, you may already have some management actions planned for a particular risk, so in this step you adjust the action to reflect any changes you've decided on to manage that risk.

5. **Take planned action(s) and monitor risk.**

   There's no point in planning actions if you don't take them, so this step is to take action, either as an ongoing action or as a response if the risk happens. You also monitor each risk to see whether it's changing and to check that any action is effective. If the action is proving insufficient or the risk has changed, the cycle goes back to step 2 to re-analyse the risk, and then on around the cycle again to decide how the risk handling should be changed.

**Book II**

**Building Your Commercial Acumen**

The following sections look at each step in more detail.

## Identifying risk

The first step in your risk assessment is to identify the specific risks that may affect your project. You should record these in a *Risk Register*, which is simply a set of forms, each one describing a risk. Don't think of having a Risk Register as bureaucratic, because you've got to be able to refer back to the information, and you can't do that if you don't record it.

Although you only identify a risk once, so it isn't a repeatable part of the cycle, remember that in the project you check for new risks periodically. This may be at the end of each stage, when you're planning the next stage, or even, in a higher risk project, at regular timed intervals.

For each risk, you need to note basic information about it but you need to be a bit balanced. If you're in a risk workshop setting, for example, and people are coming up with a lot of risks, if you stop to carefully record all of the detail about each risk, you will break the flow and possibly end up missing some of the risks. It's usually better to record just the basic information and then later come back and fill in the gaps as you think more about each risk.

### Introducing some structure

You can just think of risks at random, but you may find it helpful to bring in some structure and think through the project in a more focused and systematic way. For example, you may think about risks in terms of the type of impact, such as:

✔ **Business risk:** Things coming from outside the project; for example, lower company profits this year or government cutbacks could lead to your project budget being reduced

✔ **Product risk:** For example, the risk that the technology may not produce the desired results

✔ **Resource risk:** For example, if the development turns out to be more complicated than you anticipated, existing facilities and equipment may not be adequate

✔ **Schedule risk:** For example, the risk that because staff are unfamiliar with the new technology, tasks may take longer than you anticipate

As part of the information you are holding about each risk, you may want to include a risk category. Categories can be helpful in two ways:

✔ They can help indicate how a risk should be handled and who should be involved in managing it. For example, business risks may all need to be 'owned' by the project sponsor who is primarily responsible for monitoring them.

✔ You can make use of categories to give structure to risk identification, by taking each category heading in turn and asking what risks may affect the project in that area.

Different organisations and project and risk approaches use different sets of risk categories, and you can look on the Internet to find a few.

### Looking around for help

Don't think you always have to do everything yourself. With risk in particular, it really helps to get some different viewpoints, because different people will spot risks that you don't.

## Analysing risk

The second step in the risk cycle is analysis, when you get to really understand a risk. You need to know:

✔ What can cause the risk – it may have more than one trigger

✔ How the risk is likely to behave

✔ What impact or impacts the risk may have

✔ Whether the risk is related to any other risks

It's common in projects that people think about individual risks but fail to consider the possibility of relationships between them. For example, a single event may fire off several risks at once, or there can be a chain reaction when one risk happening has an impact that fires off another risk, and when that happens it fires off a third.

As part of your analysis, it's really helpful to assess the scale of the risk and when it can happen. In turn, that helps you think how much management of the risk you need to do, which is important because risk management will itself take time in the project and possibly cost money. The scales are normally in two dimensions – probability and impact – and you can use a Probability–Impact (P-I) Grid diagram to help (see Figure 6-2 for an example).

The P-I Grid is valuable to see where individual risks are, but also to spot patterns. You might see, for example, that although you have a lot of risks, they are mostly low probability but high impact, or that the risks are evenly scattered across the grid.

**Book II**

**Building
Your
Commercial
Acumen**

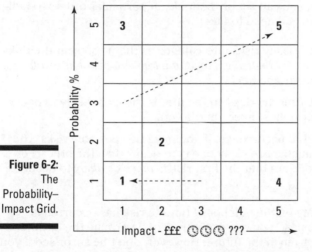

VH, H, M, L, VL
or numbers 1-5 or 1-10

Risk 1: 1 x 1 = 1
Risk 2: 2 x 2 = 4
Risk 3: 1 x 5 = 5
Risk 4: 5 x 1 = 5
Risk 5: 5 x 5 = not good at all!

**Figure 6-2:**
The
Probability–
Impact Grid.

When you have the position of each risk worked out, you can use this to help determine what action you need to take. Generally, the more you go towards the top right of the grid, the more action you need to consider. However, this isn't a numbers game, so be careful – particularly in the top left and bottom right of the grid. In Figure 6-2, Risk 3 is very low impact but very high probability. Because it's very high probability, you need to take action, even though its overall score, multiplying the impact scale by the probability scale, is only 5 ($1 \times 5$). Equally, Risk 4 probably justifies action. It's only got a severity rating of 5 ($5 \times 1$) but while it's very low probability, its impact would be devastating. For example, if you work in a large building, it will have smoke detectors, a fire alarm system, fire exit routes and fire hoses and extinguishers. With modern electrical equipment and a ban on people smoking, the probability of a fire is extremely low, but risk management action is justified because the impact is so high – life threatening – if a fire does break out.

The grid is also useful for regular risk reporting, and you can show any movement of a risk since the last reporting point with dotted lines. In Figure 6-2, you can see that Risks 1 and 5 have changed since the last reporting point, but the others still have the same evaluation of impact and probability.

### Gauging probability

Probability can be expressed as a number between 0 and 1, with 0.0 signifying that a situation will never happen, and 1.0 signifying that it will always occur. (You may also express probability as a percentage, with 100 per cent meaning the situation will always occur.)

You don't have to use the P-I Grid for recording probability and impact though. For probability, you can simply list risks in particular orders to indicate the degree of action you need to take:

- **Category ranking:** Classify risks into categories that represent their likelihood. You can use *very high*, *high*, *medium*, *low* and *very low* or *always*, *often*, *sometimes*, *rarely* and *never*.

- **Ordinal ranking:** Order the risks so the first is the most likely to occur, the second is the next most likely, and so on.

- **Relative likelihood of occurrence:** If you have two possible risks, you can express how much more likely one is to occur than the other. For example, you can declare that the first risk is *twice as likely* to occur as the second.

If you have objective data on the number of times a risk has occurred in similar situations in the past, you can use it to help determine the likelihood that the risk will occur again in the future. However, don't be surprised if you don't have such information, because most risk probability estimates just aren't like that. The lack of data makes the probability estimating difficult; it's been described as the Achilles heel of risk management.

Where you don't have objective data available, you can use personal judgements to estimate the likelihood that particular risks will occur. One technique that can help is the Delphi technique. Try also to get the opinions of experts and people who've worked on similar projects in the past.

When using objective data, you can estimate the probability of a risk occurring by considering the number of times the risk actually occurred on similar projects. Suppose, for example, that you designed 20 computer-generated reports over the past year for new clients. Eight times, when you submitted your design for final approval, new clients wanted at least one change. If you're planning to design a computer-generated report for another new client, you may conclude that the chance that you'll have to make a change in the design you submit is 40 per cent – $(8 \div 20) \times 100$.

Some computer-based risk-management tools give very precise results, but be careful because precision is different from accuracy. *Precision* refers to the detail of a number. *Accuracy* refers to how correct the number is. The computer may calculate the likelihood of a particular risk to be 67.23 per cent. However, that figure will have been determined from your answers to the questions posed by the software. If you just didn't know and entered wild guesses, don't expect the output to be accurate, even though it's very precise.

### Estimating the impact

After you identify the likelihood that a particular risk will affect your project, be sure to determine the impact if the risk does occur. That magnitude directly influences how you will decide to deal with the risk. Determine the specific effect that each risk may have on your project's product, schedule and resource performance. When evaluating these effects, do the following:

- **Consider the effect of a risk on the total project, not only a part of it.** Taking one week longer than you planned to complete an activity may cause you to miss intermediate milestones (and cause the people waiting for the results of that activity to sit idle). However, the effect on the project is even greater if the delayed activity is on your project's critical path , which means the week-long delay on that one activity also causes a week-long delay for your entire project.

- **Consider the combined effect of related risks.** The likelihood that your schedule will slip is greater if three activities on the critical path have a significant risk of delay, rather than just one.

### Being specific

Be sure to describe risks and their associated consequences as specifically as possible. For example, suppose a key piece of equipment you ordered for your project may arrive later than expected. You can describe that risk as *the delivery may be late,* or as *the delivery may be delayed by two weeks.* Just stating that the delivery may be late doesn't give you enough information to assess the likely effect of that delay on the overall project. It also makes estimating the probability of that risk's occurrence more difficult. Are you talking about a delay of one day? One month? Stating that the delivery may be delayed by two weeks allows you to determine more precisely the likely effect that the delay will have on the overall schedule and resources. It also allows you to decide how much you're willing to spend to avoid that delay.

### Deciding on an impact scale

The scale for impact in particular is one that you or your organisation as a whole must decide, because it's relative to the organisation. For example, take an impact of a loss of £1 million. Is that a problem? Well, to a small business with just three employees, that isn't just 'very high' – it's a company killer and off the scale completely. However, Nick Graham has run project training courses for a multinational company based in the UK that has an annual turnover in excess of £20 billion. What's the impact of a £1 million loss to that company? An embarrassment and an irritation perhaps, but certainly not high up the scale in terms of the financial impact.

### Considering proximity

A third useful measure for each risk, after probability and impact, is the *proximity*: how soon it can happen. Proximity information is, obviously enough, very useful in planning. Three types of proximity exist:

- ✔ **Immediate:** Some risks always have a proximity of *now*, because they can happen at any time during the project with no notice at all. An easy example is with a key team member going sick. She may walk up to you in five minutes' time and say that she's feeling dreadful and needs to go home, or that could happen in five weeks' time or in five months' time.

- ✔ **Fixed date:** Some risks are pegged to a point in time. The new rocket can't fail to launch until it's time to launch it. The team can't find that a product is more complicated to build than they thought, and so will take longer, until they get to grips with the product as they start to build it.

- ✔ **Fixed period:** Some risks will always happen a certain time ahead. Today the proximity of a particular risk is four weeks, but in five months' time the proximity of the risk will still be four weeks. That sounds weird until you consider the simple example of someone resigning from your organisation and so leaving your project. If that person resigns today, she'll leave in four weeks' time, after she's worked her four-week notice period. If she resigns in five months' time, she'll leave four weeks after that. You just hope that she doesn't have four weeks' holiday owing and a fixed period turns into now! You might even decide to check that out.

## Deciding risk handling

Recognising and evaluating risks that pose a threat to your project are the first steps towards controlling them. But you can't stop there. You also have to develop specific plans for reducing their potential negative effects on your project. You start by deciding what options you have for dealing with each one, and then you select the option or set of options that are most suitable.

### Handling all risks

As you look at the risks, be clear on the point that you're going to manage all of them, even if your choice of action for some may be to do nothing. That may sound more than a little strange until you think back to the risk cycle. As the risk goes into the management part of the cycle, you monitor it to check for changes. It may be that a risk where you decided to take no action has now changed and now does justify action. So you're still managing a 'do nothing' risk because you will continue to monitor it.

### Thinking wide

When considering what to do about each risk, it's very easy to bounce off at a superficial level, and Project Managers often come up with a single option: throw money at the risk. But often you can do a number of things to manage a risk, and some may not involve money at all, just some ingenuity. Allowing sufficient time for risk analysis and management is important, then, so that you don't just rush into the obvious management actions that may not be the cheapest or even the most effective. As you come to decide what action to take, you may pick just one of the options you've come up with or you may implement more than one action to get good control of the risk.

Record all the risk management options for each risk, albeit as concisely as possible, and include the reasons for choosing the actions that are being taken and the reasons for not selecting the others. That way, if circumstances change later on and it's necessary to review the decision, the information is still to hand. There may be some additional work to do if new options can be identified during that review, but at least, if you haven't discarded the results, it saves you repeating work that you've already done.

### Deciding on actions

When making a decision on what action(s) to take, first consider the likelihood of a risk *and* its potential effect on your project. If the potential effect of a risk is great, and if the chances it will occur are high, you probably want to develop plans to manage that risk. If both the impact and the probability are low (bottom left of the P-I Grid; see the section 'Analysing risk'), you may decide not to take control action.

When the potential impact is high but the likelihood is low, or vice versa (the top left and bottom right of the P-I Grid), you must consider the situation more carefully. In these more complex situations, you can use a more formal approach for considering the combined effect of likelihood of occurrence and potential consequence – the severity – by defining the *expected value of risk*, using exact numeric measures as follows:

Expected value of risk = Quantitative measure of the effect if it occurs × Probability it will occur

## *Understanding action types*

You can categorise options for handling risks in different ways, but here are five main alternatives:

- ✔ **Avoidance:** Act to stop the risk happening. An example is deciding not to use a new, untested procedure that you're concerned may not produce the desired project results.

- ✔ **Contingency:** This is allowing for the risk to happen, so that you can absorb the impact. Three sub-types of contingency exist:

  - • **Action contingency:** Have a plan B. If the risk is realised, take the pre-planned alternative action. If the flight to Edinburgh is cancelled because of volcanic dust from Iceland, I'll go by train.

  - • **Cost contingency:** Have some extra money in a risk budget. If the supply from the cheaper source fails, the relevant part of the risk budget is released and the item can be purchased from a better stocked but more expensive supplier.

  - • **Time contingency:** Allow some contingency time in your plan to allow for a few deliveries to be late.

- ✔ **Mitigation:** To reduce the probability that a risk will occur or to minimise the impact if it does occur. Two examples of risk mitigation are:

  - • **Minimise the probability.** Use only experienced staff on the project and so reduce the chance of serious mistakes being made.

  - • **Minimise the impact.** Have a spare engineer identified who, alongside his normal work, will attend all the project briefings and be copied in on project engineering documents. That way, if someone leaves the engineering team suddenly, this spare person can step in and join the project as a replacement. He'll still have a learning curve, but it's less steep than if he knew nothing about the project at all. He'll get up to speed faster, and the impact of the staff change will be reduced.

- ✔ **Taking no action:** This is a conscious, and recorded, decision not to take action on the risk; it isn't neglect. If the risk does occur, everyone knew what the impact would be. You might use this option if taking actions is very expensive or time consuming, and the low impact and very low probability of the risk occurring (in the present assessment of it) doesn't justify such cost or work effort.

- ✔ **Transfer:** Get someone else to take as much of the risk as possible. For example, take out insurance to cover the financial impact.

You can use the action types in combination. For example, you might choose to have some contingency in the plan to deal with a time delay, but also take out insurance (transfer) to cover the financial impact.

# Adding to or modifying plans as necessary

Having decided risk management actions after you've identified and analysed a risk, you need to build those actions into the Project Plan and Stage Plans and treat them like any other project management work. Where something has changed on a risk that is already known about and for which actions are planned or are already being taken, you need to modify those actions, depending on the review of what's now needed.

Conceptually, this step is simple enough. But do be aware that putting in the risk actions may then affect the overall plan. You'll need to make allowances for risk activity when first drafting the plan out, but later in the project risk activity could even lead to a significant update of the plan. In particular the risk management actions may:

- **Increase costs:** Such as for team member time, as well as for financial contingency, for taking actions

- **Increase time:** Because of the work involved in managing the risks, but also to build time contingency into the plan

- **Have knock-on effects:** Clearly, if the project will take more time because of contingency allowances, for example, it could affect the schedule for delivery of products during the project, which may in turn affect other projects if they need those deliverables too because of an inter-project dependency

In addition to the work on individual risk actions, there is also work to be put on the plan for the Project Manager (and perhaps others too) in order to regularly review risks and keep the risk documentation up to date. How much work is involved and how often depends partly on the criticality of the project and partly on the number of risks involved. In a very high-risk project, review will be more frequent than in a low risk project.

# Taking planned actions and monitoring risk

At the start of this chapter we made the point that it's sad when a project fails because something nasty happens that could easily have been identified up front and which could have been controlled or even prevented. Okay, but now for something even sadder. That's when risks were identified, actions planned, but then the project dies because those actions were never taken. Risks happened with nothing to stop or control them and killed the project.

This final step of the risk cycle is essential, obviously, and to be sure that it is done, it can be included in regular health checks. You normally do this checking in a project audit function . That check isn't merely on the Project Manager, though. If team members, or even the sponsor, are supposed to be taking risk-related action, project audit will check that they are and sound the alarm bells if it's being overlooked.

### Taking action on risk

Risk action may be continuous or it may be responsive if the risk actually happens. If the building catches fire, then someone is designated to call the fire brigade; that's a responsive action if the risk occurs. Other risks may need ongoing action, particularly but not solely actions to avoid or reduce risk. So every Friday you jump out of your seat in shock at midday, despite the reminder notice in the lift, because the fire alarm system is being tested to reduce the risk of it not functioning in an emergency.

### Monitoring risks

Risks should be monitored regularly and in two dimensions:

- **For change:** The first dimension is to check whether things are still the same. Has the risk increased in probability? In the light of the latest information available, is the impact greater or less than expected? Has the timing of the risk changed? Any change means that the risk needs to be re-assessed and, if necessary, the control actions changed. That's where this step cycles around to the analysing risk step.

- **For adequacy of the action(s):** Where actions are being taken, are they working? If not, the actions need to be re-considered, which in turn means that some re-analysis may be helpful because something may have been missed which led to the wrong actions being selected in the first place. Again, the cycle continues with a link back to analysing risk.

# Documenting Risk on Critical Projects

Two key documents are involved with risk management, and in all but very small projects these are both necessary and important. Even a small project should have some means of risk recording, though. The two documents are a *risk management plan* and a *Risk Register*.

## Risk management plan

A *risk management plan* lays out the strategy for how risk will be managed in your project. Develop your risk management plan in the Organising and Preparing stage of your project, refine it as necessary at the end of each stage when planning the next stage, and continually update it where needed during stages. Include the following in your risk-management plan:

- ✔ Communications and interfaces, such as with programme management or other projects that may be affected

- ✔ How risk actions will be monitored and audited

- ✔ Reporting mechanisms, such as how team members should report newly discovered risks and how they should say if they believe a risk is starting to happen

- ✔ Review points where risk will be re-assessed, such as at the end of each stage and at regular monthly intervals during each stage, unless it's getting near an end stage

- ✔ Scales to be used, such as the impact scale

- ✔ Your plan for keeping people informed about risks throughout the project

## *Risk Register*

You need a *Risk Register* or *Risk Log* in which to record risks, the action being taken on them and the responsibilities for managing each one.

The Risk Register holds the day-to-day control information for each risk that's been identified. You can adjust the contents to meet the exact needs of your project but, as always, try to keep things simple. At a minimum, you're likely to need the following information:

- ✔ **ID:** Usually a number

- ✔ **Risk title:** A short name to identify the risk quickly

- ✔ **Status:** Whether the risk is increasing, decreasing, under review or dead

- ✔ **Description:** A full description covering the characteristics of the risk and how it is likely to behave, such as whether it may happen gradually or instantly

- ✔ **Metrics:** Impact, probability and proximity information

- ✔ **Responsibilities:** Who's responsible for the risk, including taking any action on it

- ✔ **Notifier:** Who spotted the risk in the first place (that might be a good person to involve in the analysis of the risk) or who to consult if there are changes

- ✔ **Planned actions:** What actions will be taken to control the risk, or the fact that it has been decided not to take action

# Getting Some Help from Techniques

The good thing about risk management is that there are lots of techniques to help. In this last section you'll find four basic ones to get you started.

## Ishikawa (fishbone) diagram

The fishbone diagram is useful when you want to work through risk identification in a structured way. You can do this using one impact at a time, such as 'delay' or 'overspending'. Using your chosen risk categories as the primary fish bones, enter the risks as the secondary bones. Figure 6-3 gives an example with a partially completed diagram.

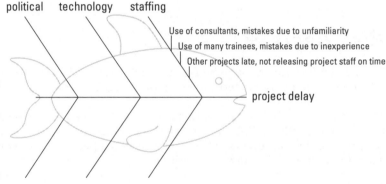

**Figure 6-3:** The Ishikawa (fishbone) diagram.

## Work flow diagram

A work flow diagram, shows all the project's products in sequence, including those coming into the project from outside. This gives a natural structure for part of the risk analysis. Simply go through the project products one at a time asking 'What could go wrong with producing this product or with this external supply?'

## Risk checklist

The risk checklist is simply a standard list of known risks grouped by category. You can buy commercial ones, but making your own for your organisation is even better. You identify all the risks you can by using other techniques, and then use the Risk Checklist to see whether you have missed anything. Don't use the checklist first, or you're likely to get focused on it and so miss a new risk that's staring you in the face but isn't on the list.

## Decision tree

A decision tree allows you to map options and cost them against the probability of them occurring. The result helps evaluate the best course of action. Figure 6-4 gives an example with two main choices of supplier. The actual cost for each then depends on whether that supplier delivers on time, early (in which case they get a bonus payment) or late (in which case there is a deduction from the cost for the inconvenience). The known history of the two suppliers allows estimation of the probability of each being early, on time or late.

Book II

Building Your Commercial Acumen

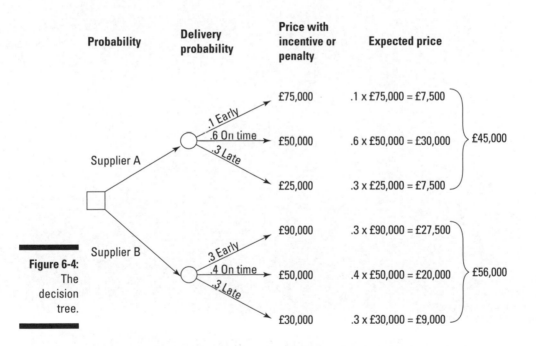

**Figure 6-4:**
The decision tree.

Multiplying the base price plus the performance incentive for early delivery by the probability of early delivery yields the expected value of the price you pay if delivery is early. You can calculate the total expected prices for suppliers A and B by totalling the expected prices if each is early, on time and late.

This analysis suggests that you can expect to pay supplier A £45,000 and have a 70 per cent chance she'll deliver on time or early. You can expect to pay vendor B £56,000 and have a 70 per cent chance she'll deliver on time or early. So you can see that vendor A is the better choice.

# Book III
# Managing and Leading Others

'I'm getting worried about the boss.'

# In this book. . .

$B$usiness revolves around people who come to work for different reasons and need to form effective work groups and teams. Emotions are always at play beneath the surface. In this book, you'll find how to develop your own leadership style so that you can ride the rough with the smooth, harnessing inevitable variations in your staff and stakeholder priorities.

Here are the contents of Book III at a glance:

# Chapter 1

# Working Together in Teams and Groups

*I*n practice, few managers work in isolation, and most have responsibilities for teams and groups of staff. Teams and groups start out as disparate collections of individuals who are gathered together for a purpose, and whose remit is to deliver specific results, resolve problems, address particular issues and create ways of working that are suitable for the work in hand. A team is two or more people who work together to achieve a common goal.

Teams offer an easy way to tap into the knowledge and resources of all employees – not just supervisors and managers – to do the work of the organisation and deliver its goals. This in turn means having teams that produce and deliver products and services, enhance business performance, contribute their own expertise for the greater good and solve the organisation's problems. A well-structured team draws together employees with different skills and knowledge, often from different functions and levels of the organisation, to help find the best way to approach an issue. Smart companies have discovered (and not-so-smart companies are figuring out) that to remain competitive they can no longer rely solely on management to guide the development of work processes and the accomplishment of organisational goals. The companies need to involve those employees who are closer to both the problems and their customers. Guess who those employees are? The front-line workers!

This chapter discusses the main kinds of teams and how they work, the impact of computer-based technology on teams and insights for conducting the best team meetings ever.

# Phasing Out the Old Hierarchy

The last couple of decades have seen a fundamental shift in the distribution of power and authority in organisations. Until recently, most organisations were *vertical* – they had many layers of managers and supervisors between top management and front-line workers. The classic model of a vertical organisation is the traditional military organisation. In the army, privates report to corporals, who report to sergeants, who report to captains and so on, up to the top general. When a general gives an order, it passes down the line from person to person until it reaches the person who's expected to execute it.

Until relatively recently, large companies such as Ford, British Airways and British Telecom weren't that different from this rigid, hierarchical model; and this remains a serious problem in some public services. Employing hundreds of thousands of workers, these organisations depended – and in many cases still depend – on legions of supervisors and managers to control the work, the workers who did it and when and how they did it. (Okay, perhaps today's legions are smaller.) The primary goal of top management was to command and control workers' schedules, assignments and decision-making processes very closely to ensure that the company met its objectives (and to ensure that workers were actually doing something!). The result of this kind of organising is, without any exception, that less gets done, more slowly, more expensively, with more errors, for fewer people.

## Downsizing organisations

The problems presented by a hierarchical model of organisation are compounded by the fact that, in many cases, supervisors and managers make little or no direct contribution to the production of a company's products or services. Instead of producing things, managers merely manage other managers or supervisors and serve as liaisons between levels, ultimately doing little more than pushing paper from one part of their desk to another. In the model's worst scenario, the levels of supervisors and managers actually impede their organisations' capability to get tasks done – dramatically adding to the cost of doing business and slowing down the response time of decision making. All those expense account lunches add up.

Although this problem was overlooked as the global economy continued to expand in the last half of the twentieth century, factors such as the economic slowdown in the late 1980s and the telecoms and dot-com crashes in the early 2000s made for quite a wake-up call for those companies with unproductive – or worse, counterproductive – middle management.

Although downsizing workforces after economic downturns has obvious negative effects on the employees who lose their jobs – and in many cases, their hopes for a comfortable retirement – this dark cloud has a silver lining. In flatter organisations a new life (and a quicker pace) comes to the following important areas:

- **Decision making:** Decisions, which may have taken weeks or even months to make in the old, bloated bureaucracy, are made in hours or minutes.

- **Communicating:** Instead of being intercepted and possibly distorted by middle managers at numerous points along its path, communication now travels a more direct – and much speedier – route from front-line workers to top management and vice versa, or to whoever the person needs to get information from. There's nothing like cutting six layers of management out of an organisation to improve communication!

Also, this transformation from vertical to *horizontal* businesses (organisations with a minimum of levels of management) has a fundamental impact on financial and organisational elements:

- **Quantifiable benefits to the bottom line:** By cutting out entire layers of management employees, many companies save money by substantially reducing the costs of personnel, facilities and expense account lunches.

- **Movement of authority and power:** This move happens from the very top of the organisation down to the front-line employees who interact with customers on a day-to-day basis. With fewer middle managers to interfere, front-line employees naturally have more autonomy and authority.

**Book III**

**Managing and Leading Others**

# *Moving towards co-operation*

More than ever before, businesses worldwide are rewarding employees for co-operating with each other instead of competing against one another. Organisations are no longer measuring employees only by their individual contributions, but also by how effective they are as contributing members of their work teams.

Coupled with this shift of authority is a fundamental change in the way that many businesses structure their work. Of course, most businesses still organise their operations by departments, divisions and so forth, but smart managers now encourage, rather than discourage, their employees to cross formal organisational lines, and set up teams made up of employees from different departments whose members work together to perform tasks and achieve common goals.

Following are benefits that your organisation can reap from promoting co-operation:

- ✓ **Reducing unproductive competition:** Promoting a co-operative, team-oriented work environment reduces the chance of your employees becoming over-competitive with each other.

 If allowed to continue unabated, over-competitiveness results in the shutdown of communication between employees and, ultimately, reduces organisational effectiveness (because over-competitive employees build and defend private fiefdoms). Besides, over-competition between employees invariably leads to backbiting, in-fighting and denigration of other people; and it can lead to bullying, victimisation and harassment.

- ✓ **Sharing knowledge:** Knowledge is power. If you're in the know, you have a clear advantage over someone who's been left in the dark – especially if your finger is on the light switch. In a co-operative work environment, team members work together and thereby share their areas of knowledge and expertise, using it to the best advantage of everyone – they don't defend it or use it as a bargaining chip.

- ✓ **Fostering communication:** Using teams helps to break down the walls between an organisation's departments, divisions and other formal structures to foster communication between organisational units.

- ✓ **Achieving common goals:** Developing teams with members from various departments encourages workers from all levels and all parts of a company to work together to achieve common goals.

# Empowering Your Teams

So if organisational structures are flatter (see the preceding section), employees gain more authority and autonomy from top management. The result: employees are more responsive to customers' needs and resolve problems at the lowest possible level in the organisation. The transfer of power, responsibility and authority from higher-level to lower-level employees is called *empowerment*.

By empowering workers, managers place the responsibility for decision making with the employees in the best position to make the decision. In the past, many managers felt that *they* were in the best position to make decisions that affected a company's products or customers. How wrong they were. Although they may have been right in some cases, their driving need to control workers and processes at all costs often blinded managers – so much so that control became more important than encouraging employee initiative.

## Recognising the value of an empowered workforce

Effective managers know the value of empowering their workers. Not only can employees serve customers better, but also by delegating more responsibility and authority to front-line workers, managers are free to pursue other important tasks that only they can do, such as coaching, 'big-picture' communicating, long-range planning, and production and service scheduling. The result is a much more efficient, more effective organisation all round.

Nissan UK runs the most productive car factory in the world, measured in terms of output per member of staff. One of the keys to this impressive outcome is that the company has given full responsibility and autonomy to the production crews (the teams) for all aspects of each car they produce. In particular, the company refers complaints from distributors and customers directly back to the crew who made the car. No quality assurance hierarchy exists; everything is the responsibility of the particular crew.

Empowerment is also a great morale booster in an organisation. Managers who empower their workers show that they trust them to make decisions that are important to the company's success.

**Book III**

**Managing and Leading Others**

## Managing your teams

If you want productive, effective and profitable groups working in harmony together, then concentrate on the following:

- Managing the task, ensuring that everybody knows what the purpose of the group is and what they're supposed to be contributing to it.

- Managing the people, ensuring that you have effective, productive and positive working relationships between everyone involved, whatever their profession, occupation or expertise.

- ✔ Managing communications between everyone involved; and managing communication between different work groups, disciplines and occupations.

- ✔ Managing individuals, to ensure that everyone gets the best possible opportunity to make the contribution required.

- ✔ Clarity of purpose and common aims and objectives, to which everyone has agreed and to which they can contribute.

- ✔ Group and team spirit, a combination of shared values, together with specific ways of working, a helpful attitude and a positive atmosphere within the group.

- ✔ Managing conflict, ensuring that you assess openly and honestly the potential for conflict within all groups. You need to pay particular attention to the nature and mix of personalities involved, the nature and mix of expertise and talent involved, and any divergence of objectives between group members, individuals and the overall objectives of the group.

Finally – finally – do make sure that the style of management and leadership is itself participative, positive and supportive! No point lies in creating work groups and expecting them to succeed if the organisation is constantly restraining and restricting the capability of those groups to operate to their full potential.

# Identifying the Advantages of Teams

Teams not only have the potential to make better decisions, they can make faster decisions too. Because team members are closest to the problems and to one another, fewer delays occur because of the need to communicate with or get approval from others in the organisation.

Teams used to be considered beneficial only for projects of short duration. However, many companies no longer follow this line of thinking. According to Peter Drucker, 'Whereas team design has traditionally been considered applicable only to short-lived, transitory, exceptional task-force assignments, it is equally applicable to some permanent needs, especially to the top-management and innovating tasks.' Indeed, the team concept has proved itself to be a workable long-term solution to the needs of many organisations.

## Smaller and nimbler

Large organisations often have a hard time competing in the marketplace against smaller, more nimble competitors. Smaller units within a large organisation – such as teams – are better able to compete. The rate and scope of change in the global business environment has led to increased competitive pressure on organisations in almost every business sector, so the importance of speed and responsiveness also increases.

As customers can get products and services faster, their expectations are constantly rising; and so organisations have to be able to meet these expectations. As they can buy products more cheaply as a result of technology improvements or global competition, they expect lower prices as well. And the expectation of quality in relation to price has dramatically increased over the years – especially with consumers' experience in obtaining more advanced electronics and computer technology for progressively lower prices. In short, customer values are changing so that they now want products and services 'any time, any place, anywhere'.

## *Innovative and adaptable*

Teams are more adaptive to the external environment as it quickly or constantly changes. Thus, a team's size and flexibility give it a distinct advantage over competing organisations structured in a more traditional way. At Xerox and Hewlett-Packard, for example, design, engineering and manufacturing functions are closely intertwined in the development of new products – dramatically shortening the time from concept to production compared with their previous, more hierarchical structure. Indeed, Hewlett-Packard now only manufactures to order; and this decision is becoming more commonplace in other organisations and industry sectors.

**Book III**

**Managing and Leading Others**

# *Setting Up and Supporting Your Teams*

When setting up a team, the first point you need to consider is what kind of team is appropriate for the situation. Three main kinds of teams exist: *formal*, *informal* and *self-managed*. Each type of team offers advantages and disadvantages depending on the specific situation, timing and the organisation's needs.

Whatever kind of team you're setting up, you need a good mix of characteristics. You need people with creative bursts of energy; people who'll question everything; and people who'll do the painstaking bits – the attention to detail, progress chasing and checking, and making sure that the team does everything on time. And you need effective team leadership!

Meredith Belbin produced a structure for the composition of effective teams, which is shown in Table 1-1.

| Table 1-1 | Members of Effective Teams | |
|---|---|---|
| *Type* | *Typical features* | *Positive qualities* |
| Company Worker | Conservative, dutiful, practicable | Organising ability, practical common sense, hard working |
| Chair | Calm, self-confident, controlled | A capacity for treating and welcoming all potential contributors on their merits and without prejudice<br><br>A strong sense of objectives |
| Shaper | Highly strung, outgoing, dynamic | Drive and readiness to challenge inertia, ineffectiveness, complacency or self-deception |
| Plant (Questioner) | Individualistic, serious minded, unorthodox | Genius, imagination, intellect, knowledge |
| Resource Investigator | Extroverted, enthusiastic, curious, communicative | A capacity for contacting people and exploring anything new<br>An ability to respond to challenge |
| Monitor-Evaluator | Sober, unemotional, prudent | Judgement, discretion, hard-headedness |
| Team Worker | Socially oriented, rather mild, sensitive | An ability to respond to people and to situations, and to promote team spirit |
| Completer-Finisher | Painstaking, orderly, conscientious, anxious | A capacity to follow through<br><br>Perfectionism |

*Source: Belbin (1986)*

In teams of only five or six members, clearly some people have to be prepared to carry out more than one role. A certain amount of discipline and commitment to the group also needs to exist, requiring members, in many cases, to do things in ways that they're not normally comfortable or familiar with.

These points apply to any team, whatever its purpose.

## *Formal teams*

A *formal team* is set up for a particular purpose and has specific goals to achieve. These goals can range from developing a new product line, determining the system for processing customer invoices or planning a company picnic. Types of formal teams include:

- **Quality improvement group and work improvement group:** A formal team assembled in order to tackle specific problems and issues relating to product and service innovation and development; specific problems and issues concerning quality, durability and accessibility; and managing customer complaints.

- **Project team:** A team drawn together for a specific purpose, and assembled for the duration of the particular project. Successful and effective project teams are crucial to the success of civil engineering and other engineering projects, the design and installation of information systems, and the development of new products and services.

- **Task force:** A formal team assembled on a job and finish basis to address specific problems or issues, very often at strategy or policy level. For example, a task force may be assembled to determine why a particular strategic initiative isn't delivering the intended results. Task forces are also a well-known and understood approach to addressing the detail required to implement new strategy and policy initiatives. A task force usually has a deadline for solving the issue and reporting the findings to top and senior management.

- **Committee:** A long-term or permanent team created to perform an ongoing, specific organisational task. For example, some companies have committees that select employees to receive awards for performance or that make recommendations to management for safety improvements. Although committee membership may change from year to year, the committees continue their work regardless of who belongs to them.

- **Command team:** Made up of a manager or supervisor and all the employees who report directly to that person. Such teams are by nature hierarchical and represent the traditional way that managers communicate tasks to workers. Examples of command teams include company sales teams, management teams and executive teams.

**Book III**

**Managing and Leading Others**

## *Informal teams*

*Informal teams* are casual associations of employees that spontaneously develop within an organisation's formal structure. Such teams include groups of employees who eat lunch together every day, form bowling teams or simply like to hang out together – both during and after work. The membership of informal teams is in a constant state of flux as members come and go and friendships and other associations between employees change over time.

Although informal teams have no specific tasks or goals that management has assigned, they're very important to organisations for the following reasons:

✔ Informal teams provide a way for employees to get information outside of formal, management-sanctioned communication channels.

✔ Informal teams provide a (relatively) safe outlet for employees to let off steam about issues that concern them and to find solutions to problems by discussing them with employees from other parts of the organisation – unimpeded by the walls (actual and metaphorical) of the formal organisation.

For example, although they're not formally constituted, dozens of informal work improvement groups (WIGS) exist at GlaxoSmithKline. The purpose of these groups is simply to enable people to get together, share information and ask for and offer solutions to problems that have occurred. Some of the groups have a regular membership; others are constituted to confront one particular problem and are then dissolved after they've addressed the matter.

*Ad hoc groups* are informal teams of employees assembled to solve a problem, with only those who are most likely to contribute invited. For example, you may form an ad hoc team when you select employees from your human resources and accounting departments to solve a problem with the system for tracking and recording pay changes in the company's payroll system. You don't invite participants from shipping to join this informal team because they probably can't provide meaningful input to solving the problem.

## Self-managed teams

*Self-managed teams* combine the attributes of both formal and informal teams. Normally established by management, self-managed teams often quickly adopt lives of their own as members take over responsibility for the day-to-day workings of the team. Self-managed teams usually contain from three to 30 employees whose job is to get together to find solutions to common worker problems. Self-managed teams are also known as *high-performance teams*, *cross-functional teams* or *super-teams*.

To save time and gain benefits, an organisation's self-managing teams must be:

✔ Made up of people from different parts of the organisation

✔ Small, because large groups create communication problems

✔ Self-managing and empowered to act, because referring decisions back up the line wastes time and often leads to poorer decisions

✔ Multi-functional, because that's the best – if not the only – way to keep the actual product and its essential delivery system clearly visible and foremost in everyone's mind

# The real world

Empowerment is a beautiful thing when it flourishes in an organisation. However, real empowerment is still rare. Many false substitutes are out there masquerading as empowerment! Although many managers tell a good story about how they empower their employees, few actually do it. When they're real and not pale imitations, empowered teams typically

- Make the most of the decisions that influence team success
- Choose their leaders
- Add or remove team members
- Set their goals and commitments
- Define and perform much of their training
- Receive rewards as a team

Unfortunately, employee empowerment, for the most part, may be only an illusion. A survey of team members showed that plenty of room for change and improvement in the working of teams still exists. Survey respondents clearly felt that intra-group trust, group effectiveness, agenda setting, meeting content and idea conformity could do with some improvement.

A great deal of research has investigated what makes effective teams. And in the overwhelming majority of cases, teams aren't fully empowered – top management is still making the strategic decisions. The studies all find that you can give much greater autonomy to teams by:

- **Making your teams empowered, not merely participative.** Instead of just inviting employees to participate in teams, grant team members the authority and power to make independent decisions.

- **Removing the source of conflicts.** Despite their attempts to empower employees, managers are often unwilling to live with the results. Be willing to start up a team, and then be prepared to accept the outcome.

- **Changing other significant factors that influence team effectiveness.** Each of these factors indicates that an organisation hasn't yet brought true empowerment to its employees. You have the power to change this situation. Do it!

# New technology and teams

In a team environment *process management information* moves precisely to where the team needs it, unfiltered by a hierarchy. Raw numbers go straight to those who need them in their jobs because front-line workers, such as sales-people and machinists, are trained in how to use that information. By letting information flow to wherever the team needs it, a horizontal self-managed company isn't only possible, it's also inevitable. Information technology-enabled team support systems include email, computer conferencing and videoconferencing, which co-ordinate geographically, as well as across time zones, more easily than ever before. The development and use of computer software to support teams is growing also. An example is the expanding body of software called *groupware*. Groupware consists of computer programs specifically designed to support collaborative work groups and processes, both in a single location and anywhere in the world.

As organisations make better use of information technology, they don't need middle managers to make decisions as often. The result? Organisations can dramatically reduce the number of management levels and the number of managers. Jobs, careers and knowledge shift constantly. Typical management career paths are eliminated, and workers advance by learning more skills, making them more valuable to the organisation.

Those managers who remain need to take on new skills and attitudes to be more like coaches, supporters and facilitators to front-line employees. Supervisors and managers no longer have the luxury of spending time trying to control the organisation – instead, they change it. Their job is to seek out new customers at the same time as they respond to the latest needs of their established customers. Managers still have considerable authority, but instead of commanding workers, their job is to inspire them.

# Chapter 2

# Tapping into Passion and Purpose

· · · · · · · · · · · · · · · · · · · · · · · · · · · · · · · · · · · · · · · · · · · · · · · ·

## In This Chapter

▶ Getting motivated with flow states

▶ Paying attention to sources of passion

▶ Discovering personal purpose

▶ Coming together with passion and purpose

· · · · · · · · · · · · · · · · · · · · · · · · · · · · · · · · · · · · · · · · · · · · · · · ·

Have you ever come across people who strike you as the living dead? They seem to lack passion and connection with the world. They're going through the motions of everyday existence with no destination in mind, simply plodding around as if life is just too much effort.

In NLP-speak, these individuals are *dissociated* from the richness of life. They operate *at effect* rather than *at cause*, which means they respond passively to events rather than proactively engaging in the experience of creating the lives they want to lead. The aim in coaching is to empower the client to be at cause. When at effect, people wait for others to give them opportunities or solve their problems. When at cause, people go out and find opportunities and solutions to their problems.

This chapter concentrates on ways to help your clients reconnect to their essential sense of purpose, which shifts them from that living-dead space to being fully alive within their own lives. I also explore the state of flow as a source of passion and purpose, and then explore coaching techniques and tools you can use to connect clients with their true sense of purpose.

## Waking Up

Any process of growth or transformation is usually accompanied by an awakening; just as in spring when nature comes alive after the winter dormancy.

NLP developer Robert Dilts talks about *Coaching with a capital C*, in which NLP coaches operate as *awakeners*, bringing people alive to their natural spirits and opening them to connections that go beyond their own identities.

Wake up clients from that disconnected zombie state by shifting focus from an individual's sense of personal identity in the here-and-now to thinking about the larger landscape of his life: invite him to ask himself what he really cares about, how does he want to connect with others, what's going to be most meaningful to him to lead life in a way that makes him happy?

# Getting in Tune with Flow States

The most productive coaching sessions happen when client and coach can access the client's *flow state,* where the client recognises how he can operate at his best. Until you tap into that flow state, your time with a client is purely task-focused and logical, lacking the creative dialogue between coach and client essential for real transformation to begin for the client.

In a flow state, people connect with what they really care about – their passions and ultimately their purpose (see the following section 'Recognising Your Life Purpose'). Being in a flow state is as if your body is on auto-pilot, unconsciously knowing exactly where it's going and not having to think or worry about anything; you just take off and get on with life in the moment. Think of Tom Hanks in the film *Forrest Gump* when he begins to run and then keeps on running right across America with grace and ease. Just as long-distance runners gets into a state of flow, the experience of flow brings a sense of easy movement right through your body and mind. You feel engaged, supple, quick and flexible.

Often you can detect a client's flow state by its absence rather than its presence. When a client isn't in a flow state, something is interfering. This interference may be linked to skills; when some people face challenges that that they don't feel competent to handle, they experience anxiety, and the flow state can't happen. By contrast, when people's skill levels exceed the challenge, they may feel bored and disconnected. Think of the flow state as the space in which your clients thrive.

In addition to skill-related issues, your clients may lose the flow state if they're:

✔ Constantly weary or experiencing low energy

✔ Over-anxious about everyday situations

✔ Unfocused in their activities – dabbling in different activities without sticking to anything

By contrast, when clients experience the flow state, they're:

- ✔ Fully absorbed in their activities and extremely focused

- ✔ Ready to carry on with the job in hand because they're having such a good time

- ✔ Alert, content and unselfconscious

## Finding your flow state

Passion is purposeful. You can experience passion as a noisy outward demonstration of what you believe in as well as a quiet internal feeling.

To see passion in action, tune into your own flow state and that of others around you. Notice that people in flow states aren't sitting back and basking passively in the sunshine; they're actively engaged in ways that create the quality of their daily lives. While these people may be working intently, they are also likely to:

- ✔ Feel thankful for the simple pleasures in life

- ✔ Quit the need to try hard at every task in order to impress others or achieve perfect results

- ✔ Make space to think and relax about non-work topics

- ✔ Enjoy what's happening in the moment

Much of coaching involves working on the ways clients go about their everyday lives rather than assigning specific tasks. Think of this as working on clients' ways of being rather than doing. As clients become more tuned into how they operate at their best, most confident self more of the time, the details of what and when they do things fall into place more easily outside of the coaching sessions.

Following are four ways to access the flow state by tuning into the place of being.

### Feeling thankful

When you pay attention to what you're thankful for in life, you can't help but filter out the bad stuff more of the time. This principle is the basis of solutions-focused coaching approaches, or *appreciative enquiry practices,* which identify what's going well and then build on that. Deliberately paying attention to what you have to be thankful for is also the basis for many general meditative practices.

A useful exercise to encourage thankfulness and your awareness of what you're thankful for is to complete a gratitude journal at the end of a day. Make a quick note of what you feel thankful for and review it periodically, especially when you're feeling down. Another good habit is to make a note of what you appreciate about others and share that with them.

### Letting go of trying hard

My colleague Elizabeth Kuhnke, author of *Body Language For Dummies* (Wiley), coaches senior executives on their personal impact and presentations at meetings. To encourage better performance, she recommends that her clients ban the word *try* from their vocabularies. But trying hard is a good thing, right? Not really.

When you try hard to do anything, your face usually forms a grimace and tension builds in your shoulders. Holding this effort in your body prevents your unconscious mind from doing its job of just allowing you to perform at your best because your conscious mind gets tangled up in all those must-try-hard pressures.

When you find yourself trying very hard at something, remember the *Pareto principle,* which states that 80 per cent of results come from 20 per cent of the effort, and that it takes four times the effort to shift the remaining 20 per cent to reach 100 per cent. A good lesson in the cost of perfection!

As a coach, when you try hard to make a session excellent, you can lose touch with staying focused on your client in the moment and thus diminish the quality of the experience for your client.

### Allowing space

The coaching session itself is a fantastic space for a client to think in a relaxed, non-judgemental way – an hour or two of pure peace and indulgence. Indeed, meeting with a coach may be the only time clients get to consider what they want for themselves between other pressures in their lives. Shifting away from the urgent pressing activities to have quiet thinking time is essential to be more effective in any role, whether as mother or chief executive.

Encourage your clients to take time for themselves outside coaching. Clients may say that feels selfish, yet by creating space they refresh and re-energise themselves, which in turn enables them to support others better.

### Enjoying the experience in the moment

You may have heard the saying, 'The past is history. The future's a mystery. The present is a gift – that's why it's called the present.' Being present to your experience in the here and now is a gift to yourself, and a great way to wake up to life.

Strange as it sounds, something good can always be found in any experience, even if it's the anticipation of the end point. Try finding the good in some experience you're really not loving (perhaps the next time you're in the dentist's chair). Decide you can choose to enjoy the experience right now, even if it's just the chance to lie back and have a little snooze and listen to the radio in the background.

Even better, take a five-minute break in the fresh air right now and look at the sky above you. Notice the sounds, sights and feelings of connecting with nature that are always around you, whatever your environment.

## Accessing the flow state

Use the following exercise to access your own flow state or help your clients to access theirs. A client can take away this exercise to work on, although you may ask some of the questions as part of a coaching session. Make copies of the questions, sit with them for a week or two and come back to make a note of whatever comes to mind for you.

No answers are right or wrong. You may like to consider these questions as an extended coaching inquiry over a period of time.

1. **What are you really thankful for in your life?** Some examples may include healthy children, kind colleagues, a reliable car, no major debts, the chance to travel to different parts of the country or world, a comfortable and warm bed, light bulbs and running water. List your examples below:

   _____
   _____
   _____

2. **When and where do you drive yourself hard?** For example, do you set very high standards of tidiness, cleanliness, target achievement or attention to details at work? List your examples below.

   _____
   _____
   _____

   Look over the examples you list above and make a note of where you can let go of trying so hard.

3. **What enables you to feel the greatest sense of spaciousness in your life?** For example, do you have any space to call your own – a spot where you can sit at home or work quietly? Do you walk in the park, woods or by the river? List your examples below:

_____

_____

_____

**4. What stops you being present?** For example, are you worrying about what happened yesterday or what will happen tomorrow? Are you connected to your email when you could be talking to your family? Contrast this with where you really experience being in the moment.

_____

_____

_____

**5. When or where do you really experience being in the moment?** For example, are you able to stop and notice the leaves on the trees, the smell of freshly baked bread, the taste of an orange, the laughter in a colleague's voice, the face of the bus driver, the feel of the ground as you run? List your examples below:

_____

_____

_____

By regularly asking yourself these kinds of questions, you can begin to shift into a flow state more of the time. When you find yourself anxious or overwhelmed, come back to your answers and decide what you need to do to get back into being thankful and enjoying the moment rather than trying too hard.

## Maintaining flow in challenging times

When clients are going though challenging times, they lose their state of flow. They may not want or even be able to talk about what's happening directly, yet a coach with good sensory acuity can notice clues in the client's physiology. Look out for tension in the neck and shoulders, colour change in the neck and face and tightening of the fingers.

NLP recognises that the mind and body are connected (the *mind-body connection*). Indeed, the body is one of the best sources of information about what's going on with a client. For example, a physical health issue may be a symptom of some underlying issue that the client hasn't yet articulated.

James was coaching Clive, the owner of a family-owned construction business, and noticed that Clive had a nervous eye twitch that worsened each time Clive talked about projects that involved his brother. James made an observation to Clive: 'I've seen that your eye twitches a little more when you talk about your brother, and wondered if that's significant?' This gentle comment highlighted the coach's observation and also left the client free to explore that subject or not if it was too painful to talk about. Clive then voiced some worries he had about his brother's capability with financial matters, which in turn opened up Clive's real issues and beliefs that coach and client hadn't addressed in earlier coaching sessions.

Of course, as an NLP coach, James is equipped to work on a topic in a coaching session content-free – that is, without talking about the specific details of a problem . So if Clive has an issue that he doesn't want to talk about, he can just name it 'Problem X' or something similar. James can work with Clive to imagine the outcome for Problem X that he wants and encourage his client to pay extra attention to his body and how it feels when the issue is resolved. James could then invite Clive to consider what needs to happen for his eye to feel relaxed once more and let James know when he has the answer.

As a coach, you can train clients to pay more attention to their physiology, so that they recognise the subtle signals that all is well – or not well. This process encourages a client's unconscious mind to support him.

 If a client consistently seems low and unable to shift from this state with coaching, he may be suffering from a physical illness or depression, in which case suggest seeing a doctor or therapist and put coaching on hold until the client feels stronger. Never push a client to override physical symptoms where the body is offering valuable information.

**Book III**

**Managing and Leading Others**

# Finding the Meaning in Your Work

Perhaps you've heard the story of the three stonemasons.

A man comes along to a building site and asks the stonemasons what they're up to. The first stonemason barely looks up and answers: 'I'm chipping away at the stone with my chisel. I do it all day, every day, and it's been going on for years.'

The second stonemason invites the man to hold the stone figures he's carved and answers: 'I'm making the gargoyles that will go over the main door.'

The third stonemason stands up, smiles and gestures expansively before answering: 'I'm building a cathedral for the glorification of God and for people to enjoy for generations to come. It's going to be truly magnificent.'

Which of the three has found meaning in his work?

In any job, stronger motivation comes when you have a sense of doing something worthwhile, something that adds value for others and makes good use of your time and talents. The third stonemason has connected with a sense of meaning.

## *Seeking value while questing constantly*

The job that engages someone today may not feel fulfilling tomorrow or satisfy an individual's desire to grow and develop. As a coach, your role involves enabling your clients to get clarity about their desires; the more you connect them to find the value in what they do, the happier they'll be jumping out of bed on a Monday morning, yelling 'Yippee, it's Monday!'.

Elements of any job can become tedious and repetitive, but one question to consider about any job is: 'How does the work I do make a difference to other people, or connect with what matters most to me?'

The hairdresser cutting the tenth customer's hair in one day can realise she's not just cutting hair, but also boosting her client's confidence. The financial services salesman filling in more regulatory papers eases the retirement worries of an aging couple when he finds the best pension product for them.

As you work with your clients, hold on to the thread that links one person in the system to another in order to see the benefits. As your clients make adjustments in their daily habits, they can focus their efforts where they have the greatest impact, choosing to do more of one thing and less of another.

## *Making sense of the tough times*

Any work has its ups and downs. You experience times when you don't feel like getting out of bed to face difficult tasks. Some days, major upsets strike – when you have to accept the death of a colleague, lose a major client, face a complete computer meltdown, lose inventory in a flood or fire, lay off staff or say goodbye to your dream job or business.

In such circumstances, staying connected with the passion that originally brought you to your work becomes paramount.

When husband and wife team Andrea and Jonathan realised their mail-order clothing business needed to be wound up, they worked with an NLP coach with an agenda to minimise their financial losses, find new jobs and keep their marriage supportive through the sale. The coach encouraged Andrea and Jonathan to come up with a list of all their positive achievements to take forward in the next chapters of their lives. These achievements included recognising:

✔ All the skills they'd developed and gained

✔ How they stuck to their core values

✔ Benefits they provided to all their employees, suppliers and customers

✔ The strength of their commitment to each other

Their coach also encouraged them to take time to mourn the things they were going to miss and to have a celebration party to thank those who worked with them as acts of closure. Photographs from the party later acted as an *anchor* or trigger to remember all the goodwill and fun they'd enjoyed during the years in business.

Through the closure process, Andrea and Jonathan came to realise that the strength of their passion for the business created a sense of meaning for other people's lives as well as their own. They were determined to keep the same energy alive in their next career moves. They also experienced a sense of relief when they acknowledged that their business had been a huge drain on their resources; they chose to revel in their new freedom from financial worries.

# Recognising Your Life Purpose

As a coach, you owe it to your clients to invite them to ask the big questions of life, including 'Why am I here?', 'What's my life about?' and 'What's my legacy?' as well as the more immediate and practical ones such as 'What shall I work on today?' and 'Is this exhibition worth attending?'

Larger self questions like 'What are you?' or 'Who are you becoming?' take your clients into the realm of questioning their identities and exploring how identity in turn relates to life purpose. You're asking clients to figure out how identity relates to the larger systems and communities in which they live. You're inviting clients to grow stronger and more powerful – just as an oak tree that extends deeper roots while reaching for the sky. These questions stretch your clients to the highest level of psychologist Abraham Maslow's famous hierarchy of human needs – the level of *self-actualisation*, where you realise your true potential in life.

**Book III**

**Managing and Leading Others**

## Noticing what energises you when the going gets tough

Life events have an uncanny way of making you re-evaluate your direction and connecting you with a stronger sense of purpose. Having a strong sense of purpose can support you through the toughest times in life, enabling you to shift beyond the anxiety or discomfort of your current situation and take a longer term view.

Madeline, a doctor whose husband died unexpectedly of a viral infection, told me about the lack of direction she was experiencing: 'I've lost my sense of purpose. My whole life was tied into being his wife. Now I'm a widow and I don't know how to behave any more.' Notice in Madeline's language that she has a new unwanted *identity* as a widow rather than her familiar role as a wife. As a wife, she knew how husband, family and colleagues expected her to behave, what was important to her and how her work fitted with the rest of her life. As a widow, she suddenly found herself in new territory, unskilled and unsure of herself, and wanted to re-establish her sense of being on the right track.

Clearly Madeline needed time and space to mourn the loss of her beloved husband, yet as a bright and determined woman, she also wanted to carve out a clear route for herself rather than dwell on her grief. We looked at the identity she wanted and how that might take shape over a period of time, without putting her under unnecessary pressure to find her new identity quickly.

Madeline eventually realised that she wanted to be a healer for less privileged communities. She decided that she'd gone into medicine originally to make a significant difference in the world. That dream had been realised only partially through her work, and she'd found her purpose more satisfying as wife and mother. Now that her children were grown, she decided to shift her work away from the general practice that no longer fired her with enthusiasm and move towards international relief programmes that filled her deeper need to connect with poorer communities.

Her first step on this journey was to contact one of her patients and volunteer her services in a local programme that supported an orphanage in India. Focusing on a short-term commitment was a safe stepping-stone, an opportunity to see how she fared as she put her new identity to the test.

## Finding and using your passion: the DASE model

You can access your passion – or help clients access theirs – by looking at the peaks or troughs of experience. In my DASE model (explored more fully in my book *Live Life, Love Work*, also published by Wiley), you explore passion from the extremes of what pleases you and what makes you mad by tapping into strong emotional states of delight (D), anger (A), sadness (S) and ecstasy (E). I use this tool to coach people to get back in touch with emotive issues that really fire up their passion. In person, the client can talk you through experiences from the past, yet he can also use the DASE model for personal reflection in preparation for a coaching session.

1. **Divide a piece of paper into four quadrants with pen or pencil.** Label the four areas Delighted, Ecstatic, Sad and Angry.

2. **Consider each quadrant on the page.** Ask yourself the following questions and make note of specific situations and experiences where your emotions were so heightened that you can still recall them.

   - **Delighted:** When were you delighted, experiencing a gentle sense of joy and feeling blessed with life? Consider times when you noticed kindness and gratitude that stopped you in your tracks.

   - **Angry:** When have you been angry or disgusted? Consider times when you were ready to fight for your rights or a cause dear to your heart.

   - **Sad:** When have you been sad, disappointed and low? What moves you to gloom and that sense of wanting to give up and hide under the duvet away from the world?

   - **Ecstatic:** When have you been *ecstatic*, experiencing the peak of exuberance and well-being? What really brings you alive and makes you jump up and down with excitement and sing from the rooftops?

3. **Review everything you wrote on your page.** Which experiences and episodes do you consider the best of times? The worst of times? Which moments stand out as really firing up your passion?

4. **Look for themes in your experiences.** For example, notice what you do when you stand up for what you care about, which in turn makes a difference for others. What happens when you get emotional? What impact does it have on your behaviour and that of those around you?

5. **Consider your sense of who you are during your most passionate and satisfying moments.** If you were to identify yourself with a role or animal, what would it be? Are you naturally a hunter or tiger, a nest builder or squirrel? Allow this role to inform your answers to activities in the following section, which focuses on defining purpose.

**Book III**

**Managing and Leading Others**

## *Defining purpose in your own words*

Successful organisations define their business purpose, their rationale for existing, as part of business planning. They often create and share great statements about their vision such as:

- ✔ 'To be the world's best quick service restaurant experience … so that we make every customer in every restaurant smile.' *McDonald's.*

- ✔ 'To create happiness by providing the finest in entertainment for people of all ages, everywhere.' *Disney.*

- ✔ 'Bringing the best to everyone we touch.' *Estée Lauder.*

Yet if you turn to a friend and say: 'What's your purpose?' or 'Why do you exist?', you're most likely to be met by a blank stare and offered a cup of tea and the chance to sit down. You can almost see the thought bubble emerge: 'Is my friend going mad?'

Not many people give much consideration to their purpose beyond saying they'd like to make a difference or help others. But you can define your personal purpose, and, in doing so, create a greater sense of meaning and direction for your life. Such meaning serves you on the days when life feels tough because you have a reason to get out of bed in the morning knowing that you can do something worthwhile.

As I explore in Book III Chapter 3, your values unconsciously drive you in a purposeful way to make an impact in the world, whether that's in bringing up healthy and happy children or taking on global peace negotiations. In the coaching context, invite clients to explore the question of their personal purpose.

The following exercise can also help you or your clients with the process of exploring and defining personal purpose.

1. **Write a statement of life purpose.** Capture your thoughts in a simple sentence that begins by focusing on your *identity*, for example:

   - *I am someone who . . .*

   - *I am a healer . . .*

   - *I am a light . . .*

   - *I'm a mum . . .*

   - *I'm a carer . . .*

   Notice that your identity may be metaphorical (as in a light or a healer) as well as real (mum, carer or other role).

2. **Add a verb and an object to your sentence that further describe what you do.** For example:

   - *I'm a polisher who shapes human gems . . .*

   - *I'm an IT whiz who designs technology . . .*

   - *I'm a waste-disposal expert who protects the environment . . .*

   - *I'm a healer of animals who helps them recover from illness and injury . . .*

3. **Add a few words to connect your identity and actions with people, places or situations.** Choose words that extend beyond yourself and the present time. Here are examples of *connection statements*.

> • *I'm a conductor who creates harmony and understanding in schools.*
>
> • *I'm a marketer who designs phone services that enable non-technical people to communicate with anyone they want.*
>
> • *I'm a homemaker who creates a welcoming environment where family and guests can recharge their batteries.*

When you're happy with your statement, put it in a place where you can see it each day – on your desk, your bathroom mirror, your personal organiser or the fridge door. You may want to add it to your business card or email signature.

# Building a Shared Vision

One person's passion creates momentum in a project or a career. Multiply that passion up into a family, team, group, organisation or nation, and it can become extraordinarily infectious and a powerful agent for change. Great organisations, whatever their size, combine and harness individuals talents in ways that acknowledge individual contribution as part of greater successes.

You can guide clients to build visions and mission statements, strategies and plans that:

✔ State core beliefs and values

✔ Recognise the organisation's contribution to employees, customers, clients, the public and other stakeholders

✔ Share the strategic direction that the organisation is heading in

✔ Present a plan of action for how to implement the vision, using the organisation's talents and resources

Why do some visions remain just a loose, intangible concept while others create enthusiastic followers who make them happen? Although many factors affect business success, great visions engage and motivate people when they incorporate a sense of passion and purpose that enables everyone to access their own passion and purpose. (Great vision statements are also likely to engage people by adopting sensory-specific language.

 Vision statements aren't limited to the business world. What would it be like to have a family vision statement or one for your school or club that included a sense of passion, values and purpose? Consider the following vision statements:

- ✔ **For a family:** To truly look out for each other in this family, listen and feel a depth of love and kindness in everything we think, do and say, whether we are physically together or far apart.

- ✔ **For a school:** To come to school to share knowledge with a passion that can be seen and heard in all our activities every single day, and which ultimately makes a difference in the world.

- ✔ **For a club:** To create an environment where everyone has a valuable part to play and feels better every time each member visits, gaining new energy to further inspire others.

Such vision statements provide a foundation of shared commitment to all the members of the group; an implicit message of what you stand for and what makes you come together.

## Merging different agendas

Ultimately, dreams and visions without coordinated actions remain just charming notions or frustrating ideals that no one ever succeeds in attaining. (See Book IV Chapter 2 for the NLP Disney strategy to coach a dream into reality.) The following section explores ways to assemble visions that are inspiring and achievable.

### Getting bigger, getting smaller: Chunking

As a coach, you need to work with your clients at different levels at different times to make grand abstract visions achievable on an everyday basis.

NLP took the idea of *chunking* from the world of IT, in which complex programs are broken into sequences, sub-sequences, lines and ultimately bits and bytes. NLP coaches talk about *chunking up* to consider big-picture information at a conceptual level and *chunking down* to tackle the details of implementing any decision.

The concept of chunking is particularly useful when people come together to implement any programme and arrive with different skills, needs and agendas. In agreeing direction and priorities for any collaborative activity or business endeavour, people need to be able to connect with the shared vision as well as recognise the detailed work beneath it.

Coaches working with teams encourage and support the natural diversity that exists within these groups to harness a mix of abilities and needs to create outcomes that the teams are looking for.

In order to steer diverse people into action, spend time building relationships and recognising each other's talents. Being able to coach others to acknowledge and listen to one another can be extremely useful. After individuals recognise their own and others' talents, they can work together to build a shared agenda by formulating their goals as well-formed outcomes. (See Book IV Chapter 2 for more on goal-setting and Book III Chapter 7 for more on chunking.)

### Confessing your strengths

The following activity encourages individuals to acknowledge their strengths – and for others in the group to acknowledge them as well. This activity is well-suited to teams, committees, small businesses and departments where people have little knowledge of each other and want to bond more closely. Try the following exercise to get a group sharing, listening and acknowledging each other.

1. **Divide the group into trios, each with a Person A, Person B and Person C.**

2. **Ask Person A to answer the question 'In what ways am I amazing?'**

3. **Person A confesses his talents and skills to Persons B and C.**

   Give Person A ample time to talk about his capabilities and share specific examples and stories.

4. **Persons B and C listen to Person A and encourage him not to be modest.**

   Persons B and C may even want to extol Person A's virtues confidently if he's naturally reticent.

5. **Person B and C make suggestions as to how Person A's talents can be used to good effect in the current group and area of focus.**

6. **The members of the trio switch positions, until each has had a turn confessing their strengths to the group.**

7. **After each member confesses his talents, the trio captures their ideas in writing.**

   In the end, each team member should have at least three areas of excellence and an outline of how to use these areas of excellence in practice to further the team agenda.

8. **Finally, bring each trio together with the rest of the group to look at the overall talents, acknowledge them and see how they can be put to good use in a practical way on the work ahead.**

**Book III**

**Managing and Leading Others**

## Knowing when to bend and when to stay tough

Passion and purpose are wonderful things, but they can bring with them a mental toughness that can verge on rigidity, stubbornness and even blinkered obsession at times. If you're too focused on what you want for yourself, you can lose touch with what other people want along the way. An inability to see others' views and needs can lead to a loss of other things that are important to you. (Try perceptual positions exercise in Book III Chapter 5 if this is the case.)

Fortunately some fundamental NLP principles can assist passionate people to navigate differences of opinion and overcome blind spots. As a coach, you can help passionate clients to develop greater rapport with other people by working on their interpersonal skills in terms of:

- ✔ **Behavioural flexibility.** NLP asserts that the person with the most flexibility in a system is the most effective. *Flexibility* means being able to do something different when what you're currently doing isn't working. As a coach, brainstorm some alternatives with your clients to come at problems more creatively. Invite them to take different *perceptual positions* with others. (I explore perceptual positions in Book III Chapter 5.)

- ✔ **Pacing and leading others.** NLP advises us to pace, pace and pace again *before* you lead. Pacing is about increasing your listening skills. You can only lead someone to your agenda when you first meet them in their map of the world. The power of listening to others' passions as well as your own can never be overrated.

Often people come to coaching after they realise that life shouldn't be so tough and that they want to make life easier. Finding the antidote to the living-dead state in which people are detached and exhausted isn't necessarily about getting more sleep; it's about becoming wholehearted about life. By enabling your clients to reconnect with a sense of passion and purpose, you can help them get back on track to the rich and rewarding lives they deserve – and make sure that they have lots of fun on the way.

# Chapter 3

# Tuning into Values

**S**ome of the biggest questions you can ask yourself in life centre on values. What do you stand for? What's most important to you? What keeps you awake at night? What enables you to sleep peacefully? What do you really want?

Values bring energy and direction; they're at the core of what makes an individual tick. When people deeply understand their values, they can create a way of operating in the world that leads them to purpose and meaning. When people live according to their innermost values, they feel satisfied that they are being true to their identities, genuinely being who they are. By contrast, when people's values are not being met, for whatever reason, they feel uneasy.

Values can change over time, depending on your experiences. People often come to coaching at moments of transition, perhaps from one job to another, as well as from one cluster of values to a revised cluster.

In this chapter, you look at how you can enable your clients to clarify their core values. They then can make whatever adjustments are necessary to honour those values in their daily lives. Acting based on values is a hugely significant piece of personal development work that you can do with a client. Together you're finding a compass for the future direction of someone's life and happiness.

## Knowing What's Important

The act of identifying your core values serves as the catalyst to shift beyond what you think you *ought to do* towards operating on the basis of what you truly *want to do*. Core values are the fundamental drivers behind your decisions and actions, which I refer to as *end values* in this chapter.

## Separating must-haves from shoulds

Most people live more in their heads than in the outside world of events. The human mind is a tricky place, filled with thoughts, gremlins and assorted voices that buzz around.

The way you interpret an event and give it meaning results in pleasure or pain. For example, when a person you care for doesn't call, you can choose how to react. Are you happy because he may be busy and enjoying himself – or sad because he's probably forgotten you? Do you think a person should or ought to behave in a particular way?

The NLP Meta Model of language states that you are continually filtering information and making assumptions using the patterns of distortion, generalisation and deletion.

In coaching, you're likely to hear clients say, 'My boss says I *should do* X' or 'My boyfriend thinks I *ought to* do Y.' The Meta Model calls these types of generalisation patterns *the modal operators of necessity*. The clients' lives seem dictated by other forces rather than the clients' own free will.

While the boss or a dear one may well have your client's best interests at heart, clients become disempowered when they always act from the position of doing what they think they ought to or should do, rather than what they really want to. Similarly, they are disempowering others by continually pushing their own interpretation of shoulds and oughts rather than giving other people freedom to decide for themselves.

As an NLP coach, tune your ears to listen for modal operators and counter the statements, for example, with 'What would happen if you didn't do this?' or 'What other choices exist here?' Push your clients to make reasoned choices.

Values work enables people to make better decisions based on what is most important to them – based on must-haves rather than shoulds. When clients call the tune themselves, they shift to a place of new possibilities. After you have clarity on values, you understand why you want to act in a certain way. The *should* and *ought to* switches to *want* and *choose*. You may still do what someone else requests of you, but when you do it from a place of choice, the internal battle ceases.

## Separating means values and end values

In working with clients to identify values, aim to distinguish between *means values*, the things that are important, yet are a means to an end, and *end values,* which are the absolute core bedrock things that need to be in place.

The following list illustrates the difference between means and end values:

✔ Money, home and work are all examples of means values.

✔ Money can create end values of security, freedom, peace and fun.

✔ Home can provide end values of safety, space and joy.

✔ Work can give end values of purpose, energy and freedom.

You generally experience end values as feelings: love, peace, freedom, self-worth, confidence, power, honesty, knowledge and joy. All are concepts that you can't touch, but you know intuitively when you have them and when you don't.

## *Focusing on core values*

The following exercise takes you through the process of establishing your initial values list. This exercise can be eye-opening for both coaches and clients.

1. **On a blank piece of paper, write down a list of your values.**

   Your answers to the following questions can help reveal values:

   - What is important to you?

   - What do you need in your life?

   - What's so critical to who you are that you'd almost forget to mention it?

   Table 3-1 gives you a selection of words to start the values conversation, but feel free to find the words that are most meaningful to you. Invite your clients to add key words to this list.

2. **After you have a list of about 12 to 15 values, see how they group and overlap; refine the values list to no more than nine items.**

   Some words may have a similar enough meaning that you can count them as one value, such as integrity/ honesty or purpose/direction.

3. **Take each word in turn and ask 'What does this value give me?'**

   Keep asking the question until you're convinced you've arrived at an *end value* – that point at which you know you (or your client) have reached a fundamental need.

   A client, Tony, first answered that his motorbike was very important to him. When his coach asked, 'What does that motorbike give you?', he replied, 'Access to the open road.' When his coach drilled further by asking, 'And when you have access to the open road, what does that give you?' Tony answered, 'It's all about *freedom*.' Freedom is Tony's end value and his prized motorbike delivers it.

**Book III**

**Managing and Leading Others**

4. **Capture this fully revised values list as the important building block for future planning, goal-setting and decision-making activities.**

Some people like to keep the list on the wall, others in their diaries or mobile phones. Find somewhere easily accessible to keep it so you can refer to it often.

| Table 3-1 | Values Words | |
|---|---|---|
| Achievement | Freedom | Peace |
| Adventure | Friendship | Pleasure |
| Affection | Fun | Power |
| Authenticity | Growth | Purpose |
| Balance | Harmony | Recognition |
| Change | Helpfulness | Relationship |
| Closeness | Honesty | Respect |
| Community | Independence | Security |
| Connection | Innovation | Service |
| Contribution | Integrity | Spirituality |
| Creativity | Learning | Success |
| Discipline | Love | Teamwork |
| Energy | Loyalty | Trus |
| Family | Order | Wealth |

# Setting Priorities

After you identify your core values (see the earlier section 'Focusing on core values'), you have a blueprint to guide the process of setting priorities and taking action.

Although this chapter's focus is an individual's values, the principles of identifying values and living them also applies to a team or larger organisation in the same way. See Book III Chapter 5 for more on coaching teams.

## Allowing time to refine values

Two people may have the same set of values, yet behave in very different ways. For this reason, you need to understand how the values translate into behaviour in everyday life and where your priorities lie.

Ollie talked about a disagreement within his family when his son and daughter-in-law were having financial problems. The daughter-in-law accused Ollie of not loving his son because he wouldn't pay his debts. Ollie argued that it was *because* he loved his son that he didn't bail him out financially. Ollie believed he was demonstrating tough love by showing his son that he needed to take responsibility for his spending. Both Ollie and the daughter-in-law were acting from positions of love, yet behaving in different ways.

### Establishing evidence of a value

You and your colleague may both say that learning is important to you. Yet when questioned, one of you may say that learning is about getting a formal qualification, while the other says that learning is about putting knowledge into practice. So who's right? Actually both of you are! Interpreting a value has no right or wrong answer.

Do the following exercise to become more specific as to *how* you know that you are honouring a value in your own way. Take each value that you identified in the earlier section 'Focusing on core values' and ask your client the following questions:

- ✔ What specifically does [this value] mean to you?
- ✔ How will you know when you've got it?
- ✔ What will you see, hear and feel?
- ✔ How will you behave?

**Book III**

**Managing and Leading Others**

After your clients know how they live specific values personally, you can also explore with them how the key people they connect with may have the same value, yet express it in a different way. Invite them to consider their key stakeholders (see Book III Chapter 5) and the values that are important to each of them.

### Working towards a hierarchy

Not all values are equally important, and often something must be missing in life before you sit up and pay attention to its importance. For instance, if your health takes a tumble, getting well moves up your priority list. If carving out a career is most important to you, wooing a partner may go on the back burner.

A natural tension exists between some values. Furthermore, a person's hierarchy of values changes according to current circumstances. The poet David Whyte has a useful way of thinking about these tensions and changes. Whyte suggests that three core relationships you engage in are with yourself, with a significant other and with work (or purposeful activity). Maintaining all three relationships is like having three marriages simultaneously (hence the title of his book *The Three Marriages*). Each relationship is dear, and you don't want to be forced into either/or decisions placing one ahead of another. Ideally, you want strong relationships in each of the three spheres.

Invite your client to place each value in order of importance and create a hierarchy of values. Write each value on a card or sticky note and then move the values around on a flat surface. Creating linear lists proves challenging to more options-oriented clients! Use a form like Table 3-2 to list your hierarchy of values.

| Table 3-2 | Prioritised List of Values |
|---|---|
| *Order of Priority* | *Value* |
| 1 | |
| 2 | |
| 3 | |
| 4 | |
| 5 | |
| 6 | |
| 7 | |
| 8 | |
| 9 | |

## Assessing values-based decisions

Values need to be lived every day, so small decisions and bigger ones must fit with values, otherwise the client feels a sense of unease. After clients have articulated a list of values, ask them to score themselves as to how they're living their values from Table 3-2. Take each in turn and invite them to give a score from 0 (low) to 10 (high) to determine how well they're doing. When they are facing a major decision such as a job change, home move or investment of time or money, ask them to look at their list of values and how this decision fits – or doesn't – with the list.

Chantal runs a marketing consultancy that includes several coaching organisations amongst its clients. She recounts how quite early in her business set-up she met someone running a coaching business who was looking for copywriting services. When explaining his products, the man said that he had no real belief in the work; his clients served as the route for him to create wealth. This statement didn't sit well with Chantal, and she realised the vital role values play in how she attracts clients.

> *For me, this man had no integrity, and I knew I couldn't work with him. Since then, I decided only to work with clients when our values are a good fit, and that's meant that during the ten years running this business I've attracted like-minded clients who are fun to work with.*

Trust is another core value that influences the way Chantal manages her staff and suppliers. She gives a clear brief with support and then trusts people to get on with the work. 'I assume people are trustworthy, and guess what? People seldom let me down. I'm honest with people, and they are honest with me.'

## Responding to violated values

Not meeting values to your standards can cause huge emotional conflicts, both internally and with other people. For example, not everybody you come across interprets honesty in the same way. Invite your client to tell you about her most uncomfortable moments, the depths of despair, and you can be sure that her values will have been violated. Ask her to tell you briefly about a bad situation and what she learnt from that about what is most important to her. In this way, you get greater clarity on her most important values and how they may get violated unless your client takes action for change.

Andrew came for coaching feeling stressed out by his role in a recruitment agency. He'd taken the job knowing that it would be unsocial hours and hard work, yet he was keen to develop new skills and to carve out a good living for himself. As he explored his values, he found that two essentials for him to feel happy were missing.

The first was fun. Andrew's colleagues were deadly serious and unsociable, and he'd come from an office where he enjoyed camaraderie and banter. Andrew realised he may not get his fix of fun in the same way at work any more, so he had to adapt to make his own fun. He began compiling funny tales based on his colleagues' quirks to amuse himself.

However, the biggest conflict of values came when Andrew realised his boss Malcolm was dishonest and had no remorse about his bad behaviour. Andrew's value for honesty amongst colleagues felt violated. Andrew felt increasingly uncomfortable about the complete lies his boss happily told about progress on clients' projects. Crunch-time came when Andrew heard his boss dishonestly promising performance bonuses for the whole team and then setting up targets that were impossible to meet. Malcolm's bullying tactics began to take their toll, depressing the work atmosphere even further.

By planning out some difficult and challenging conversations with his boss in coaching, Andrew decided his future lay in finding a more honest organisation to work with. He realised that Malcolm's bosses wouldn't act against him, so Andrew negotiated a fair severance package.

# Keeping Values Alive Every Day

An exercise in revealing values isn't a one-off activity. To feel happy means remaining alert to all the factors that are important to you and noticing what's changing.

When something just doesn't feel right, go back to your list of core values and check whether something's slipped out of alignment or if a hidden value is coming to the fore.

## Assessing whether you're walking the talk

Most coaching programmes with a client include work on values at the intake phase . As a coach, you're in a position to uphold a client's values, just as you uphold a client's overall goals and agenda.

When a client is struggling with a problem, simply ask, 'What would happen if you brought more X to the situation?' The X could be any value that the client has expressed, from joy to simplicity to energy. Another question to explore is: 'How does what you're saying here fit with your values?'

As an exercise in self-awareness, create structures to remind your clients to pay attention to their values from day to day and week to week. An example may be to get them to review how they lived their values during the day each evening, and decide what they'd like to have happen tomorrow. By developing these reflective habits, your clients take new understandings forward from coaching and let this information permeate their everyday lives.

## Dreaming bigger and better

Most of this chapter looks at values as general guiding principles to help direction. What about situations where things are already working pretty smoothly? You can also use values to explore bigger dreams and shift from what my own coach calls the 'present perfect to future perfect'.

NLP offers the as-if way of thinking to encourage bigger dreams. Step into an imaginary future as if you're already there. Explore your dream job, dream life, dream relationship or dream living environment.

The following exercise encourages clients to dream as if anything were possible. Try it on for yourself, too.

1. **Step into the future.**

   Choose a specific timeframe – six months from now, five years or whatever seems most appropriate. Place a marker on the floor and physically step into the space.

2. **Pick a context for your vision of the future.**

   Your context can be the whole of your life, or a specific aspect, such as your work or your leisure pursuits.

3. **Reassure the client that she can always honour her values and invite her to creatively explore what might make the future even more perfect than today.**

   Allow plenty of time and space for this exploration. Gently gather answers to the following questions:

   - What would you like more of?

   - What do you want less of?

   - What would you like to be best known for?

   - In an ideal world, what does your typical week look like?

   - What is most gratifying to you about the choices you've made?

**Book III**

**Managing and Leading Others**

- To what do you attribute your success in achieving exactly what you want?

- What's absolutely essential that you retain?

- In your wildest dream, what would you really like to happen?

4. **The final step is to take action based on what the client's discovered.**

Invite her to consider:

- Now that you've had time to explore, what is one first step for today that will impact on the future?

- What will you do that leads you to your dream?

# Chapter 4

# Managing Emotional States

*A*t last, people within organisations are beginning to be able to talk about emotions at work rather than trying (and often failing) to leave them in the car park. Leaders know that people need to be emotionally intelligent as well as intellectually or technically strong. Emotional intelligence involves the skill of tuning into your own emotions and those of people around you.

In this chapter, we explore emotional states and how you can encourage your clients to anchor positive states and deal with pesky gremlins who can interfere with people's resourcefulness. We also delve into dealing with fear and improving confidence.

## Saying Hello to Emotional States

The four core emotions of anger, joy, sadness and fear can each trigger an *emotional state*. An emotional state encompasses thoughts, feelings and sensations in the body. *State* describes a way of being, whether that's unhappy or peaceful, terrified or elated. In coaching, you encourage your clients to pay attention to emotional states, taking it as valuable information about what's going on for them at a deep level. For example, if someone's waking up at night in a hot sweat and going over conversations, she's clearly anxious about something that would be useful to explore. Emotions drive action and affect health; they direct attention and behaviour. If you're feeling sad or fearful, the emotion may well drive you to do something that you wouldn't otherwise consider doing.

Beware of labelling emotions as good or bad; they are what you feel in the moment and you need to examine where they lead you. For example, a touch of angry resentment may be what someone needs in order to kick-start a change he's been avoiding. By contrast, pure joy may lead someone else to take a decision with rose-tinted specs on that he later regrets.

Persistent negative emotions take their toll on clients, draining energy and creating unhealthy levels of stress. If somebody is persistently angry or sad, advise him to discuss this with hisr doctor who may refer him for therapeutic work or give medication.

Emotional ups and downs are natural; they show that you're just human. Some people love to ride through life on an emotional roller-coaster where their moods are unpredictable to others, only feeling alive at the extremes, while others prefer a steadier approach. While moods and states are similar, a state is more enduring than a mood. States are highly infectious, affecting your relationships, performance and health.

# Changing Emotional States

The good news about states is that you can change state when you feel that doing so is appropriate. In particular, the following sections cover the classic NLP approach known as *anchoring*, which enables you to access the precise states that serve you best, regardless of what's happening in the world around you.

## Checking the baseline state

To change state, you need to first tune into your *baseline state*, which is your normal, most familiar way of going through the day.

The following self-awareness exercise helps clients capture information about their baseline state and note how it shifts throughout the day.

1. **Have your client check in with himself for seven days, noting feelings at morning, noon and night.**

   Your clients may choose to write down the baseline state in words on a chart, put a colour code in his diary, drop pebbles in different jars, affix coloured sticky notes to a calendar or draw symbols such as smiley and sad faces. Be as creative as you like in co-creating this bank of information.

2. **After gathering enough information, analyse the data.**

   Have your client review the data himself prior to session so that he can answer the following:

   - What specific activities affect his baseline states for better and worse?

   - How have his states triggered behaviour?

   - What effects do various people or situations have on his states?

   - When is he at his best and his worst on a regular basis?

3. **At a subsequent session, ask questions about the client's observations and what the client might *want* to have happen differently in future.**

   If he identified that he regularly feels glum, for example, then the coaching could focus on ways to rise above that rather lonely place. Or if he finds that certain activities make him feel really good, he may want to consider how to allocate more time to those things.

4. **Design actions together that give the client the opportunity to try on new ways of behaving and being.**

   Perhaps he sets his intention to celebrate successes as he goes along and have more fun.

When clients are aware of their natural baseline states, they have a reference point from which they can consciously change how they operate. In the next section, I explore changing states through the process of anchoring.

**Book III**

**Managing and Leading Others**

## Anchoring positive states

An *anchor* is an external stimulus that triggers a particular inner state or response. You respond to anchors all the time; you know to check your phone when you hear a text message alert or to head to the kitchen when you smell dinner cooking. You may have inadvertently set negative anchors like shouting or scowling when something displeases you. You've stored these stimuli and responses in your memory bank over a period of time as you develop habits.

Memories offer powerful resources to trigger a positive shift in emotional state, and NLP taps into these with anchoring. Various NLP techniques enable you to set an anchor to create a particular state. Most usually, NLP coaches encourage clients to set an anchor such as a distinctive hand movement to trigger a particular state. Some clients prefer to use sounds and images as anchors.

The following Circle of Excellence exercise works by anchoring a positive experience enjoyed in one context to a hand movement. After an experience is anchored, clients can then fire off this anchor to change state when they're in challenging situations.

Describe the following steps and anchoring process to clients before going through the actual steps. You may want to show clients a few hand movements commonly used in anchoring.

Suggested things to say to the client throughout the following steps appear in italics.

1. **Invite the client to describe a situation that he finds challenging and where he'd like to change his emotional state.**

   *Think of the situation in which you'd like to be different and imagine a circle on the ground in front of you about one metre in diameter.*

   This imaginary circle is the client's Circle of Excellence.

2. **Stand outside the circle with the client and have him identify the positive state he wants to create.**

   *Identify your best state. Tell me what that state is in your own words.*

   Allow time for the client to describe the positive state. All you're looking for here is a couple of sentences of description or some key words.

3. **Have the client experience the positive state again.**

   *Remember a time when you were* [repeat back the client's descriptive words] . . . *Go back to it strongly . . . See what you saw then. Hear what you heard.*

   Ask the client to step inside the circle and experience the positive state even more vividly.

   *Re-live that experience. Make it vivid; be there in it with all your senses. Feel what your hands are doing. Now, hold or* anchor *that state with a hand movement at the point when the memory is most vivid.*

   After the client anchors the experience, ask him to step outside the circle.

4. **Repeat the exercise with a second experience of a positive state, anchoring the most vivid experience of the feeling with the same hand motion.**

5. **Invite the client to describe the time in the future when he wants to access this state.**

6. **After identifying the future event, ask the client to step inside the circle again as if stepping into the actual event and do the anchored hand motion.**

   *With your hand in your anchored position, move into the circle. See, hear and feel how the experience can be for you now.*

   Give the client time to enjoy and integrate the feeling of the positive state.

7. **After the client experiences the positive step, ask him to step back out of the circle.**

   *Relax . . . you've got it!*

Encourage clients to practise using this hand movement a few times between coaching sessions to remind themselves of the technique.

## Allowing negative states to slide away

Historically, the annual performance evaluations that managers gave to their subordinates dwelled on negatives, utilising a 'things you could do better' approach. Fortunately, this attitude is starting to change as more managers become trained in coaching and understand that personal transformation happens when you champion other people's strengths and successes in order to harness their potential.

As people are encouraged to pay more attention to what they're good at, the negatives slip away. Clients shift into *flow states*, finding a sense of ease and self-confidence. (Read more on flow states in Book III Chapter 2.)

When you're working with teams, the best scenario is to acknowledge and celebrate the strengths of individuals and the diverse qualities each team member brings. The power of the team is more than the sum of the individuals in it. As you notice what's working, the negatives slide away and the positive emotional connections grow.

The following exercise is based on one used by US coach Jan Elfline in her master classes. We present the exercise as a team activity, but you can adapt it for an individual coaching session by inviting your clients to talk through or write about their successes.

1. **Ask each member of the team to privately identify three personal successes and three business successes and make a brief note of them. Have them prepare to be interviewed about the successes.**

2. **Have each team member interview colleagues, asking them to share one success.**

   Have each team member interview up to six colleagues. If the team is six individuals or smaller, allow everyone to share one example each in a series of rounds.

3. **Complete six rounds of interviews, allowing each team member to share one story per round.**

   Each person should tell a story only once.

4. **Reconvene in a circle and highlight the successes of each team member.**

   Go round the group, team member by team member, and have others share a success story that relates to that person.

# Tackling Interference from Gremlins

*Gremlins* are the aspects of people's identities that may get in the way of their natural resourcefulness by playing havoc with their emotional states. Gremlins hold you back from action or criticise what you do. They're like little pesky goblins who dance around and make mischief, nagging at your clients and amplifying their insecurities.

Gremlins play on your emotions in a negative way and take on various forms. The following sections look at three examples of gremlins that often pop up.

- **The peacekeeper gremlin** avoids confrontation at any cost.
- **The perfectionist gremlin** is impossible to please because perfection is unattainable.
- **The procrastinator gremlin** wants to put off today's task until tomorrow.

 Many other gremlins are out there, so keep watch for them in coaching conversations and point them out to your clients if you sense a gremlin is lurking. While some coaching models get rid of the gremlins, the NLP approach is to honour them as an important part of your identity. When you treat gremlins as offering valuable information, you can gain wisdom from their gifts. I (Kate) prefer to treat them as inner team members who bring a different quality to my clients' goals. Clients can take gremlins out of their boxes when needed and keep them in place if not invited. The challenge is to find the positive aspect of a gremlin and keep it out of mischief unless useful.

## *Shaking up the peacekeeper gremlin*

The peacekeeper gremlin fears taking any action that may rock the boat and wants to wave the white flag at the first sign of a battle. Its job is to keep a person safely out of danger. However, 'put up and shut up' is the implicit message from the peacekeeper gremlin when taken to extremes:

- Why file for divorce when you can put up with a toxic marriage?
- Why tell a friend she's outstayed her welcome when she'll leave eventually?
- Why discipline an employee when you're changing jobs anyway?
- Why tell your boss she's being unreasonable if you can just quietly ignore her?

Peace in itself is a worthy goal, yet fear of any conflict or willingness to air a different view means you settle for a better-than-nothing kind of life.

One way to tame the peacekeeper gremlin is to learn to have courageous conversations. Clients can prepare for these emotionally with the anchoring techniques described earlier in the section 'Anchoring positive states' and by planning out the words to give feedback without confrontation (Book III Chapter 7 offers a valuable structure). When clients are in touch with their values, choosing which battles they want to fight to honour those values is easier.

**Book III**

**Managing and Leading Others**

## *Messing with the perfectionist gremlin*

Many clients recognise their perfectionist gremlins and realise that they take huge amounts of energy. Not only is perfection impossible, it causes you to agonise about and go over tasks and projects so that they never get completed. Nothing is really good enough as you seek examples of perfect lives portrayed in glossy style magazines or glowing celebrity profiles.

Of course, perfectionism may also have its roots in the past where a person perceived her efforts weren't good enough to please a parent, teacher, partner or boss. In this case, you can uncover the limiting beliefs and support your clients to create new, more empowering ones for themselves.

## *Firing up the procrastinator gremlin*

The procrastinator gremlin thrives on creating distractions, causing noise and activity that diverts you from your main focus. Procrastinator gremlins can be quite entertaining and even provide much needed relaxation or thinking time. 'Let's go shopping instead of doing that job now' or 'Let's just have another cup of tea and chat' are some appealing versions of this gremlin.

The counter-tactic for the procrastinator gremlin is to introduce more structure and bursts of focused time on identifiable activities.

Ask your clients to identify how specifically the procrastinator distracts them. What temptations does this little gremlin offer? A chance to go shopping? Spend time gossiping over coffee? A temporarily satisfying trip to raid the fridge, read a magazine or surf the net? Then invite your clients to:

- Measure the time spent on distractions.
- Decide what benefits you want to keep and what you want to let go of.
- Assign a cost to your distractions in terms of money or lost opportunities elsewhere.
- Identify ways to diminish the distractions.

When clients are procrastinating, I invite them to allocate just one power hour each day to the critical task in hand. It's not even a whole hour of work; just a commitment to spend 50 minutes of dedicated time and then take a ten-minute break. Clients who follow through with this technique have permission after one hour to stop or keep going. Most often, after starting, people spend longer on the task and get into the groove, leaving their procrastinating behind.

## Drawing your gremlins

The following exercise can help clients identify a group of gremlins that are causing trouble and decide how to get these pesky critters working for a living.

1. **Give your client a large sheet of blank paper and several coloured pens.**

2. **Invite her to identify her cast of gremlins with pictures and words.**

    Encourage your client to give the gremlins names and personalities. Start with the top three, and she may come up with two or three more.

3. **Discuss with the client each gremlin's attributes, observing all the positive benefits that they bring.**

4. **Ask the client to decide what positive role to allocate to each gremlin and find a way that each can be of service to the coaching agenda.**
    One client, Tessa, who called one gremlin Scaredy Cat, says this character is in charge of highlighting risks when big decisions loom.

5. **Identify how each gremlin may creep in unwanted and list strategies to keep each one at bay.** The Scaredy Cat gremlin can prevent Tessa enjoying parties, so she imagines tucking the gremlin in a pet-carrier on social occasions when he can be a nuisance.

# Overcoming Fear

Fear centres on the expectation of something unpleasant or undesirable happening in the future. Fear can freeze your clients to the spot or trigger frantic action to get away from the fear. Fear is a proven motivator, yet it's one that leaves people feeling drained of energy and operating below their potential.

Sometimes the fear isn't tangible or even rational to articulate – a sense that things aren't right. Although fear can keep you from achieving some goals, it can also serve as a useful warning mechanism.

To let go of fear and build confidence, clients must recognise the sensation of fear and face up to what may be unnerving them. Some common fears that people bring to coaching include:

- **Finance and possessions.** Do I have enough money? Can I buy the right car, house, clothing, treats? What if I lose my treasured belongings?

- **Loneliness and rejection.** Will anyone like/love me? Does anyone care about me? Will I lose my job?

- **Knowledge.** Do I know enough? Am I clever enough? Will others find me out?

- **Judgement.** Will I hear something critical about me that I don't like?

- **Privacy.** What happens if I tell people about a personal aspect of me? Can I hide in the wings quietly?

- **Bad experiences.** Will I repeat past mistakes yet again?

- **Courage.** How can I say what I really think and state what I want?

Ask any of the following questions in coaching sessions to explore fear:

- How are you experiencing the fear?

- Is your fear – or someone else's – driving you?

- What does your fear give you?

- What would you rather have in place of the fear?

- How will life be better for you as soon as you let go of this fear?

**Book III**

**Managing and Leading Others**

✔ What ideas do you already have for getting rid of this fear?

✔ What's one small and easy step you can take right now to release yourself from the fear?

✔ How would you leapfrog your fear?

## Championing natural confidence

When clients come to coaching saying that they have no confidence, they are generalising from one or more specific incidents to a broader sense of stuckness in which they no longer acknowledge themselves. They've lost connection with their natural, healthy state of emotional well-being.

Confidence requires the feeling that everything will be okay, regardless of events, people and circumstances. It requires you to trust yourself from your very core and not allow negative emotions to get in the way of getting on with what you want or need to do.

Sadly, no magic confidence pills and potions exist; ultimately, developing confidence is in your clients' hands.

In *Building Self-Confidence For Dummies* (Wiley), my co-author Brinley Platts and I give this definition of confidence:

> *At its heart, confidence is the ability to take appropriate and effective action in any situation, however challenging it appears to you or others.*

In order to take action, clients need to recognise themselves at their most confident. Unfortunately, under stress they delete this information. 'I'm never confident' or 'I've lost it' they say. Yet given time and space to relax and think about their previous experiences, they can find times when they were extremely confident. For example, one coaching client suffered a loss of self-confidence due to a micro-managing boss and job that required busy reactionary work, yet she had enormous confidence in setting up a charity.

As coach, encourage your clients to notice for themselves times when they felt confident. Have them describe these experiences as precisely as possible. Table 4-1 provides a form to capture these times and shows an example. Such experiences act as references that can then be anchored using the Circle of Excellence technique in the section 'Anchoring positive states' earlier in this chapter.

After clients create their set of positive reference experiences, work with them to anchor the experiences for the future or to remind them of these experiences when they are struggling.

| Table 4-1 | Confident Experiences | | |
|---|---|---|---|
| *Where was I and what was I doing when I felt most confident?* | *What assumptions did I make about myself and others?* | *What enabled me to feel confident?* | *Give a label to this state of confidence. How exactly did I feel?* |
| When I posed for my graduation photograph with my parents. | That I could achieve something difficult through my own efforts. | Knowing that my hard work had paid off. | Excited and contented. |
| | | | |
| | | | |

# Releasing phobias fast

Clients bring all kinds of insecurities to coaching that can be talked through and dealt with logically. Occasionally someone arrives with a phobic response that gets in the way of her everyday life. Her emotional state is destabilised by thinking of the thing she fears. I've had clients who fear travelling on escalators or in lifts, driving across motorway bridges and flying. Their extreme emotions create strong physical reactions including stomach cramps and panic attacks. Such fears aren't logical, and they can have a debilitating effect on everyday life. Yet when they're overcome, the clients experience a sense of freedom that's a joy to see.

### Separating emotion and memory cinematically

NLP offers a very helpful technique called the *Fast Phobia Cure* that desensitises clients from trauma or phobia. The technique works by separating – or *dissociating* – images from emotion in the client's memory. This dissociation occurs by having clients watch themselves sitting in a cinema (dissociation), while watching themselves on a cinema screen (double dissociation). The technique is also useful if someone has had a bad experience, such as doing a presentation that didn't go well.

Only use this technique in a place where clients feel very comfortable and safe and if you feel competent to keep your client relaxed and calm if she feels panicky.

After you identify a client's phobic response to a stimulus or a traumatic or unpleasant memory, go through the following with his to help him overcome his phobic responses. This technique works well sitting on a comfortable sofa in a quiet, private room.

1. **Imagine yourself sitting in the cinema, watching yourself projected as a small black and white image on the screen.** Invite your client to think about having a drink and some popcorn to get him into the experience; you could hand him a TV remote control and do the exercise imagining looking at a TV screen.

2. **Imagine floating out of the you that's sitting in the cinema seat and into the projection booth.**

3. **See yourself in the projection booth, watching yourself in the seat as well as watching the film of you on the screen.**

4. **As the projectionist, run the film in black and white, as a very tiny image.**

   Start the film at a point before you experienced the unpleasant memory you want to overcome and run it through until after the experience when you were safe.

5. **Freeze the film or turn the screen completely white.**

6. **Float out of the projection booth, out of the seat, up onto the screen and into the end of the film.**

7. **Run the film backwards very quickly, in a matter of a second or two, in full colour.**

   Experience the film from end (where you are safe) to beginning (where you also are safe).

8. **Run the film backwards and forwards several times, always stopping at a safe spot.**

   Repeat this step until you're comfortable with the experience.

9. **Test for completion.** Ask the client to leave the cinema and come back to the present time. Have him imagine a time coming up when he may experience the phobic response, such as a flight if he fears flying. Ask how he feels about it now. If he doesn't display the phobic response, then the phobia cure has been effective. You can repeat the exercise until your client is fully desensitised to the unpleasant experience.

### Identifying – and substituting – secondary gains

As a starting point to defuse the emotional over-reaction, you can support your client conversationally without tackling the phobia directly. Simply find out the phobia's *secondary gain*. What are the positive benefits your client gets from the phobia? If these benefits can all be met in other ways, the phobia may disappear of its own accord.

# Chapter 5

# Strengthening Relationships in Tough Times

........................................................

## In This Chapter

▶ Connecting with the right people

▶ Adapting your style with different people

▶ Building cohesive teams

........................................................

*W*hen you go through tough times in life, the pressure builds and inevitably impacts others around you. Under pressure you may revert to unhelpful behaviours, such as focusing on the task in hand at the expense of the relationships around you. Perhaps the hurry-up driver kicks in or the need to look for someone to blame as things go wrong. Emotions can escalate as confidence drops.

Additionally, your perceptions change under pressure because you're not firing on all cylinders. Some senses are heightened at the expense of others. You may increasingly filter information using the patterns of distortion, generalisation and deletion.

In this chapter we look at planning relationships with *stakeholders* – those people who you want or need to communicate with. Then we look at NLP tools to support better understanding between people. This chapter also explores ways to coach teams and build strong relationships that help take groups through tough times.

# Identifying the Stakeholders Who Matter

In any community in which you live or work, you connect with different people – friends, family, colleagues and others. Having strong relationships with others acts as a tremendous resource in tough times.

In the business world, *stakeholders* are those people who have a *stake* in the business or project. Business stakeholders may include:

- Customers – both internal (if you provide support services such as IT, finance, human resources or facilities) and external (where you deliver products or services).
- Employees, bosses, peers, business partners, colleagues.
- Suppliers of services and products.
- Investors and shareholders with a financial interest.
- Members of the media, including journalists and industry analysts.
- External agencies and officials, such as regulatory bodies or non-executive directors.
- Members of professional groups.

Stakeholders extend beyond an organisational context to include all areas of your clients' lives, including personal connections. Clients may not have considered friends and family as stakeholders before, but you can encourage them to consider their personal relationships, such as:

- Spouse or life partner.
- Family members.
- Friends.
- Professional supporters, such as a doctor, solicitor, financial adviser and personal coach.
- Community groups focused on specific hobbies, sports, schools, political affiliations, or volunteer and church activities.

## Mapping out the network

When coaching senior leaders in business, encourage them to build a relationship map of their key stakeholders. This process is particularly helpful when they're running complicated or challenging programmes or hold responsibility for restructuring or merging businesses with multiple stakeholder groups. The same mapping exercise works well for other clients in a personal context.

Your clients need to identify the individuals they need to be in touch with, as well as remember people they may have overlooked who can support them. Too often relationship-building gets seen as a nice-to-have activity. Yet without strong relationships in place, people suffer from a lack of support when they most need it.

The following relationship-mapping exercise also highlights where clients are spending their time and whether they're paying enough attention to building strong relationships.

To create a relationship map, take a large sheet of paper – a flip chart is ideal – and a few pads of sticky notes and follow these steps:

1. **Establish a context for identifying relationships – work/professional, home/personal or both areas of life.**

2. **Ask your client, 'Who is important to you in this context?'**

   Write names of people on sticky notes.

3. **Sort the sticky notes into groups that you can place on a wall or sheet of paper.**

   Groups may naturally form based on roles or activity areas. Example groups can include friends, colleagues, suppliers and so on.

4. **Examine the names in each group and check whether the group is complete or if people are missing.**

   Create additional sticky notes as necessary.

5. **Review each name in a group and assess the strength of the relationship.**

   Score the relationship on a scale of 1 to 10 with 10 being the strongest; the most satisfying and effective.

   To help determine a relationship's strength, ask your client, 'Looking at these names and thinking about these people, who can you count on to respond if you asked for help?' The names that come to mind first are among the client's strongest.

6. **After reviewing all the groups, invite the client to consider who the client needs to spend more time with – and who to spend less time with.**

   Are any relationships failing to serve your client well? Ask her what else she notices about the various groups and individuals.

7. **Encourage the client to come back to the map at regular intervals and review it.**

Maps develop and change over time, but clients need to actively keep stakeholders on their radars.

This exercise engages the core visual, auditory and kinaesthetic senses. Your client is looking at the names of the people, talking through the relationships and writing on notes and shifting notes to various groups.

## Informing – or influencing?

You communicate differently with people in order to deepen the relationships or achieve the results that matter most to you.

Not all relationships are equal. Clearly some people nurture your soul while others are mere passing acquaintances. Yet the interesting thing about relationships is that they don't exist in isolation; one connects with another. Spend any time on a social networking site such as LinkedIn or Facebook, and you soon realise that if you link with one person, you also link with everyone who knows that person in their network, so you form a batch of new, random relationships.

One of the major distinctions in building relationships is realising who you want to impart information to without a close involvement and who you really want to influence in order to meet a need. Table 5-1 offers my four-step Communication model. The four steps are:

- ✔ **Informing.** Supplying people with factual information.

- ✔ **Involving.** Creating a dialogue in which you invite others' opinions.

- ✔ **Influencing.** Where you seeking to persuade other people to your viewpoint.

- ✔ **Inspiring.** Raising levels of motivation in others.

| Table 5-1 | The Four-I Levels Communication Model | |
|---|---|---|
| *Level of Communication* | *Behaviour* | *Question to Ask Yourself* |
| **Inform** | Telling instructions; giving the facts | Who do I need to give information to? |
| **Involve** | Asking questions; gathering information, feedback and viewpoints | Who do I want to get information from or invite to give feedback? |

| Level of Communication | Behaviour | Question to Ask Yourself |
|---|---|---|
| **Influence** | Persuading; appealing to emotions | Who do I need to connect to at an emotional level in order for them to act? |
| **Inspire** | Motivating | What is the broader group that I could impact through my communication and behaviour? Who might choose me as a role model? |

EXAMPLE

## Shifting communication levels

When Maria's sister Jane married and moved to California, the reality of keeping in touch over the long distance meant the sisters saw each other less than they liked. As their parents grew older, Maria took on a supporting role, helping them through many hospital visits and illnesses that culminated in the death of her mother. Maria kept Jane loosely *informed* of what was happening until she began to realise that she couldn't cope alone with the responsibility of organising care for her elderly father, Peter.

Maria's coach asked whether it might help to strengthen her relationship with her sister and *involve* her in the decision-making. Maria decided to experiment with the web cam on her laptop.

In her academic work at a university, Maria was good at building teams and delegating work to researchers. She decided to work on building a stronger support team within her family. She invited her American nephews as well as her sister and brother-in-law to regular family pow-wows over the web cam with Peter included too when he was over for meals. She also booked regular Internet-based calls with

her sister to share her concerns and ask her opinion. Her level of *influence* increased.

Jane appreciated her sister's efforts and volunteered to research sheltered accommodation options online for her father. Then the whole family came across from the US to support Peter when he moved to warden-assisted care, making the trip a holiday.

Maria felt that applying lessons from her job made a difference at home too. She said: 'At work, my motto with the team is "You cannot over-communicate". I got so wrapped up in the practicalities of supporting Dad that I forgot how my communication motto is so true with the whole family as well.'

In terms of the Communication model, Maria shifted from informing to involving and thus influenced her family by increasing their emotional connections. She wasn't aware that her kindness and commitment to her family also *inspired* her work colleagues until they gave her some feedback in a peer-review process that she was a very positive role model because they saw just how much she cared for her family in addition to her high commitment to work.

**Book III**

**Managing and Leading Others**

Invite your clients to look at the people in their networks to determine the appropriate level of communication for each person or group of people. (See the earlier section 'Mapping out the network'.) Are your clients interacting with people who just need information or do they need to increase their activities to inspire or influence key people?

## Setting priorities for communication

Effective communication involves planning what you want to communicate to whom and the outcomes you seek. Specifically:

- ✔ **Audience.** Who do you need to connect with? One person, several people or a group?

- ✔ **Outcome.** What do you want to achieve? Remember *you* need to initiate and lead the outcome, based on the well-formed outcome process (see Book IV Chapter 2 for more).

- ✔ **Message.** What do you want to communicate in terms of the headline message as well as the key points?

- ✔ **Method.** What's the best way to communicate your message? Text, phone call, personal or group meeting, professional network, email, web and social media are each potentially appropriate options.

Table 5-2 summarises this simple structure and provides a worked example plus blank spaces for you to work out your communication plans.

Fred has an introverted preference and hadn't paid much attention to developing a network of contacts, other than people at his badminton club. However, when he resigned from his role as a charity worker due to stress and wanted to build up local work as a decorator and handyman, he knew he needed to talk to people to attract customers. His coach encouraged him out of hibernation and into strengthening his connections. With the help of a chart like the example in Table 5-2, he developed a communication plan to actively reconnect with friends, neighbours and ex-colleagues. As a result, Fred arranged to meet with friends at his club, did a leaflet drop in his neighbourhood and sent a flyer by email to let people know that he was available for work. In each instance, he provided specific examples of wonderful projects he'd done in his own house and garden.

| Table 5-2 | | Effective Communication Plan | | |
|---|---|---|---|---|
| *Who do I need to communicate with?* | *What is the desired outcome?* | *What is the headline message?* | *What are three key points I want to get across?* | *What is the best way to communicate?* |
| Friends and neighbours. | Create a list of potential clients for decorating and maintenance jobs. | Contact me if you need any decorating or household maintenance done so you can enjoy your weekends without doing jobs. | 1. You can trust me as a friend in your house while you work.<br><br>2. Fixed-price quotes.<br><br>3. Speedy and clean decorating and garden work. | Word of mouth.<br><br>Email.<br><br>Facebook.<br><br>Leaflet drop. |
| Colleagues at work. | Inform colleagues of the new services I'm offering. | I'm available to support office moves as well as private decorating and household maintenance. | 1. Let me sort office handyman jobs when you relocate desks or sites.<br><br>2. Available for moves at weekends.<br><br>3. I can do essential home maintenance jobs while you're busy at work. | Targeted email.<br><br>Meeting with facilities team.<br><br>Internal company website.<br><br>Notice boards. |

**Book III**

**Managing and Leading Others**

# Understanding What Makes Others Tick

In coaching you encourage your clients to understand how they relate to other people, not just themselves. As Stephen Covey, author of *The 7 Habits of Highly Effective People* (Simon and Schuster) put it: 'Seek first to understand, then to be understood.' In this section we explore the value of stepping into other people's shoes, as well as some NLP techniques for doing so.

As you read through the following sections, think of a person you'd like to get to know better; perhaps a client, colleague, friend or family member. Having a specific person in mind helps the activities come to life.

## Taking perceptual positions

The *NLP perceptual positions* help you imagine what difficult situations look like when viewed with others' fresh eyes. The term refers to the ability to imagine what others are perceiving by pretending that you are that other person. In NLP this links with the assumption that the map is not the territory, and offers a way to enrich an individual's map of the world, which may be limiting her experience.

- **First position** is your natural perspective, where you're fully aware of what you think and feel, regardless of those around you. Clients find this place the most familiar. They've come to coaching because they already have an awareness of their own perspective and the problems they face.

- **Second position** is about imagining what it's like to be another person. Some people are very good at considering others' needs and concerns; for more self-focused clients, imagining second position is a completely alien notion.

- **Third position** is an independent position where you act as a detached observer, noticing what's happening in the relationship between two other people. Good coaches naturally step into this impartial role. In coaching, encourage the client to take this position in order to gain an impartial insight into a situation, particularly to view a relationship the client has with another person.

Introduce perceptual positions to clients by having them physically move to different chairs or places in a room as you describe and discuss the three positions, asking them to notice what they experience while standing or sitting in each position.

## Scarcity rules

In Mark Twain's classic story *The Adventures of Tom Sawyer* the mischievous Tom finds himself whitewashing the fence as his punishment from Aunt Polly for his naughty behaviour. Yet he's constantly distracted by other boys who are going off to enjoy their freedom and consistently fails to bribe them to swap jobs in return for his small supply of toys and marbles.

Then Tom develops a new influencing strategy: he pretends to another lad, Ben, that he actually likes whitewashing the fence to the point where Ben is taken in by Tom's ruse and asks if he can take over. Tom pretends reluctance as Aunt Polly is so particular about the fence. Soon Ben is bribing Tom with an apple to let him whitewash. Tom eventually agrees, taking care not to show his delight.

Seeing Ben enjoy his privileged position as fence painter, several boys arrive and hand over their treasures to Tom in order to be allowed to have a turn at whitewashing the fence. Tom ends up with a pile of treasures, a perfectly whitewashed fence, and the company of other boys instead of doing the job alone. In addition to a humorous communication lesson, Tom's actions show how the *scarcity principle* influences others: 'In order to make a man or boy covet a thing, it is only necessary to make the thing difficult to obtain.'

NLP offers a number of exercises where coaches ask clients to move into various perceptual positions, including several of my favourites in the following sections. After clients master assuming the preceding three positions, they have the flexibility to imagine stepping into the shoes of any other stakeholder in the system. When doing these exercises, I might ask, 'Who else could give you insight here?' Examples of another perspective could be a family member, business guru, TV personality or spiritual leader. They can be people that the client doesn't know, as well as familiar figures.

**Book III**

**Managing and Leading Others**

## *Gazing into the NLP meta-mirror*

The *meta-mirror* is an exercise that brings together a number of different perspectives or perceptual positions. The aim is to hold up a mirror to the problem the client is confronting. Clients find answers as they realise their problems are reflections of themselves rather than about someone else. This technique allows the client to step back and see the issue in a new light – hence the idea of the mirror.

The meta-mirror helps clients to prepare for, or review, challenging situations, conversations and negotiations. When people are under pressure, this technique enables them to detach from their emotions and gain new insights as to how they can handle a situation.

The meta-mirror exercise takes four perceptual positions. As coach, invite your client to choose a relationship or situation she wants to explore and then lay out four pieces of paper on the floor to denote four positions (see Figure 5-1).

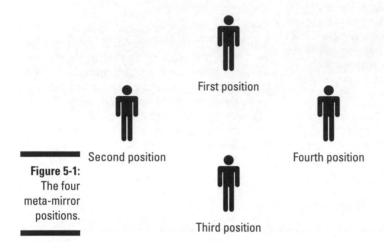

First position

Second position        Fourth position

Third position

**Figure 5-1:**
The four
meta-mirror
positions.

 Be sure to have your client break state between each position by physically moving between each. You don't want her to get stuck in one perspective! Invite the client to shake her body a little or look out of a window and tell you what the weather's like.

Talk your client through the four positions as follows:

1. **Have your client in *first position*.**

   Ask her to assume her own point of view and then look at the other person in second position.

   *Ask the client: 'What are you experiencing, thinking and feeling as you look at this person?'*

   Give the client a few minutes to talk through what's happening for her until you feel she's had a chance to express her feelings without dwelling on any negative emotion for too long.

2. **After your client shakes off first position, have the client move to *second position*.**

   Ask the client to imagine that she's that person looking back at the client in first position.

   *Ask the client: 'What are you experiencing, thinking and feeling as you look at this person?'*

The client will find this tougher than being in first position, so give her longer in this space. The exercise is for the client to imagine being in the shoes and mindset of the person she wants to connect with. Make sure that she's really taking on the idea of *being* the other person, not just being herself talking about that person. If necessary call her by the other person's name, and say: 'Okay, really being Freda now, what are you experiencing as Freda looking back at Kelly?' Expect to hear her say things like: 'She looks at me as if she's not sure how I'll react' or 'She's a decent person, just hard to talk to.' Or 'I really don't know what she wants from me.'

3. **Have the client move to *third position*, that of the independent observer looking at both people in this relationship impartially.**

   *Ask the client: 'Looking at yourself in first position, how do you respond to that "you" there?'*

   By now, the client will have got the idea of stepping out of being herself. She's in the space where she can get some insight. Give her time to observe here, and you can add questions such as: 'What are the insights about Freda and Kelly from an independent perspective?' Expect to hear answers such as: 'These people haven't given each other time to get to know each other.' 'They need to go out for a coffee and just talk it through.' 'It would be a pity if things fell apart between them for no real reason.' 'They both really want this to succeed, they just have different styles.'

4. **Have the client move to the *fourth position*.**

   Ask the client to think about how her thoughts in third position compared to her reactions in the first position and switch them around. Whatever reactions the client had in the third position, have her switch them around into her first position in her mind's eye. Don't offer any logical explanation at this point.

5. **Have the client revisit *second position*.**

   *Ask the client: 'How is this position different now? What has changed?'*

   At this point, you can expect that the situation has changed with a sense that the relationship has improved.

6. **Invite the client to come home to first position.**

   *Ask the client: 'How is this position different now? What has changed?'*

   At this point, you can expect that any stuck thoughts and feelings from the original discussion in first position have been replaced with more creative ideas to improve the relationship, and a greater understanding of the other person.

**Book III**

**Managing and Leading Others**

## Listening for metaprograms

When people are under pressure, communicating in ways that raise the chances of your words being understood and acted upon is particularly valuable. That means using similar language patterns to deepen rapport.

*Metaprograms,*are the NLP explanation for how to make predictions about people's behaviour from the way they use language.

In order to deepen rapport, you must step back and listen not just to what someone is saying, but also *how* she's saying it. Table 5-3 summarises the most common metaprograms and provides a structure to help you pay attention to how your stakeholder uses language.

The third column of Table 5-3 is particularly useful if you can initiate a phone call with someone and mark in the third column as you hear similar phrases. By figuring out another person's metaprogram patterns, you can then formulate how to respond.

As a coach, pay attention to your clients' metaprograms. You can discover many clues about how to best present new or difficult information to help them achieve greater results.

| Table 5-3 | Capturing Metaprograms | |
|---|---|---|
| *Pattern* | *Sample Phrases* | *Stakeholder's Typical Phrases* |
| Proactive | Let's go for it. | |
| Reactive | I'd like to wait and see. | |
| Options | What are the choices? | |
| Procedures | Take me through things, step by step. | |
| Toward | This is what I want. | |
| Away from | I wouldn't do that if I were you. | |
| Internal | In my opinion . . . | |
| External | Let's find out what the market wants. | |
| Global | The headline story is . . . | |
| Detail | Give me all the information. | |
| Sameness | This is just like what we did last time. | |
| Difference | Let's see what we can change. | |

Metaprograms are highly *contextual*, by which I mean you may stay at the global level of information in one context (while discussing business strategy, for example) yet wallow in detail in another (proudly extolling the virtues of your child). In order to accurately listen for metaprograms, you want to listen to your stakeholder talking about the kind of topic that is relevant to your communication need.

Also, most people have a mix of patterns, aim to listen for the style that a person leans towards most typically.

## Adapting your approach

How tempting to go through life hoping and expecting other people to adapt to your style and needs! Alas, life doesn't work that way. One thought to offer your clients is: 'For things to change, I must change,' or as Gandhi said: 'Be the change you want to see in the world.'

NLP assumes that the person with the most flexibility in the system is the one who wins. This assumption doesn't mean you need to be a pushover who bends to others' needs. Rather, you need to find creative ways to come at situations with fresh eyes and stop perpetuating behaviours that aren't working.

Situations that require people to negotiate with others demonstrate the need for flexibility. Michael is a coach who specialises in negotiating complex contracts and guides his clients to mismatch others' style of words in order to negotiate. For example, when one party is arguing logically, he recommends taking an emotional tack. When the other party comes in with an emotional argument, counter it with a rational approach. 'Flexing the style in this way proves the winning hand,' he says.

**Book III**

**Managing and Leading Others**

# Coaching Teams to Bond

The preceding sections of this chapter look at one-to-one coaching situations. However, all the principles of coaching individuals apply to coaching teams and groups too – including in business, sport, family or other settings.

Teams often come together to tackle tough issues, and a team that doesn't have strong relationships and communication falls over fast under pressure. Conversely, the team that shows its strength in tough times creates powerful relationships to take forward into other situations.

In this section, we show how you support teams throughout all the classic stages of development including forming, storming, norming, performing and finally disbanding.

# Forming: Adopting the mindset for success

At the *forming* stage, the team needs to have a mindset that focuses on success.

The following NLP presuppositions offer a great starting point for any team. In any team set-up, the coach can encourage team members to try on the following presuppositions for size and debate what they mean for the team if they're adopted as core principles from the beginning.

- ✔ **The map is not the territory.** People respond according to their own maps of the world, and everyone in the team has a different map.

- ✔ **There is no failure, only feedback**. This presupposition gives permission for the team members to risk making mistakes.

- ✔ **The meaning of the communication is the response you get.** Each team member must adapt his or her communication style in order for others in the team to understand.

- ✔ **If what you're doing isn't working, do something different.** The classic sign of insanity in teams is inflexibility! Head to Book III Chapter 7 for more on working with teams.

- ✔ **You cannot not communicate.** Even if you say nothing, people assign meaning to your silence and non-verbal clues.

- ✔ **Individuals have all the resources they need to achieve their desired outcomes.** No one needs to fix someone else.

- ✔ **Every behaviour has a positive intent.** Each person acts in a particular way for a good reason. So strive to get to the intent of an action in order to change behaviours.

- ✔ **People are much more than their behaviours.** Separate the person from his or her role and what he or she does. Then you release the natural creativity innate in the whole person.

- ✔ **The mind and body are interlinked and affect each other.** Pay attention to physical and mental well-being. I cover this in Book III Chapter 4.

- ✔ **Having choice is better than not having choice.** Give people choice if you want them to be motivated and interested.

- ✔ **Modelling successful performance leads to excellence.** Find others who have trodden a similar path and learn from them.

# Storming: Developing a shared future

As a team enters the *storming* stage, different ideas come to the fore and the team need to agree on the problems they need to solve and the theories and models they'll follow. This stage can be fraught with conflict, testing the team relationships. Here the team coach can concentrate the team's energy on three core activities:

- **Establish clear, shared goals.** The well-formed outcome process in Book IV Chapter 2 encourages teams to build goals that are specific, inspiring and achievable – ones that give the team choices and put the members of the team firmly in the driving seat. From these types of goals, people then develop clarity in what they need to do.

- **Articulate and honour a common set of values.** Strong teams know what is important to members within the team and identify and live the behaviours that reflect the shared values on a daily basis. The principle of understanding individual values also applies to teams, and simplifies decision-making.

- **Uncover limiting beliefs and develop empowering ones.** When everyone believes in the capability of the team to achieve its goals, the team can storm ahead.

The following exercise enables teams (and individuals) to be curious about their beliefs. Create a list of about ten statements and invite the team to split into pairs to explore the statements.

Use statements such as the following to get conversations started:

- *This team is like . . . because it . . .*
- *We'll be most successful if we . . .*
- *The three things that will get in our way are . . .*
- *The top issue we must consider is . . .*
- *A high-performing team can . . .*

As each pair looks at the statements, ask members to say the first thing that comes into their heads. After the paired exercise, invite the whole team to convene and ask the group:

- What beliefs might limit this team?
- What beliefs might empower this team?

Get someone in the group to capture the most empowering beliefs and circulate them to the team members for referencing later.

**Book III**

**Managing and Leading Others**

## Norming and performing: Championing great ways of operating

Through the *norming* and into the high *performing* stages of development, the team coach encourages a team to create processes and ways of behaving with each other that enable the team to stay on track for performance. Norming is the stage when people have bought into shared plans and let go of their own in order to make the team function. If the team survives long enough to get to the performing stage, it has found ways to get things done smoothly without the need for constant supervision; the team makes decisions easily, although may find itself reverting back to the storming stage, especially if new people join the team with different ideas.

The influential coach Tim Gallwey's coaching principle $P = p - I$ signifies that performance is equal to potential less interference. Team coaching sessions provide the space in which team members address the issues that interfere with performance.

High-performing teams develop deep trust, safety, openness and respect for each other. Team members demonstrate behaviours that:

- **Resolve conflict** by depersonalising issues and express shared willingness to constructively disagree in order to find the best solutions.
- **Celebrate successes** in small as well as big ways, such as a go-home-early day or lunch out together to signify a milestone reached.
- **Sustain momentum** by holding on to the goals and remembering the effect when they're achieved.
- **Avoid complacency** by regularly reflecting on what the team members are doing and inviting feedback from each other and the key external stakeholders.

By modelling the core coaching skills of active listening and asking powerful questions, the team coach shows the value of the preceding activities to the team.

## Disbanding: Moving on positively

Ultimately even the best teams experience the *disbanding* stage as the individuals go their separate ways. The project that the team got together for may be complete or the organisation is restructured.

When coaching a team through its final stages of existence, build in space for them to acknowledge and celebrate their successes, and to capture the lessons they want to take forward to their next teams.

# Chapter 6

# Dealing with Ethics and Office Politics

*E*thics and office politics are very powerful forces in any organisation. *Ethics* is the framework of values that employees use to guide their behaviour. You've seen the devastation that poor ethical standards can lead to – witness the string of business failures attributed to less than sterling ethics in more than a few large, seemingly upstanding businesses. Today, more than ever, managers are expected to model ethical behaviour and to ensure that their employees follow in their footsteps – and at the same time to purge the organisation of employees who refuse to align their own standards with those of their employer.

At its best, *office politics* means the relationships that you develop with your colleagues – both up and down the chain of command – that allow you to get tasks done, to be informed about the latest goings-on in the organisation and to form a personal network of business associates for support throughout your career. Office politics help to ensure that everyone works in the best interests of their colleagues and the organisation. At its worst, office politics can degenerate into a competition in which employees concentrate their efforts on trying to increase their personal power at the expense of other employees, and of their organisations.

This chapter is about building an ethical organisation, determining the nature and boundaries of your political environment, understanding the unspoken side of office communication, unearthing the unwritten rules of your organisation and, in the worst-case scenario, becoming adept at defending yourself against political attack.

# Doing the Right Thing: Ethics and You

With an endless parade of business scandals regarding overstated revenues, mistaken earnings and misplaced decimals hitting the daily news, rocking the stock market and shaking the foundations of the global economic system, you may often wonder whether anyone in charge knows the difference between right and wrong. Or, if they know the difference, whether they really care.

Of course, the reality is that many business leaders do know the difference between right and wrong, despite appearances to the contrary. Now more than ever, businesses and the leaders who run them are trying to do the right thing, not just because the right thing is politically correct, but also because it's good for the bottom line.

## Defining ethics

Do you know what ethics is? In case you're a bit rusty on the correct response, the long answer is that *ethics* is a set of standards, beliefs and values that guide conduct, behaviour and activities – in other words, a way of thinking that provides boundaries for action. The short answer is that ethics is simply doing the right thing. Not just talking about doing the right thing, but really doing it!

Although you come to a job with your own sense of ethical values, based on your upbringing, your beliefs and your life experiences, the organisations and leaders for which you work are responsible for setting clear ethical standards for you to operate within.

When you have high ethical standards on the job, you generally exhibit some or all of the following personal qualities and behaviours:

- ✔ Accountability
- ✔ Dedication
- ✔ Fairness
- ✔ Honesty
- ✔ Impartiality

> ✔ Integrity
>
> ✔ Loyalty
>
> ✔ Responsibility

Ethical behaviour starts with *you*. As a manager, you're a leader in your organisation, and you set an example – both for other managers and for the many workers watching your every move. When others see you behaving unethically, you're sending the message loud and clear that ethics doesn't matter. The result? Ethics doesn't matter to them, either.

However, when you behave ethically, others follow your example and behave ethically too. And if you practise ethical conduct, it also reinforces and perhaps improves your own ethical standards. As a manager, you have a responsibility to try to define, live up to and improve your own set of personal ethics.

## Creating a code of ethics

Although most people have a pretty good idea about what kinds of behaviour are ethical and what kinds aren't, ethics are to some degree subjective, and a matter of interpretation to the individual employee. One worker may, for example, think that making unlimited personal phone calls from the office is okay, but another may consider that to be inappropriate.

Instead of leaving your employees' definition of ethics on the job to chance or their upbringing, you need to spell out clearly in a code of ethics that stealing, sharing trade secrets, sexual harassment and other unethical behaviour is unacceptable and may be grounds for dismissal.

A *code of ethics* spells out for all employees – from the very top to the very bottom of the organisation – your organisation's ethical expectations, clearly and unambiguously.

A code of ethics isn't a substitute for company policies and procedures; the code complements these guidelines.

Four key areas form the foundation of a good code of ethics:

> ✔ Compliance with internal policies and procedures
>
> ✔ Compliance with external laws and regulations
>
> ✔ Standards based on organisational values
>
> ✔ Standards based on individual values

**Book III**

**Managing and Leading Others**

Any code of ethics must cover rights, responsibilities, authority and account-ability; the work carried out and the ways in which work is carried out; matters of right and wrong; compliance with the law; and a reflection of social and cultural customs and values. Running through the code of ethics is a strong vein of honesty and integrity.

Of course, a code of ethics isn't worth the paper it's printed on if it doesn't address some very specific issues, as well as the more generic ones listed previously. The following list highlights some of the areas a code of ethics needs to address:

- ✔ Conflicts of interest, especially those that occur when managers are faced with the choice of courses of action that serve their own interests at the expense of those of the organisation.

- ✔ Gifts and gratuities that can be understood or perceived to be inducements to act in a particular way.

- ✔ Financial issues, including fraud, misuse of company funds, attitudes to expenses and bonuses, and other irregularities.

- ✔ Loyalty and dedication to the organisation; this is a two-way process – you can't expect loyalty and dedication from your employees if you don't provide loyalty in return.

- ✔ Compliance with the law as it stands; and commitment to deal with employees who break the law in accordance with statutory provisions.

- ✔ Conditions in which hard and effective work can be expected, required and carried out.

- ✔ Commitment to constant improvement of all aspects of the organisation – products and services; working practices; returns to shareholders; and dealings with all stakeholders.

- ✔ Commitment to avoiding favouritism and victimisation – remember, in cases of victimisation, law courts and tribunals normally hear an allegation provided that it can be substantiated. In recent years some who've proved or demonstrated victimisation or discrimination have gained huge settlements – so apart from not being right, victimisation or discrimination can also be very expensive!

- ✔ Prohibitions against disclosing trade secrets, product and service information, or anything concerning the internal workings of the organisation without specific permission to do so.

- ✔ Expectations of the highest standards of conduct in matters concerning employee health, safety and welfare. Make sure that this extends to anyone visiting the organisation. Expose vandalism, fraud, theft and dishonesty wherever they're found; if you don't, you may be cited as an accessory after the fact if and when such a case comes to light.

✔ Commitment to exposing sexual misconduct and harassment wherever it's found – remember that not doing so may render you liable to prosecution.

✔ Commitment to establishing and upholding the principles of equality of treatment for all, regardless of ethnic origin, gender, sexual orientation, age, disability, occupation or length of service. Ensure equality of treatment and opportunity for all in specific organisational matters, especially promotions; recruitment and selection; training and development opportunities; project work and secondments; and other specific organisational issues.

✔ Paying particular attention to how technology is used. Of especial concern here are matters to do with the nature of websites accessed (such as pornography, religious and political extremism), and the content of emails (especially those that are bullying or abusive). Also, clear collective commitment is required to ensure that the organisation confidentially maintains personal and financial data and supplier and client records.

All these areas of ethics are underpinned by the ways in which you conduct yourself. So make sure that you set the same standards for yourself in all things that you expect from everyone else. And especially never make promises to anyone that you can't keep – staff, suppliers, customers and clients, or shareholders.

**Book III**

**Managing and Leading Others**

The Freedom of Information Act specifies that anyone can request to know what's being said about them or done in their name, so make sure that you commit yourself to the highest possible standards of behaviour. Additionally, the Whistleblowers' Charter states that if someone exposes wrongdoing at your organisation, you can't discipline or victimise that person as a result. So be good and be careful!

In addition to working within an organisation, a well-crafted code of ethics can be a powerful tool for publicising your company's standards and values to people outside your organisation, including suppliers, clients, customers, investors, potential job applicants, the media and the public at large. Your code of ethics tells others that you value ethical behaviour and that it guides the way you and your employees do business.

Of course, simply having a code of ethics isn't enough. You and your employees must also live according to the code. Even the world's best code of ethics does you no good if you file it away and never use it. Require your employees to read and sign a copy acknowledging their acceptance of the code; that way everyone knows what you expect of them.

## Living ethics

You may have a code of ethics, but if you don't behave ethically in your day-to-day business transactions and relationships, you call into question the purpose of having a code in the first place. Ethical challenges abound in business – some are spelled out in your company's code of ethics, or in its policies and procedures, and some aren't. What, for example, do you do if

- One of your favourite employees gives you tickets to a football match?
- An employee asks you not to discipline him for a moderate breach of company policies?
- You sold a product to a client that you later found out to be faulty, but your boss wants you to forget about it?
- Your department's financial results are actually lower than what appears in your boss's presentation to the board of directors?
- You find out that your star employee actually didn't graduate from university as he claimed in his job application?
- You know that a product you sell doesn't actually do everything your company claims it does?

You make ethical choices in your job every day, and the decisions you take have an impact on your business. Consider these six keys to making good ethical choices:

**E: Evaluate** circumstances through the appropriate filters. Filters include culture, laws, policies, circumstances, relationships, politics, perceptions, emotions, values, biases, prejudice and religion.

**T: Treat** people and issues fairly within the established boundaries. And remember that fair doesn't always mean equal.

**H: Hesitate** before making critical decisions. (Richard calls this 'wait-a-minute'.)

**I: Inform** those affected of the standard/decision that you've set/made.

**C: Create** an environment of consistency for yourself and your working group.

**S: Seek** guidance when you have any doubt. Make sure that the guidance comes from honest people who've earned your respect.

# Evaluating Your Political Environment

How political is your office or workplace? As a manager, having your finger on the political pulse of the organisation is particularly important. Otherwise, the next time you're in a management meeting you may blurt out, 'Why is it so difficult to get an employment requisition through human resources? You'd think it was their money!' only to later discover that the CEO's daughter-in-law heads the HR department.

With just a little bit of advance information and forethought, you can approach this issue much more tactfully. Being aware of your political environment can help you be more effective, and help your department and your employees have a greater impact within the organisation.

## Assessing your organisation's political environment

Asking your colleagues insightful questions is one of the best ways to assess your organisation's political environment. Such questions show you to be the polite, mature and ambitious employee that you are, and are a sure sign of your well-developed political instincts.

Give these questions, or something like them, a try:

- ✔ What's the best way to get a special item approved?

- ✔ How can I get a product from the warehouse that my client needs today when I don't have time to do the paperwork?

- ✔ Can I do anything else for you before I go home for the day?

Although asking politically pointed questions gives you an initial indication of the political lie of the land, you can do more to assess the political environment in your organisation. Watch out for the following signs while you're getting a sense of how your organisation really works:

- ✔ **Find out how others who seem to be effective get tasks done.** How much time do they spend preparing before sending through a formal request? Which items do they delegate and to which subordinates? When you find people who are particularly effective at getting tasks done in your organisation's political environment, emulate them, and apply their methods to your own goals.

- ✔ **Observe how the organisation rewards others for the jobs they do.** Do managers swiftly and enthusiastically give warm and personal rewards in a sincere manner to make it clear what behaviour they consider important? Do they give credit to everyone who helped make a project successful, or is the manager the only one singled out for praise? By observing your company's rewards, you can tell what behaviour your organisation expects of employees. Practise this behaviour.

**Book III**

**Managing and Leading Others**

✔ **Observe how the organisation disciplines others and for what.** Do your managers come down hard on employees for relatively small mistakes? Do they criticise employees in public or in front of colleagues? Do they hold everyone accountable for decisions, actions and mistakes even if someone had no prior involvement? Such behaviour on the part of management indicates that they don't encourage risk taking. If your management doesn't encourage risk taking, make your political style outwardly reserved as you work behind the scenes.

✔ **Consider how people behave towards each other, and how appropriate their conduct is.** For example, blurting out 'That's a stupid idea. Why would we even consider doing such a thing?' in a staff meeting is clearly unacceptable. Make sure that people conduct themselves professionally at all times. A more appropriate statement is: 'That's an interesting possibility. Can we explore the pros and cons of implementing such a plan?' Make mutual respect standard behaviour in your company.

## *Identifying key players*

So now that you've discovered that you work in a political environment (did you really have any doubt?), you need to determine who the key players are. Why? Because these individuals can help make your department more effective and provide positive role models to you and your employees.

*Key players* are those politically astute individuals who make things happen in an organisation. You can identify them by their tendency to make instant decisions without having to refer to people 'upstairs', their use of the latest corporate slang and their tendency to always speak up in meetings, if only to ask, 'What's our objective here?'

Sometimes influential people don't hold influential positions. For example, Jack, as the department head's assistant, may initially appear to be nothing more than a clerk. However, you may find out that Jack is responsible for scheduling all his boss's appointments, setting agendas for departmental meetings and vetoing actions on his own authority. Jack is an informal leader in the organisation and, because you can't get to the department head without going through Jack, you know that he has much more power than his title may indicate. You need to be able to influence those who act as gatekeepers to top and senior managers.

Use the following questions to identify the key players in your organisation:

✔ Which employees do others go to for advice?

✔ Which employees do others consider to be indispensable?

✔ Whose office is located closest to those of the organisation's top management and whose is farthest away? Evidence shows that the farther away you work from head office, the less influence you have.

✔ Who are the members of the inner circle? Who eats lunch with top and senior management?

As you work out who the key players in your organisation are, you start to notice that they have different office personalities. Use the following categories to help you figure out how to work with the different personality types of your organisation's key players:

✔ **Movers and shakers:** These individuals usually far exceed the boundaries of their office positions. For example, you may find a mover and shaker who's in charge of purchasing helping to negotiate a merger. Someone in charge of the physical plant may have the power to designate a wing of the building to the group of his choosing. Non-political individuals, on the other hand, tend to be bogged down by responsibilities – such as getting their own work done.

✔ **Corporate citizens:** These employees are diligent, hardworking, company-loving individuals who seek slow but steady, long-term advancement through dedication and hard work. Corporate citizens are great sources of information and advice. You can count on them for help and support, especially if your ideas seem to be in the best interest of the organisation.

✔ **Town gossips:** These employees always seem to know what's going on in the organisation – usually before those individuals who are actually affected by the news know it. Always assume that anything you say to a gossip will get back to the person your commenting on.

✔ **Firefighters:** These individuals relish rushing in at the last possible moment to save a project, client, deadline or whatever. High drama and great fanfare precede their arrival. Keep a firefighter well informed of your progress so that you aren't the subject of the next 'fire'.

✔ **Vetoers:** These people have the authority to kill your best ideas with a simple comment such as, 'We tried that and it didn't work.' Keeping them away from you is the best way to deal with vetoers. Try to find other individuals who can get your idea approved or rework it until you hit on an approach that satisfies the vetoer.

✔ **Techies:** Every organisation has technically competent workers who legitimately have a high value of their own opinions. Experts can take charge of a situation without taking over. Get to know your experts well – you can trust their judgements and opinions.

**Book III**

**Managing and Leading Others**

✔ **Moaners and whiners:** A few employees are never satisfied with whatever you do for them. Associating with them inevitably leads to a pessimistic outlook, which you can't easily turn around. Or worse, your boss may think that you're a whiner too. In addition, pessimistic people tend to get promoted less often than optimists. Be an optimist: your upbeat outlook can make a big difference to your career.

## Redrawing your organisation chart

Your company's organisation chart may be useful for determining who's who in the formal organisation, but it really has no bearing on who's who in the informal political organisation. What you need is the real organisation chart. Figure 6-1 illustrates a typical official organisation chart.

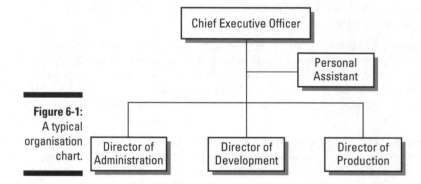

**Figure 6-1:**
A typical organisation chart.

Start by finding your organisation's official organisation chart – the one that looks like a big pyramid. Throw it away. Now, from your impressions and observations, start outlining the *real* relationships in your organisation in your mind. (But be careful! You don't always want people to know what you're up to.) Begin with the key players you've already identified. Indicate their relative power by level and relationships. Use the following questions as a guideline:

✔ **Who associates with these influential people?** Draw the associations on your chart and connect them with solid lines. Also connect friends and relatives, other clear associates and anyone who you know enjoys particular patronage or favour.

✔ **Who makes up the office cliques?** Be sure that all members are connected, because talking to one is like talking to them all.

✔ **Who are the office gossips?** Use dotted lines to represent communication without influence and solid lines for communication with influence.

✔ **Who's your competition?** Circle those employees that managers are likely to consider for the next promotion. Target them for special attention.

✔ **Who's left off the chart?** Don't forget about these individuals. The speed at which organisations change nowadays means that someone who's not featured on the chart on Friday may be on it by Monday. Always maintain positive relationships with all of your colleagues and never burn bridges between you and others throughout the company, whatever their position. Otherwise, you may find yourself omitted from the chart at some point.

The result of this exercise is a chart of who really has political power in your organisation and who doesn't. Figure 6-2 shows how the organisation really works. Update your organisation chart as you find out more information about people. Take note of any behaviour that gives away a relationship – such as your boss cutting off a colleague in mid-sentence – and factor this observation into your overall political analysis. Of course, understand that you may be wrong. You can't possibly know the inner power relationships of every department. Sometimes individuals who seem to have power may have far less of it than people who've discovered how to use their power more quietly.

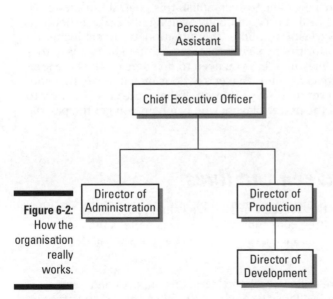

**Figure 6-2:**
How the organisation really works.

# Scrutinising Communication: What's Real and What's Not?

One of the best ways to determine how well you fit into an organisation is to see how well you communicate. But deciphering the real meaning of communication in an organisation takes some practice. So how do you determine the underlying meaning of words in your organisation? By observing behaviour, reading between the lines and, when necessary, knowing how to obtain sensitive information – that's how.

## Believing actions, not words

One way to decipher the real meaning of communication is to pay close attention to the corresponding behaviour of the communicator. People's values and priorities (that is, their ethics) tend to be revealed more clearly in what they do than what they say.

So, for example, if your manager repeatedly says she's trying to get approval for a pay rise for you, look at what actions she's taken towards that end. Did she make a call to her boss or hold a meeting? Did she submit the necessary paperwork or establish a deadline to accomplish this goal? If the answers to these questions are no, or if she's continually 'waiting to hear', the action is probably going nowhere fast. To counter this situation, try to get higher up on your boss's list of priorities by suggesting actions that she can take to get you your pay rise. You may find that you need to do some or all of the footwork yourself. Alternatively, your manager's actions may indicate that she doesn't wield much power in the organisation. If that's the case, then try to attract the attention of the power players who can help you get the pay rise you deserve.

## Reading between the lines

In business, don't take the written word at face value. Probe to discover the real reasons behind written communications. For example, a typical notice in a company newsletter announcing the reorganisation of several departments may read like this:

> With the departure of JR McNeil, the Marketing Support and Customer Service Department will now be a part of the Sales and Administration Division under Elizabeth Olsen, acting divisional director. The unit will eventually be moved under the direct supervision of the sales director, Tom Hutton.

Such an announcement appears straightforward on the surface, but if you read between the lines, you may be able to conclude:

> JR McNeil, who never did seem to get along with the director of sales, finally did something bad enough to justify getting fired. Tom Hutton apparently made a successful bid with the board of directors to add the area to his empire, probably because his sales were up 30 per cent from last year. Elizabeth Olsen will be appointed as acting divisional director for an interim period to do some of Tom's dirty work by clearing out the dead wood. Tom thus starts with a clean slate, 20 per cent lower over-heads and an almost guaranteed increase in profits for his first year in the job. This all fits very nicely with Tom's personal strategy for advance-ment – both the organisation's and his own. (*PS: A nice congratulatory call to Tom may be in order.*)

Announcements like these have been written dozens of times by so many people that they appear to be logical and valid when you initially read them. By reading between the lines, however, you can often determine what's really going on. Of course, you have to be careful not to jump to the wrong conclu-sions. JR McNeil may have simply gone on to better opportunities and the company has taken advantage of that event to reorganise. Make sure to vali-date your conclusions with others in the company to get the real story.

## *Probing for information*

In general, you can get excellent information about your organisation by being a trusted listener to as many people as possible. Show sincere inter-est in the affairs of others, and they may talk about themselves more openly. After they begin talking, you can shift the topic to work, work problems and eventually more sensitive topics. Ask encouraging questions and volunteer information as necessary to keep the exchange equitable.

Even after you've developed such trusted relationships, you need to know how to probe to uncover the facts about rumours, decisions and hidden agendas. Start by adhering to the following guidelines:

- Have at least three ways of obtaining the information.
- Check the information through two sources.
- Promise anonymity whenever possible.
- Generally, know the answers to the questions you ask.
- Be casual and non-threatening in your approach.
- Assume that the initial answer is superficial.

**Book III**

**Managing and Leading Others**

✔ Ask the same question in different ways.

✔ Be receptive to whatever information people give you.

One more thing: if you find yourself in an organisation that's rife with political intrigue, where you're always looking over your shoulder and are wondering whether the next rumour will concern you, seriously consider changing jobs! Every organisation has its share of politics, but spending too much time worrying about it is certainly counterproductive, and it can't be good for your well-being.

# Uncovering the Unwritten Rules of Organisational Politics

Every organisation has rules that are never written down and seldom discussed. Such unwritten rules pertaining to the expectations and behaviour of employees in the organisation can play a major role in your success or failure. Because unwritten rules aren't explicit, you have to piece them together by observation, insightful questioning or simply through trial and error.

Never underestimate the power of the unwritten rules of organisational politics. In many companies the unwritten rules carry just as much importance, if not more, than the written rules contained in the company's policy manual.

## Be friendly with all

The more individuals you have as friends in an organisation, the better. If you haven't already done so, start cultivating friends in your immediate work group and then extend your efforts to making contacts in other parts of the organisation. The more favourably your colleagues view you, the greater your chances of becoming their manager in the future. Cultivate your colleagues' support by seeking advice or by offering assistance.

Build a network by routinely helping new employees who enter your organisation. As they join, be the person who takes them aside to explain how the organisation really works. As the new employees establish themselves and move on to other jobs in other parts of the organisation, you have a well-entrenched network for obtaining information and assistance.

Knowing people throughout the organisation can be invaluable for clarifying rumours, obtaining information and indirectly feeding information back to others. An astute manager maintains a large number of diverse contacts throughout the organisation, all on friendly terms. The following are excellent ways to enlarge your network:

- ✔ **Walk around.** Those managers who walk the floor tend to be better known than those who don't. Return telephone and email messages in person whenever possible. Not only do you have the opportunity for one-to-one communication with the individual who left you the message, but also you can stop by to see everyone else you know along the way.

- ✔ **Get involved.** You need to meet superiors, peers and colleagues from a wide range of functions, departments, divisions and locations, so take every opportunity that presents itself to do so. Attend meetings, discussion groups, professional gatherings and problem-solving forums; and always support social and informal events.

- ✔ **Join committees.** Whether the committee forms to address employee security or simply to determine who cleans out the refrigerator in the employee lounge, take part. You get to meet new people in an informal and relaxed setting.

## *Help others get what they want*

A fundamental, unwritten rule of office politics is that getting what you want is easier when you give others what they want. Win the assistance of others by showing them what they stand to gain by helping you. When a benefit isn't readily apparent, create or allude to one that may occur if they offer to help. Such benefits can include:

- ✔ **A favour returned in kind:** Surely you can provide some kind of favour to your counterparts in exchange for their assistance. Lunch or the temporary secondment of an employee to their department is always a popular option.

- ✔ **Information:** Don't forget: information is power. Everyone desperately wants to know the latest and greatest information and gossip in an organisation – and your colleagues are no different. Be the one to give them information if you can.

- ✔ **Money:** Perhaps you have a little extra money in your equipment budget that you can allocate to someone's project in exchange for that person's help.

- ✔ **A recommendation:** Top and senior managers trust your judgement. Your willingness to recommend colleagues for promotion to a higher position or for recognition because of their extraordinary performance is a valuable commodity. The right words to the right people can make all the difference to someone's success in an organisation.

Book III

Managing and Leading Others

We're not suggesting that you do anything unethical or illegal. Don't violate your personal set of ethics or company policy to get ahead. When you provide these kinds of benefits to others in your organisation, make sure that you're within your company's rules and policies. And as a side benefit, you may actually find satisfaction in giving to others.

## Don't party at company parties

Social affairs are a serious time for those employees seeking to advance within a company. Social events offer one of the few times when everyone in the company is supposed to be on an equal footing. Don't believe it, though. Although social functions provide managers at the top with a chance to show that they're normal people and give employees below a chance to ask questions and laugh at their bosses' jokes, parties are also a time to be extremely cautious.

Beware of who you talk to and, of course, what you say. Social functions, such as Christmas parties and company picnics, aren't the time or the place to sink your career by making some injudicious comment or by making a fool of yourself. Managing most social encounters involves art and skill, especially those encounters that involve colleagues. If you have to attend such functions, then make them work to your advantage. Use these techniques at your next company party:

- ✔ Use the middle of the room to intercept individuals you especially want to speak to. As an alternative strategy for getting their attention, watch the buffet table or the punch bowl. Go for refills when the person you're seeking does so.

- ✔ Drink orange juice or mineral water. Never ever get drunk on the organisation's premises, in the organisation's time or at an organisational social function.

- ✔ Keep discussion loose and light and avoid talking about work topics with anyone other than your boss. Try to move on before the person you're speaking to runs out of topics to discuss and has a blank expression. Don't fawn or use flattery. These behaviours are more likely to lose respect for you than to gain it.

- ✔ Leave the social function only after the departure of the highest-ranking company official. If you have to leave before, let that person know why.

## Manage your manager

Successful managers know the importance of managing not just their employees, but their manager as well. The idea is to encourage your manager to do what most directly benefits you and your staff. The following tried-and-tested techniques for manager management have evolved through the ages:

- ✔ **Keep your manager informed of your successes:** 'That last sale puts me over quota for the month.'

- ✔ **Support your manager in meetings:** 'Gadsby is right on this. We really do have to consider the implications of this change for our customers.'

- ✔ **Praise your manager publicly:** 'Mr Gadsby is probably the best manager I've ever worked for.'

Although a well-controlled relationship with your manager is important, you need connections to those above your manager too. A key relationship to develop is with your manager's manager – an individual who's likely to have a very big influence on your future career.

 Volunteer for an assignment that happens to be one of your manager's boss's pet projects. If you do a good job, the senior boss may well ask you to carry out another project. Failing such an opportunity, try to find an area of common interest with your manager's boss. Bring up the topic in casual conversation and agree to meet later to discuss it in more detail. But do make sure that you maintain your own sense and appearance of integrity; don't create the impression that you're cavalier with the organisation's ranks, hierarchies and ways of working.

## Move ahead with your mentors

Having a mentor is almost essential for ensuring any long-term success within an organisation. A *mentor* is an individual – usually someone higher up in the organisation – who provides advice and helps to guide your progress. Mentors are necessary because they can offer you important career advice, as well as becoming your advocate to higher levels of the organisation – the levels that you don't have direct access to.

Make sure the person you select as your mentor (or who selects you, as is more often the case) has organisational clout and is vocal about touting your merits. If possible, get the support of several powerful people throughout the organisation. *Sponsorships* (your relationships with your mentors) develop informally over an extended period of time.

Seek out a mentor by finding an occasion to ask for advice. If you find the advice extremely helpful, frequently seek more advice from the same person. Initially, ask for guidance related to your work, but as time goes on, you can ask for advice about business in general and your career advancement specifically. Proceed slowly, or your intentions may be suspect. Always display tact and discretion in your approach to your mentor:

**Book III**

**Managing and Leading Others**

✔ **The wrong approach:** 'Mr Fairmont, I've been thinking. In the marketing department, a lot of bad rumours have been going around about you and Suzy. I could try to squash some of them if I see something in it for me. You know: you take care of me, and I take care of you. What do you say?'

✔ **The right approach:** 'Here's that special report you asked for, Ms Smith. Correlating customer colour preferences with the size of orders in the Eastern region was fascinating. You seem to be one of the most forward-looking people in this organisation.'

## Be trustworthy

Similar to having a mentor is being a loyal follower of an exceptional performer within the organisation. Finding good people to trust can be difficult, so if you're trustworthy, you're likely to become a valued associate of a bright peer. As that person rises quickly through the organisation, he can bring you along. However, whenever possible, make sure that you have many connections – when people fall, they fall very quickly and you don't want to go with them.

# Protecting Yourself

Inevitably, you may find yourself on the receiving end of someone else's political aspirations. Astute managers take precautions to protect themselves – and their employees – against the political manoeuvrings of others. These precautions can also help if your own strategies go wrong. What can you do to protect yourself?

## Document for protection

Document the progress of your department's projects and activities, especially when expected changes in plans or temporary setbacks affect them. Documenting the changes or setbacks gives you an accurate record of your projects' history and ensures that individuals who don't have your best interests at heart don't forget what happened (or inappropriately use what happened against you). The form of the documentation can vary, but the following are most common:

- ✔ Confirmation memos
- ✔ Activity reports
- ✔ Project folders
- ✔ Correspondence files
- ✔ Notes

## Don't make promises you can't keep

Avoid making promises or firm commitments when you don't want to or can't follow them through. Don't offer a deadline, final price or guarantee of action or quality unless you're sure you can meet it. When you make promises that you can't fulfil, you risk injuring your own reputation when deliveries are late, or costs are higher than expected.

If you find yourself forced to make promises when you aren't certain you can meet them, consider taking one of the following actions:

- ✔ **Hedge.** If you have to make a firm commitment to an action that you're not sure you can meet, hedge your promise as much as possible by building in extra time, staff, money or some other qualifier.

- ✔ **Extend time estimates.** If you have to make a time commitment that may be unrealistic, extend the estimate (add extra time to what you think you really need) to give yourself room to manoeuvre. If your employees deliver early, they're heroes.

- ✔ **Extend deadlines.** As deadlines approach, bring any problems you or your staff encounter – even the most basic ones – to the attention of the person who requested that you do the project. Keeping people informed prevents them from being surprised if you need to extend your deadlines.

**Book III**

**Managing and Leading Others**

## Be visible

To get the maximum credit for the efforts of you and your staff, be sure to publicise your department's successes. To ensure that credit goes where credit is due, do the following:

- ✔ **Advertise your department's successes.** Routinely send reports about successfully completed projects and letters of praise for every member of your staff to your manager and to your manager's boss.

✔ **Use surrogates.** Call on your friends in the organisation to help publicise your achievements and those of your employees. Be generous in highlighting your employees' achievements. If you highlight your own achievements at the expense of your hard-working staff, you appear tactless and boastful – and dishonest.

✔ **Be visible.** Make a name for yourself in the organisation. And performing at a level that separates you from the rest of the pack is the best way to do it. Work harder, work smarter and respond better to the needs of the organisation and your customers, and you get noticed!

# Chapter 7

# Coaching through Conflict

· · · · · · · · · · · · · · · · · · · · · · · · · · · · · · · · · · · · · · · · · · · · ·

## In This Chapter

▶ Resolving disagreements while avoiding violence

▶ Shifting away from blame

▶ Increasing team cohesion

▶ Giving and receiving feedback effectively

· · · · · · · · · · · · · · · · · · · · · · · · · · · · · · · · · · · · · · · · · · · · ·

**C**onflict – the state of opposition of ideas and interests – is an everyday fact of life that shows up in different ways. On the positive side, the energy of bouncing differing ideas back and forward allows creative solutions to emerge; the collaboration between two different styles generates wonderful results. On the negative side, conflicts lead to dramatic showdowns, physical violence and even devastatingly destructive wars.

Life would be bland without any creative tension, and expecting peace, joy and harmony at all times is unnatural. In fact, that sounds like some kind of la-la land occupied by children's toys like the Teletubbies. Yet when the battles arising from opposing views and interests escalate out of control, they not only put the parties concerned in danger, but also bring innocent bystanders into the fray.

Clients bring tales of conflict into their coaching sessions from all aspects of their lives: power struggles, money issues, relationship challenges, intellectual differences, cross-cultural misunderstandings and battles with suppliers or customers. Coaching provides a safe space to explore the creative solutions that can emerge through conflict. The battles you assist your clients in solving may be:

✔ **Internal,** involving contradictory thoughts, decisions and dilemmas going on within the client's own mind.

✔ **External,** involving the tension between the client's needs, interests and concerns and those of others the client interacts with.

In this chapter, we concentrate on ways to resolve external conflict. At the same time, each conflict situation raises questions about the client's internal conflict.

# Recognising Behaviours under Pressure

The first step in coaching clients through conflict is to support them in becoming aware of their own patterns and their typical reactions to conflict situations before exploring ways to work through differences and emerge with more creativity and resourcefulness for the future.

Invite your clients to be curious as to how they naturally react under pressure when emotions are heightened. What is their innate approach to conflicts with others? How do they deal with any conflict's underlying frustrations and the inevitable shifts of power and control? Do they naturally want to run away and hide, or do they want to fight their corner?

NLP affirms that the mind and body are inextricably linked. Stressful situations place the human body on high alert. This natural response to threat invokes what is known as the *fight or flight response*. In this aroused state, the hormone adrenalin is released into the bloodstream, and a person experiences natural physiological changes designed to increase the capacity to fight the enemy or run away.

Your clients may mention any or all the following physiological changes in conflict situations, regardless of whether they want to flee or fight:

- Heartbeat increases
- Rate of breathing speeds up
- Sweating
- Increased sensitivity to sights and sounds
- Butterflies in the stomach
- Hyperventilation leading to dizziness and tingling in fingers
- Feelings of exhaustion after prolonged anxiety

A panic attack isn't just an outburst of nerves or anger. In a panic attack, a person may exhibit any of the above symptoms and more besides, including sensations of choking, tingling and loss of reality as the sympathetic nervous system kicks into action. In particular, the shortness of breath and heart palpitations increase anxiety as sufferers fear they're suffering heart failure and thus the anxiety extends the attack.

Coaching shines a light on people's blind spots, a process that isn't always comfortable. Don't be surprised if clients facing conflict situations abandon coaching or become confrontational with you. Clients may choose to run or fight because they find the issues under discussion too challenging to work through. Just consider: by giving them the space in which they can criticise you as their coach, you're doing them the service of allowing them to express anger and anxiety that they haven't voiced elsewhere!

## Checking for patterns

After clients become aware of how they deal with conflict through coaching conversations, they can develop new strategies to work through it. If conflict is a particular issue, suggest to your clients that they keep a log of difficult relationships and what triggers conflict for them.

While clients are experiencing the intense physical symptoms of panic during conflict, clear thinking can be difficult. The following simple steps enable them to sit with the conflict, without fighting or running away.

- ✔ **Stop.** Don't fight the conflict or the feelings – and don't run away from them either. Just observe the feelings of panic, noticing the images, sounds and feelings you're experiencing in the moment.

- ✔ **Trust.** Know that feelings of panic are simply an extreme case of the normal fight-or-flight response.

- ✔ **Accept the gift.** Each experience is a chance to practise moving through conflict and develop new, useful coping mechanisms.

- ✔ **Focus on now.** Stay present in the moment, knowing that you are safe and your feelings of panic will pass.

- ✔ **Celebrate.** After the feelings pass, take a bow for staying with the situation.

**Book III**

**Managing and Leading Others**

Share these steps with your client. Some people like to keep a small card with the steps written on as a reminder. Others prefer a small object or a peaceful natural image like a beautiful sunset to help them stop panicking.

Conflict with others often arises by thoughts alone; the conflict may not have any basis in reality. For example, you may assume that a colleague isn't willing to work with you or just wants to cause trouble. NLP offers specific techniques to shift that thinking. You can help clients switch submodalities, which are the way clients represent their experiences in images, sounds and feelings, to defuse negative emotion. You can also help them gain new perspectives by having them take the perspective of the person with whom they're experiencing conflict.

# Holding on to the best outcome

In relationships with others, the ideal scenario is a win-win, where both parties get what they want. However, in a conflict, one party always loses, and most likely both parties become the losers. In conflict, you get stuck in a blame frame in which you criticise someone else and hope she changes.

In order to coach your clients to the best outcomes, check whether your questions keep them exploring the problems or shift them to seek positive outcomes. The following sections deal with specific clusters of questions you may ask during coaching sessions.

## Noticing blame-frame questions

When people are caught up in blaming others, the wrong kind of questions keep clients stuck and feeling bad about themselves.

In the following dialogue, notice how the coach's blame questions keep the client stuck in the client's own thoughts.

> **Coach:** What is your problem?
>
> **Client:** The staff are threatening a walk-out over cuts.
>
> **Coach:** How long have you had it?
>
> **Client:** It's been looming for some months now, but people have been ignoring it.
>
> **Coach:** Where does the fault lie?
>
> **Client:** It's the union rep who's been whipping up resentment amongst the staff here.
>
> **Coach:** Who is to blame?
>
> **Client:** Well, it's partly the Chancellor, who's forcing our hand with massive cuts in funding, and partly the last government for over-spending.
>
> **Coach:** What's your worst experience with this problem?
>
> **Client:** I've been having sleepless nights worrying about what's going to happen.
>
> **Coach:** Why haven't you solved it yet?
>
> **Client:** I don't know what I can do. What do you think I should do?

## Shifting to outcome-frame questions

When people concentrate on outcomes rather than problems, their thinking becomes constructive. If the coach switches to outcome-frame questions, new thinking opens up and encourages the client to begin to resolve the problem.

In the following dialogue, notice the shift in the client's thinking to take responsibility for moving forward.

> **Coach:** What do you want?
>
> **Client:** I want us to resolve this labour dispute amicably.

Check that your clients state what they want in positive terms. Using positive language harnesses the power of the unconscious mind.

> **Coach:** How will you know when you've got it? What's the evidence?
>
> **Client:** I'll see us having sensible discussions rather than being held to ransom. We'll have a series of consultations and communications, offering practical help to those we make redundant and feel that we've done the best we can with the budget.
>
> **Coach:** What else will improve when you get it?
>
> **Client:** I'll be able to sleep again at night. I'll have more energy and be better tempered at work – and at home.
>
> **Coach:** What resources do you have already that can help you achieve this outcome?
>
> **Client:** I have access to a lot of expertise in my network, and I'm generally a very calm and rational thinker, someone who's empathetic to other people.
>
> **Coach:** What is something similar that you've succeeded in doing?
>
> **Client:** I once worked on a hostile takeover project, and I planned out a whole series of consultations and communications, including outplacement support.
>
> **Coach:** What's the next step?
>
> **Client:** I'll invite the union rep to have a coffee and an informal chat with me to set up some consultations.

# Working through Differences

Conflict arises when two parties become entrenched in their own ideologies. In this section, we explore some practical NLP approaches that offer ways to shift through conflict with greater ease.

## Knowing the enemy well

The famous British military commander Field Marshal 'Monty' Montgomery kept a picture of his German opponent Rommel, The Desert Fox, on the wall of his desert campaign headquarters during the Second World War. In planning the strategy for war, he wanted to focus on his enemy in order to analyse tactics in battle through his opponent's eyes.

When negotiating through conflict, the NLP concept of *perceptual positions* can provide insight into opposing viewpoints and help you separate from your emotions in order to achieve an independent perspective (as described in Book III Chapter 5).

Take your client through the following exercise to better work with anyone with whom the client is in conflict. She needs to identify someone that she'd like to understand better, perhaps even someone she's struggled with in the past if she'd like to get a greater understanding.

1. **Lay out three pieces of paper on the floor to denote the three perceptual positions of self, opponent and independent observer.**

2. **Have the client take each position in turn.**

    When your client steps onto a piece of paper, ask the client, 'What are you thinking and feeling in this position?'

3. **As the client steps through the three positions, capture any thoughts and ideas on paper.** Be careful not to interpret the information by paraphrasing it: just capture what is said.

4. **Have the client step back to first position and relay to the client what you heard from second and third position.** Feed back what you heard and invite the client to make sense of it.

5. **Ask the client what ideas the client now has about his or her opponent.**

    Help your client identify some first steps for improving the relationship with this person.

---

# Team conflicts – and solutions

Teams and other groups can fall apart under pressure. Fortunately, team coaching can bring conflict under control before it skyrockets. Some common sources of conflict within groups are:

✔ **Lack of goals.** Teams with no goals – or confused or contradictory goals – typically experience disagreements and

dissatisfaction. As coach, you can help to bring clarity by helping to set goals as well-formed outcomes or SMART goals using a shared methodology. Turn to Book IV Chapter 2 for tools and ideas.

✔ **Role confusion.** When people don't know who's doing what and why, group members assume that somebody else is doing something that doesn't happen! As coach, you can work to ensure that all team members understand each other's roles, have clear job definitions and identify any grey areas where two roles overlap and cause potential misunderstandings.

✔ **Unclear or vague expectations**. Teams need a clear communication process so that members can express their expectations and alert the team when something isn't meeting expectations. Teams can rely on formal meetings or reporting systems to keep each other informed and share expectations. As coach, you can examine the processes in place and work with the team to set up or improve processes in order to encourage better-quality communications. (See Book III Chapter 5 for ideas to support teams shifting through the classic stages of development.) Consider sitting in on meetings and giving feedback about how the team members interact with each other.

✔ **Different styles.** Conflicts arise when different personality types and ways of working come together. They may be a mix of extrovert or introverts, commanding or collaborative tendencies, as well as containing different talents and knowledge within the group. Administering psychometric tools such as Myers-Briggs and LAB profiles offers insights into how different styles can honour each other's differences and harness these distinctions to achieve positive results.

✔ **Disagreement on methods.** Conflicts arise when the team can achieve the same result in more than one way. The team coach can remind the team that everyone is heading towards the same goal and that these differences add resilience.

## Negotiating in the best-sized chunks

Matching someone else at the right chunk-size of information eases communication. If you give an appropriate level of information, the other person can process it easily. Give too large a chunk – that is, very big-picture or general information – and she's left in the dark. Break it into too many specific details and she's swamped.

Suzanne was bemoaning the poor admin support from the office personal assistant to her coach. When asked specifically how her PA didn't support her, Suzanne kept replying in generalities: she didn't sort things, she didn't take responsibility for the financials. Suzanne is a speedy executive who doesn't like to get involved in the details of paperwork and payments. Her coach quickly realised that, in this specific context of delegating work, Suzanne operated at a global rather than detail level in terms of her NLP metaprograms. Suzanne and her coach worked on how Suzanne could slow down and patiently give very precise requests to the PA regarding the details of the admin work.

NLP takes the concept of chunking from the field of computing. *Chunking* refers to taking information and breaking it into smaller *bytes*. NLP also talks about:

✔ **Chunking up.** Going from detail to a more general concept.

✔ **Chunking across.** Taking an idea from one context to another, normally by using metaphors and stories at a similar level of detail.

✔ **Chunking down.** Getting more specific details.

When negotiating through opposing positions, chunking ideas can be very useful. Chunking up enables people to agree on certain principles even if they differ on how they're implemented.

Consider the following example of two manufacturing company directors, Clive and Sara, who are arguing about business strategy. Clive argues that they should be investing in China, and Sara is championing investment in India.

✔ **When they chunk up,** they both agree their common ground. In this case, they both see the need for overseas investment. At this level, they can also explore what other main principles they agree on.

✔ **If they chunk across,** Clive or Sara might win the other over by telling stories of other successful businesses that have invested in the respective territories.

✔ **If they chunk down into specifics** and listen to each other's plans in turn, they might explore the relative benefits and disadvantages of the different investment areas instead of dismissing the area outright.

Chunking up and down between two people isn't easy without a determined effort by both parties. People tend to get caught up in their own specific detail and find it hard to get to the common ground, which is where an independent coach can facilitate the negotiation.

# Voicing What Needs to Be Said

One of the underlying benefits of conflict is that things come into the open and each party can grow based on the new information. Conversations may finally air thoughts and feelings that have been festering beneath the surface for years.

The Johari window is a tool that illustrates that everyone has blind spots. Conflict can cut through a history of collusion and hidden information. Yet messages need to be conveyed with respect and appreciation of differences so that people can hear them.

The following sections explore techniques for getting out difficult information in useful, non-incendiary ways.

# Developing the non-violent vocabulary

To shift through conflict, your clients need to be able to communicate without fighting or running away. In order to do so, they must be persistent and stay calm when others may not be.

Practising a simple structure such as the following four-step model in a coaching session gives clients an easy tool to replicate in other conflict situations. Use this activity to rehearse a difficult conversation where your client needs to give challenging feedback.

The following four steps are based on Marshall Rosenberg's model of non-violent communication.

1. **When I saw/heard you . . .**

   Describe the specific, observable behaviour or actions that you've noticed.

   *For example, 'When I heard you raise your voice and swear at me.'*

2. **I felt/the impact on me was . . .**

   Describe your feelings objectively, including the impact the other person's behaviour or words had on you.

   *For example, 'I felt anxious,' or 'The impact on me was to want to cover my ears.'*

   Don't attribute blame to the other person. Avoid language such as 'I felt belittled/accused/suffocated', which implies a negative action on the other person's part. Instead, encourage your clients to own their feelings.

   *For example, 'I felt worried,' or 'I felt I needed more time to explain.'*

3. **I need . . .**

   Describe your underlying need in this situation. In the case of a work-related conflict, your need may be the specific requirements of the job.

   *For example, 'I need to provide good customer service.'*

4. **Can I ask you to . . .**

   Finish by making a specific request of the person and/or give guidance on how the other person can approach the situation differently in order to meet the need.

   *For example, 'If you have a complaint, please can you give me the facts quietly.'*

**Book III**

**Managing and Leading Others**

## Finessing feedback

NLP says there's no such thing as failure, only feedback, and places great value on feedback for learning. Those who've suffered with poor managers at work may associate feedback with getting told off and shy away from inviting it. Yet feedback is information that highlights both strengths and areas for improvement. Feedback is critical at home as well as in work environments, and is an essential part of the coach-client relationship. How do you know how you're doing unless you invite the other person to tell you?

In order to give feedback with respect:

- Give positive as well as critical feedback – the more positive, the better because people tend to focus on the negatives.

- Bring a constructive spirit. Avoid giving feedback when you're angry or tired, for example.

- Stick to the facts. Deal only with what you've observed and what others have recognised.

- Talk about clear, specific behaviours and be prepared to give specific examples.

- Avoid making assumptions about the person's motives or feelings.

- Don't blame the other person. You're responsible for your reactions to other people; recognise your reactions and accept your responsibility.

In order to receive feedback graciously:

- Don't argue or try to convince the feedback givers that they didn't see what they said they saw.

- Don't attempt to explain your behaviour to the giver, just acknowledge the feedback. Discussing the feedback *later* may be appropriate if you feel you want to learn more from it.

- Invite the feedback giver to provide specific examples of clear, observable behaviours. For example, ask the feedback giver something like, '*What did I do that told you I was angry?*'

- If the giver can't state the feedback in clear behavioural terms with specific examples, thank the giver but make your own judgement on the validity of the feedback.

- Listen carefully to what others have to say and thank them for their input. Your job is to determine what the feedback means to you and how you intend to use it.

✔ Stop when you've had enough. Tell the givers that you understand what they're saying or that you want some time to think about it.

If the feedback comes as part of a complaint or disciplinary process, you're right to question and challenge anything you consider unfair and exert your legal rights.

## Building the most confident voice

When people are willing to stay in the space where conflict is happening, they build the self-confidence to express what really matters to them instead of running away. With a constructive approach that looks for both parties to win, participants can increase passion, purpose and release positive energy.

Like many solopreneurs (individual entrepreneurs) selling over the Internet to global markets, Rachel's business is based from her home office. Over a period of months, she became increasingly frustrated by her poor Internet speeds, complaining that although she lived in the equivalent of Silicon Valley, she could get better Internet access in remote areas of the developing world.

After complaining for six months to her service provider and making no progress, Rachel felt that her core values – integrity, professionalism and freedom – weren't showing up in this business relationship. Instead of burying her head in the sand or turning angry, she decided to take action. She drew on her innate resources to ask: 'What can I do?' and 'What can I learn from this?'

**Book III**

**Managing and Leading Others**

Thus began a positive Internet campaign to get action on broadband speeds. From taking the first step of setting up a blog and dedicated website, interest in her campaign snowballed, taking on its own momentum for change. She became the local spokesperson, harnessing the power of social media, the press, MPs, the local authority, business leaders and key industry stakeholders.

Six lessons emerge from Rachel's campaign that can be applied by anyone looking to transform conflict into positive action:

✔ **Manage your emotional state.** Staying calm and curious enables you to work through negative interactions confidently so that you remain in a flow state (see Book III Chapter 2 for more on flow).

✔ **Focus on a positive outcome.** Know what you want and then plan and implement a strategy to get there with tenacity (see Book IV Chapter 2 for more on goal-setting).

✔ **Unlock resources.** Make the most of your own creativity, sense of fun and contacts. Look to other people to serve as role models.

- ✔ **Develop stronger beliefs.** Remind yourself often that 'I can do this' or 'I'm doing this for the greater good'.

- ✔ **Honour values.** Pay attention and respect both your own values and other people's.

- ✔ **Work with passion and purpose.** These forces can guide you to take massive action.

## Developing appreciative habits

What gets lost during conflict is the fundamental appreciation of other people, that diversity of views and cultures that enriches the experience of being human. In particular, listening at a deep level closes down in the face of anger and frustration.

As a coach, you're in a privileged position to feel empathy for your client while taking a more impartial view of the whole situation. Exercises or activities that engender an appreciation of the person, group or organisation with whom your client is in conflict can defuse the situation and make the client more flexible.

Invite your clients to reflect about the people with whom they differ. Ask questions such as:

- ✔ What are five good things that they've done?

- ✔ What are their best qualities? What are their hidden strengths?

- ✔ What are you glad that you've discovered from this situation that you wouldn't have without this opportunity?

- ✔ How can you be the catalyst for empathy and understanding here?

- ✔ What are you willing to let go of? Where could you become more flexible?

- ✔ How might you and others benefit when you look for similarities with the other party?

- ✔ Who can you become through this conflict?

Ultimately, when you provide space for your clients to raise the quality of their thinking and listening to reflect on other perspectives, you create the potential to transform conflict into co-operation. Beyond the particular troublesome situation, such lessons change how your clients behave in future interactions.

# Chapter 8

# Becoming an Engaging Leader

The great news is that you already have some skills in engaging people, and you can build on these skills to become an engaging leader with the four foundations for engaging your team members: *relating* to people; *proacting* to seek, share and critique each others' thoughts; *sensing* – switching on your senses to gather data and information; and *inter-interpreting* – interpreting and reinterpreting together.

In this chapter you find out how to enhance and effectively deploy your skills in these four foundations, and how to engage people effectively. We also show you how your improved performance as an engaging leader is linked to building your personal confidence, maintaining focus and clarity within your team, and increasing your team members' commitment.

## Recognising Your Existing Skills

The four foundations for engaging your staff are intimately connected with each other. They are sub-processes of the overall process or activity of engaging people, and to be brilliant at engaging people you have to become skilled in using these four sub-processes simultaneously.

Before we explore using each of the four foundation sub-processes in more detail, take a few minutes to reflect on situations when you were in a conversation with an individual or group of people in which one or more of the following events occurred:

✔ You were all totally engrossed in the conversation.

✔ Individual and group understanding of the subject were significantly enhanced.

✔ One or more 'aha!' moments happened: for example, when new insights were gained into the subject being discussed.

✔ The people involved experienced a strong sense of togetherness or camaraderie.

✔ A common commitment to act resulted from the conversation.

Now try the following exercise.

1. **Get a notebook and divide the page into three columns as shown in Table 8-1.**

2. **Write a brief description of the situation in which the first conversation occurred.**

3. **In the second column, list the actions that you took – briefly describe what you did or said – to make a valuable and meaningful contribution to this conversation.**

4. **Describe the effect that your contribution had on you and/or the other people involved, or the outcome of the meeting.**

5. **Repeat steps 2 to 4 for other situations that you identified.**

In the first row of the table below is an example to help you get started.

| Table 8-1 | Examples of Situations When I Used Skills in Engaging People | |
|---|---|---|
| *Brief Description of the Situation* | *Brief Description of What I Did or Said that was a Significant Contribution to the Conversation* | *The Effect that it Had on Me and/or Other People Involved, and the Outcome* |
| Weekly team meeting in which I thought that we were, as normal, meandering off the topics and wasting time. | I pointed out that we were going off-track and I questioned whether this way of holding meetings was the most effective use of our time. | Some people were initially defensive about why they had introduced new topics, but my questions prompted the team to re-evaluate how well we were holding meetings, and we agreed changes to improve the productivity of the meetings. |

| Brief Description of the Situation | Brief Description of What I Did or Said that was a Significant Contribution to the Conversation | The Effect that it Had on Me and/or Other People Involved, and the Outcome |
| --- | --- | --- |
|  |  |  |
|  |  |  |
|  |  |  |
|  |  |  |

Take a look at the notes you make in the second column: these comments are examples of the skills that you already possess in engaging people, and ones on which you can build to become an engaging leader.

# Enhancing Relating to People

Most working relationships are less stable, and sometimes more fragile, than you and other people may realise; the way that you relate to, or connect with, each other changes due to your interpretations of your experiences of working together. You find out how to enhance your skills in relating to and connecting with your work colleagues in the next four sections.

## 'Working with' and not 'doing to' people

Let's assume people want to make a positive difference or contribution to the organisation that employs them.In trying to contribute, some people may be too helpful in working with their colleagues in the sense that they take responsibility off, or undermine, them. Examples of actions – and the reasons for taking them – when you may notice colleagues (or even caught yourself) taking responsibility off people include:

✔ Interrupting a colleague and finishing his sentences by expressing what you think your colleague was going to say.

✔ Taking a task off a colleague, especially a less experienced one, because you know how to do the task better. You may indeed complete the task quicker, but your intervention stops the less experienced person from discovering how to do it correctly and may undermine his self-confidence.

These are examples of unintentionally 'doing to' rather than 'working with' people, but you may perceive that some people deliberately impose their views or actions!

Work on improving your approach to working with your colleagues by:

✔ Having and showing total respect for every individual: respect the rights that you and each person have such as:

- The right to express your views and opinions.
- The right to express how you feel.
- The right to be listened to and heard.
- The right to change your mind.

✔ Striving to get to know and really understand them. (Refer to the next section 'Having a genuine interest in others' to find out more about how to do this successfully.)

✔ Being empathetic: put yourself 'in their shoes' and try to appreciate things from the other person's perspective.

## Having a genuine interest in others

You may sometimes find that showing a genuine interest in others is difficult. For example, in a work context you may have demanding targets or results that you have to achieve, and think that you have to focus all your attention and effort on achieving those results. Focusing in on your targets has a similar effect to looking down a telescope: you can clearly see your targets but you can't see much else!

'Silo management' – which is when departments become inward looking and don't consider the needs of, or how they impact on, other departments – tends to happen when managers of departments focus on achieving their own department's targets. In doing so, managers tend to become blinkered to the needs of, or how their work affects, their peers in other departments. This effect is described in the later sidebar 'Hitting your KPIs'.

An unintended side effect of focusing on your own targets is like putting blinkers on a horse to prevent it being distracted in a race: you stop noticing and showing an interest in what's going on around you!

Practise developing a genuine interest in your work colleagues by:

✔ **Challenging yourself: 'How well do I really know each person?'** Ask yourself how well you know each person who works with you, especially the people who report directly to you. Can you accurately describe their personal circumstances, interests and hobbies, hopes and aspirations, any concerns about their work and so on? What makes them tick? If you don't know, invest time in finding out by talking to them.

✔ **Asking members of your team about whether they think that you show enough interest in them.** If your organisation has an appraisal process, invite each person who reports to you to give you honest feedback about how well you lead, support and work with them. If your organisation doesn't have an appraisal system, take the initiative to have informal conversations with each person to obtain their views about you.

✔ **Checking your plans.** Take a look at your schedule, plan or 'to do' lists for the last month and estimate how much time or how many activities were focused on people: getting to know or understand them better, train, develop, guide and support them, and so on. What insights do your findings tell you about how much of a genuine interest you show in people?

Reflect on the benefits and consequences of how often you're showing a genuine interest in people, especially if your initial assessment indicates that you're thinking about people issues less than 20 per cent of the time – depending on the size of your team.

## *Building strong connections*

When you build strong connections with your work colleagues, you also construct strong bonds and more stable relationships with them and throughout your team.

1. **Refer to Figure 8-1 and get a notebook to draw a figure to represent how closely connected you are with the people who report to you.**

2. **Draw a small circle in the centre of the page and write your name inside it.**

3. **Draw a small circle representing each person who reports to you around your circle and put their name in it, the position of each circle being closer to or farther away from your circle based on how strongly you're connected with the person.**

4. **For each close connection that you have with a person ask yourself:**

    • What are the reasons for this connection?

    • What have I done to create this connection?

    • How do I treat this person?

    • How much time do I spend with the person?

Book III

Managing and Leading Others

**5. Repeat step 4 for the connections that you have with other people who are less close.**

List the actions that you take that help you to build close connections with people, and plan actions that you're going to take to show a genuine interest in and build strong connections with all the people who report to you. Repeat this exercise for other key people who you work with.

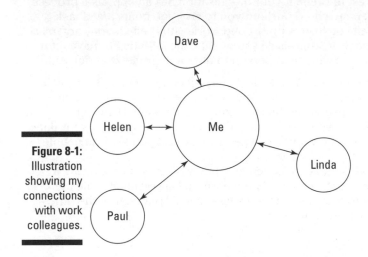

**Figure 8-1:**
Illustration showing my connections with work colleagues.

You strengthen the connection between yourself and colleagues when they sense that you have a genuine interest in, and concern for, them. Plus, when you show this kind of interest, they're highly likely to reciprocate the interest in you, and the objectives and results that you're trying to achieve.

## Being non-judgemental

You may not realise, but being judgemental – that is, forming an opinion about whether a person is good or bad – is all too easy, as is then allowing that opinion to affect adversely or unfairly how you treat the person.

Try the following exercise on leadership development programmes to explore how easy becoming judgemental with people can be:

**1. Take a few moments to think about the person you most enjoy working with: a person who perhaps does great work, is helpful, reliable, takes initiative and so on.** Does the person's face appear in your mind?

2. **Now think about the person you least like to work with: someone who perhaps causes you a lot of problems, is difficult to work with, causes you to worry about work, who you like to avoid if you can and so on.** Can you see this person's face?

3. **Now reflect on how you work with each person, and question yourself about whether you're always fair regarding how you treat these two people.**

Virtually everyone who is asked to do this exercise agrees that they quickly see that they treat people differently. A concern is that you, if you also see different people, may unconsciously be carrying baggage about each person with you: views or opinions that prompt you automatically to treat people in a certain way.

For example, if you have an opinion that a person is difficult to work with, you may go into a conversation with the person about a problem with his work expecting to have a difficult conversation: you've already formed a judgement that the person is going to be difficult! If you do so, you're likely to contribute to causing a difficult situation because you don't have an open mind and may be less objective in asking questions about the problem and listening to what the person has to say.

# Developing the Courage to Speak Your Mind

When occasionally asked to work with groups that are very dysfunctional, it's noticeable that one of the main reasons for this condition is that people don't feel able to 'speak their minds' in order to resolve problems between members of the group. For such a situation, a lot of effort is put into finding an appropriate venue that would help to create the right environment for people to open up and share their thoughts with each other.

Although the physical environment is important, the crucial factor that determines whether people open up to each other by speaking their minds is the environment created by members of the group. You discover in the earlier section 'Enhancing Relating to People' that having and showing a genuine interest in a person helps you to understand that person: this approach is a good starting point in encouraging members of any group, especially a dysfunctional group, to work better together.

## Standing out from the crowd

You have probably noticed when walking in the countryside how sheep tend to follow each other: it appears that one decides to go in a certain direction and all the rest follow in a long line. I sometimes experience a similar condition in working with management groups: one person, often the most senior manager or strongest character in the group, proposes a decision and everyone goes along with it. This behaviour often leads to the condition known as *groupthink*.

Be aware of groupthink, where the thinking behind decisions goes unchallenged in a group, leading to poor-quality decision-making.

Overcoming groupthink requires someone to have the courage to stand out from the crowd and speak his mind, to propose an alternative solution or challenge the proposed view.

Take the lead in speaking your mind in situations in which you experience groupthink, because by doing so you can:

✔ Assist the group to make more robust decisions by:

- Providing alternative and contrasting perspectives, options and solutions.

- Questioning the validity of proposals already put forward.

- Encouraging your colleagues to critique constructively, instead of automatically accepting your suggestions and proposals.

✔ Show leadership by being a role model and attempting to influence the rest of the group to follow your lead by sharing their views and critiquing the quality of thinking and decision-making.

✔ Challenge group norms of behaviour such as not questioning each other's views and encourage members of the group to strive continuously to improve how they work as a team.

Being clear about the purpose of your job, the objectives and results that senior management expects you and your team to achieve, together with having a clear understanding of the goals and objectives of your department and/or organisation, enables you to be bolder and speak your mind. This clarity helps generate confidence that the points that you want to make and the questions you want to ask are relevant.

You probably perceive that 'standing out from the crowd' by expressing your thoughts – especially if they're different to the group's view or involve critiquing the views of a senior manager or strong character – would put you in a difficult situation.

# Remaining aware of being dishonest

I don't think that you deliberately intend to be dishonest, but you may well have difficulty always being honest and saying what you really think! Complete the next exercise to check whether you do sometimes hold back.

Take a few minutes to reflect on situations in which you held back from expressing your honest views or opinions with an individual or group. The situation may be one that you experienced at work or in your personal life.

1. **Divide the page of a notebook into three columns as shown in Table 8-2.**
2. **Write a brief description of the situation in which you held back from expressing your true or honest thoughts.**
3. **Describe in the second column the thoughts that you had at the time.**
4. **Describe in the third column your reasons for not sharing your thoughts.**
5. **Repeat steps 2 to 4 for other similar situations that you identified.**

A simple example is provided in the first row to help you get started.

| Table 8-2 | Examples of Situations When I Didn't Share My True or Honest Views | |
|---|---|---|
| *Brief Description of the Situation* | *Brief Description of What I Really Thought but Didn't Say* | *My Reason for Not Sharing My Thoughts or Opinions with the Individual/Group* |
| One of the people who reports to me was again late for work by several minutes. | I thought the person shouldn't be late so often and should be better organised. | I didn't want to create a scene in which the person reacted badly and I wouldn't know how to cope with it. |

Book III

Managing and Leading Others

People hold back from sharing what they really think for two main reasons: they want to avoid being embarrassed or threatened, or they don't want another person to feel embarrassed or threatened. Many people don't want to embarrass a person because they care for them.

You may feel threatened in a situation in which you say what you really think about a work colleague's performance, behaviour or attitude to work, and the person reacts angrily, verbally or emotionally towards you. Colleagues may feel threatened by you sharing your thoughts if they then have to do something that they don't want to do, your comments reflect badly on them or they feel that their job security is under threat.

Although certain occasions exist when saying what you really think isn't appropriate or worthwhile – such as when a work colleague makes a rare minor mistake on a task – you don't want to allow standards of work and behaviour to slip by holding back. You can find tips to help in the later section 'Coping with embarrassment and threat'.

## Asking searching questions

Perhaps, like me, you've been discouraged from asking people searching questions, especially personal ones, because your parents or guardians think that doing so is impolite. You may have difficulty changing behaviour that you picked up when you were a child. The fact is, however, that as a team leader you're sometimes going to have to ask difficult questions.

In general, you're going to have one of three main aims when asking searching questions of work colleagues:

- ✔ To engage people with their own thoughts, by questioning the meaning of words, phrases and language that your colleagues are using in order to:
  - • Enable them to think things through.
  - • Clarify their thinking on the topic or subject being discussed.
  - • Prompt them to question or test the assumptions that underpin their point of view.
- ✔ To gather more information to enable:
  - • You to better understand people's points of view.
  - • You and your team to improve your understanding of the topic, subject or problem being discussed.
- ✔ To encourage and promote the activity of asking searching questions as a valuable activity in decision-making.

Practise your ability to ask searching questions by:

✔ **Being curious.** Rekindle the hunger to understand and seek the truth that young children have, as demonstrated by them asking questions such as 'Why?'.

✔ **Keeping the conversation going.** A good question can be a statement such as 'Tell me about. . .' or 'Talk me through. . .'.

✔ **Using open questions.** People feel obliged to give you more information about the topic or subject you're discussing when you ask a question starting with *what, why, where, when, how, who* or *which*.

✔ **Becoming comfortable with silence.** Many people don't like silence when they've asked a question, and ask another question or answer their own question within 20–30 seconds of asking the first question. Practise being silent for up to 90 seconds after you've asked a really good question.

✔ **Building up, not putting down.** Always have the positive intention of building up people instead of ridiculing, undermining, making them look foolish and so on in asking searching questions. People respect you when you act with integrity.

✔ **Remaining clear about your values or principles.** You're more likely to question and challenge others' views and even unacceptable behaviour in a group when you're clear about what's important to you.

✔ **Rising to your biggest challenge.** You may be the type of person who prefers to tackle the most difficult challenge straight away, or alternatively practise on less difficult situations or people first to progressively build your confidence. If you prefer the latter approach, start by asking searching questions of someone who's more receptive to being questioned or having his views challenged in order to develop your skills in framing questions.

✔ **Enhancing your ability to cope with potentially being embarrassed.** You may sometimes ask an inappropriate question such as one for which you should already know the answer. Checkout the later section 'Coping with embarrassment and threat' to find out how to handle being embarrassed.

**Book III**

**Managing and Leading Others**

## *Inviting challenge*

One of the best ways of encouraging work colleagues to become used to others asking difficult questions and challenging their views is to set an example by inviting others to question and challenge your own views.

Be a good role model for inviting challenge by:

✔ Keeping an open mind to find the best solution to a problem. You may demonstrate this approach by admitting that you may not have the best suggestion or solution to the problem being considered, but that you want to get to the best solution.

✔ Maintaining a calm composure and vulnerability to having your views or decisions questioned or challenged. You discourage colleagues from sharing their views with you when you criticise them for taking the initiative to do so.

✔ Praising colleagues who effectively question and challenge your views and decisions.

## Coping with embarrassment and threat

Expressing your thoughts and encouraging your colleagues to critique your thoughts is risky, because you may feel embarrassed or threatened. You can also develop the courage to speak your mind by being able to cope with situations that you perceive to be embarrassing or threatening.

Here are a few ways to work on being able to cope with embarrassment and threat:

✔ **Recognise that embarrassment almost always fades with time.** Think about occasions when you felt embarrassed and you often realise that the emotion fades after an hour or two, or perhaps a day or two. Rarely are occasions so embarrassing that you're left with an emotional scar!

✔ **Nurture an 'I will survive' mentality.** You're more likely to put yourself into potentially embarrassing situations when you believe that you can cope with them. Use positive language such as 'I can. . .', 'I'm good' or 'I will survive' to talk up your self-esteem, or listen to a song that motivates or inspires you to help you to feel more positive.

✔ **Assess the risk**. If you're the sort of person who tends to worry when you do something wrong, such as asking an inappropriate question or making an inappropriate statement in a meeting, assess the real risk of doing so. For example, how many people do you know who were actually disciplined or dismissed for asking questions?

✔ **Recognise that every 'cloud has a silver lining'**. You learn by being exposed to difficult situations: you may not want deliberately to create situations in which you feel embarrassed, but you can certainly profit from them!

# Sensing for Success

Switching on your senses is important – especially your visual and auditory ones – so that you can notice subtle changes or nuances in another person's or your own:

- ✔ Emotions.

- ✔ Behaviour or body language.

- ✔ Energy or enthusiasm about the issue or topic being discussed.

- ✔ Emphasis on words that reflect that certain words have significant meaning.

You can then use the information gathered in this way to better understand your work colleagues, especially their commitment towards taking a certain course of action or doing a task that needs to be done to achieve an objective. In this section you discover techniques for using your senses more effectively.

## Being in the moment

Take a few moments to relax. When you feel relaxed, turn your attention to your mind and notice how still your mind is and any thoughts that are on or come into your mind. . . .

You probably notice that your mind is still for only a few seconds before a thought jumps into it! Your active mind keeps grabbing your attention: you may sometimes find that this happens to such an extent that colleagues may occasionally notice that they don't have your attention, prompting them to enquire whether something's on your mind or even whether you're day dreaming! You yourself may sometimes notice that your attention is some-where else – that is, not in the moment – when, for example, you're in a meeting and you miss comments made by your colleagues.

'Being in the moment' is the act of bringing your attention into the here and now, and enables you to focus your total attention on the person(s) you're working with at that moment.

Practise the following techniques to enhance your ability to bring yourself into the moment:

- ✔ **Calm your mind.** Let the thoughts that clutter your mind and disturb your attention slip away, and as new thoughts jump into your mind let each of them go. You may want to find a calm place to help you practise, but you can also practise this technique in public places such as on public transport.

✔ **Be aware of a single object.** Select a single object that you can see and increase your awareness of it but don't think about it. For example, I can see the shape of an apple on the computer I'm using: I'm increasing my awareness of the detail of the shape without associating lots of thoughts about apples with it. Practise holding your attention on a single object without thoughts entering your mind.

✔ **Relax your body.** Breathe slowly and relax your body. Let the excess energy that's causing your muscles – and you – to be tense slip away as you gently exhale each deep breath. You have probably heard the saying 'healthy body, healthy mind'; now you know another one 'calm body, calm mind'!

## Seeing what others miss

'It's the little things that matter!' Such a comment is often made when describing exceptional quality of service provided by a restaurant, hotel and so on. The same is also true when you're effectively engaging a person: your work colleagues may rarely tell you how they feel and so noticing the subtle changes that other people miss, especially in a colleague's facial expressions, is crucial for you to become an engaging leader.

Try the following techniques to enhance your skills in seeing what others miss:

✔ **Keep your head up.** You can't notice subtle changes in a person's facial expressions if your radar isn't pointing in the right direction! Frequently looking at someone's eyes (without doing it so intensely that you make the person feel uncomfortable) enables you to connect with and relate to people.

People may avoid direct eye contact with you when they don't want to commit strongly to doing something.

Watch for subtle changes in a person's facial expressions, especially around the eyes, for clues about what a person is really thinking. Use subtle changes that you notice in a person's behaviour, such as a raised eyebrow, as prompts to enquire about the person's views on, for example, a statement you've just made that may have prompted the reaction. Enquire what the reaction meant instead of making assumptions.

✔ **Work your peripheral view.** Practise noticing what's on the edge of your field of vision, especially when you're working with groups. You may detect subtle changes in people's body language and behaviour that you may otherwise miss.

> ✔ **Scan in and out.** Practise focusing your vision in and out so that you can zoom in on, for example, a person and notice what's on your peripheral vision almost simultaneously.

# Listening for meaning: Getting behind language

You're most likely aware that you unconsciously ignore background noise at work, such as the soft drone of air conditioning fans. Your mind appears to tune out such noises so that you can get on with the work in hand. Although this skill is essential for good concentration, you need to develop your listening skills when talking directly with people.

Practise listening for details and meaning by tuning your hearing and attention in to the words and phrases that a work colleague's using during direct one-to-one conversations:

- ✔ 'Listen with your mind' by concentrating on trying to understand what the person means rather than primarily focusing on your own thoughts.

- ✔ Hold your attention at two levels; be 'in the moment' and attentive to the person while maintaining at the back of your mind an overview of what a successful outcome to the conversation is going to be.

- ✔ Notice subtle changes in the tone of the person's voice that indicates he's placing more emphasis on certain words and phrases: emphasis that suggests that these words and phrases have a significant meaning to the person.

- ✔ Look out for a colleague repeatedly using certain words and/or phrases in a conversation. Repeated use of the same phrase may indicate that your colleague thinks that you've not fully discussed or considered the issue. For example, if your colleague keeps on repeating the phrase 'there wasn't enough time' when discussing why a particular job wasn't completed on time with them, I suggest this probably means that he thinks that you've not considered this 'lack of time' issue to his satisfaction.

- ✔ Suspend judgement. If you interrupt someone, you've probably already decided that you know what your colleague's going to say or disagree with him.

- ✔ Listen for *how* people say things; and especially whether people are using jargon such as 'thinking outside the box', 'blue sky thinking,' and 'realising potential'. Make sure that you get people to explain what they mean in the particular situation and context.

**Book III**

**Managing and Leading Others**

✔ Listen for what people *don't* say; be alert to potentially different meanings of phrases and sentences that your colleague uses. For example, if a team member says the following sentence when explaining that he's experiencing problems obtaining information from another department: 'I tell them, but they don't take notice!' Does he mean:

- 'People in the other department deliberately ignore me.'

- 'I'm not very good at influencing people.'

- Or does he have another interpretation of the sentence?

# Being Brilliant at Building Commitment

The key to unlocking the commitment of work colleagues so that they perform tasks to a high standard is engaging them. When engaged, people take ownership of tasks and hold themselves accountable for successfully completing their work.

Work colleagues taking ownership of tasks is the difference between them being committed to doing tasks to the best of their ability and them doing their work just 'okay' simply because they're being compliant with your requests/instructions. When colleagues are only being compliant, they probably don't do their work as well as they could, unless you have a great relationship with them and they want to really please you.

In this section, you discover how to build and maintain the commitment of work colleagues to do all their tasks to the best of their ability.

## Starting from pole position

The use of a motor racing metaphor isn't meant to imply that you're in a race with your work colleagues to get what you want! As the leader of your team, however, you may feel as if you have to be (or even that others expect you to be) in pole position: as if you're in front of your team as regards setting the direction that you want your team to go in and expecting them to follow you. You may even think that you know best about what's required from your team and individual team members for them to contribute to achieving your team's objectives. While you do need to be clear about these objectives, this section shows some of the difficulties that adopting an approach of always being in pole position can create.

When managers are holding conversations with a work colleague to agree actions to complete a task, or agree a change of behaviour, when a colleague is underperforming, in real work situations or as part of leadership development programmes, . almost every manager adopts an approach that can be described as 'having the endpoint in mind', in which the managers:

- ✔ Focus on the action they want their colleague to take or the change that they want them to make in their behaviour.

- ✔ Attempt to influence the person to act or change behaviour by using what they, the manager, believes to be a logical argument or appropriate evidence of the need for their colleague to act or make the change.

This approach can backfire and fail to achieve your aims. When you adopt this approach, you're focusing on the endpoint or outcome that you want to achieve through having the conversation. Your attention is primarily on your own thoughts as you follow your plan of how you intend the conversation to proceed: you may miss or ignore important information that your colleague is sharing with you!

When you take this approach, a typical response to any comment that your colleague makes that indicates that he disagrees with your views is for you to reinforce your viewpoint by restating the need to act or change and/or by using (more) evidence that you consider appropriate. You focus on your own interpretation of, for example, your colleague's underperformance and on your own meaning or understanding of the reasons for this underperformance.

If you fail to provide sufficient reasons or evidence for taking action or making a change that your colleagues agree with, or if they interpret the evidence differently, you and they are going to have different interpretations and understanding regarding the need for them to act or change. If these different understandings persist, your colleagues probably end up with a lower commitment to act or change their behaviour than you want them to have.

Approaching conversations with colleagues by starting from pole position is more likely to result in people only being compliant with what you want them to do, instead of them being genuinely committed to act or change their behaviour. The next section presents a more effective approach.

## *Beginning from their grid position*

Instead of 'starting from pole position' (see the preceding section), a more appropriate and successful place to start conversations with colleagues to gain their commitment to act or change their behaviour is to start from their *grid position*. This approach means beginning from where your colleagues are regarding their view about the need to act or change their behaviour rather than you focusing only on the outcome that you want to achieve.

**Book III**

**Managing and Leading Others**

You're more able to gain the commitment of colleagues to act or change their behaviour when you fully understand the reasons why they do or don't do something or behave as they do.

Here's how to start from your team member's grid position:

- ✔ Focus on and find out your colleague's views or position regarding the current situation, standard of performance, need to change and so on. Strive to find out whether, and how important and worthwhile, your colleague perceives the need to act or change his behaviour.

- ✔ Be alert and attentive to notice words and phrases that appear to have significant meaning to your colleague (check out the earlier section 'Listening for meaning: Getting behind language').

- ✔ Explore the meanings that your colleague attaches to these words so that you improve your understanding of his views or perspectives by using phrases such as:

    - 'You mentioned [restate words] . . . what exactly do you mean?'

    - 'You seem to put a lot of emphasis on [restate words].'

    - 'It appears to me that [restate or paraphrase words] are significant to you.'

## *Focusing on winning together*

Your aim in engaging work colleagues to 'go the extra mile' is to work together with a common commitment to achieve optimum outcomes for everyone involved . By doing so, everyone is unified in striving to achieve common objectives that directly or ultimately benefit your organisation, you and your staff.

Focusing on you working with one member of your team, striving to achieve a common objective, requires you and your colleague to arrive at a common and shared understanding about the importance of the objective and, depending on the difficulty of achieving it, the importance of tasks and activities that have to be done to achieve the objective. You *and* your colleague are *both* likely to be committed to achieving an objective, or doing a task or activity, when you agree that it is important and worthwhile because the objective or task is meaningful.

Work with one of your colleagues to gain his commitment by agreeing that an objective, task or activity – or, perhaps, a change in his behaviour if he's underperforming – is important and worthwhile:

- ✔ Start from his grid position (see the preceding section for details).

- ✔ Explain the benefits of, for example, achieving an objective or doing a task, and the consequences of not doing it.

- ✔ Acquire a better understanding of each other's views and reasons for them.

- ✔ Gain new insights into the issue or problem, and identify more appropriate courses of action, through interpreting and reinterpreting together the views, ideas and information that you're sharing with each other.

- ✔ Notice any changes in your colleague's language during the conversation that indicates that he's accepted the need to act or change his behaviour, and that he's taking ownership and becoming committed to act or change.

  Examples include a move away from negative phrases such as 'I can't. . .' and 'I won't . . .', towards more positive responses such as 'Would it be possible for me to. . .', 'How can I/we. . .' and 'Can I. . . ?'.

- ✔ Agree some actions to take to work together more successfully (read the next section for details).

Strive to engage your colleagues to enable them to achieve their aims and objectives by working with you to achieve the team's objectives.

## Agreeing actions to drive success

Having a meaningful conversation with a colleague to gain his commitment to act or change behaviour is pointless if you don't also agree the action and a deadline for taking that action. Sometimes, depending on the situation, both your colleague and you need to take actions to demonstrate your commitment to achieving an objective and/or to working better together.

Try to be absolutely clear about actions to be taken by:

- ✔ Describing each action clearly and concisely.

- ✔ Naming who's going to take each action.

- ✔ Agreeing specific dates as deadlines for taking action; don't leave room for any misunderstandings.

- ✔ Agreeing a method and date for reviewing progress or measuring success.

**Book III**

**Managing and Leading Others**

## Avoiding meaningless language

Avoid using vague or cryptic language in any conversations in which you're agreeing actions to be taken as a result of gaining a colleague's commitment to act. Such language can cause misunderstandings and, potentially, disagreements and/or ill feeling if your colleague doesn't act as you expected him to.

Be wary of the implications of allowing colleagues to use the language set out in Table 8-3 when they're describing actions they're going to take.

| Table 8-3 | Examples of Meaningless Language |
|---|---|
| *Meaningless Language* | *Implication* |
| Hopefully I. . . | I hope but I can't be certain! |
| I'll try. . . | Is trying good enough for you? |
| I'll do it by next month. | With at least 28 days in a month, which day is meant? |
| I intend to. . . | How committed does this comment sound to you? |

## Keeping on track

One of the best ways to sustain the commitment of colleagues to take the actions that have been agreed is to recognise the progress they're making and their achievements.

Keep work colleagues on track by:

✔ Holding reviews at the time and date that you agreed. Put the review dates into your diary to prompt you to take the lead in organising and holding reviews.

✔ Asking your colleague in review meetings to take the lead in describing the progress he's made, his achievements, difficulties experienced and how he's going to overcome them and so on.

✔ Using your colleague's name when praising him to build his self-esteem, so that he hears success and praise associated with his name.

✔ Constructively challenging your colleague if you think that he's not maintaining his commitment, and providing any additional support that he needs from you to succeed.

# Book IV

# Increasing Productivity and Performance

'Are you hiding something from us, Mr Dingwall?'

# In this book...

As a manager, you have ultimate responsibility for getting people to perform at their best and removing the obstacles that might get in the way. This book offers a wealth of ideas from inspiring and motivating with clear vision and goals to the practicalities of allocating resources, managing projects, conducting appraisals, delegating and saving time wasting with emails and meetings. All without major stress.

Here are the contents of Book IV at a glance:

# Chapter 1

# Leading People to Peak Performance

Sometimes you're going to find that leading people is a joy: you admire how everyone pulls together to scale new heights of performance and teamwork. At other times, however, leading people can seem like an uphill battle as they falter and fail to deliver the performance you expect.

Throughout this chapter we employ the metaphor of climbing to help you discover how to encourage your staff to strive towards achieving peak performance by setting standards for them and acting promptly when individuals fail to achieve those standards. You find out how to tackle the thorny issues of unacceptable behaviour and performance, as well as how to use coaching to lead people to even better performance.

## Being a Great Role Model

Take a few minutes now to identify those leaders that you look up to and admire: perhaps you have direct experience of working with them or maybe you know of them only through books, magazines, television or other media.

Get a notebook and take a few minutes to capture your thoughts about each leader that you identify using the following statements as prompts:

✔ The name of the leader and the position held.

✔ The characteristics, attributes, principles, knowledge, skills or actions that you admire in this leader.

✔ The effect that this leader has had on you.

This simple exercise allows you to identify the impact that role models have had on you, and prompts you to see that you have a similar influence on your staff. You find out about the importance of setting and maintaining standards in the next two sections.

## Flying your flag on the summit

You're responsible for setting and maintaining the standards of work, behaviour and performance of your whole team and every member of it: you're the standard-bearer for your team! You want your team to rally round your standards, uphold and protect them just as an army unites around and protects its distinctive flag in battle . . . even to the last man standing!

As the standard-bearer for your team, you also:

✔ Promote and uphold your own, your team's and your organisation's values.

✔ Represent, promote and uphold the purpose, objectives and requirements of your team within your organisation to enable people to achieve the objectives and results expected of them.

✔ Create a team identity that enables your team to feel part of something special.

Be a bold standard-bearer and carry your flag high: 'fly it from the summit' so that what you and your team stand for, in terms of purpose, objectives, values and standards, can be seen by everyone in your team and all the people your team works with.

Being a leader can be extremely hard! You need to set the standards for others to follow: you have to be the person that you want others to become in terms of your team's values and standards regarding the quality of work, how members of your team work together and with colleagues in other departments and so on.

Setting the standard doesn't mean that you have to be able to do every task that every member of your team does. As people do their jobs every day, they become experts. The range of your responsibilities and the size of your team are likely to grow as you climb up your organisation's management structure and as your leadership and professional talents are recognised and appreciated, and you can't possibly be an expert in everything.

Your staff members are always watching you: your team and other work colleagues take more notice of – and tend to copy – your behaviour more than they take notice of what you say. Inspire members of your team to achieve your team's objectives by conveying your enthusiasm and commitment to succeed.

## Avoiding the crevasse of double standards

You can't expect the people who report to you to work to or maintain standards that you don't keep yourself. Therefore, you need to avoid having double standards! Developing double standards without realising it is all too easy.

Be careful of unintentionally allowing double standards:

✔ Don't make allowances for a person falling below your standard regarding an aspect of work or behaviour just because that person is highly skilled in other aspects. Some people are naturally more skilled or proficient at doing certain tasks than their colleagues, and you need to organise work to make best use of the collective talents of your team; but don't allow anyone to fall below the overall standards you expect everyone to achieve.

✔ Don't show favouritism towards certain team members. Be careful about turning a 'blind eye' towards people who fail to maintain the team's standards simply because you like them.

Noticing that the standards of work and behaviour in your team are falling can sometimes be difficult. Keep a constant lookout for early signs of standards falling because, just as a careless mountaineer can fall down a crevasse covered by snow, you need to discover problems sooner rather than later!

## Acting Before Avalanches

When avalanches happen, they carry away everything in their path and bury it in deep snow. You may find that things come crashing down around you like an avalanche if you don't notice or ignore that standards are falling in your team as regards the work itself or how members of your team are behaving. Recovering from such problems can be difficult and time-consuming. We explore why and how you should avoid work avalanches in the next two sections.

**Book IV**

**Increasing Productivity and Performance**

## Appreciating the dangers of delay

Putting off talking to someone about an unacceptable standard of work or behaviour can be all too easy, particularly if you:

- ✔ Are a busy person; you have good intentions regarding discussing the issue with the person but never get round to acting on them!

- ✔ Don't like having difficult conversations – and not many people do.

- ✔ Would be stepping outside of your comfort zone by raising the problem with the person.

Be aware of these common dangers of delaying taking action:

- ✔ **You accept a lower standard.** When people fail to meet your standard and you don't raise the problem promptly, they think that you're allowing it to happen. For example, if a person is occasionally late arriving at work and you don't raise the issue of timekeeping, that person may think that arriving late is okay. If you do not notice that the standard isn't being met, the affect on the other person is the same: she may assume you don't mind him arriving late.

- ✔ **You risk a bad apple infecting others.** If you allow one person's work or behaviour to fall below your expected standard, other team members may notice your inactivity and question why they should work to that standard when their colleague is being allowed to get away with not meeting it. For example, you may find that you've a growing timekeeping problem within your team if you don't take prompt action with a poor timekeeper.

- ✔ **Your credibility is damaged.** Members of your team who have high standards start to wonder why you don't take action: your credibility can be damaged by allowing a team member to fail to meet the team's standards.

- ✔ **Your job becomes more difficult.** Tackling the problem of unacceptable performance or behaviour becomes more difficult by not acting promptly because:

    - The problem grows due to the 'bad apple' effect mentioned above.

    - You may have to explain why you didn't act sooner; the person who's not meeting your standards may ask, 'Why didn't you raise this issue with me earlier?'.

## Applying the golden rule of 'Now'

A golden rule to adopt regarding when to raise an unacceptable standard of work or behaviour is: *Do it Now!*

When you act as soon as you notice the problem, you can avoid the dangers mentioned in the preceding section and build your self-esteem by success-fully tackling and dealing with problems with people – or people problems!

Another good general principle to adopt in leading people is to praise people in public and criticise them (constructively) in private. The following are the main benefits of adopting this principle:

✔ Praising people in public for achieving your standards means that:

   • They get the public recognition they deserve.

   • You reinforce high standards by talking publicly about a person achieving those standards.

   • Their work colleagues recognise that they also have to achieve those standards if they want to be recognised for doing a good job.

✔ Constructively criticising people who aren't meeting your standards in private means that:

   • You're treating them with respect.

   • You don't unnecessarily embarrass them in public.

Raising issues of unacceptable standards of work or behaviour straightaway may mean the following, depending on the severity of the problem and the work context:

✔ Raising the issue the minute you notice the problem, such as in a one-to-one meeting or conversation with the person.

✔ Raising the issue at a time convenient to you the same day. For example, you may decide to delay raising the issue for a few hours if you have to complete an important task by an urgent deadline.

✔ Delaying raising the issue until the earliest time at which you can have a private conversation with the person.

✔ Delaying raising the issue until the earliest time that you can gather the relevant facts or evidence to determine the severity of the problem.

Two exceptions exist to raising unacceptable standards of behaviour only in private. You need to raise the problem as soon as you notice it happening in a meeting also involving other people when the behaviour is:

✔ So severe that you can't appear to ignore it for even a minute. An exam-ple is the use of abusive personal language.

✔ Typical of the behaviour of several members of the group, and you want to discuss the behaviour in the group because the group is malfunction-ing as a result. In such situations, you may describe and discuss the behaviour without naming the last person to behave that way. A simple example is when people interrupt and talk over one another, which demonstrates that people aren't fully listening to what the others have to say.

# Leading Under-performers Towards Your Peak

You find out in the earlier section 'Flying your flag on the summit' that, as the standard-bearer for your team, you're responsible for setting and maintaining the standards of work, behaviour and performance of your whole team and everyone in it! Getting everyone in your team to own and work to your standards can be a challenge. The next four sections describe how to lead people whose performance and/or behaviour is unacceptable with regard to your standards.

## Working on commitment and capability

Your approach to working with a person who fails to meet your standards for work or behaviour is affected by your assessment of the person's:

- ✔ Capability to achieve the standard.
- ✔ Commitment to do the task to the required standard or behave in accord with your values or standards.

The capability of people to do a particular task to the standard required depends on several factors including their knowledge, skills, experience, the ability to think through complex tasks or problems, and so on. The commitment of people to do a particular task depends on the importance that they attach to the task, whether they like or dislike doing it, how easy or difficult the task is for them to do, and so on.

In some situations, you may be tempted to be satisfied when an underperforming person simply complies with your requirements, but you should always strive to gain a person's commitment to meeting the required standards because:

- ✔ Committed people are more likely to achieve the standard.
- ✔ Committed people allow you to have confidence that they're going to achieve and maintain the standard.

> ✔ Committed people are easier to manage: you don't have to monitor
> that they're meeting the standard as much as you do if they're not
> committed.

Book III Chapter8 shows you how to hold conversations to become brilliant
at building commitment.

Figure 1-1 summarises four different approaches to leading a person, whose
performance or behaviour is unacceptable, towards peak performance based
on your assessment of the person's capability and commitment to do a
given task.

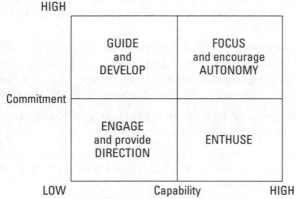

**Figure 1-1:**
Approaches
to working
with people
based
on their
commitment
and
capabilities.

*(This model is based on the original work pioneered by Hersey and
Blanchard on situational leadership. For more information on how
ituational leadership has been applied to executive coaching by Hersey
and Chevalier refer to Coaching for Leadership, 2nd Edition (Pfeiffer).)*

You can take four different approaches to leading a person. These are to:

> ✔ **Enthuse** (when someone is highly capable, but has low commitment to
> doing the task) the person by:
>
>   • Clarifying the reasons why the person isn't committed by explor-
>     ing whether she has any expectations or needs regarding the job
>     that aren't being met.
>
>   • Explaining the importance of the task and the reasons why you
>     want the person to do it.
>
>   • Recognising the person's knowledge, skills and so on that are par-
>     ticularly relevant to completing the task.

- Helping the person to understand that doing the task to the required standard will enable her to make progress towards satisfying any unmet needs or expectations that she has about the job or role in the organisation.

- Agreeing actions and deadlines, and how progress is to be measured.

- Thanking the person for using his abilities.

✔ **Engage and provide direction** (when the commitment and capability of a person to do a task are both low) by:

- Exploring whether any expectations aren't being met.

- Clarifying how the person feels about how she's doing the job, showing an interest in her sense of self-esteem and the reasons for her view.

- Looking for ways for building the person's self esteem by agreeing small steps or actions that slightly stretch her ability but that she's likely to complete successfully – with your support if necessary – so that you can recognise and praise even slight progress.

- Agreeing actions or tasks that progressively stretch the person as heris confidence increases.

- Providing on-going support to develop the person's ability and provide feedback emphasising her achievements (use the person's name when praising her).

✔ **Guide and develop** (when a person is highly committed, but has low capability to do the task) the person by:

- Explaining the main steps to complete the task.

- Encouraging the person to ask questions, and ask your own, to ensure that she clearly understands what you require.

- Agreeing milestones and deadlines when you want the person to report and discuss progress with you.

- Being available for reference.

- Praising achievements and using problems as opportunities for the person to grow and develop her capabilities.

✔ **Focus and encourage autonomy** (when the commitment and capability of a person to do a task are both high) by:

- Agreeing the objective or outcome and deadline to be achieved without discussing the method.

- Providing enough autonomy for the person to make her own decisions and take action to achieve the objective.

# Approaching cliffhanger conversations

Most leaders dislike having conversations with people whose performance or behaviour is unacceptable. We call these conversations 'cliffhangers' because you:

- Are concerned that you may lose your grip on yourself and lose control of your emotions.

- Fear that you may slip up in what you intend to say, say the wrong thing and not achieve the intended outcome.

- Expect that the conversation may sometimes be on a knife edge: tense and uncomfortable.

- Perceive that the consequences of the conversation going wrong are huge – and it looks a long way down!

Here are guidelines to help you plan how to have really meaningful and successful conversations with someone who's not doing the job to your required standard.

- Preparing yourself:

  - Be crystal clear about the standards you expect your work colleagues to achieve.

  - Be objective but non-judgemental.Book IIIChapter 8 shows that being judgemental can cause you to make the conversation difficult by, for example, expecting the person to be difficult.)

  - Switch on your senses to enable you to give the person your total attention. (You discover the benefits and how to switch on your senses in Book III Chapter 8.)

- Preparing your kit:

  - Collect all relevant facts and evidence while keeping an open mind that further relevant evidence may be shared with you during your conversation.

  - Clarify any gap between the standard expected and the current level of performance or behaviour as indicated by the evidence, while being responsive to fresh evidence being shared with you in the conversation.

  - Consider how the person prefers to be treated. For example, some people like to get straight to the point in conversations whereas others prefer to talk around and lead up to a key issue.

- • Be clear about the outcomes you want to achieve from the conversation including any actions that will demonstrate the person is capable and committed to do the task.

✔ Be wary of third party opinions:

- • Sometimes you may have to seek the views of colleagues in obtaining facts and evidence about a person's performance or behaviour such as when the person is a member of a project group that doesn't include you. Check whether the work colleagues are giving you subjective opinions or solid facts: opinions can be challenged much easier than facts.

- • Ask your colleagues' permission to reveal, if necessary during your intended conversation, that they're the source of the information. If they don't give you their permission, be wary of using the evidence: you may decide that you have to use it, but the credibility of the information may be challenged and undermined if you can't justify it.

## *Roping people into improvements*

Spend time and work with people who are failing to meet your standards so that they identify and understand the gap between their current level of performance or behaviour and your required standard. Encourage them to come up with the actions necessary to bridge this gap so that they take ownership of, and are committed to, improving. (Flip to Book III Chapter8 for how to ask searching questions, listen carefully and interpret information when agreeing the importance of a particular objective or task.)

Be smart by agreeing improvements that are 'SMART':

- ✔ **Specific.** The outcome or actions agreed need to be so clear and concise that they can only be interpreted one way.

- ✔ **Measurable.** You both clearly understand how progress will be measured such as through observation, measuring outputs, progress reviews and so on.

- ✔ **Achievable.** Agree any support that you'll provide including 'on or off-the-job' training, access to you for advice and so on.

- ✔ **Relevant.** All improvements should contribute to the individual, and/or your team and even the organisation being more successful: if not, why are you seeking an improvement?

- ✔ **Time-based.** Agree dates and times for holding progress reviews rather than propose to hold reviews in one, two or more weeks, which is too vague and open to misunderstandings about deadlines.

People tend to achieve tasks when you agree deadlines as compared to when you leave actions open-ended!

## Mapping progress towards peak performance

When working with people who fail to meet your standards, you need to demonstrate your commitment to encouraging them to achieve the required level of performance. Continue to challenge and support them following your initial conversation to discuss their performance.

Always put the date and time for conducting a progress review(s) straight into your diary system; that is, during or immediately after your conversation. This habit reminds you to hold the reviews, and forces you to think about moving or removing it from your diary and consider the implications of doing so.

Consider the following points when making decisions about the type and frequency of progress reviews to map how well a person is making progress towards the required standard:

✔ Recognising and reinforcing people's progress helps to sustain their commitment.

✔ Allowing space for people to learn from making mistakes may be risky, but 'trial and error' is an effective method of discovering how to do a job better. You may consider that taking a few well-considered risks is worthwhile to enable people who are committed to making improvements to learn through making their own decisions and taking action.

✔ Deciding whether any milestones or deadlines while completing the task are critical to achieve, and how to ensure that these are met.

# Coaching the Good Towards Greatness

When trying to enhance the performance or behaviour of their staff, many leaders make the mistake of telling people what to do: the message often goes in one ear and out of the other one! People have to take *ownership* of the need for the change and become committed to putting the effort in to sustain a change in their performance or behaviour.

Your challenge in coaching the people who report to you is to have meaningful conversations with them so that they take ownership of and become committed to making the change . . . and, ideally, to managing themselves in achieving and sustaining the improvement.

**Book IV**

**Increasing Productivity and Performance**

The role of coach can be described as:

> *Engage people in their own thinking to enable them to gain new insights and meanings that enhance their confidence and lead to better decisions, actions, behaviour and performance.*

You discover useful tips on how to coach individuals and even your whole team to be even better at what they do in the next three sections.

## Taking a time out to coach

In basketball, coaches can call a time out to discuss tactics; you can do the same and you don't even have to stop the game! You can coach individual members or the whole team as part of your normal daily activities. You may think that you don't have the time to coach people every day, but you do because each opportunity may only take a few minutes.

Be on the lookout for opportunities to coach individuals and your team everyday.

Here are a few examples of the many opportunities you have to coach members of your team towards greatness:

✔ Ask a team member who brings a problem to you to also bring options with a recommendation for how to solve the problem. Talk though the proposal and praise the person if you agree with the recommendation. If you disagree, ask relevant questions to guide the person towards your preferred action. (Dip into Book III Chapter 8 to find more on asking searching questions.)

When you've done this process a few times and are agreeing with the recommendations being put to you, help people to see that they're solving the problems, and only need to come to you if a problem is exceptional or the consequences of taking the wrong action are significant.

✔ When you notice that a task hasn't been done to the required standard, ask the relevant person to look at the task, and assess and comment on whether it meets the required standard. Ask questions to help the person spot where or how the task is sub-standard, understand the consequences of it being wrong and describe the actions to take to do the task correctly this time and in future.

✔ Catch people doing a great job by walking around and talking to them about the work they're doing. Praising people in public boosts their self-esteem and reinforces the standards that you expect people to achieve.

✔ Hold a short review of the process at the end of a team meeting to agree strengths and actions to improve how well:

- People were prepared for the meeting.

- Time was used.

- Everyone was encouraged to contribute.

- People listened to each other.

- Decisions were made and clear actions agreed.

- The team hold each other accountable for taking agreed actions following a meeting.

Be a great coach by regularly helping people to think things through for themselves.

## *Choosing the right role*

You will adopt and fulfil several different roles as a coach when working with chief executives, directors and other senior managers, often during each meeting with them. Clients often don't notice changing roles because movement from one to another is subtle in response to the issues they're raising or their emotions.

A few coaching roles, situations and when you need to consider using them are described, in Table 1-1.

| Table 1-1 | Coaching Roles and When to Use Them |
|-----------|-------------------------------------|
| Advisor | You've more knowledge and expertise than the people who report to you in certain aspects of their work. Advising involves guiding a person towards the correct or right way of doing a task where a best way exists. |
| Partner | You work together in jointly solving a problem, sharing your expertise and ideas to enhance each other's understanding of the problem and arrive at a decision that you're both committed to taking. |
| Reflector | You listen carefully and reflect back your interpretations to the person to check and clarify the meanings they're trying to convey, perhaps acting as a sounding board for their proposals and/or offering different interpretations. Use this approach to help people refine their thinking on an issue and acquire new insights into, for example, how to build a more productive working relationship with a colleague. |

*(continued)*

**Table 1-1 *(continued)***

| | |
|---|---|
| Catalyst | You prompt and probe people's thinking by asking searching questions and listening intently to notice words and phrases that seem to have significant meaning to them and, through this approach, enhance their understanding of an issue or problem and the actions that they're going to take. Useful for helping colleagues to work through what is, for them, a particularly difficult or complex problem. |
| Critical friend | You challenge someone about his thinking and behaviour while having a genuine interest in him as an individual, providing moral support and acting with integrity. This approach is powerful for helping people to enhance their self-awareness, acquire insights into their motives, attitudes and behaviours, and how their behaviour is impacting on others, and to increase their self-accountability. |

## Practising what great coaches do

Be a great coach by:

- Having a genuine interest in helping people to grow and prosper.

- Giving people your total attention when you're with them.

- Encouraging people to fulfil their potential at all times.

- Keeping your mind open to all possibilities and avoiding being judgemental.

- Asking searching and difficult questions to enhance the quality of people's thinking, explore the reasons for their actions and so on.

- Listening intently to the language people are using and noticing words and phrases that have significant meanings for them.

- Sensing whether people are showing real commitment to do what is right or necessary.

- Speaking your mind; that is, having the courage to say what needs to be said rather than ducking issues or avoiding disagreements. Be willing to challenge people's motives and behaviour.

- Reinterpreting information shared between you and individuals to create new insights and meanings about problems, and the person's self-awareness and self-knowledge.

- Being vulnerable by remaining willing to have your views questioned and challenged, and acknowledging and saying when you're wrong.

- Having humility: you're not the focus of the conversation!

# Chapter 2

# Making Goals Come Alive

### In This Chapter

▶ Confirming the well-formed conditions of a goal

▶ Increasing creativity with the help of Disney

▶ Developing new, compelling behaviours

Some people know what they want in life from an early age; they feel compelled to climb summits, step on to the stage or fly high to achieve an ambition. So tools and methods to envision the future, create strategies and follow through on plans may come naturally for them. Other people prefer to allow life to unfold in an organic way, and they never want to let goal-setting get in the way of their spontaneity.

NLP suggests that dreaming is a good thing. Coaching encourages people to shift towards their dreams by taking actions in appropriate ways. Goal-setting in some form is at the heart of coaching, even if the goal is to change the client's approach to each day rather than the fast achievement of specific plans. In fact, a reasonable goal for a client can be to allow himself more spontaneity and letting go of always having to be in control of life.

This chapter introduces three specific NLP tools that support goal-setting. You see how to take your clients competently through the classic NLP well-formed outcome process, the Disney strategy and the New Behaviour Generator. All three tools engage the creative processes by working with the senses rather than concentrating on logical problem-solving.

## Checking that Goals Are Well-Formed

Coaches understand the value of setting goals with clients. Clients' goals must be motivating and realistic, while taking clients towards the changes they most desire.

You will already be familiar with SMART principles. According to the SMART model, goals need to be Specific, Measurable, Achievable, Realistic, and Timed (hence the acronym). This approach instils valuable focus and discipline to the goal-setting process, which NLP builds on. By including sensory-specific information, as well as taking clients through a proven process, you support them to create meaningful change.

The NLP approach to making SMART goals smarter is known as the *well-formed outcome process*. This process requires you to answer a series of questions that really help you explore the hows, whys and wherefores of your desired outcome. By following this process you begin to understand your true motives for wanting your goals, and you can weigh up the pros and cons of success versus failure.

When your desired outcome meets the following criteria, it satisfies the *well-formed conditions*. For every goal or result you want to achieve, ask yourself the following seven questions:

1. **Is the goal stated in the positive?**
2. **Is the goal self-initiated, self-maintained and within my control?**
3. **Does the goal describe the evidence procedure (in other words, when will you know that you've achieved your goal)?**
4. **Is the context of the goal clearly defined?**
5. **Does the goal identify the necessary resources?**
6. **Have I evaluated whether the goal is ecological?**
7. **Does the goal identify the first step I need to take?**

The following sections explore each condition of the well-formed outcome process in detail so that you can coach anyone through these steps, including yourself.

 Take the first two steps in order and then you can jump around the stages a little. You don't need to share the questions with your client, although if you do, you're giving them a checklist that they can follow again for themselves. Always make sure that you conclude with clarity on the action needed, as in Step 7.

## *Is the goal stated in the positive?*

Creating positively worded goals is a critical foundation for the goal-setting process. Having negative goals like 'I don't want to do this warehouse work any more' can adversely affect your client's chance of success because he ends up focusing on what he doesn't want. Instead, keep the language framed in positive terms or reframe negative goals into positive ones. How much more liberating when the client declares for the first time: 'I want a job that connects with my interest in motor racing.'

The questions to ask your client are:

- ✔ What do you want?
- ✔ What would you rather have?

In addition to being positive, a goal also needs to be specific. Vague goals such as 'I want to be happy' or 'I want a successful career' are hard to quantify. People with these types of goals often lose focus. More specific goals such as: 'I want to establish a group of local friends who I can call up and invite to go to the movies with me.' or 'I want to work in an organisation that pays me £50,000 per annum and gives me professional training' are more specific and helpful.

Often people haven't ever considered what they want. Clients may come to you initially feeling the pressure of what they want to give up or get away from. With these clients, you may need to persist to get them to explore what can be better. Try words to the effect: 'Knowing that you don't want X, what's one small change you'd love – just for starters?'

# Is the goal self-initiated, self-maintained and within my control?

In coaching sessions (and in life in general), you often hear someone talk about an issue that someone else wants solved, such as 'My wife wants me to lose weight as she's worried about my health.' Your client has a far better chance of succeeding if the motivation to attain a particular outcome comes from within. For example: 'I want to feel fit and energetic so I have more bounce – for me.'

Similarly, if the goal is 'I want the directors to promote me next spring', your client needs to accept that the directors may have a different agenda and this goal isn't under your client's control at all. Instead, the client needs to set goals to put himself in the best possible situation to be promoted, knowing that the ultimate desired result is in the hands of others.

The following two questions put the client back in the driving seat:

- ✔ Am I doing this for myself or for someone else?
- ✔ Does the outcome rely solely on me?

**Book IV**

**Increasing Productivity and Performance**

When Anna came to coaching, she was extremely stressed by her work in a government department experiencing cutbacks and the fact that she was filing for divorce. Her anger centred on her ex-husband who kept visiting her elderly mother, doing jobs around the mother's house and generally playing the sympathy card. She felt that her mother and ex-husband were ganging up on her and increasing the pressure on her to return home. She felt extremely guilty, tired and confused.

Through the coaching, she recognised that her coaching agenda could focus on how to hold brave conversations with her mother and her ex-husband as well as her boss. These conversations set the record straight about her needs and decisions. She also worked on managing her emotional state when she met her ex and allowing herself to grieve for the loss of the marriage and family home.

Over the course of several coaching sessions, she broke her problems into several well-formed outcomes that put her back in control of her future. Anna said:

- ✔ 'I want to let go gracefully of my attachment to the house.'

- ✔ 'I want to have conversations with my ex-husband, during which I stay calm and focus on facts and decisions.'

- ✔ 'I want to honour the good times and fun we've had as a couple and family.'

- ✔ 'I want to tell my mother that I am 100 per cent committed to ending the marriage amicably and moving on; and I'll request that she accepts that with love and respect for me.'

- ✔ 'I want to work regular hours, leaving the office by 6 p.m.'

Read through Anna's goals a second time and notice that she can initiate her own actions for each goal, regardless of how others behave around her.

## Does the goal describe the evidence procedure?

*Evidence procedure* is another way of asking: 'When do you know that you've achieved your goal?' Most road trips have a specific destination in mind, even if the path between Points A and B is unknown.

The following sensory-specific questions invite your clients to ponder on goals that are too vague or goals with unclear outcomes:

✔ How do you know that you're getting the desired outcome?

✔ What will you be doing when you get it?

✔ What will you see, hear and feel when you have it?

In the last question, you're inviting clients to step into the experience by imagining the visual, auditory and kinaesthetic aspects of the achieved goal. With this sensory experience embedded in the memory, the unconscious mind gets to work to support the goal.

## Is the context of the goal clearly defined?

Defining the context in which you want to achieve a goal enables greater specificity. Context refers to timing, places and people. Ask your client, 'Where, when and with whom do you want to achieve your goal?' This question helps to fine-tune what you want by eliminating what you don't want.

For instance, if the goal is simply to move house, you're likely to find estate agents bombarding you with unsuitable properties in dozens of locations. You must get more specific about where you want to settle. Do you want to move together with your favourite sister? Do you need to find new housemates or live alone? Do you want to live in a specific geographical location?

By defining *when* you want something, you may identify steps that you need to take before you can have it. For instance, the goal 'I want to move house when I can afford to move into a swish new townhouse in London' may make you realise that you need to raise your income before you can contemplate moving house. Thus, your more pressing goal may be to polish your CV and contact some agencies to find a better-paid job before touring any potential new homes.

## Does the goal identify the necessary resources?

The four following questions about resources help clients identify what resources will enable them to achieve their outcomes. The questions help clients to draw on past experiences when they made use of resources that may prove useful this time around.

Resources cover a broad range of items including:

✔ Time, money, energy

✔ Skills

✔ Information sources

✔ Supportive people

✔ Equipment such as computers or machinery

✔ Positive mindset and good health

The answers to the following four questions are from Nick, a young man who wants to set up a hairdressing salon.

✔ **What resources do you have now?**

Nick: I'm very resilient. I come from a working class background, so I didn't have anything handed to me on a plate. I know that to get what I want, I can work all the hours it takes. I'm prepared to take a minimum salary myself for the first three years and top that up with my savings. I have the support of my Mum and Dad who've taken early retirement and are keen to help get me started.

✔ **What resources do you need to acquire?**

Nick: I definitely need some help on the tax and accounting side. I've never had to manage a payroll system for employees before, work with accountants or file tax documents. I'm also going to need a reliable handyman and plumber that I can call on if there are problems with the building or sinks.

✔ **Have you evidence of achieving this type of goal before?**

Nick: Well, I've worked in other people's salons for ten years, so I've seen what they've done and how it all works. I've also taken on big projects like buying and renovating my flat; that was really old-fashioned when I found it and now it's stylish and attractive – the same kind of look and feel I want for the salon.

✔ **What happens if you act as if you have the resources?**

Nick: Then I just go for it. I know I'll make some mistakes, but hopefully not major ones. I'll learn as I go along.

The final resource question – acting 'as if' the resources are available now – helps the client to recognise and shift any beliefs that may be holding him back. He can also try the outcome on for size. He may change his mind at this point, which saves him investing in a goal that doesn't fit just right.

If a client really struggles to find resources, you can try other angles. Here are some suggestions:

✔ Coach him to find another time in his life when he was resourceful and take the lessons from that.

✔ Ask him to identify someone he knows who is resourceful and what he notices about that person.

✔ Identify the resources that he definitely doesn't have, as this can lead to setting other goals to get them. For example, the person who doesn't have the necessary experience for his project may decide to get some work experience or go on a training course.

## *Have I evaluated whether the goal is ecological?*

When NLP coaches talk about *ecology checks*, they're simply asking questions to make sure that the outcome fits within all aspects of a client's life. If a client sets up a new business, what will be the effect on his health or family? What does another client stand to lose or gain by signing up for a two-year Master's degree?

Ecology checks shine a strong beam of light on any hidden agenda or *secondary gain* that the client may not have considered when setting the outcomes. A *secondary gain* or *positive by-product* refers to a behaviour that appears to be negative or problem-causing, when in fact it serves a positive function at some level.

For example, the secondary gain that a smoker obtains from their cigarettes may include finding peace, time to think or relaxation. These secondary gains need to be met through an alternative activity for the smoker to sustain a new behaviour of not smoking. He may need to enlist in some mindfulness training, meditation classes or sports activity to get the relaxation or build in a ten-minute break away from noisy children to get the peace and quiet he craves at home.

The following questions get to the heart of your clients' desires. As you ask your clients these questions, invite them to be aware of any pictures, sounds, and particularly feelings that their unconscious minds raise. Encourage them to listen sympathetically to the responses they get as their unconscious minds naturally want to protect them.

✔ What is the *real* purpose why you want this?

✔ What will you lose or gain if you get it?

After considering these questions and allowing the unconscious mind to come into play, clients may need to fine-tune their goals accordingly.

**Book IV**

**Increasing Productivity and Performance**

If a client comes with a goal that doesn't appear to serve him well, challenge him as to what he'll lose or gain. For example, if he's making a life-changing decision like leaving a well-paid job, then coaching provides the space to talk that through and see it from different perspectives, which he may have missed in the emotion of the moment. Ultimately, the client makes his own choices and as coach you can only put these under the spotlight.

## Does the goal identify the first step I need to take?

Deciding to do something and actually doing it are not the same thing. You may decide that in order to be a proficient coach you need to study with the world's best, clock up your coaching hours and become accredited. So what happens if every time you think of booking onto a formal programme, you discover something else in your schedule that takes precedence? Your goal is likely to remain just a dream.

To turn a dream into a concrete reality, you have to take that first vital step because without it, you don't build up sufficient momentum to take the next step . . . and then the next. The first step may not actually be booking a training course, but an even smaller step like checking out the scheduled dates and pencilling them into your schedule.

As a coach, you travel with your clients as they make these steps, encouraging and supporting them to act on their beliefs and desires, to stretch beyond their comfort zone.

## Balancing Dreams with Reality: The Disney Strategy

From his study of the late, great Walt Disney, NLP trainer and developer Robert Dilts created a model of creative success known in NLP as the Disney strategy, which is based on Disney's amazing ability to turn dreams into real projects. The Disney strategy enhances the goal-setting aspect of coaching to bring goals alive and ensure their viability. The Disney strategy's particularly useful with large and challenging projects for individuals and teams.

## Getting to know the various roles

*Imagineering* is the term Walt Disney coined to describe the way that he formed dreams and turned them into reality. This unique way of working created the enduring appeal of characters like Mickey and Minnie Mouse and the legacy of the film-making and theme park empire enjoyed by millions of people worldwide today.

Successful imagineering brings together three key strategies: the Dreamer, Realist and Critic roles, all of which are needed for innovation and problem-solving to ultimately reach goals. Indeed, Disney's co-workers said that three different Walts actually came to work, and they were never sure who was going to come into a meeting. Would the Dreamer, the Realist or the Critic pitch up today? No doubt this uncertainty kept everyone on their toes!

In NLP anything is achievable as long as you tackle it in small enough parts. *Chunking* refers to the level of detail or size of an information nugget. *Chunking up* means going for a larger view, while *chunking down* breaks the issue into smaller elements.

As a coach, you take your clients into each of the three ways of thinking in turn, including demonstrating the body language that suits each role.

- ✔ **The Dreamer.** In this role, you're looking to the future and thinking of the bigger picture. You want to see every piece of the story or project. To think like a Dreamer, sitting in a symmetrical and relaxed posture with your eyes looking up helps. The question being explored here is what you *want.* Table 2-1 offers questions concerning what you want to do.

- ✔ **The Realist.** The next role shifts the idea to a workable plan by chunking down a level. To think like a Realist, sit symmetrically and with head and eyes looking straight ahead and slightly forward. At this stage, you focus on the questions of *how* the plan will work. Table 2-1 offers questions concerning how to make the plan work.

- ✔ **The Critic.** The Critic's job is to check for flaws in the plan, looking for what's been overlooked by asking 'What would happen if . . .' type questions. To think like a Critic, your head and eyes look down and slightly tilted, with one of your hands touching your chin. The critic evaluates the *chances* of this really happening. Table 2-1 offers questions concerning the chance to make the plan work.

Typically you begin with the Dreamer, shift to Realist and then Critic. Sometimes you find that a client arrives with a plan he's already working on, so he's already familiar with the Realist role, yet the Dreamer and Critic roles are missing. In this situation, a team effort can often take a plan and make it much stronger and more inspirational.

| Table 2-1 | Working through the Disney Strategy Roles |
|---|---|
| *My Goal Is:* | *Answers:* |
| **Dreamer 'Want to'** | |
| What do you want? | |
| What is the purpose? Why do you want this? | |
| What will you see, hear and feel when you have this? | |
| What are the benefits? | |
| When can you expect this to happen? | |
| Where do you want this to take you in future? | |
| Who do you want to be or be like as a result? | |
| **Realist 'How to'** | |
| When will this goal be completed? | |
| Who are the key people involved? | |
| What are the steps in the plan? First step? Second step? Third step? | |
| What's the evidence that you're on track? | |
| How will you know when you reach the goal? | |
| **Critic 'Chance to'** | |
| Who will be affected? | |
| Who can make or break this idea? | |
| What would make them object? | |
| What are their needs? | |
| What are the payoffs of keeping things the same? | |
| How can you preserve those benefits when you implement the new idea? | |
| Where and when would you not want this? | |
| What's missing or needed? | |

## Coaching through the roles

You can use the Disney strategy and roles in many ways to make goals more real and achievable. You may mention one role in a quick conversation to get a client to think differently, or you may guide clients through a facilitated process lasting several hours. I use the Disney strategy with teams to set a vision for the organisation, and I use it with individuals on a range of goals.

One Scandinavian advertising agency that I've worked with recognises that its creative work must deliver business results and relies on a variation of the Disney strategy to make this happen. The Managing Director organised three different rooms in the agency for the different processes. The Dreamer space operates with standing-room only for meetings, and ideas are captured on an electronic whiteboard. The comfy chairs are allocated to the Realist space, while the Critic space features more formal hard seats and tables.

When going through the Disney roles put out three different chairs or allocate parts of a room to explore each role in turn. As Figure 2-1 shows, chairs work very well when you're coaching in a public space because you can easily sit at a table with four seats – one for you, three for your client to take in turn.

**Figure 2-1:**
An arrangement of chairs for assuming the three Disney strategy roles.

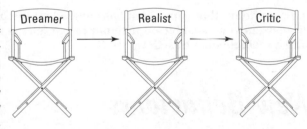

Book IV

Increasing Productivity and Performance

The following exercise encourages clients to experience the different perspectives of the three Disney roles.

1. **Invite your client to a session to work on something truly important.**

   You may want to work on the client's personal vision of life, a life-changing project or other significant goal. Of course, you can use this process for yourself too.

2. **Place three chairs in a triangular position.**

Sit alongside the client yourself in a fourth chair as you talk through the process. Figure 2-1 suggests a possible layout. However you arrange the space, keep out of the client's creative space!

3. **For each step in the creative cycle, guide the client to sit in a specific chair and change body language for each role.** Start with the Dreamer, then shift to the Realist and finally the Critic.

Thebody language for the three Disney roles is described in the earlier section 'Getting to know the various roles'.

4. **Ask the client questions relevant to a specific role and capture the client's answers.**

Use the questions and form in Table 2-1 as a guide.

5. **Have the client move to the next position and assume the next role.**

Ask the appropriate questions and record relevant answers.

6. **After the client assumes all three roles, quickly revisit each role and ask what's missing.**

An entrepreneur on a new property development was working through the Disney strategy. He realised that he was missing out by not working with other investors who had different technical backgrounds. By involving other business partners, he could build a more innovative eco-friendly scheme than he'd originally considered.

7. **When you're confident that your client has covered all the positions, review the answers you've collected together to co-create a meaningful goal with a realistic plan of action.**

# Generating New Behaviours

Change requires people to *do* things differently – things they may find difficult as they seek to achieve their goals. The *New Behaviour Generator* allows your clients to mentally rehearse new behaviours by harnessing all their senses. In this exercise, they talk it through internally, picturing it and checking their reactions until it feels right.

In the New Behaviour Generator exercise, the coach sits or stands alongside the client and directs him to change the way he sits and moves his gaze. The eye-movement patterns tie in with the idea of *eye accessing cues.* The original co-creators of NLP, Richard Bandler and John Grinder, noticed that people naturally move their eyes around according to whether they're thinking in terms of images, sounds or feelings. (See Book I Chapter 2 for more on eye accessing cues.)

In this exercise, like many in NLP, you can work content-free, which means clients don't need to tell you specifically what they want to do differently, nor even actually speak. Working content-free enables clients to stay involved with their own experiences, without any unintended distraction from the coach.

In the following sections, you can see how each round of the exercise works in turn. You may need to cycle two or three times round the steps until the client feels he's got it. In the first cycle, clients' responses can be quite vague, yet they typically become more precise with the second and third rounds.

After you become familiar with the exercise and have a sense of your client's preferred representational system, try using one part of the exercise as a quick check in with him during a coaching conversation or to reinforce an action. For example, inviting a visual client to look up and picture himself doing a particular action that he's committed to do can support him in creating new habits for success.

## *Hearing the soundtrack*

The first position of the New Behaviour Generator is the auditory one. Have the client sit and look down to his left-hand side to enable him to connect with his internal dialogues. After the client assumes this posture, ask the questions given in the example below.

In this example, Tim's been procrastinating about getting some articles written and published to promote his chiropractic business. His coach is aiming to engage Tim in what the new behaviour (writing and publishing the articles) will sound like when he's actually doing it. The coach is aiming to get Tim to identify internal sounds, such as what he's saying to himself, as well as the everyday sounds around him.

> **Coach:** Look down and to your left. Notice what you hear as you ask yourself: 'What do you want to do?'
>
> **Tim:** I want to *focus on writing an article that will be published in the professional magazines.*
>
> **Coach:** And what does that sound like?
>
> **Tim:** I hear various phone conversations with the publishers, my fingers tapping away on the keyboard, a call to an artist friend of mind who says she'll create some illustrations for me. I also hear myself saying 'On no, I have a deadline for this!' and probably lots of drafts getting ripped up.

## Seeing the movie

The second position of the New Behaviour Generator is the visual one. Ask the client to shift his gaze to his upper right-hand side and imagine what the achieved goal will look like.

In the following example conversation, the coach is aiming to engage Tim in what the new behaviour will look like when he is actually writing his article in full and glorious Technicolor – as if he's starring in the movie of his life!

> **Coach:** Listen to those sounds and look up and to your right. What does that look like, *when you are focusing on writing an article that will be published?*
>
> **Tim:** I see myself on the day I work at home, setting the timer on my watch and really concentrating, then taking a tea break, then coming back to it. I can see myself sitting in my office at the computer screen and sending the article off to another colleague who says he'll take a look. I'm looking quite scruffy in my old jeans and a warm sweater because my office can get cold.

## Feeling, touching and smelling the result

The third position of the New Behaviour Generator is the kinaesthetic one that refers to touch and feelings as well as smell and taste. Invite the client to sit comfortably, looking down and to the right to access feelings.

> **Coach:** Keeping those sounds and images in your mind, look down and to your right. What does that feel like, *when you're focusing on writing an article that will be published?*
>
> **Tim:** It feels pretty good, although a bit chilly in my office. So, I want to switch some extra heat on. I have the feeling that it's really going to happen. I can anticipate the smell of the magazine when it's published, taking it out of its plastic wrapper when it arrives through my letterbox. I feel excited to have my name in print at last and satisfied that it will promote the good name of the practice too.

Now that you've been through one cycle of the exercise, invite the client to repeat it more quickly for two more cycles, capturing any more information he notices on the way. The client now has his own sense of the new behaviour he wants. Ask him to summarise what has emerged for him that's now different and to commit to what action he'll take as a result of the exercise.

# Chapter 3

# Being an Expert at Performance Appraisal and Management

. . . . . . . . . . . . . . . . . . . . . . . . . . . . . . . . . . . . . . . . . . .

### In This Chapter

▶ Quantifying and qualifying your goals

▶ Developing a performance management and appraisal system

▶ Putting your system into practice

▶ Making sure your system works

▶ Avoiding the pitfalls of systems

. . . . . . . . . . . . . . . . . . . . . . . . . . . . . . . . . . . . . . . . . . .

**S**etting goals – for individuals, for teams and for the overall organisation – is extremely important. However, ensuring that the organisation is making progress towards the successful completion of its goals (in the manner and time frames agreed to) is equally important. The organisation's performance depends on each individual who works within it. Achieving goals is what this chapter is all about.

Measuring and monitoring the performance of individuals in your organisation is like walking a tightrope: you don't want to over-measure or over-monitor your employees. Doing so only leads to needless bureaucracy and red tape, which can negatively affect your employees' ability to perform their tasks. Neither do you want to under-measure or under-monitor your employees. Such a lack of watchfulness can lead to nasty surprises when a task is completed late, over budget or not at all. 'What? The customer database conversion isn't completed yet? I promised the sales director that we'd have that job done two weeks ago!'

Please keep in mind that, as a manager, your primary goal in measuring and monitoring your employees' performance isn't to punish them for making a mistake or missing a milestone. Instead, you help your employees stay on track and find out whether they need additional assistance or resources to do so. Few employees like to admit that they need help getting an assignment done – whatever the reason. Because of their reluctance, you must systematically check on the progress of your employees and regularly give them feedback on how they're doing.

If you don't monitor desired performance, you won't achieve desired performance. Don't leave achieving your goals to chance; develop systems to monitor progress and ensure that employees achieve your goals. And you can't measure anything except against what you set out to achieve.

# Taking the First Steps

The first step in checking your employees' progress is to determine the key indicators of a goal's success. You set goals with your employees that are few in number and *SMART* (specific, measurable, attainable, relevant and time-bound).

When you quantify a goal in precise numerical terms, your employees have no confusion over how their performance is measured and when their job performance is adequate (or less than adequate). For example, if the goal is to produce 100 sprockets per hour, with a reject rate of 1 or lower, your employees clearly understand that producing only 75 sprockets per hour with 10 rejects is unacceptable performance. You leave nothing to the imagination, and the goals aren't subject to individual interpretation or to the whims of individual supervisors or managers.

How you measure and monitor the progress of your employees towards completion of their goals depends on the nature of the goals. You can measure goals in terms of time, units of production or delivery of a particular work product (such as a report or a sales proposal), for example.

Table 3-1 offers examples of different goals and ways to measure them.

| Table 3-1 | Sample Goals and Measurements |
|---|---|
| *Goal* | *Measurement* |
| Plan and implement a company newsletter before the end of the second quarter of the current fiscal year | The specific date (for example 30 June) that the newsletter is sent out (*time*) |
| Increase the number of mountain bike frames produced by each employee from 20 to 25 per day | The exact number of mountain bike frames produced by the employee each day (*quantity*) |
| Increase profit on the project by 20 per cent in financial year 2012 | The total percentage increase in profit in the year to 31 December 2012 (*percentage increase*) |

Although noting when your employees attain their goals is obviously important, recognising your employees' *incremental* progress towards attaining their goals is just as important. For example:

- ✔ The goal for your drivers is to maintain an accident-free record. This goal is continuous – no deadline exists. To encourage drivers in their efforts, you can prominently post a huge banner in the middle of the garage that reads '153 Accident-free Days'. Increase the number for each day of accident-free driving.

- ✔ The goal of your accounts clerks is to increase the average number of transactions from 150 per day to 175 per day. To track their progress, you can publicly post a summary of the daily production count at the end of each week. As production increases, praise the progress of your employees towards the final goal.

- ✔ The goal set for your production staff is to turn customer orders around within 24 hours, without errors. You can publicly post the results for all to see; and in this case, when orders are either not turned around within 24 hours or when errors occur, you have a very quick, public and agreed point for investigation.

The secret to performance measuring and monitoring is the power of positive feedback. When you give positive feedback (increased number of units produced, percentage increase in sales and so on), you encourage the behaviour that you want. However, when you give negative feedback (number of errors, number of work days lost and so on), you aren't encouraging the behaviour you want; you're only discouraging the behaviour that you don't want. Consider the following examples:

- ✔ **Instead of measuring this:** Number of defective cartridges
- ✔ **Measure this:** Number of correctly assembled cartridges
- ✔ **Instead of measuring this:** Number of days late
- ✔ **Measure this:** Number of days on time
- ✔ **Instead of measuring this:** Quantity of late transactions
- ✔ **Measure this:** Quantity of completed transactions

You're much more likely to get the results you want when you put group performance measures (total revenues, average days sick and so on) out in the open for everyone to see, but keep individual performance measures (sales performance by employee, absence rankings by employee and so on) private. The intention is to get a team to work *together* to improve its performance – tracking and publicising group measures and then rewarding improvement in them can lead to dramatic advances in the performance you seek. What you do *not* want to do is embarrass your employees or subject them to ridicule by

**Book IV**

**Increasing Productivity and Performance**

other employees when their individual performance isn't up to par. Instead, deal with these employees privately, and coach them (and provide additional training and support, as necessary) to improve performance.

# Developing a System for Providing Immediate Performance Feedback

You can measure an infinite number of behaviours or performance characteristics. What you measure and the values you measure against are up to you and your employees. In any case, keep certain points in mind when you design a system for measuring and monitoring your employees' performance. Build your system on the *MARS* – *milestones*, *actions*, *relationships* and *schedules* – system. We describe each element of the MARS system in the following sections.

Application of each characteristic – milestones, actions, relationships and schedules – results in goals that you can measure and monitor. If you can't measure and monitor your goals, chances are that your employees never achieve them and you don't know the difference. And wouldn't that be a shame?

## Setting your checkpoints: The milestones

Every goal needs a starting point, an ending point and points in between to measure progress along the way. *Milestones* are the checkpoints, events and markers that tell you and your employees how far along you are on the road to reaching the goals you've set together.

For example, suppose that you establish a goal of finalising corporate budgets in three months' time. The third milestone along the way to your ultimate goal is that draft department budgets are submitted to division managers no later than 1 June. If you check with the division managers on 1 June and your employees haven't submitted the draft budgets, you quickly and unambiguously know that the project is behind schedule. If, however, all the budgets are in on 15 May, you know that the project is ahead of schedule and that you may reach the final goal of completing the corporate budgets sooner than you originally estimated.

## Reaching your checkpoints: The actions

*Actions* are the individual activities your employees perform to get from one milestone to the next. To reach the third milestone in your budgeting project –

submitting draft department budgets to division managers by 1 June – your employees must undertake and complete several actions after they reach the second milestone in the project. In this example, these actions may include the following:

✔ Review prior-year expenditure reports and determine the relationship, if any, to current activities.

✔ Review current-year expenditure reports and project and forecast final results.

✔ Meet with department staff to determine their training, travel and capital equipment requirements for the new financial year.

✔ Review the possibilities of new staff, lay-offs, redundancies and pay rises to determine the impact on payroll costs.

✔ Put everything onto a computerised draft budget spreadsheet using the figures from the actions already taken.

✔ Print off the draft budget and double-check the results, correcting them if necessary.

✔ Submit the draft budget to your own manager before forwarding it to the division manager.

Each action gets your employees a little farther along the way towards reaching the third milestone in the project and is therefore a critical element in their performance.

When developing a plan for completion of any activity or project, note each action in writing. By taking notes, you make concentration easier for your employees because they know exactly what they must do to reach a milestone, how far they've gone and how much farther they have to go. And each time they do reach a milestone, record it.

## Acting in sequence: The relationships

*Relationships* are how milestones and actions interact with one another. Relationships shape the proper sequencing of activities that lead you to the successful, effective accomplishment of your goals. Although sequences don't always matter, it's often more effective to perform certain actions before others and to attain certain milestones before others.

For example, in the list of actions needed to achieve the third project milestone, covered in the preceding section, trying to perform the fifth action before the first, second, third or fourth isn't going to work! If you don't work out the right numbers to put into your spreadsheet before you fill in the blanks, your results are meaningless.

## Measuring instead of counting

According to management guru Peter Drucker, most business people spend too much time counting and too little time actually measuring the performance of their organisations.

Drucker likens counting to a doctor using an X-ray machine to diagnose an ill patient. Although some ailments – broken bones, pneumonia and so on – do show up on an X-ray, other, more life-threatening illnesses such as leukaemia, hypertension and AIDS don't. Similarly, most managers use accounting systems to X-ray their organisation's financial performance. However, accounting systems don't measure a catastrophic loss of market share or a failure of the firm to innovate until the problem has already gone on too long and the 'patient' is damaged – perhaps irretrievably.

Keep in mind that you may have more than one way to reach a milestone and give your employees the scope to find their own ways to reach their goals. Doing so empowers your employees to take responsibility for their work and to benefit from both their mistakes and their successes. The results are successful performance and happy, productive employees.

## Establishing your timeframe: The schedules

How do you determine how far apart your milestones should be and how long project completion should take? You can plan better by estimating the *schedule* of each individual action in your project plan.

Using your experience and training to develop schedules that are realistic and useful is important. For example, if you give someone a deadline of two years' time, they won't take any notice of it until two or three months before the actual date. If you do need to set long-term deadlines, then make sure that you break the activities up into milestones and points of reference that you can realistically measure along the way.

## Reducing shrinkage

*Shrinkage* refers to the amount of products, equipment and supplies lost through wastage, theft, damage or breakage. Shrinkage is therefore a euphemism for sloppiness, lack of attention and, above all, an inability to set standards of performance that stick.

Many organisations are complacent about shrinkage. According to Lawrence King, managing director of the ORIS Group, a consultancy that monitors the efficiency and effectiveness of resource utilisation for its customers,

> *Some retailers especially do not even know what their shrinkage numbers are. I know of two major businesses, one in pharmaceuticals and the other in fashion, neither of which want to know how bad the problem is, because they know that they would have to do something about it if they did know. They have therefore put this problem into the 'too hard to cope with' basket. The trouble is, it does cost money to find out what the losses are. And then once you know what the losses are, you clearly have to do something about it.*

In the past, organisations thought that shoplifting and petty pilfering were the only real sources and causes of shrinkage, and so considered they had little to worry about. Shrinkage, however, occurs through staff dishonesty and information systems failure as well as through theft by customers. Part of the problem is a result of changing patterns of employment. King states:

> *Not that long ago, most retail staff were full-time. It was a career, and they worked until they drew their pensions. Now, retailers have cut their costs, there are far more part-time staff, so the manager in a typical retail outlet may be the only full-time member of staff. That may not be quite true in bigger stores of course; but the general trend is the same. There is consequently a lot less loyalty and a lot less commitment than there used to be. In addition, the pay is almost invariably lower. Retail has never been the best pay in the world, so maybe people feel that there is an opportunity to supplement low rates of pay by helping themselves a bit.*

## *Creating programmes based on desired behaviours*

Any organisation faced with a serious shrinkage problem has to be able to establish absolute standards – standards below which it doesn't slip, nor allow employees to slip. You can only address shrinkage problems under the following conditions:

- ✔ **Recognising the issue at all levels.** Recognition must be underpinned by a determination at board level to deal fully and effectively with the problem.

- ✔ **Enforcing zero tolerance for theft or fraud among staff.** No matter how senior, experienced or valued the colleague is, he must be dismissed if he's caught stealing from the business. This is the *only* way to deal with pilfering.

✔ **Making shrinkage culturally unacceptable.** Make it clear that shrinkage is an enemy of the business. Relate shrinkage rates to turnover and profitability in all staff briefings.

✔ **Rewarding the desired behaviour.** The desired behaviour is established through a combination of policies and practice. The policies very clearly state both what's required and how people are to behave and not behave. In particular, you need to focus on the conduct of everyone from the point of view of ensuring that

- We all know and understand that stealing, lying and cheating are an affront to everyone.

- You monitor all aspects of shrinkage that concern you, and make sure that you also involve all the staff.

- Shrinkage is treated from the point of view that, by stealing or lying, individuals affect not just themselves but also everyone else.

Making sure that you reward honest employees adequately for their work, so that you remove their temptation to steal, is the key to this problem. An open and honest culture needs to underpin the organisation; ensuring that employees are honest is impossible if those further up the organisation aren't. Paying attention to matters such as punctuality, commitment and enthusiasm helps to generate loyalty and engagement; and the more loyal and engaged employees are, the less likely they are to steal from their employer.

# Reading the Results

You establish your goals, you set performance measures and you obtain pages of data for each of your employees and activities. Now what? Now you determine whether your employees achieved the expected results, as follows:

✔ **Compare results to expectations.** Did your employees achieve the expected goal? Suppose that the goal is to complete the budget by 1 June. When did your employees complete the budget? It was completed on 17 May – well ahead of the deadline. Brilliant! The employees accomplished the mission with time to spare.

✔ **Record the results.** Make note of the results – perhaps put them in the files that you maintain for each employee or print them out on your computer and post them in the work area.

✔ **Praise, coach or counsel your employees.** If they did the job right, on time and within budget, congratulate your employees for a job well done and reward them appropriately: a written note of appreciation, a day off with pay, a formal awards presentation – whatever you decide.

However, if employees didn't achieve the expected results, find out why and what you can do to ensure that they are successful next time. If employees need only additional support or encouragement, coach them for a better performance. Listen to your employees, clarify their difficulties and then formulate a response; consider referring them to other employees for advice or providing your own personal examples that may be applicable to their situation. If the poor results stem from a more serious shortcoming, then retrain, or discipline, your employees.

# Appraising Performance: Why It Matters

You can find many good reasons for conducting regular formal performance appraisals with your employees and of your activities. Formal performance appraisals are just one part of an organisation's system of delegation, goal setting, coaching, motivating and ongoing informal and formal feedback on employee performance. If you don't believe us, try a few of these positive elements of performance appraisals on for size:

✔ **A chance to meet regularly:** Meeting regularly means that you know what your employees are doing and they know you're available for support when needed. When you establish regular informal meetings, you also have a much better basis for effective regular formal reviews when they happen.

✔ **A chance to summarise past performance and establish new performance goals:** All employees want to know whether they're doing a good job. Formal performance appraisals force managers to communicate performance results – both good and bad – to their employees and to set new goals. In many organisations, the annual performance appraisal is the only occasion when supervisors and managers speak to their employees about performance expectations and the results of employee efforts for the preceding appraisal period.

✔ **An opportunity for clarification and communication:** You need to continually compare expectations. Try this exercise with your manager. List your ten most important activities. Then ask your manager to list what she considers to be your ten most important activities. Surprise – the chances are that your lists are quite different. On average, businesspeople who do this exercise find that their lists overlap by only 40 per cent at best. Performance appraisals help the employer and employee to compare notes and make sure that assignments and priorities are in sync.

**Book IV**

**Increasing Productivity and Performance**

✔ **A forum for learning goals and career development:** In many organisations, career development takes place as a part of the formal performance appraisal process. Managers and employees are all very busy and often have difficulty setting aside the time to sit down and chart out the steps that they must take to progress in an organisation or career. Although career development discussions should generally take place in a forum separate from the performance appraisal process, combining the activities does afford the opportunity to kill both birds with the same stone . . . or something like that.

✔ **A formal documentation to promote advancement or dismissal:** Most employees get plenty of informal performance feedback – at least of the negative kind along the lines of: 'You did what? Are you nuts?' Most informal feedback is verbal and, as such, undocumented. If you're trying to build a case to give your employee a promotion, you can support it more easily if you have plenty of written documentation (including formal performance appraisals) to justify your decision. And if you're coming to the conclusion that you need to dismiss someone for poor performance, then you must have written evidence, including performance appraisals, that you've tried to address this performance before.

So, the preceding list gives very important reasons for conducting regular, formal performance appraisals. However, consider this statement: many companies have paid a lot of money to employees and former employees who've successfully sued them for wrongful or unfair dismissal, or for other biased and prejudicial employment decisions. Imagine how lonely you'd feel on the witness stand in the following scene, a scene that's replayed for real in courts of law and employment tribunals the length and breadth of the country:

**Lawyer:** So, Manager-on-the-spot, would you please tell the court exactly why you terminated Employee X?

**Manager-on-the-spot:** Certainly, I'll be glad to. Employee X was a very poor performer – clearly the worst in my department.

**Lawyer:** During the five years that my client was with your firm, did you ever conduct formal performance appraisals with her?

**Manager-on-the-spot:** Er . . . well, no. I meant to, but I'm a very busy person. I was never quite able to get around to it.

**Lawyer:** Manager-on-the-spot, do you mean to say that, in all the time with your firm, Employee X never received a formal performance appraisal? Exactly how was my client supposed to correct the alleged poor performance when you failed to provide her with the feedback needed to do so?

**Manager-on-the-spot:** Hmmm . . .

# Spelling Out the Performance Appraisal Process

Believe it or not, one of the most important things you can do as a manager is to conduct accurate and timely performance appraisals of your employees. As the saying goes, feedback is the breakfast of champions – make it a regular part of your management diet!

Many managers, however, tend to see the performance appraisal process in very narrow terms: how can I get this thing done as quickly as possible so I can get back to my real job? (Whatever their 'real' job is as managers.) In their haste to get the appraisal done and behind them, many managers merely consider a few examples of recent performance and base their entire appraisal on them. And because few managers give their employees the kind of meaningful, ongoing performance feedback that they need to do their jobs better, the performance appraisal can become a dreaded event – full of surprises and dismay. Or it can be so sugar-coated that it becomes a meaningless exercise in management. Neither scenario is the right way to evaluate your employees.

Have separate discussions for each of the following:

- ✔ Pay rises and bonuses
- ✔ Promotions
- ✔ Career development
- ✔ Ways to improve present performance and develop future performance
- ✔ Poor performance

Of course, in practice you can't possibly keep each of the topics totally separate from the rest. But you can prioritise; and you need to spell out to the employee the specific purpose of the present discussion.

The performance appraisal process begins on the day that your employees are hired, continues each and every day that they report to you and doesn't end until, through transfer, promotion, dismissal or resignation, they move out of your sphere of responsibility.

The performance appraisal process is much broader than just the formal, written part of it. The following steps help you encompass the broader scope of the process. Follow them when you evaluate your employees' performance:

1. **Set goals, expectations and standards – together.**

   Before your employees can achieve your goals, or perform to your expectations, you have to set goals and expectations with them and develop standards to measure their performance. And after you've done all this, you have to communicate the goals and expectations *before* you evaluate your employees – not after. In fact, the performance review really starts on the first day of work. Tell your employees immediately how you evaluate them, show them the forms to be used and explain the process.

Make sure that job descriptions, tasks and priorities are clear and unambiguous, and that you and your employees understand and agree to the standards set for them. This is a two-way process. Make sure that employees have a voice in setting their goals and standards and that you have their agreement.

2. **Give continuous and specific feedback.**

Catch your employees doing things right – every day of the week – and tell them about it then and there. And if you catch them doing wrong (nobody's perfect!), then let them know about that too. Feedback is much more effective when you give it regularly and often than when you save it up for a special occasion (which can become victimisation if the feedback is constantly negative). The best formal performance appraisals contain the fewest surprises.

Constantly bombarding your employees with negative feedback has little to do with getting the performance that you want from them and costs you their respect.

3. **Prepare a formal, written performance appraisal with your employee.**

Every organisation has different requirements for the formal performance appraisal. Some appraisals are simple, one-page forms that require you to tick a few boxes; others are multi-page extravaganzas that require extensive narrative support. The form often varies by organisation, and by the level of the employee being evaluated. Regardless of the requirements of your particular organisation, the formal performance appraisal should be a summary of the goals and expectations for the appraisal period – events that you've discussed previously (and frequently) with your employees. Support your words with examples and make appraisals meaningful to your employees by keeping your discussion relevant to the goals, expectations and standards that you developed in Step 1.

As a collaborative process, have the employee complete his own performance appraisal. Then compare your (the manager's) comments with the employee's comments; the differences that you find become topics of discussion and mutual goal setting.

4. **Meet personally with your employees to discuss the performance appraisal.**

Most employees appreciate the personal touch when you give the appraisal. Set aside some quality time to meet with them to discuss their performance appraisal. This doesn't mean five or ten minutes, but at least an hour or maybe more. When you plan performance appraisal meetings, less is definitely not more. Pick a place that's comfortable and free from distractions. Make the meeting positive and upbeat. Even when you have to discuss performance problems, centre discussions on ways that you and your employees can work together to solve them.

The tone of performance appraisals and discussions can often become defensive as you raise negative elements and the employee starts to feel that he'll get a small, or no, pay rise. Start with letting the employee share how his job is going, what's working – and what's not – then share your assessment, starting with the positive.

5. **Set new goals, expectations and standards.**

   The performance appraisal meeting gives you and your employee the opportunity to step back from the inevitable daily issues for a moment and take a look at the big picture. You both have an opportunity to review and discuss the things that worked well and those that, perhaps, didn't work so well. Based on this assessment, you can then set new goals, expectations and standards for the next review period. The last step of the performance appraisal process becomes the first step, and you start all over again.

The entire performance appraisal process consists of setting goals with your employees, monitoring their performance, coaching them, supporting them, counselling and guiding them, and providing continuous feedback on their performance – both good and bad. If you do these things before you sit down for your annual or semi-annual performance appraisal sessions with your employees, reviews will be a pleasant and positive experience, looking at past accomplishments, instead of a disappointment for both you and them.

When it comes to conducting performance appraisals, managers have plenty of things to remember. Here are a few more:

- ✔ Communication with employees should be frequent so that no surprises occur (okay, *fewer* surprises). Give your employees informal feedback on their performance early and often.

- ✔ The primary focus of performance appraisals should be on going forward – setting new goals, improving future performance – rather than on looking back.

- ✔ Learning and development should always be included as a part of the performance appraisal process (although sometimes a discussion about pay rises can be separate).

- ✔ You need to make performance appraisal a priority yourself – a part of your 'real' job – you are, after all, dependent on the performance of your employees for your own success and effectiveness.

**Book IV**

**Increasing Productivity and Performance**

## Turning the tables: Upward and 360-degree evaluations

Recently a new kind of performance appraisal has emerged. Instead of the typical downward appraisal where managers review their workers' performance, the upward appraisal process stands this convention on its head by requiring workers to evaluate their managers' performance. If you think that getting a performance appraisal from your manager is uncomfortable, you haven't seen anything yet. Nothing's quite like the feeling you get when a group of your employees appraise you, giving you direct and honest feedback about the things you do that make it hard for them to do a good job. Ouch!

However, despite the discomfort that you may feel, the upward appraisal is invaluable – who better to assess your real impact on the organisation than your employees? The system works so well that companies such as Federal Express and others have institutionalised the upward appraisal and made it part of their corporate culture. Recent surveys show that many of the world's top companies are using some form of the upward performance appraisal to assess the performance of their managers.

Also popular is the 360-degree evaluation. The *360-degree evaluation process* is when you're appraised from all sides – superiors, subordinates, colleagues and anyone from other departments with whom you happen to be working at the time. Levi Strauss & Co, for example, dictates that all employees are evaluated by their supervisors and by their underlings and peers.

The results can be quite a surprise to the lucky manager who's the subject of the appraisal, who may find that other employees see him as less caring and visionary than he thought. A study by Charles Handy many years ago found the same thing – that 70 per cent of managers and supervisors who rated themselves as caring and concerned were rated in turn as autocratic and distant by their employees.

# *Preparing for the No-Surprises Appraisal*

If you're doing your job as a manager, the appraisal holds no surprises for your employees. Follow the lead of the best managers: keep in touch with your employees and give them continuous feedback on their progress. Then, when you do sit down with them for their formal performance appraisal, the session is a recap of the things that you've already discussed during the appraisal period, instead of an ambush. Keeping up a continuous dialogue lets you use the formal appraisal to focus on the positive things that you and your employees can work on together to get the best possible performance.

Above all, be *prepared* for your appraisals!

Like interviews, many managers leave their preparation for performance appraisal meetings to the last possible minute – often just before the employee is scheduled to meet with them. 'Oh, no. Cathy is going to be here in five minutes. Now, what did I do with her file? I know it's here somewhere!' The average manager spends about one hour preparing for an employee review covering a whole year of performance.

To avoid this unprofessional and unproductive situation, follow these tips:

✒ Set time aside, make a proper appointment with the employee and stick to it.

✒ Make a clear statement to the employee: 'The purpose of this perfor-mance appraisal is as follows . . .' and stick to it.

Performance appraisal is a year-round job. Whenever you recognise a prob-lem with your employees' performance, mention it to them, make a note of it and drop it in your files. And do the same whenever your employees do something great. Then, when you're ready to do your employees' periodic performance appraisals, you can pull out their files and have plenty of docu-mentation available on which to base them. Not only does this practice make the process easier for you, it also makes the appraisal much more meaningful and productive for your employees.

EXAMPLE

## Anecdotal evidence

The following stories illustrate and reinforce the need to conduct performance appraisals thor-oughly and effectively, the results that accrue from doing so and the consequences if per-formance appraisal isn't adequate or targeted effectively.

✒ Arnold Weinstock, former chief executive of GEC, built the electrical conglomerate into the most valuable British organisa-tion in great part on the basis of weekly performance appraisals and reviews with all of his top, senior and general managers and divisional directors. Often conducted late at night or over the weekend, these performance reviews normally consisted of a one-hour telephone conversation in which Arnold Weinstock would question each top manager closely on the following areas: performance, performance targets and revenues; reasons for achievement or non-achievement; proposals for the fol-lowing week; review and commentary on longer-term plans and issues. As one man-ager said: 'Arnold knew the stuff, and you needed to know it. If you couldn't answer his questions in detail, or if you tried to flan-nel your way out of things – you didn't last.'

**Book IV**

**Increasing Productivity and Performance**

*(continued)*

*(continued)*

✔ Mark McCormack, founder and chief executive of sports representation agency IMG until his death in 2004, used to manage-by-walking-about (MBWA) as far as possible. He tried to meet up with every top and senior manager, as well as other employees in the organisation; and anyone he couldn't meet, he phoned, just as Arnold Weinstock did. Again, the purpose was to get to the detail of performance and progress, and to hammer out any problems or issues. Mark McCormack stated: 'The reason for this is quite simple. We represent the interests of some of the most famous and high-profile people in the world. If we do a bad job for them, they will simply go elsewhere; and that means we are doing a bad job for us, and for those clients and connections with whom we seek to develop business. Only by attending to performance review in this way, and in this detail, can we hope to keep everybody happy and satisfied.'

✔ The strategic human resources unit of a large UK local authority devised a system of merit pay. Merit was decided by a rigorous system of performance appraisal; and anyone meeting the merit criteria received a merit pay award. Cometh the hour, cometh the system – and after working through the performance appraisal exercise with all 53,000 staff employed by the local authority, 30 merit awards were allocated. Of the 30, almost half went to the 14 members of the strategic human resources unit that had dreamed up the system in the first place! If you're determined to introduce merit pay, do at least put the ideas out to full consultation before you go live – it will save you a fortune, and moreover, you'll get a reputation for being completely fair and transparent.

# Chapter 4

# Project Management: The Key to Achieving Results

*O*rganisations are constantly changing, and ever faster, as they adapt to new market conditions, new financial conditions, new business practices, new legal requirements and new technology. Running projects often creates the change, and as a result businesses are increasingly driven to find individuals who can excel in this project-oriented environment.

## Taking on a Project

Because you're reading this chapter, the chances are that you've been asked to manage a project for the first time or that you're already running projects and are looking to see whether you can find easier and better ways of doing things. If the project is indeed your first one, that's a challenge and may well give you the chance to excel in something you haven't done before; for many, managing a project even opens a door to a new career. Try not to think of project management as a career death threat, even if others do and they now avoid looking you in the eye when passing you in the corridor. The really good news here, whether you're completely new or have some experience, is that project management has been around for a very long time. In that time, Project Managers have come up with highly effective strategies and a range of very practical techniques.

So, hang on tight – you're going to need an effective set of skills and techniques to steer your projects to successful completion. This chapter gets you off to a great start by showing you what projects and project management really are and by helping you separate projects from non-project assignments. The chapter also offers some insight on why projects succeed or fail and starts to get you into the project management mindset.

# Avoiding the Pitfalls

By following a sound approach to the project, you automatically avoid many of the pitfalls that continue to contribute to, or cause, project failure on a mind-boggling scale. You may ask why, if good ways of doing things exist, people ignore them and then have their projects fail. Good question. People make the same project mistakes repeatedly, and they're largely avoidable. You may have come across the joke by comedian Tommy Cooper:

> *I went to the doctor and said 'Every time I do this, it hurts.'*
> *The doctor said, 'Well, don't do it then.'*

A national public project run in the UK to create a database of offenders for use by the Prison Service, Probation Service and others has attracted heavy criticism for poor management. The National Audit Office, which checks up on government departments, investigated and reported that the project was delayed by three years, and the budget was double the original, but the scope had been radically cut back. Edward Leigh MP, chairman of the powerful Public Accounts Committee in Parliament described the scheme as a 'spectacular failure' and 'a master-class in sloppy project management'.

The following list takes a quick look at the main causes of project failure. The list makes for depressing reading, particularly if you recognise some elements in parts of your own organisation. Nevertheless, the list gives a good background against which to contrast successful project management.

- ✔ **Lack of clear objectives:** Nobody's really sure what the project is about, much less are people agreed on it.

- ✔ **Lack of risk management:** Things go wrong that someone could easily have foreseen and then controlled to some degree or even prevented.

- ✔ **No senior management 'buy in':** Senior managers were never convinced and so never supported the project, leading to problems such as lack of resource. Neither did those managers exercise normal management supervision as they routinely do in their other areas of responsibility.

✔ **Poor planning:** Actually, that's being kind, because often the problem is that no planning was done at all. It's not surprising, then, when things run out of control, and not least because nobody knows where the project should be at this point anyway.

✔ **No clear progress milestones:** This follows on from poor planning. The lack of milestones means nobody sees when things are off track, and problems go unnoticed for a long time.

✔ **Understated scope:** The scope and the Project Plan are superficial and understate both what the project needs to deliver and the resource needed to deliver it. Project staff (often team members) then discover the hidden but essential components later in the project. The additional work that is necessary then takes the project out of control, causing delay to the original schedule and overspending against the original budget.

✔ **Poor communications:** So many projects fail because of communication breakdown, which can stem from unclear roles and responsibilities and from poor senior management attitudes, such as not wanting to hear bad news.

✔ **Unrealistic resource levels:** It just isn't possible to do a project of the required scope with such a small amount of resource – staff, money or both.

✔ **Unrealistic timescales:** The project just can't deliver by the required time, so it's doomed to failure.

✔ **No change control:** People add in things bit by bit – scope creep. Then it dawns on everyone that the project's grown so big that it can't be delivered within the fixed budget or by the set deadline.

That's ten reasons for failure, but you can probably think of a few more. The interesting thing about these problems is that avoiding them is, for the most part, actually not that difficult.

# *Deciding Whether the Job Is Really a Project*

Before you start to think too deeply about how to set up the project, the first thing to do is check whether it really is one. No matter what your job is, you handle a myriad of assignments every day: prepare a memo, hold a meeting, design a sales campaign or move to new offices. Not all these assignments are projects. So what makes something a project?

You can consider three easy areas to determine whether a job is a project:

- ✔ Is it a one-off job or something that's ongoing? If the job is ongoing, like producing bars of soap on a production line or taking customer orders, then it's business as usual, not a project.

- ✔ Does the job justify project controls? Project management means incurring some overheads, although we offer advice on how to keep overheads to the minimum. But the fact remains that overheads exist and some jobs are so small or straightforward that they just don't justify that degree of control.

- ✔ This last one may sound a little weird, and it certainly doesn't fit with the formal definitions; it's the question, 'Do you want to handle the job as a project?' You may choose to deal with a block of work as a project, so, in some instances, you have a choice.

## Understanding the four control areas

Different project approaches have slightly different definitions of a project; here's one:

A *project* is a temporary undertaking performed to produce a unique product, service or result.

The 'unique product' is true, but don't let that put you off setting up projects that are effectively repeated, such as organising the annual company conference. Although, strictly speaking, the task is unique each time, you will nevertheless find large areas of commonality with previous projects, and you don't need to go and reinvent the wheel. For example, you can probably adapt last year's plans rather than starting from scratch.

Large or small, projects involve the following four areas of control:

- ✔ **Scope:** What the project will deliver
- ✔ **Time:** When the project will deliver
- ✔ **Quality:** So often forgotten, but an essential dimension
- ✔ **Resource:** Necessary amounts of people, funds and other resources such as equipment and accommodation that the project needs

You need to balance these areas for each project, and you can see immediately why so many projects get into difficulties. You look at a project, think about the four control factors and say to yourself, 'They want that scope, to that quality level, with just that resource and by then? They've got to be joking!' Strangely, organisational managers often commit projects to failure by insisting on unachievable deadlines or unrealistic resources. What's even stranger is that those same managers are surprised and even angry when the projects inevitably get into difficulties and fail.

Getting the balance right in the early part of the project when you do the main scoping and planning is, obviously enough, essential. Jerry Madden of NASA, the American space agency, produced a great document called 'One Hundred Rules for NASA Project Managers'. Rule 15 is:

> *The seeds of problems are laid down early. Initial planning is the most vital part of a project. The review of most failed projects or project problems indicate the disasters were well planned to happen from the start.*

It's also useful to think about the four areas of control when dealing with change in the project. Although many other considerations may affect a project's performance, these four components are the basis of a project's definition for the following reasons:

- ✔ The only reason a project exists is to produce the results specified in its scope.

- ✔ The project's end date is usually an essential part of defining what constitutes successful performance – in many cases, the project must provide the desired result by a certain time to meet its intended need.

- ✔ The quality requirement is a vital part of the balance and may be the most important element, even though many organisational managers are preoccupied with time and cost. But what's the point of delivering an unusable heap of garbage on time and within budget?

- ✔ The availability of resources can affect which products the project can produce and the timescale in which it can produce them.

Quality can be a very important factor, and is sometimes the most important, so do think about it carefully. A project to build and install a new air traffic control system for the south of the UK was criticised for being over budget and late on delivery. As a number of people have pointed out, though, if you're sitting in an aeroplane circling while waiting to land at London Heathrow Airport – one of the world's busiest – would you rather that they'd got the air traffic control system in on time and to budget or that they'd got it right?

## *Recognising the diversity of projects*

Projects come in a wide assortment of shapes and sizes. For example, projects can:

✔ **Be large or small:**

- Building a new railway link across London, which will cost around £16 billion and take seven years to complete, is a project, perhaps linked to other projects to form a programme.

- Preparing the annual report for the department, which may take you six days to complete, may also be a project.

✔ **Involve many people or just you:**

- Training all 10,000 of your organisation's sales staff worldwide in the working of a new product is a project.

- Redecorating an office and rearranging the furniture and equipment is also a project.

✔ **Be defined by a legal contract or by an informal agreement:**

- A signed contract between you and a customer that requires you to build a house defines a project.

- An informal agreement by the IT department to install a new software package in a business area defines a project.

✔ **Be business related or personal:**

- Conducting your organisation's five-yearly strategy review is a project.

- Preparing for a family wedding is also a project – and a much more pleasant one than the five-yearly strategy review.

No matter what the individual characteristics of your project are, you can use the same four elements of scope, time, quality and resource to think it through.

## Understanding the four stages of a project

Every project, whether large or small, passes through four stages:

✔ **Starting the Project:** This stage involves generating, evaluating and framing the business need for the project and the general approach to performing it, and agreeing to prepare a detailed Project Plan. Outputs from this stage may include approval to proceed to the next stage, documentation of the need for the project, and rough estimates of time and resources to perform it, and an initial list of people who may be interested in, involved with or affected by the project.

✔ **Organising and Preparing:** This stage involves developing a plan that specifies the desired results: the work to do; the time, the cost and other resources required; and a plan for how to address key project risks. Outputs from this stage include a Project Plan documenting the intended project results and the time, resources and supporting processes to help create them, along with all the other controls that the project needs, such as for risk management.

✔ **Carrying Out the Work:** This stage involves performing the planned work, monitoring and controlling performance to ensure adherence to the current plan, and doing the more detailed planning of successive phases as the project continues. Outputs from this stage may include project progress reports, financial reports and further detailed plans.

✔ **Closing the Project:** This stage involves assessing the project results, obtaining customer approvals, assigning project team members to new work, closing financial accounts and conducting a post-project evaluation. Outputs from this stage may include final, accepted and approved project results and recommendations and suggestions for applying lessons learned from this project to similar efforts in the future.

For small projects, this entire life-cycle can take a few days. For larger projects, it can take years!

In a perfect world, projects run smoothly and always go exactly to plan. However, because you don't live in a perfect world and because your project certainly won't be running in one, you need to be flexible. When starting to think about your project, you need to allow for:

✔ **The unknown and uncertain:** Projects are rarely 100 per cent predictable. The normal territory of projects is that, to some extent at least, you're going into the unknown. Therefore, your plans need to allow for things going off track. Sometimes the uncertain areas are predictable, which falls partly into the area of risk management (see Book II Chapter 6 for how to assess and manage risks). Sometimes the areas aren't at all predictable, and that comes into the area of contingency. You need contingency; remember Murphy's Law – 'If it can go wrong, it will go wrong.' We talk about contingency in Book II Chapter 6.

✔ **Learning by doing.** Despite doing your best to assess feasibility and develop good plans at the front end of the project, you may find later on that you can't achieve what you thought you could or in the way you thought you could. When this situation happens, you need to rethink in the light of the new information you've acquired. Sometimes you can see up front that you won't know how a particular part of the project is going to work out until you get nearer to that point and better information is to hand. Don't worry about that; just point it out clearly at the beginning.

> ✔ **Unexpected change.** Your initial feasibility and benefits assessments are sound, and your plan is detailed and realistic. However, certain key project team members leave the organisation without warning during the project. Or a new technology emerges, and it's more appropriate to use than the one in your original plans. Perhaps the business environment changes and with it your organisation's whole market strategy. Because ignoring these occurrences may seriously jeopardise your project's success, you need to rethink and re-plan in light of these new realities.

# Defining the Project Manager's Role

The Project Manager's job is to manage the project on a day-to-day basis to bring it to a successful conclusion. He'll usually be accountable to a senior manager who's the project sponsor, or to a small group of managers who form a project steering committee or project board. The Project Manager's job is challenging. For instance, he often coordinates technically specialised professionals – who may have limited experience working together – to achieve a common goal.

It's important to understand that the Project Manager's position is indeed a role; it's not about status. That's true of all roles in the project and there may, for example, be very senior people working as team members (such as chief engineers and legal advisers) who are accountable to the Project Manager even though in the normal business they're very much his senior. Both team members and the Project Manager himself must understand that he has responsibility and authority in the project that comes with the role, independent of his organisational grade or rank. When the Project Manager has a clear accountability to a sponsor or steering committee, life is much easier because everyone can see that his authority comes from them. It's the same mechanism that allows a corporal on the gate of a military camp to refuse entry to a general until he's satisfied that the general's security pass is valid.

The Project Manager doesn't do any of the technical work of the project in his role as Project Manager. If he's involved in technical work it's with a different hat on – that of a team member. The distinction is important because if you're doing teamwork as well as project managing, you must be clear about both roles and only wear one hat at a time. It's all too easy to neglect the management and let the project run out of control because you're so engrossed in the detail and challenges of your part of the technical work.

The Project Manager's role requires hard skills such as planning and costing, but also soft people skills, and his success requires a keen ability to identify and resolve sensitive organisational and interpersonal issues. The next section covers the main tasks that a Project Manager handles and notes potential challenges that he may encounter.

# Looking at the Project Manager's tasks

Your role as the Project Manager is one of day-to-day responsibility for the project, and that might involve so much work that your job must necessarily be a full-time one. Or it may be that the project is smaller and less complicated and project management is just part of your job. Either way, the responsibilities are the same; it's just the scale and complexity that are different.

Here's a summary of the main tasks. Some things on the list involve consultation with others:

- Sketch out initial ideas for the project, with the justification, outline costs and timescales.

- Plan the project, including mapping out the controls that will be put in place, defining what quality the project needs and how it will be achieved, analysing risk and planning control actions.

- Control the flow of work to teams (or perhaps just team members in a smaller project).

- Motivate and support teams and team members.

- Liaise with external suppliers.

- Liaise with Project Managers of interfacing projects.

- Liaise with programme management staff if the project is one of a group of projects being coordinated as a programme.

- Ensure that the project deliverables are developed to the right level of quality.

- Keep track of progress and adjust to correct any minor drifts off the plan.

- Keep track of spending.

- Go to others, such as the steering committee, if things go more significantly off track (for example, the whole project is threatened).

- Report progress, such as to the sponsor or steering committee.

- Keep track of risks and make sure that control actions are taken.

- Deal with any problems, involving others as necessary.

- Decide on changes, getting approval from others where the Project Manager doesn't have personal authority to make a decision (for example, when changes involve very high cost).

- Plan successive delivery stages in more detail.

- Close the project down in an orderly way when everything's done.

So, the tasks will keep you very busy but also be very enjoyable if you're a Project Manager at heart.

A key to project success is being proactive. Get out in front of the project and direct where it's going. Don't follow on behind the project being reactive and having to fire-fight countless problems because you didn't see them coming.

## Staving off potential excuses for not following a structured project management approach

Be prepared for other people to oppose your attempts to use proven project management approaches. The following list provides a few examples of excuses you may encounter as a Project Manager and the appropriate responses you can give:

✔ **Excuse:** Our projects are all to short deadlines; we have no time to plan.

**Response:** Unfortunately for the excuse giver, this logic is illogical! With a short deadline, you can't afford to make many mistakes. If it doesn't matter too much when the project delivers, you don't need as good a plan as if it matters very much and time is short.

✔ **Excuse:** Structured project management is only for large projects.

**Response:** No matter what size the project is, the information you need to perform it is the same. What do you need to produce? What work has to be done? Who's going to do it? When will the project end? Have you met expectations?

✔ **Excuse:** Project management just means more overheads.

**Response:** So does corporate management, and that's essential too! But in any case, if you don't manage a project properly and it fails, how much will that cost you in wasted time, money and lost benefits?

✔ **Excuse:** These projects require creativity and new development. You can't predict their outcomes with any certainty.

**Response:** You can predict some projects' outcomes better than others. However, people awaiting the outcomes of any project still have expectations for what they'll get and when. Therefore, a project with many uncertainties needs a manager to develop and share initial plans and then to assess and communicate the effects of unexpected occurrences.

## Avoiding 'shortcuts'

The short-term pressures of your job, particularly if you're fitting in project management alongside other work, may tempt you to cut corners and miss things out. That's not the same as adjusting the project management needs to the project, but rather missing stuff out altogether that in an ideal world you would have done. Resist the temptation to cut corners, because usually doing so comes back and bites you later.

Don't be seduced into seemingly easier shortcuts such as:

- **Jumping directly from Starting the Project to Carrying Out the Work:** Sounds good, but you haven't defined the work to be done! A variation on this shortcut is: 'This project's been done before, so why plan it out again?' Even though projects can be similar to past ones, some elements will be different. Always check the plan thoroughly.

- **Failing to check progress at frequent intervals:** After all, everyone's working hard and things seem to be going okay. But just as when you're walking somewhere you need to check the map from time to time, so you need to check the project. Otherwise you won't see warning signs and may be a long way off track by the time you do eventually notice that something is wrong.

- **Not keeping the plan up to date:** That includes logging *actuals* such as the time actually taken to do things and the expense actually incurred. Yes, it takes discipline to stay up to date, but you'll never be able to control the project if you don't know where you are at the moment.

- **Not completing the closing stage:** At the end of one project, you can face pressure to move right on to the next. Scarce resources and short deadlines encourage this rapid movement, and starting a new project is always more challenging than wrapping up an old one. But you must make sure that everything is properly finished and, if necessary, handed over. You also need to check that the project has achieved what it's supposed to have done and that you and your organisation take on board any lessons, good and bad, for the future.

# Do You Have What It Takes?

You're reading this because you want to be a good Project Manager, right? Well, try a quick quiz to see what your strengths and weaknesses are.

**Book IV**

**Increasing Productivity and Performance**

## Questions

1. Do you prefer to be everyone's friend or get the job done?

2. Do you prefer to do technical work or manage technical work?

3. Do you think the best way to get a tough task done is to do it yourself?

4. Do you prefer your work to be predictable or constantly changing?

5. Do you get immersed in the detail or can you hold on to the big picture?

6. Do you handle pressure well?

7. Do you like to plan and organise the work of others?

8. Do you think you shouldn't have to monitor people after they've said they'll do a job for you?

9. Do you see a need to motivate people, or do you leave them to get on with it because they should be self-motivated to perform their jobs?

10. Are you comfortable dealing with people at all organisational levels?

## Answers

1. Good working relations are vital, but you must also deliver the goods.

2. Management is exactly that, and you move away from hands-on stuff.

3. Your role is to manage, and that includes letting others develop.

4. No project ever goes exactly to plan and, anyway, things change. That's part of the challenge and also the buzz of project management.

5. You may need to deal with fine detail, but not at the expense of losing the big picture.

6. The Project Manager needs a cool head; some times will be pressured.

7. Being an organiser and planner goes with the territory.

8. Just like with general management, you have to know that work is getting done.

9. You need soft people skills too. Projects are about people.

10. The Project Manager must deal with people at all levels – from upper management to support staff – who perform project-related activities.

# Chapter 5

# Looking at Staff Resources on Projects

S tan Portny remembers reading the following from a stressed-out Project Manager: 'We've done so much with so little for so long, they now expect us to do everything with nothing!'

The truth is, of course, you can't accomplish anything with nothing, and in the context of project resource planning, you need people as well as money. Getting the people planning right is essential both in terms of getting the right staff onto your project in the first place and then using the project staff in the best possible way. Although staff resourcing can be tricky – and many Project Managers tend to underestimate this resourcing – don't be daunted by it, but instead allow time to think it through and plan thoroughly. By the way, using project staff well isn't selfish either. Good project management includes giving team members opportunities to succeed and develop alongside you getting a successful project, and that needs careful thought and planning too.

This chapter covers the first part of the resource planning: the staff. It helps you understand the dynamics of scheduling and includes areas such as availability to show that full-time staff aren't really full time. The chapter also covers topics such as individual performance, multi-tasking and the working environment, all of which can have a big impact on your Project Plan.

You live in a world of limited resources and not enough time, which means you always have more work to do than time and resources allow. After you decide which tasks to pursue, you need to do everything possible to perform them successfully.

# Seeing Why You Need to Plan Staff Use

Before you roll your sleeves up and get stuck in to the detail of how to plan your use of staff on the project, it's helpful to be clear about *why* you need to do this planning.

## Dealing with resource conflicts

The first reason that you need to plan staff resource is that your use of staff can conflict in several ways with something else. Resource conflicts make your plan completely unworkable if you don't deal with them.

The activity plans such as the Activity Network and the Gantt Chart deal at first with the logical dependency of tasks, and they don't take account of resource availability until you add that in – the subject of this chapter.

Here are three areas of potential resource conflict, using an employee, Sue, as an example:

✔ **Multiple tasks:** We make a plan that has a number of activities including three which will take a month each. The Activity Network shows that the three can be done in parallel and each one involves Sue working full time. However, unless Sue is Superwoman and can work three shifts a day of eight hours each – 24-hour working – for a whole month, we seem to have a problem.

✔ **Calendar events:** A task is three days' duration and Sue is required to work eight hours a day. On the plan, the task is to be done from 1 to 3 January. But now we have a problem with the calendar. Because 1 January is a public holiday, there are only two working days in that period, not three, so the task can't be achieved. If we don't sort this out, our plan isn't going to work because the offices are shut on 1 January and Sue just won't be there. Oh yes, and four months ago she booked annual leave for 2 and 3 January because it's her husband's 30th birthday and she's booked a surprise trip to Paris, and although Sue appreciates that the project is quite important . . .

✔ **Other projects:** For another task, we need Sue for five days for the week commencing 8 February. Oh joy, she isn't working on any other project activity during that week and neither are there any public holidays or birthday surprises. But just when we thought it was safe to go back in the water, we find that another project also needs her for five days in the week commencing 8 February. Unfortunately, that other project has a much higher priority than ours.

The last of these conflicts reveals the messy but realistic situation that you sometimes find yourself in: sorting out resourcing between projects, not just within your own. That can take time – so allow some. You must allow sufficient time for planning at the front end of your project, because if you don't sort these problems out on the plan they'll hit you later on during the project when they'll be even harder to deal with. Picking up the last example again, Sue isn't going to be at work on 8 February even if it's on the plan in red letters, bold type and underlined. If we leave it on the plan that she'll be at work, the plan is unrealistic and the project will hit a major problem on 8 February.

Having, hopefully, convinced you that resource conflicts can cause problems and that it's important to resolve them, you may now be wondering how you actually do that. The later section 'Smoothing the resource' will help, after a closer examination of the dynamics and nature of staff resourcing.

## Making sure that people are available

Another reason you need to plan staff resource is so you can tell people when you'll need them and arrange, if necessary, for their managers to release them to work on the project. A number of people both inside the project and outside it may need to see the resource plan and agree it up front to be sure that it's acceptable and realistic. The finance manager may be more than happy to give 40 hours of finance staff time to a project. However, he may be rather less happy if a Project Manager then marches up to him at the start of the last week of the financial year when things are really busy and says, 'Okay, I need those 40 staff hours you promised, starting at 8:30 tomorrow morning.'

The staff resource plan makes everything visible, and people who are taking part in the project or who are authorising the staff hours can make sure they can meet the commitment in terms of the number of staff, the particular skills and people involved, and the dates that you actually need them. That word *commitment* is significant because you don't want empty promises that cause you problems later when the resource doesn't materialise.

## The 'we pay our staff anyway' argument

Organisations that don't track project staff resource are, to be kind and understate the point, odd. Even if they aren't interested in the cost of staff, which they surely should be, having staff hours information is useful to help assess the likely staff effort needed for future projects. But anyway, time is money, as the saying goes. The normal excuse that 'we're going to pay the staff anyway so we don't need to track their hours' just doesn't stand up to scrutiny. If the staff weren't working on this project, they could be doing something else, so it's not as if their project work comes for free. Then there is an impact on the Business Case, because if you don't record staff hours, then you leave out a major – and, in a lot of projects, the biggest – project cost.

Nick Graham was advising a major organisation that had a policy not to record staff hours. On one project, the Project Manager was looking at the Business Case and said that the project was great and would pay for itself because it would save a lot of administrative staff hours. Nick asked how she knew that, if nobody knew the number of staff hours expended on the project. The number of project hours spent could exceed the number of administrative hours saved and it could be years before the balance tipped, if it ever did. The Project Manager couldn't answer Nick's question, but the project effort was considerable and involved some very senior and expensive people, so the question was surely valid.

## Monitoring use of staff on the project

Some organisations have procedures and even systems that detail and track every resource on every project. Other organisations don't formally plan or track project resources at all (see the nearby sidebar 'The "we pay our staff anyway" argument'). However, even if your organisation doesn't require you to plan your resource needs and track your resource use, doing so is vital to your project's success. Even in terms of progress and control, how can you tell whether the project is on track if you don't know whether the actual use of staff hours on work so far is as you expected?

# Matching People to Tasks

Your project's success rests on your ability to get the right people to perform your project's work. That may be in terms of suitably qualified staff or simply just getting enough people – which isn't always so easy. You begin your project planning by looking at what you need to deliver. Next, you decide what activities you'll need performed to create the deliverables. Your third step is to decide what skills and knowledge people must have to perform the activities.

## *Working out the skill sets and knowledge that you need on the teams*

To determine the skills and knowledge that people must have for your project, you can work from the Product Definitions produced as part of your planning. You now develop that thinking as you consider the staff resource needs in more detail.

You determine the skill and knowledge requirements by reviewing what is to be built, but as with planning, don't panic if you aren't sure or simply don't know. Remember that being a Project Manager doesn't usually mean that you're a technical expert, so go and talk to other people including:

✔ Any Project Managers who've run similar projects in the past

✔ Possible external supplier companies

✔ Staff who've worked on similar projects in the past

✔ Subject matter experts

✔ Your project office, which may have plans and other documents showing staff resource on similar past projects

For most situations, you need to know two pieces of information about a task to determine the qualifications that a person must have to perform it:

✔ The required levels of proficiency in the needed skills and knowledge

✔ Whether the assignment entails:

  • Working under someone else's guidance when applying the skills or knowledge

  • Working alone to apply the skills or knowledge

  • Managing others who are applying the skills or knowledge

If you'd like to think in a more structured way about the staffing needs for each task, you can use scales such as the following two-dimensional measure:

✔ What level of proficiency is needed for the task?

  1 = Requires a basic level of proficiency

  2 = Requires an intermediate level of proficiency

  3 = Requires an advanced level of proficiency

**Book IV**

**Increasing Productivity and Performance**

✔ What's the management requirement?

a = Will be supervised, so doesn't need independent working ability

b = Needs to be able to work independently but doesn't entail managing others using the skill or knowledge

c = Entails managing others using the skill or knowledge

## Growing your people

As you think through the tasks and who you will assign them to, you'll normally need to consider staff development. You want to progress in your career, and so too do your project staff. You need to bear in mind individual needs for development and organisational needs for increasingly skilled staff, as well as the need to get the project delivered.

### Developing skills

As you look through the project tasks, you can look to see what flexibility exists for people to work on things where they can learn new skills and develop more competence in existing ones. Your efforts pay off in two ways:

✔ You help the organisation develop its skills base.

✔ You interest and motivate staff, who are enjoying what they're doing and are challenged by it.

For example, you might allocate someone to something that's new for him but where the task has got a bit of spare time, or put him alongside someone else who's already experienced.

### Using the critical path

The critical path technique, comes in useful here. If a task is on the critical path, by definition there's no spare time on it; you'll therefore usually want to assign very competent and experienced people to do the work. Equally, if a task has a lot of float (slack) time, it may be more suitable for less experienced staff. If the less experienced staff take a bit longer to do it than planned, then there won't be any time impact because of the float time on the activity.

### Explaining yourself to experienced staff

In your project, you'll want to protect the critical path and also grow your less experienced staff. However, don't now neglect your more experienced people. More experienced staff like a challenge, and if you only allocate them to the mundane tasks that all happen to be on the critical path, they're going to get bored and demotivated. Try to make sure that experienced staff get some of the more juicy project work, and where you do need them to work on something boring because it's critical or helping to develop a more junior team member, you can at least explain why and hold out the promise of something more substantial later on.

If you're now thinking that there's a lot to bear in mind when dealing with staff resource on a project, yes, there is. But that's why we dedicate a whole chapter in this book to staff resource to help you.

## Developing a Skills Matrix

Whether you're able to influence the people assigned to your project team, people are assigned to your team without your input, or you assume the role of Project Manager of an existing team, you need to confirm the skills, knowledge and interest of your team members.

If you're working on a project of any size, then it's usually helpful to document each person's skills and knowledge and verify their interests. That skills and interests information may prove really useful later when something unexpected comes up and you need to switch people between tasks or add a new task, or if you have to replace a team member unexpectedly.

A *Skills Matrix* is a table that displays people's proficiency in specified skills and knowledge, as well as their interest in working on assignments using these skills and knowledge. Figure 5-1 is an example of a portion of a Skills Matrix. The left-hand column identifies skill and knowledge areas based on two dimensions (as we suggest in the earlier section 'Working out the skill sets and knowledge that you need on the teams'), and the top row lists people's names. At the intersection of the rows and columns, you identify the level of each person's particular skills, knowledge and interests.

Figure 5-1 shows that Sue has an advanced level of proficiency in technical writing and can work independently with little or no supervision. In addition, she's interested in working on technical writing assignments. Ed has an advanced level of proficiency in the area of legal research and is capable of managing others engaged in legal research. However, he'd prefer not to work on legal research tasks. Instead, he'd like to work on questionnaire design activities, but he currently has no skills or knowledge in this area. This is one of the interests you may try to satisfy when you're considering staff growth. Or if you're trying to find more people who can develop questionnaires anyway, Ed's a prime candidate. Because he wants to work on these types of assignments, he's likely to be willing to put in the extra effort to acquire the skills needed to do so.

|  | Bill | | Mary | | Sue | | Ed | |
|---|---|---|---|---|---|---|---|---|
|  | Proficiency | Interest | Proficiency | Interest | Proficiency | Interest | Proficiency | Interest |
| Technical writing | (0,0) | 0 | (0,0) | 0 | (3,2) | 1 | (0,0) | 1 |
| Legal research | (0,0) | 1 | (0,0) | 1 | (0,0) | 0 | (3,3) | 0 |
| Graphic design | (3,3) | 1 | (0,0) | 0 | (0,0) | 1 | (3,3) | 1 |
| Questionnaire design | (1,0) | 0 | (0,0) | 0 | (0,0) | 0 | (0,0) | 1 |

Proficiency rating is expressed as (X,Y), where

X = Person's level of skill or knowledge
Y = Level of responsibility applying the skill or knowledge

**Figure 5-1:**
Listing people's skills, knowledge and interests in a Skills Matrix.

| Skill or Knowledge Level (X) | Application of Skills/Knowledge (Y) | Interest |
|---|---|---|
| 0 = No capability | | 0 = Has no interest in applying this skill or knowledge |
| 1 = Basic level of capability | 1 = Must work under supervision | 1 = Is interested in applying this skill or knowledge |
| 2 = Intermediate level of capability | 2 = Can work independently with little or no direct supervision | |
| 3 = Advanced level of capability | 3 = Can manage others applying the skill or knowledge | |

The following steps help you prepare a Skills Matrix for your project:

1. **Discuss with each team member his skills, knowledge and interests related to the activities in your project.**

   Explain that you want this information so you can take it into account when assigning team members to project tasks. However, be careful not to build up expectations that you'll be allocating each person only to the most prestigious, interesting and career-enhancing activities. Someone has to do the boring, routine stuff.

2. **Determine each person's level of interest in working on the tasks that you propose.**

   At a minimum, ask people whether they're interested in the tasks for which you've scheduled them. If a person isn't interested in a task, try to find out why and whether you can do anything to modify the assignment to make it more interesting to her.

   If a person isn't interested in a task, you can either not ask and not know the reason, or ask and (if you get an honest response) know the reason. Knowing that a person isn't interested is better than not knowing, because you can consider the possibility of rearranging assignments or at least you can show you understand, explain the importance of the activity and point out the more interesting stuff coming later.

3. **Consult with team members' functional managers and/or the people who assigned them to your project to determine their opinions of the levels of each team member's skills, knowledge and interests.**

   You want to understand the reasons why these managers assigned the people they did to your project.

4. **Check to see whether any areas of your organisation have already prepared Skills Matrices.**

   Find out whether existing Skills Matrices give any information about the extent to which team members have the skills and knowledge that you feel are required for your project's activities.

5. **Incorporate all the information you gather in a Skills Matrix and review with each team member the portion of the matrix that contains her information.**

   This review gives you the opportunity to verify that you correctly recorded the information you found, and gives the team member a chance to comment on or add to any of the information.

# Honing Your Task Duration Estimates

When drawing up an Activity Network and Gantt Chart, you should have already made some estimates of how long each activity will take. The estimates may be based on good information such as where you already know exactly who'll do that task and her level of experience. However, it may have been little more than a guess just to get the basic framework of the plan in place. Now's the time to work on the detail of the estimates and fine-tune the plan.

Changing something in your plan may have knock-on effects on other aspects, so make sure you allow plenty of time for planning.

## Documenting your estimates

Here are three basic ways to document the resource requirements and estimates:

- ✔ Make a list on paper. Given the ready availability of computer tools, this isn't a great option unless your project is very small.

- ✔ Use a project-scheduling software tool with facilities for entering people's names and work estimates against each task. Good though these tools are, they do have limitations.

✔ Work out the information on a spreadsheet and just put basic information into the project-scheduling software. Many Project Managers prefer this approach.

Either way, you need to show who you're assigning to each task and how long that task will take. Then you need to resolve any resource conflicts to make sure that the plan is workable.

If you're using a computer-based project management tool, it will almost certainly include a calendar facility, so you can avoid some of the areas of resource conflict. For example, it should already know about public holidays and so won't let you schedule work on those days unless you've overridden the default and declared particular holidays to be working days. You can even have a calendar for each person working on the project, so you can enter booked holidays and other assignments, and again the tool then prevents you allocating project work involving particular staff members on days when they aren't available. Good news for Sue's husband then (see the earlier section 'Dealing with resource conflicts').

## Factors in activity timing and estimates

Resource scheduling is inherently complicated, so don't get worried if things start to look difficult. Just work through in a methodical way and everything will come right in the end. It's tempting to focus simply on the figures when scheduling staff resource, but other factors can have an impact. Here are a few things to bear in mind as you work through the activity estimates:

✔ **Irregular availability:** Some staff may suddenly be less available than anticipated, so be aware of what their other duties are. If, for example, some of your technical staff are also involved with support, and a major breakdown of a vital piece of production line equipment occurs, they'll suddenly disappear from your project no matter what their percentage availability is on your plan. If the whole factory has come to a standstill, you can't insist that the staff come back to give their 50 per cent of the week to your project and finish fixing the production line next week.

✔ **Multiple staff:** If two or more people are working on a task and must work together on it, then the duration will depend on the one with the least availability. If part of the work can be done without everyone involved, then that impact is reduced. A simple example is where there are two people on a task, of whom one is available for part of her time and one is available for all her time. If only part of the task requires both people working together, then clearly the one who's full time can get on with some stuff when her fellow team member is unavailable.

✔ **Project dependencies:** Sometimes, work can't start until staff are released from other work such as work on other projects. So, although three of the four people on a team are ready to roll, a fourth person, who's essential, is several days late arriving because of a delay in another project. The impact of that one person's delay is that the whole team gets held up.

✔ **Speed of working:** Some staff members perform faster than others, and some organisations perform faster than others.

✔ **The team size:** If a task involves a lot of people, they tend to work more slowly than if it just involves two or three people. That's not least because of the communication and organisation needs within the team.

✔ **Working environment:** People in some working environments are hassled with noise and interruptions (such as phones ringing). Be realistic in assessing the duration of activities, and don't expect the same productivity from staff in a disruptive environment that you would from the same staff in a peaceful environment where they can focus and work with few distractions or interruptions. We offer more on this point later in the section 'Factoring in productivity'.

## Estimating required work effort

As you develop your work-effort estimates, do the following:

✔ **Think through the detail of all work related to performing the activity.** Examples include:

  • Sending out an agenda in advance of the planned meeting and booking the room and refreshments

  • Preparing and rehearsing a presentation to be given at the meeting

✔ **Consider history.** Past history doesn't guarantee future performance, but it does provide a guideline for what's possible. Find out whether similar work has been done before. If it has, review any written records to determine the work effort spent on it. If written records weren't kept, ask people who've done the activity before to estimate the work effort they invested.

✔ When using prior history to support your estimates, make sure that:

  • The people who performed the work had qualifications and experience similar to those of the people who'll work on your project.

  • The facilities, equipment and technology used were similar to those that'll be used for your project.

  • The time frame was similar to the one you anticipate for your project.

Book IV

Increasing Productivity and Performance

✔ **Have the person who'll actually do the work participate in estimating the amount of work effort that will be required.** Having people contribute to their work-effort estimates provides the following benefits:

- Their understanding of the activity improves.

- The estimates are based on their particular skills, knowledge and experience, which makes them more accurate.

- Their commitment to do the work for that level of work effort increases.

If you know who'll be working on the activity, it really helps if you can involve those people in the initial planning, perhaps in a planning workshop. If people don't join the project team until the start of the project or during it, have them review and comment on the plans you've developed. Then update your plans as needed.

✔ **Consult with experts familiar with the type of work you need done on your project, even if they haven't performed work exactly like it before.** Incorporating experience and knowledge from different sources improves the accuracy of your estimate.

Accurate estimating can be difficult, to say the least.

## *Factoring in productivity*

A good estimate is one that's close to how long a task eventually takes. If the estimates are good, then the project will stick pretty close to the plan and will be a whole lot easier to manage than if it keeps veering wildly off plan.

It's worth spending some effort getting the task durations as close in as you possibly can, because it saves a lot of corrective work, and probably time, later. A more accurate plan saves time because if project tasks don't take the time you anticipated, then you have to keep re-scheduling everything else. 'Sorry Cheng, I know I said I needed you on Week 12, but it's now going to be Week 14. Oh sorry, something else has just shifted so it's Week 11; oh wait a minute, more breaking news . . .'

### *Defining 'full time'*

Being assigned to a project full time doesn't mean a person can perform project work at peak productivity 40 hours per week, 52 weeks per year. Additional personal and organisational activities reduce the amount of work that people produce. During your project, your staff will probably:

- Take annual leave.
- Go sick occasionally.
- Read and respond to emails on non-project work.
- Talk about the football, or their holiday, or the weather. If you work in an office with other people, do you always sit straight down and start working at full capacity the moment you get in?
- Read professional journals or web feeds.
- Have organisational things to do, such as read staff notices or attend departmental meetings.

So don't ever think of staff as 100 per cent available to the project. The reality is that they won't be, and if you schedule them for five full days a week then your plan won't work. Someone working full time on a project is probably available, on average, four days a week, but watch out because it could be even less (see the nearby sidebar 'The truth is out: How workers really spend their time').

Don't use overtime when planning. Plan using normal working hours only, because that way if you come under pressure during the project you have overtime working as a fallback. If you've already planned in overtime, you've got nowhere left to run. Also be careful of how you think about overtime if you do come to use it later. Staff who are working long hours aren't usually as productive in the overtime hours as they are in the normal ones, because they get tired. But they may not be as productive in the normal hours either. If someone knows she has a really long day ahead, she'll tend to pace herself in the early part of the day.

### Making specific adjustments

In thinking about how long something will take, you need to factor in productivity. Be especially careful where you're basing estimates on how long something took on a previous project in another organisation, or even in another part of your own organisation. What matters isn't how long it took to do an earlier job *there*, but how long it will take to do the job *here*. So, you may need to make a few adjustments, and that's in three areas:

- Adjusting for the exact nature of the task
- Adjusting for your people
- Adjusting for the working environment

## The truth is out: How workers really spend their time

A number of years ago, Stan Portny read a study that determined that the typical employee spends an average of four hours of an eight-hour working day on planned project activities and work assignments. In other words, the typical employee in this study averaged a work availability of 50 per cent! The interviewers in this study spoke with people with a wide range of job responsibilities from more than 100 organisations.

Since then, Stan has found several organisations that conducted similar studies of their own operations. These organisations all found workers' project time to be about 75 per cent of total time. You may think the workers in these companies were more efficient than the ones in the previous study, but, in fact, these studies were biased. The people surveyed wanted their organisations to think that they were spending most of their time working on project assignments, and the organisations wanted to believe that their employees were doing so. Still, the organisation studies found that people spent about 25 per cent of each day doing something other than planned project-related activities!

### Adjusting for the exact nature of the task

When thinking about the task you need done in comparison with similar work done previously on another project somewhere else, consider:

- **Degree of similarity:** Is the task on your project exactly the same as the one done on a previous project, or is it more or less difficult?

- **Size:** Is the task the same size, bigger or smaller? If it took two staff two hours to pack ten boxes on a previous project, then packing 1,000 similar boxes on your project isn't going to take two staff 200 hours. For a start, your people will need a lunch break each day. On the other hand, if the box packing is quite complicated, the unit speed on your project may increase over time because your staff will get more familiar with the task, whereas on the previous project with just ten boxes they didn't have time to.

### Adjusting for your people

Consider each of the following factors when you estimate the number of hours that your people will need to complete assignments:

- **Ability to switch among several tasks:** A person's level of comfort moving to a second task when she hits a roadblock in her first one, so that she doesn't sit around stewing about her frustrations and wasting time.

✔ **Knowledge and skills:** The raw talent and capability a person has to perform a particular task.

✔ **Motivation:** Are your staff highly motivated and so likely to perform better, or less motivated – perhaps some were assigned to your project when they very much wanted to work on a different and much more interesting one – so are likely to work more slowly?

✔ **Multi-tasking:** This is the inverse of the first bullet point. When someone is constantly switching between tasks, the elapsed time of all tasks will be increased. Have a look at the sidebar 'The impact of multi-tasking' to see why.

✔ **Prior experience:** A person's familiarity with the work and the typical problems of a particular task. Trainees normally take longer than experienced team members, and make more mistakes.

✔ **Sense of urgency:** A person's drive to generate the desired results within established time frames. (Urgency influences a person's focus and concentration on an activity.)

### Adjusting for the working environment

Working conditions affect performance, and if you don't take that into account then your estimates are likely to be wrong. The area of working conditions covers an array of factors, and this point doesn't just mean avoiding Dickensian workhouse conditions. Consider also:

✔ **Availability of equipment:** Is the right equipment readily available and in good condition, or are staff having to make do with inadequate equipment or wait for a long time before they can get to use the right kit, because it is in such short supply?

✔ **The nature of other work:** Are staff involved in other work alongside the project work, for example providing support for computer systems or the production line? If they are and there are constant interruptions, performance on project activities will be severely degraded. Not only is time taken up on dealing with a support incident, but it then takes that staff member time to pick up the threads on the project task. If she's just done that and the phone rings again . . .

✔ **The quality of the environment:** Is it quiet and peaceful so that people can concentrate, or is it noisy and distracting with phones ringing and a lot of people walking through all the time? A lot of organisations have moved to open-plan offices and *hot desking* (where staff don't have their own permanent desks but are allocated one – if there's one left - when they arrive each day) to save money. However, the focus tends to be solely on reducing accommodation costs, and few organisations consider the wider dimension of staff performance.

✔ **The setup of the physical environment:** The proximity and arrangement of a person's furniture, the amount of space and the adequacy of lighting.

**Book IV**

**Increasing Productivity and Performance**

# The impact of multi-tasking

When someone is working on several tasks at once, the elapsed time of all of them will be increased. The following diagram uses the example of someone switching between three tasks that she's doing at once; you may think, 'Only three things at a time? I wish!'

If you can organise the work so that people deal with one thing at a time, then the elapsed time of each task will be reduced. If you plan well, you can tell people exactly when you will need them, confirming it as you approach that point so they can clear the decks of other work and so give you faster delivery. As the diagram shows, even just working on one thing at a time gives an improvement, with C being delivered at the same time as before, but A and B both delivered earlier. But even that doesn't account for the extra time needed to pick up the threads if a team member breaks off work on a task and then goes back to it some time later.

Each two-week task takes four elapsed weeks

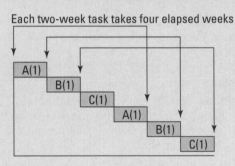

Each two-week task takes two elapsed weeks. A and B are completed earlier and C is no later than before.

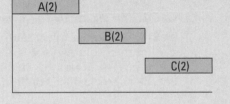

For the physical working environment, think about how you might improve it, including ways of working, and so improve productivity. When running projects involving support staff, Nick Graham set up a hot seat system. One person on the team was designated to take all of the support calls for a week. That person would be interrupted frequently, and although he or she did get some project work done, productivity was low. However, the rest of the team were sheltered and could get on without distraction unless a support problem was particularly severe and more help was needed. In the next week, a different team member was in the hot seat, so the hassle was shared out and everyone could work undisturbed most of the time.

# Taking care with historical data

When completed properly, time sheets provide the most reliable source of past experience. However, it's with good reason that time sheets are often called 'lie sheets'. Before relying on past metrics, make sure that you fully understand the information, and that includes a careful assessment of the organisational culture, which in turn affects how time is recorded.

The following time-sheet practices can cause the data on them to be inaccurate:

✔ People aren't allowed to record overtime, so some hours actually spent on an activity may never be known.

✔ People are required to send in their time sheets several days before the reporting period is over, so they must guess what their hourly allocations for the next few days will be.

✔ People fill out their time sheets just before they go home at the end of the week. They're in a hurry to get away and can't remember with any clarity what they did in the early part of the week, so they take a wild guess and put that down.

✔ People are working on some non-project stuff during the week but are supposed to be allocated full time on the project. So they spread out the hours spent on the other work among your project time codes.

✔ People copy the work-effort estimates from the Project Plan onto their time sheets each period instead of recording the actual number of hours they spend.

If any of these situations exist in your organisation, don't use historical data from time sheets to support your work-effort estimates for your current project.

In a large civil engineering company, senior managers told middle managers that if their staff were having to working overtime it was a sign of poor management. A good manager should be able to achieve things within normal working hours by working smarter not harder. Fearful of damage to their promotion prospects, the middle managers promptly instructed their staff that the total weekly hours on the time sheets must never exceed 37.5 hours, the standard week. If they'd worked more than this, the staff were to allocate the effort proportionally among the relevant codes but keep the total at 37.5 hours. All the time-sheet information was fed into a computer system from which senior managers could get reports.

A very big contract came up that was similar to a project already done, and a senior manager decided to get a report on the previous contract from the time-sheet system. That data was used as the basis of the bid for the contract, which the company easily won because its bid was significantly less than that of any of its competitors. When the project got underway, the Project Manager was puzzled that everything was taking much more work effort than shown in the breakdown of work on the bid. He went to see the Project Manager of the previous contract to ask how they did things with far fewer staff hours. The reply was, 'Oh, we didn't do it with fewer hours. What you're looking at is just the time we put on the time sheets!'

# *Accounting for availability in estimates*

If you base work-effort estimates on the opinions of people who'll do the activities or who've done similar activities in the past instead of on historical records, you have to factor in a measure of availability.

First, ask the person from whom you're getting your information to estimate the required work effort, assuming she can work at 100 per cent availability. (In other words, ask her not to worry about normal interruptions during the day, having to work on multiple tasks at a time, and so on.) Then modify the estimate to reflect availability by doing the following:

- ✔ If the person will use a time sheet that has one or more categories for non-project-specific work, use her original work-effort estimate.

- ✔ If the person will use a time sheet that doesn't have categories to record non-project-specific work, add an additional amount to her original estimate to account for her availability.

As an example, suppose a person estimates that she needs 30 work hours to perform a task (if she can be 100 per cent available) and her time sheets have no categories for recording non-project-specific work. If you estimate that she'll work at about 75 per cent capacity, allow her to charge 40 person-hours to your project to complete the task (75 per cent of 40 person-hours is 30 person-hours – the amount you really need.) Bear in mind for your Business Case, though, that you're carrying organisational work overheads in your project, not just project work costs.

Failure to consider availability when estimating and reviewing project work effort can lead to incorrect conclusions about people's performance. Suppose your boss assigns you a project on Monday morning. She tells you the project will take about 40 work hours, but she really needs it by Friday close of business. Suppose further that you work really hard all week and finish the task by Friday close of business. In the process, you record 55 hours for the project on your time sheet.

If your boss doesn't realise that her initial estimate of 40 person-hours was based on your working at 100 per cent availability, she'll think you took 15 hours longer than you should have. On the other hand, if your boss recognises that 55 person-hours *on the job* translates into about 40 person-hours of work *on specific project tasks*, she will appreciate that you invested extra effort to meet her aggressive deadline.

The longer you're involved in an assignment, the more important efficiency and availability become. Suppose you decide you have to spend one hour on an assignment. You can reasonably figure your availability is 100 per cent, so you charge your project one hour for the assignment. If you need to spend six hours on an assignment, you can figure your availability is 100 per cent, but you must consider 75 per cent availability (or a similar planning figure). Therefore, charge one work day (eight work hours) to ensure that you can spend the six hours on your assignment.

However, if you plan to devote one month or more to your assignment, you'll most likely take some leave days during that time. Even though your project budget doesn't have to pay for your annual or sick leave, one staff month means you have about 97 hours for productive work on your assignment.

# Smoothing the Resource

The resource conflicts that we explain in the earlier section 'Dealing with resource conflicts' usually apply to staff. Sometimes, though, you encounter conflicts on things like accommodation or specialised equipment but the way you'll deal with such conflicts is the same as with staff resource conflicts.

## Checking for resource conflict

To check for resource conflict, you need to look at what each person is scheduled to do in each time period, usually each day. If a person has more to do than there is time available in the day, then there is a resource conflict. That may be because the person has 16 hours' work to do in an 8-hour day, or perhaps it's 8 hours' work to do in a day that has 0 work hours because it's a public holiday.

If you're using a computerised scheduling tool, it either prevents you scheduling in a way that creates a conflict, or it allows you to schedule how you like, but then highlights the conflicts so you can work through them and deal with them.

You can create a Resource Histogram for each staff member to show whether any conflicts exist. This shows the required hours if all the work is done as scheduled, and displays that against available hours.

Going back to Sue, the overworked team member from earlier in the chapter (see 'Dealing with resource conflicts'), Figure 5-2 shows a Resource Histogram for a few of the project tasks. Sue is clearly overcommitted and for two days is needed three days per day, which is asking a bit much. To resolve these resource conflicts, it's necessary to do some *resource smoothing*, sometimes known as resource levelling. Put simply, the level of required resource needs to be got down below the level of available resource.

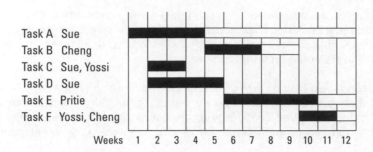

**Figure 5-2:**
A Resource
Histogram.

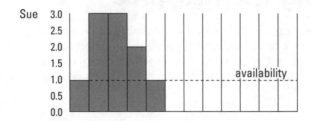

# Resolving resource conflicts – the steps

Here are some straightforward steps for resource smoothing:

1. **Check the activity dependencies and resource allocations to make sure they're correct.**

   Continuing the example from the last section, you don't want to solve the problem of Sue being overcommitted if you've put her onto the tasks by mistake and you meant to enter Sam.

2. **Adjust within float.**

   This is where the Activity Network pays dividends. You may see from your network that the earliest start date of an activity is considerably earlier than the latest start date, so you can simply slide the activity along within its float to a time when Sue has plenty of availability.

   In Figure 5-2 it looks like the start of Activity A can be delayed as late as Week 9 without causing a problem. However, you'd need to be sure that it doesn't have a knock-on effect. In this case, if Activity B was dependent on A, you would now cause problems for both Sue and the project as a whole. Again, the Activity Network will be really useful, because it shows the dependencies clearly.

3. **Adjust resource.**

   This is where the Skills Matrix (see the earlier section 'Developing a Skills Matrix') may prove extremely useful. Is there someone else who has the same skill set as Sue? If so and she has more availability at this point, can you assign one or more tasks to her instead? Or alternatively, can you put that person on the task alongside Sue to help; in other words, can you raise the line of available resource?

4. **Move tasks downstream.**

   If you've made changes but still have a resource conflict, you need to move things downstream, and the project end date will go out. In theory, three tasks can be done in parallel, but because of a resource constraint that Sue must do all three, she'll have to do them one after the other, and the impact on the end date is accepted.

Computer tools, both project-scheduling software and spreadsheets, are great for playing around to try different things. But don't forget to save a copy before you start your 'what if's'. If everything goes horribly wrong, you'll want to be able to get back to your start point. It's so easy to save the work in the middle of the 'what if's' and forget that you're overwriting your main file.

Where you have staff who aren't full time on the project, you can sometimes squeeze out a bit more flexibility by talking to them about how they allocate their work. For example, if Sam is available to your project for 50 per cent of his time, that needn't mean he just works mornings. If you have a resource conflict in the early part of a week, you could ask if he could work the first half of the week full time on your project then spend the second half of the week on his other assignments. In other words, concentrate the 50 per cent into a shorter period of time rather than have it uniformly spread. Depending on the nature of the other assignments, you may find he can be even more flexible than that and, say, work a full week for you when you really need it, then the following week work full time on the other assignments; it's still 50 per cent. Involving team members in estimating and resource planning pays off when it comes to asking people to be flexible to meet the needs of both the project and any other assignments.

## Co-ordinating assignments across multiple projects

Working on overlapping tasks can place conflicting demands on a person, whether the tasks are on one project or several. Although successfully addressing these conflicts can be more difficult when more than one Project Manager is involved, the techniques for analysing them are the same whether you're the only Project Manager involved or you're just one of many.

In general, people on any of your project teams may also be assigned to other projects you're managing or to other Project Managers' projects. If Resource Histograms (see the earlier section 'Checking for resource conflict') or other loading information is available for each project your people are assigned to, you can manage each person's overall resource commitments by combining the information.

Figure 5-3 illustrates overall loading information that shows the commitments for each person on one or more of your project teams.

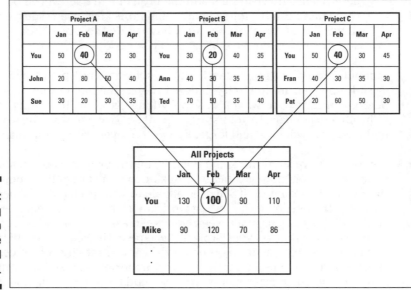

**Figure 5-3:**
Staff loading
information
to plan time
on several
projects.

With all the resourcing issues, the key to success is good plans. If you have clear plans, you not only see the problems but you also have excellent tools to hand to resolve them.

# Chapter 6

# Finding Your Motivation

*Y*our personal motivation is the force that gets you out of bed in the morning and provides you with energy for the work of the day. Have you ever wondered why you seem to be bursting with it some days, and other times it seems to desert you entirely?

Understanding how motivation works so that you can access your natural motivation to help manage the life you want with more confidence and ease is what this chapter is about. It gives you the insight you need to keep moving forward despite the challenges you face.

The most important thing you can take from this chapter is that you don't have to put up with feeling weak and unmotivated. If you deal intelligently with blocks in your natural energy source, you can restore your energy, achieve more with less effort, and feel more at ease with life, more satisfied with yourself, and more confident and powerful in the world.

## Driving Forward in Your Life

The more motivated you feel the more inclined you are to push yourself through the things that are holding you back. If you can increase your motivation, you automatically increase your confidence. In the next sections, we look at Abraham Maslow's influential hierarchy of needs to help you gain insight into what motivates you and everyone you come into contact with.

## Rising through Maslow's hierarchy of needs

One of the founders of the human potential movement, Abraham Maslow, is best known for his work on human motivation. He was fascinated by what makes some people able to face huge challenges in life, and especially what makes them refuse to give up despite incredible odds. He developed the model for which he is best known – his hierarchy of needs, shown in Figure 6-1 – to explain the forces that motivate people.

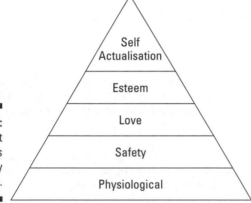

**Figure 6-1:** Looking at Maslow's hierarchy of needs.

Maslow saw men and women being constantly drawn on through life by the irresistible pull of unsatisfied needs. He grouped human needs into a hierarchy, which everyone shares and needs to satisfy from the bottom up. This model is widely taught in management development courses, but his work goes far beyond the workplace to the very heart of our humanity.

Maslow believed that you must first satisfy your basic physiological needs for air, water, food, sleep, and so on before any other desires will surface. As a member of modern society, these basic needs are largely taken care of for you, but if you have ever been short of breath under water you know and understand how this first-tier, physiological need dominates everything else until it is satisfied.

But once your physiological needs are met, you automatically shift up to the next level in the hierarchy to your need for safety, – and that now drives you. Again, modern society tends to provide safe environments, but whenever you do feel threatened, you experience an automatic anxiety response and cannot think of much else until the situation is resolved and you feel safe again.

At the next level, you have to make more personal interventions to ensure your needs are satisfied within the framework that society provides for you. Your needs for love and connection show up here; things you don't automatically get all the time. If your needs at this level are unsatisfied, and you feel isolated or lonely, you find it almost impossible to meet your higher-level needs in any meaningful way.

The next level is where your needs for self-esteem and recognition kick in. These may never have been an issue for you as you struggled to join your group, but now they can become dominant. It is no longer enough simply to belong; now you must have some power and status in the group too – drive a bigger car, become captain of the golf club perhaps, or chair of the school parent–teacher association. This is where most established adults reside most of the time today.

But thankfully, the endless striving does end, and with all your needs taken care of, you eventually arrive at the top of Maslow's hierarchy as a fully developed human being. At the exotically named *self-actualisation* stage, your major motivation becomes living and expressing what is truly most important to you in life. Often, this is where you get to give something back to the world that has supported you so royally in your journey through life so far.

Maslow's hierarchy of needs helps to explain so much of the variability in human behaviour. Different human beings will always be operating at different levels, and be driven by different needs at any given time. Your motivation level may be different on Monday from on Friday with the weekend looming. And of course, you may feel different at work from the way you feel at home. The more you understand what drives you, the better able you will be to use it to achieve the things you want in life.

## Greeting the world with grace

Maslow is often associated with motivation at work, but his insights apply equally in social situations where you can use them to help put yourself at ease.

When you find yourself in a new social group – meeting new people at a party or function, for example – you can expect to feel anxious because *at this moment* you are at Maslow's third level, needing to be accepted into this new group. When you're in this situation, the first thing to do is to accept your mild anxiety about it. There's nothing wrong with feeling or admitting that you're nervous (in case the voice inside your head starts accusing you of being a wimp).

**Book IV**

**Increasing Productivity and Performance**

Remember, everyone in the room fits into Maslow's hierarchy and is therefore feeling needy at some level. The people you're meeting who are not new to the group are operating at the second and third levels: some are anxious for acceptance, just as you are (and these people will be just as keen to be accepted by you as you are by them); some are motivated by their need for social esteem and need your respect.

Depending on the kind of party this is, you can expect to witness needy behaviours at all levels from hunger and thirst, through sex, connection, companionship, to a close approximation of self-actualisation on the dance floor. Don't judge your fellow partygoers too harshly. In fact, give everyone at the party a break, including yourself. Enjoy the spectacle!

Take on board these new factors in an otherwise ordinary and potentially dull social dynamic by paying attention to the curious and interesting display of need-motivated behaviours going on around you.

If you're curious about the people in the group and really take an interest in what's happening, you come across to others as attentive and a great conversationalist. This is more fun for you, and more fun for the people you meet. Pretty soon everyone will want you at their parties.

# Taking Charge at Work

Your personal motivation is critical to your performance and confidence in the world, but in work, your motivation is often just as important to your boss and co-workers too. This has led to motivation becoming the focus of a lot of social science research over the last 60 years, and in this section, we show you how to use some of this for your personal benefit at work.

## Looking at usable theory

Maslow's theory about human needs is universal, applying to everyone in all situations. Other important theorists, such as Frederick Herzberg and William McGregor, have focused on your motivation at work, which is important to you and to your employer. In this section, you can find out how to take more control of your motivation at work and increase this if that is what you need. You will also find a self-test to help you to measure your progress.

### Searching for satisfaction with Herzberg

Frederick Herzberg is another motivation guru frequently studied on management development courses (which means that your senior colleagues should have heard about him). His elegant theory reveals the factors that energise you at work and also those that take your natural energy away. He separates out those forces that motivate people, called *motivators*, from those that sap motivation, the *dissatisfiers*. He discovered that these forces operate in a surprising, seemingly illogical way.

Take pay as a universal example. You may think that the money you are paid provides you with motivation, and most employers act as though this is the case, but it simply isn't true in the long term according to Herzberg. Pay is a dissatisfier and not a motivator. If you aren't being paid the rate for the job, your poor pay rate can certainly make you feel dissatisfied, but surprisingly, of itself being paid over the odds doesn't motivate you any further than being paid a fair rate does (although it may bring other factors into play, such as recognition and team status).

Recognition, on the other hand, is a motivator. This is why a good job title, a word of thanks from the boss, or a mention in the in-house journal for a job well done can be so motivating.

Table 6-1 contains a list of some of the main motivators and dissatisfiers that Herzberg identified. The dissatisfiers on the left have to be carefully managed or they can create serious dissatisfaction for you, but of themselves they cannot motivate you. The factors on the right are the motivators and give you the drive you need to do your best work, but they don't come into play until the dissatisfiers have first been neutralised.

| Table 6-1 | Factors Affecting Job Attitudes |
|---|---|
| *Dissatisfiers* | *Motivators* |
| Company policies | Achievement |
| Style of supervision | Recognition |
| Relationship with boss | Work itself |
| Working conditions | Responsibility |
| Salary | Advancement |
| Relationship with peers | Personal growth |

Notice that the factors in the left column are external to the work itself and are largely imposed on you from outside. The motivators in the satisfaction column are much more personal, in that they tend to be more closely tied to the job you do. They are also more psychological, in that you have personal discretion over how much of them you feel.

If this insight starts to resonate powerfully for you, you may want to read up a bit more on Herzberg's motivation-hygiene theory before having a discussion about it with your boss. The dissatisfiers present in your work may be easy for your boss to neutralise, leaving you unencumbered psychologically to bring your motivation into play.

### Mapping McGregor's Theory X and Theory Y

Douglas McGregor's work is less well known to general managers and this is a shame as it focuses closely on management style (one of Herzberg's key dissatisfiers). McGregor brought out the effects of reactionary and over-zealous management practices and policies in his two models: Theory X and Theory Y.

*Theory X* assumes that, as a worker, you have an inbuilt dislike of working and will shirk as much as you can get away with. Therefore, you need to be controlled to ensure that you put in the effort needed, and you need to be told exactly what to do and how to do it. This can be very damaging to your natural motivation, your job satisfaction, and eventually your self-belief and confidence. Studies suggest that if your boss treats you this way, you may begin to behave as if it were true. (If this is happening to you use the feedback model in Book I Chapter 5 to make this point to your supervisor or departmental representative.)

*Theory Y* takes the opposite view. It assumes that working is important to you, as natural to you as the other parts of your life. If your work is satisfying, it becomes a source of drive and fulfilment. You become committed to it and you require little in the way of supervision.

You perform better and are more productive if you are allowed to manage your own workload, output, and so on, because you know so much better than anyone else how to get the best out of yourself. In these circumstances, your supervisor becomes a colleague you can consult when you need a second opinion and who can liaise with senior management to enable you to do the best job possible.

How do these two models compare with your own job situation? The chances are that your own supervision has elements of both Theory X and Theory Y. As ever, the onus is on you to take more control of an element of your life. Once you have knowledge you need to put it to use.

### Putting theory to the test

In this section, you see how to use the theoretical insights from the preceding sections to build your confidence as you engage with the world. And because most motivation theory is based on the workplace, you start there.

Whether you work for yourself or for someone else, you have to meet your motivational needs. Table 6-2 provides a self-test you can take in five minutes that measures your motivation response at work. If you work alone, modify the questions as necessary to suit your circumstances. Give yourself up to five points for each question – all five if you strongly agree, down to one if you strongly disagree.

## Table 6-2          Job Motivation Response Self-Test

| Value Statement | Strongly Agree (5 points) | Agree (4 points) | Neutral (3 points) | Disagree (2 point) | Strongly Disagree (1 point) |
|---|---|---|---|---|---|
| I am entirely in control of my work environment. Provided I meet my objectives, I am free to decide how much I do and what work I do next. | | | | | |
| I have established a good working relationship with my boss. He gives me the room to do my job the way I want and I usually deliver what he needs. | | | | | |
| My benefits package and general working environment are okay. When something needs to be looked at it is usually sorted out in a reasonable time. | | | | | |
| My work colleagues are generally supportive and don't get in my way. We are a good team and each of us serves the group objective pretty effectively. When issues arise, we are usually able to deal with them. | | | | | |
| I get a real buzz from the work I do. I feel closely identified with my output and put the best of myself into it. I wouldn't want it to be any other way. | | | | | |
| I feel that my employer values my work and is in touch with what is going on. They care about my career and look after things so that I don't have to worry about them. | | | | | |
| My work is very visible. People know that it is mine, and I take great pride in it. It is not unusual for people to acknowledge the good job I am doing. | | | | | |

*(continued)*

**Book IV**

**Increasing Productivity and Performance**

**Table 6-2 (continued)**

| Value Statement | Strongly Agree (5 points) | Agree (4 points) | Neutral (3 points) | Disagree (2 point) | Strongly Disagree (1 point) |
|---|---|---|---|---|---|
| I am allowed to take full responsibility for the quality of my work and for meeting my other objectives and deadlines. My boss knows that I know how to get the best out of myself and lets me get on with it. | | | | | |
| I feel that my work stretches me and allows me to grow. I have the level of challenge and variety that keeps me fully engaged without being overwhelmed. | | | | | |
| My work is an expression of who I truly am at some deeper level. Even if I were not being paid, I would still need to express myself through the kind of work I do. If I were unable to work it would be like losing a limb. | | | | | |

Use these guidelines to evaluate your score:

- ✔ **40–50:** Congratulations, you may have found your life's work. You are working in a job that gives you most of what you need not only for motivation but for your growth and fulfilment too.

- ✔ **30–40:** This is a very good score. You should be able to see the areas that are pulling you down and you can develop some goals for changing them. Use the SMART goal-setting technique to help create the changes you need.

- ✔ **10–30:** You may already know this score is not so good. You probably need to take more personal responsibility for your motivation at work, which can include changing your job or organization. Take a look at the techniques in Book I Chapter 5 to help you take more control of your work.

## Recognising the importance of achievement

Achieving results at work is not just a matter of pleasing your boss and earning a bonus. It forms an important contribution to your personal sense of significance and wellbeing as you move up the hierarchy of needs (refer to Figure 6-1) and a sense of achievement is top of the list of Herzberg's motivators (refer to Table 6-1).

As you progress at work, you need to think more about what constitutes achievement for *you*. Consider what it is you really want out of your life and your work, and then, without working any harder, you should be able to secure more of it both for yourself and your employer. This increases your sense of fulfilment and satisfaction and provides you with more motivational energy for yet more achievement.

## Going for the next promotion

Like most people, when a promotion opportunity comes up, you may want to seize the chance to get it immediately (not least because if you don't get it someone else will). But think very carefully about what the promotion may mean for you before you go for it.

It is not uncommon for a successful and happy worker to win a promotion only to become a less successful and far less happy supervisor or manager.

**Book IV**

**Increasing Productivity and Performance**

When this happens, the person can remain stuck in their new role where their poor performance rules out any further advancement and the organisational hierarchy prevents them from returning to where they were once good and happy.

If you know anyone who has been caught in this way, you understand that it is hardly a recipe for organisational achievement – much less for personal confidence and fulfilment. Armed with the knowledge of this chapter, absolutely no reason remains why it should happen to you.

Before you accept any new role, ask yourself:

- How did things play out for the previous person who held this job? Perhaps they went on to even higher things, or perhaps they were stuck in the role for a long time and didn't appear too happy in it.

- What is likely to happen to you if you remain a while longer in your current role? Is there an even better promotion coming up soon? Would your refusal to take on the promotion offered send a bad or a good signal to your management?

- How could you use the current situation to create the job you want? Would it be possible to change the new job into something that suits you better, retaining, say, some of your current responsibility? Or perhaps it would be possible to split up the new role and take only some aspects of it into your current role?

- How can you use the change on offer to let your colleagues and superiors know that you are thinking deeply about the work you do and are not just in it for the pay cheque? In the longer-term this may be the most valuable aspect of the entire situation.

Now, when the opportunity for promotion comes up, you have a far richer way of evaluating why you are interested in the new role, what it will bring to you other than money and what it will take away. And if you decide to go for it, you bring so much more to the table; making a good impression on your colleagues and leaving you with a big win whether or not you get the role.

# Chapter 7

# Relax, it's Only Work! Stress in the Workplace

*I*t's impossible to attain and hold perfection, and striving to do so positively damages your confidence. In any case, is there any fun in being perfect? You know it's horribly boring to be with 'perfect' people. So in this chapter, we look at how you can be the best you can without driving yourself insane or collapsing under the stress of trying too hard.

Keep in mind that you're a human being; you're not some sort of superhero. As a human being, you're already perfectly fine and doing your best. So as you travel through the next few pages, chuck out your 'perfect expert who must be in control of life' view of yourself and adopt a simpler, more philosophical way to move on. Already you and those around you are doing the best you can, and your best will get better as you gain more knowledge.

## Letting Go of Unreal Expectations

The poet Robert Browning said: 'A man's reach should be beyond his grasp, or what's a heaven for.' It's wonderful to have goals and dreams, the things you're going towards in your life. And we fully encourage you to aim for the stars. Yet there may be times when the goals you set, and the speed at which you want to attain them, put you under really crazy pressure. It's like expecting to be the British Prime Minister or the next President of the US when actually becoming a local councillor or standing as candidate for your favourite political party is a more than acceptable step on the success ladder. You may find you have more practical impact in your community and a better quality of life at a less senior level.

In moving forward, you may want to keep your sights closer to home too.

## Admitting that you can't be perfect (and that you don't want to be)

Liz grew up as the only child of parents who adored her. They told her she was perfect – beautiful, talented, and able to do anything she set her mind to. Yet the continual pressure on her to be top of the class, the most popular student, as well as good looking and slender became a burden as she hit her thirties. She suffered from stress-related illnesses that affected her job as a project manager for an international firm.

Expecting perfection from yourself brings problems: one is that you make unfavourable comparisons with other people all the time; another is that you set yourself on a pedestal that's all too fragile. Being on top of the pedestal at all times isn't a healthy place to be. You never have a chance to re-charge your batteries and soon wear yourself down. It's like being a pop star on tour all year, or a perpetually flowering plant. You never get a chance to just chill out if you are constantly looking for the next achievement.

Similarly, being regarded as the expert in your field is good for your ego and confidence in one way, but it can also be a very lonely position that alienates you from the rest of the team or organisation and puts you under huge pressure to solve problems single-handedly.

How can you overcome the perfection pressure? A strategy, as a coach is to step off the perfection pedestal. Listen to clients, ask questions and free people to find answers without putting themselves under pressure. In this way build on the client's innate strength.

## Focusing on perfection distracts you from excellence

Instead of 'perfection', try adopting 'excellence' as a more useful objective. When you aim for excellence, you simply go for the best, aiming high and accepting that there will be times when you don't quite reach the summit.

Substituting excellence for perfection doesn't mean you don't have high standards and expectations – you do. But it does mean you can be easier on yourself and in so doing you are more likely to succeed in what you really want to achieve.

How can you develop excellence? Think of an area of your life that's important to you. Maybe you'd like to create a happy relationship with someone significant. How will you know when you've got it? Picture what it will be like when you succeed, what will you see yourself doing, what will you be saying and feeling? Make a note of it now and write it in the present tense to make it more real for yourself. For example: 'I have a wonderful relationship with this person and I prefer to spend my time with her to being with anyone else. We have fun when we go out together and enjoy quiet evenings at home in each other's company. I am telling her that I care about her and I have a sense of contentment just being close to her.'

Getting clear about what it is that you want puts you on the way to achieving it.

# Being Generous to Yourself First

In order to support other people, be generous to yourself too. Many people run ragged putting themselves after everybody else, including their mother-in-law's dog. The result? Resentment builds, alongside ill health and unhappy relationships.

Practise being generous to yourself – give yourself the unconditional love of a parent for a child. Make time each day to be alone, even if it's only ten minutes.

When considering the requests on your time, ask yourself: What does this do for me? Does it fit with my agenda, priorities and values? Politely let go of others' demands, pressures, needs, and perceptions. You have needs too, which are just as important.

## Acknowledging your successes

Jonnie is a learning junkie. He's taken several degree and postgraduate courses and a vast array of private courses – everything from garden design and photography to software programming and business negotiation. His cupboards are stashed full of manuals, CD learning sets, and certificates. Yet he's so caught up in courses that he never has time to apply what he's learnt; in every new project he compares himself to the specialists in that field.

**Book IV**

**Increasing Productivity and Performance**

Do you ever catch yourself running so fast through everyday life that you forget to stop and realise what you've discovered and achieved? A 'done it, toss it over the shoulder' mentality is at work here. When you're always looking to the future rather than the here and now, it's easy to notice what hasn't happened and what you haven't done rather than what you've already completed. You may be piling the pressure on yourself to do more, , and your to-do lists become longer and longer. Even holidays become packed itineraries. Such competitive pressure zaps your confidence.

For your sanity pay attention to what you've achieved rather than just pushing yourself harder. So, look back over the last year and acknowledge your accomplishments and successes.

1. **Put on your success sunglasses and take out a large piece of blank paper.**

2. **Write down every success you can think of.**

   What new things have you found out? What relationships have you nurtured? How has your life moved on in some way?

   Acknowledge the everyday successes as well the big ones. Perhaps you've nursed someone through an illness, supported a friend, or completed a course of study. Perhaps you discovered the importance of time to chill out. Maybe you joined a new team at work or prepared food 365 days of the year for your family. Don't forget to count the money you raised for a charity or the jumble sales your supported at your kids' school.

3. **Keep writing until your blank page is full.**

4. **Now sit back and give yourself a pat on the back.**

   Well done. You're already a success.

At any point when your confidence dives, just take a look at your success list – remind yourself of how much you've achieved to keep positive.

## Accepting help and delegating

It takes confidence to recognise that you can't do everything yourself all the time and to let some things go. So how about relinquishing control and asking for help?

Evidence suggests that women find it harder to delegate than men, given that they take the heavier load of domestic chores in addition to working outside the home.

In either a work or home context, list the tasks you find most time consuming or burdensome (for example, updating the customer database at work or doing the laundry at home). Ask yourself:

- ✔ What would I most like to have help with or delegate to others?
- ✔ Who could help me and what's the benefit or reward for them?
- ✔ Putting time and money to one side for now, what's really stopping me accepting help and delegating?
- ✔ What will I do to get help? And when?

Whenever you're feeling overloaded, go back to your list and find something to delegate. You'll find the lighter load so much easier.

# *Overcoming Procrastination*

Question: What's your procrastination all about?

Answer: I don't know. Can I tell you later?

If confidence is about focusing your energy and acting decisively, then procrastination is the direct opposite. Procrastination scatters your energy and puts off acting at all – sometimes you avoid even deciding. You postpone and postpone. You dither about. Perhaps you have a proposal or essay to write and you keep putting it off and finding excuses for inactivity. Maybe it's the tax form to fill out, the cupboard to tidy, the difficult phone call to make, the button to sew on, the cobwebs to dust off the ceiling, or the medical check-up. It – whatever the current it happens to be – never happens.

Unless you're hyper-organised, you probably have something sitting on a 'to do' list that hasn't become urgent enough yet to do something about it. If so, you're qualified to join the procrastination club – if only club members could get a date and venue organised to meet up. Maybe next week.

Procrastination is the ultimate waiting game: waiting for someone else to take the lead; waiting for something else to happen first; and above all waiting for everything to be perfect before you do anything. Procrastination comes when you lack focus and energy. When you're high on focus and energy, the positive result you get is purposeful action.

The quick secret to bust through procrastination is to do something, anything, but just get moving.

In the next sections, we look at practical ideas to allow you to move on with confidence.

**Book IV**

**Increasing Productivity and Performance**

## Breaking the gridlock

Clients often come to coaching because they are stuck in what we call the *X then Y gridlock* scenario. They have a goal, a dream, something they want to realise, and yet it's not happening. Instead the conversation is around: 'I can't do X until Y.' These are the kind of messages we hear that signify people are putting their lives on hold. Some may be familiar to you:

'I can't do the training course until the children are older.'

'I can't turn professional until I have sponsorship.'

'I can't travel to Australia until my health is better.'

'I can't leave/change my job until my partner's business has taken off.'

'I can't buy my cottage house by the sea until I'm rich.'

'I can't get to the gym until I change jobs, and I can't change jobs until my partner finds a higher paying job.'

'I can't lose weight until my wife stops cooking delicious dinners every night.'

. . . and on it goes. The treacle gets stickier by the day. This stuck situation becomes debilitating and reduces energy. In order to achieve a big dream, most people quite rightly argue that they are limited by not having enough time, money, or energy. However, these are not the sole reasons people get stuck. Essentially, they are struggling because they haven't broken a large job into steps.

Try this step-by-step approach to breaking the pattern of gridlock for yourself and for others.

1. **Put aside the idea that you do not have enough time, money, or energy – assume the lack of any or all these elements is not the real problem.**

   Imagine that you are rich enough in time, money, or energy.

2. **State your goal or dream in a positive way and write it down.**

   For example: 'I want to move to a cottage by the sea.'

3. **Ask yourself Question 1: 'Can I do it today?'**

   If your answer is yes, everything is in place, hey presto your dream is complete. However, if it's not – and this is the most likely scenario – then proceed to Step 4.

4. **Ask yourself Question 2: 'What needs to happen first?'**

   Break out all the separate tasks you need to do to accomplish your goal.

In the example of the house by the sea, the tasks can divide into three main activities: Researching the location, Finding a more flexible job, and Getting the family's agreement.

5. **Loop around the questions in Steps 3 and 4 for each task.**

Ask yourself Question 1, 'Can I do it today?' and if not, then Question 2, 'What needs to happen first?', until you arrive at a list of activities that you can either do today or you have negotiated with yourself to do on a set date that you write in your diary.

Get the idea? In this way you have broken through the gridlock, and are moving towards your dream.

## Biting off smaller chunks

Patience and persistence are valuable qualities to help build your confidence. And when you calmly stick at things, breaking large tasks into smaller ones, you're more likely to get closer to perfection than if you rush at a job looking for a quick fix.

In order to break down your own projects into smaller chunks, follow these steps:

1. **Set your big goal.**

For example, perhaps you want to write a novel.

2. **Set a reasonable and realistic timeframe.**

Writing a novel could take a year.

3. **Break your goal down into a series of small activities to accomplish within the timeframe.**

For writing a novel, these activities may include finding a publisher, firming up the story line, and developing your creative writing skills.

4. **Set specific timeframes for each activity.**

Each novel-writing activity could take several months of work to complete.

5. **Break each activity into a series of daily habits or short projects.**

So developing your creative writing skills may translate to new habits such as attending a creative writing evening class each week and writing for an hour each day.

Organising a project into manageable tasks lets you tackle the largest task with confidence.

**Book IV**

**Increasing Productivity and Performance**

# Taking Time Off – for You

All work and no play makes for a dull life. It's also highly unproductive. If you stay at work for crazy hours, you know how your productivity dips very quickly after the main shift.

What would it be like to slow down a bit and keep things simple? The information in the next sections gives you a glimpse.

## Slowing down

You may be used to acceleration, working in top gear, tweeting and blogging as you speed from place to place by the fastest route possible and rarely stopping to think. Society today is geared to fast – fast food, fast cars, fast computers, fast results, and instant gratification. 'I want it, and I want it today.'

Yet when do your moments of inspiration come? Most often in the quiet moments when you give your brain a chance to unwind a bit: On the day you take off of work; in the shower; on the gym bike; ambling around the park; working in the garden; walking along a country lane. Rarely does your best thinking occur when you're buzzing around like a busy bumble bee in a flower patch.

Your brain may work wonders in fast mode, in logical, rational mode. But it works so much better if you give it a chance to relax at regular intervals. Perversely, going slow speeds up the results you get. Take a break, a complete break, and you come back refreshed.

Meditation offers a calm sea to support you in negotiating the choppy moments. That's why millions of people around the world now practise meditation each day. Here's a two-minute meditation you can do yourself before an important meeting or before the baby awakes – whenever you'd like to slow down gently and savour time for yourself. You may like to read it out aloud slowly to yourself or record your voice saying it and listen to the recording. Let your mind be free . . . free of any thoughts or worries. Let them go. Allow them to float away gently on the breeze. Take your awareness to your breathing. Simply notice as it rises and falls gracefully in your chest and abdomen, with no comment from the mind. Allow your thoughts to come . . . and then to go. Observe the colours and pictures around you, take in the light, and bathe your body and mind in its generous warmth. Hear the sounds in the room and beyond. Let them soften to the furthest corners of your mind, then let them go. Feel the movement of the air on your face and on your body, and bask in that cool stillness. Smell . . . taste the delicacy of the silence. Rest in that calm awareness for a few moments. And when you're ready, come back to now – refreshed, energised, and ready to move on.

# Adopting the 80/20 principle

When Kate worked in corporate advertising, she knew the rule that roughly 20 per cent of her advertising spending produced 80 per cent of the results in any campaign. The problem was always to know which 20 per cent was really working. We exeplore the 80/20 rules in the next sections.

### Explaining the split

*Pareto's law,* or the *80/20 principle,* is named after the 19th-century economist Vilfredo Pareto, who discovered that 80 per cent of the land in Italy was owned by 20 per cent of the population. He also, allegedly, noticed in his garden that 80 per cent of the peas he harvested came from 20 per cent of the pea pods.

Over the years, the same generalised principle has been applied to interesting effect in many other areas beyond land ownership and gardening. Most importantly for you, it suggests that 80 per cent of your results come from 20 per cent of your effort, and, in turn, it takes the 80 per cent of your remaining resources to shift that extra 20 per cent from 80 per cent to 100 per cent. All of that is good evidence of the real cost of perfection. To squeeze out that extra 20 per cent is going to cost you four times the effort. Some things are worth that effort and some are not.

The 80/20 rule is a rough approximation to what happens in reality, but here are some examples of where you might spot Pareto's law in action:

- Twenty per cent of your cleaning effort gets 80 per cent of your home sparkling.

- Twenty per cent of your customers bring in 80 per cent of the sales.

- Twenty per cent of the people in your office create 80 per cent of the results.

- Eighty per cent of your progress comes from 20 per cent of the activities on your to-do list.

- Twenty per cent of your clothes are worn 80 per cent of the time.

- Twenty per cent of the meeting time results in 80 per cent of the decisions.

### Adjusting the split as needed

Recently, a friend was studying for a qualification that involved writing clinical essays. Writing is not her favourite pastime and she became increasing anxious about this piece of work until she decided she could take pressure off herself. 'I'm working on an 80 per cent essay – one that will be good enough to get me the marks I need and still have time for the family and me.'

It was an eminently sensible application of the 80/20 principle – to do her best in the time she had, and then to stop rather than trying to extract the extra marks and suffer unduly in the process.

We believe that busyness is one of the biggest challenges that ordinary folks face. By aiming to do 100 per cent all the time, you dramatically lose energy and focus. If you were to apply the 80/20 rule, you could cut out 80 per cent of your activities and increase your leisure time dramatically.

Identify an area where you are struggling to achieve 100 per cent perfection. Decide on an 80 per cent result that is acceptable to you. Now allocate 20 per cent of your time to focusing on purposefully achieving this result.

# Generating Realistic Standards of Behaviour

We hope that you have heard our message that perfectionism and procrastination are both ultimately time wasters in most circumstances. They take vast amounts of your energy. Naturally, you want to be your best, and circumstances exist where you are competing to excel and want to give it your 100 per cent. The point is to get real as well as having a vision.

Most successful people recognise the benefit of keeping things simple, as in the famous acronym *KISS – Keep it Simple, Stupid.* The harder and more complex you make things for yourself, the more you are likely to make a mess when it's too tough, and lose your confidence in your ability to succeed.

## Adjusting your goals to the circumstances

You know from the previous section that 80 per cent of your results come from 20 per cent of your work. In moving towards your own vision and goals, adopt habits that stop your dillydallying procrastination and keep your energy focused. Here are some questions to ask yourself as you constantly re-evaluate your route forward.

- What's the vision now? (And reconnect with why it's important for you.)
- What am I doing that I can delegate to others?
- What am I doing that doesn't need to be done at all?
- What can I do that no one else can do to achieve this vision?

Capture your answers and refer to them whenever you need to stay on track. Refer to them at least once every month, and ideally more frequently.

## Staying positive while keeping it real

There will be times and situations when your confidence plummets due to external factors over which you have little or no control. Here are some tips for staying positive and holding it together.

- ✔ Think about a time in the future when none of this will matter.

- ✔ Plan a series of small treats for yourself, even if it will be a while before you enjoy them.

- ✔ Imagine that you are in a movie, and this is the bad bit, but you know the movie has a happy ending. Write your own happy ending.

- ✔ Go to bed early with a hot water bottle.

- ✔ Eat the best-quality, healthiest food available and drink lots of water.

- ✔ Take a walk and marvel at the sky, the air, the greenery.

- ✔ Remember everything that has gone smoothly, however small the event.

- ✔ List out the things that are perfect about this most difficult situation right now.

## Increasing your flexibility

For years, long-distance running was Joanne's favourite exercise and form of stress release. She was part of a close-knit running club, ran several miles before work through all weathers, and enlisted for competitive runs at weekends. Running at speed was a theme for all of her life in the fast lane – a high-powered job as a board director for a large firm with a demanding travel schedule. Her children rarely saw her, and her husband felt as if he was a single dad much of the time, bringing up the children on his own.

A hamstring injury enforced a break in Joanne's running schedule. On the advice of her physiotherapist, she exchanged her running routine for swimming and yoga practice at home, and clawed back more time to create an attractive environment in the cottage and relax with her husband and children at weekends. The enforced change of routine encouraged Joanne to take stock of her working life and day. She realised that she'd been stuck in a rut of the same exercise and mixing with the same group of people.

**Book IV**

**Increasing Productivity and Performance**

Once she became more flexible in her exercise routine, she allowed more flexibility and space in her life for her family, and redefined her company role. Her relationships and energy soared once more.

Think about your daily and weekly routines with an eye towards looking at areas where you may be stuck with certain habits that do you no favours. Where would some change, however small, have the most impact? Consider the routines you've developed that have become less than inspiring. Do you, for example, always mix with the same people, spend your weekends in the same way each week, or visit the same places time after time?

Examine the things you *always* do, feel you *ought* to do, or *never* do and try something different. Perhaps you've got into a boring rut. If you always eat Sunday lunch with your mother or tackle the housework every Friday morning, experiment by doing something different. What would happen if you took your mother to the beach on Sunday for a picnic or spent Friday morning playing a round of golf?

# Managing Stress in the Workplace

The level of stress in your workplace is not a fixed thing. You may have a lot of control over your job, so that you can change things easily. On the other hand, changing things in your job may be tricky. One person may find a job stressful because they find it too difficult, whilst another person may find the same job stressful because it's boring. To a certain extent, you need to try to find work that offers the right level of challenge for you.

Sometimes work is so stressful and intense that finding time to relax is almost laughable. But if you don't manage the stress and relax, your efficiency goes down, your health deteriorates and you make poor decisions. Here are some of the issues that you may face if you have chronic workplace stress:

- ✔ **Back problems:** Research suggests that back and shoulder issues are often stress-related.
- ✔ **Cardiovascular disease:** This is more likely to occur in people with demanding jobs over which they have little control.
- ✔ **Psychological disorders:** Depression and burnout have been found to be linked to high job stress levels.
- ✔ **Workplace injuries:** These are more likely if you are highly stressed.

A little bit of pressure at work is good for you. But when the pressure becomes too much, it becomes stress, which is bad for you.

You can choose from a range of methods to lower your level of stress, from personal relaxation techniques to having discussions with management about your workload. If you work for yourself, you may have even more scope for change.

## Discovering the warning signs

The following are typical warning signs of excessive workplace stress:

- **Physical symptoms:** Muscle tension, headaches, stomach problems, headaches, fatigue.

- **Psychological symptoms:** Difficulties in focusing, short temper, low morale, sleep disturbance, feeling anxious, irritability, depression, unwilling to socialise, using alcohol or drugs.

When you feel that your stress is rising take a notepad out and jot down all the warning signs that you're experiencing. Watch out for these warning signs next time you're at work, and take a few moments to reduce your stress. Use a relaxation technique that works for you, such as diaphragmatic breathing, going for a walk, having a cup of tea or listening to some calming music.

You get more work done when you're relaxed rather than highly stressed. High stress causes poor decisions, more mistakes, ineffective communication, illness and possibly even premature death. Put some relaxation into your day.

## Identifying the causes

To manage your stress at work in the long term, you need to deal with the causes of your stress. After you find out the cause, you can take appropriate action. Likely causes of workplace stress include the following:

- **Excessive workload:** You have more work than you can cope with.

- **Lack of control:** You don't have a say about how you do your work.

- **Lack of job security:** You're not sure whether you'll be working there next week.

- **Lack of support:** You don't have sufficient information and advice from either your colleagues or supervisor to help you achieve your work.

- **Poor change management:** Whenever a change takes place at work, you don't have the opportunity to engage and communicate.

- **Poor conditions:** You work in a physically uncomfortable environment.

**Book IV**

**Increasing Productivity and Performance**

- ✔ **Poor workplace relationships:** You don't have harmonious, positive relationships; instead, you may experience workplace bullying or harassment.

- ✔ **Stressful commute:** Your journey to and from work is difficult.

- ✔ **Unclear role:** You don't have a clearly defined role at work.

Go through the points above and write down which of those factors may be the cause of your workplace stress. Then either take action to reduce your stress in that area or talk to your manager. If you can't talk to your manager, seek advice from someone you know and trust. You can also see your doctor, the company's occupational health therapist or a professional counsellor.

According to Professor Cooper, a leading workplace stress researcher, control is the key to managing stress and feeling more relaxed. When you feel out of control, you feel stressed. Think about what's causing you stress at the moment and ask yourself 'How can I take a bit more control of the situation?' and then take action.

## Finding ways for you to relax

If you want to use self-help strategies to reduce your own stress levels, usethe following acronymn – TER. It stands for talk, exercise, relaxation technique.

- ✔ **Talk to someone.** If you have a certain issue causing you stress at work, you need to talk to someone about it. Talk to your friend or partner, colleague or counsellor. You can even talk to your doctor. The worse thing to do is to keep the problem to yourself and try to solve it on your own. Then you are internalising the stressor, which is unhealthy.

- ✔ **Get physical.** Taking exercise is a powerful way to relax after work. Rather than bringing all your stress home with you, go off for a run, take a brisk walk, visit the gym or play a sport. By doing some form of exercise, you put things into perspective. As you begin to relax through exercising, you start to get more creative ideas and solutions to deal with the issue. Or at least you have some time to take your mind off things.

- ✔ **Practise relaxation techniques.** You can use a variety of relaxation techniques to help deal with your stress, from meditation to yoga, or maybe just a simple 10-minute guided imagery exercise, where you sit down after work and imagine your favourite peaceful place. Doing this won't solve the problem that is causing your stress, but by getting into a relaxed frame of mind, you may be able to see the problem differently, like a challenge for example, or you may just be able to accept it and move on.

# Getting organised at work to feel more relaxed

If you're disorganised at work, you're more likely to feel stressed. Being organised helps you to relax. The section that follows offers tips for you to begin taking control of your work by becoming more organised.

Try to put the following ideas into practice to bring some order to your work:

- **Break down the big tasks.** If you have a huge task that's causing you stress, break down the job into bite-sized chunks. For example, if writing a book, break down the project into chapters and then sub-chapters. Assign days to write each section and give it the right priority. Writing a section is much less daunting than writing a whole book.

- **Delegate!** You don't have to do everything. Think about what you can pass on for others to do. Let go of your desire to control everything. Control is important but you also need to let go of some things.

- **Keep things in balance.** In a nutshell, all work and no play is a recipe for a bundle of stress. Make time to socialise, exercise, for quiet time, and time to get your creative juices flowing.

- **Manage your mornings and evenings well.** Ensure that you leave plenty of time to arrive at work so you don't start the day stressed out. Leave some time at the end of the day to plan the next day's activities and to tidy your workspace.

- **Prioritise!** This is the biggest secret of them all. Make a 'to do' list of all the things that need doing, either at the end of the day or before going to sleep, so it's not on your mind. Then, number them in order of importance. Start with the highest-priority job in the morning, which is often the one you don't want to do. However, once you've tackled it, the rest of your day will feel more relaxed. Put exercise and relaxation on your list too.

- **Say no when you can.** Agreeing to do everything will cause you to get overloaded. Practise saying no to people if you're taking on too much work. Start with things that are easy and work your way up to saying no to more challenging or demanding tasks whenever you can.

- **Take regular breaks.** Short walks, perhaps even some banter with the staff at the local coffee shop, offers exercise, a change of environment and some socialising. All great ways to relax quickly. Alternatively, if you're behind a desk, stand up every 30 minutes or so and have a stretch, a drink of water or a piece of fruit and maybe visualise a pleasant place. A little meditation would be great too.

**Book IV**

**Increasing Productivity and Performance**

## *Learning to prioritise ruthlessly*

In this section we explore the idea of developing a healthier work– life balance.

A good work–life balance is a wide-ranging concept that includes a healthy prioritising between work demands (career, vocation, ambition, financial success) and life (family, health, pleasure, leisure, socialising, spiritual development).

Here are some ways to make small improvements to your work–life balance:

- ✔ **Choose your work carefully.** Everyone is different. One person may love to work as a brain surgeon, but another may prefer to cook meals in the hospital canteen. You have your own unique talents and personality, so try to choose a field of work that you like. Choosing work that you enjoy makes your work–life balance much easier to manage. Ideally you want a job you look forward to go to each morning, and come home with a sense of satisfaction. If you're in the wrong job or career path, consider taking steps to change. For careers advice, get help by visiting www.nextstep.direct.gov.uk – use that site to get help online, on the phone or face to face. Great books on changing career paths include *What colour is your parachute?* by Richard Nelson Bolles and *The work you were born to do* by Nick Williams.

- ✔ **Know when to start and stop working.** When you're at work, work. Work hard to finish on time. But when it comes to the end of the day, stop and give time to other important parts of your life, such as family, friends and fun activities. Success entails far more than your bank balance, your position at work or how well you're known. All these are transient. Think about what people may say at your funeral – they're likely to talk about the kind of person you were and your generosity, not how many people you trampled on to get to the top of your career ladder.

- ✔ **Be passionate, not greedy.** The true joy in work comes from fulfilling your passion rather than focusing only on financial outcome. If you do a line of work that you're passionate about, you're rewarded with money as you're providing a good service. However, focusing on money alone leads to anxiety and stress as your bank balance goes up and down. You come home feeling relaxed and content if you work with passion through the day.

- ✔ **Shift your attitude.** If you're overworked and stressed out, a small shift in attitude can make a huge difference. Don't rule out career choices that result in a drop in pay. If your home and personal life are suffering due to excessive work demands, consider whether moving to a less demanding or more interesting job is feasible.

✔ **Have personal goals.** Most workplaces these days demand goals and target-setting. This strategy works so consider balancing it with personal goals. Maybe you want to take up a new sport this year, plan for a round-the-world trip in a few years' time or have at least one family holiday every year. Complete a wheel of life to help decide which area of your life to focus on. Set achievable goals, write them down and review your progress every week.

✔ **See the bigger picture.** To see the bigger picture, ask yourself 'Why am I doing this?' With a clear statement of your goals you'll be able to go into meetings with greater clarity.

If you struggle to balance your work with the rest of the demands of your life, you're not alone. Many people are overwhelmed by all the things they need to get done, both at work and at home.

You may not be able to control the amount of time you spend at work, but you do have some control outside of work. Concentrate your energy on managing that time and using your energy in that time wisely.

Here are some tips to improve the 'life' bit of your work–life balance:

✔ **Put 'life' activities into your calendar.** When you plan your week or month, put friends and family into your diary. A date with your partner at the end of the week acts as something to look forward to and makes you feel better. Looking forward to an enjoyable activity can be just as much fun as the activity itself.

For example, when you meet with your friends, take your diary so that you can plan the next get-together. Or schedule a fun afternoon trip with your kids every Sunday afternoon.

✔ **Remember the small things count.** If you can't manage to leave the office early every day, try just one night every week. If you struggle to make time to go on holiday, take a break one weekend a year. Spend half-an-hour on your hobby every week. Don't underestimate the value of small changes.

✔ **Squeeze some exercise into your day.** Exercising gives far more than the time it takes. You'll feel more alert and focused at work and have more energy at home, for your partner, family, friends and fun activities. Try waking up earlier or using your lunch hour for a 20-minute brisk walk or run.

✔ **Increase nourishing and reduce depleting activities.** Make a list of all the activities you do in a typical day. Put the letter 'N' next to the nourishing activities that make you feel energised and happy, and the letter 'D' next to the depleting activities that sap your energy. See what you can do to increase the amount of time you spend doing nourishing activities and reducing the amount of time spent on depleting activities.

**Book IV**

**Increasing Productivity and Performance**

✔ **Reconsider your chores.** Decide whether all your chores are essential. If they are, consider paying someone to help you, doing your shopping online or asking your children to do certain tasks around the home. You can even team up with a friend and do each other's tasks – for example, taking turns to drop the kids at school.

✔ **Be efficient with your time.** Make a list of all the things you need to do in town and get them done once a week. Be creative and find other ways to save time. Here are some more time-saving ideas:

  • Turn off your phone and internet when you don't want to be disturbed.

  • Do things now if you can, instead of putting them off.

  • Delegate things for others to do rather than trying to do everything yourself.

  • Do the most important things when you are fresh and have the energy.

  • Learn to say no to people's request for your time. If it's difficult for you, start with saying no to small request and gradually build up.

## Overcoming bad working habits to relax

Work attitudes are not easy to change, but as you begin to gain confidence in your ability to relax, you can discover approaches to work that just compound your stress rather than reduce it. Humans are creatures of habit, and if you can begin to mould your working life towards positive attitudes, you offer yourself the chance to ease off some of the anxieties.

To determine whether your attitudes towards work prevent you from relaxing, ask yourself the following questions:

✔ **Are you a perfectionist?** This is a common ideal that causes a great deal of stress. Notice whether you try to do things perfectly. Remember: perfection is an unreachable goal, as things can always be improved. Try listing all the disadvantages for yourself and others of a perfectionist tendency. Focus on enjoying the journey rather than only the goal. See criticism as a chance to learn rather than something to avoid all the time.

✔ **Are you negative?** Getting dragged into a complaining mode when working can be so easy. This approach drains your energy. Keep things in balance by remembering to appreciate what's going well. Phone a positive friend, make an excuse to go for a walk when your colleagues are just complaining too much, and jot down some work things you're grateful for on a daily basis.

✔ **Do you try to control everything?** If you try to control everyone and everything at work, you set yourself up for a stressful career. Change the things you can and need to change, but also learn to accept the things that you can't change. In particular, you can't control other people. Be responsible for yourself and your own actions. Lack of control doesn't mean weakness – giving others responsibility is a strength.

✔ **Do you think you're incompetent?** You may have a sense of incompetence and self-doubt about your work. You may often think that your work is inferior and judge yourself harshly. Boost your confidence by countering your own judgements. For example, if you think 'I'll never get this work done on time,' think 'I've always done it on time in the past. Let me break it down and do the project step-by-step.' I like to just do what I can and let my manager/client/interviewer decide if they like my work rather than assuming I'm doing badly. And even if the manager is unhappy about my work, that's just one opinion. Another manager may disagree entirely.

✔ **Do you try to please others all the time?** If you constantly think about others' opinion of your work, you may base your self-esteem on other people's judgements. You can end up worrying if your work is good enough and avoid contact out of fear of hearing a negative judgement. This behaviour can be linked to perfectionist tendencies. Deal with this problem by noticing this pattern of behaviour and become aware of thoughts like 'I mustn't make a mistake or others will find out I'm useless,' or, 'If I show her my work, she might think it's rubbish. That would be terrible.' Make your thinking more realistic by saying to yourself things like, 'It's okay to make mistakes. I'm a human being,' or 'If she doesn't like it, that's her opinion. I don't have to depend on her for my self-esteem.'

## *Trying other strategies to stress less and relax more*

Here are a few ideas for ways of managing stress. All of these ideas are echoed by the National Institute for Occupational Safety and Health in the US.

✔ **Crack a few jokes.** Some laughter and banter with co-workers can help you to relax during the day. Don't miss out on all the fun – take a few minutes to share a joke.

✔ **Distinguish between work and home.** Make a clear transition between your home life and work. Listen to music, do a relaxation technique such as guided imagery or self-hypnosis, pop into your local cafe or go for a walk.

✔ **Do it now!** Avoid procrastination. If you really can't stand the thought of doing a task, do it for just one minute. You'll probably feel like doing more once you've started.

✔ **Do your time and let go.** Only work for the time that you're paid to work. Then stop, leave your work behind and go home. You'll get much more done in the long run and feel more relaxed. If you can't do that, finish your work at your workplace and try not to take it home.

✔ **Don't accumulate rubbish.** Sort out your e-mail and incoming letters as soon as you get them – it only takes a few minutes.

✔ **Follow your internal clock.** Tackle your most challenging work at a time of day when you're most awake and alert.

✔ **Get enough sleep.** By working late you'll feel tired the next day and end up being even more inefficient. Give sleep a high priority, especially in the long term.

✔ **Tackle stress.** When you feel your stress levels rising, stop what you're doing. Write down what you can do to lower your stress levels, such as breaking down your problem, scheduling a break, going for a five-minute walk or challenging your negative thoughts with more positive yet realistic statements.

✔ **Try the one-touch paper rule.** As soon as a new piece of paper arrives on your desk take action, or bin it, or file it. Try to bin it if possible!

✔ **Visualise successful outcomes.** If you're worried about an upcoming event you need to deal with, visualise yourself in the situation achieving success. Then visualise the steps you need to take to be able to achieve a successful outcome. This visualisation process makes you more likely to follow the steps and relax more during the process.

# Chapter 8

# Getting Things Done with the Help of Others

*I*f you've ever observed master persuaders at work, you may feel both impressed and frustrated. You watch in awe as, with a steady stream of charisma, eloquence and ease, they engage people they want to win over, making them eager to carry out any request put forward.

If you find that your charisma quotient is modest or that your verbal skills are lacking, don't despair. Persuasive techniques are based on scientific principles that you can understand and apply to your everyday interactions. When you put the principles in this chapter into practice, others comply with your wishes almost automatically. Why? Because with global technology driving the pace, time is compressed and people barely have a moment to think. In addition, they're swamped with more information than they can absorb. They don't have time to consider their decisions and there's too much to consider anyway. As long as the choice makes sense to them, they do what you ask.

In this chapter wedescribe six simple, clear and intuitive principles based on the work of Dr Robert Cialdini, as well as significant theories and experiments in social psychology, the psychology of persuasion and the science of compliance. The research shows that people can be persuaded by appealing to a deeply rooted and limited set of basic needs and desires. If you apply these principles of persuasion, both you and the person or organisation you want to influence benefit.

Although we separate the principles and how to apply them into six sections for the sake of clarity, their impact increases when you combine them. For example, while you're establishing your authority during an informal conversation (see 'Exposing your expertise' below), you can also gain useful information about the people you want to influence. Knowing more about the other person's background, particularly his likes and dislikes, helps you uncover common ground (see 'Finding similarities') and areas where you can offer sincere praise (see 'Complimenting others'), further enhancing your persuasive powers.

However you practise the principles in this chapter, do so ethically. Not only is tricking and trapping others into doing what you want them to do morally wrong, the approach is reckless and risky.

# Highlighting Your Likeability

Renowned US lawyer Clarence Darrow summed up a key aspect of persuasion when he said, 'The main work of a trial attorney is to make a jury like his client.' In a court of law or everyday encounters, if people like you, they're much more apt to say yes to you. So, how do you persuade someone to like you?

According to research, three main factors affect your likeability:

- ✔ how attractive you are to the other person
- ✔ how similar you are to the other person
- ✔ how much you offer praise to the other person

If you want your clients, customers and colleagues to like you, you must take the time to build relationships with them. Appeal to their values, demonstrate your similarities and emphasise your association with positive points, such as your involvement in your organisation's outstanding corporate social responsibility programmes or your department's track record of superb customer service.

The following sections cover three major techniques for pumping up your likeability.

## Accenting your attractiveness

When Sir Winston Churchill was accused of being drunk, he replied, 'And you, madam, are ugly. But in the morning, I shall be sober.' Unkind but true!

Physical attractiveness goes a long way towards getting people to like you, and can increase your power of persuasion. Recall how much attention was paid to Republican vice-presidential candidate Sarah Palin's appearance during the 2008 election. Despite questions about her qualifications, and amid allegations of money inappropriately used on hair, make-up and wardrobe, Palin and her family strived to appear attractive and coordinated throughout the campaign.

People who look attractive are perceived as talented, kind, trustworthy and intelligent. They seem to draw others to them with ease. Physically attractive people with similar qualifications as less attractive individuals are more likely to be hired for the same jobs. And after they get the jobs, they typically earn more money than their less appealing counterparts.

The power of physical attraction is well known in the advertising industry. When a good looking woman promotes a product such as a car, consumers perceive the car as having a better design and as being more valuable than if the woman weren't present. By using attractive people to promote their products, advertisers create an *attractiveness bias* towards their products without the viewer being aware that the bias exists.

If you're not personally blessed with the good looks of Angelina Jolie or Orlando Bloom – and don't want to undergo cosmetic surgery or spend a fortune on beauty products – you can still make the best of what you've got. Increase your chances of persuading people that you're rather nice-looking by utilising any and all of the following strategies:

- ✔ **Dress appropriately for your shape and style.** Spending your entire salary on clothes isn't necessary; just choose well-made items that fit. Most department stores offer free measuring services and reasonable prices for tailoring.

- ✔ **Preen and prune a bit.** Make a daily effort to appear clean, healthy and polished. Get your hair cut or styled on a regular basis. A fresh 'do can make you feel amazingly confident.

- ✔ **Foster familiarity.** You naturally like people you're familiar with and find them more attractive than people you don't know. From an evolutionary standpoint, familiarity is all about safety, so do everything you can to form relationships whereby others feel safe around you. Even though you don't look like Kate Winslet or Johnny Depp, others will like you and be open to your influence.

  Some simple ways of making people feel safe around you include:

  - Actively listening to them
  - Accepting them as they are
  - Being honest, reliable and trustworthy
  - Demonstrating empathy
  - Behaving respectfully

The *mere exposure effect* is a psychological phenomenon in which people develop preferences for things based solely on their familiarity with them. In studies of interpersonal attraction, this effect is also known as the *familiarity principle;* thus the more frequently a person sees you, the more likeable you can become to them.

✔ **Keep close.** Research indicates that the longer two people are in close proximity, the greater the chance that they end up liking one another and the more likely they are to find one another physically attractive and be open to each other's influence.

Without coming across as a stalker, some of the ways you can make the most of proximity are by:

- Inviting the other person to join you for lunch or drinks after work
- Offering to share a ride home
- Suggesting you sit together if you're working on the same project
- Asking them to go to a concert, film or museum with you and some other friends

✔ **Invest time.** The more time you spend with someone, the higher the probability that you like them and find them physically attractive.

You can commute together or take lunch at the same time. You could suggest working together on a project, or join forces for a sponsored charity event. You could find out the other person's interests or hobbies and suggest that you do them together.

✔ **Play up positive personal qualities.** Research consistently shows that people with positive personality traits – such as empathy, trustworthiness or generosity – are perceived as being more attractive than those who demonstrate few of those virtues.

Characters such as Shakespeare's Bottom, DreamWorks' Shrek and the Beast in *Beauty and the Beast* all have personalities that outshine their physical flaws. Indeed, over time, their various love interests even grow to find their donkey ears, wobbling green flesh and hairy backs endearing.

If you're naturally considerate or thoughtful, share your knowledge and expertise or offer to help when someone's struggling. If you're optimistic about a project when others are sceptical, show them how they stand to benefit. When you're generous with others, they see you in a positive light.

✔ **Share experiences.** A heart-to-heart conversation or a shared experience that makes a positive impact on your life can change how you perceive someone else and how they perceive you.

Be proactive and seek out opportunities for sharing experiences. Put together a team for a sponsored event. Attend a concert, go to the theatre or visit a museum. Form a book club, put together a film society, attend a sporting event. By demonstrating your interest, you become more interesting to others.

# Finding similarities

People tend to like you because you're similar to them. Similarities create bonds and provide a platform for establishing rapport. A shared background, point of view, sense of humour, comparable lifestyles and parallel personality traits are frequently cited as reasons for liking another person.

If you want to persuade someone, search for what you've got in common and make that person your friend. Salespeople are taught to search for similarities to make their clients feel they have something in common, which helps to develop rapport, deepen trust – and make the sale.

The following sections explore some similarities you can identify or enhance in order to get closer to others.

## Common values

Discovering that you and a colleague share the same values creates a bond of trustworthiness and compatibility. Even if you don't share background, religion or lifestyle, you can probably still find some common values.

## Shared dress sense

Adopting another person's style of dress is the simplest way to create an appearance of similarity. Similar dress can serve as a shortcut to communication. If you look at all like the people you want to influence, they assume you understand them, their values and their beliefs.

## Parallel backgrounds and interests

While you may spend a lot of your energy on business-related matters, establishing a life outside of business is healthy – and helpful. You can get to know your clients and colleagues by talking about subjects other than work.

Discovering that someone comes from the same part of the country or enjoys the same pursuits, hobbies or activities as you provides grounds for liking that person. And after you like someone and they like you, persuading and influencing one another becomes easier.

Extend your interests to things that might not normally appeal to you, if they appeal to the people around you. Without meaning to sound sexist, women who are able to discuss football or the best golf club to use for getting out of the rough stand a better chance of engaging with their male colleagues and clients than those who can't differentiate a driver from a putter.

Between Facebook and other social networking tools, people can end up knowing too much about each other. Set the tone for online interactions and be selective in what you reveal about yourself. What you may see as a prank or bit of whimsy, others may view as grounds for dismissal. See *Social Media Marketing For Dummies* by Shiv Singh (Wiley) or *Facebook For Dummies* by Leah Pearlman and Carolyn Abram (Wiley).

## Complimenting others

As Abraham Lincoln said, 'Everybody likes a compliment.' Paying compliments creates goodwill and cultivates relationships. Just make sure you go about offering your praises effectively.

### Offering powerful praise

Praising others increases their positive feelings for you, and people are more prone to be persuaded by people they like. When you praise others, you're demonstrating that you're paying attention to and appreciating them.

To be successful at using compliments, limit at-work compliments to on-the-job achievements and avoid comments relating to personal appearance. Avoid commenting directly about the person and instead admire something about them. Many people are uncomfortable receiving direct compliments and feel embarrassed if the compliment is too personal. Instead, try complimenting the effect of someone's behaviour and the reasons for its positive impact.

Telling someone what a great guy they are or how much you want to be like him can be irritating and smacks of disingenuousness if not a bit of toadyism. If you tell someone you think he's wonderful, he may doubt your motives, if for no other reason than they know there are things about them that aren't so wonderful. If, however, you compliment something specific like 'I admire the way you handled that situation because you were direct without being offensive,' 'I could tell the tone and content of your presentation matched the audience's mood and expectations by their positive response,' 'I respect your ability to handle difficult conversations, because you treat people with respect while making your point' or 'I really liked the way you stood up for the team, because they've been working hard on this project without getting any recognition,' you're complimenting specific aspects of the person's behaviour that he can accept as valid.

When complimenting someone, follow these simple rules:

- ✔ **Think before you speak.** Make sure it's something true and that would benefit the listener.
- ✔ **Keep to the point.** Keep your remarks brief and avoid gushing.

✔ **Don't come on too strong.** Overwhelming the receiver will make him wonder about your motives.

✔ **Compliment an achievement not accidental good fortune.** Telling a good-looking person that they're good looking can be tiresome, because the person wonders if that's all people think of him.

✔ **Compliment in a timely manner.** Don't be the last to the post when complimenting someone. You may come out sounding like an also ran.

✔ **Stop, look and listen.** Gauge the other person's response and move on. If you continue to compliment, you may sound obsessive.

### Avoiding flattery

If praise is crudely transparent or done the wrong way, your efforts can backfire and you can be seen as sycophantic rather than sincere. Be especially mindful of:

✔ **Obvious agendas:** A statement such as, 'Good job, Charlotte! Now I need you to produce two more units by next week' may be sincere, but it also indicates that the speaker wants something in return for the compliment. A more effective alternative would be 'Good job, Charlotte! I know you're putting a lot of effort into this project and I appreciate it. Now we've been asked to produce two more units by next week. Can I count on you to make that deadline?'

✔ **The all-powerful 'but':** The word 'but' ensures that your listener negates your first statement and focuses on the second. If you say something like, 'Ted, your work has really improved, but you need to be more proactive,' which portion of that statement is Ted going to remember?

I encourage my clients to replace the 'but' word with either 'and' or a full stop. That way both sides of the message can be heard clearly without interference from the negativity 'but' implies.

✔ **False praise:** Avoid making a big show when both you and the other person know that the action being praised was actually mediocre. You just want the person to like you and you're trying to get on his good side. Furthermore, the other person is no fool; your compliment is likely to tag you as phoney. Instead, saying something like, 'So far, so good. Now that you understand what the job entails, I know you can increase your efforts to demonstrate what you're really made of.'

**Book IV**

**Increasing Productivity and Performance**

People want to believe good things about themselves; they often believe what they hear and like the person who offers the compliment, even when the praise is clearly false. Be aware of your power and only offer sincere and honest praise. Otherwise, your ethics will come into question.

# Relying on Reciprocity

Throughout history in all human societies, one of the most potent forces of influence has been based on the principle of *reciprocity*. You give something to me, and I give something similar back to you.

You may not admit that reciprocation plays a role in your interactions but empirical evidence demonstrates that when you do someone a favour, you expect the other person to pay you back in some manner.

Further research demonstrates that people feel compelled to pay back any favour they receive, no matter what the cost of the original gift or favour – and often in amounts that exceed. So don't be surprised if you get back something even bigger than what you gave in order for the other person to redress the balance.

The following sections explore how you can utilise the dynamics of giving and receiving in your efforts to persuade and influence others.

## Giving first to gain advantage

People in both the profit and not-for-profit worlds understand the advantage of being the first to give – in order to get something back.

A well-known marketing technique for giving and getting is the gift-with-purchase, in which shoppers are encouraged to make a purchase in order to receive a free gift. While a regular practice throughout business, this system is particularly prevalent in the cosmetic industry. Purchase a product and receive free samples, umbrellas or tote bags. Would you have bought any of those items if they hadn't been given to you for free? Probably not. The simple fact that you're offered a free gift in exchange for purchase compels you to buy.

Similarly, when you offer your clients free samples of your product or service, you're giving away something with the plan being to receive something of higher value in exchange later – most likely an increase in sales and referrals.

Charities understand the advantages of giving and are therefore able to persuade the great majority to put their hands in their pockets. In addition to offering little gifts such as pens, gummed address labels, lapel pins and greeting cards, charitable donations make you feel good about yourself. Also, donating to charity provides you with tax deductions; in these days of economic challenges, every little bit helps.

Of course, the things you give don't have to be physical objects. The positive dynamic that happens when you give a tangible gift also occurs when you reward someone with special recognition, extra help on a challenging project or the opportunity to leave work early on a Friday.

If someone owes you a favour, not only does he want to repay his debt, he wants to do so as soon as possible. Feeling beholden or indebted to another person is uncomfortable, and the sense of obligation is burdensome. After someone feels indebted to you, you can ask for what you want and then sit back and enjoy the spoils.

Stating 'much obliged' is a way of expressing appreciation across the globe and was first recorded in the *Oxford English Dictionary* in 1548. However, the expression translated literally means that the person saying 'much obliged' now owes the other person a favour and is obligated to pay back at some point in the future.

If you only take and don't give back, others are likely to perceive you as selfish and be less inclined to give to you in the future.

When a person gives you something, thank him with a handwritten note and follow up with an offer of your own.

While phone calls and emails are used more and more as a quick way of communicating, they don't quite cut the mustard when it comes to expressing your sincere appreciation. The time it takes to write a short note is worth the effort for the positive impression your letter leaves. While you don't need to write a long missive, you do need to be specific and sincere in your thanks. In addition, send it out promptly. Rather like fresh vegetables, a late letter becomes less attractive the longer it's left. That being said, 'better late than never' applies, because the recipient always appreciates your thanks.

Quickly come up with something you can provide in return. A meal out, a ticket to a sought-after event or a gift you know he'd particularly like are ways of keeping the relationship going.

There may be times when you'd rather not further the relationship, in which case send a brief thank-you note and leave it at that. While you want to be careful not to burn any bridges, there are just some relationships that are more trouble than they're worth. Or simply aren't worth your time and effort at all. Be polite and move on.

Whatever you do, you want to make sure that the gift you give makes the recipient feel comfortable and doesn't offend or embarrass him. Gifts should be given to honour an established relationship, not to court a new one. If someone gives you a gift that's beyond your ability to reciprocate in kind, in addition to writing a thank-you note, return his generosity with something

**Book IV**

**Increasing Productivity and Performance**

Refer to the following list when you want to give an appropriate and effective gift:

- ✔ **Make sure your gift fits with company guidelines.** Some businesses have no-gift policies or a limit on the value of gifts its employees may accept. Check with the company's receptionist or human resources department to spare you and the recipient any awkwardness.

- ✔ **Consider how the gift will be perceived.** You want to be sure that it will speak favourably of you and your organisation and will benefit the recipient.

- ✔ **Pick gifts with personal meaning.** Pay attention to what the recipient talks about and likes. That way you know what kind of gift would be appreciated.

- ✔ **Don't be skimpy.** While the gift doesn't need to be expensive, it does need to be top quality, because cheaper and lower-quality products send negative messages about the value you place on the relationship.

- ✔ **Give appropriate gifts at appropriate times.** If you send a potential client a bottle of wine or box of chocolates before the contract's signed, you may look like you're offering a bribe.

- ✔ **Include a short handwritten note.** Personal notes along with the gift show you've put extra thought into your giving.

- ✔ **Avoid inappropriate gifts.** A gift that's overly personal, such as lingerie or other articles of clothing, could insult or offend the recipient.

## *Negotiating and making concessions*

Consider this situation: you want someone to agree to your request. You know he probably won't, so you cleverly make your request larger than what you actually want, knowing that he'll turn you down, which he does. You then ask for something smaller – what you really want in the first place – and he agrees.

As long as you're adept at structuring your requests, the other person sees your second, smaller, request as a concession and is inclined to make a concession of his own. In other words, by skilfully structuring your proposals, people are much more likely to yield and agree to your second request.

When making a request, exaggerate your initial proposition enough to encourage a series of smaller reciprocal concessions that lead to your final offer being accepted. For example, if you want to sell a product or service to a potential buyer and he rejects your proposal, you can ask whether he will help you by referring people who might be interested in your offering. If you present your request as a concession following a purchase request the potential buyer just refused, he may be more willing to agree to your appeal than if you had asked for referrals at the beginning of your pitch.

If you make your first request so extreme that it's perceived as unreasonable, the other person is likely to see you as bargaining in bad faith. He may cut off further discussions entirely – or view your future concessions as fake and avoid reciprocating any concessions.

When you're negotiating, you never want to give something away without getting something in return. Use the 'If you . . . then I' formula. For example, you can say, 'If you agree to a series of programmes over the next three years, then I'll review our discount position.' By using this format you make it clear that your concession is contingent on the other person meeting the conditions you've proposed. When you're negotiating, it's good practice to give in order to get.

For more about effective negotiating practices, refer to the second edition of *Negotiating For Dummies* by Michael C Donaldson (Wiley).

# Encouraging Follow-through on Commitments

The desire to be true to your word is a central motivator of behaviour. If you make a commitment, you feel pressure from within yourself – as well as from others – to behave consistently with your decision. When you commit, either orally or in writing, to a proposal or goal, you're likely to follow through because the very act of following through conforms to your view of yourself.

People also commit more readily when they personally *own* their decisions. If you try to force your will on someone else in an effort to meet your own agenda, don't be surprised if the other person fails to follow through. The challenge is getting others to do what you want – while making the choices appear to be theirs, as I explore in the following sections.

**Book IV**

**Increasing Productivity and Performance**

## Playing to the desire for consistency

People want to appear consistent in their behaviour, and by extension, they appreciate consistency in others. People who do what they say they're going to do are highly valued individuals. You can depend on them to follow through on their promises and commitments. They seldom let you down or do surprising things.

But as you know, people aren't absolutely consistent. They say certain things and do others. That's bad enough in life outside the office, but when your career, due dates or pay package depend on the behaviour of others, inconsistency is tough to live with and can produce unfortunate consequences.

By observing how a person behaves, you discover their values, convictions and outlook. Once you have determined what motivates them as well as what holds them back, appeal to those signs. If, for example, you notice that someone's struggling to complete a project he initially seemed excited about or committed to, remind him of the pot of gold waiting at the end of the rainbow. Ask how you can help, provide your support, and encourage the other person's efforts. If he continues to struggle, ask what might be holding him back. The more information you can garner, the more resources you have to work with.

## Getting others to commit

If you want people to make commitments, rather than forcing choices on them, let the commitments be voluntary and defined in their own terms. By coming up with their own solutions and strategies, people are more inclined to commit to action than if you impose your will on them.

Empirical evidence proves that when you actively make a voluntary choice and publically announce or write down your intention, you're more likely to follow through than if you make the same choice without a public proclamation or statement.

Encourage people to write down what they say they're going to do. Whether setting a goal or agreeing a plan of action, writing down commitments is a vital psychological aid that keeps people to their word.

Committing in writing is particularly effective with people who report directly to you. For example, after one of your employees agrees that he's been slow in submitting necessary information, have him write a memo that summarises his plan for responding to the situation in the future, including whatever assistance he may need if he struggles, and send it to you. Writing and sharing the plan increases the odds that he lives up to what he puts down.

Teams that create mission and vision statements and the individuals who live by them understand the power of following through on promises. These statements are based on personal values, giving you something to own and guide your behaviour. By clearly and publically committing to your principles and promises, you put your reputation on the line.

# Following the Crowd

As any successful company leader, politician or head of a voluntary organisation can attest, if you create an environment in which enough people buy in to what you're suggesting, the rest of the group will go along too. Life is just easier that way.

Advertisers, television producers and evangelical preachers are well aware of the power of building their audiences and then getting them to buy in to their products – whether it's body lotion, a comedy programme or a chance for redemption.

Following the crowd is easy but has a downside. As the American intellectual and Pulitzer-Prize-winning reporter Walter Lippmann said, 'When we all think alike, no one thinks very much.' Additionally, when you follow the crowd, you may find yourself acting in ways you didn't expect. The following sections explore methods of working with groups effectively and ethically.

## Building your own crowd

You don't need to be physically connected to be part of a crowd. Online groups consisting of loosely linked individuals who share a passion or interest in a particular subject are popping up all over the place. Whether you're building a group of like-minded people in person or online, groups provide the opportunity to discover and feed on one another's ideas as well as influence others' beliefs and behaviours.

Groups provide a means of determining what's correct or acceptable – the more a group behaves in a certain way, the more you're influenced to comply. Groups serve as a short cut for determining how to behave, and work best in times of uncertainty. For example, if people are in an ambiguous situation, they tend to follow the example of the majority. In addition, people are inclined to follow the lead of people similar to them. Once you've got a group on your bandwagon, it's easier to persuade others to join, too. The thinking goes something like this, 'If everyone who is anyone is following her lead, why aren't I?' Most people want to be part of a special inner circle – a desire that gives you the power to persuade the masses.

**Book IV**

**Increasing Productivity and Performance**

Following the crowd can be a short cut to success – or a pathway to perdition. For the most part, you make fewer mistakes if you follow what others are doing rather than if you follow your own agenda. While mavericks may struggle with this fact, people often act in a similar fashion because they perceive it as the right thing to do. However, before following the crowd, you may want to check the values and beliefs of the people who are influencing your behaviour.

As for the people who want to lead the crowd or use group dynamics to persuade others, ethical behaviour is paramount if they're to be seen as working in the best interests of the group and not simply for their own reward. Group leaders working for the good of the group have a capacity to empathise and care for others, communicate clearly, and are committed to following through. While there are still leaders whose motives are toxic and who abuse the leader–follower relationship, rendering the group into a worse shape than when it started, most people are aware of those tactics and will abandon the leader rather than follow him. All groups need a leader – someone who can get others to follow willingly.

## Recognising and responding to peer pressure

People who are comfortable following the lead of others are particularly susceptible to peer pressure. They willingly play follow the leader, appreciating that someone else is making the decisions while all they have to do is go with the flow.

According to social psychologist Irving Janis, when members of a group have similar backgrounds, are insulated from outside options and have no defined rules for making judgments, the group can make faulty decisions. Janis called this situation *groupthink*.

If you're uncertain what course of action to take, don't be surprised if you follow the herd. Because others are acting in a similar fashion, the message being conveyed is that the choice is right. Organised religions understand this principle, as do cults.

As any leader knows, persuading your team members when they work together in a unified way is easier than coercing the unconvinced. Individuals who get along, who are loyal and who work in a united way are the foundation of a cohesive team. Additional characteristics of a cohesive team include:

- Well-defined roles and adherence to an agreed code of conduct
- Shared goals and responsibilities
- A positive team identity and pride in team membership
- Positive working relationships, built on respect and trust
- An attitude of empathy and care towards team members
- Little conflict that is handled, when it does occur, using constructive problem-solving techniques
- Group members who cooperate with each other

✔ Honest, open communication

✔ Public recognition and credit for good work, freely given

# Asserting Your Authority

Most people have a deep-seated sense of duty to authority – whether they admit it or not – and don't want to defy an authority figure's wishes. If you don't believe me, look at the research.

No matter how rebellious you may think you are, studies consistently demonstrate people's willingness to go well beyond their normal behaviour on the command of the person in charge. Without obeying the people in power, anarchy can reign. Envision your office if no one was in authority: madness and mayhem, perhaps – or everyone taking a siesta.

## Making the most of titles and positions

From the moment you're born, you're trained to believe that obeying proper authority is the right thing to do and disobeying is wrong. Authority figures from your youth taught you to do as you're told by the people in charge. These influential people include family members, nuns, priests and pastors, teachers, police officers, fire fighters – even school crossing patrols.

In the worlds of law, politics, medicine and the military, authority rules. You're expected to submit to legitimate rule and assume your place in the hierarchy of power.

Consider the following examples:

✔ A senior law partner can more easily persuade others in the firm on a course of action than a recently qualified solicitor, who probably would struggle to even get a hearing.

✔ A police officer in uniform has more influence in getting people to play by the rules than a passer-by witnessing a crime.

✔ Doctors can persuade nurses to act without questioning.

✔ In the classroom, a professor carries more weight than a graduate assistant. And while you don't bow when meeting the chancellor of an elite university, you probably stand a little taller in his presence, out of respect for his position.

**Book IV**

**Increasing Productivity and Performance**

If you currently lack a title or a position of formal authority – and the ensuing power and influence that come with them – all's not lost. You can still make your voice heard and be noticed by others when you follow these suggestions:

✔ Build strong working relationships with the people you want to influence. Pay attention to their strengths, weaknesses and what motivates them. When you're ready to influence their thinking, present your case in a way that addresses their needs.

✔ Help others. If you want your colleagues to listen to you, begin by listening to them. Support your co-workers' good ideas, help them with their work when you can, offer encouragement when they face challenges.

✔ Be an expert in your area. Take courses, read journals, attend training programmes, tweet and blog to become *the* authority in your field. If you make it known that you're up-to-date with the latest information, people will seek your opinion.

✔ Be true to your values and principles. Treat people well, don't gossip or criticise others in public, and make decisions based on the right thing to do. Act like a role model.

## Dressing like an authority figure

One of the quickest ways to gain authority is through your clothing. Uniforms denote expertise, entitlement and power. If you're wearing the clothes of your profession – a police officer's blue uniform, a judge's robes – you're seen as the authority in that area. Resisting requests from people in clothes that denote authority can be very difficult.

Someone wearing a well-tailored suit with polished shoes and classic accessories looks influential, while a person in baggy, sweaty shorts rarely does. Unless that person is Rafael Nadal after a well-won tennis match, of course.

Effective wardrobe choices can make you look more authoritative and commanding. For example:

✔ Wear jackets and blouses with shoulder pads to look broader than you really are. Choose shoes with heels or lifts to look taller. Politicians, celebrities and captains of industry know that size denotes authority, and people bow to authority.

At 5 feet 6 inches, the French president, Nicholas Sarkozy, is one of the world's most persuasive and influential men. He is also smart and understands the relationship between size and authority; he wears lifts in his shoes to make himself look taller.

✔ Accent your outfit with smart accessories. A fine watch, a good pen, and high-quality handbags and briefcases give an impression that you're a class act.

✔ Be well groomed. Polished shoes, a good haircut and well-tended nails say that you care enough to look your best.

✔ While vibrant colours liven up the ubiquitous grey, black and navy-blue suits, it's hard to be taken seriously when you're encased in fuchsia, turquoise and orange. That being said, a splash of red and gold sends out a message that you're someone to be taken seriously, because both colours are associated with power. Red symbolises all things intense and passionate, including excitement, energy and strength, while colour experts say that gold encourages communication and represents optimism, enlightenment and the promise of a positive future.

## Exposing your expertise

In today's competitive world, you have little chance of making your mark unless you demonstrate your know-how, skills and abilities. People count on the advice of experts as a short cut to helping them make good decisions. Your job is to let them know that you're the expert they want.

In order to stand a chance of influencing another person, establish your own expertise. Yes, this requires a bit of self-promotion:

✔ Display your diplomas and awards, share testimonials and publicise your credentials to help create your expert persona. If you don't have any of these things, go out and get them. Take courses and put up your certificates of completion. Do volunteer work and ask for testimonials in return for your time. Ask your clients to recommend your services on LinkedIn. It's not enough to be expert in your field; you have to show people that you are.

✔ Whoever you're speaking to, tell stories and anecdotes about your experiences relating to your area of expertise. Stories are entertaining and more interesting than a list of your accomplishments. When you tell stories and anecdotes people engage with you and remember what you say. Three different kinds of stories follow that are sure to capture your listeners' attention:

- **Facing a challenge.** In this story you tell how you overcame an obstacle to get where you are. Rather than declaring, 'I'm really good at customer service,' which sounds boastful and unsubstantiated, you could say, 'I gained my skills in customer service working at a burger bar. People would crowd around the counter calling out their orders, and it was a challenge to keep the customer satisfied.' By telling that story your listener has an image in his mind of you being good at customer service.

- **Acting creatively.** This approach turns on the eureka moment, when an idea changes everything. Rather than saying, 'I sell textbooks' which sounds pretty dull, you could say, 'Although I loved school and reading and wanted to sell textbooks, I couldn't figure out how to market textbooks in a way that would interest the customer. Then I had a brainwave: no one has a favourite textbook, but everyone has a favourite teacher. So, I hooked in the customers by working with the teachers.'

- **Making connections.** This is a good way of communicating how you pulled a group together. For example, 'Our digital games company merged with another digital games company and people were duplicating each others' efforts to create a new game for the 18- to 34-year-old male market. I convinced the teams to combine their designs and create a product together. The game they created was the best-selling game for that market during the Christmas period.'

✔ Attend conferences and conventions, which offer great opportunities to get to know others socially before buckling down to business.

✔ Make the most of golf games, tennis matches, dinner and cocktail parties. Think of these activities as chances to find things out about your colleagues, as well as to establish your own expertise.

Although you may not have a lot of time to talk about yourself, you can always establish your authority by referring to your relevant background and expertise. And never forget: failing to establish your expertise early in the game allows someone else to get the attention.

## *Taking authority and obedience too far*

Conforming to authority can be very appealing because you don't have to think. After the person at the helm gives an order, those under his command often stop thinking and start doing as they're told, even if they suspect the person in charge may be wrong, and regardless of the consequences.

*Blind obedience* to questionable activity can lead to dire consequences. Examples abound within corporations, professional firms, political parties, the medical field and any group or organisation where someone in a position of power and influence lays down the rules. The fall of major organisations such as RBS, Lehman Brothers and Arthur Andersen each shows how persuasive techniques combined with blind obedience to authority can create horrible results.

*Blind obedience* can be defined as complying with instructions without applying your personal values, morals, reason or logic to the request and potential consequences. A person acts out of ideological compulsion, obeying with neither need nor want of reason. *Deferring to authority* implies that a person understands that certain authority figures (such as judges, the police and doctors) have earned the right to exercise their power and influence. When a person defers to authority he takes into account his values and reason, and chooses to go ahead with the person's request.

# Playing Up Exclusivity

Research consistently shows that the less available an item or an opportunity, the more valuable the commodity becomes:

- Tell your colleague that he has a limited amount of time to finish a project before the contract's cancelled or given to someone else, and watch him spring into action.

- Inform a client that his favourite product is about to be discontinued, and watch the cheque book come out.

- Invite your most valued customers to a pre-sale discount shopping day, and watch them flock through your doors.

Limited time, limited offers and once-in-a-lifetime opportunities persuade people that it's a case of now or never.

## Seeking uniqueness

When you want to persuade someone to purchase your product or buy in to your ideas, highlight the unique benefits or exclusivity of what you're offering.

The more unique, beneficial and exclusive your proposition, the more inviting it is. The less available a product, service or piece of information, the more valuable it becomes:

**Book IV**

**Increasing Productivity and Performance**

- Red carpets, velvet ropes and tuxedo-clad bouncers at the entrance to a new club tell you that not just any Tom, Dick or Harry is allowed to enter. Potential customers perceive the venue as exclusive, making them long to be inside even more.

- In spite of the hype, diamonds aren't rare. However, the number of diamonds on the market at any one time is limited. Since the 1960s, a small group of companies has controlled how many diamonds are mined and where they're sold. Making diamonds difficult to purchase increases their desirability. The marketing slogan 'Diamonds are forever' encourages owners to keep their gems rather than sell them to others, which ensures new markets for additional diamonds.

✔ By limiting the number of popular handbags such as Hermès' Birkin bag, companies find that customers are willing to wait months for the chance to pay thousands to own one.

The same principles extend to information. For example, if your boss tells you something that's going to become public knowledge next week, you feel more in the know and ahead of the game than others in your department. Your manager, having shared something exclusive with you – something that may possibly benefit your career – can expect to be able to influence your behaviour in return.

Even dry and dull information, as long as it's not broadly available and supports your initiative, can be effective to share with others. When you position the information as exclusive, it becomes more persuasive than data that's widely available. If someone's unimpressed with your information or questions its exclusivity, you can assure them that what you're saying is true. If they still don't believe you, it's their loss.

Only make offers of exclusive information or opportunities to act now or lose out forever when the offer is legitimate. To do otherwise is dishonest and disingenuous, and ultimately backfires. Deceived colleagues will quickly pull away from offers that once captured them, and they will have no compunction regarding treating you as dishonestly as you treated them.

## Avoiding losses

When making economic decisions large and small, people prefer avoiding loss to acquiring gains. Studies indicate that if you tell people what they'll lose if they don't follow a particular course of action, you're more likely to persuade them than if you tell them what they stand to gain.

Noted behavioural researchers Amos Tversky and Daniel Kahneman were the first to examine and report this notion of *loss aversion*. Among many other findings, their research shows that inexperienced investors prematurely sell stocks that have done well because they don't want to lose any of their gains. In addition, because the investors want to avoid any potential for loss, they hold onto stocks that have lost value because to sell means losing on their investments officially and irretrievably. This uninformed practice often results in further losses.

When you want to persuade your team or customers to follow a certain course of action, point out what they'll lose if they don't act on the information you give them. For example, if you want to persuade your colleagues to work with you on a specific assignment, point out what they'll lose in terms of opportunities and experience if they don't go along with you – as well as what they stand to gain if they do.

# Chapter 9

# Perfecting the Art of Delegation

............................................................

## In This Chapter

▶ Accepting that you don't have to do everything

▶ Getting someone else to help you

▶ Recognising which tasks you can delegate, at home and work

▶ Mastering your delegation technique

............................................................

*H*owever much you've got to do, at some point you have to admit that you can't do everything yourself. In other chapters you'll find ways to organise all your day-to-day tasks more effectively. But as explained in this chapter, sometimes it's better to let someone else do the work for you.

Delegating is one of the key skills to master so that you can make better use of your time. You only have so many hours in your day, so if you haven't got enough time to get everything done then find someone else to do certain things for you. The more you learn to effectively delegate, the more time you free up to focus on other important tasks.

Your workload is limited by the amount of hours you have available – increase the number of hours and you increase your productivity and what you can achieve each day. One hour of your own effort achieves one hour of results. Delegate a task and one hour of effort can achieve several hours of results.

## Letting Go

You may be quite happy to let someone else help you out and do some of your work, or you may have trouble letting go of parts of your workload. Some people find it easier to delegate than others.

Reasons why you don't delegate perhaps include:

✔ No one else can do it as well as me. They won't do it right. If you want something done properly, you do it yourself.

✔ It takes too long to show someone else how to do it.

✔ If someone else does the work for me, I'll lose control of the job.

✔ I particularly enjoy this task, even if it's not the best use of my time.

✔ If I'm constantly busy I feel important and indispensable.

If you want to get more done, then delegate more – don't try to keep control of everything.

Delegation is good for other people. Your team members benefit as you develop their skills and abilities, motivation, and responsibility. The more you do, the more you improve your leadership and delegation skills. Don't micro-manage people – give them responsibility for their own work.

And don't be put off delegating just because you think that the other person isn't good enough. Give people a chance and don't expect them to get it right first time. It's worth it in the long-run when you gain an extra two hours each week to work on something that needs your undivided attention.

# Asking for Help

You don't need to do everything, although many people feel that they 'should' and don't ask for help when they need it – preferring to flounder on until it's too late or they crumble under the weight of everything they're trying to do.

One of the problems many people face is knowing when to ask for help. No one can cope with everything single-handed, so don't see asking for help as a sign of weakness. You have your own skills and abilities, other people have theirs, so make effective use of both. Stick to what you're good at and let other people do what they're good at.

Here are some signs that you need to ask for help:

✔ You're working long hours and feel you've taken on too much.

✔ You've exhausted your resources dealing with a particular problem.

✔ You're a perfectionist and feel overwhelmed trying to create a perfect solution.

You may see yourself as being reliable, capable, and able to cope with everything that your boss asks you to do or that life has to throw at you. You just get on and do things – keeping yourself busy, moving forward, juggling work, life, children, partners, friends and family. The British approach is to soldier bravely on, not admitting that a helping hand may actually be needed.

Be brave. Put your hand up if you need help – whether that's from friends, family, or a professional.

# Getting Systems in Place

In any given day you perform a number of tasks – making phone calls, sending emails, writing, data entry, meeting clients and customers – whatever is relevant to your work. Are you able to describe to someone else what it is you do? If not then you're not going to be able to delegate that task very easily. You probably don't even think about most of what you do, you just do it automatically, but would someone else know how to do it if she wasn't shown how?

Writing things down not only makes it easier to hand tasks over to someone else but is a good way to check that things are being done efficiently. What documents and checklists do you use to track your progress?

You can document what you do as you go along. As work comes in, think about all the different steps you take to process it and the various references you use. Write it all down. While you want to make life easy for yourself and better manage your time by delegating certain tasks, don't make life more difficult for the person you're delegating to.

For example, if you want someone to do your accounts, then you need to have a system for him to work with to make it easy to hand this task over. Although it does happen, no one's going to be impressed by being handed a carrier bag of receipts at the end of the year. At least put them in a different file or folder for each month and keep *all* your receipts and invoices together.

**Book IV**

**Increasing Productivity and Performance**

# Knowing What to Delegate

To be successful and effective at delegating – delegate the right tasks, at the right time, to the right people. You save yourself time by being spot on when you delegate a given task so you don't have to go back and re-delegate it.

## *Remembering the do's and don'ts*

Having established you need help and identified what you need help with, don't just dump all your jobs on to someone else. You can't delegate everything. You're always going to need to keep control of certain tasks yourself.

Do delegate:

- When you're not the best person for the job.
- Tasks that someone else can do faster, better, and cheaper than you can.
- Tasks you don't like doing yourself and that aren't your main skill set.
- Your routine tasks – freeing you up to do more complex or important tasks.
- Jobs for which you're overqualified – for example, if you're a highly paid executive why would you spend your time answering the phone rather than doing your job?
- Tasks to another department that's better able to handle the job or whose responsibility it is – for example, the human resources department can handle recruitment, and customer services may deal with customer problems and queries.
- Any tasks for which you need specialist advice – you may think that you can do it yourself but in the long run you save time and money if you get someone in with the skills to do the job in the first place.

Don't delegate:

- Anything that's confidential in nature – for example, keep personnel issues like hiring, firing, and pay-related issues as your responsibility.
- Tasks that are critical for you to do yourself.
- To someone who clearly isn't able to do the task – you're setting the person and yourself up for failure, which just reinforces the reason you didn't want to delegate in the first place.

## *Sharing the burden at work*

Don't fall into the trap of feeling you need to do everything at work. Delegating can be a useful way of freeing up more time.

- **Accounts:** If you have to do your own accounts and this is something you don't have time for or resist doing, get a bookkeeper or accountant.

Paying them for a couple of hours' work, once a month is a far better use of your time. They have the knowledge and experience and can do it faster and do a far better job than you.

✔ **Admin:** Most offices have an admin assistant to carry out routine tasks such as photocopying, printing, filing, data entry, taking calls, booking travel, and making meeting arrangements. Even if you work for yourself why not consider employing an admin assistant for a couple of hours a week? You don't need to have one full time and it would free you up to do other things.

Use *Virtual Assistants* – professionals who work from home for other businesses. They can handle all your admin requirements without the need to be there in person. They have a variety of skills depending on the work you want them to do – call handling, email, invoicing, word processing, spreadsheets, editing, presentations, and research.

✔ **Creative:** You may want to create your own website from scratch but do you really have the time to sit down and learn Frontpage, html code, and all about FTP? Get in a professional. The same applies to graphic design – even though you may be able to knock something up on your word processor with a few clip-art images, it's worth paying a professional.

✔ **Technical:** Don't waste time trying to deal with a technical issue. Pick up the phone and get in an expert – if you have an in-house IT department that's what they're there for.

## Getting help at home

If you want to enjoy your 'down' time more, you have plenty of opportunities to delegate tasks around the home by involving the rest of the family or getting someone in.

✔ **Chores:** Rope in the family to help out with the household chores. Plenty of small jobs can be done in exchange for pocket money or taxi duties. You don't have to do all the washing, ironing, and cooking yourself. Even small children can be given simple tasks to do that saves you having to do them – such as putting their toys away at the end of the day.

✔ **Cleaning:** Paying someone to come in and clean your house once a week for a couple of hours is worth its weight in gold (and so are good cleaners). Think about your hourly rate. How much do you earn, and how much would it cost you to pay someone to do your housework once a week? It frees you up to enjoy your space without feeling that your evenings and weekends need to be taken up with keeping the housework under control. You can keep on top of things more easily if the basics have been dealt with. It's much easier to keep a clean house tidy.

✔ **DIY:** We all know what a great nation of DIYers the Brits are, but how much time does it take to do even a simple thing, like painting a room? First you have the preparation time when you clear the room and wash down the walls; then you have the priming, painting, and woodwork; and finally tidying up and putting everything back. That can easily take up a whole weekend, so why not pay someone to come in and do it for you? He can do a much more professional job, far quicker than you and the cost is well worth the benefit of having a whole weekend to yourself.

Why not pay someone to come and finish up all the odd jobs you've been meaning to get around to for months? Half plastered walls, leaky taps, new plug sockets – a handyman (or woman) can get all these jobs done and out of the way in just a few hours. What you pay to get the work done is worth it for the time, effort, and energy you save, and not having the stress of half-finished jobs lying around.

✔ **Gardening:** Although you may enjoy gardening, you probably don't have too much time – other than at the weekends when you have plenty of other things that you'd like do, one of which is enjoying your garden rather than working on it. Consider paying someone to come in once a week to mow the lawn or once a month for a couple of hours to tidy things up.

Establish routines around the house – laundry gets done on certain days and needs to be in the wash basket or it doesn't get done. Blitz one room a week to keep it under control. Employ the principle of little and often to stop things piling up.

# Understanding How to Delegate

Here are some essential tips for successful delegation.

## Planning in advance

Don't dump stuff on people just because you haven't got round to doing it yourself – that's poor time management and not the way to delegate. If you want someone else to do something for you then let her know about it as soon as possible.

If you give a piece of work to someone, she may need to adjust her priorities, drop a piece of work, or delegate to someone else. Be aware of this when you make a request and don't expect your colleague to drop everything just for you.

## *Delegating appropriately*

Find the person with the right experience, skills, knowledge, and time to do the task. Ask yourself how does he work, what are his long-term goals, what sort of person is he, and is he the right person for the job? Are you delegating internally to someone else in your team or department, or externally to another professional or outside company?

When you involve the services of a professional outside of your business (or home) get a variety of prices and recommendations from friends – don't choose purely based on price. Take into account their experience, training, and professional membership.

## *Giving instructions*

When you give someone work to do, be clear about what it is you want done and when you need it done by – be specific.

- ✔ **What** outcome or results do you expect?
- ✔ **When** do you need it completed? Give a specific date.
- ✔ **How** would you like the work done, and what feedback and updates do you need along the way?
- ✔ **Why** is the work important? What are the benefits or pay-off?

Put things in writing, so you're both clear on the job description, which means less margin for error and misunderstanding.

Engage the delegated person in the process and let her know what's expected and what she can get out of it – such as recognition, promotion, financial reward, or more responsibility.

Say thank you and show your appreciation to the person helping you. People benefit from verbal encouragement and praise just as much as getting a bonus at the end of the year.

Be patient as you delegate. Whenever you delegate, you need to spend time showing someone what you want. This is time well spent as once you've spent that initial training and learning time, your colleague can then get on with the task the next time. Although you may be able to do it faster yourself, that's only because you know how to do it and you've been doing it for years. You had to learn at some point, so appreciate that others need to go through a learning curve too.

**Book IV**

**Increasing Productivity and Performance**

Show, tell, do. Repeat as many times as necessary. Get the delegated person to explain the task back to you, so you know that she's understood. Make sure that you give her all the resources necessary to get the job done – don't hold back.

Finally, make yourself available to answer any questions and provide support where necessary. Don't drop a task on someone and then run away. If she gets it wrong it may be because you haven't explained it clearly.

## Managing the delegated task

As part of your daily planning, follow up on tasks you've delegated. Keep track on the progress of the work without micro-managing the person at every step. Staying involved with the task increases the person's motivation and means you stay in control and can adjust as you go.

Put a reminder in your diary for when you want the work done and give yourself and the other person some leeway. You may want to chase her up a couple of days before you need the work so that she's still got time to get it done, if she hasn't finished it. You've then got time to review the work and give it back to her if there's still more to do or corrections need to be made.

Set certain parameters around the task – identify the other person's boundaries of responsibility and how much authority she has to get the task done. Maintain control and responsibility for the task as a whole. The buck stops with you. The other person needs to know that your support is there if she needs it while being able to get on with the task.

Communication and feedback along the way form an important part in correctly managing a delegated task.

## Achieving the best result

Don't focus on the process but the results. Be open to change. Just because you've always done something in a certain way doesn't mean that it's the only way to do it. If you've delegated a task to someone, let him use her skills and abilities to do it in her own way, as long as the end result is what you want and on time.

Review the task when it's been completed. Don't just accept a piece of work if it's not right. Provide the delegated person with feedback so that she knows she got it right, or what she needs to do to improve next time.

Be patient and don't just give up if the results are less than perfect. Stick with it – delegating really does make a difference to managing your time more effectively.

# Chapter 10

# Organising Your Time and Your Tasks

*In This Chapter*

▶ Planning how to spend your time

▶ Breaking time into productive blocks

▶ Establishing which tasks you need to do, and in what order

▶ Ticking off your tasks on action lists and checklists

▶ Removing the clutter from your work space

*I*n this chapter we show you ways to structure and organise your time in the most effective way so that you get focused but also remain flexible. If you can't do everything, you need to know how to identify your most important tasks and what needs to be done first.

In this chapter you discover how to tackle those never-ending to-do lists and create something that's more realistic, productive, and actually works.

## Structuring Your Time

Successful time management isn't rocket science; it goes hand in hand with effectively organising your time. The following sections help you think about the best ways to plan and spend your time.

### Creating blocks of time

Divide your day into blocks of time. Not only does doing this make it easier to plan and organise your day in advance, you also make better use of your time. Focusing on one task at a time is much more efficient than switching from one task to another as things pop into your head.

If you have regular tasks that you do every week, block out the same time each week. For example, if you do your accounts on a weekly basis, block out an hour or so on a Friday morning or Monday afternoon, or book time out a couple of days before the end of the month.

### Setting aside communication time

Create blocks of time in which you handle communications – emails and outgoing phone calls. Don't fall into the trap of tackling emails and calls in dribs and drabs, otherwise you get sucked into spending longer than you intended. Set aside designated time, lay down a time limit, and stick to it.

Although it's not usually practical to set aside blocks of time for incoming calls, you can minimise the disruption of the constant brrrring. Switch on your answerphone or turn off your mobile for the time when you need to focus, then return calls later (during your designated time for making outgoing calls).

Book IV Chapter 12 gives you much more detail on how to deal with your emails quickly and easily.

### Blocking out focused time

Some jobs, such as writing a report or proofreading a newsletter, require your complete concentration. To ensure that you can give the task the attention it requires, block out time in your diary.

If you just leave doing a task to when you feel like it, you find other things take priority. But if you've already scheduled in the time for the task, there's less reason to put it off or be interrupted by other work coming in. Your time is already committed.

If you need some quiet, creative time, go somewhere different, away from the distractions of your normal workspace. For example, getting up early and working from home for a couple of hours enables you to get more done away from the distractions of the office.

### Factoring in circumstances

Unless you're clairvoyant, you can't plan for every eventuality. For example:

- ✔ Your boss turns up and asks you to do an urgent piece of work by the end of the day.
- ✔ You come up against a problem and it takes time to fix. For example, your computer crashes just at the critical moment and you lose everything you've been working on. You have to wait a day or so for the repair, or you have to rely on your backups. (You do back up, don't you?

✔ A report you're writing needs a vital piece of information and you can't get hold of the person who can provide it because he or she is away on holiday until next week.

✔ You get a call reminding you about a piece of work you'd forgotten about and you need to get it done now.

✔ You underestimate how long a task takes.

In addition, bear the following in mind when blocking out time in your diary:

✔ When you book a meeting in your diary, the time involved isn't just about the meeting itself. You may have preparation work to do, travel time, and after the meeting, follow-up and minutes or a report to produce. Block out time for both pre- and post-meeting work as well as the event itself.

✔ Be aware of the energy requirements of different days (see the following section 'Working with your natural tendencies'). If you've had an intense day of meetings, book in some time for admin work or for catching up. Training courses and workshops can be mentally and physically demanding – whether you're the one giving them or participating.

✔ When you get back from holiday, set aside at least the first half-day for dealing with your emails and paperwork, otherwise you fall straight back into work mode and never catch up. Try not to book up a heavy day of meetings for your first day back, so that you have time to catch up or check in with your staff or colleagues.

Your aim is not to have a full diary. You can guarantee that if you've allocated all your time, your boss comes along with a high priority task and you then need to drop everything and re-jig your plans to fit the new work in. You need space between your blocks of time, not only for unexpected tasks but for breaks too. Don't try to cram too much in on one day.

## *Working with your natural tendencies*

We all like to work in different ways. When planning your time, work to your strengths and create a structure that best fits your natural tendencies.

Know when your most productive time of day is and when you prefer doing certain types of tasks and plan around those times:

✔ **Early bird:** Some people work best first thing in the morning, which can be a good time for creativity. If you find you're more efficient and productive in the morning, use the morning to do tasks that require you to be at your best or need your concentration. Don't set aside time to work

**Book IV**

**Increasing Productivity and Performance**

on a complex report or something that requires your concentration in the afternoon when you're more likely to hit the post-lunch slump, or in the evening when you're tired.

Try getting up an hour or so earlier to make the best use of your productive time of day. But don't burn the candle at both ends and go to bed late as well!

✔ **Night owl:** Some people get steadily more alert and effective as the day goes on. Perhaps you struggle to get going in the morning and feel as if you're just ticking over, but are turbo-charged after lunch and into the evening. You may find you focus best late at night, when it's quiet. If this is you, plan your day around your tendencies. Don't try getting up at 6 a.m. to write a report if you know you can do it better and quicker at 2 p.m.

Also think about how the week pans out for you. Certain days of the week may make better sense when scheduling in particular tasks. For example, you may hit the ground running on a Monday morning but be ready to go home by Thursday. Alternatively, you may find you have a peak of activity on a Friday when you're keen to clear things out at the end of the week and go home with a clean slate.

Try not to fight your natural tendency to schedule work when you feel at your best. If you're tied to traditional office hours then when you start and finish work may not be entirely your decision. But many employers now offer more flexible working patterns, and you can choose how you spend your time before and after work. Of course, if you work for yourself you have more flexibility around when you work.

## Doing varied tasks, little and often

Your mind can easily become bored if you spend too long on a particular task. So don't plan to sit down for hours on end focusing on just one task in a long, intense session. Break a task down into small bites and work through little and often.

The longer you spend doing one thing, the more ineffective you actually become. You're more efficient and productive when you do short bursts of activity:

✔ You won't get so distracted if you know you've only got a limited amount of time on which to work on a task.

✔ Time out during a task refreshes you. Your mind has a chance to process things and you can come up with new thoughts and solutions, particularly if you have a difficult problem to deal with or a mental block.

✔ Having a time limit – such as 10, 20, or 30 minutes – can increase the rate at which you work, so you actually get more done.

✔ Working on a difficult or odious task for just a short period of time doesn't seem as bad as having to do it all in one go!

And while you're blocking out short amounts of time for tasks, you can also introduce a bit of variety to spice up your day. Injecting a bit of variety into your everyday work helps you keep interested, energetic, and motivated.

Consider the following ideas:

✔ Mix high-energy or intense tasks with something less demanding. Work hard, and then sit back a bit. Spread out your energy.

✔ Switch from a task that requires you to be analytical to one that requires you to work more creatively. Think about engaging the left and right sides of your brain as you work. You'll find you're able to focus better.

✔ Can you do the same thing in a different location? Working from home or working at a different office from time to time can add variety to your working environment, keeping your mind stimulated.

## Scheduling in 'me time'

Spending all day sitting at your desk, hunched over your computer keyboard, or with the phone attached to your head, leaves you tired, both physically and mentally.

Include breaks in the structure of your day:

✔ Do some stretches.

✔ Step away from your desk and walk around the office, or even better, get outside for some fresh air.

✔ Grab a healthy snack or a drink of water.

✔ Take some quiet time and just relax.

Building 'me time' into your day is just as important as fitting in the million and one jobs you have to do.

## Organising Your Tasks

The following sections have one key, unifying theme – lists. Forget relying on your memory to tell you everything you need to do, or working amid piles of scribbled to-do lists – in the following sections, I show you how using simple lists helps you to manage your workload effectively.

**Book IV**

**Increasing Productivity and Performance**

## Binning to-do lists

If you're like most people, you have a to-do list. Your list likely consists of an A4 sheet of paper (or several) or perhaps a document on your computer. You continually add tasks to the list and occasionally cross things off.

Actually I don't like using to-do lists and I suspect others don't either. Such lists can be a bit of a double-edged sword. Although they're a useful tool when used correctly – and they create structure in a busy day – the items on the list have a tendency to be things you *want* to do and not things that actually get done.

Your to-do list then becomes a source of frustration and stress. You constantly add tasks, and end up demoralised and overwhelmed as the list grows longer and longer and you never seem to get to the end of it.

My advice? Ditch the to-do list, and instead, use action lists (see the following sections). An *action list* comprises tasks you're going to action rather an endless list of jobs that you'd get round to . . . if only you had the time.

## Deciding what belongs on your action list

Identify your overall goals – both personal and business. When putting together an action list, you need to keep a close eye on how tasks fit in with your goals. By focusing on your goals you can identify the important tasks and ignore the trivial tasks that are likely to lead you off in the wrong direction or distract you from your main purpose.

Ask yourself what you want to achieve in the next week or the next month. Then take each task in turn, and ask how it fits with your goals for the short and long term.

Your lists need to be manageable. One thing is certain – you're never going to be able to do everything on your list if you just keep adding to it. There really aren't enough hours in the day. Don't give yourself a hard time and set unrealistic expectations about what you're capable of doing in the time available.

Get into the habit of reviewing and updating your lists regularly. Otherwise they end up becoming useless and more of an effort than an effective tool if they're forgotten or ignored.

## Prioritising your tasks

It's rarely possible to get everything done that you'd like to, so you have to make choices about what you need to work on. When you have a limited amount of time available you make a choice about what to work on immediately and what to leave until later – you *prioritise* your tasks.

You may choose to reorganise your filing system because it'll make finding things easier and you'll have a great sense of satisfaction when it's done. However, if you've chosen to do this instead of doing the report that your boss needs by the end of the day, you need to rethink your priorities.

Prioritising your tasks is essential. However many tasks you have on your list, you can establish a logical order in which they need to be done.

Putting things off is a common reason for inefficiency. Well, prioritising blows procrastination out of the water. You have to tackle those important tasks first, rather than put them off in favour of easier, more enjoyable ones.

### Finding a method that suits you

Develop a method to organise your tasks in order of importance. Keep things simple with just three or four levels of priority.

You can split up tasks by using different systems such as:

- ✔ Must do, need to do, can do.
- ✔ High, Medium, Low.
- ✔ 1, 2, 3.
- ✔ A, B, C.
- ✔ Red, Amber, Green.

Don't make *all* your tasks high priority. Unless you've only got three things on your list, you won't manage to do them all.

Recognise the difference between an urgent task and an important task that shouts very loudly. For example, say you have three reports to write. Report A is due in two days and you haven't started it yet – that's *urgent*. Report B is due in two weeks and is *important* to a client your company is working with. Report C is also due in two weeks, but a colleague keeps asking for updates and pushing you to get on with it. Stick to your guns and do Report A first because that's the most urgent task. B and C are equally important but as your colleague is chasing C, you may decide to work on that one next.

When trying to decide how crucial a task is, don't belittle the important things in your life like your partner, family, friends, and your health. Make sure that you're prioritising time for them too.

### Working down the hierarchy

After you prioritise your tasks, you can work through them in order:

1. Always try to do the highest priority tasks first. Don't leave them to the last minute – get them out of the way as soon as possible.

2. Make sure that once you've cleared the *urgent* tasks you start to spend more of your time working on the *important* tasks. If you make this switch then they won't become urgent in the first place.

3. Finally, when you've ticked off the urgent and important tasks, tackle the unimportant tasks. These are your lower priority tasks.

Generally, you work through tasks in this order. However, don't feel constrained by your prioritised list. Sometimes, in the course of your working day, you can pick and mix tasks. For example, you may check emails before making an important phone call because the person isn't yet in the office.

The important thing to remember is that, at the end of the day, you must have completed *all* the high priority tasks you scheduled for that day. If you didn't, you need to ask yourself what stopped you:

✔ Did you prioritise the task correctly? If not, can you see where you went wrong and remedy it for the next time?

✔ Were you distracted or interrupted?

✔ Did you simply put the task off? Had this task become high priority because you've left it to the last minute?

At the other end of the list, you may find that you're not getting through the lower priority tasks. Don't worry – these trivial tasks have a natural tendency to become even less important and can finally be crossed off the list all together. Let the natural course of time dictate what falls off the bottom of the list. Anything serious or urgent finds its way to the top of the list.

As you get better at prioritising you'll start to recognise certain tasks that you're just not going to have time for and they won't even make it onto the list.

## Setting up action lists

Avoid *listitis* – creating lists for the sake of it. You may feel as though you're being organised, but not if you don't actually do anything with the list. Rather than having different lists scattered all over the place, stick to just two lists: a Master List and a Daily Action List.

### Creating your Master List

Your Master List helps you to keep track of everything you want to get done. Put all the daily, weekly, and monthly actions on your Master List, as well as tasks and projects for the future that are part of your longer-term goals.

Write things down on your Master List as a placeholder and a reminder for things that don't need doing immediately.

Table 10-1 shows an example of a Master List.

| Table 10-1 | Master Action List |
|---|---|
| **Task** | |
| Check emails (daily) | |
| Follow-up with all clients | |
| Update website | |
| Complete monthly newsletter | |
| Develop new project | |
| Update account | |
| Update tax information | |
| Complete audit | |
| Organise clients' files | |
| Sort through filing tray | |
| Read industry publications (weekly) | |
| Book up seminar | |
| Arrange training course for Q3 | |
| Carry out staff annual assessments | |

When your Master Lists gets too messy, or when most of the actions have been transferred, completed, or have become redundant, then rewrite it. It helps to keep the list fresh and easier to work with.

### Making a Daily Action List

The aim of a Daily Action List is that you're actually going to tick off every single item. For your action list to work, you need to be sensible when estimating how long each task will take (don't worry; this comes with experience).

Make time for a planning session each morning. Refer to your Master List and pick out the things you're going to get done that day. Write your tasks on your Daily Action List.

Don't make the mistake of listing out 20 things you need to do and then realising that they can take anything from 30 minutes to an hour to complete. Be realistic; you just don't have enough time in the day for everything. If you only have five things on your list and you cross them all off, that's far more effective, satisfying, and sensible than having a list of 20 items and only doing half of them. Action lists are all about getting away from the traditional, endless to-do list.

Table 10-2 shows a sample Daily Action List.

| Table 10-2 | Sample Daily Action List | |
|---|---|---|
| *Task* | *Priority* | *Time* |
| Check emails | 2 | 1 hour |
| Call John at xyz Company | 1 | 15 minutes |
| Order new supplies | 1 | 30 minutes |
| Finish Monthly Report | 2 | 2 hours |
| Prepare presentation | 2 | 1 hour |
| Write article | 3 | 2 hours |
| Collect dry cleaning | 2 | 30 minutes |

Note that the 'Priority' column helps you decide the order in which you need to do the jobs (see the earlier section 'Prioritising your tasks'). The 'Time' column gives you an idea of how long each task takes (see the earlier section 'Structuring your time').

Your list doesn't have to be just about work; after all, you can't always get your personal actions done outside of the 9–5 slot. Include everything you need to do in the day.

Keep referring to your Daily Action List throughout the day. Make sure that you complete the most important tasks by the end of each day. Don't get distracted if something new comes up during the day – jot it down on the Master List rather than adding it to your Daily Action List.

## Creating checklists

In addition to crossing off the tasks on your Master and Daily Action Lists (see the preceding section), creating checklists for general and regular tasks helps you get organised, focused, and on track. Ticking off jobs gives you a sense of achievement and progression.

Create a template checklist on your computer. The advantage of using a computer-based template is that many of your tasks are the same from day to day or week to week. You can manage the checklist on your computer, or better still, print out the list and tick things off by hand. There's something quite satisfying about putting pen to paper.

Table 10-3 is a very simple checklist for a week. Simply tick off the tasks as you complete them.

| Table 10-3 | Sample Weekly Checklist | | | | | |
|---|---|---|---|---|---|---|
| *No* | *Task* | *M* | *T* | *W* | *T* | *F* |
| 1 | Accounts | ✔ | | | | ✔ |
| 2 | Emails | ✔ | ✔ | ✔ | ✔ | ✔ |
| 3 | Filing | ✔ | ✔ | | | ✔ |
| 4 | Weekly report | | | | ✔ | |
| 5 | Clear inbox | ✔ | ✔ | ✔ | ✔ | |

You can use similar checklists for your regular monthly tasks.

An erasable whiteboard can be a useful, larger, more visual reminder and planning tool. Try dividing into different sections:

✔ Blogs

✔ Business

✔ Calls

✔ Emails

✔ Finance

✔ Personal

The headings stay the same from week to week, but the actions change. At the beginning of the week write up all the weekly actions and then update it each day, crossing out or erasing the tasks you complete.

Create sections that are relevant to the way you work and under each section write your actions on a daily basis. If you don't have a whiteboard, a large sheet of paper on a notice board does the job.

Give yourself a reward at the end of the week if you manage to tick off all your tasks. These don't have be big rewards but the equivalent of a gold star – a little time for yourself at the end of the day, leaving work early.

# Investing Your Time Instead of Spending It

Average salespeople often spend their time foolishly doing unproductive 'busywork' – and then they wonder where their day went, why they accomplished so little, and why they never seem to have time for the fun stuff they'd really like to do or enough money to buy the lifestyle they wish for. The key word in that sentence is *spend*: they *spent* their time instead of *investing* it. And doing so makes all the difference.

The words *spending* and *investing* connote very different ideas. When you spend money, you probably think of the loss of that money rather than the benefits you'll enjoy from whatever it was you spent your money on. On the other hand, the word *invest* signifies a payment from which you will derive a return; you don't focus on the momentary loss of money, but rather on the gain of the product or service that you will receive. Similarly, when you spend your time instead of investing it, you focus on lost time rather than on personal gain.

If you've never put a monetary value on your time before, do it now. To determine what your time is worth, take your hourly rate and follow this simple equation:

Gross Income/Total Annual Working Hours = Hourly Rate

To see the value of this equation, suppose that your annual income is £30,000 and you work 40 hours a week for 48 weeks a year (allowing 4 weeks off for holidays). That means that the value of each hour in your working week is £15. In straight-commission sales, if you spend just one hour each day of each working week on unproductive activity, you spend about £3,750 a year on nothing. And that's exactly what you have to show for your wasted time, too – nothing. When you choose not to manage your time, you may end up wasting 12 per cent of your annual income or more. And this amount doesn't even account for all the future business you lost because you spent time instead of investing it. If you're a regular, full-time employee, that £3,750 is money your employer may as well burn for all the productivity they get for it.

# Beware of Fluffy Time!

We need to warn you about a killer disease infecting almost every business start-up, small business, and salesperson alike. This insidious disease creeps in and slowly suffocates you without you really noticing. Worse, it even makes you feel like it doesn't exist and gradually poisons you to death. Beware of fluffy time disease!

What does the fluffy time disease look like? Well, it starts with a salesperson getting ready to launch her new venture. She thinks of all the things that have to be done, such as logo design, stationery print, and office establishment, then getting furniture for the office and buying computers and phones, and so on. She's busy focusing on what's called *creation of product*. Then she refines the creation of product. Then she does some more planning and some talking and some meetings with people who might be helpful/useful one day. And then an awareness of needing income creeps in and provides a gentle push into creating some enquiries, but that needs adverts, so that needs planning and design, so that consumes more time.

Do you see the picture gradually unfolding? You always have an abundance of stuff to do and your 'to do' list can never be completed. Somewhere among the action, though, has to be income generation. You have to go and sell something! Fluffy time is consumed every day with everything that is seemingly needed but really is not. Fluffy time is those phone calls, or those moments (that become hours) when you're planning (thinking or daydreaming?). And those days when you plan to leave the house at 9 a.m. but actually do so after 10; when you mean to be really proactive until you open your e-mail box and are consumed for three hours dealing with replies and following links in the name of finding out; when you decide to make some phone calls to generate leads but don't really know who to phone so sit and make a target list that takes three hours because the data is all over the place.

# Making Time to Plan Time

People who don't practise effective time management often complain that they don't have time to plan their time. But if you don't make time for planning and self-improvement, you may as well plan to earn the same income that you earn today for the rest of your life. By taking the time to plan, you save as much as 20 to 30 times the amount of time that you expend in the planning process.

In the following sections, we go into more depth on categorising your activities.

## Undertaking urgent activities

Urgent activities are *only* those activities that you must complete today. If you clutter your mind with things that should be secondary activities (the things you don't have to do today), you can end up neglecting your immediate activities or not giving them the full, focused attention they require.

Ask yourself these questions to determine the immediacy of your activities and prioritise them by either the amount of relief you'll feel in getting them done or the amount of goodwill or income they'll generate:

- ✔ If I can achieve only three or four activities today, which ones should they be? What if I can only accomplish one?
- ✔ Which activities will yield the most immediate rewards?
- ✔ Which activities will complicate my day tomorrow if I do not accomplish them today?
- ✔ Which of these activities can I delegate to someone else in order to leave myself more time to generate more business or enhance my personal relationships?
- ✔ Which activities, if I postpone them, will damage my relationships with others?

Have your urgent activities in front of you at all times. If you can't see what you need to accomplish today because you've buried your urgent activities under other less important work, those activities can get lost in the shuffle and you can lose sight of your goals.

## Sorting important activities

Identifying your important group of activities is usually easier than identifying urgent ones. Some important activities may be almost-but-not-quite urgent, so put them at the top of your important activity list. As you do for immediate activities, prioritise your important list so you finish what's most important first.

Important activities may include meeting your sales manager to review your targets and to ask for help and clarification on whom best to talk to in a particular client's organisation, for example. Clarifying these details and meeting your manager are both important, but schedule them into a non-prime selling slot and with plenty of time before actually visiting the client in question.

Other important activities may be to meet a potential contact who could be a great source of referrals. Developing good relationships with these types of people is important but recognise that selling is about selling – not just looking like a salesperson. Thus you need to put selling and results first. So meet a source of referrals if they can produce immediate potential clients that might, say, be sold to over this next month or quarter, but make the meeting happen when you have a sales call already in the area.

Paperwork traps people into a belief that it must be dealt with, so they often look at it and then put it on another pile to be sorted out later. Often the paperwork then doesn't get dealt with until a lot later, and is quite possibly found to be out of date. Putting paper on another pile for the future and not getting around to it shows that you didn't actually miss it. You didn't do it and didn't lose out, so why not just throw it away in the first place? You need to develop your decision muscle. Make a habit of asking questions such as 'Do I need this now?' If the answer isn't a resounding 'Yes', then throw the piece of paper away. You'll eventually realise that your procrastination and poor decision strength only smother you with work and stress. Be ruthless and learn to throw papers away. 'Touch it once' is the motto. Pick up paperwork only once. Decide its importance and deal with it by passing it on or filing it. Don't read it and put it in a pile to be looked at again later.

## Deciding on secondary activities

Identifying which tasks fall into the secondary category is difficult: You may think everything needs your attention (if it didn't, it wouldn't come your way, right?). But such thinking simply isn't true. Other people pass many unimportant activities to you to take care of – activities that have a funny habit of working themselves out if you just give them a little time. By putting those activities in your secondary category, you may be able to avoid spending time on these chores when you need to be investing time in your immediate activities.

Secondary activities are *relatively* unimportant activities. For example, think about the number of times an associate has come to you for help with a problem, only to reveal that it wasn't your assistance she wanted after all? She just wanted you to take on the problem as yours. What begins as a favour thus ends up being a real chore. Her worries become your worries – and she's off having a relaxed two-hour lunch, knowing you'll take care of it. Or, secondary activity might be where you're planning a sales launch or marketing event such as a mini-exhibition or party and you get yourself dragged into planning the room layout or organising the catering. Doing so really isn't your job and doesn't need your valuable selling time.

## Making time for unplanned happenings

Planning your time efficiently can prevent some emergencies from happening in the first place, but always have an alternative approach to your most important activities just in case an emergency arises. Planning ahead and being prepared will keep you from panicking and completely trashing your schedule, and that of others, when emergencies do arise.

**Book IV**

**Increasing Productivity and Performance**

If you have children, you know that occasionally they're ill or get hurt, or they forget to tell you about vital events that you need to attend. If you have a whole day of report writing to get done and school phones asking you to collect your child, do you have a back-up person, such as a grandparent, who's willing to care for her? If not, organise it now. Save all your report data onto a portable memory stick so that you can grab your laptop and your daily planner, and head for the door at a moment's notice. Or e-mail your files to yourself at home so they can be waiting for you when you arrive.

Have back-up plans in place for transportation as well. If your car breaks down, does a colleague live nearby who can give you a lift in? Or if you're on a bus route, do you have a schedule handy? Do you have a taxi company's number in your address book? Better yet, do you have a few vital numbers stored in your mobile phone so that if a situation arises, wherever you are you can contact the right people? Preventing emergencies from happening isn't always possible, but you can be less of a victim and be organised so that the event passes without major fall-out.

# Accounting for Your Time

Just as you separate work tasks into three categories, you need to separate your life time zones into three areas in order to effectively organise yourself. You need to

- ✔ Investigate your yesterday.
- ✔ Analyse your today.
- ✔ Discover your tomorrow.

In the following sections, we show you how to do it.

## Investigating your past

Start by taking some time to write down what you do with each of the 168 hours in your typical week. If you're like many self-management beginners, you probably have some seriously time-wasting habits, but you can easily eliminate those habits when you become aware of them. Try to be as honest and thorough as possible.

Keep a daily record of your typical routine for seven days. Print out on separate sheets of A4 paper a daily planner from your Microsoft Outlook diary or similar. We mention Outlook because frankly we live in a Microsoft-dominated world and most people use it, but it could be the diary in another program – just choose a day per page view.

The record sheets will help you establish an accurate record of everything you actually do – including the habits you may need to change. The best way to keep such a log is to jot down the time you spend moving through your daily routine: Three hours running errands, five minutes looking for a purchase agreement, half a day scouring around for a misplaced phone message, ten minutes trying to get refocused after an interruption, and so on. After completing this time log for seven days, you'll be amazed at how much time you cannot account for and how much time you waste on relatively unimportant activities. This is the fluffy time we talked about earlier in the chapter, and seeing it visually can be a frightening exercise! In fact, you'll probably feel so guilty after only one day that you'll be tempted to fill in the blanks. You'll look at it and say, 'I know I've done more than that!' but truthfully you will have recorded what you've done, and either you haven't done much or you haven't done much of any great worth.

## Analysing your today

If you use the word *productivity* when you refer to time planning, time planning won't be such a mystery to you.

People frequently say that they just can't plan their time or that they just can't seem to keep up with everything they need to do. The answer to their time management problems is to do the most productive thing possible at every given moment.

The concept of being productive at every moment is so simple that many people don't understand it. So, no matter what you're doing, ask yourself, 'Is this the most productive thing I can do at this time?' Doing so makes you focus upon results, and productivity equals results achieved – and in selling, that is pretty much your top priority. You need to do a few simple things to answer that question:

- Keep a list of important tasks.
- Keep an appointment calendar.
- Know what your time is worth.

To increase your productivity, you must learn – by doing the most productive thing at each moment – how to increase the value of each hour. If doing so sounds simple, that's because it *is*. You increase the value of each hour by constantly asking yourself that same question: 'Is what I'm doing right now the most productive thing I can do?'

Some salespeople spend all their time getting organised and getting ready for persuasion situations that never come about. To them, getting organised itself has become the game. Sometimes people overvalue the organising stage because they're afraid of facing rejection or failure, so they hide from seeing the public. In some cases the salesperson makes organisation a focus because he lives in a misconception that you can't take action until everything is perfect. But that situation's a recipe for disaster, as we live in a very imperfect world. In most cases, though, salespeople who make organising the end rather than the means just don't appreciate the difference between productivity and organisation. To many salespeople, time planning revolves around just buying a time-planning device, program, or binder and filling in the squares. Of course, those tasks are necessary. But they're just a small part of a very big picture. Time planning actually starts with goals because setting goals is the only way you can tell what the most productive tasks are at any given moment.

## Discovering your tomorrow

Assume that your goals and priorities are in line. You know what you want and how you want to get there. Your goals are all in writing and your priorities are set. Start your daily time planning at night before you go to bed. Go through your time planner and lay out the day to come. Get a handle on your top six priorities, as well as whom you'll see or call, for the next day. Then add any personal areas you also need to cover the next day. Writing down or entering the next day's top six priorities shouldn't take more than 10 to 15 minutes. When you've mapped out the next day, forget it and go to bed.

We suggest doing next day's planning last thing at night because it helps you sleep better. Restless sleep is caused by the stress resulting from trying to remember everything you need to remember for the next day. Thus writing it all down just before you retire for the night lets the brain relax and switch off safe in the knowledge that it cannot forget because you've already sorted it.

At the beginning of the day you've just mapped out, the most productive thing possible may be a 20-minute workout at 6.00 a.m., or breakfast with your family, or working in the garden, or any of a thousand other things that may be important to you and your goals and priorities. You have many choices throughout your day. Only *you* know if what you're doing is the most productive thing in relation to the goals you want to achieve.

People grow up being told what to do for the first 20 or so years of their lives – at home, at school, and sometimes even at work. So the fact that some people lack a certain amount of self-discipline when they go into a career such as selling, which leaves people almost entirely to their own resources, isn't surprising. We'd like to have a pound for every time we've heard a salesperson say, 'I went into sales so I could be my own boss', or 'I went into sales so no one would tell me what to do', or 'I went into sales for more free time'. All those reasons are great. But the people who hold those reasons had better develop a strong degree of self-discipline for doing what needs to be done. If they don't, they'll soon be back in a job where someone's telling them what to do because being their own boss is the weak link and their productivity slumps.

To get started with an effective time-management method, don't try to plan for every minute of the day. Being inaccurate is too easy when you forecast time for task completion. Instead, start by planning just 75 per cent of your total work time. That way, you allow for interruptions, delays, and unexpected emergencies. As your work planning improves, you can increase to planning 90 per cent of your day. But never plan for 100 per cent – if you do, you won't leave room for the unexpected, and you'll just frustrate yourself when you can't accomplish your designated goals.

Remain flexible. Not much is black and white in the world of selling; many areas of grey exist. By staying flexible, you can maintain your equilibrium and move on to greater things. Don't lock yourself into a time-management programme so rigid that you don't have time for anything else.

Winners always plan their time. To increase your productivity and your income, you must plan your time like a professional. Professional salespeople are very conscious of the value of their customers' time, as well as their own. All sales professionals must make daily decisions on priorities. Some are major, some are minor – but all are factors in the management of time. Every professional salesperson needs a systematic approach to setting priorities.

Over the years, we've noticed that successful people who run large companies and build fortunes don't spend much more time working than anyone else. The difference is that they get more productivity out of each hour of every day. They don't try to do too much at once and, because they don't, they are more productive at accomplishing the day's most important goals.

# Knowing When and Where to Plan

If you want to manage your time wisely, you need a planning device of some sort. Whether you prefer the pen-and-paper route or the high-tech one, find an option that works well for you. Use contact management software that includes a calendar section so you have both your contact information and meeting schedule all in one place. Many of these programs will even flag you if you try to enter a meeting that conflicts with another event you already have scheduled, which can help you save face with clients instead of having to call them to reschedule. Some contact management software is even available online so you don't have to be concerned about your laptop crashing and losing all your valuable information. Others are customised to the specific needs of salespeople with forms for travel itineraries, charting activity and productivity, meeting notes, expense reports, and so on. Take some time to find one you think you'll be comfortable using. If you're not comfortable with it, you don't use it and you defeat your purpose of planning.

In daily time planning, keep track of *all* activities *as you go*. Don't wait until 4.00 p.m. to try to remember what you did at 9.30 a.m. Be truthful. Don't play around with numbers or fake anything just so you can check it off. And don't overwhelm yourself with writing down every detail of your working day. You're not trying to write a book. Just note the key events and any information you simply wouldn't want to forget.

Do your planning where you conduct your business. If you wait until you get home, you won't have that phone number or other detail you need to record and you'll only half-plan. If doing so means you sit in your car to plan, so be it – you're just joining the rest of us in sales where the car doubles as a second home! You may need triggers to remember everything you need to plan and those triggers are most available to you at your place of business.

# Organising Your Work Space

Disorganised office space is the most common cause of wasted time and lost income. Believe it or not, clearing your desk also helps to clear your mind. When your mind is clear, you're more able to focus on one task at a time. And all you can accomplish is one thing at a time, anyway, so why try to do more. So where do you start? Try the tips in the following sections.

## Keep only immediate activities on your desk

Keep everything but your most pressing tasks out of sight. And keep everything you need for accomplishing the immediate tasks somewhere nearby (in a place you'll remember), so you don't waste time running here and there looking for what you need. Develop two simple habits:

- Touch a paper once, dealing with it or throwing it away.
- File everything that you need but don't need now in a proper filing system.

These two simple habits can save you much time and effort.

# Take charge of your time

If you suffer innumerable interruptions, close your door. If you don't have a door, try earplugs or a headset attached to an MP3 player to isolate yourself. Maybe your company will allow you to put a sign on your door saying something along the lines of: 'Unless you are a client with a large need, or have a fantastic lead for me, please let me do what I need to do to find those people.' As a last resort, consider posting a snarling Doberman near your desk!

Develop your ability to focus on your work. Let your colleagues or family know that sometimes they simply cannot interrupt you. Don't answer your telephone – let voice mail be your receptionist for a while.

Make yourself less accessible. If you need to, set up a specific time of day for your associates to freely walk into your office; make all other times off limits. If an associate drops by at a bad time, don't be afraid to look at your watch and say, 'I'd love to catch up with you, but let's do it at 3.00.' If what he has to tell you is important enough, he'll be happy to schedule the time. If it's not that important, he'll beg off, and you'll have saved yourself from spending time listening to him.

And if interruptions from team members are an issue, we strongly recommend that you read a terrific book called *The One Minute Manager Meets the Monkey* by Ken Blanchard, published by HarperCollins Business.

# Handle phone calls wisely

If the phone is not a necessary tool of your immediate business, learn to ignore it or turn off the ring tone, or tell your colleagues that you are not in and will not be accepting calls.

Do *not* be ruled by the phone. Unless you are expecting an urgent call, turn it off and come back to messages. You won't lose out but will gain from your own feelings of self-satisfaction and accomplishment when you've successfully done lots of jobs because you stole an hour or two from a hectic day.

Also make sure that when you're actually using the phone, your conversation is relevant to the tasks ahead. If you have to take a call, manage the content of the call. Keep it on track for your business. When the other party gets off the subject, or when the other party stays on the subject but is long-winded, try these techniques:

**Book IV**

**Increasing Productivity and Performance**

✔ **If you initiate the call, tell the person, 'I have three things to cover with you'.** If he starts to get sidetracked, you have the right to bring him back to one of your three topics.

✔ **If the other party initiates the call and you don't have a lot of time to give him, let him know him call is important, but that you were just heading out the door.** He doesn't need to know it was to get a glass of water. Get the basic information he needs to tell you and make an appointment to call him back if a call back is really necessary. Unless you're dealing with an irate customer whose assembly line has completely stopped because of your equipment, most people will be willing to accept a call back. If they can't wait, it's an emergency and you'll have to handle it on the spot.

✔ **Call a known long-winded person just before lunchtime or just before he goes home for the day.** If doing so isn't possible, start your call by saying, 'I'm really pressed for time, but I just wanted to let you know something' or 'I'm on my way to an appointment, but I wanted to touch base with you'.

# Chapter 11

# Making the Most of Meetings

Meetings can be a great way of keeping track of projects, reviewing progress, solving problems, and discussing new opportunities. Meetings can include seminars, workshops, training, and any situation where more than one person is gathered in one room.

However, some meetings can be real time-wasters. This chapter guides you towards making the most of meetings and avoiding wasting time.

## Do We Really Need Another Meeting?

Before arranging or attending a meeting, consider whether it's the most effective use of everybody's time. Can the information be communicated by email or a written report? What do you actually want to get out of the meeting? Meetings need to be relevant and appropriate. Don't hold a meeting just for the sake of it and don't attend a meeting unless it's relevant to you. If in doubt, ask.

Holding a meeting means that a number of people spend a certain amount of their limited time in one place. The result can be a loss of productivity if the meeting is unhelpful. The outcome of the meeting should at least go some way to balance the input of time and effort.

# Choosing the Right Type of Meeting

If you're organising the meeting, decide on the type of meeting you need. People don't necessarily have to be in the same room in order to meet. These days teleconferencing and web conferencing can be arranged and can save a huge amount of time and money in travel when several people, or large distances, are involved.

## Face to face

If you're working in a team, face-to-face meetings can be useful. If you all work in the same office, or within a short distance from each other, a face-to-face meeting is easy to arrange.

If you're part of a work team that's located in different offices or even different countries, then organising a face-to-face meeting may be difficult. However, such meetings still need to happen in order to help team members gel with each other. Although meetings held over the phone can work, meeting face to face may be the only chance that people can get to know other members of the team.

## Tele/Web conferences

Teleconferences or web conferences enable people to meet and discuss key objectives without having to be in the same room or even the same country. Teleconferences are held as a live group call over the phone, using speakerphones at each end of the line, with or without the use of video cameras. Web conferences take place over the Internet with the use of a broadband phone connection and web cam.

Setting up team project meetings or training sessions using group conference call facilities, or over the Internet, is easy. These teleconferences can include presentations and notes online in 'classroom' format. Everyone is able to share notes and write up comments on the screen without being physically present.

Group teleconference calls don't allow for any visual cues so you need to handle these meetings carefully to ensure that everyone gets a chance to speak, that you document key points, and make follow-up actions clear.

# Planning the Meeting

When it's your responsibility to organise the meeting, before you even start arranging it, think about what you hope to achieve and put your objectives down in writing.

You need to know why you're meeting and that you're involving the right people. A successful meeting depends on selecting only the people who need to be there to achieve the overall objective.

Think carefully about who needs to be involved in the meeting when making decisions or providing the right information. Remember these considerations when planning a meeting:

- Don't invite people unnecessarily – you're just wasting their time if they don't really need to be there.

- Don't invite two people with the same roles if only one person is needed to provide the information or make decisions.

- Give people enough notice. Don't expect people to be able to attend at the drop of a hat – unless it's a real emergency. You can give a couple of days' notice for an in-house, project-based meeting or a few months for a full-day meeting, workshop, or training session. The key to managing your own, and everyone else's, time is planning – particularly when it comes to meetings.

- Decide on a suitable location, how long the meeting needs to be, and, most importantly, have an agenda.

- Confirm things ahead of time such as the meeting venue, attendees, speakers, agenda, equipment, and hand-outs. Create a checklist so that you know everything is covered and confirm all final arrangements with attendees a couple of days before.

- Get to the venue or meeting room in good time on the actual day to check everything out.

- Have a plan B in case certain key people don't turn up, or something goes wrong, or isn't working. Decide at what point it's necessary to cancel the meeting.

If you need to have a large meeting or event, get a professional event organiser involved to deal with all the logistics and to free you up to focus on other aspects of the meeting – such as the attendees and content.

# Running the Meeting

If a meeting is going to be effective, you need to run it properly.

## Agendas

*All* meetings need an agenda, no matter how big or small, short or long the meeting is. An agenda helps to keep the meeting on track and to time.

The agenda needs to include the start time, end time, and objectives and outcomes for the meeting. Send it out to everyone that's due to attend ahead of time as soon as you confirm the date (or at least a week beforehand), so people have time to prepare. If additional information is required send it out with the agenda. If you need people to bring information to the meeting or carry out any pre-work, make this clear in the agenda. Sending an agenda out also enables you to check that everyone's still able to make it.

If you're organising a workshop or seminar, people want to know the agenda in advance or at least have an overview in order to decide whether to attend.

Start on time. Even if you have a few latecomers, don't let them delay things. Don't try to cram too much into a meeting. Keep on track. The person responsible for running the meeting needs to keep to the agenda, keep to time, and bring people back on track if they go off on a tangent. Make sure that everyone gets a chance to speak, and don't let one person dominate the meeting. Leave time at the beginning and end of the meeting for introductions, discussing the agenda, and summarising the agreed follow-up actions. Always let people know when the meeting is due to finish and don't allow meetings to over-run.

Allow time for breaks and refreshments. If it's a full day's meeting don't forget that you need to provide lunch or have an appropriate break for people to get their own.

At the end of the meeting agree on the next date to meet if you need a follow-up meeting. Fixing a date with everyone in the same room is easier than spending time chasing people up afterwards.

## Taking notes

If you need to keep a record of the meeting delegate someone to take notes (or *minutes*). Depending on the type of meeting these can be formal or informal notes. If you hold regular meetings then create a template that can be used at each one thus saving time typing up the same information each time. Notes for board meetings always need a formal structure (including the date, location, and what was discussed) because these need to be kept on record.

Create handouts for the meeting to share information. Flip charts can be really useful for noting down key points, brainstorming, and capturing key actions, and can then be used to type up the notes.

Any follow-up actions coming out of the meeting need to be properly minuted with the specific action, agreed dates, and responsibilities noted.

Send out the follow-up notes as soon as possible after the meeting – certainly within a couple of days – so that any actions can be dealt with. If you need confirmation or approval of any meeting minutes or notes send out a draft first, and send the final copy after any comments or changes have been made.

If you've come away with an armful of handouts and leaflets, as soon as you get back to the office sort them into the four categories:

- ✔ Action
- ✔ Read
- ✔ File
- ✔ Bin

Don't dump the handouts into the 'leave it for later' pile – you know what happens to that!

If you agreed to do something or contact someone at a later date, put a note in your diary.

Get feedback after the meeting. Feedback provides valuable information for planning future meetings and helps you to see if the meeting met the planned objectives. Hand out a feedback form as part of the meeting agenda or follow-up with attendees after the meeting.

# Getting to Your Meetings on Time

How often do you arrive late for a meeting or find yourself rushing to arrive just in the nick of time? You can ensure that you always arrive on time for your meetings by planning sufficient time at either end.

Aim to arrive a few minutes early even for in-house or local meetings. Respect the organiser and the other attendees. Arriving early means you have a few minutes to settle yourself in and prepare what you need to say.

## Calculating travel time

If you need to travel to a meeting, start by planning backwards from your scheduled arrival time. Aim to arrive at least five to ten minutes early if the meeting is less than an hour away – whether that's on foot, by bus, train, or car.

When road or rail travel is involved you don't know what unexpected delays may occur. Delays can include heavy traffic, stopping for petrol, queues at ticket offices, and leaves on the line!

Travelling during peak commuting times means busier roads, and packed buses and trains. Longer travel times need more leeway at either end.

Many training and networking meetings usually have a half-hour time slot for registration. However, don't assume that if registration starts at 9.30 a.m. and the meeting starts at 10.00 a.m. you can arrive at 9.55 a.m.! Aim to arrive for 9.30 a.m. By the time you've parked, walked to the location, found where you're meant to be, registered, and got a cup of coffee it's probably 9.45 a.m. You now have time to talk to the other people before settling down, relaxed, and ready to start.

If you're taking the bus or train aim to catch an earlier one than you need. If you happen to miss that, you know that you've still got plan B: the second train or bus that will still get you there on time.

## Leaving in good time

Don't stress yourself out before you even begin heading off to a meeting. Make sure that you set off for your meeting in good time. If it takes you an hour to drive to the location of the meeting, leave ten minutes early.

Even if you have lots to do before you leave, don't leave things to the last minute. Give yourself a good five or ten minutes to get out of the house or office and on your journey. It may take you that long to gather all your papers together, find your keys, switch on the answer machine, find your mobile, and so on.

If you have an early start the following day, get out everything you need the night before. Put everything in your briefcase or bag that you need for the meeting ahead of time. That way you can get up and go without rushing around at the last minute.

# Networking Meetings

Business owners attend networking meetings and here you have the opportunity to talk to your colleagues and peers, develop alliances, and build your business and relationships. The meetings are often held over breakfast, so you still have a full day at work, or in the early evening so you can go straight from the office.

Hundreds of different networking groups meet around the country aimed at different types of business from small to large. More women-only networks are springing up aimed at busy working mums, so they can juggle networking with the demands of children and family.

Make sure that the events you attend relate to your business. If possible get a list of potential attendees before you arrive, so you have an idea of who's going to be there and who you want to talk to, which saves time when you get there.

If you regularly attend networking events, think about what you plan to get from the proceedings to make sure that it's an effective use of your time, such as:

- ✔ Meeting new contacts.
- ✔ Getting new ideas.
- ✔ Brainstorming with colleagues.
- ✔ Finding out about new developments.
- ✔ Developing existing relationships.
- ✔ Finding suppliers.
- ✔ Growing your business.

Networking meetings aren't about doing business. No one likes to have a sales pitch in the first few minutes of meeting you. Networking is about making connections and building relationships.

Don't give out your business card to anyone and everyone – only do so if you're asked for it and if it's relevant. Equally, don't automatically collect cards for the sake of it.

Enter the useful business cards into your contact system as soon as possible when you get back to the office. Include the date and place that you met and any relevant notes about the person and his or her business.

Send a follow-up email or phone your new contact within a couple of days of the meeting to continue your initial discussion or arrange a subsequent meeting. Add the person to your mailing list so you can keep in touch.

**Book IV**

Increasing
Productivity
and
Performance

# Chapter 12

# Dealing with Your Emails

*M*odern technology is designed to make our lives easier and to make us more productive. Email is a great way to communicate with people around the world, easily, effectively, and more quickly than the traditional methods of communication. However, emails need to be handled sensibly, so that they don't become something else that sucks up your time.

In this chapter, we take you through setting up a smooth, efficient email-processing system – from deciding when to check emails and using tools and techniques to manage messages, to dealing with the inevitable backlogs that build up when you take a break from work.

## Dedicating Time to Your Emails

Do you constantly check your inbox for new messages throughout the day? When you hear the email alert go, do you switch from whatever you're doing and go and check the latest message?

Emails can be a great time waster and provide a constant distraction throughout the day. If you're going to make the most of your day then one way to increase your productivity is to manage the amount of time you spend on emails.

## Checking your email periodically

Only check your emails every so often throughout the day – perhaps first thing, late morning, and again in the afternoon.

Set your email system to only check for new messages periodically (say every two hours or so) or disconnect yourself from the Internet except when you want to download emails. In most applications you can change the settings by clicking Tools on the top menu, and then Settings.

Emails are rarely so urgent that you need to respond to them immediately, unless an instant response is expected as part of your job.

## Setting aside time for emails

If you need to spend time responding to emails, set aside time in your schedule to do that and make sure that you put a limit on the amount of time you spend, otherwise you're likely to end up distracted and sidetracked, and spending more time than you intended.

When you're on 'email time', don't jump straight in and start responding to the first one, unless you have only a few new messages. If you have more messages than you can comfortably deal with in half an hour or so, take a few minutes to scan through and sort them into urgent/action, non-urgent, and reading.

Limit yourself to 30 minutes at a time, or work to clear the existing action emails for as long as it takes (within reason!) without addressing any new emails. Leave those until next time.

 You must factor in the expectations and needs of your clients, customers, and/or colleagues. How quickly do you really need to respond to emails? Does your work require you to respond immediately or can you wait a few hours or maybe even until the next day? If an email requires a lengthy response, send a confirmation email to let the sender know that you've received her email and will reply shortly.

# Managing Your Inbox

Find a way to control your inbox and you'll find it a lot easier to manage the volume of email that comes in on a daily basis. Use various systems and tools and your inbox won't become such an overwhelming source of stress and frustration. Create good mail-handling habits so you have more time available.

## *Organising your incoming mail*

Being organised is the key to time-efficient email processing. Here are some simple things you can do to sort your new messages quickly and easily.

### *Setting up folders*

Filters and folders can be very useful tools in helping you to manage your inbox. Just like paper filing, you categorise your emails, which helps you prioritise them and easily see what actions you need to take.

To start off with, create the following folders:

- ✔ Action
- ✔ Newsletters
- ✔ Priority
- ✔ Reading
- ✔ Reference

Then make additional folders for specific projects or clients.

### *Filtering emails*

After you set up your folders, you can introduce filters in your mail program that automatically sort your incoming mail into the correct folder, making it quicker and easier to deal with your inbox.

You can define filters based on the sender or subject. For example, say each day your client The Red Company sends you an email that you must respond to quickly, and a company called Business News sends you an email newsletter that you're in no rush to read. You can tell your email program to put all messages from Jim@theredcompany.co.uk into a folder called 'Red Company', and all messages from news@businessnews.co.uk into your Reading folder. Then you can easily see at a glance when you have a message from the Red Company you need to deal with, and you can ignore the new message in the Reading folder for now.

### *Using multiple email addresses*

Why not use a different email address for different types of email? Create one specifically for business, one for personal, one for all your newsletters, and one for less important things. It's also advisable to create one you use where you think that you might get spammed – for example, when you sign up for product information on a website.

Using different email addresses may sound complicated but it helps with the sorting process. You can set your mail system to pick up multiple accounts and then check the important ones regularly and the less important ones, less often. For example, non-essential newsletters can go to one email address that you check now and again, and work-related emails can go to your main account that you check regularly.

# Following email etiquette

Don't just consider your own time management when dealing with emails – spare a thought for the recipient too. Follow the pointers below to make sure that you don't frustrate, bore, or offend with your emails.

✔ **Auto responder:** If necessary, set an auto responder so that people who email you can automatically be notified that you've received their emails and you'll get back to them within a specified time.

✔ **Addressees:** Only send an email to the person who actually needs to read it. Don't copy in everyone unless you need to: use the cc and bcc fields appropriately. Use the cc field to copy in someone who may want to read the email for information, and the bcc field when you send an email out to a number of users and you don't want to reveal the email addresses to all recipients.

✔ **Capitals:** Don't use capitals – this is seen as SHOUTING in the online world.

✔ **Content:** Keep emails short and precise, and watch your spelling, punctuation, and grammar. Avoid the use of jargon or abbreviations unless you know that the reader is familiar with the topic. Make sure that your meaning is clear, and include the original email when you reply to make it easier to follow the thread of a discussion. Remove any unnecessary previous messages and ensure that the Subject field contains something relevant. Finally, re-read your email before you hit Send.

✔ **Delivery:** Emails aren't 100 per cent guaranteed to reach their recipients, especially with spam filters getting more and more efficient/aggressive/selective. You can't be sure that your email has been delivered and there can also be a time delay in pressing Send and it turning up in the recipient's inbox. If it's urgent, pick up the phone.

You can also look into getting a tool which checks your email for the key flags that it identifies as spam and provides a rating. A spam filter is useful if you send out a regular newsletter or mailing to your contact list and is often built into newsletter and email distribution tools.

✔ **Hoaxes/chain letters:** *Never* forward hoaxes or chain letters. They waste everyone's time. Bill Gates is *not* going to give you money for forwarding that email as part of Microsoft research. And virus warning messages are probably hoaxes or contain viruses themselves. (Make sure that you have virus protection installed on your computer)

✔ **Length:** Don't waffle on in an email – keep to the point. Longer emails are more difficult to read.

✔ **Request Read Receipt:** If you want to know that an email has been received, set the Receipt requested option. But you may not automatically get a receipt if the recipient chooses not to send confirmation of reading. Don't set this as the default – it's not necessary.

It's easy to set up a new mail address in Hotmail, Yahoo, Gmail, or your email provider. You can then forward most of these email accounts on to one preferred email account.

You can also 'Send mail as' so you can reply in, say, your Gmail account but as if you're in your Hotmail account. This makes it easy to handle various accounts from one email application such as Outlook or Thunderbird.

## Using templates

Take a look at the types of emails you send out on a regular basis and think about using a template to speed up your response. You can make a template for each different type of email that you can use over and over again, rather than creating it from new each time. This saves you time and effort.

You can create your template in a word processing programme, and then just cut and paste the text into your mail system as needed.

Use the template as the basis for your email, but make sure that you personalise the message in some way. You don't want to send a stilted and impersonal email that makes your use of a template obvious to the recipient.

## Clearing the clutter

Although the Internet is great for finding information, if you're anything like me, you just love signing up for things – special offers, bulletins, newsletters, forums, and so on. As a result, you end up on more and more mailing lists, and receiving more and more emails, which take up more and more of your time to wade through.

Make sure that every few months you go through your inbox or reading and newsletter folders and unsubscribe from communications you haven't read or that are no longer useful.

There's no point in cluttering up your inbox with things that you're never going to get round to reading. If you haven't made time to read the communication in the week it arrives, the chances are you won't get round to looking at it or, if you do, then the information is already out-of-date. And if you need to find the information the email contains, you can probably access it on the original website or find it through a search engine.

**Book IV**

**Increasing Productivity and Performance**

## Avoiding spam

Unfortunately, you can't avoid receiving any spam at all, but you do have a few ways of dealing with it once you start receiving it.

The best way to avoid spam is to be selective about who you give your email address to. For example, posting your email address on a website guarantees that automated email grabbers can pick up your address, and then send spam to it. Publishing your address on various directories or public listings also increases the risk of receiving more and more spam.

Thankfully most email providers have a junk and spam filter option that automatically sends email it identifies as potential spam into a separate folder or just deletes it. You can usually opt to do the same with emails that come from an address you don't recognise.

You can also find spam filters that plug into your mailbox and filter out the spam for you. Most of these filters need initial 'training' so they can identify what is spam and you need to check the spam folder regularly to make sure that valid emails aren't being marked as spam.

Protect yourself from viruses, which are invariably passed in spam messages by installing good virus protection such as McAfee, Norton, CA AntiVirus, or AVG Anti-Virus (free).

# Dealing with an Email Backlog

You probably dread coming back from holiday to hundreds if not thousands of emails in your inbox. Your heart sinks at the prospect of spending hours doing little else but dealing with all those emails. Fear not – here are a few ideas to help you minimise and deal with the backlog.

## Preparing before time out

Before you take any time away from work, cancel any email notifications you receive, such as messages from email groups. You can do this for all Yahoo! groups and most online discussion/networking groups. This reduces the volume coming through in the first place so you have fewer messages to deal with.

# Handling the deluge when you return

To start with, set aside an hour to go through your inbox. Yes, I know that it's probably going to take much longer than that but at least you make a start.

You can tackle the backlog by performing a number of scans:

1. **First scan: Go through quickly and eliminate the spam and any email you know that you don't need to read.**

   Don't read or respond to any emails on this scan. Use the Sort function to sort your email by sender or subject, which makes it easier to delete the junk.

   You don't have time to read everything so delete anything that doesn't require your attention or have information you absolutely *must* have. Don't save it 'just in case'.

2. **Second scan: Pick out all the priority emails you need to respond to first.**

   Place these urgent emails in a separate 'Action' folder. Then set aside time in your diary to respond to your 'Action' emails – do this in that first hour as you should still have a reasonable chunk of the first hour left; if not, set aside more time later in the day.

3. **Third scan: If your filters haven't already sorted out reading emails, now is the time to place them all in the appropriate folder(s).**

   Depending on the volume of emails, you should be able to complete these first two scans in the first hour. Do the third scan too if you still have time; otherwise leave this stage until the next time you're scheduled to work on your email.

4. **Fourth scan: Deal with any remaining emails.**

   Less urgent action emails can now be dealt with. What's left? If it's not action or reading – it's probably not urgent so can be deleted.

Only after you've safely dealt with the backlog that came in while you were away can you apply the same process to the new emails that have come in.

Another method you can use to process your bulging inbox is to create a 'Backlog' folder. Copy all the emails currently in the inbox into this folder. Deal with your inbox in the usual way from now on, and set aside a few minutes each day, or a half an hour a couple of times a week, to deal with the backlog using the scanning method. This way you won't get bogged down with mass of emails in your inbox: you can deal with the new emails and then handle the backlog separately.

**Book IV**

**Increasing Productivity and Performance**

# Index

• N •